W9-BWD-069

The Best in Children's Books

Written and edited by
Zena Sutherland

The Best in Children's Books

The University of Chicago
Guide to Children's Literature
1973–1978

The University of Chicago Press
Chicago and London

ZENA SUTHERLAND is associate professor in the Graduate Library School at the University of Chicago. She is also the children's book editor at the *Chicago Tribune*.

The University of Chicago Press, Chicago 60637
The University of Chicago Press, Ltd., London

Printed in the United States of America

Library of Congress Cataloging in Publication Data

Sutherland, Zena.
The best in children's books.

Reviews which originally appeared in the Bulletin of the Center for Children's Books.
Includes indexes.
1. Children's literature—Book reviews. I. Chicago. University. Center for Children's Books. Bulletin. II. Title.
Z1037.A1S92 [PN1009.A1] 810'.9'9282 79-24331
ISBN 0-226-78059-7

87 86 85 84 83 82 81 80 54321

Contents

Acknowledgments

The critical evaluations used in this book are based on the judgments of the members of the *Bulletin of the Center for Children's Books* advisory committee: Yolanda Federici, Sara Fenwick, Isabel McCaul, Hazel Rochman, Robert Strang, and the editor, Zena Sutherland, who is grateful to the members of the advisory committee and to Frances Henne and Alice Brooks McGuire, who were instrumental in establishing the *Bulletin,* to the Graduate Library School which sponsors it, and to the many members of the university and the laboratory schools who have given advice in specialized subject areas.

Introduction

When the Center for Children's Books was established at the University of Chicago in 1945 one of its goals in setting up a collection of trade books written for children was the evaluation and analysis of books in terms of uses, appeals, and literary quality. The *Bulletin of the Center for Children's Books,* which grew out of a memorandum that circulated within the Graduate School of Education, now is sponsored by the Graduate Library School and has international circulation.

Review copies of all children's trade books are sent to the center by publishers. Once each week, members of the advisory committee meet to examine the books and discuss the reviews prepared by the editor. The committee comprises teachers and librarians in public and private schools and libraries. When the editor or the committee feels that the subject matter of any book should be evaluated by an expert, the resources of the University of Chicago faculty are called upon, with teachers in the university's laboratory schools and in the college and divisions participating.

Books for children and young people of all ages are reviewed, and occasionally an adult book that may be of particular interest to adolescent readers is included. It is clear from the reading level index that some spans are heavily represented. There are many more citations listed for grades 4–6, for example, than for grades 4–7; however, material may also be found for the 7th grade reader in such groups as 5–7, 6–9, or 7–10. The book has not been planned as a balanced list in respect to an individual grade or age, or to subject or genre. The editor's selections have been made primarily on the basis of literary quality, with representation of subjects as a secondary consideration. The goal—a list of the best books published in the years 1973–78.

Why is it important to select children's books with discrimination? For one thing, the years in which such books are appropriate are fleeting, although some books can gratify readers of any age. There are so many activities and competing interests that fill children's time today that only the most inveterate readers read more than half a dozen books yearly beyond those required by their schools.

Second, studies of the adult reading population show how easy it is to fall into the pattern of reading only superficial material. Children exposed to flimsy mass market books, comics, and pedestrian series books will not necessarily proceed to good literature. It is possible for a child to acquire discrimination, but it isn't likely to happen unless some adult—a parent, a teacher, a librarian—suggests better books, encourages the ownership of books, and discusses good books with enthusiasm and understanding. It is incumbent on adults who are concerned with children's reading to select and counsel wisely, to appreciate the importance of both the content of books and the reading habit itself, and to comprehend what the elements of good children's books are.

In many ways, the literary criteria that apply to adult books and children's books are the same. The best books have that most elusive component, a distinctive literary style. A well-constructed plot; sound characterization with no stereotypes; dialogue that flows naturally and is appropriate to the speaker's age, education, and milieu; and a pervasive theme are equally important in children's and adults' fiction. Authoritative knowledge, logical organization of material, and accuracy are major considerations in informational books for any age.

In books for children, there are additional considerations based on limitations of comprehension and experience. Comparatively few children enjoy a story without action or conflict, however delicate the nuances of style, and most young readers abjure the tedious presentation of information in the guise of conversation. For very young children, it is important that a book not contain so much information as to confuse them. The vocabulary need not be rigidly controlled, but it should not include so many terms that the reader is discouraged. The concepts must be comprehensible—for example, a reader in the primary grades is not spatially sophisticated—and the subject appropriate. Format (type size, distribution of print, placement on page) and illustrations should be consistent with the level of the text, and maps or diagrams should be very carefully placed and labeled.

Because children are forming concepts of themselves and their society and are testing and acquiring ethical values, it is imperative that the books they read foster and nurture opinions and attitudes that are intelligent and flexible. Will the books they read serve to do this? The best ones will. Adults should be wary, however, of their own bias and should evaluate very carefully the author's values and assumptions lest agreement with their own ideas be confused with objectivity.

Each book must be judged on its own merits, and each book should be chosen—whether for an individual child, a library, or a classroom collection—with consideration for its strength even though it may have some weaknesses. This has been a precept in critical evaluation of books for the *Bulletin*. It is often illuminating to compare a book with other books by the same author or with similar books on a subject, but the judgment of each book is made on that book alone. With the spate of publication of children's books, selection is difficult. It is our hope that through this bibliography and its indexes, readers may more easily find the best in children's books.

Suggestions for using this book

The reviews included here have been selected by the editor from those already published in the *Bulletin of the Center for Children's Books.* Save for a few titles coded as "Additional" or "Special Reader," all of the books listed here had received a rating of "Recommended." Since some of the late titles of 1972 were not available for inclusion in the previous edition, they have been included here as books of distinction. The practice of using an asterisk to denote books of special distinction was not instituted until September 1975 (the first issue of volume 29), and is therefore missing from some earlier titles which surely merit such recognition. The reviews are listed alphabetically by the author's name and are numbered in sequence to facilitate the use of the six indexes at the back of this book.

Of the indexes, only the *title index* does not refer the reader to the number assigned each book but gives the last name of the author.

The *developmental values index* is based on the analysis of each book for those elements that illuminate some aspect of achieving maturity, solving problems, or establishing relationships at any developmental stage in the life of a child or young reader. The developmental values covered range from the young child's acquisition of environmental concepts or adjustment to a new baby in the family, to the adolescent's attitudes toward his or her role in marriage.

The *curricular use index* suggests books for incorporation into the school curriculum, or for supplemental reading in relation to curricular units. Lennart Nilsson's *How Was I Born?* (no. 952), for example, is included under "Sex Education" in the curricular use index, whereas it is cited under "Reproduction" in the subject index.

The *reading level index* is arranged progressively by grades following the books for preschool children, which are listed by age. Books for independent reading begin with first grade, usually age six. The reading levels are given in a span that is intended to suggest probable use rather than to impose limits. A volume of poetry, for example, may be graded 4–6, indicating widest use in grades 4, 5, and 6; it may, however, be read aloud to younger children, used independently by proficient readers in grade 3 or even grade 2, or be read by older children or adults. The levels of reading difficulty have been determined by the *Bulletin* advisory committee after consideration of the vocabulary, the length and complexity of the writing, subject interest, latent content, organization of material, and the appropriateness of content, difficulty, and format to the maturity of the intended reader.

The *subject index* entries include both fiction and nonfiction. Nonfiction books about Africa, for example, are grouped according to subject matter into various subheadings under the general heading "Africa." Fictional stories set in that region will be found under the "Africa, stories" subheading.

The *type of literature index* makes it possible for the reader to find citations for all of the books of poetry, all of the mystery stories, and so on, that have been selected to be grouped together. The temptation to break this index down into fine categories has been sternly resisted, lest the book become inordinately massive. It is hoped that the separate indexes give ample access to the material in the volume.

Many of the books listed are from countries in the United Kingdom. The appended list of publishers includes British titles available in the United States. It could be said that this bibliography reflects the best in American children's literature and, to the extent that information about British and American copublished books is available, some of the best in British children's literature.

Reviews of Books

1 **Aardema,** Verna, ad. *Behind the Back of the Mountain;* Black Folktales from Southern Africa; retold by Verna Aardema; illus. by Leo and Diane Dillon. Dial, 1973, 85p. Trade ed. $4.95; Library ed. $4.58 net.

4-6 Dramatic pictures in black, white, and grey are bold and stylized, with a high sense of design. The tales they illustrate are folk legends from half a dozen language groups of South Africa; trickster tales, witches outwitted, talking animals and magical skymaidens, stories of love and charity and hunger that reflect the concerns of people who live close to the land and are governed by the mores of their cultures. The writing style is smooth, and some of the tales are particularly suited for storytelling although all come from the oral tradition. A glossary and a list of sources is appended.

2 **Aardema,** Verna, ad. *Why Mosquitoes Buzz in People's Ears;* A West African Folk Tale; retold by Verna Aardema; illus. by Leo and Diane Dillon. Dial, 1975. 74-2886. 27p. $6.95.

K-3 A "why" story from Africa is retold with verve in a picture book
* that should delight young listeners and adult readers—especially those who may use it for storytelling—equally. A mosquito tells a whopping lie to an iguana who, muttering, fails to respond to the greeting of a friendly snake. The snake goes into a rabbit hole and frightens a rabbit . . . and this chain of events leads to an owlet accidentally killed and its mother failing to hoot and wake the sun. No sun? The lion calls a meeting of all animals, the chain is unraveled, and the mosquito is condemned. The cumulation will appeal to listeners, and the youngest children especially will enjoy the descriptions of sound (the snake moves "wasawusu, wasawusu . . .") and the surprise ending. The illustrations are magnificent, stylized and patterned pictures of animals, strongly-composed double-page spreads with plenty of white to set off the distinct forms and separate their parts, bold colors used with restraint and nuance. A handsome example of good bookmaking.

3 **Aardema,** Verna, ad. *Who's in Rabbit's House? A Masai Tale;* retold by Verna Aardema; illus. by Leo and Diane Dillon. Dial, 1977, 77-71514. 25p. Trade ed. $7.95; Library ed. $7.45 net.

4-7 yrs. A humorous Masai animal tale is told here as a performance by Masai villagers, and the characters are shown as people wearing animal masks. The story: Rabbit sits in her doorway every night to watch the other animals drinking at the lake. One night she comes home to hear a voice inside her house, behind a barred door, saying "I am The Long One. I eat trees and trample on elephants. Go away!" Jackal offers to burn the house to get The Long One out; Rabbit protests. Leopard attacks the roof; Rabbit sends him away. Frog, who's been amused by these and other abortive attempts, tries scaring the mysterious intruder, who proves to be a caterpillar. Rabbit goes back to sitting in her doorway, while Frog sits on a log, croaking with laughter. The illustrations, double-page spreads rich with color, are beautifully composed, although young children may be confused by the fact that there are three images of Jackal, for example, shown on the page that refers to a single jackal. The story is deftly told, with the action and humor that appal to children, and the text is extended by the vitality of the illustrations.

4 **Adams,** Richard. *Watership Down.* Macmillan, 1974. 444p. $6.95.

7- Winner of the 1972 Carnegie Medal, *Watership Down* is a monumental book in every sense, including that of sheer bulk, but readers who are captivated by this fresh and vital fantasy will end their reading reluctantly. Adams has created a whole entity, a fantasy world as convincing as Middle Earth or Wonderland. There are stories—legends told within the book—that are pages long and do halt the action, but they add, on the other hand, to the authenticity of an adventure tale about rabbits that has overtones of social comment, distinctive characterization, an intricate but sturdy plot, and a wonderfully flowing style. Incited by the fears of one rabbit, Fiver, who is prescient, a group led by the heroic Hazel (and he does truly develop as a heroic character) leave the doomed warren and go off to found a new rabbit community. Their way is beset by difficulties, especially when they escape after a stay in a regimented community and are pursued by the militant rabbits whose way of life they scorn. They are aided in their efforts to find mates by a seagull they've rescued (whose speech patterns are perhaps the one grating note in the book: "No fight, but vatch, vatch, always vatch. Ees no good," as though the bird were a foreigner speaking English.) The descriptions of the Berkshire countryside are poetic, but the most enthralling aspect of the story is surely the magnitude of the rabbit world, with its cultural patterns, tradition, folklore, language, and vigor.

5 **Adamson,** Wendy Wriston. *Saving Lake Superior;* A Story of Environmental Action. Dillon, 1974. 74p. illus. $5.95.

6-9 With few exceptions, the many books about pollution have dealt with aspects of the problem on a broad basis; here the text, after describing the history of the region and changes of the land over millennia, focuses on the varied causes of pollution in Lake Superior and on a grass-roots effort to make changes. The chief offender, Reserve Mining, dumps into the lake the equivalent of 30,000 automobiles each day (67,000 tons of taconite tailings per day) and insists it cannot afford to change although other companies' plants have on-land waste disposals. Although judgment against Reserve Mining was appealed and has been in litigation for seven years, the governmental agencies and the citizens' groups that spurred investigation are still working to save the world's largest lake. The writing style is straightforward and well-organized; the author is the Librarian of the Environmental Library of Minnesota. Some informative photographs are included, and an annotated bibliography is appended.

6 **Adkins,** Jan. *The Craft of Sail;* written, designed and illus. by Jan Adkins. Walker, 1973. 64p. $5.95.

6- Despite the visual handicap of text that appears handprinted and is often crowded, this is an excellent book on sailing. It moves from basic physical principles of air pressure and flow to an explanation of the points of sail, describes nautical terminology, and has detailed coverage, in text and illustrations, of the structure of boats, kinds of sails, and fittings in sailboats. The second part of the book is devoted to the techniques of sailing (including mooring and docking) and to such ancillary but necessary topics as knots, rope coiling, charts and navigation, anchoring, et cetera. Solidly packed with information, this is not for the casual reader but for a serious student of the craft of sail.

7 **Adkins,** Jan. *Toolchest;* written and illus. by Jan Adkins. Walker, 1973. 48p. Trade ed. $4.95; Library ed. $4.85 net.

5- Meticulously illustrated with drawings that show exact details of tools, hardware, wood grains, and techniques, this is a superb first book for the amateur carpenter. Adkins explains the uses of each tool, the ways in which each variety of saw or chisel is fitted for a particular task, such procedures as dowelling, gluing, or cutting a tenon and mortise, and he describes the uses for each kind of nail and screw. This most useful book concludes with advice on the care of tools. A fine piece of craftsmanship, both in example and in execution.

8 **Adler,** David A. *Redwoods Are the Tallest Trees in the World;* illus. by Kazue Mizumura. T. Y. Crowell, 1978. 77-4713. 33p. (Let's-Read-and-Find-Out Books). $5.79.

2-3 Another fine book in an outstanding series of science books for younger readers, this has a clear, simple text that is nicely integrated with the illustrations. Both text and picture captions give measurements in meters as well as feet, and—like other books in the series—the text has been carefully compiled to provide just enough information for primary grades readers without deluging them with facts. Adler discusses the climate in which redwoods grow, their size and longevity, the ways in which they reproduce and grow, and their usefulness in building, a usefulness which has led conservationists to establish a Save-The-Redwoods League.

9 **Adoff,** Arnold. *Black Is Brown Is Tan;* illus. by Emily Arnold McCully. Harper, 1973. 32p. Trade ed. $4.95; Library ed. $5.11 net.

K-3 Charming pictures share and augment the warmth and affection of a story that is a poem about an interracial family. "Black is brown is tan/ is girl is boy/ is nose is face/ is all the colors/ of the race/ is dark is light/ singing songs/ in singing night/ kiss big woman hug big man/ black is brown is tan," it begins, and goes on to celebrate the differences of color and the love that is pervasive. The family plays and works, scolds and teases, and through it all there is an ebullience and a joy.

10 **Adoff,** Arnold, ed. *Celebrations; A New Anthology of Black American Poetry;* comp. and ed. by Arnold Adoff. Follett, 1977. 76-19888. 285p. Trade ed. $7.95; Library ed. $7.98 net.

5- A noted anthologist has selected poems that celebrate aspects of black life, and that means life itself in its universal applications as well as the special pride of blackness. The book is divided into twelve sections, although there is no table of contents to indicate that poems are grouped under such headings as "The Idea of Ancestry," "The Southern Road," "Myself When I Am Real," or "A Poem for Heroes," and there is a continuity to the whole. Eighty-five poets are represented; biographical notes are appended, and the author-title index shows both the range from great to less known writers as well as the care and discrimination of the selection process.

11 **Adoff,** Arnold, ed. *My Black Me;* A Beginning Book on Black Poetry. Dutton, 1974. 83p. $5.50.

3-6 "Power to the poets," writes Adoff in his foreword, and in this anthology of poems by black writers the proud, joyful note of his message is exemplified by the closing lines of the first selection, Lucille Clifton's "Listen Children"; "We have always loved each other/ children/ all ways/ pass it on." There are poems that speak in protest, but as a collection the poems are a positive affirmation of blackness, and they have been wisely chosen for younger readers. Notes on the poets and an index are appended.

12 **Adoff,** Arnold, ed. *The Poetry of Black America;* Anthology of the 20th Century. Harper, 1973. 552p. Trade ed. $12.50; Library ed. $9.89 net.

7- A most impressive anthology that includes the work of major and minor poets; the selection has been thoughtful and such poets as Langston Hughes, Robert Hayden, Countee Cullen, and Nikki Giovanni are represented by a satisfying number of poems. The material is arranged chronologically by authors' birth dates, and the book is a celebration of blackness and of poetry. Biographical notes and an index are appended.

13 **Adoff,** Arnold. *Tornado!* illus. by Ronald Himler. Delacorte, 1977. 76-47241. 44p. Trade ed. $6.95; Library ed. $6.46 net.

3-5 * Himler's black and white pictures, as effective in depicting a huddle of frightened faces as in the scenes of boiling black clouds and their ominous funnels, are as evocative and dramatic as Adoff's linked poems. The lines are spoken by a child; they describe the family's apprehension, their preparations for safety, and their observations of the aftermath of the tornado. The poetry is direct, vivid, and immediate, yet it is colored throughout by the sense of comfort that those whithin a family give each other and by the sense of determined courage of those whose lives and property have been damaged. It ends, ". . . no old tornado/ I don't care how bad/ is stronger than the people on the land." An epilogue gives background information on tornadoes and on the Xenia tornado of the poems.

14 **Adoff,** Arnold. *Where Wild Willie;* illus. by Emily Arnold McCully. Harper, 1978. 76-21390. 22p. Trade ed. $6.95; Library ed. $6.79 net.

K-2 Willie could be a boy or a girl; neither the text of the free, rhythmic poem nor the scrawly, color-washed line drawings establishes anything other than the facts that Willie is young, a child who stays out late and joyously explores the neighborhood, a child whose parents are concerned but not frantic. The poem describes with lilting fluency Willie's rambles and then the voices from home speak for themselves, an antiphonal arrangement in which the two draw closer until Willie comes home. The ending is especially warm, for there are no reprimands, no punishment: "willie / is you / willie / is me / willie is / com / in / home / to be / wild

/ willie / willie / wild / willie / be / free / be / free / willie / wild / willie / be / free."

15 **Aiken,** Joan, et al. *Authors' Choice 2*. T. Y. Crowell, 1974. 246p. illus. $6.95.

6- Each of the eighteen stories in this companion anthology to *Authors' Choice* is prefaced by some commentary written by the author who chose the tale or book excerpt. Several of the selections are science fiction, including the touching "The Star Beast" by Nicholas Stuart Gray; several are about animals; one of the most delightful, chosen by the late Honor Arundel, is from a journal of 1908 by a girl of twelve, "The Book of Maggie Owen." Expectably diverse, the book is enjoyable in itself and interesting because of the selectors' comments.

16 **Aiken,** Joan. *The Faithless Lollybird;* illus. by Eros Keith. Doubleday, 1978. 77-72999. 255p. $6.95.

6-9 A diverting collection of Aiken stories has her usual frothy mix of realism and fantasy, lightly seasoned by whimsy and sentiment. Some of the tales, like "The Man Who Pinched God's Letter" or "Moonshine in the Mustard Pot," are realistic and touching, if not always restrained; some, like "The Cat Who Lived in a Drainpipe," are blandly fanciful; and tales like "Cat's Cradle," are wholly fantastic. The style is light and polished, the humor sophisticated.

17 **Aiken,** Joan. *The Far Forests; Tales of Romance, Fantasy, and Suspense*. Viking, 1977. 77-356. 154p. $7.95.

8-
* A collection of sophisticated, witty tales for mature readers, this has the polished style that's Aiken at her best; it hasn't the exaggeration that is enjoyed by some of her younger readers in books like *Nightbirds on Nantucket* or *The Whispering Mountain* but it has just as much imagination and humor. And a touch of the macabre. And magic, and diversity.

18 **Aiken,** Joan. *Midnight Is a Place*. Viking, 1974. 287p. $6.95.

6-9 The year is 1842, the place is a huge, grim house—Midnight Court—outside an English manufacturing town, and the protagonist is a lonely boy, Lucas, who lives with his dour guardian and his aloof tutor. Lucas, who has longed for a friend, is dismayed when the new arrival at Midnight Court proves to be a small French girl, Anna-Marie, child of the man who had lost his fortune on a gambling bet made with the grim guardian. While the basic plot is patterned, Aiken weaves about it a marvelously intricate and convincing story that has both the romance and an awareness of a need for social reform that are Dickensian. Her style, however, is her own, rich and distinctive, and the story of the struggles of Lucas and Anna-Marie after a fire razes Midnight Court and they are forced to work in the factories and sewers of the town enables her to bring in some marvelously villainous characters and to use the period argot she handles so deftly.

19 **Albert,** Louise. *But I'm Ready to Go*. Bradbury, 1976. 76-9949. 230p. $6.95.

6-9 There have been many stories for children and young people that describe with sympathy the problems of those who are retarded or have learning disabilities. Few of them have the potential for touching and teaching the reader as does this novel in which the protagonist is a fifteen-year-old girl who suffers from teasing by others, the differences of which she is so keenly aware, and her own feelings of inadequacy and apprehension. For Judy is intelligent. She cannot understand why learning and understanding are so hard for her, but she is determined to find a niche, to achieve something that will gain the respect of others. She decides that she will go into New York by herself and get an audition that will—surely—bring her fame as a singer. But New York is confusing, there are preparations she should have made (back-up music); and she is dismissed quite summarily when she turns up with no experience and no appointment. Yet she's achieved something, she's taken a step on her own and is surprised when her sister, whose role has seemed that of an adversary, is stimulated enough by Judy's idea to suggest that they practice together, she as guitarist and Judy as vocalist. Since Judy's problems in fitting into the family patterns have been stressed, the outcome is a logical one in the structure of the story. The characterization is convincing, the writing style smooth, but the book's strength certainly lies in the sympathetic, moving, and credible picture of a handicapped person.

20 **Alderson,** Brian, comp. *Cakes and Custard;* Children's Rhymes chosen by Brian Alderson; illus. by Helen Oxenbury. Morrow, 1975. 75-24523. 156p. Trade ed. $9.95; Library ed. $7.96 net.

4-7 yrs. One of the best collections of nursery verses to come along since
* the Briggs' *Mother Goose,* this has splendid illustrations and rhymes chosen by an astute expert in children's literature. Alderson has included, in addition to Mother Goose rhymes, street chants and his own childhood favorites; he states in his prefatory note that he has felt free to make changes, and the changes he has made give a fresh fillip to the familiar. Oxenbury's illustrations are deft, delicate, and humorous; for example, the framed vignette for "Eight o'clock is striking / Mother may I go out?" shows a miniskirted adolescent peering in at Mum, hair in

curlers, raptly glued to the telly. The colors are soft but strong, the draughtsmanship elegant. This British import is a prime example of good page layout and good bookmaking.

21 **Aleksin,** Anatolii Georgievich. *Alik the Detective;* tr. from the Russian by Bonnie Carrey. Morrow, 1977. 77-24121. 192p. Trade ed. $6.95; Library ed. $6.43 net.

5-7 Translated from the Russian, a comic adventure story is told by Alik, who is a mystery buff. He and five others in his class have formed a literary club in honor of a local author, Gleb Borodayev; one of the six is the author's grandson and namesake and is prevailed on to take the others to visit the cottage where Borodayev wrote. Trapped in a cellar by an inexplicably hostile caretaker, the children escape through Alik's ingenuity. Some passages are a bit long-winded, but Alik's solution, based on deduction, is credible, the story has suspense and humor, and the children emerge as vividly distinct characters.

22 **Alexander,** Lloyd. *The Cat Who Wished to Be a Man.* Dutton, 1973. 107p. $4.95.

5-6 When his cat Lionel begged to be turned into a man for just a little while, the old magician relented, but exacted a promise that Lionel would return home without delay. Alas, neither foresaw that Lionel (a Billy Budd among thieves) would fall in love, would resent and fight against injustice, would rid the town of Brightford of its mercenary mayor. Nor did they know that the magician's spell-making would break down and Lionel remain a man. The plot is not highly original in basic concept (innocent strength overcoming entrenched and malefic interests) save for the cat-into-man twist, but the style, the humor, the play on words, the rumbustious characters, and the pace of the action are delightful.

23 **Alexander,** Lloyd. *The First Two Lives of Lukas-Kasha.* Dutton, 1978. 77-26699. 213p. $8.50.

5-7 Save for the magical device that precipitates Lukas-Kasha in and
* out of his second world, this is more an adventure tale than a fantasy, and it's Alexander at his best. A contented young vagrant, Lukas volunteers to participate in a showman's trick on market day . . . and he wakes to find himself in a strange land where he is acclaimed king. His coming has been prophesied by the bumbling court astrologer, his courtiers flatter but ignore him, and his Grand Vizier is obviously the real power in the land of Abadan. Flattered by being addressed as "Center of the Universe" or "Wonder of the Age," Lukas at first revels in kingship—but as soon as he begins to take his responsibilities seriously, the vizier's

enmity is exposed. His life in danger, Lukas flees, accompanied by a renegade and satrical poet and a slave girl, Nur-Jehan, a defiant captive from Bishangar, the enemy country. From there on, it's high adventure as the three fugitives make their dashing way to Bishangar, where Lukas outwits the pursuing vizier and realizes he has come to love the slave, who proves to be Queen of Bishangar. It looks set for a traditional ending, but Lukas is suddenly returned to his original world; saddened by his loss, he goes off to search for new adventure. What gives the story its final high gloss are the depth and nuance of the serious conversation and the transfusion of pithy ideas into the derring-do setting, ideas that are universally applicable. That's the frosting; it crowns a confection of polished style, well-paced plot, and engaging wit.

24 **Alexander,** Lloyd. *The Foundling and Other Tales of Prydain;* illus. by Margot Zemach. Holt, 1973. 87p. $4.95.

4-6 Six stories of the mythical land so beautifully conceived by Alexander are written with vivid grace and humor; some of the characters will be familiar to Prydain fans as related to major figures in the cycle: Eilonwy's mother as a young Princess of Llyr, as independent as her daughter; Dallben the enchanter as a child; Doli of the Fair Folk. Each tale stands alone, a small gem, and the humor and romance are echoed in the soft, deft black and white Zemach drawings.

25 **Alexander,** Lloyd. *The Town Cats and Other Tales;* illus. by Laszlo Kubinyi. Dutton, 1977. 76-13647. 126p. $7.50.

4-6 * Each of the eight tales in this collection is fresh, witty, and written in polished, deceptively light style; beneath the magic and humor and entertaining dialogue are perceptive insights into the foibles of creatures, feline or human. It's the cats who are wise in these original fairy tales, getting rid of a bullying official, soothing irate gentlemen who want their portraits to surpass reality, helping a pair of young lovers overcome a father's obduracy, or tricking a foolish master into behaving sensibly. Alexander at his best.

26 **Alexander,** Lloyd. *The Wizard in the Tree;* illus. by Lazlo Kubinyi. Dutton, 1975. 138p. $7.50.

4-6 Having spent many ages trapped in a tree, the wizard Arbican was not in the most pleasant of moods when Mallory found him. All he wanted was to get away to the distant Land of Heart's Desire to which every other wizard had fled years ago. He sneered at Mallory's tales of magic and wizards as nonsense invented by humans, but he found his own powers were failing and it was Mallory, a small orphan who worked as a slave for the redoubtable Mrs. Parsel, who repeatedly came to his rescue. The two became embroiled, in the course of this fresh and funny fantasy, with the acquisitive Mrs. Parsel and the malevolent Squire Scrupnor to whom she toadies. The dupes and villains of the tale are robustly Dickensian, but there are no set characters; the writing is vigorous and the characterization sly, the plot an inventive embroidery of the battle between good and evil.

27 **Alexander,** Martha. *I'll Be the Horse If You'll Play With Me;* written and illus. by Martha Alexander. Dial, 1975. 75-9207. 28p. Trade ed. $4.95; Library ed. $4.58 net.

3-6 yrs. A sequel to *Nobody Asked Me If I Wanted a Baby Sister* is just as beguiling as the first book. Remember how Oliver tried to give away baby Bonnie? It ends with Oliver riding Bonnie (pillow-enthroned) around in his wagon, envisioning himself reclining on the pillow while Bonnie pulls the wagon. Well, now Bonnie *is* pulling the wagon—and giving Oliver her new crayons—and always being the robber in playing cops and robbers. She's tired of her role, cranky, and snappish with her younger brother. But then he says "Scott big boy!" So (full circle) Bonnie relaxes on the pillow and Scott pulls. A funny comment on the pecking order is at the same time reassuring about growing past the stooge-stage. The light touch in the writing and in the precise little drawings is just right.

28 **Alexander,** Sue. *Witch, Goblin, and Sometimes Ghost; Six Read-Alone Stories;* pictures by Jeanette Winter. Pantheon Books, 1976. 76-8657. 61p. Trade ed. $3.95; Library ed. $4.99 net.

1-2 Although these brief tales of friendship for beginning independent readers do not flow quite as smoothly as Lobel's stories of frog and toad, they have the same ingenuous quality, a quality reflected in the dumpy, engaging figures of the witch, ghost, and goblin. The book is useful as additional material for the beginning reader, and the stories reflect familiar everyday experiences and emotions. Goblin has trouble flying his kite until he realizes that no kite will fly if there is not wind; he looks forward to his birthday, convinced he will then know the answers to such puzzling questions as why the wind blows and how mountains get to be so big—and is disappointed at not waking to instant knowledge but appeased when his friends give him an encyclopedia.

29 **Aliki.** *At Mary Bloom's;* written and illus. by Aliki. Greenwillow, 1976. 75-45482. 29p. Trade ed. $6.95; Library ed. $5.94 net.

K-2 Lively drawings add to the humor of an engaging story that has animals as an appealing subject, a repeat pattern that is not abused by being overdone, a warm friendship between a child and an older neighbor, and a pervasive enjoyment of creatures—any kind of creature, especially any kind of new creature. A child's mouse has babies. She decides to call her neighbor but she knows that when the telephone rings the magpie will call, the monkey will shriek, the dogs will bark, et cetera. "So I'll call." And the magpie calls, the monkey shrieks, the dogs bark . . . but when she brings her mice to Mary Bloom's, she is expected, and the only response from the menagerie and from Mary (her own baby tucked under her arm) is joy. Mary bakes a cake, and they all celebrate the new babies. Great fun.

30 **Aliki.** *Corn Is Maize; The Gift of the Indians;* written and illus. by Aliki. T. Y. Crowell, 1976. 75-6928. 34p. $5.95.

2-4 Simply told but quite comprehensive, illustrated with brisk, informal drawings, the text gives information about how the plant we use today originated (insofar as is known), how it is husbanded and harvested, and how it is used by people for food, medicine, cosmetics, and many other products. Aliki describes, also, some of the ways in which the grain is processed, from hand-grinding to electrically-run milling.

31 **Aliki.** *The Long-Lost Coelacanth and Other Living Fossils;* written and illus. by Aliki. T. Y. Crowell, 1973. 26p. Trade ed. $3.75; Library ed. $4.50 net.

2-4 Both the text and the illustrations show clearly the excitement that gripped scientists when the discovery of a coelacanth was reported in 1938. Written with clarity, the simple text gives a clear explanation of how fossil finds enable naturalists to recognize living fossils, and mentions some of the familiar creatures that—although they may have changed in size—are essentially the same as their ancestors of millions of years ago.

32 **Allan,** Ted. *Willie the Squowse;* illus. by Quentin Blake. Hastings House, 1978. 78-1716. 57p. $5.95.

3-5 A prize-winning entry in a London *Times* competition for a children's story, this is a fresh fantasy that has an O. Henry touch, and the scribbly, comic line drawings are a nice foil for the matter-of-fact telling of the tale. The squowse is son of a mouse and a squirrel, trained as an acrobat but separated, by chance, from his unhappy trainer. Willie lives in the wall that joins two houses; in one, a contented old couple puts their dividends into a hole in the wall, and, in the other house, the mother of a large, poor family becomes convinced that there's a miracle operating: twice a day she holds cheese near the wall, trying to catch a mouse (Willie) and each time a hundred-dollar bill appears. So the poor get rich, the elderly couple never knows their money is gone, and

Willie finds his trainer. There may be layers of meaning beneath the bones of the story, but they're elegant bones and nicely patterned, and they stand sturdily on their own.

33 **Allard,** Harry. *It's So Nice to Have a Wolf Around the House;* illus. by James Marshall. Doubleday, 1977. 76-48836. 28p. $5.95.

3-5 yrs. According to the jacket, "this story . . . has something serious to say to children about being good, being bad, and being forgiven." The story is so flagrantly and engagingly silly, however, that few children will be likely to resent the message. An elderly man and his elderly pets decide they need a fresh face about the place. Cuthbert Devine, wolf and bank robber, pretends to be a dog when he applies for the post, and the old man is too nearsighted to spot the deception. Cuthbert proves to be a treasure, hardworking and cheerful and devoted; when the old man sees an article about the bank robbery, he realizes he's been duped. Cuthbert faints and goes into a decline; sobbing, he says that he's always wanted to be good but never had a chance because everyone expected wolves to be bad. Supported by the old man, Cuthbert confesses to the police, is let off because he's reformed, and the story ends with all hands (and paws and fins) enjoying life in Arizona, whither they've moved because of Cuthbert's health. The illustrations have a robust inanity to match the story.

34 **Allen,** Samuel, ed. *Poems from Africa;* illus. by Romare Bearden. T. Y. Crowell, 1973. 205p. $4.50.

7- "Poetry," says Samuel Allen in his excellent preface, "is one of the best roads to understanding," and in this impressive compilation of African poetry he proves it. The book includes poems from oral tradition, love songs and poems that celebrate the Creator, poems that speak of love, death, and war. In both these poems and those of our time there is a vein of lusty humor: "Keep it dark! / Don't tell your wife / For your wife is a log / That is smouldering surely!" says a sage of the Zezuru. The section of poems from the oral tradition is followed by sections geographically rather than chronologically divided, and among these are lyric poems, social commentary, poems that sharply etch the confrontation between black and white in Africa and in other countries. Some of the selections are tender or reverent; many are bitter; all are strong and evocative. This is an outstanding addition to the publisher's series of poetry books, useful for its sociological implications as well as for the discriminating choices of poems. A section of biographical notes on the poets is appended, as are title, first line, poet, and translator indexes.

35 **Ambrus,** Victor G. *Mishka;* written and illus. by Victor Ambrus. Warne, 1978. 77-084602. 24p. $6.95.

K-2 A blithely silly tale has illustrations in brilliant color; amply spaced on the oversize pages, the pictures have a vitality and humor that brought the book the Greenaway Medal in England. Mishka is an eight-year-old who has learned to play "The Blue Danube" on his fiddle. Seeking work at a circus, Mishka is rejected as a fiddler but accepted as odd-job man, and his jobs are menial. But glory comes at last when the elephant trainer is ill and Mishka offers to take his place; standing on his head—atop the head of a seated elephant—and playing his one tune, Mishka delights the crowd. Naturally, he becomes the star turn and the once-sneering ringmaster is demoted to elephant mucker-out. Improbable as the outcome is, it adds the success of a small person to the lure of the circus background to appeal to a young audience, and the writing style has a bland directness that contrasts nicely with the exuberance of the pictures.

36 **Amon,** Aline. *Reading, Writing, Chattering Chimps;* text and drawings by Aline Amon. Atheneum, 1975. 75-9524. 118p. $7.95.

5-7 A fascinating report on several programs in which scientists have trained chimpanzees to communicate through the use of signs or symbols, this is written in a brisk, informal, but dignified style and is illustrated by photographs of the chimps. One animal described at length is Washoe, who learned to sign short, structured sentences by hand gestures; another was taught through the use of plastic symbols, and a third through operating a computer. Amon discusses the limitations of the chimpanzee, physical handicaps to communication such as the shape and size of the pharynx, so that they cannot make the same sounds as a human does. There's every evidence in the book of the chimpanzee's intelligence and sense of humor, and the text is lucid in explaining training methods and the evolution of each animal's growing ability to use increasingly complex language. A list of sugggestions for further reading is included.

37 **Amon,** Aline. *Roadrunners and Other Cuckoos;* written and illus. by Aline Amon. Atheneum, 1978. 78-6648. 87p. $7.95.

6-9 In an easy, often conversational style, Amon describes some of the many and varied species of the cuckoo family: the bustling roadrunner, the parasitic species that lay their eggs in other birds' nests, the vile-smelling hoatzin of South America, the inefficient but amicable groove-billed anis. There is no rigid pattern, but in the course of discussing the various species, the author gives facts about courting, mating, nest-building, brooding, and anatomical structure; she also discusses anatomical differences that have led to problems in classification. The illustrations are deft, often slightly comical, in black and white. A chart that gives classification and such characteristics as range, habits of nesting, and habitats is appended, as are a bibliography and a relative index.

38 **Andersen,** Hans Christian. *The Complete Fairy Tales and Stories;* tr. by Erik Christian Haugaard. Doubleday, 1974. 1101p. $15.

4-6 Erik Haugaard is the sort of translator about whom every editor dreams, thoroughly at home in both languages and a writer who understands—as is evident from the fine books he has written—how to write for children. It's valuable to have Andersen's complete works in one volume, it's doubly valuable when they have been translated in a style that is colloquial, flowing, and having the cadence of the oral tradition. Andersen's notes for his stories are included, and the introduction by Haugaard makes perceptive comment on the author's style, on the Victorian translators who "had a tendency to make a kiss on the mouth, in translation, land on the cheek," and on the requirements of translation itself.

39 **Andersen,** Hans Christian. *The Woman with the Eggs;* adapted by Jan Wahl; illus. by Ray Cruz. Crown, 1975. 26p. $5.95.

K-3 Perhaps the most familiar dream-of-glory tale in children's literature is retold in a simply but smoothly written adaptation. The woman who goes to market, daydreaming about how her basket of eggs will be only the first step in accumulating a fortune, who tosses her head with haughty pride, and who breaks every egg that was in the basket on her head is shown in pictures that have vitality and humor, with clear, strong colors that make the book as attractive for group use as it is for reading aloud to a single child.

40 **Anderson,** Lonzo. *Arion and the Dolphins;* illus. by Adrienne Adams. Scribner, 1978. 77-16564. 28p. $7.95.

2-3 In a simple, graceful retelling of a Greek legend, Anderson communicates a sense of bubbling joy, and the lightness is echoed in Adams' pastel-sunny watercolor paintings of sea and sky, of the ebullient boy Arion and the leaping dolphins who are his friends. Interior scenes have exquisite details of Grecian costume and architecture. Hearing of a music contest in far-off Sicily, the boy musician sails from Corinth; his singing and his lute-playing enchant the audience as mush as they do the sailors, and Arion wins the prize: all the gold he can carry. On the voyage home, the greedy crew plan to kill him for the gold. Arion jumps overboard and is carried home by the dolphins. In Corinth, he tells the king, who sternly takes the gold from the crew when they arrive, threatening that they will never know when death will strike them. Arion, knowing that the king plans no retribution, laughs, and he slips away to swim happily with the dolphins.

41 **Anderson,** Mary. *Step on a Crack.* Atheneum, 1978. 77-22767. 180p. $7.95.

6-9 While the deductive powers and psychological insight of Sarah and her friend Josie seem overstated, the problem they solve is fascinated, and the story Sarah tells is deftly structured. Her mother is loving and sensible, and there is no conflict between them. Why, then, does she have recurrent nightmares about killing her mother? Why is each nightmare followed by the compulsive shiplifting of a worthless trinket? And why, when Mother's sister Katrin comes to visit, does Sarah begin to walk in her sleep? Their tenacious research brings Sarah and Josie to the discovery that sadistic, irresponsible Katrin is Sarah's real mother and that all of the dreamed revenge is a response to a traumatic childhood incident. Well written, the story has suspense and momentum, and Sarah accepts her adoptive mother's belief that "we are all victims of victims, none of us villains."

42 **Angier,** Bradford. *Ask for Love and They Give You Rice Pudding;* by Bradford Angier and Barbara Corcoran. Houghton, 1977. 77-354. 151p. $6.95.

7-9 Written in the form of journal entries, this is Robbie Benson's story; seventeen, he's almost friendless. He has a luxurious home with his grandparents, his mother is drying out in Europe, his father has disappeared years ago. So what good are a fat allowance and a Fiat? Especially since the one girl Robbie really wants to date has made it clear (14 times) that she's not interested. Reading an old journal of his father's, Robbie is fascinated by his father's long, bittersweet love affair with a college sweetheart. Robbie does finally get a date with the elusive Vicki, meets and enjoys her family (even getting a crush on her mother) and learns, painfully, that you cannot buy affection. He hadn't even realized that that was what he had been trying to do. Robbie tracks down and visits his father, a disturbing experience for both of them, after his grandfather dies. There's no instant rapport, but Rob does begin to see his parents as people with their own problems and to realize that he is now adult and can not only be emotionally independent but can even—possibly—help the adults in his life rather than expecting always to receive help. The writing is casual, the characters adequately drawn, the relationships credibly developed, and the style convincingly that of a young man who is at once isolated and arrogant.

43 **Annett,** Cora. *How the Witch Got Alf;* illus. by Steven Kellogg. Watts, 1975. 74-8808. 47p. $4.95.

3-4 Kelloggs's beguiling little donkey is nicely matched to the affable, silly protagonist of Annett's lightly nonsensical story. Observing the demonstrations that the cat, dog, and canary get from the Old Man and the Old Woman, and pondering on the fact that he is even more deserving than they because he works, Alf the donkey tries to imitate. He sings. It is not appreciated. He tries curling up in Old Woman's lap. He, she, and the chair collapse. He jumps up on Old Man and licks his face. Response, but the wrong kind. So, sure that he is unlovable, Alf runs away, but not far; he climbs to the roof of the house and hides. The subsequent noises convince the old couple there's a witch about, and the antics of Alf should amuse young readers as much as the ending satisfies them. The writing style is breezy, the ambience sunny.

44 **Annixter,** Jane. *Trumpeter;* The Story of a Swan; by Jane and Paul Annixter; illus. by Gilbert Riswold. Holiday House, 1973. 64p. $3.95.

5-7 Although Olor and his mate, Asa, are named there is no anthropomorphism or embroidery in this story, which serves not only as a life-cycle tale, but as an implicit plea for conservation. This gives a considerable amount of information about migratory patterns, courtship and mating, and flock behavior, and the text is written with respect for the creatures of the wild and with an appreciation of the beauty of that environment. The narrative is realistic, with enough variety and action to sustain the momentum of the text.

45 **Anno,** Mitsumasa, illus. *Anno's Alphabet;* An Adventure in Imagination. T. Y. Crowell, 1975. 53p. $6.95.

5-7 yrs. Presumably alphabet books are for children learning the first tool of reading, but this alphabet book, like Leonard Baskin's, is for anyone who enjoys a beautiful creation. The letters are shown as a solid pieces of rough, grained wood; the facing pages show objects beginning with each letter (no words), and each page has a different frame of flowers and animal forms, delicately drawn in black and white. The letters and facing objects are in strong but muted colors, and they are varied and distinctive: an exquisitely scrolled lock, an old map, an odd nutcracker, a tube of orange paint on an easel, a meticulously detailed pen point. Nice to have a child's first alphabet be an introduction to art.

46 **Anno,** Mitsumasa, illus. *Anno's Counting Book.* T. Y. Crowell, 1977. 76-28977. 26p. Trade ed. $5.95; Library ed. $6.95 net.

3-6 yrs. * When a picture book artist tries to introduce too many concepts, the book usually suffers. Here, however, Anno has so adroitly incorporated concepts in a wordless counting book that they reinforce each other. The watercolor pictures show a bare, snowy landscape for zero (unusual in itself) and on each page that follows, the same landscape—with one house, one bird, one tree; then two birds, two buildings, two trees, two adults, two children, etc. The concept of sets is introduced: adults and children, two kinds of trees. The church clock shows 2, 3, and 4 o'clock on succeeding pages. In the margin a Cuisenaire block tower mounts, cube by cube; after there are ten, a new pile begins—ending with twelve in toto. The landscape shows the seasonal changes through the cycle of a year. The book is instructive, attractive, and appealing because of the game element.

47 **Anno,** Mitsumasa, illus. *Anno's Journey.* Collins/World, 1978. 42p. Trade ed. $6.95; Library ed. $6.91 net.

5-7 yrs. * As always, Anno's draughtsmanship and composition are impressive, his balance of mass and detail wise, and his use of color restrained. Here he moves from an open landscape to village to town to city, and reverses the procedure, in a wordless book that pictures European settings and inhabitants. The pages are filled with small delights: a bridge that is straight out of a Van Gogh painting, a building marked "Anno 1976," some quirks of perspective, some marvelously comic details in the activities of the people in the streets or on the roofs of buildings. The book is full of wit, action, and beauty.

48 **Archer,** Jules. *Superspies; The Secret Side of Government.* Delacorte, 1977. 77-72640. 250p. $7.95.

7- As scandals and esposés have occurred, much of the information about the unsavory investigative activities of government agencies Archer describes has been revealed in the news media. Here it is all brought together, with special emphasis on the spying (past and present) of the FBI and the CIA. Archer gives corroborating evidence for his statements and, although his writing style is solid and somber, he's organized a mass of dramatic material with logic and care. A bibliography, with starred items that recommend material for further reading, is appended.

49 **Archer,** Jules. *You and the Law.* Harcourt, 1978. 78-52812. 178p. $7.95.

7- Archer uses accounts of actual cases to illustrate and dramatize legal problems and the procedures of the law and the courts. The text, addressed to the reader, describes the rights, obligations and processes in cases of false arrest, police brutality, suing or being sued on an issue of rights, being the victim of a violent crime, et cetera. Even on what it's like to be in prison. The writing style is a bit heavy but the book is very informative, with well-organized material and a substantial glossary, bibliography, and index.

50 **Ardizzone,** Edward. *Ship's Cook Ginger;* written and illus. by Edward Ardizzone. Macmillan, 1978. 78-7518. 48p. $7.95.

2-3 Like earlier stories about Tim, this has a breezy, nonchalant way of dealing with children's involvement in crises: Tim and his friend Ginger are allowed to stay on board Captain McFee's ship when Tim's parents are called back from the trip, and what could be more natural than Tim's manning the wheel and saving the ship when the crew is decimated by illness? Ginger pinchhits as ship's cook for the same reason; while his raspberry-sardine sandwiches and putting mustard in coffee to make it hot are not quite believable, they furnish the sort of humor younger readers enjoy. It's a blithe tale of action and accomplishment, and the illustrations indicate that, for Ardizzone, age cannot wither nor custom stale. . . .

51 **Arrick,** Fran. *Steffie Can't Come Out to Play.* Bradbury, 1978. 78-4423. 196p. $7.95.

8-10 Blonde, beautiful, tired of life in a small town and of her family's poverty, fourteen-year-old Stephanie dreams of becoming a model. She runs away, and when she reaches New York she's delighted when a kind and handsome man helps her, even gives her a bed for the night. She promptly falls in love with him and is ready to do anything her protector says. Her protector says "Hustle," since he's a pimp. Most of the book is an explicit exposé of a life of prostitution; interspersed with the episodes about Steffie are episodes about two policemen who patrol the district she's in and who—suspecting that the new girl is younger than she looks—try to find a way to help her. Fortunately for Steffie (who tells the story, save for the material about the police), she's sent to a halfway house after her pimp is hospitalized, and her parents take her home. She's still fourteen, but she's old. Candid, frightening, and poignant, the story demands credulity in Steffie's naiveté, but if the reader accepts that, her plight is believable, since the characterization and motivation are consistent.

52 **Asbjørnsen,** Peter Christen. *The Squire's Bride;* illus. by Marcia Sewall. Atheneum, 1975. 74-19316. 27p. $5.95.

3-5 A version of a Norwegian folktale is based on the H. L. Broekstad translation and is illustrated with pencil drawings that have warmth, vitality, and a great sense of the comic. The pictures suit the tale admirably, since the story of an obdurate peasant girl who outwits an equally determined elderly suitor ends on a note of comedy. The story, which is as good for storytelling as it is for reading aloud or alone, gives the reader that special pleasure of being in on the joke, since only the squire assumes that the bride who is being forcibly summoned and dressed for the wedding is the girl; everyone else knows it's a horse.

53 **Ashe,** Arthur. *Getting Started in Tennis;* by Arthur Ashe with Louie Robinson; photographs by Jeanne Moutoussamy. Atheneum, 1977. 77-5199. 102p. $6.95.

5-9 Ashe gives a great deal of sensible advice clearly and sequentially, with separate chapters on forehand, backhand, volley, serve, and footwork as well as chapters on equipment, tactics, strategy, court conduct, diet, and practice. He begins with such basics as how to choose a racket and he cautions readers that a beginner should concentrate on form rather than power. Many of the chapters are followed by questions and answers, and the text—which includes scoring and rules for play—concludes with a glossary of terms. A clear and useful how-to book.

54 **Ashley,** Bernard. *All My Men.* Phillips, 1978. 78-12683. 159p. $8.95.

6-8 There were many things about his new home that made Paul unhappy. Instead of lively London, they were in a dull small town; instead of the attention he was used to as an only child, he found his parents too busy with their grocery store to have time for him; instead of his friend's voice calling for "all my men" to join in a ball game, there were no friends at all. Paul's eagerness, when he starts school, to avoid the dull boys like Arthur and to be accepted by a natural leader (and bully) like Billy is so acute that he does things that make him ashamed—but he does them. Anything to appease Billy and get on his team. Paul steals candy from the store for Billy; he accommodatingly lies when he's made a goal and Billy, the goalkeeper, asks him to agree that the ball had swerved out. Assigned to work on a school project with Arthur, Paul becomes intrigued by Arthur's grandfather, who teaches him how to use a camera; then he becomes interested in the project itself; he also becomes interested in one of the girls in his class, Lorraine. She is present when Billy swaggers on the scene while Paul is taking some shots to use on the project, and he becomes so incensed by Billy's interference that he gives chase. And that's how Paul learns what a coward a bully can be, and when he realizes fully how skewed his values have been. Ashley writes a nicely balanced story with good pace, but there's a universal story of self-conflict and self doubt that is perceptively introduced and that gives the book depth and significance.

55 **Asimov,** Isaac. *The Birth of the United States 1763–1816.* Houghton, 1974. 274p. illus. $5.95.

6-10 A sequel to *The Shaping of North America* is written in the same easy, flowing, and informal style; again Asimov's fresh viewpoint gives vitality to a portion of our history that will be familiar to most readers. The insertion of birth dates after the first mention of almost every figure is slightly distracting but may be useful. The text covers the crowded years between the Treaty of Paris to the end of the War of 1812; it doesn't give the reader the broad picture of trends, movements, and the lives of ordinary citizens that Daniel Boorstin does in *The Landmark History of the American People: From Plymouth to Appomattox* but it's far less dry and just as informative as most history texts. A table of dates and a relative index, both extensive, are appended.

56 **Asimov,** Isaac. *The Golden Door; The United States from 1865 to 1918*. Houghton, 1977. 77-21385. 241p. illus. $8.95.

7- In the fourth book of his history of the United States, Asimov explores the years of massive change in the period that began with the post-Civil War ferment and ended with the close of World War I. As always, he crowds his text with people, dates, and events; as always, his erudition, perception, and periodic irruptions of informality in writing style triumph over the weight of the material. And, in this book, over the handicap of very small print. A chronology and an index are included.

57 **Asimov,** Isaac. *How Did We Find Out About Atoms?* illus. by David Wool. Walker, 1976. 75-3910. 62p. Trade ed. $5.95; Library ed. $5.85 net.

5-7 In an excellent introduction to atomic structure, Asimov discusses the earliest theories about atoms, the diligent search for elements in the 18th century, the discovery by Proust of the law of definite proportions, and Dalton's investigations of the linkage between the two. Subsequent chapters describe atomic weight and distribution in compounds, the problem of isomers and the research in bonding, and—with the discovery of Brownian motion and the invention of the field-emission microscope—the opportunity of seeing atoms and their internal structure. Logically organized and lucidly written, this is a good example both of the science book that is authoritative but not too technical for the layman and of the scientific method. An index is appended.

58 **Asimov,** Isaac. *How Did We Find Out About Comets?* illus. by David Wool. Walker, 1975. 74-78115. 64p. Trade ed. $4.95; Library ed. $4.85 net.

4-6 There's less Asimov wit here than pervades his series of "Words from . . ." or history books, but the writing style is not formal; the clear explanations and authoritative manner are, as always, impressive. After a brief survey of the theories about comets in ancient times, the text covers the building of a body of knowledge by scientists of the past and present, the composition and orbits of comets, and the deviations that have brought new theories held by contemporary astronomers. The diagrams are adequate; an index is appended.

59 **Asimov,** Isaac. *How Did We Find Out About Nuclear Power?* illus. by David Wool. Walker, 1976. 76-12057. 64p. Trade ed. $5.95; Library ed. $5.85 net.

5-7 With his usual clarity, Asimov describes the accrued knowledge that, over a century, made it possible for scientists to perfect techniques of nuclear fusion and fission. The material is chronologically arranged, so that the reader can understand how each new discovery about atomic structure contributed to the body of nuclear knowledge, and can appreciate how discoveries in science may be based on the work of predecessors. The author concludes with a discussion of controlled nuclear fusion that could give new resources to an energy-starved world. Phonetic guides (some seeming unnecessary, like "EL-eh-ment") are provided with the body of the text; an index is included.

60 **Asimov,** Isaac. *Mars, the Red Planet;* diagrams by Guilio Maestro; illus. with photographs. Lothrop, 1977. 77-24151. 222p. Trade ed. $7.95; Library ed. $7.35 net.

7- Since Asimov always packs an incredible amount of information into his books, and since *Mars* includes some advanced and detailed astronomical facts, this is hardly the book for a beginner; however, even a beginner could assimilate much of the material, since it is logically organized and lucidly descriptive. The author incorporates historical material about discoveries and theories of the past, but the major emphasis in the text is on aspects of Mars' motion, distance, size, mass, rotation, and satellite system. These are always seen in relation to similar aspects of other planets, with many charts and diagrams (separately listed for easy access) that synthesize expanded textual information. A glossary and an extensive index are appended.

61 **Avery,** Gillian. *Ellen and the Queen;* illus. by Krystyna Turska. Nelson, 1975. 74-10287. 80p. $4.95.

3-5 A story set in Victorian England is illustrated with charming black and white sketches that have meticulous costume details. Since her mother was lodgekeeper for the Earl, Ellen was convinced that she would see the queen on the occasion of a royal visit; her classmates were irritated by her boasting and dubious about her prospects. Well, Ellen did see Queen Victoria. She saw her by peeping out from under the bed where she and the daughter of the house were hiding, and so she knew the answer to the question that had come up in the schoolyard: did fine ladies have l-e-g-s? Ellen knew, but she couldn't ever tell! In a brief book Avery does a fine job of establishing character and incorporating period atmosphere; the style of writing is keyed to the setting and the dialogue is skillfully appropriate both to the time and to the ages and education of the village children.

62 **Axelbank,** Albert. *Soviet Dissent:* Intellectuals, Jews and Detente. Watts, 1975. 74-13635. 105p. illus. $5.88.

7- A mature and objective assessment of the growing dissidence in the U.S.S.R. focuses on particular well-known individuals like Solzhenitsyn and Nureyev but also discusses official attitudes, both the reflection of the philosophy of control and the expressions of opinion about outside influence. Axelbank also describes the attitudes of politicians in the United States and those special areas of conflict like Soviet Jewry or writers and other creative artists. Timely and thoughtful, a candid and provocative book, skillfully written by an eminent journalist. Extensive chapter notes, a bibliography, and a relative index are appended.

63 **Babbitt,** Natalie. *The Devil's Storybook;* stories and pictures by Natalie Babbitt. Farrar, 1974. 101p. $4.95.

4-6 Ten short stories about a middle-aged, vain, and rather paunchy devil are imaginative, varied, and engagingly illustrated. There's some variation in the solidity of the plots, but the quiet humor and vitality of the writing style are ubiquitous. In one story the Devil meets his match, a cantankerous goat; in another he tries in vain to send two citizens of Hell, former thieves, to steal a heavenly harp, and in one of the more sophisticated tales, "Perfection," he finds a devilish solution for his annoyance with a human being who is always sweet, calm, and understanding.

64 **Babbitt,** Natalie. *Tuck Everlasting*. Farrar, 1975. 75-33306. 139p. $5.95.

4-6 A fantasy written in flowing, natural style is deftly constructed,
* firmly based on a realistic foundation, and strong in dialogue and character establishment, save for one malevolent character. However, if the villain is a bit too villainous, he is the one exaggeration that sets off the other, wholly believable characters. And the Tuck family, who have drunk the waters of immortality, *are* wholly believable. The parents and two sons who, by accident, had found a hidden spring, have hidden their longevity by separation and isolation from others; they have a secret reunion every ten years. When ten-year-old Winnie Foster stumbles across them, the Tucks take her home for a night so that they can explain

their predicament, and they all become fast friends. When a slick evil man who has been tracking down the Tucks takes advantage of the situation and endangers the family, Mrs. Tuck shoots him and is jailed. Then Winnie helps plan the rescue and escape that will take her friends away forever—unless she decides to drink the water herself. A very good read, indeed, with an unexpectedly poignant ending.

65 **Bach,** Alice. *The Most Delicious Camping Trip Ever;* pictures by Steven Kellogg. Harper, 1976. 76-2956. 48p. Trade ed. $5.95; Library ed. $5.79 net.

K-2 Bach and Kellogg are both at their best in a humorous sequel to *The Smartest Bear and His Brother Oliver* (reviewed in the October, 1975 issue); here the two cubs are reluctantly packing for an overnight camping trip with Aunt Bear. Oliver, dubious about subsisting on found food, wants to take provender; Ronald wants to take more scientific equipment than he can carry. Solution: taking food in jars and crocks that can later hold specimens. Aunt Bear surprises them both, and the trip is more pleasant than they had expected. What Bach manages to do is invest the animal characters with strong personalities through their actions and words. The dialogue is witty, the writing style smooth, and the soft brown drawings on cream pages imbued with comic zest and bucolic charm.

66 **Bacon,** Margaret Hope. *Rebellion at Christiana.* Crown, 1974. 216p. $5.95.

7-10 A little-known episode in American history is made vivid in a fine book that is solidly based on research. In 1851 a group of escaped slaves who had settled in Chistiana, Pennsylvania resisted an attempt at capture by a Maryland slave owner, some of his friends, and a deputy United States Marshal. The rebellion was led by one of the slaves, William Parker, who escaped; others (black and white) who were, or were accused of being, involved, were put on trial. The first charge was treason, for this was a test of the compromise legislation, the Fugitive Slave Law of 1850. The verdict was a victory for the antislavery forces. Bacon's account of the rebellion and the trial is fully detailed; parts of the events are told again in excerpts from William Parker's autobiography. A stirring story. A divided bibliography and an index are appended.

67 **Bacon**, Martha. *In the Company of Clowns.* Atlantic-Little, Brown, 1973. 153p. illus. $5.95.

5-8 An adventure tale set in Italy early in the eighteenth century, the story of a twelve-year-old orphan is richly colored, filled with action, and vivid in characterization. Gian-Piero is bored with being a convent scullery boy, and when he is the victim of a fraudulent sale on the part of a strolling player, he has no hesitation in taking off and following him. He meets the Harlequin of the troop, who convinces Gian-Piero that he can find—and be acknowledged by—his unknown father. The way to Venice and the putative parent is filled with the doings of the rapscallion band of players and the uninvited minx, Ginestra. A lively book, witty and romantic in the picaresque vein.

68 **Bailey,** Maurice. *Staying Alive!* By Maurice and Maralyn Bailey; drawings by Peter A. G. Milne; maps by Alan Irving. McKay, 1974. 192p. $6.95.

6- For 117 days a small life-raft and a rubber dinghy were the world of the Baileys, a British couple who had given up their jobs and their home to go yachting. Their yacht had sunk after being struck by a whale, they had had less than an hour to collect stores, and they were sure that, in that part of the Pacific, they would soon be picked up. Seven ships, in the course of their long months' battle to survive, were sighted and did not see them; the eighth, a Korean ship, rescued the gaunt pair who had lived primarily on raw sea turtles and fish. This true and dramatic story is told alternatively by each of the authors and is based on the log they kept. It's a saga of endurance and resourcefulness, candid in discussing the relationship between two people under great tension, dispassionate and detailed in describing the storms, the damage to their craft, the hunger and illness with which they coped.

69 **Baker,** Betty. *At the Center of the World;* Based on Papago and Pima Myths; illus. by Murray Tinkelman. Macmillan, 1973. 53p. $4.95.

4-6 Illustrated with grave, romantic pictures that reflect the mood of a
* long and beautifully written story that incorporates some of the myths and legends of the Pima and Papago, this is a fine source for storytelling as well as reading aloud or reading independently. The myths tell the story of Earth Magician's creation of the earth and its creatures, the animal-gods who came first and helped guide his work, and of Eetoi, son of Earth and Sky, who gave life to the people made of red earth. "And his people settled near him at the center of the world," the story ends. A superb interpretation.

70 **Baker,** Betty. *Dupper;* illus. by Chuck Eckart. Greenwillow, 1976. 75-44155. 147p. Trade ed. $6.95; Library ed. $5.94 net.

4-6 The other prairie dogs think Dupper is rabbit-brained. His mother
* thinks he has a sensitive stomach. Why should a nice prairie dog like Dupper make such a fuss over some scratchings he's made on

a tin can covered with mud? But this becomes Dupper's consuming interest, for he is a creator, an artist who sees pictures in his scratchings and beauty in clouds and shadows. He is also a concerned member of the community, for it is he who makes the long journey to find the distant Great Ants who can drive away a rattlesnake that threatens the prairie dogs' colony. And on his journey (which is successful) Dupper discovers petroglyphs. Scratchings like his own! And so Dupper, the artist, the one who dares to be different, is encouraged and continues his work. This is a rare animal story: it has sensitively drawn characters who speak but who do nothing that a prairie dog, an ant, or an owl would not do; it has moments of humor and moments of poignant tenderness; it has a sturdy plot and is written in polished style.

71 **Baker,** Betty, *Partners;* illus. by Emily Arnold McCully. Greenwillow, 1978. 77-18253. 56p. (Read-alone Books) Trade ed. $5.95; Library ed. $5.71 net.

1-2 Three Native American tales of the Southwest are retold with great simplicity and understated humor, and are illustrated with crayon drawings that capture both qualities. The text, carefully gauged for the beginning independent reader, describes the trickery of Coyote, whose wiles are usually matched by those of his partner, Badger. One tale is about the chore of putting stars in the sky (Badger places them slowly and correctly, Coyote flings them up with abandon), another is about hunting for food (Coyote sneaks off with a prairie dog after tricking Badger, but Badger also gets his fill), and the third—probably the most familiar—is the tale of the two crops: Badger does all the work, Coyote asks for everything above ground and gets no potatoes; when he decides he'll ask for everything below ground with the second crop, Badger plants melons and Coyote gets none.

72 **Baker,** Betty. *Settlers and Strangers; Native Americans of the Desert Southwest and History As They Saw It.* Macmillan, 1977. 77-4925. 88p. illus. $7.95.

4-9
* Most of Baker's excellent historical survey is set in what is now Arizona and New Mexico, beginning with the first wave of travellers who walked, thousands of years ago, across the land bridge from Asia. While there are names and dates, this is primarily a narrative that explores the way people lived, what they believed, how they responded to changes in the environment, to the resources of their land, and to each other. And, sadly, to the Spanish and Yankee troops and missionaries who took their lands. The text is direct and authoritative, dramatic in what it says rather than how it is written; it concludes with a description of some of the problems native Americans face today. Top-notch. An index is appended; a map precedes the text.

73 **Baker,** Betty. *The Spirit is Willing.* Macmillan, 1974. 135p. $4.95.

5-7 There was no feminine liberation movement in Arizona at the end of the nineteenth century, but there might have been with a few more citizens like Carrie. Her friend Portia was properly romantic, as a girl of fourteen ought to be, but not Carrie. She craved excitement—and lacking any, created her own. Nice girls just don't go into saloons, not even to see an Indian mummy, but Carrie did. And while many girls are interested in spiritualism, very few are acknowledged as mediums because they are nice, sensible creatures, the writing style is vivacious, the characters come alive, the details of period and locale are vivid, and the author has created a family and a community that are believable and enjoyable.

74 **Bales,** Carol Ann. *Chinatown Sunday; The Story of Lilliann Der.* Reilly and Lee, 1973. 1973. 32p. illus. $5.95.

3-5 Like Ms. Bales' earlier book, *Kevin Cloud,* this is based on tapes made by a child who here describes her life and her family, and it has fine photographs; the author spent enough time with the Der family so that they were at ease, and the pictures lack the posed, self-conscious look of many photo-documentaries. Since ten-year-old Lilliann Der, who is the protagonist, has no trip to give variety, this has less action than Kevin's description of an urban Chippewa family, but it has the same colloquial flow as Lilliann prattles about her family and how they came to the Chicago area, her friends in a suburban school, her ability as a batter, her favorite holidays, and the customs and traditions that her family observes as Chinese Americans and devout members of the Chinese Christian Union Church.

75 **Bales,** Carol Ann. *Tales of the Elders; A Memory Book of Men and Women Who Came to America as Immigrants, 1900–1930;* written and photographed by Carol Ann Bales. Follett, 1977. 76-19886. 160p. Trade ed. $6.95; Library ed. $6.99 net.

6- A dozen monologues written by Bales and based on interviews give a broad and varied picture of the immigrant experience. In each case the account is prefaced by some background information, and almost all accounts include reminiscences about life in the old country, reasons for emigrating, anecdotes about the voyage, and the struggle to establish oneself in a new country, learn the language, get a job, weather the depression era, and adjust to a new culture. One woman describes being in an internment camp for Japanese Americans, a man recounts the difficulties of establishing a union in the clothing industry. The book is impressive as a picture of an era in our history as well as being a forceful and touching reminder of the diversity of our heritage, the courage of the immigrants, and the image of the United States as a haven for the poor and the oppressed.

76 **Bang,** Molly, comp. *The Buried Moon and Other Stories;* comp. and illus. by Molly Bang. Scribner, 1977. 76-58238. 63p. $5.95.

4-6 Five tales of magic are told in high style, with a good sense of the oral tradition, and in one case, "The Wolf in Disguise," adroitly blending the Grimm Brothers' "The Wolf and the Seven Kids" and a Japanese version of the story. The title story and "William and Jack and the King of England" are English, the first a witchy tale of the moon trapped by evil creatures and the second a sturdy traditional tale of brothers, a mother's blessing, a magical object, and a princess won. The two other stories are from China and India, the latter a stately tale from the *Mahabharata* and the former a brief, rather breezy tale of magic and vengeance. There's nice variety of source and style, and the dramatic black and white illustrations are softened by grey tones, strong in use of light and shadow and in the contrast between delicate details and textural masses.

77 **Bangs,** Edward. *Steven Kellogg's Yankee Doodle;* written by Edward Bangs. Parents Magazine, 1976. 75-19190. 31p. illus. Trade ed. $5.50; Library ed. $4.96 net.

2-4 The words (without chorus repetition) of "Yankee Doodle" are used as a launching pad for illustrations that extend the story with humor and panache, as Kellogg's small patriot exuberantly waves a flag, watches a military skirmish, and heads home frantically after some teasing soldiers have frightened him. The crowded scenes are full of action; although not as precise in the use of line, Kellogg's style here is reminiscent of Peter Spier's: pages filled with small figures, good period details in costume and architecture, and nice bits of humor. Kudos to all, not least for acknowledging the contribution of Bangs, who served in the colonial forces. The flag shown throughout the illustrations is one used in 1777.

78 **Banks,** Lynne Reid. *My Darling Villain.* Harper, 1977. 76-58718. 238p. Trade ed. $6.95; Library ed. $6.79 net.

7-10 Kate is fifteen, her brother Alastair is older; their father, an actor, is disappointed because his son prefers garage work to further education. It is only after Kate has been through some sobering experiences that she understands her brother's feelings about class differences and snobbishness, for she has met Mark, the "villain" of the title. Mark's lower class, he rides a motorbike, he's come into Kate's life as one of a rowdy group that crashed her first party;

he's all the things her parents disapprove of, although they are careful not to say that. They also disapprove of Kate's affection for Leo, who lives next door, although they approve of Leo himself. A nice man, but too old for Kate. And Jewish. Oh, *they* wouldn't mind, but Leo's parents would. Kate is torn between Leo and Mark, but realizes after Mark has had a bike accident, that it is he she cares for. The accident conveniently draws Mike's and Kate's family together, a weak ending for a book that makes some strong points. In fact, the author's perception of the adolescent's problems are the strongest part of the book, although dialogue and characterization are competent. Despite the fact that she uses (several times) phrases like "Jewish blood" or "this Jewish shrug" there is a clear effort to be candid about religious and class prejudice.

79 **Banks,** Lynne Reid. *Sarah and After; Five Women Who Founded a Nation*. Doubleday, 1977. 76-16250. 183p. $6.95.

7- Sarah, Hagar, Rebecca, the sisters Leah and Rachel, and Dinah are the women whose lives are described in a novel based on the Bible but fictionalized enough so that the book is more a continuing story than an adaptation. What Banks does extends the facts of the Old Testament by making her characters, male and female, people of passion and fallibility; Rebecca's motivation for deceiving her husband by sending Jacob to usurp Esau's birthright, or Leah's, in taking her sister's place on Rachel's wedding night, are given validity by the vivid recreation of their personalities and problems.

80 **Barkin,** Carol. *Slapdash Cooking;* by Carol Barkin and Elizabeth James; illus. by Rita Flodén Leydon. Lothrop, 1976. 75-45183. 128p. Trade ed. $5.50; Library ed. $4.81 net.

5- While the authors stress timesaving recipes, the ones they provide are also fairly inexpensive and decidedly healthful; the desserts are all fruit dishes, for example. Instructions are clear, complete, and informal. Each recipe is preceded by information on the number of servings, actual cooking time, and the amount of time required in the kitchen; basic ingredients and equipment are listed, and they are followed by instructions for preparation and cooking. A useful book for beginners as well as for experienced cooks looking for ways to save time.

81 **Barkin,** Carol. *Sometimes I Hate School;* by Carol Barkin and Elizabeth James; photographs by Heinz Kluetmeier. Raintree, 1975. 75-20143. 32p. Trade ed. $6.60; Library ed. $4.95 net.

K-2 Full-color photographs of good quality face each page of text; the amount of print on each page is minimal, with plenty of white space and large type. This is one of a series of books in similar format, books intended to help the young child bridge the gap between the home and school environments. The book accentuates the positive, but the child who is the protagonist doesn't like a substitute teacher and he sulks (the text is in first person) and his friend says *he* hates school. But the new teacher, a man, turns out to be fun (nothing sexist here, he teaches the class to make cranberry sauce) and by the time the popular Ms. Kimball (uh-huh, "Ms.") comes back, everybody—although glad to see her—realizes they're going to miss Mr. Coleman, too.

82 **Bartel,** Pauline C. *Biorhythm.* Watts, 1978. 77-17585. 77p. illus. $4.90.

7- In a survey of the natural rhythms of life forms, Bartel explains the research findings that substantiate the fact that each individual is affected by physical, emotional, and intellectual cycles that occur for specified periods of time. She describes some of the experiments that have established a body of knowledge about biorhythms and some of the results that have been documented in industry when such knowledge has been applied, particularly in the cutting down of accident rates. The text gives instructions for calculating one's own biorhythmic pattern, and suggests ways in which such awareness of critical days can help each of us adjust to increased or decreased abilities. Finally, Bartel makes some predictions about use of biorhythmic patterns in the future, and includes a chapter on "Biorhythm Obituaries of Famous People." A clearly written book about an interesting and fairly new frontier in biology includes a bibliography and an index.

83 **Barth,** Edna, ad. *Cupid and Psyche; A Love Story;* pictures by Ati Forberg. Seabury, 1976. 76-8821. 64p. $6.95.

4-6 Beautifully illustrated with wash drawings (black, white, and rust) that incorporate Grecian motifs and that are handsomely arranged on the pages, this version of the mythical love story (its first written version attributed to Apuleis, the author's note states, and "said to represent the progress of the human soul toward perfection,") is polished and moving. It describes the love of Cupid for the lovely mortal, Psyche, whom he weds, and the vengeful jealousy of his mother Venus; it contains the device that so frequently appears in myth and folktale: the wife who loses her husband if she looks at him; it continues the tale to describe Psyche's despair, Cupid's contrition, and the reunion in which Venus forgives all and Psyche becomes a goddess.

84 **Bartoli,** Jennifer. *Nonna;* illus. by Joan Drescher. Harvey House, 1975. 74-25423. 43p. $4.79.

K-3 There's little story line here, but the text gives a warm, gentle picture of the closeness of a large Italian-American family, and of the grandparent's death as seen from a child's viewpoint. Nonna had lived nearby, her children and grandchildren had gathered at her home every Saturday, and the grandson who tells the story describes how much Nonna is missed, how empty her house seems. Although there have been many recent books about losing a beloved grandparent, this is the first that very calmly and naturally discusses burial and the disposal of property. Nothing macabre here, the emphasis being on how loved Nonna was and how much the memories of her are treasured. Primarily for reading aloud, the book may also be enjoyed by independent readers.

85 **Baskin,** Leonard, illus. *Hosie's Alphabet;* words by Hosea, Tobias and Lisa Baskin. Viking, 1972. 52p. $4.95.

4-6 yrs. Not since Milton Glaser's illustrations for Conrad Aiken's *Cats and Bats and Things with Wings* has there been such a display of virtuosity in a picture book. Leonard Baskin's range of techniques is as impressive as his pictures are dazzling. Children may not appreciate the humor in typography, but they should be enchanted by the pictures; some of the phrases ("Cadaver-haunted vulture," "Omnivorous swarming locust") may be sophisticated and some of the creatures unfamiliar, but the book should pull its readers up to its level, and any adult art lover will be enthralled.

86 **Bason,** Lillian. *Those Foolish Molboes!* illus. by Margot Tomes. Coward, 1977. 76-42459. 47p. $4.99.

2-4 Mols, a peninsula in Denmark, has been a butt of noodlehead stories for over two centuries. Like the fools of Chelm, the Molboes are blandly and cheerfully stupid: they hide their precious churchbell in the sea so the enemy (in a faraway war) won't get it, and they mark the spot by putting an "X" on the side of the rowboat. A second story is familiar in the folklore of many countries: the dolts who get confused when counting because each forgets to count himself. In the third tale, the Molboes buy a small boat and confidently wait for it to grow big like its mother. The illustrations, alternately in color and in black and white, show the slightly scruffy peasant figures with comic flair; Tomes uses deft touches to suggest awkwardness or bucolic origin: red noses, large hands, sabots. The tales are simply told, perhaps over-explained, but the humor should appeal equally to young readers or to a read-aloud audience.

87 **Bate,** Lucy. *Little Rabbit's Loose Tooth;* illus. by Diane De Groat. Crown, 1975. 75-6833. 27p. $5.95.

3-5 yrs. A very tactful handling of the question of tooth fairies adds to the benign charm of this picture book about a small rabbit with understanding parents. Little Rabbit tries to use her loose tooth as an excuse for avoiding carrots and eating conveniently soft strawberries. It doesn't work. When the tooth does come out, it's in a spoonful of chocolate ice cream. "What should I do with it?" she asks; her mother says, "You should take it out of your chocolate ice cream." Then there's the under-the-pillow bit. Little Rabbit says she does not believe in tooth fairies, but she wavers and, after much discussion, she asks her mother to remind the tooth fairy about the tooth under the pillow. Then she has second thoughts. Just in case there isn't a tooth fairy will Mommy sneak in and look? And leave a present if there isn't one? Mommy will. "You don't have to tell me," says Little Rabbit, "You could just sneak." The illustrations are pleasantly detailed (Little Rabbit wears pants but has a rakish bow over her ear) and the writing has a bland, understated humor.

88 **Bates,** Daisy, comp. *Tales Told to Kabbarli;* collected by Daisy Bates; retold by Barbara Ker Wilson; illus. by Harold Thomas. Crown, 1972. 101p. $4.95.

5- When Daisy Bates, an Irishwoman who devoted many years of her life in Australia to recording Aboriginal lore, died in 1951, her notes were unpublished. Barbara Ker Wilson's retelling of the tales of the Dreamtime, the period when men first inhabited the earth, has a sturdy directness; there is nothing interposed between the story and the reader. The tales reflect the Aboriginal culture and its mores and traditions, and give both legends and history of the people to whom Daisy Bates was Kabbarli, the white grandmother. The illustrations are starkly effective in dramatic black and white.

89 **Batterberry,** Ariane (Ruskin). *The Pantheon Story of American Art for Young People;* by Ariane and Michael Batterberry. Pantheon Books, 1976. 75-22249. 159p. illus. $14.95.

6- The Batterberrys begin with "The Art of the North American Indian" and consider the representative work of such regions as the southwest or the plains, then examine the art of white settlers of different nationalities, and continue chronologically throughout the volume. A large book, profusely illustrated, this is limited in accessibility to the contents by the lack of an index; it occasionally includes a conjectural statement such as, "His painting . . . must have been a perfect likeness . . ." and it gives short shrift to some subjects, such as 20th century architecture, which is covered in two pages. Nevertheless, the book is impressive: the authors are knowledgeable, they write smoothly, and they incorporate into their discussion not only artistic commentary but also comments on cultural matrixes and cross-influences in art history.

90 **Batterberry,** Ariane (Ruskin). *Pantheon Story of Art for Young People;* Rev. ed.; Pantheon Books, 1975. 74-24717. 159p. illus. $12.95.

5- A revised edition of the 1964 title which was published under the name of Ruskin, this oversize book is profusedly illustrated with reproductions of excellent quality, many in full color. The writing style is simple and informal, the information given with authoritative knowledge; the author discusses details of pictures as well as giving general facts about artists, trends in art history, and the cultural matrices out of which artists or trends emerged. The revision brings the book up to date, although there is comparatively little material on today's artists; the chapter on "Art in America" is dissappointingly brief, but the book as a whole gives a broad view of art history and communicates the author's pleasure in, and appreciation of, her subject. There is no index.

91 **Batterberry,** Michael, ad. *Primitive Art;* ad. by Michael Batterberry and Ariane Ruskin. McGraw-Hill, 1973. 191p. illus. $9.95.

7- Stunning in every way, this newest in the publisher's "Discovering Art" series is illustrated with a lavish array of color photographs of art objects and architectural splendors, well-placed and captioned. The text, which covers the primitive art of Africa, Australia and Oceania, Mexico, Peru, Eskimos, and the North American Indian, is written in a graceful style and with firm authority; division of material is by tribes, and the authors describe art objects both as creative works and as objects related to their cultures, giving historical and sociological background that makes the discussion more meaningful. This would be worth having for the beauty of the photographs alone, or for the text alone; together they enhance and expand each other. A divided list of the illustrations, giving locations, and an index are appended.

92 **Bauer,** Marion Dane. *Foster Child.* Seabury, 1977. 76-54291. 192p. $6.95.

5-7 Great-grandmother, who had raised twelve-year-old Renny (Lorraine) was in the hospital, and Renny was put into a foster home run by the Becks, where among the other children was a small girl whose mother was emotionally disturbed, Karen. Mrs. Beck was an easy-going slattern who deferred completely to her husband, a handsome man, sternly pious. Renny was frightened and guilty after an episode in which Mr. Beck—ostensibly comforting her during an illness—caressed her. Frightened of what might happen next, guilty because she enjoyed his petting, and worried because of what might happen to little Karen, Renny ran home, taking Karen with her. But an aunt had cleared the house of furniture and put Great-grandmother in a nursing home. The book ends on a hopeful note, since Karen's mother, who has improved, comes home and takes Renny in. Bauer's characterization is remarkable in vividness and depth; the other children in the Beck home are distinctively drawn. The story has pace, candor, and pathos that never becomes maudlin, and the writing style and dialogue are skilled.

93 **Bawden,** Nina. *Carrie's War.* Lippincott, 1973. 158p. $4.94.

4-6 A story of two children, evacuated from London during the Blitz and sent to a small Welsh town, is told with consummate skill and deft characterization. Twelve-year-old Carrie and her younger brother were lodged with dour Mr. Evans and his nervous, timid sister. Carrie despised Mr. Evans and pitied Miss Evans, while young Nick accepted their peculiarities with calm resilience. Both children found their real happiness in visiting the farm where Mr. Evans' invalid sister lived, a place run by a warm, compassionate woman; Carrie especially enjoyed it because another London child, Albert, was quartered there and Albert (a wonderfully rational and intelligent character) became her special friend. With the death of the invalid and Mr. Evans' inheritance, the happy household was broken up. Not until she visited, years later, with her own children, did Carrie learn all the intricacies of that unhappy time. The story is taut in construction, notable for its cast, compassionate in its treatment of the harsh Mr. Evans as it is of the gentle retarded man who lived at the farm.

94 **Bawden,** Nina. *Devil by the Sea.* Lippincott, 1976. 76-13177. 228p. $6.95.

5-6 Hilary is nine, and when she and her younger brother see the old man who behaves so strangely go off with another child, Poppet, they don't later connect the incident with the fact that Poppet is found murdered. Pegerine, the younger brother, insists that the old man is the devil; Hilary—who has the reputation of a mendacious troublemaker—is ignored when she tries to talk about the man and then is punished for lying. She is being watched. Watched and waited for. And eventually she is caught by the devil—and saved by the police. The characterization is superb, from the hostile, unhappy Hilary to such minor characters as her eccentric old aunt or her bitter yet romantic older half-sister; the plot is beautifully structured, with fine timing and well-sustained suspense. The book was first published in England in 1958 as an adult novel.

95 **Bawden,** Nina. *The Peppermint Pig.* Lippincott, 1975. 189p. $5.95.

4-6 Nine-year-old Poll is the youngest of the four children who move from London to a Norfolk village in an absorbing turn of the century story. Father has gone to America, having taken the blame for a theft he did not commit, a sacrifice made to protect his employer from the bitter knowledge that his only son had robbed him. Mother and the children go to live with relatives, Mother resuming her work as a dressmaker. There is no major plot line to the story of Poll's year, but none is needed when the author is as skilled as Nina Bawden: her characters come alive, the dialogue has a natural spontaneity, and the milestones in the family's year are described with vitality and polish: Poll's bout of scarlet fever, Theo's feud with a local boy, Mother's efforts to eke out a living, and above all the short life of Johnnie, the peppermint pig, the runt of the litter who became a beloved pet.

96 **Bawden,** Nina. *Rebel on a Rock.* Lippincott, 1978. 77-10686. 158p. $7.95.

5-8 Jo is one of four children who go with their mother and stepfather to the imaginary land of Ithaca, a country ruled by a dictator. Jo is puzzled by her stepfather's involvement in the underground movement: he seems to be sympathetic, yet he praises the accomplishments of the régime. Jo herself becomes involved when she meets the son of a banished leader and is implicated in his arrest, to her sorrow. Bawden creates the rocky citadel of an Ithacan village most vividly, her well-structured plot has suspense, and her characterization is excellent, save for the rebel's son, who is so ingenuously conceited as to be not quite believable. Among the book's bonuses are the casual treatment of the two younger children, who are black and adopted; the affection between Jo and her stepfather; and the intricate shifts in relations among the several members of Jo's family.

97 **Bayley,** Nicola, illus. *One Old Oxford Ox.* Atheneum, 1977. 77-77866. 24p. $6.95.

K-2 In a counting book that goes from 1-12, Bayley's framed, lushly intricate, and imaginative pictures face phrases that are based on the first letter of each spelled digit: "o" for one, "t" for two and three, "f" for four and five, et cetera. It will be the unusual child who can appreciate or relate to "Eight eminent Englishmen eagerly examining Europe" or "Twelve typographical topographers typically translating types," despite the appeal of the animal characters, but any child can enjoy the beauty of the illustrations.

98 **Baylor,** Byrd, comp. *And It Is Still That Way; Legends Told by Arizona Indian Children.* Scribner, 1976. 76-42242. 85p. illus. $6.95.

2-4 Stories from several Native American tribes are grouped under the headings "Why Animals Are That Way," "Why Our World Is Like

It Is," "Great Troubles and Great Heroes," "People Can Turn Into Anything," "Brother Coyote," and "There is Magic All Around Us." The stories were told the compiler by children in Arizona, and their names and tribes are provided. All the stories are simply told, some with the abrupt directness of a young child, others with a true sense of the storyteller's cadence, and together they make a good cross-section of folktale types.

99 **Baylor,** Byrd. *The Desert Is Theirs;* illus. by Peter Parnall. Scribner, 1975. 74-24417. 27p. $6.95.

2-4 Peter Parnall's first book in full color may draw mixed reactions from his admirers; the composition and line of his work are no less spare, and the colors are clean hues used with restraint, but they do focus attention on themselves. The text is, like that of other Baylor books, a prose poem of lyric simplicity; it is infrequently marred slightly by attributions of purposiveness that add a note of anthropomorphism (". . . birds . . . sing . . . because they're where they want to be . . ." or, "The Papagos begin their ceremonies to pull down the rain. Every plant joins in.") but the whole is a graceful, stately tribute to the "strong brown Desert People" whose gentle courtesy toward the other life-forms of the desert, whose love and understanding for the land they occupy, and whose nature myths contribute to a harmonious way of life.

100 **Baylor,** Byrd. *Hawk, I'm Your Brother;* illus. by Peter Parnall. Scribner, 1976. 75-39296. 44p. $5.95.

3-5 All that Rudy had ever wanted was to fly; although he had been told many times that people cannot fly, he dreamed and hoped. Perhaps, he thought, if he were brother to a hawk, he might learn. So he stole from its cliffside nest a young hawk and kept it on a string. The bird grew tame, but always it watched the sky and strained against its bond. Then the boy knew he must let the bird go, and—watching it soar in the wind, hearing its wild cry—the boy felt he had captured the joy of flight. And his people knew that there was something different about him. In the poetic simplicity of the writing, Baylor echoes the quietness of the desert and she captures the essence of the desert people's affinity for natural things. Both are reflected in Parnall's spacious illustrations, as clean and poetic as is the writing.

101 **Baylor,** Byrd. *The Other Way to Listen;* illus. by Peter Parnall. Scribner, 1978. 78-23430. 27p. $7.95.

3-5 In the spare and elegant veinings of his spacious black and white drawings, Parnall uses yellow for an effective contrast. The words are spoken by a child, who remembers his conversations with the old man who could hear the cactus flowers blooming or the rock murmuring to the lizard perching on it. There was no way, he said, to teach such listening, but one must feel that each object or creature is important, and one must be silent and patient. The child tried and tried to no avail, and then one morning, singing to the hills, heard the hills sing too. And, as the old man had said, it wasn't surprising at all, but seemed the most natural thing in the world. The lyric tone, the stately pace, and the quiet mood of the book will not appeal to every reader, but it may well enchant the nature-lovers among them.

102 **Baylor,** Byrd. *They Put on Masks;* illus. by Jerry Ingram. Scribner, 1974. 48p. $5.95.

3-5 A poetic text describes the masks used by some Indian tribes, chiefly those of the Southwest, in their ceremonial rites and dances, giving details about the way the masks are made as well as about how they are used. The illustrations are effective and interesting although they do not make the impact of the Bahti pictures that illustrated earlier Baylor books. The text incorporates some of the beautiful song poetry that is used by the masked dancers, but it does more than that; it explains how the masks evoke the spirits of those they portray, how wearing a mask invests the person with the powers of the god or the creature he has become.

103 **Baylor,** Byrd. *The Way to Start a Day;* illus. by Peter Parnall. Scribner, 1978. 78-113. 27p. $7.95.

3-5 While the format is that of a picture book, the concepts in the poetic text of this handsome volume are more appropriate for independent readers who can grasp the historic and ritual values of Baylor's thoughts. The way to start a new day is to go outdoors and face the sun, making it welcome for the new day by your song or gift or blessing, as the cavemen did, and the Peruvians who chanted at dawn in their sun temples, and the people of Egypt and Africa and China. And, she concludes, if you greet the sun "you'll be one more person in one more place at one more time in the world" who is saying hello to the sun and letting it know you are there; that's the way to start a new day. Parnall's geometric composition, his brilliant colors, and his precise and elegant use of line reflect the strength and lyricism of the writing.

104 **Beatty,** John. *Master Rosalind;* by John and Patricia Beatty. Morrow, 1974. 221p. Trade ed. $5.95; Library ed. $5.11 net.

7-9 Living alone with her grandfather, Rosalind often found it useful to dress as a boy when she was away from home, for this was Elizabethan England, and rogues were often on the highways. Taken forcibly to London by one of them, Rosalind got away and joined the players' company of the Globe theater, where—since no women were then permitted on stage—she played girls' parts as other "boys" did. A wicked cousin was searching for her all the while, knowing that she stood between him and a title. Rosalind, who didn't know it, feared the mysterious man who had been asking about her. Eventually the matter is cleared by the intervention of Sir Robert Cecil and some of the rogues Rosalind had met when she first came to London; the cousin is punished and Lady Rosalind is pardoned by the Queen. Although many real characters appear (Shakespeare, Burbage, Cecil, Essex, and Elizabeth) this is not concerned (except peripherally) with matters of great historical import, but it gives an interesting picture of the theatrical world, the criminal element, and court circles in the period. Characterization is shallow and occasionally stereotyped, but the plot is vigorous and the protagonist lively and courageous.

105 **Beatty,** John. *Who Comes to King's Mountain?* by John and Patricia Beatty. Morrow, 1975. 75-11997. 287p. Trade ed. $5.95; Library ed. $5.11 net.

6-9 This is one of the best of the many stories that celebrate the Bicentennial, a historical novel that is based on thorough research and that explores a facet of the American Revolution that is comparatively little known: the divided loyalties of Scottish southerners. The time is 1780, the place South Carolina, the protagonist fourteen-year-old Alec MacLeod. Like his father, Alec is loyal to King George, although he does not hate his maternal grandfather (as his father does) for his devotion to Prince Charles, whom he considers the rightful king. Alec burns to serve his idol, Jamie Gilchrist—but he sees Jamie's cruelty, and that of Tarleton and Sumter, and he changes, offering his services to the patriot Francis Marion, the Swamp Fox. There is no glorification of war here, nor do the authors depict the men and women on either side as all good or all bad. The events are exciting, the fiction and history nicely meshed. The Beattys do a good job of handling language (with one exception) since many of the Scottish settlers spoke Gaelic rather than English.

106 **Beatty,** Patricia. *The Bad Bell of San Salvador.* Morrow, 1973. 253p. Trade ed. $5.95; Library ed. $5.11 net.

5-8 He answered to the name of "Jacinto," but the boy promised himself that some day he would escape his Mexican captors, rejoin his tribe, and be known by his true Comanche name, Spotted Wild Horse. Thirteen, rebellious, refusing to accept the Catholic religion of his *patrón,* Jacinto was sent away to California with a band of settlers; there he resolved to steal a horse and get back to his own people. Again unruly, the boy was punished by being sent to live with and serve the Swiss priest who served the small, new community; while he helped cast the bell for the church, Jacinto never made concessions about his religious convictions and was the more appreciative of the priest's understanding because he was almost an outcast in the village. The story has good pace, lively incidents, and credible characters, but its major strength is the vigorous re-creation of the 1840's in California, a period in which the wealthy patrons ruled large tracts of land in almost feudal style, and converted Indians helped protect the lands and herds against local marauding Indian tribes.

107 **Beatty,** Patricia. *By Crumbs, It's Mine!* frontispiece by Loring Eutemy. Morrow, 1976. 75-31574. 254p. Trade ed. $6.95; Library ed. $5.81 net.

6-8 In a story set in the Arizona Territory in 1882, fourteen-year-old Damaris Boyd is given a knock-down hotel by a man whose conscience troubles him because he has taken the family's money from Mr. Boyd in a poker game. So Damaris, with her mother's help and that of a series of friends and relatives, becomes a hotel-keeper. Papa has gone off to join a gold rush, and Damaris finally decides that the family can't get along without him and, with two friends as trail companions, she goes off to find him. Although some of the characters seem overdrawn, they are depicted with humor; Damaris' achievements are believable, the story line is fresh, and the details of period and locale are colorful. Sources explored in the author's research are cited in an appendix.

108 **Beatty,** Patricia. *How Many Miles to Sundown.* Morrow, 1974. 222p. Trade ed. $5.95; Library ed. $5.11 net.

5-7 A companion volume to *A Long Way to Whiskey Creek* (reviewed in the June, 1971 issue) in which Nate Graber, a Yankee boy, helped Texan Parker Quiney bring his brother's body home for burial. There's less anti-Yankee feeling in this second story of the Southwest in the 1880's but just as much rich language and humor. This time it's Nate who gets help; Parker is ill, but his thirteen-year-old sister Beeler (Beulah Land Quiney) and her younger brother feel obliged to return the favor done their family, they say. Actually, Beeler (a tough, bright, bossy girl of thirteen who wears pants and totes a gun) is delighted by the chance to get away from home. The story follows their trip through Texas, New Mexico, and the Arizona Territory as the three hunt for Sundown, the last place Nate's father had mentioned. When they get there after numerous adventures, including an encounter with Billy the Kid, a roving circus troupe, Apaches, and diverse salty characters, they find that Sundown is a saloon. The story line is adequate, but it's eclipsed by the period language, the humor, and the vitality of Beeler Quiney.

109 **Beisner,** Monika. *Fantastic Toys*. Follett, 1974. 19p. illus. Trade ed. $4.95; Library ed. $4.98 net.

K-3 Marvelously mad and intricate ideas for toys are described in a text that has the aura of a low-keyed sales catalog, and the tone is a good foil for the extravagance of the concepts and the illustrations. Some of the toys: a child-size set of alphabet letters, to be matched by each player with a small set of letters; an inflatable flower on which one can climb; a huge balloon for painting large pictures on (after which you can let the air out and send the balloon to an aunt who has never seen a zoo); or a row of huge dolls with a wind-up mechanism that operates a multiple jump-rope for several children. Fun!

110 **Bellairs,** John. *The Figure in the Shadows;* drawings by Mercer Mayer. Dial, 1975. 74-2885. 155p. Trade ed. $5.95; Library ed. $5.47 net.

5-7 A sequel to *The House with a Clock in its Walls* (reviewed in the November, 1973 issue) has the same cast: orphaned Lewis, a timid boy who has found a very happy home with his uncle; Uncle Jonathan and his neighbor Mrs. Zimmerman, both benevolent sorcerers; and Lewis' friend Rose Rita, who has all the nerve Lewis wishes he had. Lewis hopes the old coin he's found in a trunk is an amulet, but it doesn't seem to help him with the class bully. It is magical, however, and it is evil; using it, Lewis evokes the shadowed figure of a ghost and puts himself in great danger. Again here, as in the earlier book, Bellairs combines effectively an aura of brooding suspense and the down-to-earth characters of Mrs. Zimmerman and Jonathan, whose attitude toward magic is practical. Smoothly contrapuntal, often amusing, and adroitly constructed and paced.

111 **Belting,** Natalia Maree. *Our Fathers Had Powerful Songs;* illus. by Laszlo Kubinyi. Dutton, 1974. 27p. $4.95.

4-7 Selected and translated into English, poems from one Canadian Indian and several American Indian tribes are illustrated by softly drawn, imaginative pictures in black and white. Like other Indian poetry, these reflect a closeness to and reverence for nature and a quiet joy in the dignity of men and the power of the gods. The collection comprises nine poems, one each from the Apache, Cochiti, Diegueno, Kwakiutl, Luiseno, Mandan, Navaho, Papago, and Wintu cultures.

112 **Belting,** Natalia Maree. *Whirlwind is a Ghost Dancing;* illus. by Leo and Diane Dillon. Dutton, 1974. 28p. $7.50.

4- A collection of poems of North American Indians is illustrated with striking stylized paintings. Using acrylics and pastels, the

Dillons created muted, glowing colors and have incorporated tribal motifs in their pictures, echoing the dignity, beauty, and reverence of the poems. Sources and locations are ascribed to each selection (i.e. "Yana, California," or "Shoshoni, Nevada and Utah") and the poems are primarily related to myths of creation or explanations of natural phenomena, some very brief, as in "Icicles are the walking sticks of the winter winds," and others substantial narrative poems.

113 **Benchley,** Nathaniel. *Beyond the Mists.* Harper, 1975. 75-9389. 152p. Trade ed. $5.50; Library ed. $5.11.

6-9 Imaginative, exciting, convincing in evocation of a period, historically supportive, this is an adventure story told by an eleventh-century Norseman who goes a-Viking to the New World. Gunnar Egilsen begins with a reader-catching, "I hear they've finally conquered England," and reminisces about his first raid at the age of seventeen, other voyages, and then his participation in the explorations of Leif Eriksson. Woven through the tale are Gunnar's love story, the creeds and superstitions of the time, and several strong characterizations of companions of the voyages. Period details and historical background are smoothly integrated in a robust tale.

114 **Benchley,** Nathaniel. *Bright Candles; A Novel of the Danish Resistance.* Harper, 1974. 256p. Trade ed. $5.50; Library ed. $5.70 net.

7-12 Jens Hansen looks back to the time when he was sixteen, an adolescent schoolboy who's just become seriously interested in a girl and who is disturbed by the fact that his father seems to accept so placidly the German occupation that has just begun. In describing his own participation in the resistance movement, Jens gives a vivid picture of the dogged, quiet heroism of the Danes, the devious sabotage they practiced, the desperate effort to save Danish Jews, and the day-to-day encounter with the occupying forces. In the depiction of Jens' father, Benchley shows a segment of the Danish people seldom included in stories of World War II: the moderate men, slow to anger, who sincerely believed in accepting German rule—until some excess precipitated their active participation in the struggle. The first-person format makes the story both credible and immediate. Style, dialogue, characterization, and setting are treated with consummate skill.

115 **Benchley,** Nathaniel. *George the Drummer Boy;* pictures by Don Bolognese. Harper, 1977. 76-18398. 61p. (I Can Read Books). Trade ed. $4.95; Library ed. $4.79 net.

1-2 The start of the American Revolution is seen from the viewpoint of a young British soldier in a book for beginning independent readers. George, a drummer boy, is baffled by the stealthy night departure for the town of Concord. Waylaid by a band of Minutemen at Lexington, the British are drawn into the first battle. George is not happy; "I knew that was a bad idea. Look what they started." He does no fighting, and all he wants is to get safely back to Boston. While the story has one remark ("Two hundred years ago, Boston belonged to England,") that may need clarification, it should appeal to readers who have heard or read tales of the Lexington-Concord fray from the American viewpoint, since it has such aspects as George and his friend wondering if the lights they saw in the spire of the Old North Church might not have been a signal. Much of the story is told through dialogue, which adds a note of humor, and of course the book has plenty of the action young readers enjoy.

116 **Benchley,** Nathaniel. *Kilroy and the Gull;* pictures by John Schoenherr. Harper, 1977. 76-24309. 118p. Trade ed. $4.95; Library ed. $4.79 net.

5-7 Kilroy, a young killer whale, is caught and brought to a Marineland aquarium, where he watches a dolphin do tricks in a training program. Bored and restless, irritated by the hostility of the dolphin, missing his friend Morris the seagull, Kilroy decides he can do any trick the dolphin can do. He's a bit baffled by the humans, since all his efforts to communicate with them fail, although they are apparently intelligent beings. Kilroy's pleased when Morris shows up and, with the seagull's help, he tricks the humans into letting him go back to sea. There Kilroy discovers that it isn't as easy to operate alone as it was while he was a member of a pod. The book ends with a marvelous chapter in which a group of scientists jeers at one of their number who is convinced the whales are trying to establish communication—and then they are all convinced, capering madly as the whales leap in formation. "Gulls," Morris says enviously, "could never get people to do tricks like that." There is humor in the story, but the whales' behavior is based on research, even the whale-seagull friendship, and the book has many provocative ideas that are deftly blended with the brisk narrative.

117 **Benchley,** Nathaniel. *A Necessary End; A Novel of World War II.* Harper, 1976. 75-37105. 193p. Trade ed. $6.95; Library ed. $6.79 net.

7- This is the story of Ralph Bowers, told in diary form, describing his service on a subchaser, both in training and in a Pacific combat zone, during the last months of World War II. It's completely convincing, a vigorous and perceptive account of the homesickness, the fear, the camaraderie, the clowning as well as the tension among crew members and officers. It's not a message book, not a glorification of war or a bitter indictment. The characters are vibrantly real, the pace brisk; since Ralph has aspirations as a writer, the long, detailed entries are logical.

118 **Benchley,** Nathaniel. *Snorri and the Strangers;* pictures by Don Bolognese. Harper, 1976. 76-3290. 63p. (I Can Read Books) Trade ed. $3.95; Library ed. $3.79 net.

1-2 Snorri, born in America over a thousand years ago, lived in a small community of descendants of the Norwegians who had come to Iceland, then to Greenland, then south to the lonely, unknown continent. The story describes the meeting with native Americans who, at first friendly, became hostile and were repelled by one doughty woman when the men of the community were frightened off. Simply told from Snorri's viewpoint, illustrated with exuberantly scrawly drawings, the tale, based on fact, has enough action to interest beginning independent readers; it has some humor, and it has an unusual setting that can help extend young children's ideas of long-ago history.

119 **Bendick,** Jeanne. *The Consumer's Catalog of Economy & Ecology;* by Jeanne and Robert Bendick; illus. by Karen Watson. McGraw-Hill, 1974. 160p. Trade ed. $7.95; Paper ed. $4.95.

7- Diagrams and trendy collage pictures illustrate a loosely organized book of tips about wise purchases, with a textual emphasis on preservation of a balanced ecology and of energy resources. The book does not attempt to cover all subjects; as the preface explains, housing, cars, and insurance are topics too complicated and large to cover, but it gives advice on food, clothing, furniture, recreational equipment, kitchen appliances, et cetera. Included also are general tips on watching labels, contracts, and advertisements, sales, and so on. The text is written in brief paragraphs with headings in heavy type, and the writing style is breezy and informal. A list of sources of information and a relative index are appended.

120 **Bendick,** Jeanne. *How Animals Behave.* Parents Magazine, 1976. 75-11613. 64p. illus. $4.96.

2-4 This is not the usual birds migrate—bears hibernate—bees swarm book but a discussion of behavior as a series of responses, individual or group, to sensory stimuli, or to the words or acts of others. Bendick points out that for some animals behavior is based on experience or reasoning, while all animals respond in some degree because of instinct. She stresses the facts that all animal forms, including human beings, have differing potentials, explaining that people display the most sophisticated behavior, and that animals, acting either through instinct, for self-preservation, or in reaction to the behavior of others, are not being "wise" or "good" or "mean," but are behaving in a manner that is consonant with their species' patterns. Lucid, sensible, and objective, this is a good introduction to a complex subject.

121 **Bendick,** Jeanne. *How Heredity Works; Why Living Things Are As They Are.* Parents Magazine, 1975. 74-4472. 64p. illus. $4.59.

2-4 Good integration of text and illustrations helps in a clear presentation of the topic. Bendick divides the text into short topics, reiterates, asks open-ended questions (these tend to be repetitive) and provides some good bases for discussion. Without going into the intricacies of DNA and RNA, she explains that genes within cells for all species of living things contain instructions, that each species reproduces its kind, that inherited traits don't always show up in the next generation (again, no exploration of the complexities of recessive and dominant genes) and that environment can influence individuals. Lucid and crisp, a good introduction. And index is appended.

122 **Bendick,** Jeanne. *The Mystery of the Loch Ness Monster.* McGraw-Hill, 1976. 76-18083. 128p. illus. Trade ed. $5.95; Library ed. $5.72 net.

6-8 Less personal than the Cookes' *The Great Monster Hunt,* and more objective, this is also less formal in writing style. Bendick provides the same information about early sightings, the stirring of wide belief and of scientific investigations that began in the 1930's, and the apparent corroboration by computer-sharpened photographs, experiments with sonar and echo-sounding equipment, and underwater television cameras of *some* kind of creature living in the cold waters of the loch. She concludes with a run-down of the kinds of creatures that may have been observed, and the discrepant evidence or conflict in theory about each. A bibliography and an index are appended.

123 **Berger,** Melvin. *Jigsaw Continents;* illus. by Bob Totten. Coward, 1978. 77-6730. 46p. $4.97.

3-5 In a continuous text, amply illustrated with drawings that show the relations between drifting continental plates and such disasters as earthquakes or volcanic eruption, Berger explains the theory of plate tectonics. Text and illustrations show clearly how the present land masses could have fitted together, and include some of the clues scientists have to corroborate the theory that the earth originally had one giant land mass. The explanation isn't comprehensive, and the material might have been better organized, but the book fills a real need; while there have been some excellent books for older readers, there has been little available on continental drift for the middle grades. A brief index is appended.

124 **Berger,** Melvin. *The New Water Book;* illus. by Leonard Kessler. T. Y. Crowell, 1973. 111p. $4.50.

4-6 A treatment of the subject that is comprehensive in scope, simple in style, lucid in explanation, and given added interest by the inclusion throughout the text of home demonstrations, helpfully illustrated and clearly outlined. The text discusses the composition of water, its three states (liquid, solid, and gas), and some of the unusual properties of water; it describes the need for water in plants, human beings, and other animal life; it surveys water in agriculture and industry, describes the water cycle, and discusses the water supply and water pollution. A reading list and a relative index are appended.

125 **Berger,** Melvin. *Oceanography Lab.* Day, 1973. 126p. illus. $5.95.

4-6 A competent survey of the work of oceanographers, in the publisher's "Scientists at Work" series, presents information in a simply written text organized in brief chapters. The book describes an oceanographic laboratory, preparations for a sea voyage, work in the laboratory, and some of the many projects on which oceanographers work. The text makes it clear that there are many specialties, many scientists from other disciplines who are concerned with marine problems or phenomena. A good introduction for the middle grades, dignified enough in tone to be used by the slow older reader. A brief bibliography and an index are appended.

126 **Berger,** Melvin. *Time After Time;* illus. by Richard Cuffari. Coward, 1975. 74-83012. 45p. $4.69.

2-4 There have been many books written for children on the subject of time, and this is one of the best. Simply and clearly, Berger discusses a broad range of subjects: the inner time sense of living things, the natural phenomena that bring night and day and the four seasons of the year, various time-measuring devices, and how to make a shadow-stick clock; he concludes by bringing up some intriguing open-ended questions about time. Only once does the text lapse from natural happenings to one that is created by human beings (in discussing seasonal phenomena, Berger includes "Hay is cut and stored,") but the rest of the continuous text is consistent and coherent. Nicely illustrated, too.

127 **Bernheim,** Marc. *In Africa;* by Marc and Evelyne Bernheim. Atheneum, 1973. 90p. illus. $5.50.

K-3 A photo-documentary surveys the variety of life-styles in Africa and introduces to young children the geographic contrasts and the beauty of the continent. The text is continuous, but the book has five sections that portray ways of life; "If you live in the desert," one begins, and shows the nomad life, and the others survey the patterns of a coastal village, a city, a savannah, and a forest community. The pictures are of good quality and well-chosen, the text is brief and consists primarily of statements that expand the information given by the photographs. Very simple, very effective.

128 **Bernstein,** Joanne E. *When People Die;* by Joanne E. Bernstein and Stephen V. Gullo; photographs by Rosmarie Hausherr. Dutton, 1977. 76-23099. 36p. $6.95.

K-3 Written by a specialist in early childhood education and a psychologist, illustrated by well-chosen photographs, and addressed directly to children, this is a discussion of death that is sensible, fairly comprehensive, and tender without being somber or mawkish. Intended to answer most of the questions children ask, it describes the cycle of life, burial customs, religious beliefs about afterlife (making it clear, as few books do when written for younger children, that there is variation within religious groups and that some people may belong to such groups but not share religious convictions), normal life span versus early death by accidents or severe illness, and reactions to bereavement. The book ends on an encouraging note, assuring the reader that time does heal, commenting on how one can enjoy pleasant memories or treasure family resemblances and taste. The text ends, as it begins, with "There is a time to be born, a time to live, and a time to die." Books about death, old age, and grief have been proliferating in recent years; this is one of the best.

129 **Bernstein,** Margery, ad. *The First Morning; An African Myth;* retold by Margery Bernstein and Janet Kobrin; illus. by Enid Warner Romanek. Scribner, 1976. 75-27705. 45p. $5.95.

2-3 A simplified retelling of an African myth about natural phenomena explains how light came to the world. A fly, mouse, a spider make their way to the king of the land above the sky, which was then in darkness, and pass three tests because the fly has eavesdropped on the king's plans. In the third test, the animals must choose between a box containing darkness and one that contains light. They scamper off with the box of light, open it, and are disappointed to see a rooster; but the rooster crows, the sky grows light, and the rooster has called up the sun "every morning from that day to this," the story ends. The tale incorporates several familiar folktale elements; it is told in a simple, direct style; it has the appeals of small creatures triumphing over large ones and a wish granted. The illustrations are black and white, starkly dramatic. The very white paper, the large, clear print, and the spacious pages add to the book's appropriateness for young independent readers.

130 **Berson,** Harold, ad. *Kassim's Shoes;* ad. and illus. by Harold Berson. Crown, 1977. 77-4688. 29p. $5.95.

R
K-3

A Moroccan folktale is nicely retold and is illustrated with clean-lined drawings that are distinctive for their restrained use of color, their humor, and their geometrically patterned frames that use motifs typical of the region. Since all his neighbors and fellow vendors, disliking Kassim's tattered shoes, buy him a new pair, he tries diligently to get rid of his comfortable, loved old shoes. Each time he throws or puts them somewhere, a minor disaster occurs to one or more of the donors. Example: hidden in a tall palm tree, the shoes blow down in a wind and hit a donkey carrying melons, the melons bounce around, and all the market wares are tossed about or broken. So—out go the tight new shoes, and everybody's happy.

131 **Bible.** *Noah's Ark;* illus. by Peter Spier. Doubleday, 1977. 76-43630. 40p. $6.95.

K-3
*

Save for a poem, "The Flood," written by Revius, who lived in the 16th and 17th centuries, this has no text. The poem, translated by Spier, begins "High and long / Thick and strong / Wide and stark / Was the ark," and ends, "Back on land / Through God's hand / Who forgave / And did save / The Lord's Grace / Be the praise!" The pictures are delightful; filled with humor and action and painted in soft tones, they show in precise detail the building of the ark, the animals flocking in paired procession (although Noah is fending off a swarm of bees who wish to join the chosen two), and then the rains. The cities are deeper and deeper beneath the waters as they rise, and Noah keeps busy feeding his creatures. The ark is marooned on Ararat as the waters recede, the dove flies back with a green branch, Noah cautiously lets down the ramp. There's a picture of the deserted interior, all in a colossal mess, as the pair of snails end the exodus; then a final double-page spread with a superrainbow, Noah's house and garden, and the words, ". . . and he planted a vineyard." This is a deft visual pairing with another double-page spread that precedes the title page, with slaughter and arson as soldiers leave a city, while the facing page shows Noah's peaceful home, and ". . . But Noah found grace in the eyes of the Lord." Nifty.

132 **Bible.** *The Story of Christmas;* ad. and illus. by Felix Hoffmann. Atheneum, 1975. 75-6921. 31p. $6.95.

3-6 yrs. * Although this picturebook version of the Nativity eschews Biblical language, it adheres closely to the original, and it is illustrated with beautifully composed pictures that have both dignity and a homely warmth. Hoffmann uses large masses of color with restraint and delicacy; the text begins with the appearance of the Angel Gabriel to Mary and concludes with the Holy Family's return to Nazareth after the death of King Herod.

133 **Bierhorst,** John, ed. *Black Rainbow; Legends of the Incas and Myths of Ancient Peru;* ed. and tr. by John Bierhorst. Farrar, 1976. 76-19092. 131p. $7.95.

8- * This is what every such collection of traditional literature for older readers should be: it is prefaced by an erudite and informative introduction; it is chronologically arranged insofar as possible; it is followed by notes on sources, a reading list, a glossary of terms, and a guide to pronunciation. Above all, it consists of stories that are selected with discrimination and retold with skill. The tales are grouped into "Legends of the Incas," "Myths of Ancient Peru," "Myths That Have Survived," and "Modern Fables and Animal Tales," and they give a vivid picture of both the cultural and historical milieu from which they came and of the style and humor of Andean storytelling.

134 **Bierhorst,** John, ad. *Songs of the Chippewa;* ad. from the collections of Frances Densmore and Henry Rowe Schoolcraft, and arranged for piano and guitar by John Bierhorst: pictures by Joe Servello. Farrar, 1974. 47p. $6.95.

4- Dramatic illustrations face each page of music in a collection of songs based on those gathered in the nineteenth and early twentiety century by Henry Rowe Schoolcraft and Frances Densmore. The words are given in English or, if in the original, a translation is provided; the notation is given for the melodic line with simple chords for piano or guitar accompaniment. The songs are simple and dignified, often tender, always aware of—and responsive to—the beauty of nature and the powers of the spirits. Notes on sources are appended to this interesting addition to any collection of music for children.

135 **Bitter,** Gary G. *Exploring with Pocket Calculators;* by Gary G. Bitter and Thomas H. Metos; photographs by Thomas H. and Jeffery T. Metos. Messner, 1977. 77-351. 64p. $6.64.

4-7 Following a brief historical review of devices and machines for efficient computing (from the abacus to the first electric-powered adding machine) the text describes the operations of a four-function pocket calculator, giving many examples and problems in a clear, succinct style. The authors add a few samples of tricks that can be done with a calculator, suggest some of the machine's uses (comparison shopping, calculating measurements for a carpentry project), and describe some of the special calculators that are available on the market. Photographs and diagrams are nicely integrated with the text; an index is appended.

136 **Block,** Irvin. *The Lives of Pearl Buck; A Tale of China and America.* T. Y. Crowell, 1973. 169p. $4.50.

7- As a subject for biography, Pearl Buck would be fascinating either for the role she played as a fine and prolific writer, as a humanitarian, or as a person whose life in China was filled with color and drama. Therefore any book about her would be interesting; her biographer here has woven the facts of her life into a book that also truly conveys the warmth and vitality of her personality. There is some discussion of Buck's major works, but the strength of this smoothly-written and balanced biography is in the picture of the development of a forceful and compassionate fighter for justice from the small daughter of American missionaries in a China that was a beloved home for the first half of Pearl Buck's long life. A selective reading list and an index are appended.

137 **Blood,** Charles L. *The Goat in the Rug;* by Charles L. Blood and Martin Link; illus. by Nancy Winslow Parker. Parents Magazine, 1976. 75-19192. 30p. Trade ed. $5.50; Library ed. $4.96 net.

K-3 Like *Pelle's New Suit* and *"Charlie Needs a Cloak,"* this follows each step in the manufacture of an article made by hand. Here it's a Navajo rug, and the story is told by Geraldine, the goat whose hair is used to make the rug. From the sharpening of the scissors that clip the hair to the finished product, all processes are described; the weaver buys nothing except some dyes, Geraldine having unfortunately eaten all the plants that had been collected to make natural dyes. The writing style is blithe and brisk, the pictures echo the light humor of the writing, and the book stresses the craft that goes into the whole procedure.

138 **Blume,** Judy. *Blubber.* Bradbury, 1974. 153p. $5.95.

4-6 Linda wasn't the fattest girl in the fifth grade classroom but she was the butt of most of the teasing, especially after she gave a report on the whale and talked about blubber. That's when Wendy (as described by Jill, who tells the story, Wendy's the queen bee) started calling Linda "Blubber," and after that the teasing became persecution. When Jill defended Linda, locked in a supply closet, and let her out, Wendy and her sycophantic set turned on Jill, and she found out what it was like to be a taunted outsider. Realistically, no miracles happen. The social relationships settle down, but Linda is still an outsider and Wendy still arrogant. The change is in Jill, whose sense of values shifts to include the compassion that understanding another's position brings. The plot is nicely balanced by Jill's friendship with reliable Tracy Wu, her support and sympathy from understanding parents, her relationship with an erudite younger brother, a Hallowe'en escapade, etc. A good family story as well as a school story, this had good characterization and dialogue, a vigorous first-person writing style, and—Judy Blume demonstrates again—a respectful and perceptive understanding of the anguished concerns of the pre-teen years.

139 **Blume,** Judy. *Forever*. Bradbury, 1975. 74-22850. 199p. $6.95.

7-10 Katherine had liked Michael when they met at a party, she was delighted when he asked for a date, and she knew it was only a question of time until they became lovers. Kath, who has her eighteenth birthday during the course of the book, tells her story most convincingly; she does not feel ashamed when she goes to a birth control clinic, although she tells nobody but Michael. They are deeply in love, wholly committed. Forever. And then, due to parental insistence, Kath goes to work in a summer camp and finds she is attracted to another man. And that's it—the end of forever. No preaching (Blume never does) but the message is clear; no hedging (Blume never does) but a candid account by Kath gives intimate details of a first sexual relationship. The characters and dialogue are equally natural and vigorous, the language uncensored, and depiction of family relationships outstanding.

140 **Bodecker,** N. M. *Hurry, Hurry, Mary Dear! And Other Nonsense Poems;* written and illus. by N. M. Bodecker, Atheneum, 1976. 76-14841. 118p. $5.95.

2-5 Copenhagen's gift to the United States, the Great Dane of children's poetry, has done it again. Witty pen sketches add to the ebullient fun of the poems, a few of which have serious moments but rely on their rhythm and humor for immediate appeal. And under the surface of that easy appeal are (at least, in some poems) some perceptive commentaries on human behavior. A few poems are sheer nonsense, some play with words, all are delightful to read aloud. Sample verse, and one of the shortest: "House Flies." "What makes / common house flies / trying / is / that they keep / multiflieing."

141 **Bodecker,** N. M., tr. *It's Raining Said John Twaining; Danish Nursery Rhymes;* tr. and illus. by N. M. Bodecker. Atheneum, 1973. 28p. $4.95.

K-2 Absolutely delightful drawings with precise and comic details illustrate an adept translation of nursery rhymes that are Danish in origin and universal in appeal. The verses have a jaunty rhythm and rhyme, and the translator-artist has used personal and place names that will be familiar to English-speaking children: "Squire McGuire, how much is your lyre?" or the John Twaining of the title verse, and his friends John Penny, John Oats, John Square, etc.

142 **Bodecker,** N. M. *Let's Marry Said the Cherry and Other Nonsense Poems;* illus. by the author. Atheneum, 1974. 79p. $4.95.

4-6 Daft and delicately detailed line drawings illustrate a collection of nonsense verses that are adroit and amusing, and that should appeal especially to readers who enjoy word-play. A poem called "Booteries and Fluteries and Flatteries and Things," includes the lines, "For the crocodiles are watching from the crockery / and the mocking birds are scowling in the mockery / and someone's sure to trick you in the trickery / to make you laugh and hiccup in the hickory . . ." Sheer ebullience, the poems are too much alike in mood to be best enjoyed in a sitting, but the book is fun in brief forays.

143 **Bødker,** Cecil. *Silas and Ben-Godik;* tr. from the Danish by Sheila La Farge. Delacorte/Lawrence, 1978. 78-50459. 191p. $7.95.

5-7 * In a sequel to *Silas and the Black Mare* (reviewed in the December 1978 issue) the two boys take off together, Silas on his mare and the village boy, Ben-Godik, on his shaggy horse. As they travel about, Silas earns money as a performer and Ben-Godik as a woodcarver, and their adventures include rescuing a small boy from the wicked Horse Crone, avoiding the thieves who have hidden a sack of silver ore, and catching a tame bear that has gotten loose and terrorized everyone in a marketplace. Bødker's style has pace and vigor; it is smoothly translated, and moves skillfully from incident to incident. Period details are smoothly incorporated, and the characters are sharply defined.

144 **Bødker,** Cecil. *Silas and the Black Mare;* tr. from the Danish by Sheila La Farge. Delacorte, 1978. 77-86303. 153p. Trade ed. $6.95; Library ed. $6.46 net.

5-7 Silas appears in dramatic fashion, drifting aimlessly in a small boat, and the horsetrader Bartolin first thinks the boy is dead; but Silas is hale enough to work a shrewd bargain and win the black mare, Bartolin's horse. A series of adventures culminates in a long and stirring episode in which all the characters of previous incidents are brought together: Bartolin, the small band of performers from whom Silas had run away, the crippled boy who has helped him, the peddler who has thrashed him, and even the black mare which had been stolen from him. There is no deep characterization, but the characters are well-defined and colorful, the dialogue has vitality, and the story is nicely knit together.

145 **Bødker,** Cecil. *Silas and the Runaway Coach;* tr. from the Danish by Sheila La Farge. Delacorte/Lawrence, 1978. 78-50465. 245p. $7.95.

5-7
*
In the third book in the "Silas" series by a Hans Christian Andersen Award author, the doughty adolescent is again on his own. He leaves the village (to which he and Ben-Godik have returned) by chance, riding desperately to stop the careening horses who have run wild with a coach carrying a wealthy family. Alexander Planke and his wife, grateful to their rescuer, insist that Silas stay with them. While he frets at city clothes and formal manners, Silas is curious—as always—and stays long enough to learn to read and to become involved in another encounter with the Horse Crone and with the men who have stolen his horse and one of Planke's. Again, the pace of the story and the resourcefulness of the protagonist are appealing; because Silas is, in this story, settled in one place rather than on the road, there is a bit more cohesion of structure.

146 **Bomans,** Godfried. *The Wily Witch and All the Other Fairy Tales and Fables;* illus. by Wouter Hoogendijk; tr. by Patricia Crampton. Stemmer House, 1977. 76-54196. 205p. $6.95.

4-7
*
A brilliant translation of the collected tales of a popular and prolific Dutch author, published in the Netherlands under the title *Groot Sprookjesboek.* Crampton has kept the easy flexibility of the storyteller's conversational tone and the pithiness of his quirky wit. Although Bomans uses some familiar patterns of the genre, he almost invariably gives them a new twist; at times it is sardonic or sophisticated, as in "Princess Steppie," in which her peremptory royal father finds something wrong with every suitor who bids for the hand of the beautiful Steppie—who dies unwed. Parallel with this strain is a compassion for human foibles, and pervading almost every tale is a sense of fun, a relish for the ridiculous.

147 **Bond,** Michael. *Olga Carries On;* illus. by Hans Helweg. Hastings House, 1977. 77-8710. 127p. $5.95.

3-5 More anecdotes about the engaging guinea pig whose vivid imagination leads her into tale-telling in which she lets her high esteem for guinea pigs in general, and herself in particular, have full sway. Such as her own explanation for the way the French language started: one of her ancestors conceived the idea during the Wars of the Roses, when people across the channel grew an enormous rose hedge to keep the English out. Yet Olga has some charitable instincts toward her three companions, and is willing to share the glory—real or imagined—when she sees that one of them needs a boost to morale. Like Bond's Paddington, Olga is a well-defined and engaging character; and the lively style and humor of Bond's writing, with each chapter a discrete episode, make the book fun to read aloud or alone.

148 **Bond,** Michael. *Paddington on Top;* illus. by Peggy Fortnum. Houghton, 1975. 75-17026. 124p. $4.95.

3-5 Paddington's in good form in this latest collection of anecdotes about the Peruvian bear who lives with a London family, and the illustrations, small sketches with a marvelous economy of line, are also amusing. Each chapter is a separate incident, and Bond's tried-and-true formula works very nicely as Paddington gets into trouble and (somehow) out again; secretly taking a lesson in waterskiing, being called to testify by mistake, ordered to attend school and making a nervous wreck of the teacher. Paddington's bland, literal, amiable, gullible, and quite endearing.

149 **Bond,** Michael. *The Tales of Olga da Polga;* illus. by Hans Helweg. Macmillan, 1973. 114p. $4.95.

4-5 The creator of Paddington uses the same format for Olga da Polga, episodic chapters loosely strung together and just right for reading aloud to children for whom the vocabulary is too difficult to cope with alone. Olga is a guinea pig who thinks like a human being, and who talks to other animals, but who—unlike Paddington—does not communicate with people; she behaves like a guinea pig and is treated like one. Here the humor is not so much in Olga's adventures, since she is hutch-bound, but in her personality. Complacently confident of her own charms and given to outrageous invention when it suits her purpose, Olga's tales are told to other animals with such assurance that they believe her impromptu fibs readily. Not as much action here as in the Paddington stories, but the humor and vitality of the writing make Olga and her tall tales highly amusing.

150 **Bond,** Nancy. *A String in the Harp.* Atheneum, 1976. 75-28181. 370p. $9.95.

6-9
* In a most impressive first novel, Bond deftly blends fantasy and realism; realism predominates, but it is a successful setting for the fanciful element that affects the everyday life of twelve-year-old Peter and his family. His father, grieving for the wife who died the

year before, has taken a year's professorship in Wales. None of the three children prefers it to their Amherst home, but Peter antagonizes his father and upsets his sisters by his surly hostility. Then Peter finds a key, and the key enables him to see the past, for it is the lost tuning key for Taliesin's harp. Peter struggles, first to hide his visions and then to convince the others, are completely believable, and the story gains momentum when a museum curator presses for the key, Peter resisting because he is convinced that he must return it to the proper place. And what that place is, the key must tell him. The interweaving of Welsh background, the intermittently-told story of Taliesin, and the problems of family adjustment is adroit. The characters are drawn with depth, changing and growing in their maturity and in their understanding of each other.

151 **Bonsall,** Crosby Newell. *Mine's the Best*. Harper, 1973. 32p. illus. (I Can Read Books). Trade ed. $1.95; Library ed. $2.79 net.

1-2 A delightfully funny and fresh story for beginning independent readers can also be used for reading aloud to younger children. Framed pictures expand the story of two small boys who discover that they have identical balloons and are instantly hostile. As they argue about which one is best, both balloons are shriveling; when a girl goes by carrying a new balloon just like theirs, the boys are just as quickly allied as they were embattled. They go off, arms around each other agreeing that theirs was the best. Icing on the cake: in the background, throughout the book, there are children of all shapes and sizes with the very same balloon.

152 **Bornstein,** Ruth. *Little Gorilla;* story and pictures by Ruth Bornstein. Seabury, 1976. 75-25508. 28p. $6.95.

2-4 yrs. Short and sweet, a song of love which, slight as it is, is beguiling. Everybody loved Little Gorilla from the day he was born (catalog of Little Gorilla-lovers follows) until one day "something happened . . . Little Gorilla began to grow (next page, with appropriately looming pictures) and Grow (animals staring) and Grow . . ." And he was big, and everybody came and sang and danced and wished him a happy birthday and still loved him. So the message to the audience is clear: love goes on. The drawings are simple, large-scale, rather cartoonish in technique; they aren't handsome, but they fit the text very comfortably.

153 **Boston,** Lucy Martin. *The Stones of Green Knowe;* illus. by Peter Boston. Atheneum, 1976. 75-44143. 118p. $5.95.

4-6 Although this may have a special appeal to Green Knowe fans, it stands on its own as an intriguing time-shift fantasy, deftly blending the real and the fantastic in a story about a child of the twelfth century. Roger d'Aulneaux watches the building of his family's stone manor house with pride; he finds two ancient stones nearby and discovers that through their magic he can move in time to see the other children of Green Knowe's future. Like other Boston books, this is written with grace and conviction, so that the meetings of the children of many generations is no less real than the love of their home or the Norman setting.

154 **Bourne,** Miriam Anne. *What is Papa Up To Now?* illus. by Dick Gackenbach. Coward, 1977. 76-51272. 63p. $4.99.

2-3 Sally, Benjamin Franklin's small daughter, describes Papa's excitement and pleasure at each discovery he makes while experimenting with electricity. While the fiction has a base in fact, this is more fictional than biographical. Sally's industrious prattle conveys an impression of Franklin's eager interest in scientific phenomena, but it focuses primarily on the experiments, and it does so with an appreciation of the logical simplicity needed in making scientific information comprehensible to the primary grades reader. The illustrations have good period details and great vitality and humor.

155 **Bova,** Benjamin. *End of Exile.* Dutton, 1975. 75-6748. 214p. $7.95.

5-8 The great space ship was in danger; all the fifty-seven young people who were left knew that there were ghosts of the dead in the Ghost Place, that the ship was hurtling toward a blazing star, that the machines had stopped working and the food supplies were low. And Linc knew that somewhere in the ship their mentor, Jerlet, still lived, although the high priestess Magda and the malevolent Monel refused to admit it. In this final volume of Bova's trilogy, "Exiled," Linc finds the dying Jerlet and learns that the ship is headed for a benevolent planet; against the wishes of the ignorant and superstitious survivors, Linc repairs the broken machines and lead his agemates to a safe landing and a new life. This has everything a science fiction fan might want: conflict, suspense, technical information, drama, and a satisfying, realistic ending. It's interesting to compare this with the Nelson book reviewed in the January, 1976 issue, which is about another society in which only the young have survived.

156 **Bova,** Benjamin. *Man Changes the Weather.* Addison-Wesley, 1973. 159p. illus. $4.95.

5-8 Prefaced by a hasty peek at the past, Bova's text describes the ways in which man has—deliberately or accidentally—changed his world's atmosphere; some of the book discusses such planned activity as rainmaking, some of the efforts to control violent phenomena of weather, and some (a considerable portion) to pollution. The final chapter poses the need for international weather control and the problems it might entail. Appended material includes a list of government weather modification programs and an index. The writing style is brisk and informal, the organization of material logical, and the information authoritative and interesting. This book pairs nicely with the author's fictional *The Weathermakers*.

157 **Bova,** Benjamin. *Through Eyes of Wonder; Science Fiction and Science*. Addison/Wesley, 1975. 74-13893. 127p. illus. Trade ed. $5.75; Library ed. $4.32 net.

6- An eminent writer of science fiction and science books describes the influence of science fiction in his life, defends the genre with conviction and a degree of passion, and discusses the parallels between science fiction writing and scientific developments. Although there is in the text a degree of repetition and rambling, it is interesting both for what it sets out to do and for the information it gives about the early days of science fiction publishing and the changes in attitude toward the genre in the literary world.

158 **Bova,** Benjamin. *Workshops in Space;* illus. with photographs. Dutton, 1974. 67p. $6.95.

6-9 Bova explains why putting men on the moon was only the first phase of space exploration and how the knowledge gained from the Apollo missions has already been put to use in the operation of Skylab. He discusses the Apollo-Soyuz mission planned for 1975, a joint project of the U.S.A. and the U.S.S.R., as a scientific and political step forward; he describes the information that has been garnered from technical apparatus about geological, agricultural, meteorological, and other problems. In closing, Bova discusses the costs of space flights and how they may be alleviated in the future by the reuseable space shuttle. The writing is crisp and knowledgeable. An index is appended.

159 **Bowman,** Kathleen. *New Women in Medicine*. Creative Education/Childrens Press, 1976. 76-4918. 47p. illus. $4.95.

5-7 Seven brief biographies are included in this volume, one of a series of "New Women in . . ." that also has volumes on women in the fields of art and dance, entertainment, media, politics, and social sciences. The tone of the biographies is admiring but not adulatory, and the author discusses career preparation with emphasis on problems the doctors and others (one subject is a nurse-midwife, one a microbiologist, another a professor of endocrinology, etc.) have had as women, both in reaching their goals and in being accepted once they were practicing medicine. None of the women quoted is starry-eyed about her profession, but all of them express deep satisfaction while being aware of obstacles, and many of the biographies have successfully combined a career and family life.

160 **Brady,** Irene. *Beaver Year;* written and illus. by Irene Brady. Houghton, 1976. 75-38907. 40p. $5.95.

3-5 A story of the life cycle of the beaver is told through the development of two kits from birth to their founding of a new beaver colony as yearlings. The writing is, despite the fact that the kits are called Cassie and Paddle, without anthropomorphism; although the approach is patterned, the narrative form and authenticity of details give the book substance. Brady's black and white sketches, softly drawn and realistic, are remarkable for their texture.

161 **Brady,** Irene. *Wild Mouse.* Scribner, 1976. 76-14912. 22p. illus. $5.95.

2-4
* Brady's drawings bring out fully the appeal of the tiny white-footed mouse, with its big bright eyes, and of the even tinier newborn in its litter of three. The text is written in diary form, as the author watches the development of the babies from blind, helpless newborn nurslings to frisky, sixteen-day-olds. The writing has humor and affection, yet it's light, brisk, and informative; it's simple enough for independent reading and is also the sort of book that the preschool child enjoys poring over after it's been read aloud.

162 **Branley,** Franklyn Mansfield. *A Book of Planet Earth for You;* illus. by Leonard Kessler. T. Y. Crowell, 1975. 74-30408. 89p. $6.95.

3-5 A continuous text, comprising some material that has been treated in separate, shorter Branley books, describes the earth as it might be observed from the mythical extragalactic planet Omega. The author discusses the composition, motion, rotation, orbit, and precession of Earth, all in his usual direct and lucid style; this is preceded by a brief recapitulation of ancient theories and how it was proved that the world is round. While there is neither table of contents nor index, the book should be valued for the fact that it gives a clear and comprehensive summary of Earth in contrast to, and in relation to, other parts of the solar system. Readers will surely enjoy the credit line given "Professor X2174(YY)" as Chairperson of the Extra-Omegan Studies Group. Professor (YY), it points out, has been a member of a commune for the past ninety-six years.

163 **Branley,** Franklyn Mansfield. *Color; From Rainbows to Lasers;* illus. by Henry Roth. T. Y. Crowell, 1978. 76-46304. 87p. $8.95.

6-10 Since color is based on light, Branley begins with a history of scientists' theories about light, from the early Greek philosophers on. Some of the topics that follow the second chapter, which describes the color spectrum, are the psychology and physiology of color, the basic colors and color printing, color and light (the pigmentation of eyes, sea colors, rainbows, etc.) and the measurement of colors. The text is written in a serious, straightforward style; throughout the book Branley suggests home experiments. A few titles are suggested for further reading; an index is provided.

164 **Branley,** Franklyn Mansfield. *Eclipse; Darkness in Daytime;* illus. by Donald Crews. T. Y. Crowell, 1973. 33p. (Let's-Read-and-Find-Out Books). $3.75.

2-4 In his usual capable fashion, an eminent astronomer explains the phenomenon of the total solar eclipse, defining terminology and explaining why it is possible for the moon to obscure the larger sun. There's some discussion of the effect of the eclipse on animals and on the people of ancient times, and a home demonstration project that will enable the reader to see the image of the eclipse in safety. Succinct, lucid, and authoritative, the text is attractively illustrated.

165 **Branley,** Franklyn Mansfield. *The End of the World;* illus. by David Palladini. T. Y. Crowell, 1974. 41p. $5.50.

5-9 As it must to all worlds, death will come to the planet Earth. An eminent astronomer discusses the ways in which the explosion of the moon and the cooling of the sun—although billions of years in the future—will so affect the surface and atmosphere of our world that life cannot be sustained. Informative, depressing, authoritative, and fascinating, the book is illustrated with imaginative and dramatic pictures.

166 **Branley,** Franklyn Mansfield. *Shakes, Quakes, and Shifts; Earth Tectonics;* illus. by Daniel Maffia. T. Y. Crowell, 1974. 33p. $5.50.

5-9 After discussing some of the ways in which the earth moves and changes, Branley describes the theory of plate tectonics and some of the corroborating evidence for the concept (proposed years ago, received with disdain, and more recently accepted) that the continents were one land mass billions of years ago, that they drifted apart and will continue to do so; that they move on huge segments, or plates, on which land masses float and collide. While Branley always writes lucidly and authoritatively, here he discusses a topic perhaps too broad and complex to be covered adequately in a text so brief and without division. A bibliography and an index are appended.

167 **Branley,** Franklyn Mansfield. *Think Metric!* illus. by Graham Booth. T. Y. Crowell, 1973. 53p. Trade ed. $4.50; Library ed. $5.25 net.

4-6 A distinguished scientist, writing in the expectation of an adoption of the metric system in this country, explains how the system works and describes its advantages over our present system of measurement both in terms of efficiency and of translation. The text begins with historical background, goes on to the establishment of the metric system, and presents translation problems that can familiarize the reader with the metric system. A chart that compares English and metric measurements for many terms is appended. While the writing style is clear and the explanations lucid, this is a book so filled with solid paragraphs of facts that it seems heavier than most of Branley's books, perhaps in part due to the fact that the text is continuous.

168 **Branscum,** Robbie. *The Three Wars of Billy Joe Treat.* McGraw-Hill, 1975. 75-10917. 90p. Trade ed. $5.95; Library ed. $5.72 net.

5-7 Set in a rural Arkansas community during World War II, this is the first-person story of thirteen-year-old Billy Joe, who assumes a large share of the farm work when his older brothers go off to fight. But Billy Joe has wars of his own; one is against the new teacher, a most harsh and peculiar man, and the other is against Ma. Dissatisfied with his portion at meals, Billy Joe vows he'll eschew the family table until Ma invites him to sit down to a man's share of food. Ma is just as stubborn as Billy Joe, but she finally concedes. The teacher is something else again, and Billy Joe discovers that the surly Mr. Marshall is a spy. Despite the fact that the teacher-spy facet of the story is not convincing, the book has the unmistakable authenticity of setting and dialogue that lend credence to any book, and the characters—especially Ma—are strong.

169 **Breinburg,** Petronella. *Doctor Shawn;* illus. by Errol Lloyd. T. Y. Crowell, 1975. 24p. $5.95.

K-2 Large-scale drawings in bright colors show the imaginative play of a group of children in an English story that is a sequel to *Shawn Goes to School.* Like the first book, this pictures a universal and familiar situation in which the protagonist is a black child; like the first, the story is the right length and complexity for a read-aloud audience, although the large print may tempt some beginning independent readers. Mother has gone shopping, adjuring Shawn and his older sister not to make a mess; their game of "playing hospital" involves two friends and a growing number of props, but Mother takes it with a smile when she returns. The style is direct and informal, and there's no sex stereotyping: Shawn is the doctor and his sister the nurse because the last time they played the roles were reversed.

170 **Breinburg,** Petronella. *Shawn Goes to School;* illus. by Errol Lloyd. T. Y. Crowell, 1974. 24p. $4.50.

3-5 yrs. First published in England, a story by a South American author and a Jamaican illustrator describes a child's first day at school—as told by his older sister. The style is very simple and direct, the pictures bold but also simple, with vigorous use of color. Shawn cried, a full-throated roar of dismay. But the kind, smiling teacher said there were "lots of nice kids," and Mom pointed out the toys, Shawn's sister the swing, and a friendly classmate the donkey, a real one, for riding. The story ends, "Shawn smiled a teeny weeny smile." But the smile tells all. This is the sort of book we need more of, the light, firm treatment of a universal experience in a story with minority group protagonists.

171 **Brenner,** Barbara. *Lizard Tails and Cactus Spines;* photographs by Merritt S. Keasey. Harper, 1975. 75-6297. 84p. Trade ed. $5.95; Library ed. $5.79 net.

4-7 Photographs of desert creatures make it clear that, although the book is cast in narrative form, the emphasis is on informative aspects of the story rather than on the fictional vehicle that carries them. Pip goes to Arizona for the summer to visit his sister, who is working as a botanist at a research station. Already curious about lizards, he spends a happy summer observing and recording not only the lizards but their ecosystem. Brenner combines Pip's adventures and conversations with facts about the desert and its creatures so smoothly that the book is truly a coup, a completely successful mesh of fiction and fact.

172 **Brenner,** Barbara. *On the Frontier with Mr. Audubon.* Coward, 1977. 76-41601. 96p. illus. $6.95.

5-8 * Thirteen-year-old Joseph Mason describes his travels down the Mississippi River and in the southern swamps and forests and cities. As pupil-assistant, Joseph helped shoot specimens of birds never before pictured in guide books, helped paint some of the details or background, and suffered with Audubon through poverty, illness, and homesickness. Whether describing life on a flatboat or on the crowded docks of New Orleans, the narrative (based on thorough research) is lively and natural, and through Joseph's eyes Brenner draws a perceptive, candid picture of the great artist who had been jailed for debt, branded a wastrel, and gone from a pampered childhood in France to near-penury in America. Joseph's journal is a fictional device, but the facts it records are documented, and it gives a memorable picture of the artist and his work.

173 **Brenner,** Barbara. *Wagon Wheels;* illus. by Don Bolognese. Harper, 1978. 76-21391. 64p. (I Can Read Books) Trade ed. $4.95; Library ed. $4.79 net.

1-3 A fine frontier story for beginning independent readers describes the experiences of a black family which comes from Kentucky to Kansas in the 1870's. The story is told by one of the three boys; the writing is simple and direct, yet it has a narrative flow and gives a vivid picture of both the hardships of pioneer life and of the love and courage of the family. The book is based on fact: Nicodemus, Kansas, was a black community and there really was an Ed Muldie who journeyed there and who left the younger boys in the hands of eleven-year-old Johnny while he went ahead to find better land; there really was a famine in Nicodemus that ended because of the kindness of some Osage Indians, and the three boys really did strike out alone to join their father, following his directions and having a happy reunion.

174 **Brewton,** Sara Westbrook, comp. *Of Quarks, Quasars, and Other Quirks; Quizzical Poems for the Supersonic Age;* comp. by Sara and John E. Brewton and John Brewton Blackburn; illus. by Quentin Blake, T. Y. Crowell, 1977. 76-54747. 113p. $6.95.

5- A diverse and discriminating selection of poems of our time, most of which are pointed and funny. There are many parodies, and there's much trenchant commentary; some of the best-known poets are Belloc, McCord, Merriam, Nash, Starbird, and Updike, and they—and other poets—poke fun at advertising, scientific jargon, organic produce, transplants, and water beds. It's a tart, refreshing anthology.

175 **Bridgers,** Sue Ellen. *Home Before Dark.* Knopf, 1977. 76-8661. 159p. $6.95.

6-9 After years as a migrant laborer, James Earl brings his family to settle down and work on the tobacco farm inherited by his younger brother Newt. Fourteen-year-old Stella is particularly pleased; she's anxious to have a better life, to make something more of herself than her timid, fearful mother has. Stella admires Newt's brisk wife, is admired by two boys and learns to care for one of them, and resists (eventually succumbing) the genuinely affectionate overtures made by her stepmother after her mother's death and James Earl's rather hasty second marriage. The plot is not outstanding, but the characters are solid, the dialogue true, and the setting and motivation most convincing.

176 **Briggs,** Raymond. *Father Christmas.* Coward, 1973. 28p. illus. $4.95.

K-3 From England, a book in comic strip style by a Greenaway Award winning author-illustrator portrays Christmas Eve as Santa sees it. Dreaming of tropic weather, he grumbles his way through the preparations for a long, cold night of work: feeding the animals, loading the sleigh, packing a snack. He grumbles at chimneys, catches cold, wearily distributes gifts, and rides home to a steaming bath and a solitary Christmas dinner. Last frame: looking at the reader, Father Christmas grumbles, "Happy blooming Christmas to you, too!" It's original, it's engaging, and the pictures are delightful.

177 **Brooks,** Jerome. *The Testing of Charlie Hammelman.* Dutton, 1977. 77-7493. 144p. $6.95.

7-10 Charlie, who tells the story, is a high school junior. His father has a traveling job and is home only once a week; Charlie knows his father is industriously unfaithful and that his mother suffers; he also knows that his father wants him to be thin and athletic. Charlie's plump, shy, and so terrified of being seen naked by other boys that he's taken R.O.T.C. as an alternative to swimming. But there's a new rule; everybody must take a swim test. This horrifies Charlie so much that he sees a psychiatrist (once) and actually tells his best friend. Never, never, does Charlie expect help from a girl, but on a weekend trip to visit a girl who's working at a camp, Charlie finds that Shirley understands him, loves him, and encourages him to the point where he can talk to his father and he can strip in the locker room. And it all works out! Sometimes funny, often tender, this is—despite some passages that lag—a true and touching story of an adolescent. It is permeated throughout by the boy's grief over the death of a favorite teacher, and it deals much more kindly than many contemporary adolescent novels with adults: Charlie's father tries to change, the psychiatrist is kind and constructive, and the teacher, seen through Charlie's memories, is clearly a person of warmth and integrity.

178 **Brooks,** Jerome. *Uncle Mike's Boy.* Harper, 1973. 226p. Trade ed. $4.95; Library ed. $4.43 net.

5-7 Eleven-year-old Pudge is still trying to adjust to his parents' divorce and to the fact that his father drinks and his mother is now withdrawn, when the death of his small sister, hit by a runaway truck, tragically deprives him of his closest companion and his refuge. "Having her around to reassure was like having someone around to reassure him." His father's brother, Uncle Mike, is the adult to whom Pudge turns; Uncle Mike has lost his wife and child and understands the boy's loneliness and insecurity. What he does for his nephew, in Pudge's subsequent visits, is help the boy to understand the causes of his parents' unhappiness, to adjust to

Sharon's death and his own guilt (if he had been taking better care of her, she wouldn't have been hit, Pudge feels), to accept his mother's remarriage, and—most important—to become independent. A lonely man himself, Uncle Mike resists the temptation to let Pudge be dependent on him. The relationship between the two is drawn with warmth and sensitivity; indeed, all of the relationships in the story are perceptively seen. A somber book, at times touching.

179 **Brown,** Marcia Joan. *All Butterflies;* An ABC; woodcuts by Marcia Brown. Scribner, 1974. 26p. $5.95.

3-5 yrs. Handsome woodcuts in muted colors show creatures of all kinds in realistic or fanciful situations; save for a few pictures in which they would be inappropriate (the Arctic, the ocean depths) butterflies of varied shapes and colors appear on all the pages. Each of the double-page spreads uses words for two letters of the alphabet: "All Butterflies, Cat Dance, Elephant Fly? Giraffes High." Some of the pictures have a grave serenity, other are vigorous or humorous. Moderately useful as an alphabet book, graphically delightful.

180 **Brown,** Roy. *Find Debbie!* Seabury, 1976. 75-25511. 160p. $6.95.

7- Debbie Shepherd has disappeared. But where could she have gone, a psychotic child who cannot talk but screams for hours, who eats garbage and bites people? Her mother is almost ill, her twin brother Ian uncommunicative, her father haughty. Jack Shepherd stays away from his family and he sneers at Inspector Bates when the detective comes too close to the truth. Not every answer is supplied in this taut mystery story, but there's enough to satisfy the reader by the time it comes to its tragic end. Characterization is strong, and the author has skillfully depicted the behavior of Debbie, the burden borne by a family living with such a child, and the attitudes of our society toward mental illness. And he does all this without in the least interrupting the impetus of a cracking good mystery story, first published in England under the title *The Siblings.*

181 **Bryan,** Ashley, ad. *The Adventures of Aku; Or How It Came About That We Shall Always See Okra the Cat Lying on a Velvet Cushion, While Okraman the Dog Sleeps Among the Ashes;* ad. and illus. by Ashley Bryan. Atheneum, 1976. 75-44245. 70p. $7.95.

4-6 Illustrated with dramatic, stylized pictures in black and white or in black, red, and gold, this synthesis of African folktales into one story that contains other tales is smooth and effective. Basically it is a "why" story that explains the different ways people treat dogs and cats, but it also contains many familiar folklore patterns: the child who comes magically to a lonely, childless person; the dolt who forgets his errand; the crafty creature (Spider Ananse, in this case) who is outwitted; the kind deed rewarded, and others. Bryan's style is direct and colloquial in the best storytelling tradition. The child, Aku, who foolishly buys a dog, a cat, and a bird when given gold dust to buy food, is rewarded for his kindness by the bird, a bewitched ruler. He gives Aku a magic ring, Aku becomes a chief and falls in love with Ananse's niece, who has been sent by her uncle to steal the ring. She succeeds, Aku sends his cat and dog to retrieve the ring and the dog proves useless while the faithful, clever cat brings home the magical ring. And that's why Cat sleeps on a velvet cushion, and Dog sleeps among the ashes.

182 **Bryan,** Ashley, ad. *The Dancing Granny;* ad. and illus. by Ashley Bryan. Atheneum, 1977. 76-25847. 54p. $5.95.

K-3 In an adaptation of a folktale from the Antilles, Granny Anika bests that pervasive traditional character, Spider Ananse, pictured as a tall, vigorous man in Bryan's drawings. The illustrations look like pages of preliminary sketches; flyaway line drawings of dancing figures (usually several on a page) in which the broken or parallel lines suggest movement. For Granny Anika loves to dance. She dances as she works in her garden, and crafty Ananse soon sees that if he can dance her away, he can (and does) steal her vegetables. Four times she tries to resist; four times the music and the rhythm of his singing capture her until she cartwheels off for miles. And then she clutches Spider Ananse and forces him to dance with her, "And if Spider's still singing, then they're still dancing." The style has cadence and vitality, and a pithy humor.

183 **Bryan,** Ashley. *Walk Together Children; Black American Spirituals;* selected and illus. by Ashley Bryan. Atheneum, 1974. 53p. $6.95.

3-5 Full-page woodcut prints, strong and dramatic in black and white, illustrate a collection of spirituals (also printed from wood blocks). Only the melodic line is given, so that even young readers who have no musical training can pick out the notes; some songs have several verses, others only one or two. An attractive book that can be used with younger children or by older readers has a preface that gives interesting background information.

184 **Buchwald,** Emilie. *Gildaen; The Heroic Adventures of a Most Unusual Rabbit;* illus. by Barbara Flynn. Harcourt, 1973. 189p. $4.95.

4-6 Unlike the other rabbits, Gildaen has a thirst for adventure, so it is natural that he agrees to help a bewitched creature go off on a mission to find out who or what he really is. Gildaen calls him

Evon, this boy who is not sure he is a boy and who can change his shape at will. When the two run into a band of criminals they find one member, Hickory, who is loyal to the king who has ostracized him. He joins Evon and Gildaen in their self-appointed task of saving the young king from destruction by the sorcerer Grimald, who already has control of the monarch. Evon changes himself to a woman, and Hickory hides in the nearby woods. After several adventures that are dangerous and in which Gildaen proves that he is indeed heroic, the sorcerer is thwarted, Hickory restored to the king's good graces, and Evon finds his identity—a white witch. As for the adventurous rabbit, he decides that home is best—if he can periodically visit his companions—and he fares very well as a returning hero with tall tales to tell. The writing has pace and color, the plot is fresh and imaginative although it uses the traditional fairy tale devices, and the story is sparked with humor.

185 **Bulla,** Clyde Robert. *Keep Running, Allen!* illus. by Satomi Ichikawa. T. Y. Crowell, 1978. 77-23311. 27p. Trade ed. $6.95; Library ed. $6.79 net.

3-5 yrs. Softly colored, realistic paintings with fine detail illustrate a pleasant fragmentary story about a small boy. Allen is the youngest of four, and in order to keep up with his sister and brothers as they dash about investigating neighborhood phenomena he's always on the run. He trips on a shoelace just as the others race over the brow of a hill, and discovers how pleasant it is to lie in the sun and watch small creatures. His siblings retrace their steps to urge him on, but they succumb too, and the slight but nicely told tale ends, "They stopped talking and just looked at the sky. They all lay in a row, and it was the best time Allen ever had."

186 **Bulla,** Clyde Robert. *Shoeshine Girl;* illus by Leigh Grant. T. Y. Crowell, 1975. 75-8516. 84p. $5.95.

3-5 * Sarah Ida, not quite eleven, has come to spend the summer at Aunt Claudia's because she and her mother haven't been getting along. Sarah Ida is hostile and uncooperative, especially because she wants pocket money and her aunt has been told not to give her any. She gets a job shining shoes, becomes proficient and loses some of her surliness, and even becomes friendly with her employer, Al. When Al is hit by a car, Sarah Ida carries on alone at the shoeshine stand. The more she is depended on and approved, the more she thaws. When it is finally time to go home, she is touched when Al gives her a medal he's kept and loved since his boyhood—and Sarah Ida decides she's ready to face and solve any problems that await her. This is a quiet story with little drama but it's psychologically sound, well-structured, and satisfying in its realistic development of the changes in its protagonist.

187 **Bunin,** Catherine, *Is That Your Sister? A True Story of Adoption;* by Catherine and Sherry Bunin. Pantheon Books, 1976. 76-60. 45p. illus. $4.95.

K-3 Catherine, six, chatters amicably about the adoption of herself and her younger sister Carla (both black, but different shades of black) into a white family with two boys. She is candid about her feelings: bothered when people say she doesn't look like her sister or her mother, wondering about her natural mother, slightly annoyed by how little most people understand about adoption, and baffled by the fact that they can't understand that her *real* parents are her adoptive parents, that they and their four children are a family who—like any family—bicker a bit and love each other very much. Candid and appealing, the book includes many informal photographs of all the Bunins.

188 **Bunting,** Glenn. *Skateboards; How To Make Them, How To Ride Them;* by Glenn and Eve Bunting. Harvey House, 1977. 76-55528. 39p. illus. $5.59.

5-9 Skateboarding has grown from a fad to a sport, with all the fanfare of organized competition, its own terminology, and a formal organization. The first section of the book gives instructions for making wooden skateboards, describes differences in size, shape, and composition of skateboards and how they affect performance, and offers suggestions for maintenance. Most of the book is devoted to photographs and descriptions of basic and advanced figures, with a few pages that discuss safety. Like any book of this kind, the instruction offered needs to be supplemented by practice and personal instruction. The two-column format crowds the pages, but the directions given throughout the book are clear, and—given the popularity of this new sport—the book should be useful.

189 **Burch,** Robert. *The Whitman Kick.* Dutton, 1977. 77-23384. 116p. $6.95.

7-10 Writing for older readers than he usually does, and doing it very well indeed, Burch tells the story of Alan's last two years of high school through Alan. Newly inducted into the army, Alan remembers . . . he and Amanda had been friends since sixth grade, sharing a love of poetry, and they were just beginning to become physically aware of each other in their junior year. Amanda's socially ambitious mother ruled that her daughter must stop seeing Alan; in part she considered him personally undesirable, in part she disdained him because—as the whole town knew—his mother had gone off and had been living with another man. When trying to outwit Amanda's mother by setting up an arranged double date, Alan loses his love, for she briefly falls for the other boy. The affair is soon over, but Amanda is pregnant. When she comes to Alan for a friend's comfort, he rejects her. Bitterly she points out that his weakness is in never being able to forgive, and he remembers this when his mother returns; at first hostile, he relents in time to save the relationship. And in time, he thinks of Amanda with love. Forgiving, he stops en route to the induction center to send her a fine copy of *Leaves of Grass* in memory of their shared love of Whitman's poetry. The love story is nicely balanced with family relationships, the characterization and dialogue are excellent, and the book gives a poignant, credible picture of adolescence and of a small Georgia community in the 1940's.

190 **Burch,** Robert. *Wilkin's Ghost;* illus. by Lloyd Bloom. Viking, 1978. 78-6293. 152p. $7.95.

5-7 After a long absence, the three brothers of *Tyler, Wilkin, and Skee* are back; it is thirteen-year-old Wilkin who tells the story, set in rural Georgia in 1935. The "ghost" who frightens Wilkin when he's alone in the woods proves to be Alex Folsom, an older boy who has come back to the area although he left under suspicion of being a thief. Wilkin is convinced that Alex has changed, talks a storekeeper into giving him a job, and helps him find lodging. One of his bonds with Alex is their common dream of riding the railroad and seeing the world. Wilkin's family situation is depicted with warmth and affection, and Burch gives an excellent view—flavored by details of locale and period—of both the local community and the farm family. Wanderlust impels Wilkin, nevertheless, to agree to Alex's plans to run away—but just as they are about to go off, Wilkin discovers his friend had indeed been a thief in the past and has, even more recently, done some shoplifting and has committed another theft and let another boy stand accused. And so the train goes off into the night and Wilkin sadly turns back. The plot is not a strongly dramatic one, despite the ending, but the writing style, setting, characterization, and dialogue more than compensate.

191 **Burchard,** Marshall. *Sports Hero; Phil Esposito;* by Marshall and Sue Burchard. Putnam, 1975. 74-21083. 95p. illus. $4.69.

3-4 Nicely gauged for young hockey fans, with big print and plenty of white space, simple vocabulary and photographs of Esposito in action. The text describes the high-scoring Esposito's boyhood devotion to the game, his years on a farm team and with the Chicago Blackhawks, and—in a greater detail—his record with the Boston Bruins, as leading scorer, contributor to a Stanley Cup victory, and participant in the Team Canada games with U.S.S.R.

192 **Burnford,** Sheila. *Mr. Noah and the Second Flood;* illus. by Michael Foreman. Praeger, 1973. 64p. $4.95.

7- A cautionary fable about man's destroying the world through pollution is written in a deceptively bland style and with moments of wry humor. Descendants of the first Noah, Mr. and Mrs. James Noah and their three sons live in contented isolation on a mountain top, hospitably entertaining animals—and, once a year, the Bank Manager brings them a gold brick from royalties on a patent covering toy arks. Mr. Noah reads that the world is getting warmer and the waters are rising, so he sets about building another ark and collecting animals. Having sent his sons out to collect wives and beasts, Noah decides, seeing the environmental detritus on the creeping water, that tools are an abomination and that mankind is a species not worth continuing. He sends his sons to join the extraterrestrial emigration, and, as the ark floats off, placidly decides to let evolution take its course without the human race on earth. The theme has been used in other, recent variations, but the treatment is new and the writing style is graceful; the action of the story bogs down a bit in the long process of animal-gathering and food preparation (ten years) but it picks up at the end, and the story closes with some decisions made and the future a question mark.

193 **Burningham,** John. *Come Away from the Water, Shirley.* T. Y. Crowell, 1977. 77-483. 22p. illus. Trade ed. $6.95; Library ed. $7.95 net.

K-2 On one page, realism; on the facing page, a child's imaginative fancies. Shirley and her parents come to the beach; her mother gives periodic instructions, such as, "Don't stroke that dog, Shirley, you don't know where he's been," or, "You won't bring any of that smelly seaweed home, will you Shirley." The parents sit in folding chairs, with no sign of Shirley. She is on the facing pages, rowing a dog out to a pirate ship, battling the crew, escaping with a map, digging for treasure, standing—triumphant and jewel-draped—in her vessel. Then a meek little Shirley goes, as she has come, along the beach with her parents. It's fun, and the pictures have Burningham's usual humor, economical line, and effective composition; the humor of the nagging remarks may be lost on the picture book audience and the wordless fantasy sequence demands some familiarity with pirate tales.

194 **Burningham,** John. *Mr. Gumpy's Motor Car.* T. Y. Crowell, 1976. 75-4582. 30p. illus. Trade ed. $7.95; Library ed. $8.95 net.

4-7 yrs. A sequel to the Greenaway Award book, *Mr. Gumpy's Outing,* follows much the same pattern. This time it's an aging touring car instead of a boat, but the action is much the same: the vehicle is crowded with children and animals, there's a spot of trouble, but all ends happily. Here the passengers at first refuse to get out and push when the car gets stuck, but their help is necessary, and a concerted effort gets the car out of the mud; the ride is followed by a swim, and everyone goes home. Placid but pleasant, the slight plot is adequate enough for young listeners, the message is as mild as it can be, and the sprightly pictures (some in black and white, some in color) have a comic flair.

195 **Burningham,** John. *Time to Get Out of the Bath, Shirley;* written and illus. by John Burningham. T. Y. Crowell, 1978. 76-58503. 22p. Trade ed. $6.95; Library ed. $6.79.

K-2 Again, as in *Come Away from the Water, Shirley,* Shirley is seen as protagonist of her splendid, active daydreams on pages that face the mundane reality of a mother who grumbles about taking baths more often, dropping clothes all over the floor, leaving the soap in the bathtub, and on and on. Shirley, meanwhile, is sailing out through the drain to adventure with tilting knights and crenellated castles, and playing water games with the king of her imaginary land. This is a shade less effective than the first book, perhaps because here mother and child are in close proximity whereas at the shore they were physically separated, but it is still very amusing in concept and execution, the bland maternal monologue a contrapuntal foil for the adventurous journey. The illustrations (pale bathroom scenes facing the brighter hues of dreamland) are deft and humorous.

196 **Burton,** Hester. *Riders of the Storm;* illus. by Victor G. Ambrus. T. Y. Crowell, 1973. 200p. $4.95.

6-9 In the sequel to *The Rebel* (reviewed in the September, 1972 issue) in which a radical Oxonian, Stephen, became a victim of the French Revolution when he went to Paris to help, Stephen and his radical friends ride out another storm in England. Stephen has come to Manchester to teach millworkers' children, and his political and reform attitudes provoke the anger of the local conservatives. Persecuted, he and his friends face charges of treason and possible deportation, but they discover that British justice prevails—at least it does with canny counsel. Well written, more tightly structured than *The Rebel,* and fast-paced, this is both an exciting story and a sturdy study of corruption and mob violence in a time of political stress.

197 **Byars,** Betsy C. *After the Goat Man;* illus. by Ronald Himler. Viking, 1974. 126p. $5.95.

5-7 Figgy's grandfather had been adamant about giving up his home and land for a superhighway, and the media had made the most of the taciturn old man, called the Goat Man because he'd once had very tame goats. Now Figgy, who lived alone with the Goat Man, was worried because his grandfather had disappeared. The two friends he'd made since moving into the relocation settlement, Ada and Harold, went with him to the old homestead to look for the Goat Man. Harold, a fat and unhappy boy who has a major role, goes—with nervous courage—to ask the old man, who is making a last stand, with gun, at his old home, to come with him after Figgy broke his leg. For Harold, a turning point. He had coped with an emergency, had played the heroic role of which he'd daydreamed, had seen with new insight the pathos of the Goat Man's ruined life. Byars builds her characterization with exposition and with deft dialogue in fine balance; her writing style flows smoothly and the plot is tightly structured and convincing.

198 **Byars,** Betsy C. *The Cartoonist;* illus. by Richard Cuffari. Viking, 1978. 77-12782. 119p. $6.95.

4-6 Alfie's refuge is the attic room where he draws cartoons and dreams of fame, where he escapes his mother's vacuous nagging, where he can forget that Mom is disappointed in him because isn't like his brother Bubba. An athlete, a delinquent, a clown, Bubba is married and is an expectant father. Alfie and his sister are equally horrified to learn that Bubba plans to move back home with his wife. Mom is overjoyed. It doesn't even bother her deeply that Alfie sits locked in the attic, refusing to eat, refusing to come downstairs, refusing to give up his haven. As it happens, Bubba changes his plans, but the period of solitude has had an effect on Alfie: he sees more clearly now that he must give up daydreams and accept the realities of his situation. The ending is not strong, and the book is more an exploration of a situation than a developing story line, but Byars pulls it off because of the smooth writing style, the natural sounding dialogue, and the clear-cut characterization.

199 **Byars,** Betsy C. *The 18th Emergency;* illus. by Robert Grossman. Viking, 1973. 126p. $5.95.

4-6 First of all, you can tell quite a bit about a boy when his nickname is "Mouse." And when Mouse incites the vengefulness of the school's bully, you know he is petrified with apprehension. Mouse's friend Ezzy has survival plans for emergency situations (being bitten by a tarantula, or being threatened by an octopus) but none for Imminent Beating by Large Boy. Most of the story is concerned with Mouse's fear of this eighteenth emergency, his efforts to avoid it, his feeble attempts to get adult sympathy; when he comes to the inevitable, Mouse surprises himself by his stalwart acceptance of the fight. The writing style is more staccato than it is in other books by Betsy Byars, the treatment lighter, but the perceptiveness is just as sharp and the lesson (not in the least didactic in presentation) is clear: reality is more bearable than fear.

200 **Byars,** Betsy C. *The Lace Snail;* illus. by Betsy Byars. Viking, 1975. 74-32376. 28p. $4.95.

K-2 In a surprisingly successful blend of quiet tenderness and contemporary, often slangy, dialogue, Betsy Byars has written a witty picture book, appealing despite the slight story line. The illustrations are spacious, with animals in strong, dark green and a contrasting note of delicate, lacy black on white. How does Snail make lace, the other creatures ask? She doesn't know, it just happens; to each one asking for some lace, she gladly gives it for as long as it lasts, spinning it out behind her in an intricate trail. A sample of the dialogue: the crocodile, gloating over a delicate lace hammock, says, "I love it. I love it. I LOVE it! And you can give me a push every time you go by, all right? Everybody can give me a push. Everybody BETTER give me a push, if you get what I mean."

201 **Byars,** Betsy C. *The Pinballs.* Harper, 1977. 76-41518. 144p. Trade ed. $5.95; Library ed. $5.79 net.

5-7 The camaraderie of those joined in misfortune is as evident, as touching, and often as wryly amusing here as it is in Marjorie Kellogg's *Tell Me That You Love Me, Junie Moon.* Of the three children in a foster home, Carlie is the oldest, an adolescent whose brittle and sophisticated toughness hides an aching need for love. She's been brutally treated by a hostile stepfather; Harvey is thirteen, confined to a wheelchair because both legs were broken when his father (alcoholic, missing the wife who had run off to join a commune) accidentally ran over him; eight-year-old Thomas J is lonesome for octogenarian twins (hospitalized) who have taken care of him since he was abandoned at the age of two. It's Carlie who has called them all pinballs, people who just get sent somewhere to be out of the way. No choice about their lives. But, with loving patience on the part of their foster parents (beautifully understated) and with a growing affection for each other, the three children gain security and enough assurance to feel that they do have some control about the direction of their lives. This could have been sugar soup, but Byars does a superb job of creating vivid characters who change convincingly in reaction to each other. The exposition is smooth, the dialogue excellent.

202 **Byars,** Betsy C. *The TV Kid;* illus. by Richard Cuffari. Viking, 1976. 75-27944. 123p. $6.50.

3-4 In all the moving around Lennie had done, there was one way to forget his rootless state, to keep in touch with familiar people. Television. He watched too much, he had long daydreams about winning contests, he knew all the characters, announcers, and singing commercials. Living alone with his mother at the motel she had inherited, Lennie knew Mom was right, he ought to settle down and study—but the daydreaming was too strong a pattern. Then, prowling around an empty vacation home, Lennie heard a patrol car and hid in the crawl space under the house. Bitten by a rattlesnake, he was hospitalized, and in that long nightmare of pain and fear he came to appreciate the difference between his dream life and reality. All that stuff on TV wasn't real or important. This is a most sympathetic study of a child whose flight from reality ends in a convincing way. That it is a narrative with suspense and color is the more remarkable because there is only one dramatic incident, there are few characters to give variety, and the major part of the book is given over to Lennie's internal monologues.

203 **Byars,** Betsy C. *The Winged Colt of Casa Mia;* illus. by Richard Cuffari. Viking, 1973. 128p. $5.95.

4-6 Uncle Coot tells the story of his nephew's visit to Casa Mia, the Texas ranch to which Coot had retired after he quit as a movie stunt man. Grim and taciturn, Coot feels little in common with his visitor, a bookish boy who hero-worships the man he's seen only in movie thrillers. This sober background serves as the context for an odd bit of fantasy: a colt that is born with wings. The boy is enthralled but Coot is rather irritated by the strangeness of the situation; when Coot rescues the colt after it has disappeared, two things happen: the boy and the man recognize the affection that has grown between them, and the colt flies. The style is smooth, the structure spare, the characterization good although not probing; the combination of realism and fantasy is believable in the context, but it somehow lacks impact—perhaps because, with two aspects of the plot, (the relationship between boy and man, and the story of the winged colt) each robs the other of drama although in a literary sense they combine well.

204 **Byfield,** Barbara Ninde. *Andrew and the Alchemist;* illus. by Deanne Hollinger. Doubleday, 1977. 76-7694. 103p. $5.95.

4-6 In a sprightly fantasy, eleven-year-old Andrew is newly orphaned, destitute, and miserably cold and hungry when he is found by the Venerable P. C. Delver, Adept. Delver takes Andrew as his apprentice, and both are protected by cheery Mrs. Strawspinner and her daughter Sassie, who run a sweets-and-savories business in the shop above Delver's cellar, appropriately filled with crucibles, retorts, cauldrons, and awesome secrets. Delver is imprisoned, suspected of sorcery by the king's evil prime minister—or so the P.M. says. But when the two children brave danger to rescue the old alchemist, it proves to be the evil P.M. who has stolen royal jewels. Naturally, justice is meted out and this pseudo-medieval romp ends with Andrew and his friends firmly entrenched in the royal favor. The characters are lampooned just enough to be amusing, the writing style is brisk, the plot nicely paced. It's hard not to enjoy a book that reads as though the author had fun writing it.

205 **Byfield,** Barbara Ninde. *The Haunted Ghost;* written and illus. by Barbara Ninde Byfield. Doubleday, 1973. 36p. $4.95.

3-5 A sequel to *The Haunted Spy* is related by the ex-spy himself, now comfortably established in the castle of Sir Roger de Rudisill, his friend the ghost. Sir Roger complains of haunting dreams, and suspicious circumstances lead the two experts to investigate. A merry spoof with a modern touch (pollution, but our heroes take care of the factory that is the culprit) is told in a light style, with added amusement in the illustrations and in the very idea of a haunter haunted.

206 **Byfield,** Barbara Ninde. *The Haunted Tower;* written and illus. by Barbara Ninde Byfield. Doubleday, 1976. 75-11999. 44p. $5.95.

3-5 Fourth in a series of books about the retired detective Hannibal Stern and the four-hundred-year-old ghost, Sir Roger de Rudisill, who share a moated castle in amity. When a darkened train pulls into the station without its expected passenger, the Crown Prince Brulph, who is to be crowned on Midsummer's Day, Hannibal is asked to guard the tower in which the crown lies in state. He sees a ghostly hand remove it, reports the theft, and is himself suspected. With Holmesian aplomb, Hannibal solves both mysteries, appearing with the crown and the prince. There is a logical (well, as logical as such fantasy ever gets) explanation, and there are visual clues to the mystery. The illustrations echo the light touch of the writing but are not as deft; in particular, they are awkward in depicting the fog that plays a large part in the proceedings.

207 **Caines,** Jeannette Franklin. *Abby;* illus. by Steven Kellogg. Harper, 1973. 32p. Trade ed. $3.95; Library ed. $3.79 net.

3-6 yrs. A story told in dialogue is simple, amusing, and disarmingly sweet and natural. Abby is a very small black girl who is looking at her baby book and asks, "Ma, where did I come from?" "Manhattan." "How old was I when you and Daddy got me?" "Eleven months and thirteen days." Abby's older brother comes in, she makes overtures, he is busy, she feels rejected; he weakens, and sits down with her. When he leaves, Abby suggests they adopt a boy for Kevin. The story is charming in itself, and as a story about adoption, it is far more effective than most.

208 **Calhoun,** Mary Huiskamp. *The Battle of Reuben Robin & Kite Uncle John;* illus. by Janet McCaffery. Morrow, 1973. 30p. Trade ed. $4.50; Library ed. $4.14 net.

K-3 Vigorous illustrations add humor to a tallish tale that is written with the cadence of speech, nice for reading aloud and for storytelling. A lively, elderly man, called "Kite Uncle John" because he taught all the children how to fly kites, had found a superlative string for kite flying—but when his kite was made, he saw that Reuben Robin had also discovered the string, in fact was using it for nest-building. John took the string, the robin fussed; John flew the kite, the robin followed, scolding. Kite Uncle John ran himself breathless trying to outwit the competitive bird, who rode the kite, pecked at the string, and finally just took it in his beak and hung on. The problem is solved to the satisfaction of both parties in a rollicking, light-weight, pleasant story.

209 **Calhoun,** Mary Huiskamp. *Euphonia and the Flood;* pictures by Simms Taback. Parents Magazine, 1976. 75-19274. 28p. Trade ed. $5.50; Library ed. $4.96 net.

K-3 A breezy tall tale has humor, action, and some word play to appeal to the read-aloud audience; it is illustrated with busy drawings, awkward but vigorous. Euphonia, a brisk maiden lady in leg-of-mutton sleeves and sunbonnet, has a motto: "If a thing is worth doing, it's worth doing well" and this recurs throughout the story, as Euphonia, her broom Briskly, and her pig Fatly careen along in a flooded creek, rescuing animals whether they want rescuing or not. Just before the waterfall, they turn in to shore (they've been riding just to see where the flood was going) and join Farmer Stump at the picnic tables he's set up. Calhoun is a capable and experienced storyteller, and her writing has a cadence that makes her stories useful for telling as well as for reading aloud.

210 **Calhoun,** Mary Huiskamp. *Medicine Show; Conning People and Making Them Like It.* Harper, 1976. 75-25417. 136p. illus. Trade ed. $6.96; Library ed. $6.79 net.

6-9 A conversational, breezy, but well-researched survey of the quacks and confidence men—and some women—who toured the United States from the mid-19th century to the 1940's. Much of Calhoun's story is based on the reminiscences of her son's father-in-law, Cliff Mann, who was part of a touring family from the age of eight. This is both a history of the medicine show and some of its most illustrious or infamous stars, and an explanation of the way in which the confidence man operates; it is rife with color, with the jargon of the trade, and with dramatic and humorous anecdotes about the "doctors," the fake royalty, and the musicians and other performers who amused the crowds until the serious business of the pitch came along. A divided bibliography, a glossary of terms, and an index are appended.

211 **Calhoun,** Mary Huiskamp. *Old Man Whickutt's Donkey;* illus. by Tomie de Paola. Parents Magazine, 1975. 74-12289. 38p. Trade ed. $4.95. Library ed. $4.95 net.

K-3 Engagingly funny pictures complement the rustic flavor of a sort of hillbilly version of the LaFontaine fable about the man who ends a journey carrying his beast of burden. Here it's Old Man Whickutt and his boy (grandson) and his donkey who go off to the mill with a sack of corn. The sack slides, the donkey rears, and the old man says, "Derned fool donkey! Acts as addled as a hen with its head off," and he slings the sack under the donkey's belly. Comments of passersby elicit various other methods, and the ending has a bit of new embroidery. The colloquial conversation, the regional idiom, and the humor of the pictures make this as much fun for the readers as for their audience.

212 **Cameron,** Eleanor. *The Court of the Stone Children.* Dutton, 1973. 191p. $5.50.

5-7 A nice concoction of mystery, fantasy, and realism adroitly blended in a contemporary story in San Francisco. Nina and her parents had recently come from a small mountain town, and the lonely girl hated the apartment, hated the city, almost hated her father for bringing the family. Through a chance acquaintance, an understanding and sensitive boy, Nina found the small museum where a ghost from the past became her friend and sought Nina's help in clearing the reputation of her father, declared a traitor by Napoleon. The fact that with all of this, Nina finds a new apartment with a view and is set on the path of her profession (museum curator) and that the story is not overburdened but enriched is a tribute to the author's skill. The characters are interesting, the plot threads nicely integrated.

213 **Cameron,** Eleanor. *Julia and the Hand of God;* illus. by Gail Owens. Dutton, 1977. 77-4507. 168p. $6.95.

4-6 In *A Room Made of Windows,* Julia was older than she is here; in fact, the story—which begins with Julia's eleventh birthday—focuses on Julia's, and her mother's dissatisfaction with their accommodations and concludes with their delight in finding a new home and its room "made of windows." For Julia, her brother, and their widowed mother live with crotchety, critical Gramma, who dotes on brother Greg and carps at Julia. Cameron is adroit at weaving plot and subplots together, and Julia's story emerges as a perceptive family story as well as an excellent piece of period fiction, highlighted by the excitement and drama of the raging fire that sweeps Berkeley. Characterization and relationships are drawn with depth and consistency, and the book has a compelling narrative flow.

214 **Cameron,** Eleanor. *To the Green Mountains.* Dutton, 1975. 75-6758. 180p. $6.95.

5-8 * Kath hadn't seen her grandmother's mountain home since she was four, but she dreamed of it still, longed to leave Ohio and the detested hotel life and escape to the cool and spacious Vermont hills. Kath's father is a ne'er-do-well who, on his infrequent visits from his farm, ignores her; he is supported by his wife, who manages a hotel with the capable help of Grant, a black man. Grant and his wife Tiss are Kath's close friends, and she is upset both because there is censure of her mother for helping Grant with his plans to read law and by the fact that Tiss resents his studying. Only after a difficult decision to divorce her husband and an adjustment to Tiss's tragic accidental death does Kath's mother decide to return to Vermont, and the book ends with the journey. This is surely the best of Eleanor Cameron's realistic fiction: her characters are vivid, they are affected by—and affect—each other and the course of the story; relationships are intricate but not confusing; the dialogue is smooth, the story line both fluid and cohesive.

215 **Caras,** Roger. *A Zoo in Your Room;* illus. by Pamela Johnson. Harcourt, 1975. 74-24322. 96p. $5.95.

5-8 Sensible advice on housing, feeding, and caring for pets is tempered by cautionary reminders about safety for the child, respect for pets, and not keeping creatures that are endangered species. The book is organized in a useful fashion: for birds, for example, Caras describes appropriate captive-bred species to buy, enclosures, food, and "tips," suggestions for keeping birds safe and content. The final chapters discuss different kinds of terrariums. There is an occasional florid note (". . . nature had already made her decision.") but the writing is, on the whole, brisk and direct. A bibliography and an index are appended.

216 **Carew,** Jan. *The Third Gift;* illus. by Leo and Diane Dillon. Little, 1974. 32p. $5.95.

3-5 An African tale by a Guyana-born author has a rich, poetic quality that is echoed in the brilliant colors and intricate patterns of the handsome illustrations. A prophet who had led his people from famine to a land of plenty decrees that when he dies, the tribe's young men must climb the Nameless Mountain, and that he who climbs the highest shall bring a gift to his people. Three times in the tribe's history, a gift is brought to the people; first they are given the gift of work, then the gift of beauty, then the gift of fantasy, of imagination and faith. "So," the story ends, "with the gifts of Work and Beauty and Imagination, the Jubas became poets and bards and creators, and they live at the foot of Nameless Mountain to this day." The writing style is rather grave and ornate, not as direct as most traditional folklore is, which may limit its appeal to some readers and be an added attraction for those who enjoy poetic prose.

217 **Carle,** Eric. *All about Arthur (an absolutely absurd ape).* Watts, 1974. 27p. illus. $5.95.

3-6 yrs. A combination of photographic and woodcut techniques is used to illustrate an alphabet book that catalogs the friends made by Arthur who left Atlanta because he felt all alone. In Baltimore he met a bear named Ben, in Cincinnati Cindy the cat, et cetera; each animal has an extravagantly alliterative description ("In Jacksonville, he met a jaguar who could juggle. His name was John. A jolly judge had just released John from jail.") that should amuse children because of the appeal of absurdity. There's no liaison, simply a cataloging, but the combined appeals of interesting pages, each of which has a large photograph of a letter from a signboard, nonsense, and animals should be attractive as well as instructive to the audience for alphabet books.

218 **Carle,** Eric. *The Grouchy Ladybug.* T. Y. Crowell, 1977. 77-3170. 39p. illus. Trade ed. $6.95; Library ed. $7.95 net.

4-6 yrs. Carle's story is about a ladybug, but he also manages to get across the idea of bullies being cowardly (if one stands up to them) and to introduce the concept of comparative size. The story line is simple: a grouchy ladybug refuses to share the aphids on a leaf with another ladybug, then offers to fight a series of creatures ranging from a yellow jacket to a whale. Each time her pugnacious offer to fight is accepted, the grouchy ladybug says, "Oh, you're not big enough," and flies off. Tired and hungry, she eventually accepts the other ladybug's leavings. The pages are set back, graduated in size, and the concept of time is also introduced, with a nice twist at the end; whereas other creatures were encountered on the hour, it takes almost an hour just to fly past the whale. A fresh approach is developed with ingenuity, and the bold, colorful paintings are particularly effective, with larger and larger print used as the size of the pages increases.

219 **Carlson,** Dale Bick. *Girls Are Equal Too; The Women's Movement for Teenagers;* illus. by Carol Nicklaus. Atheneum, 1973. 146p. $6.25.

6-9 A discussion of what causes sexist attitudes and how females are discriminated against in their personal, academic, professional, and social roles is written with vigor, a polemic rather than a diatribe, and in a sharp, humorous style. While all of the attitudes toward, and treatment of, girls and women are sadly true, they seem slightly exaggerated here because there is so seldom a mention of the exceptions. (Some parents do give girls scientific toys, some teachers do encourage female students to become architects or economists, etc.) Yet what Ms. Carlson propounds is basically true; from the cradle on, traditionally, girls have been encouraged to become appendages rather than people—and the author briskly notes that some people may prefer to do housework but they should have options, that some career women may prefer to do all the grocery-shopping and cooking, but they shouldn't be expected to do it. If this accomplishes nothing else, which is not likely, it may at least disabuse some teenagers of the notion that being attractive is a career and that not being pretty is a disaster. A bibliography is appended.

220 **Carlson,** Natalie Savage. *Marie Louise's Heyday;* illus. by Jose Aruego and Ariane Dewey. Scribner, 1975. 75-8345. 30p. $6.95.

3-5 yrs. Marie Louise is a mongoose and the children she takes care of are possums, but they might as well be human beings, because the fun of the story is in the childlike behavior that should bring giggles of recognition from small listeners. Having declared it is her heyday and pondered the delicious possibilities of where and how to eat her favorite food (banana) Marie Louise is not delighted when called on to babysit five possum children whose mother has been called away on an emergency. The playful five exhaust Marie Louise, they won't eat the lunch their mother has left, they eat poisonous berries and require medication. Too tired to eat, the babysitter goes home and to bed; next day, she is surprised by a visit from her charges complete with compliments and a bouquet. Relishing her banana and gazing at her flowers, Mary Louise decides that *this* is her heyday. The light, wry approach adds piquancy to the tale, the dialogue is sprightly, and the illustrations—economical line, small pictures nicely placed and spaced, comic expressions on the animal's faces—fit the page as deftly as they echo the mood of the story.

221 **Carpelan,** Bo. *Dolphins in the City;* trans. from the Swedish by Sheila La Farge. Delacorte/Seymour Lawrence, 1976. 75-8001. 145p. $5.95.

6-9 A quiet, brooding person himself, fourteen-year-old Johan was patient and affectionate toward the retarded Marvin, whom he had met when vacationing on the island where Marvin and his mother lived. Now the islanders have come to Helsinki; Marvin gets a low-skill job and his mother becomes a charwoman, but they are desperately unhappy in the cold and alien city. The book ends on an encouraging but realistic note; it is not an exciting story but it is deeply perceptive and thoughtful, a study in human relations and fine analysis both of the narrator, who has normal problems, and of the deeply troubled Marvin.

222 **Carrick,** Malcolm. *The Wise Men of Gotham;* adapted and illus. by Malcolm Carrick. Viking, 1975. 74-10832. 41p. $6.95.

4-6 First published in England, a selection of tales from a chapbook version of *The Foles of Gotyam* is adapted and illustrated with vigorous, busy pictures, some in color and some in black and white. Almost every culture has a set of tales like these, a collection of stories about the noodleheads of a particular town. The retellings are blithe and bouncy, the pictures captivating in their humor and vitality. The silly Gotham folk love spring, so they capture a spring bird, the cuckoo, so that it will always be spring; when a huge eel eats all the fish in the net, they punish him by putting him in the river to drown; the blacksmith burns down his forge to rid it of wasps.

223 **Carroll,** Lewis. *Poems of Lewis Carroll;* comp. by Myra Cohn Livingston; illus. by John Tenniel, Harry Furniss, Henry Holiday, Arthur B. Frost, and Lewis Carroll. T. Y. Crowell, 1973. 149p. $4.50.

5- How nice to have so much of Carroll's delightful daftness in one volume, with poems from Wonderland, ciphers and riddle-poems, the famous "Hiawatha" parody, odd bits of humorous verse, and the saga of the Snark. The editor's biographical introduction and notes on the poems make the book all the more interesting and useful to Carroll buffs. An index is appended.

224 **Carter,** Dorothy Sharp, ad. *The Enchanted Orchard; And Other Folktales of Central America;* selected and ad. by Dorothy Sharp Carter; illus. by W. T. Mars. Harcourt, 1973. 126p. $4.75.

5-7 Handsomely illustrated, this excellent collection has wide variety, a fluent and colloquial style in the retellings, and a section of notes that give backgrounds and sources. The tales include myths and legends from early Indian cultures, animal tales and "why" stories, and some ghostly tales. All of the selections are quite brief, and the anthology reflects broadly the diversity and mores of Central American cultures.

225 **Carter,** Dorothy Sharp, ad. *Greedy Mariani; And Other Folktales of the Antilles;* illus. by Trina Schart Hyman. Atheneum, 1974. 131p. $5.50.

4-6 One of the most delightful collections of folktales to appear in a long, long time, these stories from the West Indies are illustrated with black and white drawings that are handsome and dramatic. The stories are entertaining in themselves, but they are made delectable by the adapter's style, which captures to perfection the conversational tone of the oral tradition, extracts every ounce of humor from the stories, and handles deftly the use of other languages in dialogue.

226 **Causley,** Charles. *Figgie Hobbin;* illus. by Trina Schart Hyman. Walker, 1974. 48p. Trade ed. $4.94; Library ed. $4.85 net.

3-4 The delicate details of Hyman's illustrations, raffish or serene in mood, add to the appeal of a small collection of poems that range from nonsense verse to selections that have the poignancy of a ballad. A few of the poems are just rhyming fun; others are more substantial, and the collection includes some narrative poems.

227 **Cawley,** Winifred. *Gran at Coalgate;* illus. by Fermin Rocker. Holt, 1975. 75-6944. 211p. $6.50.

6-8 Worried about an exam, Jinnie becomes ill and is sent to her grandmother's for a rest. Gran's town, Coalgate, is a mining community in northern England; the time is the 1920's; a background issue is the imminent General Strike. Jinnie's father is strict, conservative, and out of sympathy with the miners, so she is unprepared for the sentiment she encounters at Coalgate. She's also unprepared for her Aunt Polly, who is clearly having an affair although she is married, and who is just as clearly flaunting it and making her son Will miserable. Jinnie is allowed by her beloved Gran to do all sorts of things her Dad would disapprove of, even to go to a dance, and there she sees a flapper doing the Charleston. Awful! Delightful! There are light moments and there is social commentary in the story; there's some high drama, although the book is on the whole rather sedate, a period piece given vitality by the sharp characterization and the color of the local speech patterns. The print is wretchedly small.

228 **Chance,** Stephen. *Septimus and the Danedyke Mystery.* Nelson, 1973. 137p. $4.95.

6- The Reverend Septimus Treloar is an engaging and gentlemanly cleric-detective, former member of the CID, who investigates the mysterious incursions into St. Mary's Danedyke, although he cannot imagine what there is in the church that thieves want. Septimus and the two young people who are helping him in the investigation are caught and held prisoners on a boat, but engineer both an escape and the capture of the culprits who have stolen a valuable religious relic; the story ends with a suave bit of blackmail by the parson, who forces the absent leader of the thieves to make a sizable "voluntary" contribution to the church. Lively style, good construction, better characterization than there is in most mystery stories, and a brisk pace contribute to the value of a tale with well-maintained suspense.

229 **Chance,** Stephen. *The Stone of Offering*. Nelson, 1977. 77-1485. 191p. $6.95.

7- Once again the Reverend Philip Turner, writing under the name of Chance, has his ex-policeman clergyman, the Reverend Septimus Treloar, stumble into a mystery which he solves. This time Septimus is climbing the Welsh hills when he runs into an old wartime friend, Colonel Sanderson, who starts him on the trail. The resentment and hostility expressed by the villagers against a proposed plan to flood their valley for a dam that will bring electrical power is understandable, but why, he wonders, the element of magic and propitiatory sacrifices of live creatures? When Septimus realizes a child's life is threatened, he speeds the pace of investigation and takes a chance on his own life. The author has an elegant style that permits his own erudition to emerge through his characters in believable fashion, and he creates convincingly both the rural setting and the colorful local characters; the raveling of the plot is occasionally cumbersome, but not enough so to slow the pace or lessen the suspense.

230 **Charlip,** Remy. *Handtalk; An ABC of Finger Spelling & Sign Language;* by Remy Charlip, Mary Beth, and George Ancona. Parents' Magazine, 1974. 42p. illus. $4.95.

3- Why, one wonders, did nobody ever think of doing this before? It's for the deaf and those who live or work with them, it's for children who are intrigued by any kind of sign language, and it may have a significant influence on children's attitudes toward those who are aurally handicapped. Handsome color photographs show the signs for letters (and some of the shorthand signs for words) and almost every page shows a word in handtalk (angel, bug, crazy, etc.) with all the letters given on early pages and the interpretation left, after that, to the reader. The whole alphabet is printed separately inside the book jacket for easier reference. It's attractive, informative, amusing, and long overdue.

231 **Charlip,** Remy. *Harlequin; And the Gift of Many Colors;* by Remy Charlip and Burton Supree; illus. by Remy Charlip. Parents' Magazine, 1973. 36p. Trade ed. $4.50; Library ed. $4.19 net.

K-3 Based on the factual story of the origin of the commedia dell'arte character's costume, this is illustrated in soft, soft colors, the first scenes of a small boy alone in his room a dramatic contrast to later pages, swirling with the action of a festival. Too poor to have a costume for the carnival, Harlequin sadly tells his friends he will not be there. Each of the children brings a piece of cloth from his own costume, and Harlequin's mother painstakingly sews them on his own cloths until he is a rainbow figure, clothed—the story ends—"in the love of his friends." The writing style is subdued, but the story has enough conflict-resolution and the perennial appeal of a granted wish to compensate.

232 **Charosh,** Mannis. *Number Ideas Through Pictures;* illus. Giulio Maestro. T. Y. Crowell, 1974. 33p. $3.95.

2-4 Informal but dignified, simply written, a text that presents such mathematical concepts as odd and even numbers, square numbers, triangular numbers, and some of the ways in which these can be combined and manipulated. The pictures are clear and helpful (save for one in which there is too little color differentiation) using pictures of cats or houses or buttons to illustrate the text. Like other books in the series, this is notable for the appropriateness of scope and vocabulary as well as for the way in which it approaches mathematical ideas; there is, however, one point in the text in which, after combining odd and even numbers in several ways, the procedure is reversed ("We can now show without pairing that 17 is an odd number: 17 = 10 + 7 = even + odd = odd," . . .) which seems rather abruptly to imply an understanding of division.

233 **Cheki Haney,** Erene. *Yoga for Children;* by Erene Cheki Haney and Ruth Richards; illus. by Betty Schilling. Bobbs-Merrill, 1973. 39p. $4.95

3-5 Simplified instructions for a group of exercises that imitate animal postures are illustrated by drawings that are mediocre in quality but are adequately clear as instructional diagrams. General advice includes the facts that there should never be any strain and that the child should rest after each exercise. The book can also be used by adults working with younger children.

234 **Cheng,** Hou-tien. *The Chinese New Year;* scissor cuts by the author. Holt, 1976. 76-8229. 29p. $5.50.

4-6 Cheng Hou-tien describes the events of each of the days of the Little New Year, the five-day celebration of the New Year that follows, and the three-day Festival of Lanterns that takes place ten days later, with the first full moon of the new year. The Chinese New Year, a movable holiday, falls between January 21 and February 20, and has been celebrated for five thousand years; the book concludes with an explanation of the twelve-year cycle of animal signs. Cheng is a master of the art of papercutting and his illustrations, each page cut from a single sheet of paper in intricate style, are handsome but, as printed on the page, give no real sense of the medium since they could as well have been painted.

235 **Chesnutt,** Charles W. *Conjure Tales;* retold by Ray Anthony Shepard; illus. by John Ross and Clare Romano. Dutton, 1973. 99p. $4.95.

5-9 Tales from Chesnutt's *Conjure Woman;* published in 1899, the stories had first appeared separately in the *Atlantic Monthly*. These early stories by a black author are vigorous and humorous, full of action and drama, yet they reveal fully the injustice and cruelty of slavery. Ray Shepard has retold the tales brilliantly, with the true cadence and flow of the oral tradition.

236 **Child Study Association of America.** comp. *Courage to Adventure;* Stories of Boys and Girls Growing Up with America; selected by the Child Study Association of America/Wel-Met; illus. by Reisie Lonette. T. Y. Crowell, 1976. 75-29159. 277p. $8.95.

4-6 An anthology that covers the years of national growth from revolutionary war times to the present consists primarily of excerpts from books, although there are some short stories from magazines and two sets of lyrics ("The Erie Canal" and "Oh, Susanna"). The material is chronologically arranged, chosen with discrimination, and varied; it's a nice change for the bicentennial year to have a book that focuses on two hundred years rather than one period that was two hundred years ago.

237 **Child Study Association of America.** *Families Are Like That!* illus. by Richard Cuffari. T. Y. Crowell, 1975. 73-21647. 142p. $6.50.

2-4 Cuffari's simply composed line drawings illustrate a selection of stories, or excerpts from books, that have been chosen with discrimination. Family life and relationships are the theme of the book, and the stories have variety in style, setting, and plot. Included are ten stories by Rose Blue, Emma Brock, Carolyn Haywood, Marion Holland, Doris Johnson, Joan Lexau, Patricia Miles Martin (two), Ruth Sonneborn, and Janice Udry.

238 **Childress,** Alice. *a HERO ain't nothin' but a Sandwich.* Coward, 1973. 126p. $5.95.

6-9 "I hate for people to lie on me . . . Why folks got to lie and say I'm on skag, say I'm a junkie? My grandmother say, 'You a dope fiend.'" He's not, Benjie insists, he can do without the stuff any time he wants. But to the despair of his family and his best friend, he can't. Benjie is thirteen. Parts of the story are told by Benjie, others by his mother, grandmother, stepfather, friend, school principal, etc. It is Benjie's stepfather who is the true hero; despite Benjie's resistance to his overtures, Butler Craig keeps offering love and security to the boy, and in the end wins his trust. Whether or not he has convinced Benjie (who is attending a rehabilitation center) to hew to the line is moot, since the book ends with Butler waiting to see if Benjie will show up for treatment. This is not only a moving if harrowing story but also a literary triumph; only a playwright as experienced as Childress could achieve such drama and such conviction in a book that consists of short monologues.

239 **Childress,** Alice. *When the Rattlesnake Sounds;* drawings by Charles Lilly. Coward, 1975. 75-10456. 32p. $5.95.

5-9 A play based on the summer in which Harriet Tubman worked as a laundress in a New Jersey resort hotel. There is little movement in this one-act drama, but a wealth of poignant dialogue, for the two girls working with Harriet had volunteered at a church meeting to put every penny of their earnings, beyond what they needed for food, toward the antislavery cause. One, Celia, has been plaintive about the hard work, but as Harriet Tubman talks about attaining her own freedom and her vow to dedicate her life to helping other slaves escape bondage, Celia is strengthened and cheered. The title refers to Harriet's consoling Celia about her fear by saying, "Child, you lookin at a woman who's been plenty afraid. When the rattlesnake sounds a warnin . . . It's time to be scared." Despite the lack of action, the play is moving because of its subject and impressive because of the deftness with which Childress develops characters and background in so brief and static a setting.

240 **Christopher,** John. *Wild Jack.* Macmillan. 1974. 147p. $5.95.

6-9 The first of a new trilogy is set in the 23rd century, in an England where (as in other Christopher books) a new kind of society has emerged after the breakdown of the civilization we know today. Clive is the pampered son of an influential city dweller, contemptuous of the savages that live outside each of the isolated cities of the world. Falsely accused of criticizing the authorities, he is sent to an island prison, escapes with an American and a Japanese boy to the Outlands and is picked up by Wild Jack, a rebel in the Robin Hood tradition. By the time the book ends, Clive has realized that he prefers the freedom and the self-reliance of the Outlands to the chauvinism of the cloistered city. A colorful setting, a wholly conceived society, strong characters, and plenty of action will leave readers, especially science fiction buffs, waiting for more.

241 **Chukovsky,** Kornei. *The Silver Crest; My Russian Boyhood;* trans. from the Russian by Beatrice Stillman. Holt, 1976. 75-32248. 182p. $6.95.

6- Kornei Chukovsky was both an authority on the language of childhood and a children's author. This account of his late childhood has the same qualities of candor and humor that have made his poetry popular. Son of an unwed mother, the eleven-year-old Kornei was evicted from school on a slim pretext because he was socially undesirable. The ploys he tries in order to stay in school and keep his friends, the misery he feels when he fails in the former and is little more successful in the latter, are as touching as they are comical. The setting is unusual, the period details vivid, yet everything that Kornei feels when he loses the silver school crest from his cap is universal.

242 **Chwast,** Seymour, illus. *The House that Jack Built;* designed and illus. by Seymour Chwast. Random House, 1973. 23p. $1.25.

2-5 yrs. A clever variation on the familiar nursery rhyme is achieved by a series of stiff pages, each leaf a larger square than the preceding one. "This is the malt that lay in the house that Jack built," is on a page just a bit over an inch square, the next page is 2½ inches square, and so on until the last, fullsize page. The pages are bound in the lower left-hand corner, so that the backgrounds of the larger pages are always visible and make a complete picture; the characters cumulate on the pages just as they do in the text. Funny pictures, tried-and-true text, an inventive concept.

243 **Clapp,** Patricia. *Dr. Elizabeth; The Story of the First Woman Doctor.* Lothrop, 1974. 157p. Trade ed. $4.95; Library ed. $4.59 net.

6-10 As she did in *Constance,* the author uses first person to gain immediacy in a fine biography of the first woman to get a medical degree in the United States. The difficulties Elizabeth Blackwell had in being admitted to medical school, in getting post-graduate training, and in being accepted as a practitioner have been described in other biographies, but—seen from her own viewpoint—gain an added dimension here. One reason this is so is that Dr. Blackwell is not pictured as an early convert: an older friend suggested it, and the young schoolteacher was not at first enthralled. Her problems, her triumphs, and her encouragement of other women who entered the medical profession are interesting and admirable. The use of the first person is convincing and it avoids the adulatory tone so often found in third person biographies. An epilogue describes Dr. Blackwell's last years; a bibliography is appended.

244 **Clapp,** Patricia. *I'm Deborah Sampson; A Soldier in the War of the Revolution.* Lothrop, 1977. 76-51770. 176p. Trade ed. $6.50; Library ed. $5.61 net.

5-8 Clapp adds a new dimension to the story of the young woman who, disguised as a man, served as "Robert Shurtlieff" in the Continental Army during the Revolutionary War. For Deborah tells her own story and, in describing her childhood and youth, and the death of the young soldier she had expected to marry, gives reasons for her enlistment. She is candid about some of the problems she has during her service, hiding her identity by retreating to the woods when necessary, and becomes used to seeing her comrades relieving themselves or bathing. The writing style is vigorous, the historical details accurate and unobtrusive, and the language and concepts consistently appropriate for the period.

245 **Clark,** Ann Nolan. *Year Walk.* Viking, 1975. 197p. $6.95.

7-9 The setting and the protagonist are unusual in a story about Basque sheepherders in Idaho. The author gives a vivid picture of both the Spanish Basque community from which sixteen-year-old Kepa comes and the vicissitudes of his first year in America, in 1910. There's a love interest as a minor theme, but the book's appeal to readers will rest primarily on the details of Kepa's long, often lonely travels. Because the old man who is training him becomes ill, Kepa must finish the year by himself, caring for a flock of over two thousand sheep on a journey that totals hundreds of miles. Ann Nolan Clark gives the story pace and variety, believable characters, and a convincing evocation of time and place.

246 **Clark,** Mavis Thorpe. *The Sky Is Free.* Macmillan, 1976. 76-15171. 173p. $6.95.

6-9 First published in Australia, this tightly structured story concerns two runaway boys who meet and decide to travel together. Sam is angry at his family, Tony has run away from an orphanage; they decide to cross the desert and go to Opal Town. They have no money, no equipment, no food, no friends. Caught stealing groceries, they are given a probationary term helping an elderly miner, Bob; Sam is aware that Tony desperately craves some opal and he is sure that his friend has stolen some. He's also sure of the reason: Tony feels rootless and is convinced that he can track down his family (he was a foundling) if he has enough money. In the end, Tony's ethical sense prevails: he leaves the opal for old Bob, steals off to free some wild camels that have been caught for export, and leaves town. Sam insists *he* has freed the animals, knowing that Tony would be prosecuted by the irate stockade owner and knowing he himself will be sent home. So each boy has gained enough maturity to make a sacrifice for a friend, in an unexpectedly touching ending to a story that reflects the flinty, harsh life of the opal mining country. Characterization, dialogue, and setting are of equally high quality.

247 **Clark,** Mavis Thorpe. *Spark of Opal*. Macmillan, 1973. 215p. $4.95.

6-9 First published in Australia, this story of a family's problems in eking out a living as opal miners is realistic in approach, written with vitality, and remarkable for the evocation of its harsh and distinctive setting. Liz, who is fifteen, is the protagonist; she and her mother are anxious to leave and move to Adelaide so that they can be near a good school. Her father hopes for just one lucky strike before they go, her younger brother resents having to leave his friend Steve. Even Liz is unhappy at the thought of leaving her friend Kathy, and hopes that the house in Adelaide will be big enough so that Steve and Kathy can live with the family. While the book has a sturdy plot that centers on the finding of a good "parcel" of opals, and the plot has suspense and satisfaction, it is given depth both by the family's affection for Steve and Kathy, who are aborigines, and by the object lesson they learn in their unwarranted prejudice against a Greek neighbor.

248 **Clarke,** Joan. *Early Rising*. Lippincott, 1976. 76-17874. 252p. $7.95.

5-8 A lovely period piece, this is set in an English vicarage in the 1880's, where Erica and her brothers and sisters are being brought up by a widowed father and a loving staff. Erica is the Jo March in this family, an independent romping child who is excitable and vehement. When an older half-sister, Beatrice, comes to keep house for the brood, Erica refuses to see, so anxious is she for a mother substitute, that Beattie is domineering, biased, and often untruthful. Eventually Erica sees Beattie clearly, but by then she has had a year abroad, she has had a proposal, and she has firmly decided on a college education. The book is filled with lively incidents, the characters come alive, and the style is light and fluent.

249 **Clarke,** Pauline. *Torolv the Fatherless;* illus. by Cecil Leslie. Faber, 1978. 190p. $5.95.

6-9 First published in England, this fine historical adventure tale is set in Saxon England during the reign of Ethelred the Unready. A Viking waif is accidentally stranded when the ship leaves while he is (against instructions) ashore. Brought up in the household of an elderly earl, Torolv becomes a loved foster child; as he grows, the boy shifts his allegiance, and by the time the earl dies fighting

Vikings at the Battle of Maldon, there is no question of his loyalty to the English forces. Like Sutcliff, Clarke has the ability to blend historical details so deftly into her narrative that they seem effortless. While the book has many characters and incidents (identified in the author's concluding notes) that are real, they are not wooden insertions but vivid parts of the whole.

250 **Cleary,** Beverly. *Ramona the Brave;* illus. by Alan Tiegreen. Morrow, 1975. 190p. Trade ed. $5.50. Library ed. $4.81 net.

3-5 A sequel to *Ramona the Pest* is equally diverting, written with the ebullient humor and sympathy that distinguish Cleary's stories. Ramona is as convincing a first-grader as a fictional character can be, trying to be compliant but too independent a child to be conforming. She's bored by her first-grade teacher and relieved to learn her older sister felt the same way; she's thrilled by having a room of her own but ashamed of the fact that she's nervous when alone at night; she's pleased when her father calls her his spunky girl and entirely satisfied with herself when she does something that proves it. This is a perfect book for installment reading to younger children as well as a pleasure trip for independent readers.

251 **Cleary,** Beverly. *Ramona and Her Father;* illus. by Alan Tiegreen. Morrow, 1977. 77-1614. 186p. Trade ed. $6.50; Library ed. $6.01 net.

3-5 Another warm, funny, pithy story about Ramona, now in second grade, has some problem situations, large and small, but it is the engaging candor of Ramona, expressed in Cleary's impeccably authentic dialogue and exposition, that gives validity to the book. Daddy loses his job and there are resultant strains on family finances and relationships, but life goes on. In any household containing Ramona it could hardly do otherwise.

252 **Cleaver,** Vera. *Trial Valley;* by Vera and Bill Cleaver. Lippincott, 1977. 76-54303. 158p. $7.95.

6-9 The protagonist of *Where the Lilies Bloom* is now sixteen, not quite ready to fall in love but aware that two young men, Thad and Gaither, are smitten. Mary Call is still proud, strong, and independent; she refuses help from her brother-in-law, Kiser, and ekes out a living by gathering plants, "wildcrafting," with the help of a younger brother and sister who complain that she is a tyrant but rely on her love and judgment. Mary Call's love goes out to a small, abandoned boy, Jack, who clings to her rather than to her sister and brother-in-law, who are anxious to adopt the child. When Jack is lost, Mary Call realizes that she could never marry Thad, who is less concerned with the boy's welfare than with

Mary Call's safety. She insists that Jack live with Kiser and Devola; she accepts Gaither's continuing help in managing her affairs, she feels a responsibility to her siblings, yet Mary Call isn't quite ready to give up her dreams of a better life, a chance for her to move on alone. She's standing at the brink. The writing style is fluent, the dialogue excellent save for a tendency to lean heavily on local idiom, which gives color to the book but results in Mary Call sounding at times like a young, poetic philosopher and at times—when she uses the idiom—like an educated hillbilly. But the overall effect of the story is still impressive; the setting is vividly evoked, the characters come alive, the relationships are perceptive.

253 **Clement,** Roland C. *Hammond Nature Atlas of America.* Ridge/Hammond, 1973. 225p. illus. $17.95.

7- An oversize book profusely illustrated with beautiful color photographs and useful location maps is designed, as the editor's introductory section makes clear, for the automobile age, for neophyte naturalists who can use the text and the maps when they visit sites throughout the United States. Although this does not pretend to be comprehensive in coverage, it gives a considerable amount of information on such topics as rocks and minerals, trees, wildflowers, birds, insects, et cetera. The writing varies from section to section, occasionally ornate, but written by subject experts and therefore authoritative; the maps are particularly useful, both the range maps and such maps as those on climate and temperature, rainfall and sunshine, or public lands—topics that are not covered in the text. A glossary, a list of books suggested for reading (many of which are guides or handbooks), and an index are appended.

254 **Clifton,** Lucille. *Amifika;* illus. by Thomas DiGrazia. Dutton, 1977. 77-5887. 26p. $5.95.

4-6 yrs. Amifika's Daddy was coming home, having finished his military service. How could his Mama make space in their two rooms? He overheard her tell a cousin, "We'll just get rid of something he won't miss. Lot of stuff around here he won't even remember." Amifika didn't remember his Daddy—so would Daddy remember him? Probably not, so Amifika hides lest he be thrown away to make space; he falls asleep outdoors and wakes to find he is being carried in his father's warm and loving arms. A gentle and moving story is told with conviction and simplicity and is illustrated with black and white pictures that have no hard lines but a soft, rounded quality befitting the circle of warmth that is Amifika's family.

255 **Clifton,** Lucille. *Don't You Remember?* illus. by Evaline Ness. Dutton, 1973. 26p. $4.95.

3-5 yrs. It was very irritating to Denise Mary Tate, who was four years old. She wanted to go to work with her father, who kept saying, "Next time," but when she said it was now next time, he seemed unable to remember what she said. Her mother, too; she'd promised to bring home a cake from the bakery where she worked, a cake that said "Tate" on it. She never remembered; Tate remembered everything. One morning her parents and brothers woke her, and there was the cake, and she was allowed to have coffee, and she was going to work with Daddy. She'd forgotten, they teased, that it was her birthday. But she hadn't, because she remembered everything. A charming black family story, lightly and affectionately told, is illustrated by Evaline Ness at her best.

256 **Clifton,** Lucille. *Everett Anderson's Friend;* illus. by Ann Grifalconi. Holt, 1976. 75-32251. 20p. $5.95.

K-2 The free-flowing lines of Grifalconi's uncluttered pen and ink drawings echo the simplicity and directness of Clifton's verses. Everett Anderson, a small black boy who is the protagonist of earlier Clifton Books, is delighted to see a new family move in across the hall but disappointed, at first, when he learns that all the children are girls. He thinks Maria is too proficient at playing ball, he thinks three (two male friends and he) are just the right number, and he thinks things would be better if Daddy were there. But it's nice to be welcomed when you've lost your apartment key—and Maria's mother distributes tacos and kisses—and Maria proves to be a compatible fourth in Everett Anderson's group of friends. The writing style is light; the concerns, however, are those that loom large to an only child.

257 **Clifton,** Lucille. *The Times They Used to Be;* illus. by Susan Jeschke. Holt, 1974. 40p. $4.95.

5-6 Most books that awaken adult nostalgia are not quite as appealing to young readers, but this brief story has enough warmth and vitality and humor for any reader. "Mama, Mama, tell us about when you was a girl," it begins, and Mama tells. She was twelve years old, it was 1948, and her best friend Tassie (who, to her grandmother's dismay, wasn't saved) wanted to run off and find her father because she needed help. "I done become a sinner," she explained, "Sin done broke all out in my body." Turned out that Tassie's granny hadn't told her about menstruation, but her friend's mother came to the rescue. Woven through the story are bits about Amos and Andy, the end of segregation in the army, Satchel Paige getting up to the major league, all a fluid collage of the period and of a black family's life.

258 **Clymer,** Eleanor (Lowenton). *Luke Was There;* illus. by Diane de Groat. Holt, 1973. 74p. $4.95.

4-7 One of the greatest fears of children is that they will be abandoned, and Julius has good reason for his unhappiness. His father had left, and so had his stepfather; when his mother was hospitalized, he and his small brother went to a children's home. Luke, a black social worker, is the first person to win Julius' confidence, and when Luke goes (he is a conscientious objector and must take another job) Julius is disconsolate. He runs away, begs, commits petty theft, and comes back to the Children's House only when he finds a deserted boy of seven who needs a home. To his surprise, Julius is welcomed back, is not reproached by the staff, and even finds Luke, who has taken time off to look for him. The story ends with Julius and his brother home again with their mother, but Julius—who tells the story very convincingly—has not forgotten Luke, who was there when he was needed. Both in the depiction of the small, lost boy who clings to Julius and of Julius' little brother, who felt that he had been doubly abandoned when Julius ran away, there is a logical influence that makes Julius' growing understanding credible. The story is well-written, the hero Luke is sensitively characterized, and it is a relief to read a story in which both the stepfather and the authorities at a children's home are sympathetically portrayed.

259 **Clymer,** Theodore, ed. *Four Corners of the Sky; Poems, Chants, and Oratory;* illus. by Marc Brown. Little, 1975. 75-8893. 48p. $6.95.

5- A collection of short poems, chants, quotations from speeches, and songs from many native American cultures is handsomely illustrated with drawings that use various techniques but include many tribal motifs. The pages occasionally overwhelm the print with use of design and color. The textual excerpts are brief, and—while there is grouping of material—there is no organization, or none easily discernible; there is no table of contents or index; a bibliography is provided. Each selection has tribal identification, and the poems and chants are often beautiful and always interesting. A minor flaw: some selections are followed by explanations which are in the same type face but with size and leading reduced, and some readers may assume such comments to be part of the text.

260 **Coatsworth,** Elizabeth Jane. *Marra's World;* illus. by Krystyna Turska. Greenwillow, 1975. 75-9520. 83p. Trade ed. $5.95; Library ed. $5.11 net.

4-6 A strange and memorable story, this, with something of the evanescent quality of the foggy, mystical aura of the final scene. Living with a taciturn father and a hostile grandmother, Marra is a lonely child; she is dreamy, hapless, slow at her studies and the butt of her classmates' ridicule. She knows her mother was strangely silent, but her father will say no more about the wife who left him. Life changes for Marra when a new girl at school becomes her friend, and her friend's mother helps the child learn some skills, makes her new clothes, offers affection and approval. In the final scene, Marra and her friend Alison are in a boat, lost in the fog; Marra calls to her mother for help, and a grey seal steers the boat to the landing. Both girls immediately forget the episode, but Marra has a new sense of being loved. The story line is tenuous in ending, but that is amply compensated for by the creation of mood and setting, by the definitive characterization, and by the fluidity of the writing style.

261 **Cobalt,** Marin. *Pool of Swallows.* Nelson, 1974. 140p. $5.25.

6-10 A sophisticated and amusing mystery-ghost story is set in a rural community on the English coast, and the tale is outstanding in evocation of setting and in the use of local dialect. The Swallows are three pools on the Babbacombe property, and there's long been a dark suspicion that there's something fey about the Swallows just as there have long been rumors that the Babbacombes have dark powers. A series of peculiar happenings occur; cows are sucked down in a vortex in the usually placid water, there's an exodus of animal life, and the Babbacombe house seems to have been taken over by particularly destructive, noisy poltergeists. There's a love interest, humor, and delightful characterization; there's also a logical conclusion that explains the peculiar events in this well-paced story.

262 **Cochrane,** Louise. *Tabletop Theatres;* illus. by Kate Simunek. Plays, Inc., 1974. 48p. $4.95.

5-8 First published in England, this gives directions for making four kinds of stages, puppets, and costumes, and includes scripts for plays. For the Elizabethan stage there is a play about Merlin and Arthur as a boy; the traditional characters are used in a Punch and Judy theater, a superficial adaptation of Molière's *A Doctor in Spite of Himself* is given for a picture-frame stage, and the open stage script is contemporary, a play about ocean divers. The instructions are clear and most of the materials inexpensive and easily obtained; characters include both hand-puppets and marionettes. While the caliber of the scripts is pedestrian, the book gives a considerable amount of basic information that will enable readers to improvise and adapt other material.

263 **Coerr,** Eleanor. *Sadako and the Thousand Paper Cranes;* paintings by Ronald Himler. Putnam, 1977. 76-9872. 64p. $6.95.

3-5 Eleven years old, Sadako Sasaki was a lively, impetuous child whose whole family shared her pride in her ability as a runner. When her first dizzy spell came, Sadako didn't tell anyone, but soon it was impossible to hide her weakness. The diagnosis: leukemia. Sadako had been only two when the bomb struck Hiroshima, but she had seen many later cases of leukemia victims. If she could make a thousand paper cranes, the legend went, she would be well. So Sadako began—but she lived only long enough to make 644. After her death, her classmates made more, and she was buried with the thousand cranes. Touched by the bravery and cheerfulness in the letters she had written them, they instigated the collection of enough money to raise a statue to Sadako in memory of her and other victims of the bomb, the epilogue explains. The story is told tenderly but with neither a morbid nor a sentimental tone; it is direct and touching. Himler's black and white drawings capture both the vitality that is Sadako's outstanding quality, and, later in the story, the poignancy of the loving family's efforts to make her last days as happy as they can.

264 **Cohen,** Barbara. *Benny.* Lothrop, 1977. 77-242. 154p. Trade ed. $5.95; Library ed. $5.21 net.

4-6 Set in New Jersey in 1939, this is both a nicely honed period piece and a warm family story. Benny is twelve, and he loves playing baseball. But his sister is doing her mother's work while Ma recuperates from a hysterectomy, and older brother Sheldon studies constantly for a scholarship exam, so it's Benny who has to work in the family store. Pa just can't see that playing ball is important, although he eventually relents—and even comes to a ball game. Benny stops feeling sorry for himself when he realizes how unhappy Arnulf, a German refugee, is. It isn't just that he's homesick, but that his Jewish mother is dead—and his father and stepmother, neither of them Jewish, don't want the stigma of having a Jew in their home. It's Benny who finds Arnulf when he runs away; for once, even Sheldon stops sneering and appreciates the fact that Benny has compassion and common sense. The writing style is smooth, the characters and the period wholly convincing.

265 **Cohen,** Barbara. *Thank You, Jackie Robinson;* drawings by Richard Cuffari. Lothrop, 1974. 125p. Trade ed. $4.50; Library ed. $4.14 net.

4-6 An unusual baseball story gets off to an attention-getting start with, "Listen. When I was a kid I was crazy. Nuttier than a fruitcake . . . I was in love with the Brooklyn Dodgers." Fatherless, Sam had never seen a baseball game until he met Davy. Davy was sixty, black, and the cook in Sam's mother's restaurant. Sam describes the trips to Ebbets Field with Davy, and sometimes with Davy's daughter and son-in-law; he is casual and candid about their discussions of race and the problems created when they travel together to other ball parks. The book ends on a poignant note, with Davy in the hospital after a heart attack and Sam bringing him a baseball (procured after considerable effort) signed by Jackie Robinson. The story has vitality and integrity, the characters are beautifully drawn, and the writing has pace; the book is never maudlin, but it's truly touching. And, for the baseball fan, there are Sam's eager descriptions of games on record, every detail of which he has memorized.

266 **Cohen,** Miriam. *When Will I Read?* illus. by Lillian Hoban. Greenwillow, 1977. 76-28320. 28p. Trade ed. $6.95; Library ed. $6.43 net.

4-6 yrs. Some children in the class could read, but Jim couldn't yet, and he yearned to. The teacher pointed out that he knew what the "Don't let the hamsters out" sign said. But he'd always known that, that wasn't reading. And then somebody tore the sign; it said "Do let the hamsters out." Jim rushed to the teacher to tell her, and she smiled. Jim was reading! "I waited all my life," Jim marveled, "Now I can read." A multiethnic classroom, a loving teacher, a child who wants to read, amusing antics of Jim and the other children, natural sounding dialogue: who could ask for anything more? The illustrations, despite the girls-and-dolls, boys-and-trucks sequence, are fetching and funny, echoing the humor and bonhomie of the story.

267 **Cole,** Joanna. *A Chick Hatches;* photographs by Jerome Wexler. Morrow, 1976. 76-29017. 47p. Trade ed. $6.95; Library ed. $5.94 net.

K-3 A simply written account of the development from egg to embryo to fetus to chick is made more meaningful by the accompanying photographs, some in color and almost all enlarged. The writing is matter-of-fact, but the pictures of the developing fetus make the recurrent miracle of reproduction vividly clear. The coverage and tone are much like those of Selsam's *Egg to Chick,* which is designed for the beginning independent reader.

268 **Cole,** Joanna. *A Fish Hatches;* illus. by Jerome Wexler. Morrow, 1978. 78-13445. 39p. Trade ed. $6.95; Library ed. $6.67 net.

4-7 yrs. Photographs of excellent quality, many of them enlarged, expand the usefulness of a text that describes, very simply, the fertilization, gestation period, and hatching of a trout egg. The information supplied is accurate and lucid, although it gives no indication of how fertilization occurs naturally; the process occurs here by human intervention in a fish hatchery. The title gives no indication of the fact that the text goes beyond the birth process and provides information about anatomical structure and about how a fish breathes and moves through water. Despite these minor flaws, the combination of direct, simple writing and fine photography plus a good format for young children (spacious pages, good layout) makes an unusually good introduction to fish biology.

269 **Cole,** Joanna. *My Puppy Is Born;* with photographs by Jerome Wexler. Morrow, 1973. 38p. Trade ed. $4.95; Library ed. $3.94 net.

3-6 yrs. Big, clear photographs and a pared-down text show the birth process and the first weeks of a litter of miniature dachshund puppies. The pups, blind and weak, open their eyes and stagger about, suck their mother's milk, begin to explore their world, and are ready to be taken home and loved by a child when they are eight weeks old. This is a wonderful opportunity for the child who has never seen the miracle of birth: to see the sac emerging, the mother biting the cord and licking the newborn pup, and the helplessness of infant life. It's also a lesson in being gentle with animal babies, and it's charming in portrayal of the beguiling puppies.

270 **Cole,** William, comp. *A Book of Animal Poems;* illus. by Robert Andrew Parker. Viking, 1973. 281p. $8.95.

4- Attractive line drawings illustrate an anthology that is broad and discriminating in its selections, which—the editor notes in his brief preface—are not intended to represent every form of animal life, but the best poems he could find. Most of the poems are by contemporary authors, and the choices tend to be less familiar works: Randall Jarrell's "In and Out the Bushes" but not his familiar self-portrait by the bat poet, Theodore Roethke's "The Heron," but not his "The Bat" or "The Kitty-Cat Bird." The poems are arranged by type of animal; some are humorous, a few narrative, most lyric. A lovely collection.

271 **Cole,** William. *What's Good for a Three-Year-Old?* illus. by Lillian Hoban. Holt, 1974. 26p. $4.95.

2-3 yrs. A companion volume to three other *What's Good for a . . .* (four, five, or six-year-old) books also has the children offering their opinions. Here a group of boys and girls of three are assembled for a birthday party. Their replies include funny faces, blowing out matches, toy trucks and trains, seesaws, tricycles, etc. All of this is in facile rhyme, and at the end of the party there were "Paper things that make a BANG! / And *you know* what song they sang." Ending: a satisfactorily noisy parade to the front door. The dialogue abounds with things both pleasant and familiar; the text has rhyme, rhythm, and humor; the illustrations are both lively and engaging.

272 **Collier,** James Lincoln. *The Bloody Country;* by James Lincoln Collier and Christopher Collier. Four Winds, 1976. 75-34461. 183p. $6.95.

6-9 As they did in their other story of the American Revolution, *My Brother Sam is Dead,* the Colliers focus on a small geographical area and use it to explore the conflicting loyalties and abrasions between groups of colonists. Here the setting is a Pennsylvania valley community whose residents, emigrants from Connecticut, are persecuted by the Pennamites, older residents who claim the land and who use the help of the British and of a local Indian tribe to drive the newcomers away. Ben Buck, whose family is one of the Connecticut group, tells the story of his father's struggle for survival, the deaths in the valley, the efforts to rebuild homes, the flooding of the town, the exodus. And Ben describes the growing desire for freedom that lead the family slave and his friend, Joe Mountain, half black and half Mohegan, to strike out on his own. Most of the book is based on fact; the community is Wilkes-Barre. The story is dramatic and convincing, the characters drawn with depth and vigor, and the book especially valuable for its exploration of issues and philosophy in a way that enhances the narrative impact of a fine example of historical fiction.

273 **Collier,** James Lincoln. *Inside Jazz.* Four Winds, 1973. 176p. Trade ed. $5.95; Library ed. $5.92 net.

7-10 How can one define jazz and differentiate it from other kinds of music? Collier does it as well as one can in print by analyzing the rhythmic variations, the use of legato phrasing and syncopation, the improvisation and free phrasing, the interdependence in ensemble performance. The major part of the book is devoted to a history of jazz and jazz musicians, heady and nostalgic stuff for the addicted fan, intriguing for anyone. Collier puts less emphasis than did Studs Terkel, in *Giants of Jazz,* on the contributions of individual composers and performers, but he does discuss trends and influences, the way jazz people lived, and the effects of the record industry on jazz. A divided and annotated bibliography of jazz records and a relative index are appended.

274 **Collier,** James Lincoln. *My Brother Sam is Dead;* by James Lincoln Collier and Christopher Collier. Four Winds, 1974. 216p. $6.50.

6-9 Based in large part on actual events, the first-person story of a

Connecticut family during the Revolutionary War is told by Tim, a young Adolescent whose father is not sympathetic toward the Patriot cause but whose chief purpose is to maintain a neutral attitude. Tim is grieved because his older brother has joined the Patriot army after a fight with their father; he cannot feel a commitment to either side, and after his father has been imprisoned for selling cattle to the British (although it somehow befalls that he dies on a British prison ship) Tim urges his brother Sam to quit and come home. But Sam feels loyalty to his country comes first—and he is executed by General Putnam as a cattle thief, a charge that is untrue. So Tim sees the long years of tragedy, confusion, hunger, and despair go by with more conviction about the folly of war than he ever has about the Tory or the Patriot viewpoint. The authors explain that they have used contemporary speech patterns because "nobody is really sure how people talked in those days," and while the modernity is occasionally obtrusive, it is never really jarring. Well-paced, the story blends fact and fiction adroitly; the characterization is solid and the writing convincingly that of a young boy concerned more with his own problems and family in wartime than with issues or principles.

275 **Collier,** James Lincoln. *Rich and Famous; The Further Adventures of George Stable.* Four Winds, 1975. 75-14040. 155p. $5.95.

6-9 A sequel to *The Teddy Bear Habit,* just as funny and perhaps a bit more sophisticated. George is now thirteen, and his agent is still trying to whip up some business; there's a sponsor interested in using George's talent (voice and guitar) on a show that will present him as the apple-cheeked, all-American, small town boy next door. And, of course, make him rich and famous. George, who tells the story, lives in Greenwich Village and is used to junkies and con men; he takes it for granted that his father will go off on a trip with a woman. He does not take it for granted that just as the pilot's being planned, he'll be sent off to live in the home of relatives he dislikes, and to whom he lies heroically in order to get into Manhattan twice a week. The ending is a bit lurid (dope-pushing and attempted murder) but the whole is so cheerful a spoof of agents, television and advertising circles, and the Power of the Sponsor that it overshadows the ending.

276 **Collier,** James Lincoln. *The Winter Hero;* by James Lincoln Collier and Christopher Collier. Four Winds, 1978. 78-7609. 152p. $5.95.

6-9 Like the other historical novels by the Collier brothers, this is fiction skilfully based on fact, and an appended note makes clear which is which. The story is based on Shays' Rebellion, and

Daniel Shays is an important figure in fourteen-year-old Justin's account of his participation in that campaign. As is true of the earlier books, the story has a dramatic plot and good style, historical information nicely integrated into the plot and the dialogue, and that final element that marks the best in historical fiction: it gives the reader an understanding of the personal conflicts, the practical needs, the ideological principles, and the background that contributed to an event. The political oppression and financial burdens suffered by Massachusetts citizens in 1787, seen through Justin's eyes, are as vivid as his descriptions of confrontations between farmers and government troops.

277 **Colman,** Hila. *Rachel's Legacy*. Morrow, 1978. 78-12783. 190p. Trade ed. $6.95; Library ed. $6.67 net.

7-10 A story within a story frame is told by Rachel, one of the three daughters of a widowed Jewish woman who had come from Russia to East Side New York in the early 1900's. Mama and her older sister Esther were timid, clinging fearfully to the old ways; younger sister Ida adjusted with happy celerity to being an American; Rachel—who had a good brain and a protective instinct that drove her to work doggedly to provide the others with material comforts—was independent, hungry for culture, and ready to accept new ideas. The book gives a vivid picture of an immigrant family and of the period, it's well-written, and it has strong characterization. The framing story adds little: Rachel's daughter, destitute and living with her unemployed father after Rachel's death, decides not to contest a legal maneuver that will deprive her of money stipulated in her mother's will, for after going over her mother's history, she feels that she would rather be poor than cause a family rift, that she is rich enough in her heritage of courage. The fact that the author uses Yiddish terms without explaining them is a mild but recurrent irritant.

278 **Colman,** Hila. *The Secret Life of Harold the Bird Watcher;* illus. by Charles Robinson. T. Y. Crowell, 1978. 71p. Trade ed. $5.95; Library ed. $5.79 net.

3-4 Contentedly solitary, nine-year-old Harold (an only child whose parents both work) watches birds, indulges in hours of dreamy, imaginative play, and longs to be a hero. He doesn't really need friends, he feels, but he'd like his parents to stop worrying about him and he'd like his classmates to have a higher opinion of him. On a class outing, alas, it is Harold who falls into the river and another boy rescues him and becomes a hero. But Harold has his turn; he's so angry at a man who is shooting the ducks he's loved to watch quietly, that he trips the man and runs off with his gun.

What brings Harold satisfaction, however, is not being a bona fide hero, but a secondary result: visited by the boy who'd rescued him from the river, Harold discovers that sustained imaginative play is more than twice as much fun with two. He's found a friend who likes to pretend as much as he does. Harold's heroic act is believable, his concern for the environment laudable, and his acceptance of being different a strong appeal in a smoothly written story.

279 **Colman,** Hila. *Sometimes I Don't Love My Mother.* Morrow, 1977. 77-23445. 190p. Trade ed. $6.95; Library ed. $6.43 net.

7-12 A recent high school graduate and an only child, Dallas is doubly crippled by her father's death, for they had been closer than she and her mother. First, there is her grief; second, there is the fact that her mother clings to her, so that Dallas can't go to college, can't even see her friends without her mother joining them. Torn between protective pity and strong resentment, Dallas finds it hard to declare her independence; she eventually does so, in logical fashion, but not before both mother and daughter have explored the intricacies of a taut emotional conflict. Colman, while sympathetic toward her young protagonist, makes the reader see clearly the internal conflict of each, and, while they are reacting to a stress situation, there is enough that is universal so that any reader can identify with the typical identity-search of adolescence.

280 **Colwell,** Eileen, comp. *The Magic Umbrella and Other Stories for Telling;* drawings by Shirley Felts. McKay, 1977. 76-53970. 160p. $6.95.

4-7 Although Colwell's annotations are for storytellers, giving background information and telling time, and suggesting the appropriate age range for the audience, this varied selection of tales and poems can also be used by children for their own pleasure. The book includes Greek and Norse legends, such storytellers' classics as "Molly Whuppie" and "The Woman of the Sea," and more recent selections like "Zlateh the Goat" or a section of Serraillier's poem, "Everest Climbed." Expectably excellent.

281 **Conford,** Ellen. *Felicia the Critic;* illus. by Arvis Stewart. Little, 1973. 145p. $4.95.

5-7 Why did people get so irritated by her remarks, Felicia wondered? She was only using common sense and telling the truth. Her mother suggested gently that Felicia might do better to turn to constructive criticism, so she eagerly seized on the idea. She wrote a list of suggestions for the harassed policeman at a school crossing, and she couldn't resist jotting down some ideas on her aunt's new children's book and the arrangements at a cousin's wedding. While all of this embarrassed her family, some of it worked; when Felicia decided to keep her own counsel in a newly-formed girls' club the members of which had complained about her criticism, disaster struck. Why, the girls complained, hadn't Felicia seen the pitfalls and criticized? Fresh and funny, the story has enough variety to be interesting depite the narrow focus of the plot; the relationships with family and friends are seen with a bright and keen eye, and the dialogue is completely natural.

282 **Conford,** Ellen. *Hail, Hail Camp Timberwood;* illus. by Gail Owens. Little, 1978. 78-18715. 151p. $6.95.

5-7 Convincingly told by thirteen-year-old Melanie, this is the story of her first summer at camp. An only child who's never been away from her parents, Mel is homesick, but not for long; she is smitten by romance, she learns to ride and is elated to find she's good at it, she struggles to learn swimming (at which she remains terrible) and she makes friends—including the small brother of her darling Steve. And she learns that the advice she's given little Dougie applies to her: nobody else can fight your battles for you if you want to be self-reliant. Nothing unusual happens in the story, but it all rings true, it's told at lively pace and in an easy, natural style, and it has unforced humor.

283 **Coolidge,** Olivia E. *The Statesmanship of Abraham Lincoln.* Scribner, 1977. 76-14863. 237p. illus. $7.95.

8- Coolidge's ability to bring a period and its people and events to life are as evident as her painstaking scholarship in this perceptive, analytical study of Lincoln's years in office. Inexperienced, held in contempt by many in his own newly-formed party, the new President slowly gained popularity with the voters as he struggled with inept military men, experienced politicians who assumed they could control him, and his own need to decide priorities among the serious issues of war, of slavery, and of long-term and short-term goals. A section of photographs is bound in; a chronology and a full relative index is appended.

284 **Cooper,** Susan. *Greenwitch.* Atheneum, 1974. 147p. $5.50.

5-7 The third volume in a sequence of five (*Over Sea, Under Stone; The Dark is Rising*) is the most cohesive of the three, bringing together Will Stanton, protagonist of the second book and the three Drew children of the first. The Drews, visiting again the Cornish village where they had first learned of the forces of evil, the Dark, are not aware that their uncle is one of the powers of Light or that Will, seventh son of a seventh son, is another—one of the Old Ones who must fight to keep the Dark from rising. The Greenwitch is a figure constructed each year by the villagers for an ancient rite, but they do not know that she comes alive and is under the aegis of Tethys, the White Lady of the ageless sea. The realistic pedestal of the story is slight but firm, the weaving of magic intricate, and the whole permeated by a remarkably strong sense of inexorable evil in a fantasy that adroitly uses the setting as a foil for the classic struggle between good and evil.

285 **Cooper,** Susan. *The Grey King;* illus. by Michael Heslop. Atheneum, 1975. 75-8526. 208p. $6.95.

5-7 * The fourth book in the sequence that began with *Over Sea, Under Stone* (the whole sequence has the same title as the second book, *The Dark is Rising*) is set in Wales. Will Stanton, eleven, is aware, as one of the Old Ones, the immortal beings who serve the Light that guards the world, that he must pursue his quest against the rising of the Dark, the evil forces of the universe. Recuperating from illness at the home of Welsh kin, Will meets a strange boy, Bran, who accompanies him on his battle against the malevolence of the Grey King. Intricate yet cohesive, strong in its creation of a magic world that meshes closely with reality, this is a compelling fantasy that is traditional in theme and components yet original in conception.

286 **Cooper,** Susan. *Silver on the Tree.* Atheneum, 1977. 77-5361. 269p. $7.95.

5-7 * In the fifth and last volume of the cycle "The Dark Is Rising," young Will Stanton, last of the magical Immortals, engages in a final, desperate struggle with the Dark, the powers of evil. Bran, who first appeared in *The Grey King,* and the three Drew children of an earlier book help in the quest for the silver sword, the silver on the tree (mistletoe) and the six Signs of the Light by which the Dark can be vanquished. Intricate but beautifully woven fantasy incorporates many elements of the legends of the British Isles in a story that concludes with the triumph of the Light, the return of King Arthur, and Bran, who proves to be Arthur's son, refusing to depart with the king because he has come to feel he belongs with those for whom he feels "loving bonds," ties even stronger than the High Magic of the creatures of Light. Cooper captures a true sense of mission, but this is more than a quest; it is a tale of adventure and a complex, seamless weaving of ancient lore and contemporary scene.

287 **Corbett,** Scott. *Bridges;* illus. by Richard Rosenblum. Four Winds, 1978. 77-13871. 122p. $6.95.

5-7 Corbett's history of bridge-building is confined to Western Europe and the New World, and he does a quite competent job of describing changes and improvements in construction over the centuries while incorporating material about famous bridges and bridge-builders. The text begins with a discussion of the logs and vines used by primitive cultures as bridges, continues with the massive contributions of Roman engineers, and concludes with the newest advances, such as the box-girder bridge. Illustrations are interesting, although chiefly they show the finished bridges; diagrams of steps in construction might have aided in comprehension of the processes of construction. The writing is clear, the material well organized; the appended index includes the listings for types of bridges but not such terms as aqueduct, arch, conduit, voussoir, etc.

288 **Corbett,** Scott. *The Hockey Girls.* Dutton, 1976. 75-33804. 104p. $6.50.

4-6 The announcement that there will be a sports program for girls at Wagstaff High causes dismay among a group of first year girls, especially Irma, the protagonist, who has no interest in athletics. An elderly, popular English teacher, Miss Tingley, is the coach for field hockey, and she really whips the team into shape. They think. They lose their first game 11-0, in part due to the fact that their coach has a broken leg and the substitute is ineffectual. But Miss Tingley comes back, the team is stimulated, and Wagstaff High wins the return match. The story has some elements of the formula sports story, with two rivals (Irma and Fran) learning to cooperate for the good of the team and one unenthusiastic player who, at a crucial moment, dashes in to help save the game, but there is enough humor in the writing and the sprightly dialogue to compensate amply, and the story has good game sequences as well as explanations of rules and techniques of play.

289 **Corcoran,** Barbara. *Axe-Time, Sword-Time.* Atheneum, 1976. 75-29468. 204p. $6.95.

7-10 The head injury she had had as a small child had left Elinor with no less intelligence, but with a malfunction that kept her from reading or spelling well. Mother insists that Elinor should stay in school for an extra year so that she can get into college. It isn't what Elinor wants, but it's hard to break away, especially since Mother is bereft because Dad has walked out. The story is set in the period of World War II, and Elinor, elated by her success as an airplane spotter, lonely because her brother and her boy friend have enlisted, breaks the silver cord and gets a war plant job. Elinor's problems are not those of all readers, but most adolescents face similar situations: adjusting to, and accepting, one's own limitations; establishing independence from parents; and learning, as Elinor does, to accept people with other—even disparate—interests and backgrounds. The writing is subdued but not sedate, the characters and relationships perceptively depicted.

290 **Corcoran,** Barbara. *The Clown.* Atheneum, 1975. 75-8759. 188p. $6.50.

5-8 A fast-paced adventure story has a strong plot, an unusual setting, sympathetic characters strongly drawn, suspense, love interest and a vigorous writing style. The orphaned daughter of an American diplomat, Liza is in Moscow with a tiresome aunt and uncle who need her help, since she has lived there and speaks some Russian. Aunt May is called home, and Liza uses her uncle's passport and clothes to smuggle out of the country a Russian clown who is in danger for political reasons. Having seen Grigol in a performance, Liza had followed him, learned that he was in peril, and offered her help. The details of the planning and execution of the escape are intriguing and convincing, and the end of the story is satisfying but not pat. A doughty and believable heroine, a cracking good book.

291 **Corcoran,** Barbara. *A Dance to Still Music;* illus. by Charles Robinson. Atheneum, 1974. 180p. $6.95.

6-8 Margaret had become deaf after an illness the year before; she'd felt uncomfortable with her classmates at home in Maine, but now—having moved to Key West—she was totally isolated. Remembering her deaf grandfather's harsh voice, she wouldn't even talk. When her mother announced that she was going to remarry and that Margaret would be sent to a special school, she ran away, headed for Maine. Stopping to rescue a wounded fawn, she met Josie, an older woman who was brisk and efficient, asked no questions, but accepted Margaret as a guest on her houseboat and helped care for the fawn. Josie gradually brought her young friend to agree that she would attend a workshop for the deaf on a Florida campus, and Margaret tentatively ventured to speak again, her mother reluctantly agreeing to the new program. The setting is interesting and the characterization good; although one minor character, a daft woman, seems overdrawn, the major characters are convincing, especially the protagonist and her mother—not a bad woman, but lacking in understanding.

292 **Corcoran,** Barbara. *Hey, That's My Soul You're Stomping On.* Atheneum, 1978. 77-13499. 122p. $6.95.

7-9 "Rachel knew exactly how her father felt. Smothered." She also knew that she was being sent to visit her grandparents because her parents were having bitter quarrels. Sixteen, she arrives at a modest Palm Springs motel to find that the residents are all, like her grandparents, elderly people. The one friend she makes is the beautiful Ariadne, staying at another motel with a fashion-plate mother. Rachel hasn't expected to be so involved with all her grandparents' friends, but she's deeply concerned about them and about Ariadne, who proves to be emotionally disturbed. So she learns about caring—and by the time her dependent mother is in Reno, Rachel volunteers to be with her. She still judges her parents, but she can accept them and accept the responsibility that love entails. A familiar theme, but Corcoran has given it a fresh slant. The characters are strongly drawn, the narrative smooth, and Rachel's reactions and fears emerge naturally via letters to an only brother in Europe.

293 **Coren,** Alan. *Arthur the Kid;* illus. by John Astrop. Little, 1978. 77-26989. 73p. $5.95.

4-6 Even if he does claim the Seminoles as "Wyoming's largest Indian tribe," in this spoof of a Western desperado tale, the author, editor of *Punch,* seems quite at home in the milieu. He's written a very funny story about a gang of three who are miserable failures at every crime they try to perpetrate; only when they come (by mistake) under the leadership of ten-year-old Arthur the Kid (they thought when someone answered their ad for a boss they were getting *the* Billy the Kid) do they achieve success . . . but of another kind. Coren lays it on a bit, but that's quite in keeping with the exaggerated syle of humor he uses.

294 **Coren,** Alan. *Buffalo Arthur;* illus. by John Astrop. Little, 1978. 78-6398. 70p. $5.95.

4-6 In the blithe, mock-swashbuckle style that made *Arthur the Kid* so amusing, Coren tells another story of the Far West. Set in Arizona a century ago, this is a tale of cattle rustlers who are decimating the stock on Dan Dundee's ranch. The sheriff refuses to help, so Dan puts an ad in the Buckeye Bugle, and a certain "Buffalo Bill" answers it. Who steps off the train? That indomitable small sleuth, Arthur, who explains he's the *other* Buffalo Bill, Arthur William Foskett. Naturally, after using his brain, Buffalo Arthur retrieves the cattle and catches the thieves. After a few Arthur stories, the reader will know what to expect—but then, the expectable can be fun if one reads the book tongue-in-cheek, as written.

295 **Coren,** Alan. *The Lone Arthur;* illus. by John Astrop. Little, 1978. 78-6459. 72p. $5.95.

4-6 Coren moves to yet another site of the Old West, Dodge City, in telling yet another tale about the ten-year-old detective, Arthur, who appears in each book and saves a group of baffled characters from their desperate plight. This time it's three gullible cowboys who buy a California ranch, sight unseen, from a Dodge City charlatan. The "ranch" proves to be a collapsed shed in a stretch of sand; undaunted, the cowboys open a restaurant. When they come back from a vacation they've taken to celebrate the restaurant's success, the men find they've been robbed of their savings. Again, the sheriff says he can't handle the job; again, the victims advertise; again (hear that fanfare of trumpets?) Arthur answers the ad, stepping off the stagecoach to announce that he's the Lone Ranger. Armed with a magnifying glass, our hero goes hunting for clues, and before you know it he's tracked down the guilty pirates (yes, pirates) and sunk their ship single-handed. Why not? Arthur can do anything.

296 **Corey,** Dorothy. *Tomorrow You Can;* illus. by Lois Axeman. Whitman, 1977. 77-12789. 30p. Trade ed. $4.25; Library ed. $3.19 net.

2-5 yrs. In a multiethnic book, young children are reassured about their potential for accomplishing tasks that are difficult or impossible at some stages of growth. The text is arranged in facing pages and is very simple: One side, "Today," and the other, "Tomorrow," or one side, "Today you can't," and the other, "Tomorrow you can." At the end, there are more specific comments about being bigger and stronger. The pictures show such familiar activities as drawing, putting clothes on, or swinging alone. This doesn't have the smooth progression of the author's *You Go Away,* but it can be equally useful in helping young children adjust to a universal problem.

297 **Corey,** Dorothy. *You Go Away;* pictures by Lois Axeman. Whitman, 1976. 75-33015. 29p. Trade ed. $3.75; Library ed. $2.81 net.

3-5 Although simple enough for the beginning reader, this is primarily for reading aloud to preschool children. It iterates the idea that people who go away—whether it's a baby being tossed into the air, a little brother hiding under the bed, Daddy going off with a basket of laundry, or Mother leaving a child with a sitter at a sandbox—come back. The text moves from a brief distance and a brief time to longer times and distances, concluding with parents going off with luggage, "far away." Each time, reassuringly, "I come back!" The pictures have ethnic variety, the text can help extend concepts of time and distance as well as helping children adjust to the realization that having a parent leave does not mean one is being abandoned.

298 **Cormier,** Robert. *The Chocolate War*. Pantheon Books, 1974. 253p. $5.95.

8- The setting is a Catholic high school for boys, the treatment of the school power structure grimly realistic in this stunning story about moral courage and moral corruption. The chocolates are meaningless in themselves, but the drive to sell boxes of chocolates to raise money for the school brings out every aspect of the power of a sadistic teacher, the influence of bullies and gangs, and—most depressing—the collusion between the cruel and dishonest Brother Leon and the leader of the secret society that controls student behavior. The plot is original, the style powerful, the characters and their intricate relationships wholly convincing. One boy, secretly ordered (one in a long series of secret gang ploys to provoke the teachers) to refuse to sell candy, is so incensed at all of the chicanery and brutality that he goes on refusing even after the order is rescinded. He gets sympathy from a few—but he can't beat the system. The chocolate war ends in victory for the establishment, the bullies and Brother Leon. A sobering, dramatic, and timeless story.

299 **Cormier,** Robert. *I Am the Cheese*. Pantheon Books, 1977. 76-55948. 224p. $7.95.

7-12 A gripping novel, beautifully crafted, is written on three levels
* that merge as the story progresses, building into a dramatic whole that has suspense and a tense poignancy. Adam Farmer describes, in a taut present tense account, his bicycle trip to Vermont to see his father. It is clear that Adam is excited, apprehensive, and determined—and it comes as an odd shock to the reader when his narrative is first interrupted by a question-and-answer column that seems to be a psychiatric interview. The interview sessions continue to pierce the narrative flow, and they lead to the third level, Adam's reminiscences that are evoked by the sessions. What Cormier brings off in brilliant fashion is that these sessions (which quickly establish themselves as psychiatric probes) and the memories do two things simultaneously: they clarify Adam's problems, the reasons for his trip and his anxiety, and at the same time they create suspense because it is not clear how the timing fits, when and where the interviews take place, but it is clear that a crisis is looming. As the story progresses, the facts about Adam's childhood emerge: his father had changed the names of the family members and had created a fictitious background in order to

protect them all from retribution because of testimony he had given at a government hearing. As for the ending: it would be unfair to readers to divulge it, but it is stunning.

300 **Couffer,** Jack. *African Summer;* by Jack and Mike Couffer; sketches by Charles Callahan. Putnam, 1976. 76-7917. 96p. $6.95.

6- A record of a summer spent on an island in an East African lake is recorded alternatively by Jack Couffer, there to film a television series, and by his thirteen-year-old son, who came along with his friend Charles. Some of the sequences describe filming episodes (some dangerous, some amusing) and others adventures with the wild creatures of Kenya or the tame performers, chiefly lions, brought in by the television crew. The writing styles are informal, the setting fascinating, and the double lure of filming and animals should capture readers.

301 **Cowan,** Rachel. *Growing Up Yanqui.* Viking, 1975. 75-16334. 158p. $6.95.

7- Her family background was more of an influence than the ambience of an upper-middle class, conservative WASP community, and Rachel Cowan, with her husband Paul, had worked in the Civil Rights movement before joining the Peace Corps. What she learned in that organization was little that was not depressing: the lack of understanding of peoples with whom it worked, the carping and superiority, and the internal bickering. But she and Paul learned a great deal from the families with whom they lived and worked in Mexico and Ecuador, and they are concerned critics of our country's policies and practices in Latin America. Sympathetic toward Latin America and the Cuban Revolution, a personal documentary that is intense and partial, the book is well-written and has vitality and intimacy that come from personal observation and involvement. An extensive divided bibliography and a chronological table of events (based on Richard Walton's *The United States and Latin America*) are appended.

302 **Coy,** Harold. *Chicano Roots Go Deep;* foreword by José Vázquez-Amaral. Dodd, 1975. 75-11434. 210p. $5.95.

7-12 Although some of the material in this excellent survey of Chicano history and the Chicano movement of today is covered in Coy's earlier book *The Mexicans,* the format is different (the first book was in epistolary form) and the emphasis here is on Mexican-American relations in the past and the problems of Chicanos in the United States. The author uses several generations of a Mexican-American family to reflect both Mexican history and Chicano cultural heritage, and his text is comprehensive, knowledgeable, and sympathetic. A glossary of Chicano expressions, an impressive divided bibliography, and a relative index are appended.

303 **Craft,** Ruth. *The Winter Bear;* illus. by Erik Blegvad. Atheneum, 1975. 74-18178. 23p. $5.95.

3-5 yrs. Blegvad's at his best in this British import, the delicate but strong precision of his winter scenes complemented by the soft nuances of the colors. The rhyming text is restrained and polished, telling the details of a wintry day's walk by three children. The youngest spots an object in the branches of a tree, and pokes it down. What a find! A toy bear. They take it home and lovingly wash, dry, and dress the little derelict. Simple as the story is, it conveys the feeling of a cold, brisk country walk and of the contrasting warmth and bustle of home.

304 **Craig,** M. Jean. *Little Monsters;* illus. with photographs. Dial, 1977. 76-42936. 39p. Trade ed. $6.50; Library ed. $6.29 net.

2-4 Seventeen small creatures, deceptively ferocious in appearance, are shown in large-scale photographs (many in full color) facing pages of text. There are two kinds of bats, several larval forms, some fish, some insects, a chameleon, a lizard, a shell, a star-nosed mole. All fascinating, and the text gives just enough information about structure, habits, and habitat to complement the photographs. An appended note points out that these creatures aren't monsters at all, since they are natural and real, and nothing real is monstrous.

305 **Crary,** Margaret. *Susette La Flesche: Voice of the Omaha Indians.* Hawthorn, 1973. 174p. $5.95.

6-9 A fictionalized biography, well documented and carefully indexed, gives a vivid picture of the way in which American Indians were persecuted, as well as an interesting one of the staunch and dedicated Susette La Flesche. At Omaha, she had had excellent schooling and she felt that she must speak out for her friends in the Ponca tribe who had lost their lands and been sent to Oklahoma. The record of broken treaties, appeals ignored, warped news releases, and the petty tyranny of agents is familiar, but the courage and persistence of a nineteenth century Indian girl—in a time when Indians were not legal persons and an Indian woman had no rights—add poignancy to the story. Susette La Flesche met some of the major reformers and cultural leaders of the time in the course of her lecture tours, and many of them joined with her and other Omaha leaders in working for the legislation that finally, in 1881, restored their homes to the Ponca Indians.

306 **Crayder,** Dorothy. *She and the Dubious Three;* illus. by Velma Ilsley. Atheneum, 1974. 186p. $6.95.

5-7 A lively sequel to *She, the Adventuress,* in which Maggie traveled alone to Italy, invited by her Aunt Yvonne (very Auntie Mame). Here, Maggie becomes suspicious on the train to Venice: several clues point to the fact that the baby across the aisle is not the child of the hippie couple he's with. Ergo, he must be kidnapped! Maggie meets the hippies again in Venice, also a detective who was on the train, also two people she's met during her previous adventure; so there's a heavy dose of coincidence and an all-on-stage ending. Still, she's as engaging and doughty a heroine as before, and the Venetian setting adds interest to the appeal of a somewhat intricate but amusing suspense story.

307 **Crayder,** Dorothy. *She the Adventuress;* illus. by Velma Ilsley. Atheneum, 1973. 188p. $5.50.

4-6 That was the way Maggie thought of herself: She, the Adventuress, a reluctant traveler from Iowa en route to Italy. As long as her parents had agreed that she must accept her aunt's invitation, she might as well think of it as glamorous adventure. Maggie makes two friends on shipboard: Jasper, a stowaway, and the delightful elderly woman who is her cabin mate, and she actually does become involved in an exciting adventure when one passenger asks her to do him a favor and she finds that she is carrying a stolen Da Vinci picture. The story is lively, the pace sustained, and Maggie an intrepid heroine. The book also makes sea travel sound enticing, and it's an experience few air-age children have enjoyed in our air age.

308 **Cresswell,** Helen. *Absolute Zero.* Macmillan, 1978. 77-12675. 174p. $6.95.

5-7 A second novel in the cycle that began with *Ordinary Jack* has the same sophistication and ebullience, although it stretches credulity a notch further. When Uncle Parker wins a contest and goes off on his prize cruise, he and his wife leave their terrible, wonderful four-year-old with Jack and his family. There's no question of the havoc created by little Daisy, but almost as much damage is done by the Bagthorpe family's instant conviction that if Uncle Parker can win a slogan-writing contest, so can they. And the Bagthorpes never do anything by half. In all the ferment and competition, the star proves to be Jack's dog, Zero, and the combination of the vicissitudes of owning a canine star and also being chosen "The Happiest Family in England" when they are dedicated bickerers brings the happiest of bedlams to acerbic life.

309 **Cresswell,** Helen. *Bagthorpes Unlimited.* Macmillan, 1978. 78-3561. 180p. $6.95.

5-7 In a third hilarious story about the entertainingly daffy English family of *Ordinary Jack* and *Absolute Zero,* Grandma decides that she needs the comfort of having all her dear ones gathered about her. Since the Bagthorpe children cordially detest prissy Aunt Penelope and Uncle Claud and their two precocious children, Esther and Luke, it's only to be expected that they'd mount a campaign of insidious sabotage. Maggots introduced into a box of chocolates, for example. Since nothing ever happens quietly at the Bagthorpe home, readers can expect cataclysm and reprisal, hue and cry, perhaps even young William's attempt to set a world record for a nonstop drum tattoo. Undaunted, Grandma decides to set a record for the longest daisy chain in the world, a project that—as usual—brings disaster and publicity. Again, a deft and polished comedy with an all-star cast.

310 **Cresswell,** Helen. *The Bongleweed.* Macmillan, 1973. 138p. $4.95.

4-6 One fanciful concept is firmly rooted in reality in an English story in which a mysterious plant grows in a magical, rampaging fashion. Becky Finch is the daughter of the head gardener of Pew Gardens, working for a botanist named Harper whose house and the Finches' has a common wall. The Harpers' young house guest Jason becomes—after a period of hostility—Becky's colleague in defending the plant she calls the "bongleweed," a botanical sport that reaches two feet only two days after planting. The bongleweed takes over, its tropical lushness defended by Becky and her father against her mother's fury at the interloper that is taking over the garden. The problem solves itself when the first snow falls. The story is imaginative in conception, written in polished, easy style; the dialogue and characterization are excellent.

311 **Cresswell,** Helen. *A Game of Catch;* illus. by Ati Forberg. Macmillan, 1977. 76-46991. 44p. $5.95.

3-5 Cresswell's matrix for a time-shift fantasy is a realistic story of two children who are spending a few days with an aunt before leaving England for Canada. Kate and Hugh walk through a deserted museum and Kate is sure that she hears other children's laughter. Nobody else sees the two children from an 18th century painting who later play a game of ball with Kate on the skating pond—but when Kate sees the painting a second time, the girl is holding the ball Kate had thrown her at the end of the game. When she'd first seen the picture, the boy was holding the ball. The style is polished, the plot soundly structured, and the story nicely appropriate in length and complexity for middle-grades readers.

312 **Cresswell,** Helen. *Ordinary Jack.* Macmillan, 1977. 192p. $6.95.

5-7 * The first of a trilogy, this English story is a romp from cover to cover; it occasionally verges on slapstick, but the characters are so deftly daft and the dialogue so witty that it never goes past the verge. The Bagthorpe family is nutty, for starters; they're like the cast of *You Can't Take It With You* in that each goes his or her own talented way—except Jack, ordinary Jack, who is the protagonist. His brother and sisters have assorted talents, so do his parents, but Jack has none. So—his uncle, who lives next door (with a charming four-year-old daughter who starts fires) takes over, and the two work up elaborate plans whereby Jack, stage-managed by Uncle Parker, will convince the others that he has prophetic powers. A joy.

313 **Cresswell,** Helen. *The Winter of the Birds.* Macmillan, 1976. 75-34278. 244p. $7.95.

6- * First published in England, a story that is told from three viewpoints is beautifully put together. First, the musings of a lonely old recluse, Mr. Rudge, who sees the steel birds who come at night, on long wires, to strike and slash. Second, the journal kept by young Edward Flack, foster son to a timid father and a curt, domineering mother. Third, the narration by the author. Into the working class neighborhood of St. Savior's Street come Mrs. Flack's meek older brother and the loquacious, expansive, radiant Patrick Finn, who has just rescued the brother after a suicide attempt and has decided to come along with him to visit Mrs. Flack. For Edward, who has been training himself to be heroic, Finn is a true hero—and Cresswell makes him a convincing one. Always able to cope, always cheerful, Finn deals with bullying boys firmly and with their victim, Mr. Rudge, gently. He gives Mrs. Flack's brother courage to start a new sort of life, he charms Mrs. Flack, he thinks of a scheme to get rid of the winter birds of steel that terrify Rudge and Edward, and he is a catalyst for community action. The characters and dialogue have enormous vitality, the story is cohesive despite its tripartite nature, and the writing style has consummate craft.

314 **Crews,** Donald. *Freight Train;* written and illus. by Donald Crews. Greenwillow, 1978. 78-2303. 19p. Trade ed. $6.95; Library ed. $6.67 net.

3-5 yrs. * A pared-down description of the cars included in a small freight train also serves to identify black and the primary and complimentary colors. There's a track with a red caboose at the back, next are an orange tank car, a yellow hopper car, a green cattle car, a blue gondola car, a purple box car, and the black tender and engine. They are almost-solid blocks of color, with just enough detail to make them look real; they are in frieze form, running along the track that is at the foot of all pages; the train gathers speed, moves in and out of a tunnel, passes cities and crosses trestles . . . and then it's gone. Very simple, very attractive, it's a fine first train book.

315 **Crowe,** Robert L. *Clyde Monster;* illus. by Kay Chorao. Dutton, 1976. 76-10733. 26p. $5.95.

4-7 yrs. A small, awkward, engaging monster, Clyde was, to his parents' pleasure, growing uglier every day. His only problem was that he was afraid of the dark; when he told his parents why (people might get him) they explained carefully that people didn't harm monsters anymore than monsters harmed people. So Clyde trotted off to his cave, reassured. Well, he did ask that they leave the rock door open just a bit. A soothing and amusing bedtime tale is nicely illustrated by humorous pencil drawings in black, white, grey, yellow, and blue.

316 **Cumberlege,** Vera. *Shipwreck;* illus. by Charles Mikolaycak. Follett, 1974. 31p. Trade ed. $4.95; Library ed. $4.98 net.

3-5 A British author bases a short, vivid story on a shipwreck she saw during her childhood, and the incident—seen here from the viewpoint of another child—has a remarkable authenticity of detail and mood. Waking in the early dark of a cold, stormy morning Jim hears the lifeboat gun and sees his father, a member of the crew, go off. The new powered boat hasn't come yet, and Jim feels that it can never be as exciting as the oared launching of the old boat, but the experience of watching the crew struggling against the wind to reach the vessel in distress, of seeing a drowning, makes the boy realize what a boon it will be to have a lifeboat that can make speedier rescues. Cumberlege's description of the tension, the fear, and the final exhaustion of the day is beautifully matched by the strong, sensitive illustrations.

317 **Cunningham,** Julia. *Tuppenny*. Dutton, 1978. 78-7449. 87p. $6.95.

6-8 Readers who know Cunningham's earlier books, particularly *Dorp Dead,* will recognize the dark, occult strain and the grave compassion that appear here in a story about a strange girl, Tuppenny, who wanders into the lives of three couples in a small town. Each has lost a daughter: Victoria Standing had run away; Dorrie Mason had drowned; retarded Josie Herd is in an institution. Silent, mysterious, and forceful, Tuppenny brings changes for all of them and then slips off as quietly as she had come to town, her arrival and departure recorded by silent, unhappy Jessica Standing, the "other" daughter, the rejected child. She has been quick to love and trust Tuppenny, and her role in the story is strangely minimal. What Tuppenny does is make all of these parents face facts; Mrs. Standing admits she had hated as well as loved Victoria, and having confessed that to Tuppenny, she knows herself and loses her hate. Mrs. Herd understands her deep need and brings Josie home; as for the Masons, they confess the murder of their child and disclose their insanity. Victoria returns, and a new relationship with her parents is established. All Tuppenny's doing, and when this human catalyst disappears, the reader knows little more than was known at her coming. A therapeutic force? An avenging angel? Cunningham is so compelling a writer that one is content to accept the mystery and symbolism, the violence of the past of her characters, and the transmutation from evil to good that her protagonist effects. A strong, strange story.

318 **Currell,** David. *The Complete Book of Puppetry.* Plays, Inc., 1975. 73-19484. 206p. illus. $14.95.

6- A Council Member of the British Puppet and Model Theatre Guild, Currell has written a comprehensive book that can be used by young adults and adults for making and operating puppet theatres, and that can serve as a browsing source for younger readers. Even without an index, the book has reference use. The text, illustrated profusely and well with diagrams and photographs, describes the traditional puppetry of countries throughout most of the world, and the uses of puppetry in education. Chapters on various types of puppets (glove, rod, shadow) include information of making, operating, and staging puppets; the book closes with advice on related puppetry techniques and on the puppet show itself: script, dialogue, rehearsal, music, performance, et cetera. As an example of the thorough coverage, the chapter on the marionette lists, in the table of contents, about 100 separate subjects. The print is unfortunately small; the writing style is direct and clear. A list of puppetry organizations in many countries, sources of suppliers in the U.S. and England, copyright and safety regulations, and an extensive divided bibliography are appended.

319 **Curry,** Jane Louise. *The Watchers.* Atheneum, 1975. 75-8582. 235p. $6.50.

5-7 Thirteen-year-old Ray, unable to get along with his stepmother, comes to stay with his mother's kin in Twillys' Green feeling bitter and resentful. He finds himself in an extended community in a pocket of the West Virginia hills, a warm, loving family that accepts him as one of their own—yet Ray knows there is something odd about the family. When he sees the avaricious local storekeeper curiously excited about Ray's fossil find, the boy first suspects that there is something about the stone carving that is both arcane and important. This is a two-level story: the family fights against the depredation of the land and, like their ancestral Watchers, who are incorporated as a fantasy element, they fight as guardians of a sacred site. The two themes are adroitly meshed, and the author has created a colorful set of characters, a well-constructed story, and a vivid setting.

320 **Curtis,** Edward S., comp. *The Girl Who Married a Ghost and Other Tales from the North American Indian;* comp. and photographed by Edward S. Curtis; ed. by John Bierhorst. Four Winds, 1978. 77-21515. 115p. $9.95.

5- Selected from the massive collection of Curtis' material, these nine tales, minimally edited, are told with considerable narrative flair. Representing six geographical regions, the folktales show cultural and literary variety, and they are complemented by the posed, romantic pictures taken by Curtis and selected by Bierhorst. A handsome piece of bookmaking, a good selection of stories to read alone, read aloud, or use as a source for storytelling.

321 **Cusack,** Isabel Langis. *Ivan the Great;* illus. by Carol Nicklaus. T. Y. Crowell, 1978. 77-26593. 45p. Trade ed. $5.95; Library ed. $5.79 net.

2-4 You think a story about ethical concepts can't be funny? Try this one. Robby, who has just turned nine, has always been a model child, truthful and polite. When he acquires a parrot (Ivan) for his birthday, Robby hears the bird speak—nobody else does. He gets a lecture on lying. Then he tells his mother that a small girl named Australia has his lunch-box; his mother calls the school, finds no child by that name, and gives Robby another lecture. Yet when he lies about having been invited to a birthday party (he hasn't) Mother seems to understand he's saving face. Then he hears Mother tell a caller she can't join a bridge group because she doesn't play—but he knows she does. All of these matters are discussed at length with Robby's mentor, Ivan, who is a garrulous and conceited character whose speech is peppered with fibs, pretentious quotations, sophisticated logic, and humor. When a small girl comes to the door and says she is Australia, but that it's an invented name and can she have some brownies, Robby's mother knows he was telling the truth—and, for the first time, she mutters, "I could have sworn I heard that bird say something." A nice blend of realism and fantasy, and a palatable presentation of food for thought.

322 **Cutler,** Ebbitt. *I Once Knew an Indian Woman;* illus. by Bruce Johnson. Houghton, 1973. 69p. $3.95.

7- First published in Canada in 1967, this short novel about an Iroquois woman the author met during her childhood vacations was awarded first prize in the Canadian Centennial Literary Competitions. It is told as a first-person reminiscence, written in a quiet, conversational style with very little dialogue; it captures both the tempo of life in a resort village and the colorful personalities of some of its characters, particularly that of Madame Dey, the protagonist. Proud, independent, self-reliant, and compassionate, Madame Dey was low in the village caste system but it was she who cast a mantle of dignity on a tragic situation when a stranger drowned. The curé didn't appear when notified, the hotel refused to take the corpse. "They can't just leave him there like that for his parents to come and find him," she said, and carried the body from the station platform where it lay to her own house, laid out the corpse, and lighted candles, so that the grieving parents would find their son properly cared for. Through the heavy burden of her own troubles she understood the needs of others, and she cared enough to make an effort for strangers. Very impressive, very sophisticated.

323 **Cutler,** Ivor. *The Animal House;* illus. by Helen Oxenbury. Morrow, 1977. 77-4468. 30p. $6.95.

K-2 One morning the Diamond family wakes to find that the wind has blown their house away. Dennis Diamond, father, works at a zoo and is inspired to concoct a house made of animals (with an amusing scene in which Dennis busses the head keeper in his gratitude for loan of some animals) and it works beautifully. Large beasts form the walls, snakes obediently stretch clothesline-straight so that birds can perch on them and spread their wings for a rainproof roof, and Artificial Diamond (mother) cooks by firefly "heat." Next morning the animals are gone, but the house is back, washed up near shore. So the adaptable Diamonds hitch the house to a rock, and live happily in their gently rocking home. Nonsense, but inventive nonsense, freshly imaginative and funny, told in a bland style that's a good foil for the absurd story and the inventive pictures, softly executed and admirably detailed. Oxenbury achieves a great deal with remarkable economy of line.

324 **Cutler,** Ivor. *Elephant Girl;* pictures by Helen Oxenbury. Morrow, 1976. 75-38755. 22p. Trade ed. $4.95; Library ed. $4.95 net.

2-5 yrs. Amusing and deft drawings have the same mock-ingenuous humor as the text, a palatably nonsensical fantasy that reflects the quality of a child's imaginative play. A small girl, digging in her garden with a spoon, unearths an amicable elephant who permits the child—her name is Balooky Klujypop—to scrub him—his name is Pansy—and hold him up to the sun to dry. With one hand. Then he gives her a ride and then she grants his request and buries him cosily in the earth again. Length, style, and humor are nicely gauged for the very young audience.

325 **Czaja,** Paul Clement. *Writing with Light; A Simple Workshop in Basic Photography.* Chatham/Viking, 1973. 96p. illus. $5.95.

6- There are many books that explain the functioning of a camera or the techniques of photography. This book does that, but it offers more: for the beginner, it teaches ways to make images—writing with light—without a camera or with a simple and inexpensive one the reader can make, and it teaches the reader to use his eyes, to be aware of light and changes in light. Later chapters of the book describe developing and printing procedures; throughout the text there is an emphasis on awareness, on using photography to communicate. While there are many pictures, and most of them are handsome, there are few pictures that illustrate specific comments of the text or that clarify textual explanations, a minor flaw in a book that is otherwise impressive,

326 **Dana,** Barbara. *Crazy Eights.* Harper, 1978. 77-25645. 194p. Trade ed. $7.95; Library ed. $7.89 net.

7-10 "When the shrink up here first talked to me about writing," Thelma begins, "I thought he needed help." Thelma's final act of despair had been to set fire to a building in which her older sister was to be married. Sure that Jennifer (as vacuous as their mother) was marrying for the wrong reasons, as unhappy about her relationship with her timid father as she was about her mother's domineering and carping, Thelma has been a loner. She writes her story in retrospect at the quiet insistence of a therapist at a private school for young people who are emotionally disturbed; through therapy and the friendship of an understanding teacher, Thelma finds comfort and security. Both the pattern of her increasing stability and the pattern of a fragmented family are built with logic and sensitivity, in a book with sharp characterization and a trenchant style alleviated by moments of wry humor.

327 **Danziger,** Paula. *The Cat Ate My Gymsuit.* Delacorte, 1974. 92p. Trade ed. $4.95; Library ed. $4.58 net.

6-8 "I hate my father. I hate school. I hate being fat," Marcy begins. Marcy is thirteen, she dislikes the boredom of her classes, she dislikes herself. Embarrassed about her size, she always has an excuse (like that of the title) to give her gym teacher. Her father is indeed a tyrant and an insensitive bully. What changes Marcy's life is a teacher: young, bright, sympathetic, innovative, Barbara Finney makes learning English fun and helps her students to like themselves and each other. Marcy even gains a new friend, Joel. When Ms. Finney is dismissed by the principal, irate because of teaching methods he doesn't understand and because she won't say the Pledge of Allegiance (she feels there isn't yet liberty and justice for all) Marcy and her friends protest and are suspended, their parents become involved, and Marcy's mother for the first time has the courage to go her own way, supporting the teacher although her husband refuses to go to the hearing, will not let her use the car, and hopes that Ms. Finney will be fired. He's against bleeding-heart radicals. The book is written with skill, it handles an important issue realistically and brings it to a logical conclusion, and it is competent both in characterization and in the interaction among its characters.

328 **Danziger,** Paula. *The Pistachio Prescription.* Delacorte, 1978. 77-86330. 154p. $6.95.

6-8 The quotation from Camus that precedes the story tells all: "In the midst of winter, I finally learned that there was in me an invincible summer." Thirteen-year-old Cassie, who tells the story, has asthma, is a hypochondriac, and eats pistachio nuts compulsively when anything goes wrong. And almost everything does, she thinks. But Cassie's elected president of the freshman class, she acquires Bernie, she has the stalwart support of her friend Vicki, who won't let Cassie retreat into coddling fears, and she manages to cope with a nagging mother, parental quarrels, and a hostile, competitive sister. When Mom and Dad separate, the sisters unite protectively against Mom's sniping; Cassie begins to understand that the situation is irrevocable, that she can live through the years before she is able to leave home, and that she can even abjure pistachio nuts. Not unusual in theme, this is unusually well done; the characterization and dialogue are strong, the relationships depicted with perception, and the writing style vigorous.

329 **Darke,** Marjorie. *A Question of Courage.* T. Y. Crowell, 1975. 75-8756. 208p. $5.95.

7-10 A fine story about woman's suffrage is set in Birmingham and London, where young Emily Palmer has become more and more involved in the cause. A working girl, Emily had lost her job when she was arrested for joining the local leader, Louise Marshall, in putting her banners up on a private golf course. She goes to London, as does Louise, and eventually is jailed and force-fed; she also falls hopelessly in love with Louise's brother, and—although he is interested in her, clearly—the story ends with the imminence of the first world war. This is informative and an excellent supplement to the many books about the leaders of the suffrage movement, but it's also an absorbing story, with good characterization and dialogue.

330 **Davis,** Burke. *Newer and Better Organic Gardening;* illus. by Honi Werner. Putnam, 1976. 75-42028. 95p. $5.95.

6-9 A useful book for the beginning gardener stresses the use of natural fertilizer and the avoidance of insecticides, fungicides, and artificial fertilizers. Davis discusses the relative merits of mulch and compost, giving full information for both; he lists specific plants that repel insects and can be used to protect other plants (basil and tomato, for example); he gives exact, separate instructions for planting and tending a dozen common vegetables. The writing gets a bit rhapsodical at times, but it is for the most part practical and direct. The appended material includes a bibliography, some sources of information, a planting table, zoned frost charts, and an index.

331 **Davis,** Burke. *Runaway Balloon; The Last Flight of Confederate Air Force One;* drawings by Salvatore Murdocca. Coward, 1976. 75-29060. 46p. $5.95.

4-6 A fictionalized account of a true incident of the Civil War is given in a casual, humorous style. Impressed by the observation balloon of the Federal troops, General Joe Johnston sent out an appeal to Confederate womanhood for silk to make a balloon for the cause. When the patchwork bag and its basket was ready, the general pressed for a volunteer—and young John Randolph Bryan stepped forward. His first trip was brief, albeit successful; on his second flight, the reluctant Lieutenant Bryan thought he was going to make a watery landing after the balloon escaped from the men holding its ropes, so he jettisoned everything. And that's how a naked young man in a peculiar vehicle, of which a dubious Confederate colonel had never heard, had to explain the Whole Thing.

332 **Davis,** Ossie. *Escape to Freedom; a Play About Young Frederick Douglass.* Viking, 1978. 77-25346. 89p. $7.95.

6-9 A noted black actor and playwright dramatizes the life of Frederick Douglass, using some characters who shift from part to part and incorporating a fair amount of music as background, although this cannot be called a musical. The young slave Fred is shown yearning for the education he's denied, managing to learn to read and well aware that it is through literacy that his chance for freedom lies. Since Davis is a good craftsman and the material is inherently dramatic, the play is eminently satisfying both structurally and emotionally.

333 **Dawood,** N. J., ad. *Tales from the Arabian Nights;* ad. from the Arabic; illus. by Ed Young. Doubleday, 1978. 77-16886. 320p. Trade ed. $12.95; Library ed. $13.90 net.

5-8 A publisher and translator, Dawood has based this version of the familiar tales (actually, there are a few that have never before been included in versions intended for children) on three versions in the original Arabic. In this version, most tales end with a promise about the next story; the language is modernized but flavorful, not as embellished as that of the Williams-Ellis version, for example, and rather easier to read. Darkly romantic paintings are in full color, and very handsome they are, albeit less delicate than the Baynes illustrations for the Williams-Ellis version, which have the stylized beauty of Persian miniatures.

334 **De Angeli,** Marguerite. *Fiddlestrings.* Doubleday, 1974. 143p. illus. $4.95.

4-6 A turn-of-the-century story about eleven-year-old Dailey de Angeli, torn between his interest in playing the violin and his exuberant talent for friendship and adventure. Dai's father is invited to take charge of entertainment at the new Steel Pier in Atlantic City, and Dai leaves his baseball team with reluctance, but looks forward to a summer of fun. Most of the story is about Dai's ploys at Atlantic City, the balance about Dai's stay with an aunt in Philadelphia, where he is sent so that he can have a better musical education. The book has a happy blend of pranks, music, family affection, and period detail; the writing style is smooth. Marguerite de Angeli has a special talent for making her children convincingly of their time and, at the same time, children of any time, anywhere.

335 **De Angeli,** Marguerite. *The Lion in the Box;* illus. by the author. Doubleday, 1975. 74-33676. 63p. $4.95.

4-6 There is, in this Christmas story based on a true incident in the life of the author's friend Lili, something reminiscent both of Taylor's *All-of-a-Kind Family* and of the direct simplicity of *Little Women.* There were five children in widowed Anna Scher's family in this turn-of-the-century tale. Mama did night cleaning in Madison Avenue buildings, and the children were either watched by a neighbor or took care of themselves and each other when she was away. There is no sentimentality in the cheerful poverty of the story, as the Schers prepare as best they can for Christmas. The paper star they make as a tree decoration is described so that readers can make it, too, and what little the family has they share with neighbors. The high point of the story is the arrival of a box big enough to hold a lion, a box that holds all sorts of treasures: toys, food, clothing, a doll house, cooking utensils. All of these were actually sent to the family by a real Mrs. Stix who had talked to Mama while her husband was at a business meeting in an inner office. Appropriately old-fashioned, the pictures and the story have a perennial fairy-godmother appeal.

336 **Degens,** T. *The Game on Thatcher Island.* Viking, 1977. 77-24166. 148p. $6.95.

6-8 Harry, eleven, knew perfectly well that the older boys—especially the Morrison brothers—who had asked him to join their "war games" on the island were bullies, but he was thrilled when they invited him to join them. He hadn't expected to be saddled with a younger sister and with the "Fresh Air" boy from New York who had come for a fortnight. And he knew it would be necessary to lie, to tell his mother they were going on a picnic. Harry didn't understand that he was meant to be the victim. The gear that he and Sarah and John brought with them is ripped and thrown about; Sarah and John are tied and their mouths taped, are put in a pit and bombarded with lighted matches. Harry rescues them, catches one of the Morrisons and tricks him into the pit. And then the three "nice" children treat him exactly as they have been treated. They go off, with no thought of telling parents, with some guilt feelings for having sunk to the Morrisons' level, and with some confusion about why it had all happened. Degens pulls no punches: young people can be cruel, and cruelty can engender a reciprocating violence. She is also realistic in perceiving the small deceptions people use to hide their fears or to gain status; Harry and John have lied to each other, covering what they think are their own weaknesses. The story is dramatic and fast-paced, with good characterization and dialogue.

337 **Degens,** T. *Transport 7–41-R.* Viking, 1974. 171p. $5.95.

7- The year is 1946, the place is the Russian sector of a vanquished Germany, and the story is told by a girl of thirteen whose parents have put her on the train to Cologne, her papers stating falsely that she is being repatriated to her home zone. Self-reliant and self-absorbed, the girl is concerned only with her own safety, as are most of the other refugees, but she is drawn to the old couple in her car. The wife is very ill, her husband very protective; as the long days go by—for the train is halted more than once for dangerous inspections—the young girl and the old man share a secret. The wife has died, and they must hide this so that the body can reach Cologne and the man keep his promise to his dead wife, that she will be buried at home. By the end of the journey the girl has come to realize that it is good to be needed, that the stance of independence she had taken would have brought nothing but loneliness, and that she needs the old man as much as he needs her. The characterization of the occupants of the crowded boxcar is incisive and perceptive, and the author makes the tension and suspense of the journey remarkably real.

338 **Deiss,** Joseph Jay. *The Town of Hercules; A Buried Treasure Trove.* Houghton, 1974. 183p. illus. $5.95.

5-8 Author of an adult book, *Herculaneum,* published in 1966, Deiss lived for four years in that ancient city. His text is as much about the people who lived there (some real characters, some imagined) as about the sophistication and beauty of the architecture, the artifacts, and the art. Discussion of particular buildings includes facts about their function: for example, a description of the baths or the amphitheater is given added interest by a description of bathing customs or the drama of the period. The book is profusely illustrated with photographs of sites and objects, with full captions. There is in the writing style an occasional but infrequent evidence of writing down to younger readers, but this is a minor flaw in a book with so fascinating a subject written by one with such familiarity and enthusiasm as Deiss has.

339 **De Larrabeiti,** Michael. *The Borribles.* Macmillan, 1978. 77-12743. 240p. $6.95.

6-8 A fantasy in the Tolkien tradition pits a picked group of Borrible guerrillas against the whole might of their foes, the Rumbles. Borribles are waifs who live in secret in the more crowded districts of London; Rumbles are large, mole-like creatures of the countryside who, the Borrible leader maintains, are threatening invasion. Nine ardent volunteers steal out of London, since the worst fate that can befall a Borrible is to be seen and caught by ordinary people, and have a glorious adventure, creating disaster and death amongst the Rumbles. They encounter treachery when they return, losing some of their number; fortunately, they never learn that their mission was spurious, that their own leader's goal was mercenary. The combination of a well-structured and exciting plot, the orginality of the conceived world, and the vitality and humor of the tough, street-wise dialogue make this an outstanding book.

340 **Deming,** Richard. *Metric Power; Why and How We Are Going Metric.* Nelson, 1974. 144p. illus. $5.95.

6-10 "Actually, it is all over but the shouting, because the battle has been won," says the author, writing of our country's long record of resistance to adoption of the metric system. Industries that once fought bitterly are now converting, many schools teach the metric system as well as the old one (and some teach only the metric measurement) and in many industrial and scientific areas it is used exclusively. Every major country but the United States can exchange products and information based on metric standards. We must convert—although there will be a period of confusion and expensive change—and the author points out that one group of beneficiaries will be the school children whose period of learning will be shortened because of the simplicity and uniformity of a decimal system with standard prefixes. Deming gives a history of the development of systems of measurement and of the controversy in the United States, explains the metric system and its advantages clearly in a well-researched text, and gives many examples of the effects that conversion will have on business and on the individual. Tables of metric units, conversion tables, a bibliography, and an index are appended.

341 **Deming,** Richard. *Women; The New Criminals.* Nelson, 1977. 76-40209. 191p. $6.95.

7- A study of female criminals is objective and thoughtful, written for mature young adults in a serious style. Deming is a careful writer, pointing out the fallacies that can be found in statistics (for example, the ways different states codify and tabulate crimes) and the subjectivity that can be found in individual analyses. Giving some historical information, he discusses the increase in violence in recent years, particularly in the traditionally "male" crimes committed by women, and causes in the rise of female criminality, and the relationship between the latter and the changing roles of women in our society. Separate chapters describe the delinquent girl, women in prison, and other specific problems in female criminality; Deming concludes that female criminality will, since present trends so indicate, rise until it approximates the rate of male criminality, and that there will be a decrease of sex discrimination in sentencing. Alas, the print is as solid as the research. A bibliography and an index are appended.

342 **De Paola,** Thomas Anthony. *Bill and Pete;* written and illus. by Tomie de Paola. Putnam, 1978. 78-5330. 28p. Hardcover $7.95; Paperback $2.95.

K-2 Drama on the Nile! What begins as a pleasant if zany home-and-school story ends with a lurid adventure, as a small crocodile is saved from a terrible fate—becoming a suitcase—by his toothbrush. The toothbrush is a pink, helpful bird named Pete; he's already helped Bill learn to spell his name by suggesting "Bill" instead of the more difficult "William Everett." Bill is seized by an evil man, Pete picks the lock of the cage with his bill, and the evil man is frightened away when Bill sneaks into his bathtub. The story is told with brisk simplicity, and the pictures of Bill and other crocodiles learning their alphabet (each beast with his own accompanying toothbrush-bird) add humor to the action.

343 **De Paola,** Tomie. *"Charlie Needs a Cloak"*; story and pictures by Tomie de Paola. Prentice-Hall, 1974. 28p. $4.95.

4-6 yrs. Charles is a shepherd whose cloak is ragged, so he shears his sheep, washes and cards the wool, dies it and spins it into cloth, and makes a beautiful new red cloak. The text is minimal, the story will give children an idea of the processes of handwork required to make cloth, but the story alone is static. What it needs, and gets from the illustrations, are action and lightness. Charlie's sheep are obstreperous: in every picture there's a sheep in the way, making the shepherd trip, or tugging at a skein, or standing obdurately on the cloth while Charlie tries to cut it.

344 **De Paola,** Tomie. *Nana Upstairs and Nana Downstairs;* written and illus. by Tomie de Paola. Putnam, 1973. 28p. $3.95.

K-3 This is one of the best of the several stories for very young children that shows the love between a child and a grandparent, and pictures the child's adjustment to death. Like Lundgren's *Matt's Grandfather*, this stresses the affinity between the very young and the very old; unlike any of the other stories, it includes a great-grandmother as well as a grandmother. Small Tommy calls his ninety-four-year-old great-grandmother "Nana Upstairs" because she is bedridden; downstairs her daughter is busily keeping house, she's "Nana Downstairs." When great-grandmother dies, Tommy learns about death and, years later, he is better prepared when Nana Downstairs dies in her old age. The book gives a tender—but not overly sentimental—picture of the child's relationships with his grandmothers, the quiet tone given relief by touches of humor—as when Tommy sees his older grandmother tied into a chair to enjoy a rare time of being out of bed, and he wants to be tied in, too. "So every Sunday . . . Nana Downstairs would come up the back stairway and tie Nana Upstairs and Tommy in their chairs, and then they would eat their candy and talk."

345 **De Paola,**Tomie. *The Popcorn Book;* written and illus. by Tomie de Paola. Holiday House, 1978. 77-21456. 28p. $6.95.

2-4 Twin boys, seeing a television commercial about popcorn, ask their mother's permission to make some. While one assembles ingredients and does the cooking, the other reads aloud from a reference book. This doesn't give botanical facts as precisely as does Millicent Selsam's book on the subject, but it does give interesting facts, it has a minimal story line, and it adds humor by having the zealous cook surprised by a torrent of popped corn.

346 **De Paola,** Tomie. *The Quicksand Book.* Holiday House, 1977. 76-28762. 28p. illus. $6.95.

K-3 A deft blend of fact and fiction is illustrated with ebullient paintings framed in enormous leaves that remind the lap audience of the jungle setting and that provide a corner for silent action that gives a third dimension. A small jungle girl falls into quicksand; a small, bespectacled jungle boy takes his time about rescuing her, presenting charts about quicksand and how to get out of it while the girl slowly sinks. He does get her out, and there is a cheerfully retaliatory ending. Meanwhile, a monkey is seen in the verdure; on the corners of pages, he bustles silently about, setting up a tea table complete with goodies and a vase of flowers. The boy, who has stumbled into the quicksand, is shrieking for help; the girl calmly promises to pull him out when she's had her tea, saying "Now, now. Remember what you told me! Just keep calm . . ." And the information about quicksand is accurate, too. Very nice.

347 **De Paola,** Tomie, ad. *Strega Nona;* retold and illus. by Tomie de Paola. Prentice-Hall, 1975. 75-11565. 30p. $6.95.

K-3 In this picturebook version of an Italian folktale, Tomie de Paola has used soft colors, simple line, and medieval costume and architecture in his spaciously composed, humorous pictures. The tale of Strega Nona ("Grandmother Witch") is told in modest but fluent style, and the familiar theme of a self-filling magical object is used to good effect. Strega Nona's pasta pot, her helper Anthony has secretly noted, produces pasta when the right verse is said, stops at another verse; what Anthony carelessly ignores is the fact that Strega Nona also blows three kisses to the pot. Having boasted to the townspeople that he can produce pasta galore, Anthony says the magic verse when Strega Nona is away. Predictable, funny result: Anthony doesn't know how to stem the tide, and a river of pasta flows through the town. Strega Nona returns and saves the day, and she suggests a poetically just punishment instead of the vengeful hanging Anthony's neighbors propose: the poor lad has to eat all the pasta he's evoked—an ending children will probably enjoy tremendously.

348 **DePauw,** Linda Grant. *Founding Mothers; Women in America in the Revolutionary Era;* wood engravings by Michael McCurdy. Houghton, 1975. 75-17031. 228p. $6.95.

7- A scholarly exploration of women's roles and their participation in business, their duties at home, their efforts as civilians or soldiers in the war effort (on both sides) and of the lives of black and native American women has reference use, gives many facts, and is given variety by the inclusion of primary source quotations. It is, however, written in a rather ponderous style and may be limited in appeal to some readers because each chapter is so packed with details and—often—names. A bibliography, divided by chapters, and an index is appended.

349 **Des Jarlait,** Patrick. *Patrick Des Jarlait; The Story of an American Indian Artist;* as told to Neva Williams. Lerner, 1975. 74-33523. 57p. illus. $5.95.

6-9 Although Des Jarlait's story, transcribed from taped interviews, is told in a rather flat style, it is cohesive in form and engrossing in the picture it gives of Chippewa Indian life. Des Jarlait describes customs, ceremonies, children's games, and the ways in which his people hunted and gathered crops; he speaks modestly of the artistic talent that became increasingly evident through the years in which he attended a series of government schools and for which he received a scholarship to study art in Arizona. His love of the Minnesota countryside and his pride in his people permeate the book and are evident in the reproductions of his bold, dramatic pictures in brilliant watercolor.

350 **Dickinson,** Peter. *Chance, Luck & Destiny.* Atlantic-Little, Brown, 1976. 75-28403. 254p. $8.95.

7- Dickinson uses a bit of presto-chango panache in an orderly collage of stories, discussions, quips, poems, case histories, and adages. Even a flow chart on "what else might have happened to Little Red Riding Hood." He uses portions of the Oedipus story as a thread throughout the text, which examines the three aspects of the title, discussing coincidence, superstition, tarot cards and astrology, myths, witchcraft, and other topics of the occult, the accidental, and the improbable. Nicely illustrated, written with wit and vigor (and one touch of sexism, " . . . houses from which men go off every day to their offices, children to their schools and women to the shops. . . .") and filled with an intriguing variety of subjects.

351 **Dickinson,** Peter. *The Dancing Bear;* illus. by David Smee. Atlantic-Little, Brown, 1973. 243p. $5.95.

6-9 An adventure story of the time of the Byzantine Empire, this has strong characters, historical interest, and enough action for two books; it moves ponderously at times, perhaps because there is so broad a canvas that the details obscure the composition. Nevertheless, the story of a slave boy and his trained bear is exciting; it begins in 558 A. D. when the Huns sacked Byzantium.

Silvester the slave, his young mistress, and Holy John, a religious fanatic, escape with the trained bear. They save the life of a wounded Hun en route, take the man to his tribe and receive its gratitude, later escaping to a Slav stronghold where Silvester receives manumission and marries the Lady Ariadne. An epilogue describes those portions of the story that are historically based.

352 **Dickinson,** Peter. *The Gift.* Little, 1974. 188p. $5.95.

5-9 Dickinson does a masterful job of combining adventure with the theme of telepathy, adds local color, perceptive depiction of characters, and a liberal dash of suspense in a well written and skillfully paced mystery story. Only Davy's Welsh grandmother and his sister knew that he had inherited the gift of reading minds; Granny knew from her own experience that it could be a curse, and Davy often tried to block his thinking, since the reception of others' thoughts was involuntary. Then the boy was startled by receiving a stranger's thoughts, vicious and psychotic, and he followed the man; thus he began the unraveling of a mysterious criminal plot in which his own father was involved as a scapegoat, a plot that meant danger and confrontation and death. Davy's father is strongly drawn, a weak man who is not evil but is almost amoral, who loves his children enough, when faced with decision, to give up his hopes of easy success, to tell his story to the police. Dickinson makes Davy's gift completely credible.

353 **Dillon,** Eilis. *Rome Under the Emperors.* Nelson, 1975. 75-23245. 186p. illus. $6.95.

6- In the format used so successfully by Alfred Duggan to recreate an historical period, Dillon describes in narrative form four Roman families of 110 A.D., those of a senator, a businessman, a farmer, and a stallholder. The writing is lively and colloquial, the use of present tense adding a sense of immediacy to the text. Historical personages and imaginary ones mingle and reappear in the four accounts, and the whole gives a vivid evocation of the bustling city, the social life and social classes, the customs and institutions, attitudes toward slavery, and the pervasive awareness of Roman supremacy in the ancient world.

354 **Ditzel,** Paul C. *Railroad Yard;* illus. with photographs. Messner, 1977. 77-12758. 64p. $6.64.

4-6 Profusely illustrated with photographs, this is a brisk, straightforward description of the step-by-step procedures of the checking, repairing, assembling, and despatching of freight cars in railroad yards. The book is minimally weakened by an occasional irrelevancy ("After taking a sip of coffee from his 'Big Daddy' mug, Jerry pushes buttons . . .") and by the fact that photographic captions are in the same type face and size as the text, but it gives a great deal of information about the mechanized and human operations of a railroad yard in sequential fashion. A glossary of railroad terms and an index are appended.

355 **Dixon,** Paige. *May I Cross Your Golden River?* Atheneum, 1975. 75-6943. 262p. $7.95.

7-10 Everything's rosy in Jordan's world on his eighteenth birthday: his girl is coming to the family party, he likes the the lawyer for whom he works; he's looking forward to college and law school; he enjoys his mother and three brothers, only occasionally wondering about the father who'd left them. But at the party his leg gives way. It's nothing, it passes. Too much tennis, perhaps. The next day he's out driving with his girl, Susan, and has to turn the wheel over to her. So Jordan goes to a doctor, who sends him on to Mayo Clinic. Amyotrophic lateral sclerosis, "Lou Gehrig's disease," a progressive and incurable illness. Jordan and his family must adjust to the knowledge of certain death, and this adjustment is handled by the author with conviction and dignity, with sympathy and no sentimentality. Jordan learns to hoard his strength, to appreciate some of the people he'd taken for granted, to see others, like shallow and self-centered Susan, in their true light. Bitter at first, he becomes resigned and lives as well as he can as long as he can. Solid characterization, warm family relationships, and a smooth writing style balance the pathos of the inexorable theme.

356 **Dobrin,** Arnold. *I Am a Stranger on the Earth; The Story of Vincent Van Gogh.* Warne, 1975. 75-8105. 95p. illus. $7.95.

5-7 A serious and candidly written biography that is illustrated by many reproductions of the artist's work, some of them in full color, is marred slightly by the placement of illustrations, i.e., some are not referred to in the text, or appear facing pages that describe other works that are not reproduced. However, Dobrin has fulfilled the major obligations of a biographer: balanced treatment, accuracy, almost no fictionalization, and a text that conveys the essence of the subject's personality. A brief bibliography, a list of the locations of originals of the book's illustrations, and an index are appended.

357 **Dodd,** Wayne. *A Time of Hunting.* Seabury, 1975. 75-4779. 128p. $6.95.

6-9 In a moving story set in the Depression Era, adolescent Jess learns to value life in all living creatures. Jess had loved hunting; he was saving money earned by selling pelts to buy back a hunting dog his father had tried and returned. But several things happen to Jess: he falls in love and becomes more sensitive to how other people feel and then to how other creatures feel; he shares the grief of a classmate whose father dies; he finds it more and more difficult to look at an animal he's killed with pride but is instead filled with compassion. And so Jess decides that he won't buy the hunting dog, and that he'll bury the last animal he's killed rather than skin and sell it. This is not a message book; Jess makes his decision for himself and does not condemn his father, who is an ardent hunter, but his change of attitude is gradual and believable, achieved thoughtfully and not without pain. The writing is taut but smooth, serious but not heavy, and the several elements of the story are nicely balanced in treatment.

358 **Domanska,** Janina. *Din Dan Don It's Christmas;* illus. by the author. Greenwillow, 1975. 75-8509. 31p. Trade ed. $6.95; Library ed. $5.81 net.

3-6 yrs. * Against black pages, the framed and stylized pictures with their border decorations and their medieval figures glow like the paintings of an old illuminated manuscript, and the circular designs of the end pages are reminiscent of the hand-cut paper circles that are a notable Polish folk art. The pictures show the story of the first Christmas, but with Domanska's variations; the people wear peasant costume, the buildings have onion domes, and the animals participate in the journey to the manger, of those who follow the star. The text is rather still and formal, beginning, "The speckled duck plays the bagpipes. Din dan don she plays. The gander and the turkey beat the drums. Din dan don they beat."

359 **Donovan,** John. *Family*. Harper, 1976. 75-37409. 116p. Trade ed. $5.95; Library ed. $5.79 net.

6- * Can one say a novel is in first person when the narrator is an ape? Sasha, one of the apes in an experimental laboratory, is so convincing a voice that he seems a person—yet he remains, always, always, a primate, an intelligent being that is used by man. Suspecting that each ape in the project group will be killed at some point, Sasha tries to convince others to run away, but only three others go with him. The story of their flight, the refuge they find, the one understanding human being they encounter, and their final surrender to the inevitable, are serious in tone and convincing; there are some passages that move slowly, as Sasha ponders history or problems of the ape community, but the drama of the situation and the cohesion of the plot are impressive, and the style and characterization of the story most effective.

360 **Doty,** Jean Slaughter. *The Crumb.* Greenwillow, 1976. 75-33648. 122p. Trade ed. $5.95; Library ed. $5.11 net.

5-7 Crumb is Cindy's pony, and caring for him is so expensive that she's delighted when she gets a part-time job at the Ashford stables. Jan Ashford is relieved to share the work of teaching young riders and caring for the animals; she confides that she's looking forward to the day when Alex, to whose horses she's kindly given stable room after his own establishment burned, leaves and she can expand her business. Cindy doesn't trust Alex; there's his odd way of treating his superb horse, Cat Burgler, and a mysterious incident in which he used a hypodermic needle on some horse, she couldn't see which one. The story ends with a dramatic conclusion to the mystery, and it has good pace and color; its strongest appeal may be more in the authenticity of background than in the suspense, although the latter is maintained well. What Doty conveys is a sure sense of being at home in the fictional world she describes. In a way, she's the child's Dick Francis.

361 **Dowden,** Anne Ophelia Todd. *The Blossom on the Bough; A Book of Trees;* illus. by the author. T. Y. Crowell, 1975. 74-6192. 71p. $7.50.

6-
* Surely Ms. Dowden has no peer in botanical drawing; her pictures have the beauty and precision of Audubon's bird paintings, and the color reproduction is marvelously faithful in hues and shadings. While less formal in style than a textbook, this can serve as a beginning text in botany since it gives much general information about the structure and classification of plants, pollination and reproduction, and facts about the usefulness of all plant life in ecology, in giving people oxygen, food, and lumber, in preventing soil erosion, and in sheer aesthetic pleasure. The pictures can be used for identifying species, and several chapters are devoted to forest regions in the United States. A list, divided by forest regions, of common trees, and an index that gives scientific and common names are appended.

362 **Dowden,** Anne Ophelia Todd. *State Flowers;* written and illus. by Anne Ophelia Dowden. T. Y. Crowell, 1978. 78-51927. 86p. Trade ed. $7.95; Library ed. $7.89 net.

6- Dowden's precise and beautiful paintings are the outstanding feature of this book but it is also useful because the text that accompanies each picture gives some botanical information and cites the year each flower was adopted and the statutes that each state enacted. The one weakness of the book is that, in those cases where two states have made the same flower their legal emblems, there are not separate entries or even a cross-reference. Information about the violet, the state flower of Illinois, for example, cites both Illinois and New Jersey (for which the violet is also the state flower) statutes. It is true that the table of contents and the index give access to this information, but the reader misses the New Jersey entry if he or she turns first to the alphabetically arranged text. A small book, this is useful both because of its handy size and because the pictures are excellent for identification. Common and scientific names are provided.

363 **Dragonwagon,** Crescent. *When Light Turns Into Night;* illus. by Robert Andrew Parker. Harper, 1975. 74-2634. 28p. $4.95.

K-2 A twilight paean is illustrated in subdued colors, the economy of line and subtlety of composition evoking a sense of space and isolation in the rural scenes. The text is a child's long soliloquy that begins, "There's that time of day again / when light turns into night / and I have to go away / away away away / My mother wipes her hands upon her skirt and says / be back in time for dinner. . . . " The child goes off through the fields and lies in a meadow, looking up at the darkening sky; she feels a kinship with the windblown grass and thinks large thoughts of faraway people and her own identity. Her mother calls and the child goes home to the warmth and love of a communal dinner, to enjoy the differences of people and the closeness they all share. This is too quiet and perhaps too introspective for some children or for some times—but it's a poignant and evocative reflection of a thoughtful mood that is just right for that time when a child is subdued and wondering.

364 **Dragonwagon,** Crescent. *Wind Rose;* pictures by Ronald Himler. Harper, 1976. 75-25414. 31p. Trade ed. $4.95; Library ed. $4.79 net.

4-6 yrs. A prose poem of mother love is illustrated by soft black and white drawings that capture the warmth of the text. The young mother describes how, lying with her husband inside her, wrapped close and touching everywhere, "we had too much love for two / and that was the night we thought of you." Both parents share in the joy of feeling their child move in the womb, the excitement and the labor of birth, the wonder of seeing their infant child. Save for the statement "It didn't hurt," of a delivery at home and apparently without anesthesia, the story flows with smoothness, directly and simply describing the anticipation and satisfaction of having a child. The baby is named Wind Rose because "the wind rose warm and wild on the day that you were born."

365 **Drummond,** A. H. *The Population Puzzle; Overcrowding and Stress Among Animals and Men.* Addison-Wesley, 1973. 143p. illus. $4.50.

7-10 With some of the world's population already suffering from the effects of overcrowding and the anticipation of further population density, this survey of the experimental findings of scientists working with animals in situations of crowding is timely and enlightening. Most of the experiments described here have used rats as laboratory animals; while the author does not imply that discovered facts will necessarily apply to human beings, he does correlate those facts with what is known already about the adverse effects of population density on people: the tension, the criminal behavior, the need for personal space, the inhibition of personal potential. Brisk and well-organized, a provocative book that convinces by its assemblage of facts rather than by pronouncement. An index is appended.

366 **Du Bois,** William Pène. *The Forbidden Forest;* written and illus. by William Pène du Bois. Harper, 1978. 56p. Trade ed. $7.95; Library ed. $7.89 net.

3-5 A World War I story like no other, this bit of palatable nonsense is told in Pène du Bois' usual bland style and illustrated with his usual distinction. Presenting three heroic figures (a bulldog called Buckingham, a boxing champion called Spider Max, and a large veiled "woman" called Lady Adelaide who proves to be a kangaroo) being received with honors at an Australian port, the author goes back in time to tell their story. It's a tale of pursuit, escape, danger, combat, and balderdash, and it ends with a Cinderella note: Lady Adelaide is the only female whose huge foot fits the enormous pink slipper a reporter has found at the scene where Adelaide escaped a firing squad (part of the sequence that stopped the war and made heroes of the three friends) by jumping straight up into the air and over the wall. The scenes of martial destruction are rather flashy, and the ending is abrupt, but there's plenty of action, plenty of humor, and a pacific message inherent in the spoof.

367 **Dunbar,** Robert E. *Mental Retardation;* illus. with photographs. Watts, 1978. 78-8689. 63p. $4.90.

4-7 Dunbar, a former faculty member at a medical school, gives some historical information about treatment of the retarded and insane in the past, discusses ways in which retardation can be recognized, some of its causes, the handicaps (deafness, for example) that may accompany retardation, educating and mainstreaming the retarded child, and preparing the retarded for adult life. He concludes with a brief survey of some of the ways in which retardation can be anticipated, alleviated, or prevented, and with a description of the rights of the retarded. There are some small flaws in the book; an early reference to people being afraid of the child who can't talk clearly, another to parents who "no longer have to feel shame about having a child who is retarded," the use of both "the mentally retarded has" and "the mentally retarded have," but on the whole the book serves well both as a vehicle for general information about the retarded and as a platform for the author's purpose of encouraging acceptance of, and respect for, those handicapped by mental retardation. An index is provided.

---

368 **Dunlop,** Eileen. *Elizabeth Elizabeth;* illus. by Peter Farmer. Holt, 1977. 76-46578. 185p. $6.95.

5-7 First published in England, this excellent first novel is a time-shift story set in an unoccupied country house in Scotland. Elizabeth, twelve, is staying with her aunt, Kate, while her parents are abroad. She had loved Kate when she was younger, but Kate has become brusque, distant, and preoccupied with her work at the big house, where she is engaged on a project of historical research related to her teaching at Oxford. Elizabeth finds a mirror that takes her into the eighteenth century and into the body of another Elizabeth, a daughter of the mansion family. Slipping back and forth from role to role, Elizabeth realizes that she has become obsessed by a beloved older brother who, after her death (in 1779) became cruel and depraved. In a dramatic dénouement, Kate rescues her niece, and each learns again how much she loves the other. Perceptive in its depiction of characters and relationships, this compelling story is taut with suspense, solid in structure, and deft in its merging of fantasy and realism.

369 **Dunlop,** Eileen. *The House on Mayferry Street;* illus. by Phillida Gili. Holt, 1977. 77-5744. 204p. $6.50.

7-10 First published in England under the title *A Flute in Mayferry Street,* this beautifully crafted story is basically realistic but has a fantasy element adroitly woven in. Eleven-year-old Colin and his sister Marion, an invalid since an accident several years before, become intrigued by scraps of evidence that indicate there is a hidden treasure somewhere in the house, a truck that had disappeared at the time of World War I. Their mother is a widow, and they have little money; since Colin yearns for a flute so that he can join the school orchestra, he is enthralled when he hears mysterious flute music and delighted when his sister hears it also. Save for this and the fact that Marion has some psychic presentiment, the story focuses on her emotional lethargy and on the pursuing of clues. What Dunlop achieves is remarkable, a deft blend of percipient characterization, evocative atmosphere (Edinburgh), sound motivations and relationships, good pace, and a fluid, polished style that keeps the narrative vigorous.

370 **Edmonds,** Walter Dumaux. *Bert Breen's Barn.* Little, 1975. 75-2157. 270p. $6.95.

7-10 Edmond's period piece, set in upstate New York at the turn of the century, is a long, quiet story with strong characters and a well-knit plot, its strength lying in the felicity of details, the full picture it gives of a bygone way of life. Tom Dolan is thirteen when he sees the sturdy old barn of the Breen property and decides that the one thing he wants in life is to take the building down and put it up on Dolan land. His father had run off years before, leaving Tom's mother with three children and no money. Tom works in a mill (twenty-five cents a day) and saves his money; eventually he buys the barn, coping with bullies who are sure that Bert Breen had left a treasure cached on the property. Tom finds the money and adjusts to prosperity, but it is the rebuilding of the barn that is important to him, and the day of the barn-raising is as vividly depicted as a Brueghel canvas. There's no preaching of virtue here, but the story is permeated with the homely virtues of industry and honesty, although Edmonds invests them with neither sentimentality nor glamor. Sedate, but a good, solid read.

371 **Egypt,** Ophelia Settle. *James Weldon Johnson;* illus. by Moneta Barnett. T. Y. Crowell, 1974. 41p. $3.95.

2-4 A biography of the versatile Johnson concludes with the lyrics of "Lift Every Voice and Sing," the most famous of the many songs he wrote in cooperation with his brother or with Bob Cole. Teacher, lawyer, diplomat, field secretary for the NAACP, James Weldon Johnson is best known for the songs and books he wrote. The text is simply written, most of it devoted to Johnson's childhood and the early part of his career, but it touches on his major contributions and it avoids the adulatory tone that would be so easy to adopt with a subject so deserving.

372 **Eiseman,** Albert. *Mañana Is Now; The Spanish-Speaking in the United States;* illus. with photographs. Atheneum, 1973. 184p. $6.25.

7- "Tomorrow will not do; mañana is now," concludes the text of a book that surveys with firm and detailed objectivity the history of Spanish-speaking people in our country, of the discrimination with which they have been treated, of their problems, and of those measures that have been taken by them, or on their behalf, to achieve redress of their grievances. The histories of the Hispanic people from Mexico, Puerto Rico, and Cuba are given separately, with good background and a candid appraisal of the situation today. Well written, well organized, and certainly needed. A list of important dates, a list of books suggested for further reading, and an index are appended.

373 **Ellentuck,** Shan. *Yankel the Fool;* written and illus. by Shan Ellentuck. Doubleday, 1973. 100p. Trade ed. $4.95; Library ed. $5.70.

4-7 A charming humorous tale, episodic in structure, is told in an easy, colloquial style in the oral tradition. Yankel is known to be the village fool, and he stumbles from one contretemps to another as he is contemptuously dismissed by his fellow citizens. In desperation he has turned to a life of crime when a wonder-working Rabbi comes to town and manages to convince everyone that Yankel is an unrecognized sage and scholar. For independent reading, for reading aloud, and as a source for storytelling, this is one of the nicest noodlehead tales in a long while.

374 **Elliott,** Donald. *Alligators and Music;* illus. by Clinton Arrowood. Gambit, 1976. 76-1569. 67p. $8.95.

5-7 The alligators are the performers, as shown in witty, pseudo-sedate black and white drawings, in a book in which each instrument in an orchestra sings its own praises. The text does provide information about the composition of a symphony orchestra, but it will probably appeal even to those readers who are not music lovers, because it is very, very funny. Example: the oboe says, in part, "I wonder, often, why I feel so mournful. The sounds I produce make me sad. In fact, *everything* seems to make me sad!" Or the double bass: "Those violins! They think they're so important!" The violin: "The whole orchestra is only a background for me . . . why aren't most symphonies composed for violin alone? . . . But is it possible I am wrong, that the others are really necessary? . . ." Each group of instruments is preceded by a descriptive page. Delightful.

375 **Engdahl,** Sylvia Louise. *Beyond the Tomorrow Mountains;* illus. by Richard Cuffari. Atheneum, 1973. 257p. $6.95.

6-9 A sequel to *This Star Shall Abide,* a science fiction story set in the future, this takes the young protagonist Noren farther along the path of education for leadership. In a remnant-civilization, the scholar-leaders have to keep secret from the villagers their technological and scientific knowledge. Here the action springs from a crisis situation in which Noren must go to help found another city on the forbidding other side of the Tomorrow Mountains, an experience that tests Noren's courage and faith. More than most science fiction writers for young people,

Engdahl's books are concerned with individual motivation and ethical conduct; the writing style is often heavy and therefore the book moves slowly, but it offers depth and provocative ideas for the mature reader who wants more than just action.

376 **Engdahl,** Sylvia Louise. *The Subnuclear Zoo; New Discoveries in High Energy Physics;* by Sylvia Engdahl and Rick Roberson; illus. with diagrams, charts and photographs. Atheneum, 1977. 77-1686. 100p. $5.95.

7- A survey of old and new knowledge about the structure of matter focuses on particle physics, "called high energy physics because of the kind of experiments needed to find out about particles without seeing them." (This is made more explicit a dozen pages later.) A discussion of subnuclear particles leads to a description of the ways in which scientists can observe the unobservable through bubble or spark chambers, or can identify types of particles by the manner in which they behave. The text also discusses particle interaction and antiparticles, among other ways of classifying particles, and concludes with some conjecture about unsolved aspects of particle physics, including the tantalizing question of what the fundamental particle really is. The writing style is direct, the explanations clear if not comprehensive. An index is appended.

377 **Epstein,** Samuel. *Dr. Beaumont and the Man with the Hole in His Stomach;* by Sam and Beryl Epstein; illus. by Joseph Scrofani. Coward, 1978. 77-8236. 61p. $5.49.

4-7 The Epsteins have made an absorbing story out of one of the most famous incidents in American medical history. William Beaumont, an army doctor, was called to attend a nineteen-year-old Canadian voyageur, Alexis St. Martin, who had been accidentally shot in the stomach. Beaumont never expected his patient to live, But St. Martin did—although the hole in his stomach never healed. Given this medically marvelous opportunity, Beaumont used St. Martin as a guinea pig for years, dipping different types of food into the hole to gauge digestion rate, drawing off gastric juices for analysis, using his findings to gain fame. St. Martin and his wife were restive under the doctor's demands for his patient's accomodating presence, and the Canadian finally went home and refused to come back to be further exhibited and poked at. But Beaumont became famous, learned almost as much about nutrition in the early nineteenth century as is known today. As for St. Martin, he lived—still with the hole in his stomach—to be eighty-three. A selected bibliography is appended.

378 **Erdoes,** Richard, ed. *The Sound of Flutes and other Indian Legends;* pictures by Paul Goble. Pantheon Books, 1976. 76-8660. 132p. $5.95.

5-7
*
For a quarter of a century, Erdoes has been listening to Indian tales; the collection here is from storytellers of Plains Indian tribes, some tales remembered and some transcribed from tapes by Erdoes. Goble's illustrations, stylized and handsome in color or in black and white, are used both as full-page pictures and as marginal ornamentation, and the stories have variety and vitality. They include historical material (the death of Sitting Bull), dignified legends, brief humorous tales, *pourquoi* tales, and stories of creation. A fine collection.

379 **Erdoes,** Richard. *The Sun Dance People;* written and photographed by Richard Erdoes. Knopf, 1976. 218p. Trade ed. $4.95; Library ed. $5.49 net.

8-
*
A comprehensive and detailed examination of Pueblo history and of Pueblo Indian life today is permeated with Erdoes' knowledgeable sympathy for the Native American and a tart candor in his references to the Spanish and American impositions of their own cultures and lack of understanding of the stable, harmonious cultures they have disrupted. A *very* impressive book. The writing is not objective, but it is dignified yet dramatic; the bibliography and index are extensive.

380 **Ericson,** Stig. *Dan Henry in the Wild West;* tr. by Thomas Teal. Delacorte/Lawrence, 1976. 76-5595. 93p. $5.95.

6-9 First published in Sweden in 1971, this smoothly translated story describes the first experiences of adolescent Dan Henry (so written on the emigrant contract made out by an English official who'd thought Daniel Gustafsson would be hard to pronounce) in the United States in the 1870's. Dan had met Martin Nilsson en route and gladly accepted an offer to join him and go to Uncle Charles in Minnesota. They found Martin's uncle and his family living in a cabin; the farmhouse had been hit by lightning and burned. Save for Martin's tragic death as accidental victim in a shootout, the story focuses on the hard lives of frontier dwellers. This has more depth than many such stories, both in characterization and in depicting the conflicting goals of the immigrant Dan, who enjoys being part of a family and having a measure of security yet longs for freedom. In the end he goes off and joins the music corps of a military unit. This is the first of a trilogy that won Sweden's highest children's book award.

381 **Eskenazi,** Gerald. *Hockey.* Grosset, 1973. 157p. illus. $4.95.

6-9 Profusely illustrated with action pictures, this survey of a sport that is attracting increasing numbers of fans is well-organized and comprehensive, written in a breezy, informal style. The text describes the evolution of the game, the first organized teams in Canada and the United States, and then the individual teams and players, grouped under the headings, "The Dropouts," "The Dynasties," "The Great Expansion," and "World Hockey Association," and includes information about the Stanley Cup and about changes in game rules. Although this would be more useful if it had an index and included statistics, it's nevertheless a book that is informative and should prove entertaining, especially to confirmed ice hockey fans.

382 **Estes,** Eleanor. *The Coat-Hanger Christmas Tree;* illus. by Suzanne Suba. Atheneum, 1973. 79p. $5.50.

4-6 "I don't believe in doing something just because a million other people do it," their mother had said, "Now just don't nag me any more about trees." But Marianna and her brother, ten and eleven, still longed for a Christmas tree; even Marianna's friend who lived on a boat had a Christmas tree. Stealthily the children brought discarded trees home and put them in the back yard—and were ordered to throw them away. When Marianna had the idea of making an artificial tree from coathangers, however, her mother was delighted and even contributed a string of lights. So, in a way, Marianna had her tree. The plot isn't strong, but the characterization is convincing, and the story is appealing in the same way that the books about the Moffats are: gentle, cozy, realistic, achieving a sense of family life and home atmosphere that frame and permeate the small events of the action.

383 **Estes,** Eleanor. *The Lost Umbrella of Kim Chu;* illus. by Jacqueline Ayer. Atheneum, 1978. 78-59156. 86p. $7.95.

3-4 Nine-year-old Kim Chu's parents were busy at their restaurant, so it was Grandmother who was there each day when Kim came home, Grandmother who was disapproving when Kim borrowed her father's umbrella one day. It looked like an ordinary umbrella, but in the handle there was a secret compartment that held a scroll that had been given to Father by the people of New York's Chinatown. The umbrella disappeared while Kim was at the library; she decided she'd spotted the culprit and she followed him by El train and ferry to Staten Island. Her friend Mae Lee turned up on the ferry and both girls played detective, solving their case triumphantly. Even stern Grandmother was pleased when Kim told her the dramatic story at the family dinner table.

The plot is developed logically and at a good pace; the writing style is deceptively simple and ingenious, and the gentle humor of a believable adventure is echoed by the deft pen and ink drawings.

384 **Evslin,** Bernard. *Greeks Bearing Gifts; The Epics of Achilles and Ulysses;* illus. by Lucy Martin Bitzer, Four Winds, 1976. 76-16039. 324p. $9.95.

8-
*
As he did in *The Green Hero,* Evslin gives fresh life to old legends, for his version of the epic deeds and of the Greek pantheon combines a fluent, witty style that can be as delightfully irreverent as it is sonorous. His men and gods, women and goddesses, have distinct personalities; his battlecries are stirring. Just let the reader be lulled by the cadence of poetic prose, and Evslin tweaks the ear with such surprises as, "Screaming like Harpies, Athena and Hera flew back to Olympus, flung themselves before Zeus, and tried to get Aphrodite disqualified for illegal use of hands," or, "It is a true auspice, oh King, and must be obeyed. You know me well enough to realize I would never allow myself to appear in any dream that was not of the utmost authenticity." The book, first published as two stories in paperback, can bring clarification to readers who have hitherto been confused by the names and events of the epics, and it's also extremely diverting.

385 **Evslin,** Bernard. *The Green Hero; Early Adventures of Finn McCool;* illus. by Barbara Bascove. Four Winds, 1975. 74-23851. 181p. $7.95.

6-9
*
In a sophisticated and witty retelling of Finn McCool legends, Evslin has constructed a sequential narrative from which storytellers may use separate chapters as source material. Most of the tales are concerned with Finn's struggles against his enemies, the witch sisters and the mighty chieftain Goll McMorna, who had slain Finn's father; the cycle concludes with Finn's victory over Goll and his assumption of the role of chieftain of the Fianna. Evslin is especially adept at using contemporary phrases or concepts (A witch speaks to Finn's love Murtha, who sees only a pelican which she addresses politely as Mr. Pelican. Says the bird, "*Miss,* dear.") so that they are not awkward but amusing. The events are not changed from other versions, but the yeasty style gives them new vitality.

386 **Ewen,** David. *Orchestral Music; Its Story Told through the Lives and Works of its Foremost Composers.* Watts, 1973. 312p. illus. $9.95.

7-
Second in a "Mainstream of Music" series (the first was *Opera;* still to come are *Vocal Music* and *Solo Instrumental and Chamber*

Music), this has reference use despite the fact that it is not all-inclusive. The major part of the book is devoted to chapters that discuss the work of major composers—from one to four per chapter—with authority and clarity, with major trends, changes in form of composition, analyses of individual compositions, and distinctive individual contributions included. The first chapters describe orchestral instruments, the way they developed, how they are used in contemporary orchestras, and the beginnings of orchestral music—both the background and the sixteenth century emergence of orchestral forms as they have persisted—with variations—to today. Like other Ewen books, this is packed with information yet not so solidly that it impairs the style. A glossary and an index are appended.

387 **Ewen,** David. *Solo Instrumental and Chamber Music; Its Story Told Through the Lives and Works of its Foremost Composers.* Watts, 1974. 278p. illus. $9.95.

8- A companion volume to the author's *Opera and Orchestral Music* is, like them, arranged chronologically by chapters that discuss the lives and the works of composers, major and minor. The introductory section describes intruments and musical forms in general terms, but these subjects recur throughout the book, with a particular form often explained in considerable detail; Ewen is concerned both with particulars and with such broad topics as trends and influences. Erudite and serious but written with enough skill so that the book is not dry or heavy, this is lucid enough for the general reader, dignified enough for the specialist. Many photographs and drawings of musicians are included; a glossary and a relative index are appended.

388 **Ewen,** David. *Vocal Music; Its Story Told Through the Lives and Works of its Foremost Composers.* Watts, 1975. 74-34115. 260p. illus. $10.95.

7- As he has done in other books about musical subjects, Ewen provides a rich, full, and knowledgeable history by focusing on major composers, discussing the men (no women) who write vocal music in terms of their distinctive contributions and of their response to, or innovations on, the trends of their times. The book is given color and variety by the biographical information, the length of which varies in relation to the importance of the composer; information about musical forms, changes in notation, influences of—and on—other composers is woven throughout the text, which is chronologically arranged. The book is both impressive and enjoyable. A glossary and an extensive index are appended.

389 **Facklam,** Margery. *Wild Animals, Gentle Women;* illus. with line drawings by Paul Facklam and with photographs. Harcourt, 1978. 77-88961. 139p. $5.95.

6-9 Facklam describes the work of ten women who work with wild creatures as observers, trainers, research scientists, or zoo personnel. Each section includes information on how the subject became interested in the field and/or trained for it, and some facts about the creatures being studied. Since the material itself is dramatic (making friends with a gorilla, swimming into a cave filled with sharks) and the text is competently written, the book should appeal to a broad range of readers. Each section is prefaced by a handsome line drawing of the animal and includes a photograph of the subject or (in one case) subjects. A final chapter discusses choosing a career working with animals; a bibliography, an index, and a list of "Organizations to Help You Learn about Animal Watching" are appended.

390 **Farber,** Norma. *As I Was Crossing Boston Common;* illus. by Arnold Lobel. Dutton, 1975. 75-6520. 26p. $6.95.

K-3 "As I was crossing Boston Common, not very fast, not very slow, I met a man with a creature in tow." Thus begins a linked parade of creatures with odd names, from angwantibo to zibet. The words are spoken by a turtle; the whole text has a slow, stately pace, just right for the speaker, and a poetic cadence. The grave, faithfully detailed illustrations are in soft, pale green and buff; each creature bears a label, each picture has a touch of humor, and the repeat frieze of bordering houses changes in appropriately inch-along fashion. A descriptive listing is appended. Only one question arises: how many children old enough to be interested in odd (and sometimes difficult) names will be caught by what looks like an animal alphabet book?

391 **Farber,** Norma. *Six Impossible Things Before Breakfast;* drawings by Tomie De Paola and others. Addison-Wesley, 1977. 76-40264. 43p. Trade Ed. $6.95; Library ed. $5.21 net.

3-5 An entertaining potpourri of stories and poems, each of the six illustrated, in black and white, by a distinctively different artist, has zest and humor. In a folk-like tale, a forgotten batch of dough rises to the sky, irritating the almost-eclipsed moon; in a less effective fanciful tale, a woman blows bubbles that never break but fill her home. One of the poems is about riding a unicorn, another is a Bunyanesque hero tale; a narrative poem describes the plight of a New Yorker who's left her shopping basket on a bus, and the last poem is a dialogue between an indulgent royal father and his drooping daughter. Varied, breezy, and useful for reading aloud to younger children.

392 **Farber,** Norma. *This Is the Ambulance Leaving the Zoo;* illus. by Tomie de Paola. Dutton, 1975. 28p. $5.95.

4-6 yrs. There's always room for an alphabet book that uses a fresh concept, and this does. At first it seems like a book about vehicles, as the ambulance roars away from the zoo, while a bus stops to let it pass, cars pile up, drivers are balked, and the emergency signal flashes. But the path of the ambulance is marked by other sights, and it eventually arrives at the underpass, choked by traffic, where the veterinarian lives, et cetera. Then, adding cumulation to the appeals of action, variety, vehicles, and animals, there's a rundown reversal: the patient (a yak) leaves". . . the VETERINARIAN who lives just beyond the UNDERPASS choking with TRAFFIC snarling and unsnarling at the sound of the SIREN clearing the ROTARY . . ." Delightful pictures, bright idea, attractive book.

393 **Farber,** Norma. *Where's Gomer?* illustrated by William Pène du Bois. Dutton, 1974. 26p. $6.95.

K-3 A happy romp to all readers as they follow the distrait ponderings and apprehensions of the crew of the Ark, for Gomer son of Japheth son of Noah is missing at embarkation time. "O tempest and flood! O watery ways / of dismal darks and desolate grays! / O deluge! O umpteen nights and days / without Gomer!" His mother has been weeping into the stew, his father peering from the prow, and the animals have been remembering their not-always-amicable encounters with the boy. The ending is satisfying and mildly surprising, the poetry has bounce and humor, and the illustrations—showing all hands in nautical dress—are lovely and funny and just right.

394 **Farmer,** Penelope. *The Story of Persephone;* illus. by Graham McCallum. Morrow, 1973. 45p. Trade ed. $4.50; Library ed. $4.14 net.

4-6 The legend of the goddess Demeter and her beloved child, the mythic explanation of the seasonal changes, is told in dramatic style. Both the vitality of the illustrations and the sophistication of the writing give this retelling of the Greek legend more impact than Margaret Hodges' *Persephone and the Springtime;* while it is for slightly more mature readers than the audience for Sarah Tomaino's *Persephone: Bringer of Spring,* Farmer's style may pose difficulties for some readers. Compare her description of Hades: ". . . he, too, fell passionately in love. Obsessed by Persephone, determined to have her, he watched continually, invisible. A black rock, a hawthorn tree, a cloud on the hillside," with Tomaino's simpler presentation, in which Hades simply appears and sweeps

Persephone into his chariot, or with Penelope Proddow's poetic brevity in *Demeter and Persephone,* beautifully illustrated by Barbara Cooney. McCallum's pictures have vigor and drama, but they do not achieve the subtle contrast and effective composition of Ati Forberg's illustration for the Tomaino version, or the elegance of Cooney's pictures. Farmer devotes more attention to the involvement of the Olympian dwellers than do the others, and the often-lyric prose contributes also to achieving more of a sense of majesty than is found in the other versions.

395 **Farmer,** Penelope. *William and Mary; a Story.* Atheneum, 1974. 160p. $5.95.

5-7 In an adroit blending of fantasy and realism, two children share the experience of being transported to other times and places. William is the only pupil who is staying through the holidays at the boarding school where Mary's father is headmaster; relying on each other's company, the two children find that whenever they are together and looking at a scene they may find themselves there (they can't control it) but that it happens only when they are holding the half-shell William's father had sent. All through the book William hunts for the other half of the shell, and only at the end when he finds it does he admit that he had hoped it would bring his parents—as it does. Farmer excels in the dramatic composition of a book such as this: strongly defined characters, a sustaining theme, a convincing antiphonal structure of real-unreal, and, as background, a strong evocation of place.

396 **Farmer,** Penelope. *Year King.* Atheneum, 1977. 77-3165. 232p. $6.95.

8- A subtle and intricate story for sophisticated readers, set in the English countryside, has a compelling sweep and depth as it explores the tenacious struggle of a nineteen-year-old to free himself of the self-doubt engendered by the dominating personalities of his twin brother and his mother. Lew retreats to the family cottage where he lives alone, has an affair with an American girl, and—periodically—has strange spells during which he seems to enter his brother's body, sharing even intimate tactile sensations. The story, explicit in its descriptions of anger, passion, and fear, ends with a confrontation between Lew and his twin while they are on an underground expedition; it's a dramatic conclusion to a taut and polished story with deep psychological implications.

397 **Farrar,** Richard. *The Birds' Woodland; What Lives There;* drawings by William Downey. Coward, 1976. 75-28304. 26p. $4.99

3-6 Beautifully detailed pen and pencil drawings in black and white show the birds discussed in the text in so meticulous a way that the pictures can, despite the lack of color, almost serve for identifying species. The text explains how each bird forages within a given territory and how the different ways they move and the different sub-areas in which they hunt food enable them to coexist within the woodland. The author concludes with some brief, sensible basic advice on birdwatching.

398 **Fassler,** Joan. *Howie Helps Himself;* illus. by Joe Lasker. Whitman, 1974. 29p. Trade ed. $3.95; Library ed. $2.96 net.

1-3 Although a prefatory note addressed to adults suggests that Howie's disability is probably cerebral palsy, the nature of his handicap is not specifically stated in the text. He's presented as a boy in a wheelchair who goes by special bus to a special school, whose limbs are too weak to do many things other, physically normal children can do. At times Howie is frustrated, but most of the time he's a happy child, loved and loving. The climax of the story comes when Howie, after long effort, manipulates his wheelchair by himself. Readers may wonder why he wheels his way to Daddy down the long, empty classroom when the hug at the end of the trip (in a subsequent picture) shows the beaming faces of teachers and classmates, but this is a minor flaw in a book that should make normal children understand better the problems of the handicapped and may make permanently handicapped children feel that they aren't wholly ignored (i.e. anathema) in the literature for children.

399 **Faulkner,** William J. *The Days When the Animals Talked; Black American Folktales and How They Came to Be;* illus. by Troy Howell. Follett, 1977. 76-50315. 190p. Trade ed. $7.95; Library ed. $7.98 net.

5- Although the title gives no indication of it, the book contains not only animal tales but, in a separate section, a series of anecdotes about his days of slavery told by Simon Brown to Faulkner, an eminent black folklorist. The several forewords and introductions are addressed, clearly, to adult readers, while the reminiscences and the folktales (the chief character is Brer Rabbit) are scaled for younger audiences. Whether Faulkner has a flair for folklore or fidelity in retelling the versions of those from which he heard the tales is immaterial; they are richly dramatic and compellingly told.

400 **Feelings,** Muriel L. *Jambo Means Hello; Swahili Alphabet Book;* pictures by Tom Feelings. Dial, 1974. 48p. Trade ed. $5.95; Library ed. $5.47 net.

2-4 A companion volume to the Feelings' *Moja Means One;* a Swahili counting book, this gives a word for each letter of the alphabet (the Swahili alphabet has 24 letters) save for "q" and "x", and a sentence or two provides additional information. A double-page spread of soft black and white drawings illustrates each word; for example. "V, vyombo are utensils (vee-oam-bow). A craftsman makes utensils for the village. Carved wooden bowls and ladles and pitchers made from gourds are useful and decorative objects for the home." The picture shows such a craftsman making one object and surrounded by others. The text gives a considerable amount of information about traditional East African life as well as some acquaintance with the language that is used by approximately 45 million people.

401 **Fegely,** Thomas D. *Wonders of Wild Ducks;* illus. with photographs. Dodd, Mead, 1975. 75-11443. 80p. $4.95.

5-9 Good photographs and careful organization of material add to the reference use of a book that stresses conservation throughout the text. Fegely gives general information about duck species, habits of courtship and mating, flyways (with several maps), and the predators or forms of pollutants that threaten duck populations. The major part of the text describes about two dozen types of ducks, with added details about breeding, nesting, appearance, care of the young, et cetera. The writing is dry, brisk, and direct; an index is appended.

402 **Fenner,** Carol. *Gorilla Gorilla;* illus. by Symeon Shimin. Random House, 1973. 50p. Trade ed. $4.95; Library ed. $5.39 net.

3-5 Dramatic illustrations in black and white show the gorilla, in a narrative that is really informational rather than fictional, growing from birth to adulthood. The gorilla clings to his mother, gains independence, learns to fend for himself, and watches with awed interest the behavior of the tribe's leader. Captured and put in a zoo, the gorilla languishes at first; then he adjusts and finally is stirred by the new female gorilla that has been put in the next cage to drum his declaration of maturity as the leader of his tribe had done. The facts are accurate, the story-line rather extended; the writing is simple and direct, with a touch of the poetic.

403 **Fenner,** Carol. *The Skates of Uncle Richard;* illus. by Ati Forberg. Random House, 1978. 78-55910. 46p. Trade ed. $4.95; Library ed. $5.99 net.

3-4 Three years before, Marsha had seen skaters on television, but it
* wasn't until recently that she'd seen a black figure skater. Nine now, she yearned for ice skates, half afraid she'd be inept, half dreaming of herself as a great skater. She did get skates for Christmas, but they weren't the lovely white skates she'd hoped for; her mother had saved Uncle Richard's ugly old hockey skates. A bitter disappointment, and it took a long time before Marsha

tried them out. She was awful. Her ankles turned, she kept falling down, it was no fun at all. Then Uncle Richard appeared and he understood, he really understood her dream; he helped her get started and then he told her she must stand up and reach high, she must skate proudly. He told her she was a natural skater, and when he had left her, she glided proudly, "on the skates of Uncle Richard, taller and taller and taller, never falling down," the story ends. Fenner has an easy, natural writing style that has convincing dialogue and a smooth narrative flow; the story is nicely constructed and the author's perceptive sympathy is understated. Marsha doesn't accomplish miracles on the ice, no instant spins or axels, but readers are left with a warm feeling that she's only begun to see her dream come true.

404 **Fenten,** D. X. *Indoor Gardening;* illus. by Howard Berelson. Watts, 1974, 61p. $3.45.

4-7 Although this gives much of the same information as does Anita Soucie's *Plant Fun,* it gives facts about a greater variety of plants and does not go into as great an amount of detail about each. A brisk, straightforward, and informal style and adequate illustrations provide enough instruction for the beginning plant collector on such aspects of plant care as light, temperature, pruning, soil, humidity, et cetera. This is general information, without—for example—specific recipes for potting-soil extras like humus and bonemeal. Separate chapters deal with foliage plants, flowering plants, food plants, and cacti, with a final chapter on gift plants. Not comprehensive, but a good introduction, with an appended bibliography and an index.

405 **Fenton,** Edward. *Duffy's Rocks.* Dutton, 1974. 198p. $5.95.

6-8 Duffy's Rocks is a Pittsburgh suburb where Timothy Brennan lives with his grandmother; his mother is dead, his father has gone off and not been seen for years. Timothy knows that Gran hears from his father, but she won't tell him anything; one day he steals a look at the latest letter and decides to track his father down. He goes to see his father's wife in New York only to find that she'd been deserted the year before; he finds a girl who'd worked with his father and been in love with him, but she hasn't seen him for months. Resigned to the fact that the man he has longed for is lost to him, Timothy goes back to the hated dullness of the grimy suburb and finds that his grandmother, who had doted on her son, knows that he's a wastrel and had wanted the boy to grow up unlike his father, but wanted him to keep his father's image a shining one. The plot isn't dramatic, but it is strong and realistic, and the book is unusual both in its portrayal of a Catholic family and of the prejudice they have toward non-Catholics. Style, characterization, and the details of locale and period (the depression years) are outstanding.

406 **Ferguson,** Dorothy. *Black Duck;* illus. by Douglas K. Morris. Walker, 1978. 77-77543. 30p. Trade ed. $6.95; Library ed. $6.85 net.

2-3 Delicately detailed, realistic line drawings illustrate a description of a black duck and her seven ducklings. Simply written and rather sedate, the text gives a modest amount of information about other creatures of the salt marsh community as well as about the feeding habits, natural enemies, and behavior of the species. The book covers the ducklings' first year and concludes with their independence and their mother's search for a new nesting site.

407 **Ferry,** Charles. *O Zebron Falls!* Houghton, 1977. 77-9986. 213p. $7.95.

7-10 Like Burch's story, this is set before and during World War II, and concerns the problems of an adolescent in a small town. This is Michigan, though, and sixteen-year-old Lukie discovers, as did Amanda in the Burch book, that she has romantic feelings about her life-long friend. Billy is black, an outstanding and popular student at Zebron High, and it is he who gently points out to Lukie the problems they would have as a couple. So Billy, like Alan, goes off to war. Here, too, the author gives a vivid picture of a small town and laces into the story a family problem: the hostility between Lukie's father and his brother, and the resentment that Lukie often feels her father is expressing toward her. The last few pages are a bit of a letdown, as there is a graduation night sequence with saccharine overtones, but the rest of the book is sturdy, well-paced and competently written.

408 **Field,** Edward, comp. *Eskimo Songs and Stories;* selected and tr. by Edward Field; collected by Knud Rasmussen; illus. by Kiakshuk and Pudlo. Delacorte, 1973. 103p. $6.95.

4-7 Although this does not substitute for *Beyond the High Hills* with its splendid photographs by Guy Mary-Rousseliere, there are more poems here from the same collection by Knud Rasmussen, and the illustrations by two Eskimo artists are handsome and are used to good effect on the clean pages. The poems are rhythmic and vigorous, reflecting the cultural patterns of the tribes of the Hudson Bay area yet having universality, revealing the beliefs and the mores of the society in poem-chants that are simple and beautiful, occasionally humorous, often touching.

409 **Finlayson,** Ann. *Greenhorn on the Frontier;* illus. by W. T. Mars. Warne, 1974. 209p. $4.95.

5-8 A lively and convincing frontier story is set in the period just before the American Revolution. An English brother and sister, Harry and Sukey Warrilow, have walked weary miles through the forests of Pennsylvania to the acreage Harry had bought from John Penn. During their stop in Pittsburgh they had gained an enemy, Girty, and a friend, McBain; after they built their cabin they also became friendly with an Indian who later warned them that Girty was coming to seize their land, having entered a pre-emptive claim under Virginia authority. The little-known struggle for land between Pennsylvania and Virginia gives, as do the frontiersmen's reactions to delayed news of rumblings against the British from the seaboard, a solid historical basis to a story that has sturdy characterization and good pace, with Sukey's hatred of slavery and her love affair with McBain (who frees his two slaves to please Sukey) as minor themes.

410 **Fisher,** Aileen Lucia. *Do Bears Have Mothers, Too?* by Aileen Fisher and Eric Carle. T. Y. Crowell, 1973. 24p. illus. $4.95.

K-2 A collection of poems addressed to animal young by their mothers is illustrated by pictures that take full advantage of the oversize pages. The pictures—large in scale, bright, handsome, executed in a combination of collage and other media—are excellent for group use as well as for individual lap-lookers. The poems are breezy and fresh, with moments of humor and a permeating mood of mother love. Sample: "Cygnets, you must practice early/not to be unkempt or surly/Swans have quite a reputation/we are known in every nation/For our grace and comely beauty/To uphold this is your duty." A beguiling book.

411 **Fisher,** Leonard Everett. *Alphabet Art: Thirteen ABCs from Around the World;* written and illus. by Leonard Everett Fisher. Four Winds, 1978. 78-6148. 64p. $8.95.

5- This doesn't give as much information as does Ogg's *The 26 Letters,* but it is beautifully illustrated (dark red and white scratchboard pictures, double-page spreads showing 13 alphabets in dark red on white) and it gives information about historical background. The 13 ABCs are Arabic, Cherokee, Chinese, Cyrillic, Eskimo, Gaelic, German, Greek, Hebrew, Japanese, Sanskrit, Thai, and Tibetan; following an introductory discussion of ancient alphabets, the separate alphabets are presented in a three-part format: a picture that carries a text in that alphabet, with such phrases as "Hudson Bay Company" in Eskimo, "Man, Myth, and Greece" in Greek, or "O, the jewel in the lotus" in Tibetan; a page of information; and the two-page chart of the alphabet, with the English equivalent—when appropriate—in the corner of each box showing a letter.

412 **Fisher,** Leonard Everett. *The Blacksmiths;* written and illus. by Leonard Everett Fisher. Watts, 1976. 75-26684. 47p. $3.90.

5-7 Black and white scratchboard illustrations show tools, processes, and techniques of the colonial smithy; the text is divided, as it is in all the books in this useful series, into a section that gives historical background about the role of the smith in the colonies, and a somewhat longer section that describes the equipment, procedures, and products of the blacksmith's forge. A list of terms and an index are appended.

413 **Fisher,** Leonard Everett. *The Warlock of Westfall;* written and illus. by Leonard Everett Fisher. Doubleday, 1974. 119p. $4.95.

5-7 Somber yet dramatic, the stark black and white illustrations in Fisher's distinctive style are particularly well suited to the taut and brooding atmosphere evoked in this tale of witch-hunting in colonial America. The setting is the small village of Westfall, where an old, crotchety man is accused by a group of boys and hanged by the villagers, easily aroused in those hysterical times. The tense conclusion, in which the same credulous hysteria brings about the abandonment of the village, is conceived with a fine sense of theater. Both the mood of the times and the physical atmosphere are skillfully evoked in a stirring and convincing story.

414 **Fisk,** Nicholas. *Grinny*. Nelson, 1974. 124p. $4.95.

5-7 First published in England, a science fantasy that is firmly meshed with reality, written with a flair for dialogue, and—although it uses a device familiar to readers of the genre, the planetary visitor masquerading as a human being—unusual in plot. It's unusual because the dea ex machina (U.F.O. type) is a sweet little old lady who presents herself at Tim's door. She's Great-Aunt Emma; she says to Tim's mother, "You remember me, Millie!" And Millie remembers. It's Tim's younger sister who first suspects the ever-beaming Emma and calls her "Grinny," and at first Tim, who tells the story in his diary, thinks Beth is being nine-year-old silly. Beth and Tim, with the help of a friend, outwit the menacing Grinny, and (because the phrase "You remember me" has hypnotized each adult) the children's conquest is logically without adult help. The nicely crafted story has suspense, action, and a frisson here and there.

415 **Fitzgerald,** John D. *The Great Brain Reforms;* illus. by Mercer Mayer. Dial, 1973. 165p. Trade ed. $4.95; Library ed. $4.58 net.

4-6 The Great Brain is Tom, the older brother of J.D., who tells the story as he did in four earlier books about the clever manipulator who repeatedly has succeeded in tricking his friends and his brothers into schemes out of which Tom makes a profit. Here Tom gets his long-overdue comeuppance when, after yet another ploy, J.D. and all the other boys hold a mock trial. Sentence: a year of ostracism, but the sentence is suspended when the Great Brain promises to reform. The writing is light and lively, the humor of the story echoed in the illustrations.

416 **Fitzgerald,** John D. *The Return of the Great Brain;* illus. by Mercer Mayer. Dial, 1974. 150p. Trade ed. $5.95; Library ed. $5.47 net.

4-6 Like earlier books about the Great Brain, Tom Fitzgerald, this is a series of anecdotes told by his younger brother. Tom, whose avarice and cunning had caused him to be put on probation by a jury of his peers in *The Great Brain Reforms,* is finding it hard to play his usual con games on his friends (and his brother) without backsliding, but he manages nicely to keep just this side of swindling: he also contributes to the solution of a crime. His only failure: trying to cure a friend of a severe case of first love. Lively, funny, warm, and perceptive, this is both a good period piece and a timeless picture of boyhood.

417 **Flanagan,** Geraldine Lux. *Window Into a Nest;* by Geraldine Lux Flanagan and Sean Morris. Houghton, 1976. 75-17028. 96p. illus. $7.95.

5- A nesting box with open back was built against a window, the
* window was covered with black cloth, and the cloth could be stealthily pulled aside for observation and photography. Thus the authors were able to record minute details of the events of chickadee family life: the furnishing of the nest, as the birds imitated nest-cupping, the patterns of egg-brooding, the incessant activity of feeding seven chicks (including solving such problems as coping with an oversize, uncooperative caterpillar), and the preparation for flight. Flanagan and Morris describe all these activities, but they make them more interesting and comprehensible by discussing purposes, problems, and some of the behavior that could not be recorded on film.

418 **Fleischman,** Sid. *The Ghost on Saturday Night;* illus. by Eric Von Schmidt. Little, 1974. 57p. $3.95.

3-5 A blithe and tallish tale is set in a west coast town at some time in the past and told by ten-year-old Opie, whose efforts to earn enough money for a saddle were spurred by Aunt Etta's promise that if he could get one she would buy him a horse. When Opie earned a ticket to Professor Pepper's ghost-raising, he never expected to have an adventure, rescue money stolen from the town bank, and get a saddle. In part this is due to Opie's quick thinking, in part to Aunt Etta's stout common sense. The style is admirable: light, breezy, convincingly that of a child of ten; the author deftly puts into a quite short story just the right balance of action, humor, and quick characterization.

419 **Fleischman,** Sid. *Humbug Mountain;* illus. by Eric von Schmidt. Atlantic-Little, Brown, 1978. 78-9419. 149p. $7.95.

4-6 Another hilarious tall-tale adventure concerns a roving newspaper publisher of frontier times. Wiley, who tells the story, is irritated now and then when Pa goes off by himself, but otherwise he's proud of Pa. And Ma. He even gets along with his sister Glorietta. Bound for Grandpa's planned town, Sunrise, the family finds only swampy Dakota Territory land and Grandpa's old riverboat —occupied by two desperadoes and what appears to be a ghost. The plot is full of salty characters, quirks of fate (the Sunrise land is retrieved—as it had been lost—when the river changes its course and places the property back in Dakota Territory after having placed it, briefly, in Nevada) and outwittings of rascals. Grandpa shows up; Pa proves to have disappeared periodically because he's been writing the trashy series that is Wiley's favorite reading, and the hero of those stories, Quickshot Billy, appears in person. A flavorful romp.

420 **Fleischman,** Sid. *McBroom and the Beanstalk;* illus. by Walter Lorraine. Atlantic-Little, Brown, 1978. 77-22177. 40p. $5.95.

3-5 "Why, I couldn't hold my head up," says McBroom, when his family urges him to enter a contest for liars. Why, hair would grow on fish before he'd trifle with the truth! All McBroom fans will recognize the humor of this auspicious beginning of another McBroom story, especially when it's followed by the children's discovery of a giant footprint and then—due to the vaunted fertility of McBroom soil—by a huge stalk that grows from a discarded bean. A version of Jack and the beanstalk? Not at all, this top-heavy vine collapses, grows right down the road and into town, and traps two bank robbers. Fleischman gets a nice touch into the ending of another yeasty tall tale told in blithe style.

421 **Fleischman,** Sid. *McBroom Tells a Lie;* illus. by Walter Lorraine. Atlantic/Little, 1976. 76-8396. 48p. $4.95.

3-5 To old admirers of the Tall Tale Teller Extraordinary, McBroom, even the admission of a lie, with which he begins this story, should be amusing. Well, he admits he told a lie once, but not until the end of another tale full of whoppers does he say what the lie was. By that time McBroom's children have saved the marvelously fertile farm from going to a demanding neighbor by producing a crop of tomatoes as he'd required. Overnight, and in a dust storm. How? Wellll . . . seems that the children built a machine powered by popcorn exploding from the heat of some sunlight that had once frozen in a sudden cold snap, and they gathered fire flies and the firefly-light made the tomatoes grow. The lie? Well, McBroom said the neighbor's cow had mistaken the popcorn for snow and had frozen to death. Not true. All she did was catch a terrible cold. It's more of the same, but fans don't care, and to first-timers, it won't be a repeat performance.

422 **Fleischman,** Sid. *McBroom the Rainmaker;* illus. by Kurt Werth. Grosset, 1973. 42p. $4.99.

3-5 Another braggadocio tall tale from the indomitable farmer McBroom whose lush land grew things so fast that a crop in one day was considered slow-growing. Plagued doubly by a drought and by giant mosquitoes, McBroom brought rain by chasing a raincloud and planting onion seeds in a wagon filled with the wonderful McBroom soil. When the thirsty mosquitoes attacked the Instant Giant Onions, their tears finally brought rain to the parched earth. Sheer ebullient nonsense, the fun is augmented by the lively Werth drawings.

423 **Fleming,** Alice, comp. *America Is Not All Traffic Lights; Poems of the Midwest;* illus. with photographs. Little, 1976. 75-25651. 68p. illus. $5.95.

5- Fleming has chosen with discrimination poems that have a great diversity of mood, subject, and style, and the photographs that illustrate the poems have been selected with equal care. Among the poets represented are Brooks, Dickinson, William Rose Benét, Sandburg, and Sherwood Anderson; among the selections are an Osage chant, a funeral lament, lyrics that reflect the cities and the prairies, and poems about people.

424 **Fleming,** Alice. *Contraception, Abortion, Pregnancy.* Nelson, 1975. 74-10268. 92p. $5.95.

9-12 Fleming's discussion of the subjects is candid and objective; she advances no viewpoint and makes no judgments about mores. The text describes the reproductive process, birth prevention methods, and the various abortive techniques, stressing legality and safety. In discussing pregnancy, the author again stresses proper care and safety during the prenatal period and the health of mother and child during and after labor. The writing is direct and straightforward, comprehensive and informative. A relative index is appended.

425 **Fleming,** Alice, comp. *Hosannah the Home Run! Poems about Sports;* illus. with photographs. Little, 1972. 68p. $4.95.

5- Well-chosen photographs illustrate a charming and varied anthology, with selections from English language poets from Izaak Walton and John Gay to Richard Armour and Gregory Corso. Approximately twenty sports are reflected in poems that range from the light humor of Armour and Nash to the beating insistence of William Carlos Williams' "The Yachts," or Edwin Hooey's dramatic "Foul Shot." A very nice collection, one that may well catch the interest of—perhaps even convert—a reader who has eschewed poetry heretofore. A section of brief notes on the authors is appended.

426 **Fleming,** Alice. *Trials that Made Headlines.* St. Martin's, 1975. 146p. illus. $6.95.

7-10 Ten trials in American history that were landmarks in influencing our judicial system are described in a book that is objective in approach and is written in a straightforward style that makes the drama of the events the more vivid by contrast. Fleming begins with the Boston Massacre trial, emphasizing John Adams' strong sense of justice in defending the men his cousin, Samuel Adams, was agitating against; she concludes with the efforts toward scrupulous impartiality at the Nuremberg trial. Other trials discussed are "The President vs. the Press," a libel trial of the Jeffersonian era, the Amistad case, the trials of John Brown, the Haymarket riot and Triangle fire cases, Andrew Johnson's impeachment trial, the Scopes case, and the Sweet trial. A bibliography is appended.

427 **Fleming,** Thomas J. *Benjamin Franklin.* Four Winds, 1973. 166p. Trade ed. $5.95; Library ed. $5.62 net.

6-10 Author of other books on Franklin, among them the adult title *The Man Who Dared the Lightning* (Morrow, 1971), Fleming has added new depth and vigor to a familiar subject of biographies. The facts that are usually glossed over in books for young readers, such as Franklin's penchant for dalliance, are given in a brisk and graceful style; there are many quotations from Franklin's writings and many anecdotes and bits of information not usually included in other books and giving evidence of thorough research. Above all, the vigor and informality of the writing make this a pleasure to read. An index is appended.

428 **Folsom,** Franklin. *Red Power on the Rio Grande; The Native American Revolution of 1680;* illus. by J. D. Roybal. Follett, 1973. 144p. $5.95.

7-10 A history of the Pueblo Revolution of 1680, slightly and ably fictionalized, gives the Indian point of view. Since all of the records are Spanish and events have usually been heretofore seen from the conquerors' position, this—the author states—is a reinterpretation based on knowledge of the Pueblo culture and ethos, an attempt to single out a neglected hero, Popé, an effort to compensate for the biased accounts of the past. Folsom succeeds; the text makes a convincing case for a people whose way of life was disrupted, who were persecuted for observing their own religion and forced to work at hard labor, who had to pay taxes to a detested victor, and who finally made a desperate attempt to salvage their own way of life under the leadership of the Tewa medicine man, Popé. Although the revolution was successful, it was not permanent—but the people who were reconquered by the Spanish when they returned were stronger in defense of their rights because of the revolution. The writing style is solid and occasionally stolid, but the drama of the events carries the book, and the representation of the Indian viewpoint is welcome. A pronunciation guide, a list of source materials, and an index are appended.

429 **Forman,** James. *The Survivor.* Farrar, 1976. 76-2478. 272p. $7.95.

8- Just as many Jewish families in Germany felt more German than Jewish, so did David Ullman's family think of themselves as Dutch citizens who were also Jews. That was before the Germans came. In the long and detailed story of the Ullmans are all the apprehension, danger, persecution, and manic prejudice that are traced in Meltzer's book, on the Holocaust. David's sister Ruth works for the underground, his grandfather commits suicide, his mother dies of exposure, and he (with his father and brother) goes to Auschwitz. Only David survives, and the grim, powerful story ends with the war over and David setting out for Palestine to find a younger sister and an uncle. This is not more real than Meltzer's Holocaust, but it is just as intensive an examination, just as convincing although fictionalized and with a narrower scope. The print is, unfortunately, very small.

430 **Foster,** Genevieve (Stump). *The World of William Penn;* illus. by the author. Scribner, 1973. 189p. $5.95.

4-7 A convert when he was sixteen to the Society of Friends, William Penn was cast off by his father and was imprisoned in the Tower of London for his beliefs. This is not a full biography, although the last pages summarize the events of Penn's declining years, but a broad view of happenings throughout the civilized world in the year in which he was most active as a Quaker and was establishing the settlements of Pennsylvania. Like other Foster books, this "World" moves, shuttle-fashion, from episodes in Penn's life to events in England and the Continent, the Far East and colonial

America. Like the others, it is engrossing as a broad view of history; unlike the earlier books, it is not oversize and therefore a bit easier to handle. An index is appended.

431 **Fowke,** Edith, comp. *Ring Around the Moon;* illus. by Judith Gwyn Brown. Prentice-Hall, 1977. 76-44207. 160p. $6.95.

3-5 No, not a children's version of the Anouilh play, but a compilation of riddles, rhymes, rounds, and songs—including "answer-back" songs—selected by an eminent Canadian folklorist. All the material is in the oral tradition, and is profusely and deftly illustrated by small sketches that are, like the text, printed in dark brown. The divided list of sources and references, the bibliography, and the index are printed in unfortunately small type, as are the lyrics and musical notation (the melody line only) for songs; nevertheless, the collection contains a substantial amount of varied, interesting, and often amusing material.

432 **Fox,** Michael. *Sundance Coyote;* illus. by Dee Gates. Coward, 1974. 93p. $4.95.

5-7 The description of an animal's life from birth to mating is a familiar device in informational books; few authors write with the sure knowledge (and with an unsentimental sympathy) of Michael Fox, a psychologist specializing in animal behavior. His coyote is given a name but there is otherwise no anthropomorphism, and the narrative form is used with skill as Dr. Fox describes the early training of coyote cubs, their social behavior, coping with predators—including man—and their mating patterns. The text is sprinkled with minor errors ("Countless insects, such as desert plants . . .", "Smaller predators . . . prayed on insects . . .", "The teeth of the trap . . . sunk deep into his ankle.") but they affect neither accuracy nor mood of the writing.

433 **Fox,** Michael. *The Wolf;* illus. by Charles Frace. Coward, 1973. 95p. $4.95.

5-8 Although the narrative framework of the text and the use of names for a family of wolves lend a fictional aura to the text, this is a book that is primarily informational. It follows the wolves Shadow and Silver from the birth of a litter through the first year of their cubs' lives, giving a sequential picture of the care and training of the cubs, the ways in which the young learn to avoid danger, hunt, and acquire the approved patterns of behavior. The author, an authority on animal behavior, is particularly explicit about the familial affection and the sharing that exist among wolves, animals whose behavior belies their reputation for ferocity. The writing style is dry but the material is interesting and the details authoritative.

434 **Fox,** Paula. *Good Ethan;* illus. by Arnold Lobel. Bradbury, 1973. 24p. $4.95.

K-2 As Ethan went off to play, his mother said, "Ethan?" What did I *mean* when I said 'be a good boy'?" "I can't walk across the street," he answered. What a predicament for an obedient child, when a new ball bounces across the street and lies there, tantalizingly visible but not reachable. Ethan's polite requests of passersby get varied responses but no action, and he finally conceives an ingenious method of retrieval. In this part of the book the story moves into the improbable with blithe assurance, as Ethan climbs wires, swings from tree to tree, descends via wisteria vine to the other side of the street. The style of writing is bland and humorous, the story just the right length, complexity, and structure for the read-aloud audience: the brownstone-milieu pictures have a debonair simplicity.

435 **Fox,** Paula. *The Slave Dancer;* illus. by Eros Keith. Bradbury, 1973. 176p. $5.95.

6-9 Set in 1840, this historical novel is a departure for Paula Fox, the distinguished writer of contemporary stories that are remarkable for their perceptive characterization and style. *The Slave Dancer,* too, is remarkable—but in quite a different way. It is the story of fourteen-year-old Jessie, impressed into service on a slave ship so that he can play his fife. To his horror, Jessie discovers that he is a slave dancer, his piping meant to keep the wretched black captives jigging in order to maintain their health—the motive mercenary rather than humanitarian. Jessie and a slave his age escape after a shipwreck and are taken in by a black man who sends each of them safely on his way—but this is after a four-month voyage on which Jessie has learned the horrors of the slave trade and the depravity and avarice of the crew. It's a grim story, but powerful in its tragic drama, vivid in characterization, and searing in its indictment of slavery.

436 **Freedman,** Russell. *Getting Born;* illus. with photographs; drawings by Corbett Jones. Holiday House, 1978. 78-6673. 37p. $6.95.

2-4 There is nothing in this text that hasn't already been presented in books for children, but Freedman has pulled material together neatly, describing in a direct and simple writing style the reproductive patterns of various kinds of animal life: the trout and the molly, which differ in the way they lay eggs; the seahorse, whose offspring are spawned by the male parent; the frog, with its metamorphosis from tadpole; a snake, a turtle, a chicken, a cat, a dolphin, and a horse. Diagrams are clear, and photographs—some of which are magnified—are well placed. Neither a table of contents nor an index accompany the continuous text, but they are not really needed.

437 **Freedman,** Russell. *How Birds Fly;* illus. by Lorence F. Bjorklund. Holiday House, 1977. 77-555. 64p. $6.95.

4-6 Illustrated by soft pencil drawings, meticulously detailed, a simple, lucid text moves logically from those features of bird anatomy that contribute to the ability to fly, to general principles of flight, and then—in brief chapters—to separate aspects of birds' flight: getting lift, gliding or flapping, taking off or landing, etc. Freedman also discusses the differences between different kinds of birds and their flying speeds. A glossary and an index are appended.

438 **Freeman,** Barbara Constance. *A Haunting Air.* Dutton, 1977. 77-2810. 158p. $7.50.

5-7 In a ghost story set in contemporary England, a child of the past proves to be the sad little ghost who croons the haunting air heard by Melissa and her neighbor. The story is told in retrospect by Melissa; she was twelve when she and her father moved to Bellwood, renting the two top floors of the house owned by crisp, elderly Miss Clayfield. The neighbor, a widow with a single child, helps Melissa solve the mystery of the singing; Hanny had been a servant's illegitimate child and she'd longed for a baby to come to the people her mother worked for. She had wanted a baby to love and care for. In the dénouement of the story, Melissa confronts the slattern who was Hanny's mother, a woman who spitefully tries to take her ghost-child away. The story is deftly constructed and developed, the characterization adequate, and the pace even; the blending of realism and fantasy is adroit.

439 **Freeman,** Don. *Bearymore;* story and pictures by Don Freeman. Viking, 1976. 76-94. 36p. $6.95.

K-2 Told by the circus ringmaster that his unicycle riding act is stale, Bearymore prepares for his hibernation in a depressed state. Worried, he tosses and turns, gets up to try new stunts but remembers that his friends the performing seals already did them, and gives up, setting his alarm clock for April. The bear wakes to an April shower and recalls that his unicycle is still outdoors. It's muddy out, so Bearymore crosses the yard via laundry line, using the umbrella for balance and protection. On the way back it occurs to him that he can ride the unicycle—and there's his new act: a unicycle on a tightrope! Brief and blithe, with uncluttered pictures of appealing circus scenes, the story—one of Freeman's best in a long time—is nicely told and has the appeals of a wish granted and of achievement.

440 **Freeman,** Don. *Will's Quill;* story and pictures by Don Freeman. Viking, 1975. 74-32382. 28p. $6.95.

K-2 The story of Willoughby Waddle, a country goose who goes to Elizabethan London, is one of the nicest Freeman books in a long time. Soft, bright paintings have intriguing details of costume and architecture, and they are full of action. After several mishaps typical of the newcomer to any city, Willoughby is befriended by a bearded gentleman who proves to be an actor; when the goose sees his friend attacked on stage, he rushes to the man's defense, disrupting the play. Later he plucks one of his own quills to help the man write, and with the fine new quill the play is finished and, with a flourish, signed "William Shakespeare." The dialogue is a bit heavy with "Gadzooks" and "Forsooths" but the plot is adequately structured, and both text and illustrations have plenty of humor and action.

441 **Freschet,** Berniece. *Bernard of Scotland Yard;* illus. by Gina Freschet. Scribner, 1978. 78-9584. 45p. $7.95.

K-3 In a sequel to *Bernard Sees the World,* the mouse leaves his Beacon Hill brownstone after hearing from a visiting English aunt that her son, a Scotland Yard Inspector, is on the trail of a jewel thief. Hastily constructing a balloon, our hero flies unerringly to Trafalgar Square, goes to the Yard to see his cousin, and is appointed a temporary Inspector. Hoping to catch the Mole Gang (suspected of a series of diamond robberies) the cousins go to a masked ball. Bernard follows the thieves after they have successfully taken the jewels of most of the women, and hears the gang plot their last heist; the crown jewels. Needless to say, the plot is foiled. What's more, Bernard is knighted. What's still more, he wins the heart of a lovely damsel he'd met at the ball. Nicely detailed drawings in soft black and white illustrate a tale that is blandly told—a nice contrast to the wildly improbable events and pace of the plot—providing a comic note.

442 **Freschet,** Berniece. *Bernard Sees the World;* pictures by Gina Freschet. Scribner, 1976. 76-1323. 48p. $5.95.

K-3 Despite the sedate background of a Beacon Hill home where his family had lived for generations, Bernard (a mouse) read so much about other places in the world that he decided to travel. So off he went, via rides picked up on a skateboard, a bicycle, a rowing shell, a ship, and a rocket to the moon. After reentry and splashdown, Bernard made his way home—as he had promised, in time for Christmas—and added his tiny moon rock to the holiday decorations. That was enough travel for him; at least, it was until he began reading about Australia . . . and there the story ends. The black and white drawings seldom have vitality but they have ingenious details and are nicely integrated with the text. The writing is blandly direct, the pace is brisk, the settings offer variety, and the improbable ease of Bernard's stowaway journeying is made quite credible.

443 **Freschet,** Berniece. *Year on Muskrat Marsh;* illus. by Peter Parnall. Scribner, 1974. 51p. $4.95.

3-5 The impeccable drawings of Peter Parnall show the flora and fauna of a Minnesota marshland; the clean, precise black and white pictures are lovely in themselves and they harmonize nicely with the style of the continuous text, which has the same qualities of accurate details and poetic interpretation. There is less focus here than in most of the author's books, the text moving steadily through the cycle of a year and describing the creatures who feed and mate, prey or play, migrate and return, nest and breed. There is—perhaps deliberately—no sense of time division, but an even flow of small events that gives a rounded ecological picture.

444 **Fritz,** Jean. *And Then What Happened, Paul Revere?* illus. by Margot Tomes. Coward, 1973. 45p. $5.95.

3-5 Hear ye, hear ye! Historical fiction, done to a turn. A description of Paul Revere's ride to Lexington is funny, fast-paced, and historically accurate; it is given added interest by the establishment of Revere's character: busy, bustling, versatile, and patriotic, a man who loved people and excitement. The account of his ride is preceded by a description of his life and the political situation in Boston, and it concludes with Revere's adventures after reaching Lexington.

445 **Fritz,** Jean. *Can't You Make Them Behave, King George?* illus. by Tomie de Paola. Coward, 1977. 75-33722. 48p. $6.95.

3-5 Demonstrating that a monarch's lot is not necessarily a happy one, Fritz presents the biography of King George III, a ruler who was determined to be a good king but who had the not uncommon royal viewpoint that whoever disagreed with him was "a traitor or a scoundrel." So King George, tidy and thrifty, amiable father of fifteen, resolutely moral, was disturbed by his wayward subjects in the New World. Fritz gives both a cozy, slightly comic view of the monarch, a tone picked up by the artist, and a view of the American Revolution that may help children understand that there is more than one approach to historical events. The research is thorough but doesn't obtrude, as the author uses source information with skill and writes with humor and perspective.

446 **Fritz,** Jean. *What's the Big Idea, Ben Franklin?* illus. by Margot Tomes. Coward, 1976. 75-25902. 47p. $6.95.

3-5 The usual breezy, entertaining Fritz style masks the usual meticulous Fritz research in a brisk biography that is informal and informative. The adroit and amusing illustrations have interesting period details and are nicely integrated with the text, which focuses on Franklin's multifaceted career but also gives personal details and quotes some of his pithy sayings. Enough background information about the colonial affairs is given to enable readers to understand the importance of Franklin's contributions to the public good but not so much that it obtrudes on his life story. Although the text is not punctuated by references or footnotes, a page of notes (with numbers for pages referred to) is appended; the references are not always clear.

447 **Fritz,** Jean. *Where Was Patrick Henry on the 29th of May?* illus. by Margot Tomes. Coward, 1975. 74-83014. 47p. $5.95.

3-5 Jean Fritz really has an approach to history that is unique: she makes it fun. In this biography of Patrick Henry, the prose sails blithely along almost with the conversational tone of storytelling but all the research is there, not showing up as dry facts but incorporated into the story. A delightful addition to the Bicentennial Year and all the years thereafter.

448 **Fritz,** Jean. *Who's That Stepping on Plymouth Rock?* illus. by J. B. Handelsman. Coward, 1975. 74-30593. 31p. $5.95.

3-5 What's to write about? You'll be surprised. Plymouth Rock hasn't
* just sat there in the harbor doing nothing. It's been broken in half, broken again and cemented, parts enshrined in two places, reunited, moved, and enshrined again. And it all began in 1741 when one elderly man, pressed, said he thought he remembered hearing that the rock was, indeed, a landmark. There is no proof that the Pilgrims ever landed on it. Jean Fritz, whose meticulous research buoys rather than burdens her books, has written another lively, amusing, and informative little gem.

449 **Fritz,** Jean. *Will You Sign Here, John Hancock?* illus. by Trina Schart Hyman. Coward, 1976. 75-33243. 47p. $6.95.

3-5 Wealthy, extravagant, and vain, young John Hancock was one of Boston's leading fops. But, as shrewd and sloppy Samuel Adams saw it, anyone with such winning ways and such a lot of useful money was valuable to the Patriot cause. Hancock soon became identified by the British as one of the insurgent colonials, especially when—as president of the seceding colony of Massachusetts—he attended the Continental Congress. As its president he signed first the new Declaration of Independence, having practiced his signature beforehand. Hancock hoped to become commander in chief of the army, but it is perhaps as well he did not, for his first engagement as a major general was a failure, and he soon retired to a more suitable role, lavishly entertaining French officers; later he was elected governor of Massachusetts eleven times. As always, Jean Fritz writes with a light touch that belies the serious scholarship of her research and makes the conceited but good-hearted Hancock a truly believable man. The sly humor of Hyman's illustrations effectively underlines the tone of teasing affection, although—a fact that will undoubtedly go unnoticed by young readers—the artist incorporates a caustic personal comment in one pictorial detail.

450 **Fritz,** Jean. *Why Don't You Get a Horse, Sam Adams?* illus. by Trina Schart Hyman. Coward, 1974. 47p. $5.95.

3-5 Samuel Adams didn't care how he looked, didn't care if he had to walk everywhere, only cared about his thoughts on colonial independence. Unkempt, Samuel stumped around Boston talking to all who would listen; he wouldn't ride, not even when he was chosen as a delegate to the Philadelphia meeting. Well, he'd ride a coach—but not a horse. Even when Paul Revere later warned Sam and John Hancock that the British were coming, Sam wouldn't ride a horse. John Adams suggested that riding was good for one's health, was a convenient way to get about, was the fastest way to travel—and Samuel wasn't convinced, not until Adams pointed out that if a declaration of independence were signed, they would be not just revolutionary leaders but statesmen of a new nation. And who ever heard of a statesman who couldn't ride horseback? And that's how Samuel Adams was talked into riding a horse; with padded drawers to ease the pain, he rode again to Philadelphia toward a role in history. A postscript by the author gives additional historical details, but her story very effectively describes the start of colonial dissent as she deftly and humorously pictures the reluctant rider. The illustrations have a corresponding blend of raffish, funny details and historical accuracy.

451 **Froman,** Robert. *Less than Nothing Is Really Something;* illus. by Don Madden. T. Y. Crowell, 1973. 33p. Trade ed. $3.75; Library ed. $4.50 net.

2-4 An addition to an excellent series of first-concept mathematics books for primary grades readers is illustrated with lively drawings and clear diagrams. The author uses the ideas of being in debt, swimming downward in water, and the more familiar positive and negative readings on a thermometer to explain the idea of minus numbers. A board-and-counter game called "Plus and Minus" is used to show, with several examples of playing and scoring, how plus and minus numbers can be added and subtracted. The writing style is simple and clear, the text hewing admirably to the line.

452 **Gackenbach,** Dick. *Do You Love Me?* story and pictures by Dick Gackenbach. Seabury, 1975. 74-34104. 45p. $5.95.

K-2 * There's a spacious look to the pages of this book, with ample white space, clean-lined drawings with little shading, and clear tones of brown or grey. In sum, a poster-like simplicity that fits the modesty of the story. A small child who lives on a farm, Walter has one sister much older than he. He has nobody to play with, so he takes tender care of some insects in a jar and a turtle. When he accidentally kills a hummingbird, Walter runs to his sister for help, but it's too late. His sister explains that one cannot hold everything one loves but must show respect even for animals' wishes. Sadly, bravely, Walter releases his bugs and his turtle; with joy and respect he tentatively holds the puppy his sister brings him. It *likes* to be held! At last, something loves him, something can be cuddled, something plays with him. There's nothing didactic in the way the lesson about respect for all creatures is presented, the ending is satisfying, the writing style is direct, and the depiction of the affection between the small boy and his older sister is tender without being sentimental.

453 **Gackenbach,** Dick. *The Pig Who Saw Everything;* written and illus. by Dick Gackenbach. Seabury, 1978. 77-12741. 37p. $6.95.

K-3 A plump, pink pig is shown investigating his environment in clean, simple drawings of black/white/red barnyard surroundings. His older friend Esther cannot understand why Henry is so curious, but she doesn't protest when a farm boy leaves the sty door open and Henry trots off. He sees several kinds of animals, and the strangest of all is a large beast with hard body and round legs. With a roar, it swallows the farmer and tears off through a gap at the end of the world. Young children should enjoy their superior sophistication in realizing that Henry's "world" is the barnyard and his huge creature an automobile. And when he comes home to report to Esther on the strange pig with wings (geese) and the ones with black faces (sheep) it can give children a provocative conception of what it means to see the world from another viewpoint.

454 **Galdone,** Paul. *The Gingerbread Boy*. Seabury, 1975. 74-11461. 36p. illus. $6.95.

3-6 yrs. The cumulation and repetition of a folk favorite are appealing as ever; the story is adequately told; the illustrations are wonderfully vigorous and funny: nobody's ever drawn a slyer fox than Galdone, or a wilder-eyed horse pursuing the runaway gingerbread boy, or a more plumply old-fashioned farm wife than the old woman who baked the gullible runaway.

455 **Gans,** Roma. *Caves;* illus. by Giulio Maestro. T. Y. Crowell, 1977. 76-4881. 33p. (Let's-Read-and-Find-Out Books). $5.95.

2-4 The author, a specialist in childhood education, writes with direct simplicity about the ways in which caves are formed, the range of size from a small animal's lair to an enormous cavern, and the lure of cave exploration to amateurs (spelunkers) and scientists (speleologists) alike. Save for the fact that a reader may infer that all caves are inhabited by bats, the text is clear in distinguishing between information that applies to all caves ("The temperature in caves stays about the same all year round.") and that which may be a feature of some caves ("In some caves water trickles from place to place.") Nicely gauged in extent and difficulty for a young independent reader, the book describes stalactites and stalagmites, cave tunnels, and the blind fish that inhabit the water in some caves.

456 **Gans,** Roma. *Millions and Millions of Crystals;* illus. by Giulio Maestro. T. Y. Crowell, 1973. 33p. $3.75.

2-3 One of the editors of this distinguished series of science books for primary grades readers, Roma Gans is a specialist in childhood education; she introduces the topic of crystalline structure in a text that is simply and logically constructed and is carefully gauged for the very young independent reader. The book describes some familiar crystals, explains how the grouping of atoms produces the regular structure of crystals and gives examples of how these groupings vary from crystal to crystal. Very easy to read, very difficult to write, very deft.

457 **Gans,** Roma. *Oil: The Buried Treasure;* illus. by Giulio Maestro. T. Y. Crowell, 1975. 74-7353. 33p. $4.50.

2-3 Very simple, very much to the point, and geared to the scope of children's understanding, this is a good introduction to the subject; while it does not go into the ramifications of supply and cost, it can be used as background for understanding a topic most young children hear about on television news programs repeatedly. Gans explains how oil deposits were made in prehistoric times, how oil is sought and drilled for, and how it is used in many manufactured products (clothing, food, cosmetics, paint, etc.) The illustrations are attractive, some merely decorative, others extending the text.

458 **Gardam,** Jane. *Bilgewater.* Greenwillow, 1977. 77-2890. 212p. Trade ed. $6.95; Library ed. $6.43 net.

7-10 Bill's daughter, "Bilgewater" to all the boys at the school where her father was a Housemaster, had been aware all her seventeen years that she was ugly. Why shouldn't she be called Bilgewater instead of her real name, Marigold? The story she tells of her first romancing, her first friendship, her first brush with haute couture, and her discovery that she was (after having had trouble reading most of her life) bright enough to be admitted to Cambridge, is touching, funny, and brilliantly written.

459 **Gardam,** Jane. *The Summer After the Funeral.* Macmillan, 1973. 151p. $4.95.

6-9 More intricate in structure than Gardam's earlier books, this has the same felicitous percipience and fluency, the characters seen with a slightly amused, slightly ironic affection. Here the major part of the story is devoted to the gentle, lovely Athene whose older brother and younger sister have gone off, as she has, after their father's death. Their mother has arranged their summer plans by bullying, wheedling, and manipulating friends and relatives. The younger girl unhappily puts up with her hearty, ebullient hosts; Sebastian has cannily chosen an Anglican retreat in Scotland; Athene meanders from host to host, managing to fall in love twice. And all the time their mother is bustling around looking for a new home and imposing on others. The threads are deftly pulled together in a satisfying and logical conclusion to a story written with grace and wit.

460 **Garfield,** Leon. *The Golden Shadow;* by Leon Garfield and Edward Blishen; illus. by Charles Keeping. Pantheon Books, 1973. 159p. Trade ed. $5.50; Library ed. $5.99 net.

7- As they did in *The God Beneath the Sea,* Garfield and Blishen have woven Greek legends together in a continuous tale. Here Heracles is the central figure, and all the legendry is bound by the character of an old storyteller who wanders through Greece hoping to meet the gods of whom he sings. Here again the prose is trenchant and sophisticated, the legends retold with lusty, vivid detail and illustrated in stunning black and white pictures by Keeping.

461 **Garfield,** Leon. *The Sound of Coaches;* with engravings by John Lawrence. Viking, 1974. 256p. $5.95.

7- Garfield at his picaresque best, telling in high dramatic style and with a keen appreciation of period the story of a foundling child whose foster father is a coachman. Young Sam is anxious to become a driver himself, and his path seems assured until he has an accident. Drifting in London, Sam becomes stagestruck and is drawn into a minor role in a Shakespearian company by the boastful, pretentious Daniel Coventry. Always searching for facts about his real parents, Sam has a double surprise when he learns who his father is. There's also a love interest; Jenny is a mendacious, salty little character who proves as loyal as she is vulgar. The book is a delight: robust characters, marvelously rich dialogue, vivid creation of the period, and a vigorous writing style.

462 **Garner,** Alan. *The Stone Book;* illus. by Michael Foreman. Collins/World, 1978. 78-7965. 60p. $6.95.
Garner, Alan. *Granny Reardun;* illus. by Michael Foreman. Collins/World, 1978. 78-8141. 61p. $6.95.

3-5
*
Many of Garner's books for older readers are superbly written but too intricate for many children; with *The Stone Book* he begins a cycle of related short novels for younger children and combines a profound depth and compassion with simpler writing and an intriguing story. The four stories are set in Cheshire, and both the setting and the dialogue, rich in local idiom, give color to the writing. In the first book, set in the past (four generations past) the young daughter of a stonemason wants to learn to read, but yearns—even if she can't read it—for a prayerbook to carry to Chapel, as the other girls do. Instead, her father takes her deep into a cleft in the hill, where she can read the record of the rocks: figures, and marks of the tide, and a handprint just the size of her own. And footprints. The handprint proves to be one her father made when he was her size, and she feels the joy of knowing that past generations have been in the same place. The other girls press flowers in their prayerbooks, but what Father makes Mary is a stone book that's even more wonderful, for the split stone shows the marks of an ancient fern. *In Granny Reardun,* Joseph is Mary's son, a boy who is raised by his grandmother because his mother can't afford to bring him up. All through the village Joseph sees evidence of the work of his grandfather, the stonemason; he helps the old man with his work, but he has no wish to carry on the tradition and asks to be apprenticed to the village smith. To his surprise, Grandfather is pleased at his initiative and Joseph is lightheaded with joy. The first book is set in Victorian times, but it and the second have a timeless quality; they are elemental, honest, touching vignettes of a simple life lived by good people, and they are small gems.

463 **Garrigue,** Sheila. *All the Children Were Sent Away*. Bradbury, 1976. 75-33600. 171p. $6.95.

3-5 Based on the author's experience of traveling, in 1940, to Canada as an English evacuee, this describes the journey of eight-year-old Sara. Along with hundreds of other children, she boarded the *H.M.S. Duke of Perth,* but she was the only child who'd been put under the care of stern, dictatorial Lady Drume by her mother. That was Sara's cross to bear, for Lady Drume didn't like the Cockney children, Maggie and Ernie, who became Sara's friends. "Guttersnipes," she pronounced them, and forbade Sara to play with them. Tough, wise, and courageous, the Cockney children helped Sara fight her fear and loneliness, and her disobedience in associating with the two brought drastic results that made her hate Lady Drume. After her arrival in Vancouver, however, Sara found that the elderly woman had reasons for her tyrannical behavior, and she even came to be fond of her when Lady Drume arranged a reunion with the other children. There are action and variety in the shipboard sequences, a vivid evocation of the period, and sturdy dialogue and characterization.

464 **Garrison,** Christian. *The Dream Eater;* illus. by Diane Goode. Bradbury, 1978. 78-55213. 27p. $8.95.

K-2 Based on a Japanese legend, this is illustrated with handsome paintings, flowing in movement and richly detailed, in the style of an Oriental scroll. Small Yukio has a bad dream, but each time he approaches an adult to tell about it, the man or woman has a bad dream, too, to talk about, and sends Yukio away. Disconsolate, he wanders to the bank of the river; there he rescues a strange creature who tells the boy he is a baku, an eater of bad dreams. The grateful baku goes back to the village with Yukio, and hungrily devours each person's bad dream. Soon all are dreaming of lovely things; they are happy and the baku, replete, is content. Nicely told, briskly paced, and beautifully illustrated.

465 **Gauch,** Patricia Lee. *The Impossible Major Rogers;* illus. by Robert Andrew Parker. Putnam, 1977. 76-51233. 61p. $5.95.

4-6 A biography of Robert Rogers, the wily leader of a band of rangers in the French and Indian War of the eighteenth century, is written in a casual, conversational style. It's a good way to make history appealing to readers, although there are some passages in which Gauch's chatty tone or casual syntax are obtrusive. Rogers was not above smuggling or passing counterfeit money, and he eventually landed in an English jail, but as a soldier/scout he accomplished missions that did indeed seem impossible and that were laudable for the tenacity and ingenuity they displayed. Parker's scrawly line and deft tonal treatment create roughness and vitality in illustrations that echo the vigor and bravado of the subject.

466 **Gauch,** Patricia Lee. *On to Widecombe Fair;* illus. by Trina Schart Hyman. Putnam, 1978. 76-48151. 27p. $7.95.

K-3 Based on the familiar folksong, Gauch's story extends the plot of the lyrics but has the same jaunty, rollicking tone. And Trina Schart Hyman captures all the rustic humor in deftly composed pictures of the Devon countryside that have vitality; the text is framed and decorated. Double page spreads are alternately in black and white and in color, and this handsome example of book-making closes with the music and lyrics that tell the story of the troop of cronies who celebrate the fair and wear out the horse that transports them.

467 **George,** Jean (Craighead). *Julie of the Wolves;* illus. by John Schoenherr. Harper, 1972. 170p. Trade ed. $4.95; Library ed. $4.79 net.

5-8 Thirteen-year-old Miyax (Julie is her English name) is alone on the Arctic plain, hidden, watching carefully the behavior of the wolves nearby, hoping that she can learn their ways of communicating and get some food. She is almost starving, having run away rather than submit to an arranged marriage, and she slowly, patiently learns to talk to her wolves and is treated as another child of the leader whom she has named Amaroq. The central portion of the book goes back to cover Miyax's story up to that time, when she has run away, planning to get to the United States and visit a pen pal. Part III picks up the story of Miyax and the wolves, and brings her to a camp where she finds that the beloved father she had thought dead is alive. But he has changed; he has a white wife and has forsaken the Eskimo ways. The story ends with Miyax slipping off to resume her journey, a child caught between cultures. The setting is beautifully evoked, the scenes in which Miyax learns the language of the wolves dramatic and compelling. Taut in structure, poignant in implication, an absorbing story.

468 **George,** Jean Craighead. *The Wounded Wolf;* illus. by John Schoenherr. Harper, 1978. 76-58711. 32p. Trade ed. $4.95; Library ed. $5.49 net.

2-4 Schoenherr's realistically detailed animal drawings are effectively evocative, in black and white, of the stark rocks and snowy wastes of the Arctic setting, and an effective foil for George's stripped but poetic text. Her descriptions of animal behavior are meticulously faithful, and she builds into a simple story a strong element of suspense, as a wounded wolf, surrounded by creatures waiting for his death, is saved by the food brought him by the leader of the wolf pack. Although this can be read aloud to younger children for whom the publishers indicate the book is designed (K-3) it seems more appropriate for readers who can understand such phrases as "stoic owl," "penetrates the rocky crags," or "they toll with keen excitement," and appreciate their imagery.

469 **Gerson**, Mary-Joan. *Omoteji's Baby Brother;* illus. by Elzia Moon. Walck, 1974. 45p. $5.95.

3-4 It isn't always the youngest child who feels dethroned when a new baby comes along, and the universality of the situation should awaken readers' sympathy for the Yoruba boy, Omoteji. He refused to play with a friend on the first day of his mother's ordained isolation with the new baby, but announced importantly that he must go to market and help the other women there. But they teased him and asked if he had nothing better to do; then each of the adult members of his family spurned his attempt to help, to feel that he was making a contribution. Then Omoteji had a wonderful idea, a present for the newborn child, and when the naming-day came he was proud and happy. The illustrations are attractive although muted in hues, the story is sedate but engaging, with the authenticity of cultural details that stems from the author's observances during a three-year stay in Nigeria.

470 **Gersting,** Judith L. *Yes-No; Stop-Go;* by Judith L. Gersting and Joseph E. Kuczkowski; illus. by Don Madden. T. Y. Crowell, 1977. 76-46376. 33p. $5.95.

3-5 Cartoon-style illustrations include some clear diagrams that extend an equally clear text that introduces the concept, in mathematical logic, that there is a distinction between "and" and "or" situations. The authors also include suggestions for building models of the examples they've given, using easily available materials to build a set of train switches that can be manipulated by hand to simulate alternative situations and their solutions. In only one instance is the text susceptible to misinterpretation, and that is when the authors use the word "statement" for both a simple and a compound statement.

471 **Getz,** Arthur. *Hamilton Duck's Springtime Story;* story and pictures by Arthur Getz. Golden Press, 1974. 24p. (Golden Books) Trade ed. $1.95; Library ed. $5.27 net.

2-5 yrs. Big pages, large scale illustrations that use to advantage the cartoonist's economical line, and a story that is just right for the small child just learning about the seasons of the year. Hamilton Duck wakes one morning to hear a bird singing of spring and finds other seasonal signs to cheer him. Napping, later that day, he wakes to a brisk breeze and a flurry of snow. Snow? No spring? Then he realizes that the snow is pink and fragrant; he's been sleeping under a blossoming apple tree. "Spring had really come," the story ends. Simple, with fresh pastel colors and enough action to carry the tale, this is nice for reading aloud to individual children but especially well suited—because of the scale of objects—to use with preschool groups.

472 **Gidal,** Sonia. *My Village in Hungary*. Pantheon Books, 1974. 86p. illus. $5.67.

4-6 In the pattern of other books in this excellent series, the text is in first person, with Zoltán Sardi describing his family and friends, life in his village (Gölle, in southwest Hungary), and—through conversations and classroom scenes—something of the history of his country and facts about its cultural and economic facets. Profusely illustrated by photographs of good quality, the book is informative and interesting, weakened somewhat by the repeated use of unnatural translation in the dialogue: "*Igen*. Yes. *Nagjon jó!* Very good!"

473 **Ginsburg,** Mirra, ad. *How the Sun Was Brought Back to the Sky;* adapted from a Slovenian Folk Tale by Mirra Ginsburg; illus. by Jose Aruego and Ariane Dewey. Macmillan, 1975. 74-19060. 29p. $6.95.

3-6 yrs. Five plump yellow chicks, dismayed because for three days there has been no sun, only grey clouds, decide they will go off to find the sun and bring it back to the sky. They go to one animal after another, ride a mountain-top cloud to the moon, and are directed to the sun's house, accompanied by all the animals they've met. The sun sadly says the clouds have kept it out of the sky and it's forgotten how to shine; the animals clean and burnish the sun, and it fills the sky; the animals slide down the rays to earth. Silly, merry, and sunny, the story is matched by the artless insouciance. of the vigorous, colorful pictures.

474 **Ginsburg,** Mirra, tr. *How Wilka Went to Sea;* tr. and ed. by Mirra Ginsburg; illus. by Charles Mikolaycak. Crown, 1975. 73-78877. 128p. $6.95.

4-6 Nine Finno-Ugric and Turkic folktales are beautifully illustrated by soft, dramatic pictures with precise costume details. The tales abound with witches, giants, and wizards who are inevitably outwitted by the daring of youth or the wisdom of age; many of them attest to the close family relationships within the rural cultures from which they emanate. The title story is almost a situation comedy, a series of disasters from which stubborn, hapless Wilka emerges triumphant; the most dramatic story—although it has less action and violence than others—is "The Beautiful Birch," a tale with a stunning ending.

475 **Ginsburg,** Mirra, tr. *The Lazies; Tales of the Peoples of Russia;* tr. and ed. by Mirra Ginsburg; illus. by Marian Parry. Macmillan, 1973. 70p. $4.95.

3-5 Fifteen humorous stories about lazy people or animals are illustrated with line drawings that achieve a remarkably funny and effective strength for the economical use of line. The tales are typical of the genre; usually the lazy creature either learns a lesson and changes or there is a just—often harsh—punishment for indolence. The source of each tale is given, and the collection should be particularly useful as a storytelling source, since the selections vary in length.

476 **Giovanni,** Nikki. *Ego-Tripping and Other Poems for Young People;* illus. by George Ford. Lawrence Hill, 1974. 37p. $4.95.

6- Illustrated with vigorous black and white pictures, a book of poems selected by the author (from her published works) as being especially appropriate for young people. Some of the poems are about children, tender or impassioned, some are about Giovanni's childhood; some of the poems are angry and some an ebullient explosion of love or pride; all of them are a celebration of blackness.

477 **Gladstone,** M.J. *A Carrot for a Nose;* The Form of Folk Sculpture on America's City Streets and Country Roads. Scribner, 1974. 72p. illus. $9.95.

5-8 Photographs and drawings, lavishly used and fully captioned, show in alluring detail the range of folk sculpture found out-of-doors: weathervanes, carousel animals, gravestones, trade signs, snowmen and scarecrows, and—among the most decorative—manhole covers. The text is written in a casual, conversational style and is both entertaining and informative; the book is intriguing in itself but also useful for those interested in American history, in art, or in the relationship between creative expression and the culture and/or period from which it emanates.

478 **Glazer,** Tom. *Eye Winker, Tom Tinker, Chin Chopper;* Fifty Musical Fingerplays; illus. by Ron Himler. Doubleday, 1973. 89p. $4.95.

K-6 Fifty songs are accompanied by directions (sometimes cursory) for fingerplay and other interpretative motions, the music in simple arrangements for piano with guitar chords provided. The illustrations are frolicsome, always attractive but not always indicative of the action suggested to accompany the song. Even without the fingerplay, this is a compilation of songs that anyone working with young children, particularly in groups, should find useful, and older children who can play piano or guitar can use the book for the music alone.

479 **Glubok,** Shirley. *The Art of America in the Early Twentieth Century;* designed by Gerard Nook. Macmillan, 1974. 48p. $6.95.

5-8 In a period during which artists were breaking away from traditional patterns of style, especially in painting, much of the art in America reflected the changes in our society both by the subjects of works of art and by the freedom of artistic expression. Glubok has chosen for discussion and reproduction a single work by each of over thirty artists—painters, sculptors, photographers, architects—and she discusses, briefly, the work of the artist and the reproduction shown. While the pictures are in black and white, they do show the breadth and variety of work done in the first four decades of the century.

480 **Glubok,** Shirley. *The Art of China;* designed by Gerard Nook. Macmillan, 1973. 48p. illus. $6.95.

4-6 A survey of the art objects of a country the art heritage of which spans more than four millenia is necessarily brief; this does not attempt to be inclusive but serves nicely as an introduction to art forms. The material is more or less in chronological arrangement but stresses form and relates objects to their contemporary cultures. Designed with discrimination, the book is—like its predecessors—both handsome and informative, and it should lead readers to further examination of Chinese art.

481 **Glubok,** Shirley. *The Art of the Plains Indians;* designed by Gerard Nook; photography by Alfred Tamarin. Macmillan, 1975. 75-14064. 48p. $7.95.

4-7 As are all of the books in this series, this is handsomely designed, with restrained use of color (appropriately, earth colors) as backgrounds for some pages. In discussing the arts and crafts of the Plains Indians, the author relates creative expression to the rituals and beliefs of the tribes from which the objects illustrated came. Each illustration carries a label denoting source, and the objects are not only impressive in themselves but give, in conjunction with the text, a geat deal of information about the way the tribes lived: what they ate, how they dressed, how they worshipped. Glubok also gives, simply and sympathetically, some of the sad history of the relationships between the Plains Indians and white settlers.

482 **Glubok,** Shirley. *The Art of the Vikings;* illus. by Gerard Nook. Macmillan, 1978. 78-6849. 48p. $8.95.

4-7 White and cool colors are used as backgrounds for handsomely laid out pages that carry the text and photographs describing and illustrating the art of the Viking period. There are a few examples of architecture and artifacts, but most of the work that is discussed consists of carving (wood, metal, or stone), or of jewelry. As is true of earlier books in this handsome series, the text is direct and informative, giving facts about the objects described and about the way of life into which the artistic examples fit.

483 **Glubok,** Shirley. *The Art of the Woodland Indians;* photographs by Alfred Tamarin. Macmillan, 1976. 76-12434. 48p. $7.95.

4-6 An addition to Glubok's useful series of books about the arts and crafts of Native American cultures focuses on the forest dwellers of the eastern United States and Canada. As in other Glubok books, the illustrations of art objects, articles of clothing, weapons, musical instruments, et cetera, are carefully placed in relation to the text which describes them and relates them to the tribal cultures from which they emanate. The photographs and reproductions are of good quality, the format dignified, the writing style direct, a bit dry, and unassuming.

484 **Glubok,** Shirley. *The Mummy of Ramose; The Life and Death of an Ancient Egyptian Nobleman;* by Shirley Glubok and Alfred Tamarin. Harper, 1978. 76-21392. 82p. illus. Trade ed. 6.95; Library ed. $6.79 net.

6-9 Based on the life of one of the chief counselors of Amenhotep III, a remarkably informative and well-researched text is lightly fictionalized but has no invented dialogue. The book begins on the day Ramose dies; an old man, he has relinquished his power upon the accession to the throne of Amenhotep IV, who—worshipping the sun god—changed his name to Akhenaten. Through reminiscent flashbacks on Ramose's last day of life, the authors give facts about dynastic families, the planning of tombs, many aspects of ancient Egyptian life as it was lived by the rich and many of the beliefs and customs shared by all levels of the society. When Ramose dies, the text gives a detailed and explicit account of embalming and mummification as well as facts about burial and mourning practices and the rituals and beliefs associated with death. This has much more polish and more vitality than Glubok's *Discovering the Royal Tombs at Ur.* The pictures have been chosen and placed with care; a selected bibliography and a relative index are appended.

485 **Glubok,** Shirley. *Olympic Games in Ancient Greece;* by Shirley Glubok and Alfred Tamarin. Harper, 1976. 75-25408. 116p. illus. Trade ed. $5.95; Library ed. $5.79 net.

5-8 The authors describe an imaginary Olympiad of the 5th century B.C. and include background material that is historical or anecdotal to give variety to their account. Maps and drawings show details of the site, and photographs of sculpture or pottery that show athletes in action add interest. Glubok and Tamarin write in a rather dry style, but their anecdotes about rivalry, chicanery, and vengeance provide color and the historical information gives depth to the text. A list of important dates (up to the Montreal games) and an index are appended.

486 **Goble,** Paul. *The Friendly Wolf;* by Paul and Dorothy Goble; pictures by Paul Goble. Bradbury, 1975. 74-77664. 27p. $6.95.

3-5 Little Cloud and his sister wander away from the tribe during berry-picking and get lost; they shelter in a wolf's den and then beg him to help them find their way home. The wolf agrees to help them, even lets little Bright Eyes ride on his back, and brings them close enough so that they can see the home teepees. The tribe, in gratitude, walks to the hilltop and brings their gifts and their friendship to the wolf—and the wolf has been their friend to this day. The story is not unusual in theme nor is it told with grace, but it is adequately told. The strength of the book lies in the illustrations, handsome in design and composition, and incorporating authentic and beautiful art motifs of the Plains Indians. Goble uses a great deal of color but not too many different colors in any one of the double-page spreads, so that the small details (each tiny leaf, each red berry) are not obscured.

487 **Goble,** Paul. *The Girl Who Loved Wild Horses;* written and illus. by Paul Goble. Bradbury, 1978. 77-20500. 27p. $8.95.

K-2 The clean lines and brilliant palette of Goble's style are somewhat softened by some variations (abstractions of black clouds, a crayon rainbow) to illustrate a tale in the folk tradition. An Indian girl who loves horses is with them as much as her duties permit; when a storm frightens the herd into a stampede, she goes off with them. Both the girl and the horses are enchanted by a wild horse. Found by her people, the girl visits them—but she goes back to her horses and to the proud, wild stallion. Each year she returns to visit, bringing a colt as a gift—and then, one year, she is missing. She is never seen again, but after that when the people see the stallion, he has a beautiful mare at his side. This is less specific than many of the tales about human-animal mating; it is simply and fairly effectively told, but it is the pictures that carry the book.

488 **Goble,** Paul. *Lone Bull's Horse Raid;* by Paul and Dorothy Goble; illus. by Paul Goble. Bradbury, 1973. 54p. $5.95.

5-8 Lone Bull, who tells the story, is a fourteen-year-old Oglala Sioux of the late nineteenth century; like other boys, he yearns to win honor and status by capturing a horse from the enemy, the Crows.

The text is solidly written but permeated with the excitement and suspense that Lone Bull feels. Both in the handwriting and in the stunningly detailed, colorful pictures the Gobles' account is given added validity by the authenticity of detail and by their respect for the culture they portray. A list of additional readings about horse raiding and tribal battles among North American Indians is appended.

489 **Godden,** Rumer. *Mr. McFadden's Hallowe'en*. Viking, 1975. 75-20483. 127p. $5.95.

4-6 Despite the fact that it is clear, long before he does so, that the crusty Mr. McFadden is going to succumb to eight-year-old Selina's determined ministrations and that he will deed the land for a park to the village, the author has managed to sustain the slow unwinding of the plot by polished style, good characterization, affectionate humor, and just enough sentiment to be bearable. Injured, Mr. McFadden accepts Selina's help when nobody else will come near him. A solitary, dour man, he has not been a good neighbor but has been tolerated. However, when the village is left a plump bequest for a park and McFadden refuses to sell the land (in the perfect spot, a central location) the citizens are outraged. Selina's mother has to shop for the old man; her father is dropped from the park committee. There is—and readers will probably be satisfied if not surprised—a happy finale after Mr. McFadden has relented and Selina honored for her influence. There's also enough about doughty Selina and her cantankerous pony to balance the book and make it truly a story for children.

490 **Godden,** Rumer. *The Rocking-Horse Secret;* illus. by Juliet Stanwell Smith. Viking, 1978. 77-25489. 87p. $6.95.

4-6 This has all the ingredients for a highly palatable story, and in Godden's deft hands the result is felicitous. A lonely, only child; a beloved toy that the child yearns to call her own; haughty sisters who claim an estate that rightfully goes to a kind young man; a threat of losing a home—and a happy, logical ending in which a child produces a lost will that solves all problems. Living alone with her mother, caretaker of old Miss Pomeroy's house, Tibby dreamed of having the rocking horse in the old nursery; when Miss Pomeroy died, her nieces were ready to sell everything in the house—and then Tibby produced the will (hidden in the rocking horse) that made young Jed, the handyman, the heir, and that meant Tibby and her mother could stay on forever. Nicely constructed, beautifully told.

491 **Goffstein,** M. B. *Family Scrapbook;* written and illus. by M. B. Goffstein. Farrar, 1978. 78-51435. 42p. $5.95.

K-3 Simple stories, simply told, but they have a warmth and sweetness that is effective and affective. Save for one tale, which is about Giacometti and seems out of place in this collection of family stories, the half-dozen vignettes give some highlights in the life of a family with two children. They are told by the older, a girl, and have the directness typical of a child's viewpoint; they describe a birthday, a ride in a truck, attendance at a Yom Kippur service, an unexpected and welcome visitor . . . and the illustrations have the same homely, cozy feeling.

492 **Goffstein,** M. B. *My Noah's Ark;* written and illus. by M. B. Goffstein. Harper, 1978. 77-25666. 25p. Trade ed. $5.95; Library ed. $6.44 net.

4-7 yrs. A woman in her nineties looks back to her childhood, when her grandfather carved an ark and some animals, to which her father added other beasts. As a young mother, she told her children Noah's story and told them how her grandfather had said, ". . . behind a closed door, his voice booming like God's: 'Make it three hundred cubits long.'" Now everyone associated with her memories of the ark is gone, but those memories warm the old woman like sunshine. The jacket quotes Goffstein: "You should work and work until it looks like you didn't have to work at all." And that is what this gentle, loving book does; the text is stripped of verbiage but gravid with sentiment, and the small, spare drawings are framed and static.

493 **Goins,** Ellen H. *Big Diamond's Boy.* Nelson, 1977. 76-54877. 160p. $6.95.

5-7 Albert Harvey, "Big Diamond," is a shiftless, lazy gambler whose intimidated wife accepts uncomplainingly the ups and downs of family finances, and up to a point agrees with Big Diamond's dictum that no wife of his will work. And both she and their son Cotton, Albert Junior, go along with the idea that education is a waste of time, for Big Diamond is carefully teaching his small son the arts of his extensive knowledge of gambling. Cotton adores his father, believes everything he says, and refuses to learn anything in those periods when, during their migrant life, he does go to school. It takes a long, long time for Cotton to understand his father's obduracy and irresponsibility, but eventually he does so. His mother defiantly goes to work, refuses to leave her job or sacrifice the education of Cotton's older sister—and even Cotton comes to realize that he must get an education, that he actually enjoys learning. So Big Diamond goes off alone (to make a fortune again) and his boy, grieving, stays with his mother. The book gives a good picture of the rural south during the depression era, it has some strong characterization (especially the jovial, blustering Big Diamond) and the writing style is competent. Cotton's devoted imitation of his father's sloth is not quite credible, however, since it goes on for years while he and the other two members of the family suffer the consequences of living with a gambler.

494 **Gonzalez,** Gloria. *The Glad Man.* Knopf, 1975. 75-2541. 160p. Trade ed. $4.95; Library ed. $5.99 net.

4-6 Melissa's goal in life is to play for the St. Louis Cardinals, although she'll settle right now for making the school team. She and her owlish younger brother find the "Glad Man" (he used to sell gladiolas and other flowers) living in an old bus near a dump and decide to rescue him when his home is threatened by municipal authorities. Melissa organizes community support, including her parents and teacher, in a renovation crew. The baseball aspect is almost submerged by the "Glad Man" theme, although Melissa does make the team, but the treatment is well-balanced, with some believable school episodes, warm family relationships, lively dialogue, and writing that has pace and humor, all compensating for a not too impressive plot.

495 **Goodall,** John S., illus. *Creepy Castle.* Atheneum, 1975. 74-16836. 31p. $4.95.

4-6 yrs. A medieval adventure is portrayed in a book without words, with alternate half and full pages used to change the scene economically and cleverly. Two mice approach the castle, followed by a stealthy, evil figure (another mouse) who locks them in. Our hero thwarts bats and a menacing dragon, pushes his fair lady out of a window and into the moat. He follows her; they are rescued by a frog, who ferries them to safety on his lily pad. They creep up on the villain, dump him into the pond just as he is about to shoot an arrow at a placid fowl, and caper ecstatically home. The story is clear, the plot sturdy, the pictures exciting and romantic. Great fun.

496 **Goodall,** John S., illus. *An Edwardian Christmas.* Atheneum, 1978. 77-4580. 61p. $7.95.

all ages Goodall's small books, always wordless, are usually embellished by the details of an Edwardian setting; here he's surpassed himself in creating an English Christmas in a nostalgic county/country setting. Family members come to the manor, the children gather holly and mistletoe to help decorate the church, there are Christmas services and family breakfasts, walks in the snow, carolers, a musical evening, and a costume party upstairs that is echoed by the dancing in the servants' hall below. The class structure is clear both in the upstairs-downstairs pictures and in the charitable visit to a cottager. The book may pique children's curiosity, but it should evoke sentimental sighs from the older audience. The paintings, all double-paged, are full without being too busy, nicely composed and detailed, and the restrained use of color contributes to the mellow mood; the night scenes are especially attractive, with Christmas card snow falling on blue shadows.

497 **Goodall,** John S. *Naughty Nancy.* Atheneum, 1975. 31p. illus. $4.95.

3-5 yrs. Using his now-familiar format of vertical half-pages that, when turned, change the whole implication of an illustration, Goodall portrays the bridal day of a mouse in a wordless picture book. Nancy is the flower girl (or flower mouse) at her sister's wedding, and she pulls off one prank after another: rolling up the red carpet that's just been unrolled, riding the bride's train, jumping on the wedding cake, sliding off the roof of the marquee, hiding in the newlyweds' trunk. The adventures are easy to follow; the action is less a story line than a situation punctuated by Nancy's ploys, the story ending with the trunk lid open and Nancy emergent. Plenty of action and humor is in the engaging illustrations, which picture a well-to-do household replete with servants, elaborate preparations, and the lavishness of a well-to-do English household of the past.

498 **Goodall,** John S., illus. *Paddy Pork's Holiday.* Atheneum, 1976. 75-28278. 59p. $4.95.

3-5 yrs. Like other Goodall books about a lively pig, this has half-pages inserted between each set of full pages, so that turning the half-page changes the picture. Goodall is one of the more adept creators of such wordless picture books; his story line is always clear, and his tales abound in humor and action. Here Paddy goes off on a hiking trip, is passed up when he tries to thumb a ride with an elegant gentleman but picked up by a friendly family in a caravan. He sets up a tent, goes for a swim, is caught in a storm, climbs a tree and falls into a coal car of a passing train, inadvertently is pushed on a concert stage while wearing a scarecrow's clothes, and eventually reaches home in fine fettle.

499 **Gordon,** Sol. *Girls are Girls and Boys are Boys; So What's the Difference?* illus. by Frank C. Smith. Day, 1974. 28p. $4.95.

3-4 A psychologist and director of a family research program, Gordon moves from a debunking of sexist ideas about the characters and roles of boys and girls to the area of sex education, describing sexual intercourse, menstruation, nocturnal emission, and masturbation. The writing is direct, informal, and candid; the author makes no judgments, pulls no punches, and he concludes with the fact that all human beings are of equal value and should have equal opportunities—pointing out that both boys and girls can have many interests. This doesn't explore either physical differences or social attitudes very deeply but it serves well as an introduction.

500 **Graham,** Ada. *The Milkweed and Its World of Animals;* by Ada and Frank Graham; photographs by Les Line. Doubleday, 1976. 74-18801. 103p. $5.95.

6-9 Written in a direct, informal style, this describes in considerable detail the vast numbers of creatures, primarily insects, that feed on various parts of the milkweed or that use it for laying eggs, as a base for spinning webs, and as an anchorage for cocoons. The authors also describe ways in which people use the milkweed, from collecting edible parts of the plant to gathering the milkweed for lining clothing. Through such descriptions, illustrated by good magnified photographs, they also give a clear picture of much of the ecology of a meadow, excluding only larger forms of wildlife.

501 **Graham,** Ada. *Whale Watch;* by Ada and Frank Graham; illus. by D. D. Tyler. Delacorte, 1978. 77-20532. 120p. Trade ed. $6.95; Library ed. $6.46 net.

5-8 An excellent survey of the dwindling whale population of the oceans describes both the intensive slaughter and the inadequate protective legislation that have led many conservation groups to protest the killing of whales. The Grahams discuss the various kinds of baleen and toothed whales, including their physical differences, habits and habitats, reproductive patterns and care of young; they also describe whales in captivity and some of the information that has been gained by research scientists working with these mammals. The illustrations are excellent; a list of sources and an index are appended to a text that is well written and nicely organized.

502 **Graham,** Lorenz. *Hongry Catch the Foolish Boy;* pictures by James Brown, Jr. T. Y. Crowell, 1973. 32p. $3.95.

K-3 Like the other tales from *How God Fix Jonah (Every Man Heart Lay Down, David He No Fear)* this single-story picture book edition has the soft and colorful cadence of African speech patterns that adapt Biblical language. There is an appealing tenderness in the story of the young prodigal who comes home to be welcomed by his father and who is envied by his oldest brother until their father's explanation touches him, too. The illustrations are bold in design but distracting because of their page-filling detail.

503 **Graham,** Lorenz. *Return to South Town.* T. Y. Crowell, 1976. 75-33712. 247p. $6.50.

6-9 Fourth in the series that began with *South Town,* this describes the return of David Williams to the small town his family had left fifteen years earlier after bitter racial hostility. David, finishing his medical training at Bellevue in New York, has decided he wants to be a general practitioner in Pocahontas County. While he finds many changes: integrated schools, friendships between black and white, the disappearance of Jim Crow laws, he discovers that there are still some "rebbish" white people who do not welcome a black doctor to South Town; unfortunately, one of them controls policy at the nearest hospital. David buys land, builds offices, finds new friends but has difficulty getting a state license. Every problem is eventually solved. The text moves slowly, and the writing style is not distinguished, but the book gives a good picture of life in a small southern town today and of the changes that have occurred in recent years.

504 **Graham,** Lorenz. *Song of the Boat;* illus. by Leo and Diane Dillon. T. Y. Crowell, 1975. 74-5183. 37p. Trade ed. $6.50; Library ed. $7.25 net.

K-3 Remember Graham's touching *Every Man Heart Lay Down?* In this story there is the same cadence and structure of language, the poetic English of African tribesmen: "Flumbo look him small boy. He say, 'The road I walk be long. It be long past the legs of my small boy.'" But his small son, Momolu, not only keeps the pace, but helps his father find just the right tree for making a boat that will replace the canoe broken by an alligator. Both the story and the style are beguiling, and the finely detailed illustrations, based on the style of African woodcuts, are strong and dramatic, bold in composition but intricate within the masses of figures.

505 **Gray,** Genevieve S. *Ghost Story;* illus. by Greta Matus. Lothrop, 1975. 64p. Trade ed. $4.50; Library ed. $4.14 net.

3-5 Bet you've never read one like this, a very funny ghost story that's delightful to read alone or aloud. The ghost family occupying a derelict mansion is irritated when their domain is invaded by junkies. Papa Ghost says, when the first one comes, "This character moved in on our territory. Looks like he could leave us alone." Mama Ghost, "she don't like it either. 'He's a bad influence on the kids. Besides, he clutters up the place. I like a neat house.'" Then come some graduate students interested in extrasensory phenomena. The junkies think it's a stakeout and take off, the ghost family does its best to perform so well they'll frighten the students away, but to no avail, and they all achieve a balanced situation: the ghosts happily haunt, the students happily observe. Zesty style and a fresh approach. The illustrations tend to combine blob-like figures and much handprinting of "plosh," "boing," "Whoosh," "ickle," and "aaaaaaaiiiiieeee" but comic strip-inured readers won't object.

506 **Gray,** Genevieve. *Send Wendell;* drawings by Symeon Shimin. McGraw-Hill, 1974. 28p. $4.95.

K-3 Shimin's people are always drawn with love, and here the illustrations capture the warmth and affection of a black family in which six-year-old Wendell is the errand boy. Wendell's older brothers and sisters always have some good reason why they can't do small chores for Mama. So good-natured Wendell trots off each time. One day he is rewarded; he is the first to see Mama's brother when he comes on a visit from California. Self-assured and full of vitality, Uncle Robert sees that Wendell is an engaging and agreeable child; it is arranged that Wendell will be the nephew to go west and help with Uncle Robert's farm when he is older. His sister says the usual "Send Wendell," the next day when Mama asks her to do an errand, but this time it is Wendell who has something else to do, he's writing a letter to Uncle Robert. Low-keyed, realistic, and gentle, this affable family story gives a picture of goals and relationships at the child's level.

507 **Greenberg,** Barbara. *The Bravest Babysitter;* illus. by Diane Paterson. Dial, 1977. 77-71516. 24p. Trade ed. $5.95; Library ed. $5.47 net.

4-6 yrs. Heather comes straight from hockey practice to babysit with Lisa; Lisa's pleased, because Heather is cheerful, inventive, and self-reliant, but not—Lisa discovers—when there's thunder. Heather tries hard to mask her fear, but Lisa sees through her efforts and suggests a series of occupations to keep her babysitter busy. By the time the storm ends and Lisa goes to bed, it's clear that there's been a role reversal. A good child-babysitter relationship and genuine kindness on Lisa's part are assets in a story that is nicely told and that has a fresh viewpoint in dealing with the handicap of fear. The illustrations are in pastel tones and, while not cluttered, are filled with small details (figured wallpaper, patterned rugs, floral print on clothing) that make them a bit busy.

508 **Greene,** Bette. *Morning Is a Long Time Coming.* Dial, 1978. 76-42933. 288p. $7.95.

6-9 While this doesn't have the dramatic impact of *Summer of My German Soldier,* to which it is a sequel, it has the same authenticity; the jacket copy explains that Greene wrote the book because "I needed to explain my life to myself." Patty, on graduating from high school, uses gift money to go to Europe despite her parent's objections. Her sadistic father, in fact, objects to the extent that he cuts her out of his will and says the Jewish prayers for the dead for her. Patty's love affair in Paris and her search for the mother of her German soldier are interesting enough to hold the reader, the writing style has vitality and conviction, and there is percipient depth in characterization, but the book is weakened somewhat by the extensive referrals to events of the earlier story and by the fact that the narrative breaks rather sharply between events before and after the ocean voyage.

509 **Greene,** Bette. *Philip Hall Likes Me. I Reckon Maybe;* pictures by Charles Lilly, Dial, 1974. 135p. Trade ed. $4.95; Library ed. $4.58 net.

4-6 First love has come to eleven-year-old Beth Lambert, who could be the best student in school if she didn't let Philip take first place. "Beth, honey, you is so smart about most things. How come the good Lord made you dumb about Philip Hall?" Mama asks. There are times when Beth is furious, sure that Philip does like her but won't say so, and times when he doesn't even act like a friend; not until Beth has decided to do her best and beat him (and she does) does Philip admit that he likes her. Sometimes. Woven through and around Beth's innocent romance are some very funny episodes of life in rural Arkansas, warm family relationships, and a good picture of community life. The writing style is deceptively casual, characterizations and dialogue are sound, and the protagonist (who tells the story) a resourceful, lively girl whose charm and vitality come through clearly in the deft, realistic illustrations.

510 **Greene,** Bette. *Summer of My German Soldier.* Dial, 1973. 230p. $5.95.

6-9 A World War II story, set in a small Arkansas town, is told by twelve-year-old Patty. Treated coldly by her parents, the child is homely and lonely, her comfort coming from a black housekeeper and a grandmother in Memphis. When a German prisoner of war comes into her father's store, Patty succumbs to his gentle politeness; later the man escapes and Patty hides him in an unused room over the family garage. She knows what would happen if her father, who beats her with a strap when he punishes her, would do if he knew that a Nazi soldier were being hidden by a Jewish child, but she cannot turn against the man who has become a loving friend. While this never achieves the tender quality of the relationship in *Tiger Bay,* it is a believable situation, and the quality of other characters and relationships is remarkably vivid and convincing.

511 **Greene,** Constance C. *Beat the Turtle Drum;* illus. by Donna Diamond. Viking, 1976. 76-14772. 119p. $5.95.

4-6 This is Kate's story, but it is about her younger sister Joss. Joss has a loving heart, a gift for friendship; she and Kate are close friends even though Kate knows Joss is their parents' favorite. Joss is almost everyone's favorite. Her dream comes true on her eleventh birthday when she gets a horse, and one day she and Kate tie the horse to a tree and climb another tree to picnic; Joss falls from the tree and breaks her neck. Because the author has so powerfully drawn the special quality Joss has, especially as seen through Kate's eyes, the conclusion of the story has tremendous impact. Kate lives through the period of numbness, the pain of her own and her parents' grief, the service, and the ambivalent reaction to condolences in a daze. She knows things will get better, but ends, "It's the now that hurts."

512 **Greene,** Constance C. *The Ears of Louis;* illus. by Nola Langner. Viking, 1974. 90p. $5.95.

3-5 It was no consolation to Louis, whose big ears made the boys at school tease him, when his mother said Clark Gable had big ears and always got the girl. Louis didn't want to get the girl, he wanted to play football even though he was small. One person who didn't care was his friend Matthew, who *liked* Louis' ears because they were all pink when the sun shone through them, another was his friend Mrs. Beeble next door, with whom he played poker. Louis finally realizes that some of the teasing is just standard operating procedure—and as for the bullies, they stop calling him "Sugar Bowl" when they find that Louis is a buddy of the older football players. The problem/solution aspect of the story is firmly realistic and satisfying, but it's the sympathetic characterization, the ease and humor of the writing style, the perception shown in relationships (particularly between Louis and Mrs. Beeble), and the felicitous dialogue that make the book enjoyable.

513 **Greene,** Constance C. *I Know You, Al;* illus. by Byron Barton. Viking, 1975. 75-9741. 126p. $5.95.

5-7 At last, a sequel to *A Girl Called Al,* and it's every bit as entertaining, as warm, as perceptive. Again the story is told by Al's staunchest friend (her name is never used) and has just enough about the narrator to balance the comments on, and conversations with, Al as she faces the problems in her life: being the only girl in the class who hasn't yet begun to menstruate, being too plump, not liking her mother's suitor, and meeting the father she hasn't seen for eight years. Al's father invites her to his wedding, and *that* entails tremendous decisions about clothes as well as attitudes. Throughout the story, as the narrator copes with a younger brother, as Al grumbles about her mother's friend, as both of them rebuff the class in-group, there's evidence of supportive friendship between the girls and of a perceptive sympathy on the part of the author.

514 **Greenfeld,** Howard. *Books; From Writer to Reader.* Crown, 1976. 76-15991. 211p. illus. $8.95.

7- * An admirable book both for the material it contains and for the superb illustrations and format, this is one of the most comprehensive and lucid texts on the subject. Greenfeld discusses the roles of each participant in the book-making process and of the steps in production, literary and physical. Illustrations include reproductions of manuscript stages, reports, financial forms, contracts, layout, type faces, preparations for illustrations, and the work of the designer as well as facets of color printing, order forms, and reviews. The facts are authoritative, the arrangement of them is logical, and the writing is smooth and knowledgeable. A glossary, a bibliography, and an index are included.

515 **Greenfeld,** Howard. *Chanukah;* designed by Bea Feitler. Holt, 1976. 76-6527. 39p. $5.95.

6- A dignified retelling of the episode in Jewish history that is commemorated by Chanukah, the Festival of Lights. Greenfeld describes the persecution ordered by Antiochus in his attempt to eradicate Judaism and Hellenize his kingdom, the resistance movement led by Mattathias and his son Judah, and the three-year struggle that culminated in victory by Judah's troops. Celebrated by the rededication of the Temple, the eight-day holiday is observed today as a joyous occasion in December in which candles are kept lit in memory of the lamps that burned for eight days on one cruse of oil. The use of "B.C.E.," before the Common Era, in dating, may puzzle some readers.

516 **Greenfeld,** Howard. *Gertrude Stein;* A Biography. Crown, 1973. 147p. illus. $5.95.

7- Of the four biographies of Gertrude Stein published recently this is the most sensitive in evoking Stein's personality and most thorough in analysis of her as an author. Greenfeld concentrates on the years in Paris, creating vividly the atmosphere of cultural ferment in which Gertrude Stein played so large a part. A lucid book. A list of books by Stein, a bibliography of books on Stein or her period, and an index are appended.

517 **Greenfeld,** Howard, *Gypsies.* Crown, 1977. 77-23746. 111p. photographs. $6.95.

7- Greenfeld, in his usual meticulous fashion, explores Gypsy life in a book that contains both well-researched background and objective commentary about contemporary Gypsies. Persecuted, romanticized, tenaciously keeping themselves aloof from the Gaje, non-gypsies, for whom they feel mistrust and contempt, the wandering people have clung to their own mores and traditions, their own code of ethics. Greenfeld describes the Gypsy way of life: birth, marriage, and death; superstitions and health practices; occupations; the system of justice; sex roles, and many other aspects. He closes with a chapter that discusses the Gypsies today, focusing on the efforts in many countries to integrate them, often by restrictive legislation, into the community. Greenfeld is a serious writer; his style, while sober and direct, is not stiff, and it is neither lightened by humor nor colored by personal comment. A bibliography and an index are appended.

518 **Greenfeld,** Howard. *The Impressionist Revolution.* Doubleday, 1972. 111p. illus. $5.95.

7- The author's introduction explains that he has limited his discussion to four major figures: Claude Monet, Camille Pissaro, Pierre-Auguste Renoir, and Alfred Sisley. Other impressionist painters and some of their predecessors and followers, their critics and proponents, do enter this detailed and knowledgeable history of the rebel group whose work was for years reviled and ridiculed by contemporary art critics and judges, and sneered at by the public. The book gives adequate coverage to the artists' personal lives, but focuses on their theories, techniques, and innovations, and on the way they influenced and sustained each other through the long years of poverty and rejection. An important book and an interesting one, with many reproductions in black and white and one section of color reproductions.

519 **Greenfeld,** Howard. *Sumer Is Icumen In; Our Ever-Changing Language.* Crown, 1978. 78-15166. 47p. $5.95.

7-12 As serious as most of Greenfeld's books, and more scholarly, this traces the influences that enriched and tightened the language that began with Teutonic imposition on a Celtic-speaking people, was further changed by Viking and Latin invaders of the island, and amplified by the French language elements that came with the Norman Conquest. Greenfeld describes the kinds of words, throughout the text, that illustrate each influence, and discusses the importance of the printed book and of translations that helped expand the English language. Several chapters are devoted to such topics as slang, euphemisms, the use of proper nouns (Sandwich, Silhouette) as common words, the inclusion of words from other languages ("ginger" from Sanskrit, "cigar" from Spanish, the German "sauerkraut") and the future of the still-changing language. Crisp writing on a subject that should fascinate all word-lovers. A bibliography is appended.

520 **Greenfeld,** Howard. *They Came to Paris.* Crown, 1975. 75-2413. 176p. illus. with photographs. $6.95.

8- * The creative ferment of Paris in the years just after the first world war has been touched on in several of Greenfeld's biographies; here he pulls together the highlights of movements in art, music, literature, and dance in an engrossing survey of the major personalities who loved, quarreled, met at Gertrude Stein's salon and at Sylvia Beach's bookstore, who applauded or decried new ideas at concerts, cafes, and exhibitions. The author conveys vividly the intensity and excitement of those years and, in fluent prose, describes the cross-currents in the lives of French intellectuals and others, many of whom were American expatriates: Pound, Hemingway, Fitzgerald, Stein, Ford, Anderson, Antheil, Beach, and Dos Passos. A well-researched feast for the reader interested in literature and other arts. A bibliography and an index are appended.

521 **Greenfield,** Eloise. *Mary McLeod Bethune;* illus. by Jerry Pinkney. T. Y. Crowell, 1977. 76-11522. 33p. $6.95.

2-4 Written with a simple, natural flow, this biography for younger readers does not have all the fascinating details of the life of the great educator, but it gives salient facts and is nicely balanced in treatment. The illustrations, rather scribbly pencil drawings, do not do justice to a woman who grew beautiful as she grew old, but they are adequate. The story of Mary McLeod, the only child in a poor family (seventeen children) who could go to school and who, through her devotion and courage, became a figure of national importance as an educator and a black leader, is always thrilling; Greenfield has wisely chosen not to laud, but to let the facts speak for themselves.

522 **Greenfield,** Eloise. *Rosa Parks;* illus. by Eric Marlow. T. Y. Crowell, 1973. 33p. $3.75.

2-4 Like Louise Meriwether's *Don't Ride the Bus on Monday,* this covers Rosa Parks' childhood, her historic stand that precipitated the Montgomery bus strike, her increasing participation in the civil rights struggle, and the Supreme Court decision that ended the Jim Crow rule in transportation. Here, however, the writing has more vitality, and the author's use of other incidents, earlier in Rosa Parks' life, that had evoked her resentment, makes the stand this quiet, self-contained woman took more convincing.

523 **Greenfield,** Eloise. *She Come Bringing Me that Little Baby Girl;* illus. by John Steptoe. Lippincott, 1974. 27p. $5.95.

3-5 yrs. Kevin had asked Mama to bring a boy home from the hospital and was not pleased when she came home with a girl. Aunt Mildred unwrapped the baby, and "It was a girl, all right, 'cause her fingers were way too small. She'd never be able to throw my football to me." Neighbors and relatives came to see the baby and ignored Kevin, even Uncle Roy didn't swing him around the way he always did, and Kevin didn't like the way Mama and Daddy looked at the baby. "Like she was the only baby in the world." Kevin's pangs of dethronement are assuaged by Mama's reminding him that she was a baby girl once, that Uncle Roy had loved and protected her, and that Kevin was now a big brother like Uncle Roy. The story ends with Kevin showing off his sister to his friends. There have been many books like this, in which a child's jealousy is overcome and he or she accepts a sibling, but there's always room for another when it's well done, and this is: the story catches that wistful pathos of the child who is feeling displaced. Although the conversion is suspiciously easy, it's not unbelievable, and Steptoe's vibrant pictures (too bold in style for good close viewing, but marvelous at a distance) catch the tender mood of the text.

524 **Greenfield,** Eloise. *Sister;* drawings by Moneta Barnett. T. Y. Crowell, 1974. 83p. $4.95.

5-7 Doretha is thirteen, black, and confused by her ambivalence about herself; her adolescent groping for security is exacerbated by her feelings about the older sister she has always adored and imitated. Now she doesn't want to be like Alberta—flippant when she isn't aloof, rude to their mother, who thinks Alberta is headed for trouble. Leafing through her diary, Doretha remembers . . . and each memory of the past four years (treated as chapter episodes) reveals something about her and about the people she has loved. When the story ends, as it starts—in the present—Doretha has a better sense of who she is and where she's going. Despite the fragmentation of the literary format, the story reads smoothly, and the variety of the episodes compensates for the absence of a strong story line. The book is strong nevertheless, strong in perception, in its sensitivity, in its realism.

525 **Gregor,** Arthur Stephen. *Amulets, Talismans, and Fetishes;* illus. by Anne Burgess. Scribner, 1975. 74-26002. 120p. $6.95.

6-10 A fascinating discussion of the magical, superstitious, and religious uses of amulets, fetishes, talismans, etc. from ancient times to today. Gregor writes with polished facility and with broad coverage; although he points out repeatedly the credulity behind the belief in magical objects or rituals, he does not sneer but concludes that belief itself can achieve, at some times and in some measure, the very goal the wearer or practitioner desires. Throughout the text, the author mentions those symbols and practices that persist today: wearing an ankh, carrying a rabbit's foot, using symbols on flags, using a religious figure in an automobile, wearing birthstone rings. A glossary, a bibliography, and an index are included.

526 **Griese,** Arnold A. *At the Mouth of the Luckiest River;* illus. by Glo Coalson, T. Y. Crowell, 1973. 65p. Trade ed. $4.50; Library ed. $5.25 net.

4-6 The story of an Athabascan Indian boy of a century ago is effectively illustrated with black and white pictures that reflect the isolation of the setting and the drama of the plot. Tatlek, who uses sled dogs to help in his hunting, is crippled and fatherless, anxious to prove that he is a man, puzzled by the animosity of the medicine man who says that using the dogs (a practice Tatlek has learned from Eskimo traders) will provoke the anger of the spirits, the yegas. When the medicine man warns that he has been told by an owl that the Eskimos are coming to kill the tribe, Tatlek and his friend go off by dogsled to spy on the Eskimo camp and so learn that the medicine man has lied to both sides. He races back to tell his people: will they believe him or the medicine man they fear? And if they do not believe him, Tatlek knows he will be reviled. The story is told in a rather heavy writing style, but it has suspense enough to compensate for this, and it is very successful in creating mood and atmosphere and in incorporating cultural details unobtrusively.

527 **Griese,** Arnold A. *The Way of Our People;* illus. by Haru Wells. T. Y. Crowell, 1975. 74-23086. 82p. Trade ed. $5.95; Library ed. $6.70 net.

4-6 Stark, clean illustrations in black and white, softened by smoky grey, echo both the isolated vastness of the setting and the sturdy dignity of an Alaskan Indian community. The story, set in 1838, describes a critical period in the life of an adolescent boy; it is written with restrained vigor, the characters are strong, and it gives a convincing picture of the mores and legends of the Anvik community. Kano, who has just been admitted to the circle of manhood, knows that he must conquer his secret fear of being alone in the forest or become an outcast. He turns to the Old One for help, and the solitary old forest-dweller does give Kano enough experience and comfort to cope with a crisis when it comes, so that he wins the respect of Anvik.

528 **Griese,** Arnold A. *The Wind is Not a River;* illus. by Glo Coalson. T. Y. Crowell, 1978. 77-5082. 108p. Trade ed. $6.95; Library ed. $6.79 net.

4-6 Based on a real incident of World War II, this is the story of an ethical dilemma in the midst of an exciting adventure on the small Aleutian island of Attu, last of a chain of islands off the coast of

Alaska. Susan and her brother Sidak are the only persons in their village who get away when a troop of Japanese soldiers take over Attu Village. Their father is away; their mother is dead; the grandmother who had taken care of them has just died. The children decide they will leave early for the summer fishing camp, but once they are there, Susan decides that they must go back to attend church—and that's when they see the soldiers. They get back to camp safely but find an enemy soldier, wounded and unconscious. They save the man's life, but then they must decide what to do with him, for a Japanese scouting party comes and goes without finding their camp. Taro, the soldier, has promised not to call out and has kept his word. When Susan and Sidak leave to get help, they are picked up by a submarine crew; Taro has promised not to tell his superior officer about the children and again they find that his gratitude has been placed above military duty, and they feel relieved that they, too, had kept to the old ways of kindness Grandmother had taught them. The story has suspense and drama, it's well told, and the achievements of the children are believable.

529 **Griffin,** John Howard. *A Time to Be Human.* Macmillan, 1977. 76-47468. 102p. illus. $6.95.

7-10 In *Black Like Me,* Griffin described his experiences with black and white people in the South in 1959; a white man, he had medical treatment to darken his skin. Here he reviews some of the experiences of 1959 and goes on to discuss events in the civil rights movement since that time, changes in attitudes in both races, and the learned prejudice that has not changed. This is a cogent and moving plea for change, based on Griffin's analysis of racism; he discusses Nazi philosophy and candidly explores in himself and other whites the ingrained bias that they find difficult to recognize and that black people recognize all too well. "If hopeful signs are dim," he concludes, "at least they exist."

530 **Griffiths,** Helen. *Just a Dog;* Illus. by Victor Ambrus. Holiday House, 1975. 74-19025. 160p. $5.95.

5-7 A mongrel pup's story is set in Madrid, although the setting is irrelevant, since this could be the story of any stray. The dog is loved by a boy whose parents will not let him keep her, she roams the streets and fends for herself, occasionally produces a litter, finds that some people are gentle and some harsh; eventually she is rescued from the dog pound by a family that has known and fed her, and is really taken in as a pet for the first time. Licensed, vaccinated, named, and loved. Periodically in the story there are episodes in which the human beings she encounters are described, but for the most part the author maintains the dog's viewpoint with remarkable consistency. Realistic, often moving, the story is written with a sensitivity that never lapses into sentimentality.

531 **Grillone,** Lisa. *Small Worlds Close Up;* by Lisa Grillone & Joseph Gennaro. Crown, 1978. 77-15860. 61p. illus. $7.95.

5-8 A series of photographs taken by a scanning electron microscope shows the marvelous intricacy of natural and man-made products. The text is divided into objects that are animal, vegetable, or mineral, and the text—although dry in style—gives a considerable amount of information about structure and function; often the authors use increasing magnification in a set of photographs to show increasingly minute details.

532 **Grimm,** Jakob Ludwig Karl. *The Bearskinner;* illus. by Felix Hoffman. Atheneum, 1978. 77-92742. 30p. $8.95.

K-3 Although Hoffman died before he had prepared the finished art for this version of an old tale, his brush drawings and preliminary color sketches have tremendous vitality and grace; the version used is that of the Grimm brothers. A soldier makes a bargain with the devil: for seven years he must not wash or cut his hair, he must always wear the skin of the bear he has just killed, and he must not pray. The devil's coat is his—and it has a pocket that provides an endless supply of gold. When the soldier, now called "Bearskinner," does a kind deed for an old man, the man offers one of his daughters in marriage. In traditional form, the youngest of the three daughters agrees to marry the bearish, uncouth stranger after his seven years of bondage are up. When he then appears, shaved and handsome, beautifully dressed, the youngest sister happily embraces him, the older sisters rush off in a jealous rage, and all the amenities of the folk tradition have been observed: reward for kindness, reward for filial devotion, penalty for haughtiness, and faithfulness to a vow.

533 **Grimm,** Jakob Ludwig Karl. *The Brothers Grimm Popular Folk Tales;* tr. by Brian Alderson; illus. by Michael Foreman. Doubleday, 1978. 77-17748. 192p. $8.95.

4-6 There's always room for a new version of an old tale when the tale has been carefully translated, simplified with grace and flair, and illustrated beautifully. Here, Brian Alderson has chosen thirty-one folk and fairy tales, including most of those that are best known; Michael Foreman provides a black and white sketch for the beginning of each story and a full-page, full-color painting for each. The paintings are either in the romantic or the grotesque mood; they are varied, imaginative, and deft in composition and use of color. The adaptations are fluent; despite the simplification that should enlarge the reading audience, Alderson has kept the flavor of the originals and has enhanced them by subtle introduction of the phrasing of the true storyteller.

534 **Grimm,** Jakob Ludwig Karl. *Clever Kate;* ad. from a story by the Brothers Grimm by Elizabeth Shub; pictures by Anita Lobel. Macmillan, 1973. 62p. $4.50.

2-3 A simplified and nicely told adaptation of the story of the foolish wife who took everything her husband said literally, and who—being a noodlehead—did one stupid thing after another. For example, when her husband told her not to go near the box of yellow buttons (gold coins) he'd buried, she didn't. But she told some peddlers to dig up the box. The recovery of their small fortune is due less to Kate's cleverness than to her fatigue, but it's a happy ending to an amusing tale, and the illustrations, light and charming, use color, floral frames, and peasant dress to capture to perfection the mood of the story.

535 **Grimm,** Jakob Ludwig Karl. *The Complete Grimm's Fairy Tales;* Introduction by Padraic Colum; Folkloristic commentary by Joseph Campbell; illus. by Josef Scharl. Pantheon Books, 1974. 864p. $12.95.

4-6 A reissue of the 1944 publication, based on the Margaret Hunt translation, which was and is a standard edition of the collected household tales. A discussion of folk literature, with examples from the Grimm's stories, adds to the value of the book.

536 **Grimm,** Jakob Ludwig Karl. *The Donkey Prince;* ad. by M. Jean Craig; illus. by Barbara Cooney. Doubleday, 1977. 75-45477. 43p. $6.95.

2-3 An adaptation of a tale from Grimm is told in a fluent writing style and is illustrated with delectable paintings in full color. Cooney is skilled at introducing small details like the little donkey's amiable smile or a spray of flowers, yet not letting them dominate the spacious composition of the pages; she also introduces texture effectively. The little donkey is born to a childless royal couple by the magic work of a wizard—but because the king has cheated him, the wizard gives him a strange son. Ignored by his parents, the donkey wanders off to a castle where there is a beautiful princess. She learns to love him, and of course when she tells him, he emerges as a handsome prince, and of course they live happily ever after. A charming version of a traditionally patterned tale.

537 **Grimm,** Jakob Ludwig Karl. *Grimm's Fairy Tales; Twenty Stories;* illus. by Arthur Rackham. Viking, 1973. 128p. $6.95.

4-6 A selection of stories from the Rackham edition, long out of print, comprises some of the best-known Grimm tales: "Tom Thumb," "Jorinda and Joringel," "The Bremen Town Musicians," "Rumpelstiltskin," "The Twelve Dancing Princesses," and others. The illustrations include some full-color plates, some black and white drawings, some silhouettes. More romantic and conventional than Sendak's interpretation, Rackham's pictures have a beauty and—in some pictures—a vigor that are perennially delectable.

538 **Grimm,** Jakob Ludwig Karl. *Grimms' Tales for Young and Old;* tr. by Ralph Manheim. Doubleday, 1977. 76-56318. 633p. $12.50.

4-6
* Translated from the 1819 edition by a winner (for his translation) of the National Book Award, this unillustrated edition of the Grimms' tales is comparable to, but simpler than, the Pantheon edition based on the Hunt translation. Although some of the titles are given in different forms, they are in the same order, two hundred tales and ten children's legends. Examples of Manheim's simpler style compared to the older edition: he begins "Hansel and Gretel" with, "At the edge of the forest lives a poor woodcutter with his wife and two children," whereas the other reads, "Hard by a great forest dwelt a poor wood-cutter with his wife and his two children." For "King Thrushbeard," Manheim translates the start as, "A king had a daughter who was unequalled for beauty, but she was so proud and thought so much of herself that no suitor was good enough for her." Hunt's translation, revised by Joseph Stern, "A king had a daughter who was beautiful beyond measure, but so proud and haughty withal that no suitor was good enough for her." Clearly, for those who like a "withal" here and there to flavor the writing, the older edition may be preferred, while the Manheim translation is easier to read and therefore extends the audience-potential. Both are very good.

539 **Grimm,** Jacob Ludwig Karl. *Hansel and Gretel;* by the Brothers Grimm; tr. by Charles Scribner; illus. by Adrienne Adams. Scribner, 1975. 74-14080. 27p. $6.95.

3-5 A version of the familiar story is adapted adequately, with small variations that deviate from other versions. The illustrations are handsome, particularly the night scenes; Adams is skilled at using color to create atmosphere: the trees loom, a greenish light sifts through the dark forest. When the children escape, it is into a sunny, open landscape of lake, sky, and clouds. The paintings are deftly composed and dramatic, closely fitted to the incidents of the story.

540 **Grimm,** Jakob Ludwig Karl. *The Juniper Tree and Other Tales from Grimm;* in two volumes; selected by Lore Segal and Maurice Sendak; tr. by Lore Segal with four tales tr. by Randall Jarrell; illus. by Maurice Sendak. Farrar, 1973. 332p. 2v. $12.95.

4- A milestone, a tour de force, a joy to see, this two-volume edition of some of the stories from the Grimm brothers' collection includes some familiar tales and others that are less well-known. The translations have been made from several early editions, and both those of Jarrell and of Lore Segal are direct and fresh, unexpurgated and unsweetened. The illustrations are superb: beautiful, imaginative, appropriate, tender and terrible—as though the tales had been waiting for Maurice Sendak to interpret them. For children and adults.

541 **Grimm,** Jakob Ludwig Karl. *King Grisly-Beard;* tr. by Edgar Taylor; illus. by Maurice Sendak. Farrar, 1973. 24p. $3.95.

K-3 A delightful picture book version of the familiar tale of the disdainful princess who is taught humility by her husband. Maurice Sendak does not just add funny (and lovely) pictures, but interprets and expands the story so that it achieves a robust shrew-taming humor, and he uses three devices that should appeal to children: his leads are played by children, briefly introduced in audition pictures that precede the story proper, by one-line balloon captions within the drawings, and by the inclusion of a small, vocal dog in every set of illustrations.

542 **Grimm,** Jakob Ludwig Karl. *The Sleeping Beauty, from the Brothers Grimm;* ad. and illus. by Trina Schart Hyman. Little, 1977. 75-43769. 43p. $7.95.

4-6 Gracefully retold, the story of the princess who slept for a hundred years until waking—as prophesied—from her enchantment, is illustrated by Hyman at her best. Her best means appropriately romantic scenes, humorous touches, a rich palette, and a deft accommodation of line and perspective to handsome composition.

543 **Grimm,** Jakob Ludwig Karl. *Tom Thumb;* illus. by Felix Hoffmann. Atheneum, 1973. 30p. $5.25.

K-2 The familiar tale of the tiny, perfect child who has a series of adventures and returns safely home by using his wits is illustrated delightfully with large-scale, beautifully composed pictures with a sturdy peasant flavor, the strength softened by fine detail. First published in Switzerland, the story is faithful to the original version and the pictures (some in black and white, some in full color) add immeasurably to this picture book version.

544 **Grimm,** Jacob Ludwig Karl. *The Twelve Dancing Princesses;* retold from a story by the Brothers Grimm; illus. by Errol LeCain. Viking, 1978. 78-8578. 29p. $8.95.

4-6 In a version that adheres to standard translations, this edition of a favorite Grimm tale is illustrated in rich fashion, with paintings and page frames that are intricately and beautifully patterned, romantic in mood, and superb in the use of color and the delicacy of costume and architectural details. With advice from a wise old woman and the help of a cloak of invisibility, a poor soldier solves the riddle of the dancing princesses—why are their shoes worn through each morning?—and chooses the eldest for his wife because, he says, "I'm not as young as I was."

545 **Gripe,** Maria. *Elvis and His Secret;* with drawings by Harald Gripe; trans. from the Swedish by Sheila La Farge. Delacorte/Seymour Lawrence, 1976. 75-8000. 199p. Trade ed. $6.95; Library ed. $6.46 net.

Elvis and His Friends; with drawings by Harald Gripe; trans. from the Swedish by Sheila La Farge. Delacorte/Seymour Lawrence, 1976. 75-8002. 199p. Trade ed. $6.95; Library ed. $6.46 net.

4-6 While it is possible that children old enough to cope with the vocabulary may need persuasion to read about a child of six, those children who have already been captivated by the small, solitary figure that appeared in *Julia's House* always hovering on the outside of any action, will be a ready audience. These two books about Elvis are touchingly poignant and imbued with a wry humor. Elvis has been named for Elvis Presley by his flighty, self-preoccupied mother, who constantly impresses on the child that he is a nuisance, that he is annoyingly different from other children, that he looks a mess, in fact, that he is a burden to her. Serious, naive, and logical, the resilient six-year-old tries to please but is puzzled when he repeatedly fails. In *Elvis and His Secret,* Elvis becomes a close friend of Peter, the "Night Daddy" who took care of Julia, and his supportive affection helps Elvis realize the very important secret that "Elvis is Elvis," that he has his own identity and can accept himself. Both books establish the tender understanding between Elvis and his grandfather; in *Elvis and His Friends,* Elvis starts school (his mother carping every step of the way, more concerned with her appearance than with her child's adjustment) and meets an understanding teacher and a new friend, Annarosa. What is most remarkable about these books is the consistency with which the author describes everything that happens from Elvis's viewpoint. The stories are written with perception in a style that is both ingenuous and graceful.

546 **Gripe,** Maria. *The Glassblower's Children;* illus. by Harald Gripe; tr. by Sheila La Farge. Delacorte, 1973. 170p. $4.95.

4-6 Moving from the field of realism in which she has been a distinguished contributor, Maria Gripe proves equally skilled in writing fantasy. There's a touch of Henry James in her portrayal of the wicked governess who bullies two children who have been stolen from their parents by a wealthy, childless Lord who had hoped, unsuccessfully, to make his languid Lady happy. The story starts in the humble home of the glassblower, a fine artisan who has seen ominous signs of the danger to his children; he and his wife seek the aid of a good witch who proves to be the sister of the malevolent governess. Set in the Gothic mood, the tale of the struggle between the sisters is a saga of good and evil. Style, mood, and tempo are adroitly integrated, and the illustrations—reminiscent of Leonard Everett Fisher's scratchboard work—effectively support the story.

547 **Gripe,** Maria. *Julia's House;* with drawings by Harald Gripe; tr. from the Swedish by Gerry Bothmer. Delacorte, 1975. 116p. Trade ed. $5.95; Library ed. $5.47 net.

5-6 A sequel to *The Night Daddy* is in the same format, with chapters written alternately by Julia and by Peter, the young man who stays with her each night while her mother is on night duty as a nurse. Julia is older now, her affection for Peter complicated by some ambivalence about their relationship. This is a less cohesive book than the first one, with Julia's loyalties divided between Peter and her teacher and friends at school, with Peter's interest caught by a small, silent boy who watches him; each is a little jealous of the other's divergent interests. There is just enough of this conflict to impinge on the major plot line, the threatened demolition of Julia's house. Albeit less cohesive, the writing evinces such a genuine understanding of a child's concerns, it is so fluent and perceptive, that the book makes an incisive impact.

548 **Groch,** Judith. *Play the Bach, Dear!* Doubleday, 1978. 77-76960. 191p. $6.95.

4-6 Eleven-year-old Hilary takes piano lessons, but she knows she plays badly and she detests the thought of her imminent recital. Her teacher, Miss Orpheo, scolds; she pleads for more practicing; she urges Hilary to relax. No improvement. In fact, she's the last person in the world that Hilary would expect to come to her rescue at the dreaded recital, but it is Miss Orpheo who—by disappearing into the piano—saves the day at the recital. But *had* she been in the piano? Or was it practice and self-confidence that made Hilary play so well? An original and very funny story, told in andante tempo and with brio.

549 **Gross,** Ruth Belov. *Snakes.* Four Winds, 1975. 74-13227. 63p. illus. $6.95.

3-5 Although the text is coded by the publisher for reading aloud (and it can be used that way, or used for browsing by a pre-reader who enjoys the photographs), it seems more appropriate for the independent reader who is interested in details of the subject. Some of the illustrations are in color and can be used for identification; some are in black and white. Gross describes reproduction inadequately (there's only a passing reference to mating and no diagrams of a snake's anatomy) but gives quite full information about behavior and habitat, and she provides a special section on poisonous snakes. The writing style is direct and crisp, with short sentences and large print, and with the text arranged in short chapters to facilitate reading ease.

550 **Grosser,** Morton. *The Snake Horn;* illus. by David K. Stone. Atheneum, 1973. 131p. $4.95.

5-7 It was a tartöld, an old musical instrument made in the form of a snake, and one of his father's musician friends had brought it to Danny. What happened when he played it was frightening: the Snake Horn brought into Danny's room its original owner, a 17th century musician. Very deftly, the author weaves this bit of time-warp fantasy into a story of today. Danny's father is a jazz musician (and isn't it nice to see one pictured as a responsible father and husband) who picks up a few ideas from the time traveler. And vice versa. Danny's friends are of all ethnic backgrounds, his major interest in life is football, although girls are beginning to be interesting, and the story has a nice balance of all these interests. Very now, very merry, very well done.

551 **Gurney,** Gene. *The Launching of Sputnik, October 4, 1957; The Space Age Begins;* by Gene and Clare Gurney. Watts, 1975. 75-5545. 86p. illus. $3.90.

5-8 A review of the work of early rocketry experts (in Russia, Germany, and the United States primarily) gives some background for the descriptions of the successful V-2, Sputnik, and Redstone rockets' structure and their missions. The Gurneys discuss the secrecy that surrounded the construction and launching plans for the first Sputnik, announced in 1956, a year before it was sent into orbit; they also discuss the rivalry between the U.S.S.R. and the U.S. in rocket and bomb research. A brief last section describes the ways in which the information gleaned from space satellites has been useful to mankind. A bibliography and an index are appended. The writing is not too technical; the book is dignified and informative, although it is written in a dry and rather heavy style and is uneven in organization.

552 **Gutman,** Bill. *Duke; The Musical Life of Duke Ellington.* Random House, 1977. 76-8138. 184p. illus. $6.95.

7-10 As the title makes clear, this is a musical rather than a personal biography. There is brief mention of Ellington's parents and his childhood, only a passing reference to a marriage that soon ended in divorce, and one photograph that includes Ellington's son, by then a man of middle age. The bound-in pages of photographs otherwise focus on Ellington and his band or other musical colleagues, as is fitting for a book that describes the musical influences on Ellington, comments on musical forms, and gives, in thoughtful detail, the stages of his career as pianist, entrepreneur, showman, bandleader, and composer. The book is useful as a contribution to musical history in the United States, and fascinating in the colorful depiction of the life of travelling musicians. There are comments included that make clear the problems black musicians had on the road, and there is massive evidence that Duke Ellington's position as one of our great men of music is as recognized abroad as it is at home. An index and a partial discography are appended.

553 **Gutman,** Bill. *Hank Aaron.* Grosset, 1973. 87p. illus. Trade ed. $3.99; Paperback ed. $1.50.

3-5 Less fictionalized than May's *Hank Aaron Clinches the Pennant,* written for the same age group, and with more vitality of style, this is otherwise much the same, with coverage of Aaron's childhood, his years in black baseball leagues and on the major League farm club circuit, his career highlights as a major league superstar, and some information on his personal life and his role as a black player. Several pages of statistics are appended. The approach is dignified enough to make the book useful, also, for slow older readers.

554 **Gutman,** Bill. *Modern Women Superstars;* illus. with photographs. Dodd, 1977. 77–6503. 112p. $5.25.

4-7 One of a series of sports biographies designed to appeal to the slow older reader, this has good sized, well-spaced print, an undemanding vocabulary, and fairly short sentences. It is, however, not written down and is reportorial rather than laudatory, emphasizing each woman's dedication and rigorous training rather than her accomplishments, although those are of course included. The six women described are Nadia Comaneci, Chris Evert, Dorothy Hamill, Kathy Kusner, Cindy Nelson, and Judy Rankin, so the book has variety. An index is appended.

555 **Guy,** Rosa. *Edith Jackson.* Viking, 1978. 77–28098. 187p. $8.95.

8-12 Edith, who appeared in the author's *The Friends,* is now seventeen; although she and her three younger sisters live with a foster mother, it is Edith who feels responsible for the others, who vows that when she is of age she will work and provide a home for them. They will not be separated. But they are: one sister runs off with their foster mother's lover; one is taken in by a white couple whose daughter is her best friend. Edith becomes the reluctant protégée of Mrs. Bates, a black woman lawyer, and falls in love with the woman's nephew. For Edith it's love—for James it's just another easy conquest. The story ends with Edith's discovery that she is pregnant; she turns first to Phyllisia, who welcomes her—and then, sitting in a welfare agency office, Edith suddenly walks out and telephones Mrs. Bates to tell her she is going to have an abortion. And Mrs. Bates simply says she is coming, she'll be with her soon. That's how the story ends, but what is left unsaid (and is clear) is that Edith has admitted to herself that the encouragement Mrs. Bates has offered, and her help, will be accepted. Proud and strong, Edith had been insisting on getting a job and holding the family together—which meant accepting the role of mother to her sisters—and now she can admit that she can change her life if she will focus on her own needs. The characterization is excellent, the writing style smooth, and the depiction of an adolescent torn between her need for independence and achievement and her feeling of responsibility (which has pushed her into protecting the sisters who don't want protection) strong and perceptive.

556 **Guy,** Rosa. *The Friends.* Holt, 1973. 203p. $5.95.

7-10 "Her name was Edith. I did not like her," Phyllisia begins, and describes the slovenly, cheerful girl who is the only friendly person in class. Phyl and her sister have just come from the West Indies to Harlem, where their blustering, domineering father has a restaurant. Lonely, she turns to Edith even though she is ashamed to be seen with her, and she learns to be ashamed of herself when she insults her friend in front of others. Bereavement and paternal bullying have almost broken Phyl's spirit when a meeting with Edith, whom she has ignored, make her realize what true friendship is and give her the courage to have a showdown with her tyrannical father. The characters are memorable, the story powerful in its candor, vigor, and insight.

557 **Habenstreit,** Barbara. *Men Against War.* Doubleday, 1973. 210p. $4.50.

7-10 A survey of protest from earliest colonial times to today includes religious groups that did not believe in killing, men and women who protested as individuals against all war or against particular wars, organizations for peace, peaceful resistance in the black power struggle, and conscientious objectors in our time. The book is a useful adjunct to a study of American history, the material is interesting in itself, and the text is written in an informal and enthusiastic style. A list of books suggested for further reading and an index are appended.

558 **Hahn,** James. *Recycling; Re-Using Our World's Solid Wastes;* by James and Lynn Hahn. Watts, 1973. 66p. illus. $3.95.

4-7 A timely and informative text discusses the problems of the mountains of solid waste materials that accumulate in our world, the ways in which individuals can help in collecting and sorting metals, glass, paper, and plastics, and the ways in which such materials are processed in recycling plants. The authors also describe the ways in which garbage can be recycled, used for land fill, or used in energy recovery systems. Well organized and capably written, the book may well stimulate reader's participation in the recycling process; it is unfortunate that the print is small and solid in appearance. A glossary and an index are appended.

559 **Halacy,** Daniel S. *The Energy Trap.* Four Winds, 1975. 143p. illus. $6.95.

7-10 A sober and sobering assessment of the situation in which the world is today, with population and pollution and demands for energy increasing, while available energy sources dwindle and future attempts to meet demands impose additional problems of further pollution, enormous cost, and problems of disposal. A gloomy picture, but it is presented in matter-of-fact fashion; the prospects of using solar energy or geothermal sources as well as of a mandatory return to a simpler standard of living are explored, and Halacy presents some cogent arguments for action now. Despite minor flaws (a chart on oil production that refers to numbers showing thousands of barrels per day—but has no numbers; the dubious opening sentence which states that a desire to harness "all the energy sources in the environment" is "one of the strongest drives man is born with") the book is valuable:

competently written, with material logically arranged, and with corroborating data incorporated. An index is appended.

560 **Hall,** Elizabeth. *From Pigeons to People; A Look at Behavior Shaping.* Houghton, 1975. 75-17030. 130p. $6.95.

6-10 Meticulously organized, written with clarity, and authoritative, this is a forceful yet objective introduction to the subject of behavior modification. Hall describes the work of psychologists in studies of positive, negative, and intermittent reinforcement; she discusses the differences of opinion—even controversy—about the effectiveness or the justification for shaping human behavior. The research projects described are fascinating, and the book may, especially because of the examples it gives of modifying one's own behavior, prove to be benignly provocative. A glossary and a relative index are appended.

561 **Hall,** Elizabeth. *Why We Do What We Do; A Look at Psychology.* Houghton, 1973. 184p. illus. $5.95

6-9 A very good overview of psychological processes and animal behavior is clarified by descriptions of experimental research. Hall emphasizes individual differences in such areas as responses and reactions; her discussion of conditioning and reinforcement during learning is particularly lucid. While the text contains an occasional conclusion that seems unwarranted, the book as a whole is sensible, well-organized, and authoritative. It includes chapters on motivation, emotions, learning, memory, thinking, and personality. A glossary and a relative index are appended.

562 **Halmi,** Robert. *Zoos of the World.* Four Winds, 1975. 72–87078. 117p. illus. $6.95.

5-7 Although there are many other good books about zoos, this well-organized discussion of the subject has a somewhat different emphasis, focusing on the improved zoos and game parks of today and on some of the facts that have been established about the comfort, happiness, and health of animals by careful and concerned zoo personnel. Reviewing the animal collections made in antiquity and the early zoos that were established, Halmi describes some of the inadequate zoos of today (Central Park in New York) and some of the great ones (San Diego) as well as the huge game parks that no city can afford within its boundaries. He also stresses the zoo as an educational experience for adults and children, and discusses such problems as feeding, escaped animals, preservation of endangered species, mating and breeding in captivity, and learning what environment is conducive to an animal's security. An index is appended.

563 **Hamblin,** Dora Jane. *Buried Cities and Ancient Treasures.* Simon and Schuster, 1973. 287p. illus. $7.95.

7- A description of the author's travels through Turkey on an archaeological ramble is illustrated with photographs that are as enticing as the text. The discoveries that are being made in Turkey by contemporary archaeologists are fascinating in themselves, but a less capable writer might have given a dry account; Hamblin is witty, enthusiastic, and knowledgeable, and she writes with polished ease. A divided bibliography and an extensive index are appended.

564 **Hamilton,** Gail. *Titania's Lodestone.* Atheneum, 1975. 74-19491. 200p. $6.50.

6-8 Fifteen-year-old Priscilla is the only member of the family who is really anxious to settle down in their ancestral home in Maine; her peripatetic parents and brother are content to stay in a small Massachusetts town where their car has broken down. After years of roaming Europe, Priscilla is ready to melt into American life and she worries about her gypsy-like parents. Her mother (Hazel, who dubs herself Titania and counts on her lodestone to help in times of trouble) wears peculiar clothes, her father has a ponytail, they have taken up residence in an abandoned, half-built castle. Priscilla is surprised when her mother's lectures on transcendental meditation prove popular, and slowly she realizes that local people are ready to accept those who are different. The characterization, the relations within the family, and the attitudes of the townspeople are drawn with variety and perception, and Priscilla's growing understanding and perspective are gradual and believable.

565 **Hamilton,** Virginia. *Arilla Sun Down.* Greenwillow, 1976. 76-13180. 248p. Trade ed. $7.95; Library ed. $6.71 net.

7-9 Arilla Adams is twelve, daughter of a black mother and a father who has black and Native American origins; she feels overshadowed by her brother Jack (Jack Sun Run) who is dramatic, attractive, and assured. Arilla is not sure of anything, not claiming the Indian heritage in which Sun glories, not sure how her father (who periodically disappears) feels about them all, not convinced that her brother doesn't hate her. But she sorts things out, and with perspective comes a new confidence and security. She is almost ready to tell her true name, Arilla Sun Down. Arilla tells her story with interpolated flashbacks to early childhood, and the latter may present some difficulty to readers, since she uses language in an odd way: "She patting making baby to feel so sleeping," or "Can't seeing his face, brown shade." Yet

Hamilton is a genius with words; once accustomed to the pattern, the reader hears the singing quality. What is outstanding in the story is the depth and nuance of the author's perception of the young adolescent, the brilliant characterization, and the dramatic impact of some of the episodes.

566 **Hamilton,** Virginia. *Justice and Her Brothers.* Greenwillow, 1978. 78-54684. 217p. Trade ed. $7.95; Library ed. $7.63 net.

7- Virginia Hamilton is one of our great stylists, and in this story of eleven-year-old Tice (Justice) Douglas and her brothers, who are identical twins of thirteen, her prose carries readers through a slow beginning to a compelling and quickening movement of events that have a quality of inexorable force. Tice is afraid of one of the twins, Thomas, whose teasing has a cruelty and anger she cannot understand, while she feels that her other brother Lee (Levi) protects her. She begins to be aware that there is a strange empathy between the boys; it seems a telepathic communication. Then, guided by a neighbor who is psychic, Tice becomes aware of her own psychic powers—and as soon as she does, the full force of Tom's malevolence, the full disclosure of the brutal invasion he makes of his twin's mind, and the nature of the battle between them become evident. The story is fleshed out with other action (Tice's participation in a snake hunt) and other characters (warm relationships between Tice and her parents, who are supportive and strong) and with a vivid evocation of the rural setting. It concludes on a hopeful, if tantalizing note, as the three children and a fourth, son of the woman who has helped Tice find her powers, look to a future in which they will be together, knowing they are different from other people. ". . . she was content," Tice muses, "to be different as long as she was not alone. She would never be alone again."

567 **Hamilton,** Virginia. *M. C. Higgins, the Great.* Macmillan, 1974. 278p. $6.95.

6-8 Thirteen-year-old M. C. helps take care of the younger children while his parents work, steals off to play when he can with Ben, whose "witchy" family are pariahs, and sits in splendor atop the forty foot pole he has set up so that he can survey his domain, the mountain that his family owns. M. C. dreams of getting his family away from the danger of the slow-moving spoil heap (left from strip mining) that threatens their home, dreams that the folklorist who visits them will offer Mama a fortune to leave and become a recording star. His initiative is awakened by another wanderer, a girl who comes from "outside" and helps M. C. realize that he can take the initiative, that one helps mold his own fate. The characterization, the creation of setting, the establishment of mood, and the writing style are all superb; Virginia Hamilton has never written more beautifully. Her style is both intricate and graceful, with nuances of meaning that more mature readers may appreciate, but which are not essential for the average reader's comprehension.

568 **Hamilton,** Virginia. *Paul Robeson;* The Life and Times of a Free Black Man; illus. with photographs. Harper, 1974. 217p. Trade ed. $5.95; Library ed. $6.79 net.

7- Virginia Hamilton does full justice to the great artist whose political views and sympathy for the Soviet Union caused disruption of his career in this country. Robeson had been a participant in the Harlem Renaissance, and his quick emergence as a talented actor and singer led him to give up his legal career and devote himself to the arts. Both the warmth of his personality and the passion of his convictions are made piercingly clear in a well-researched and sympathetic biography that gives adequate attention to Robeson's family life but that focuses on his political ideology, his struggles as a black artist, and his role in our society. A section of notes, an extensive bibliography of sources, and an index are appended.

569 **Hamilton,** Virginia. *Time-Ago Lost;* More Tales of Jahdu; illus. by Ray Prather. Macmillan, 1973. 85p. $4.95.

3-5 A sequel to *Time-Ago Tales of Jahdu,* in which a small black boy comes to stay each day with Mama Luka until his parents are through work. And each day Mama Luka tells Lee Edward stories about the hero figure, Jahdu, tales in the folk tradition. The Jahdu stories are told with consummate skill, and the framing narrative has a warmth and substance that are a firm base for the tales. Mama Luka is worried becuase she has been told she will have to move, and Lee Edward is so upset that he seeks—and gets—reassurance from his father. Relieved, Lee Edward is inspired to concoct and tell his parents a Jahdu-tale of his own. Skilled writing, taut structure, and deep affection between the child and the adults of his world, a "fine good place called Harlem" make this a distinguished book.

570 **Hamilton,** Virginia. *W. E. B. DuBois; A Biography;* illus. with photographs. T. Y. Crowell, 1972. 218p. $4.50

7-10 Carefully researched and documented, sympathetic toward the subject yet candid about his failings, this is a sober record of the long career of William Du Bois. The biography concentrates on his adult life, giving a detailed account of the teacher, writer, and political activist and very little about his personal life. This lacks the warmth that characterizes Virginia Hamilton's fiction, but it makes a particular contribution in placing the events of Du Bois' life not just in the stream of black history but against the background of what was happening in the United States and how it inevitably affected what was happening to William Du Bois. A section of chapter notes, a selective bibliography of writings by and about the biographee, and an extensive relative index are appended.

571 **Haney,** Lynn. *Ride 'em Cowgirl!* photographs by Peter Burchard. Putnam, 1975. 74-21085. 128p. $6.95.

5-9 Pretty and softly feminine? Tough and courageous? The young women and girls described here are both, and the book gives lively accounts of the training and the performance of female rodeo participants as well as a good deal of information about the events themselves. The author is sympathetic and objective, informal in her writing style, and—quoting frequently the comments by contestants—successful in conveying the atmosphere of the rodeo and the life style of the women who are "on the road." Haney discusses earnings (and the differences between what men and women earn) and provides information about the Girls Rodeo Association as well as a list of events, a glossary of terms, and an index.

572 **Hanlon,** Emily. *It's Too Late for Sorry.* Bradbury, 1978. 78-4422. 222p. $7.95.

7-10 Kenny, a high school student, is pulled two ways. He and Phil had been best friends since fourth grade, and now Phil was jeering at Kenny for his devotion to the football team and for his interest in Harold, the retarded adolescent who had just come from years in an institution. As Harold's neighbor, Kenny saw him often, especially after Kenny's girl, Rachel, became interested in helping Harold. And they did help him; Harold became more adept socially and was devoted to his new friends. "Mental Lover," Phil jeered, and went on teasing Harold whenever they met, calling him "retard." When Kenny and Rachel broke up, Phil showed up again; he convinced Kenny to try grass, and under its influence Kenny went to a dance where he saw Rachel and Harold dancing, and turned on his retarded friend viciously. It was too late to be sorry when Kenny learned that Harold had run away, had then been beaten up by a gang, and was hospitalized. Like the adolescents in Zindel's *The Pigman,* Kenny has learned that one lives with the consequences of one's actions. The author, a former teacher of retarded adolescents, draws a touching picture of Harold, loving and responsive, although her comments on institutionalizing the retarded are a bit obtrusive. Save for Phil, who seems overdrawn, the characterization is good; the dialogue flows naturally, and the book has a balanced structure.

573 **Harnett,** Cynthia. *The Writing on the Hearth;* illus. by Gareth Floyd. Viking, 1973. 318p. $6.95.

7-10 A story set in fifteenth-century England is an admirable example of good historical fiction: the historical characters (distinguished from those that are fictional in an author's note) on the periphery, so that attention is focused on the protagonist, the period details unobtrusively incorporated, the story line solid, the characters and dialogue firmly drawn. Young Stephen has been permitted to attend the first free school because his father had served the Earl of Suffolk, and he hopes to become an Oxford scholar. An Oxford master who visits Suffolk Hall describes a strange design on the hearth, and this symbol is related to the web of intrigue in which Stephen becomes embroiled.

574 **Harris,** Christie. *Mouse Woman and the Mischief-Makers;* drawings by Douglas Tait. Atheneum, 1977. 76-25846. 115p. $6.95.

4-6 In a companion volume to *Mouse Woman and the Vanished Princesses,* Harris retells seven stories about the narnauk Mouse Woman, a tiny supernatural creature who is in the pantheon of many tribes of the Northwest Coast Indians. Children will probably enjoy especially "Mouse Woman and the Tooth," since its protagonist Mouse Woman is a girl-narnauk, as mischievous then as she is in all the other tales in which she is older and enjoys, in her efforts to set everybody's affairs right, using magic and trickery. The black and white illustrations are impressive, having the precision of Fisher's scratchboard work with some of the drama of early Keeping illustration. Sources for the tales are cited.

575 **Harris,** Christie. *Mouse Woman and the Vanished Princesses;* drawings by Douglas Tait. Atheneum, 1976. 75-23147. 155p. $6.95.

4-6 Six legends of the Northwest Coast Indians are about princesses who vanish, and in each the Mouse Woman is a major character. She is the smallest of the narnauks, the supernatural beings who trick (or steal) people, and she often assumes the shape of a mouse; it is her role to rescue the princesses. One is tricked by the evil arrow-maker who leaves her to be eaten by birds of prey; another, the captive of the Prince-of-Bears, bears him twin sons who can change from human to bear; a third is taken by Great-Whirlpool Maker. Mouse Woman's intercessions are successful more because of wisdom than magic, although she uses both. The stories, which are long and intricate, are based on *Tsimshian Mythology* by Frank Boas and on John Swanton's *Haida Texts and Myths.* The retellings seem overextended, but the book is an excellent source for storytelling.

576 **Harris,** Christie. *Once More Upon a Totem;* illus. by Douglas Tait. Atheneum, 1973. 195p. $5.95.

4-7 Three stories based on legends of Indians of the North West Coast are illustrated with bold, dramatic designs that incorporate the motifs of totem carvings. The first tale is one used by several tribes, an explanation of salmon migration, "The Prince Who Was Taken Away by the Salmon," a long story that explains many cultural patterns of the tribes of the Northern Nations. The second tale, "Raven Traveling," is one of the many legends of a major trickster character, an episodic version that focuses on Raven as a glutton; the third, "Ghost Story," reveals the acceptance of a spirit world in a narrative about a young prince who learns to slip out of his body, join the ghosts, and rescue those who have just died, bringing them back to life. The writing merges the folk style and some modern idiom quite successfully.

577 **Harris,** Rosemary. *Sea Magic; and Other Stories of Enchantment.* Macmillan, 1974. 178p. $5.95.

5-7 Ten legends, each from a different country, are retold in dramatic style. While the stories lack the humor that adds zest to Harris' own books, they are colorful and varied; although there is magic in the tales, and magical beings, the strong characters are human beings, whether they are fighting enchantment or their own frailties. These tales are more difficult to read than is most folk literature adapted for children, but they are well worth the effort for those who can appreciate the rich convolutions of the writing style.

578 **Hart,** Carole. *Delilah;* illus. by Edward Frascino. Harper, 1973. 63p. Trade ed. $3.95; Library ed. $3.79 net.

3-4 Written in a casual, staccato style, short chapters that are distinct episodes give some of the small adventures in the life of a cheerful, rather slapdash ten-year-old. No sexism here: Delilah loves basketball and drumming, her parents both have jobs and take turns doing housework. While the lack of a storyline and the choppy style may seem drawbacks to some readers, the book has some strong assets: Delilah is an engaging character, her relationship with her parents is warm and friendly, the incidents are realistic, and the writing has a casual humor that is appealing.

579 **Härtling,** Peter. *Oma;* illus. by Jutta Ash; tr. by Anthea Bell. Harper, 1977. 76-58719. 95p. Trade ed. $6.95; Library ed. $6.79 net.

3-5 The story of an elderly German woman and her relationship with a small grandson, who comes to live with her when his parents are killed, won the 1976 German Children's Book Award. The writing is direct and rather bland, with interpolated musings (in italics) by

Oma, stressing her viewpoint; in dialogue and exposition her viewpoint is subordinated to that of young Kalle. The two cope with the differences and conflicts imposed by poverty as well as by a situation that has brought striking changes in the lifestyle of each. The book gives a realistic picture of a resilient, courageous older person; while the story line isn't strong, the establishment of milieu and the development of the grandparent-child relationship are.

580 **Haskins,** James S. *Barbara Jordan;* illus. with photographs. Dial, 1977. 77-71522. 192p. $7.95.

7 In describing Barbara Jordan's career, Haskins gives a vivid picture of her vigorous and forceful personality, achieving this not by effusive prose but by letting her words and her accomplishments tell the story. Her record of "firsts" is impressive: the first black woman to become a Texas senator, to sit in the House of Representatives in Washington, to serve during House impeachment proceedings, to give the keynote address at a Democratic National Convention. The writing is balanced, objective, and candid, and it gives fascinating information about political realities, particularly at the state level, as well as about the subject. An index is appended.

581 **Haskins,** James. *Fighting Shirley Chisholm;* illus. with photographs. Dial, 1975. 74-20384. 211p. $5.95.

7-12 A biography of the first black woman to serve in the United States
* Congress gives a good balance of personal and professional material, is written with vigorous admiration, and is candid about incidents not included in other Chisholm biographies written for young people. All her biographers have made it clear that Shirley Chisholm is honest, courageous, and forthright; Haskins stresses the decisions she has had to make about paramount causes: would she take a stand on an issue as a black or as a woman when the stands conflicted, for example. Like Brownmiller' *Shirley Chisholm,* for slightly younger readers, this is a lesson in political structure and in the necessity for practical compromise to achieve idealistic goals.

582 **Haskins,** James. *Religions.* Lippincott, 1973. 157p. $4.95.

6-9 A measured and objective survey of five faiths: Buddhism, Christianity, Hinduism, Islam, and Judaism. The text gives both the historical developments of each religion, including modern practices, sects within them, and founders or major leaders, and also discusses some of the differences in their attitudes about questions of ethical behavior and mores. The descriptions are not comprehensive, but they include major holy days and ritual practices. The writing is serious and straightforward; the book serves as a good introduction to the subject. A bibliography and an index are appended.

583 **Haskins,** James. *Street Gangs, Yesterday and Today;* illus. with prints and photographs. Hastings House, 1974. 155p. $6.95.

8- A sober and sobering history of street gangs from colonial times to the present is based on newspaper accounts and sociological studies. Well-researched and organized, written in strong, direct prose, the book makes clear the facts that street gangs are not a new phenomenon, that there have long been ties of political and criminal nature, and that there are no easy solutions. Haskins points out the conditions of loneliness, poverty, low status, and class distinctions that are conducive to the formation of gangs, to the aggrandizement by members in choosing names and uniform clothing, and to the fierce loyalty within the gang and hostility toward other gangs. A glossary of early gang slang, a bibliography, and an index are appended.

584 **Haskins,** James S. *Who Are the Handicapped?* Doubleday, 1978. 76-2777. 109p. illus. $5.95.

8- Haskins takes a long and sober look at the position of handicapped members of our society, discussing the attitudes of the past and the present, and describing some of the ways "normal" people help or further handicap them now or can further help them in the future. Separate chapters focus on the different types of handicaps, with special emphasis on handicapped children. As in other books by this author, the evidence of careful research is equalled by the high quality of organization and lucidity of the text. A glossary, an index, and an extensive divided bibliography are appended.

585 **Haskins,** James S. *Your Rights Past and Present; A Guide for Young People.* Hawthorn Books, 1975. 74-6665. 122p. $5.95.

7-12 This is not a handbook on the rights of children and young people, but a survey of the development and present status of the rights of youth in five areas: labor, school, justice, in the home, and in choosing a home. In the chapter, "Youth and Rights at Home," for example, the author discusses the first recognition of such rights during the nineteenth century, with intervention by the state in cases of child labor and physical abuse, and with a growing body of cases in which children were removed from homes with deleterious situations. A need, Haskins points out, exists still for healthy alternative housing for children who are taken out of their homes. There has also been a growing body of case law in which courts have decided that parents who are able to do so must provide minor children with a college education. Children still have no control over moneys they may earn—nor over their personal property. In only a few states is it possible for a minor to make a will, and Haskins points out that this is a complex problem and that, like other questions of control, this is one that may well change in the still-shifting area of parent-child relationships and rights. Haskins is tempered and thoughtful, neither defensive nor accusatory, and he concludes by pointing out the fact that many young people are satisfied with the rights they have but should be aware that not all young people are satisfied or, indeed, have those rights, and that all young people's rights are endangered if those rights are denied to any person. A bibliography and an index are appended.

586 **Hauff,** Wilhelm. *The Adventures of Little Mouk;* tr. and ad. by Elizabeth Shub; illus. by Monika Laimgruber. Macmillan, 1975. 74-4420. 34p. $6.95.

4-5 A freely adapted version of the original German fairy tale is illustrated with richly colored pictures in which Laimgruber has used the Turkish setting for including ornate architectural and costume details. Mouk is a dwarf who goes into the world to seek his fortune. His first position is unrewarding, but as he leaves, a friendly dog helps him find a stick and some shoes with magical properties; he next becomes a trusted messenger at the king's court but is accused of having stolen the treasure he has dug up with the help of the magic stick. Sent away in disgrace, Mouk stumbles on a way to take his revenge on the ungrateful monarch, flies off on his magic shoes, and lives ever after in solitary and comfortable circumstances, lonely but respected. The translation is fluent, and the story has many of the attributes of folk literature: the weak overcoming the strong, magical objects, punishment for injustice, the intervention of an animal, and plenty of action.

587 **Haugaard,** Erik Christian. *A Messenger for Parliament.* Houghton, 1976. 76-21737. 218p. $6.95.

7-9 Oliver Cromwell was only a plowman in 1630, when the teller of this tale was born and was named for him, for the young Oliver's shiftless father much admired the strong-willed, contentious Master Cromwell. Young Oliver's life, seen in retrospect when he is an old man in America, changed completely when his beloved mother died in 1641 and he went with his father as camp followers of the Parliamentary Army. Haugaard does a fine job in this historical fiction, focusing attention on the vicissitudes of Oliver's life and on the ordinary people he meets but relating the lives of such people to the cross-currents and fierce allegiances of a divided country. The fictionalizing is used for fiction; Haugaard never falls into the pit of inventing adventures for the historical characters. The writing style has vigor, the plot is well-constructed and paced.

588 **Hautzig,** Deborah. *Hey Dollface.* Greenwillow, 1978. 78-54685. 151p. Trade ed. $6.95; Library ed. $6.67 net.

7-9 Valerie, who tells the story, had met Chloe when they became students at a private school for adolescent girls in Manhattan. Val is interested in boys, but not ready for a sexual relationship; she is puzzled and upset by the discovery that there are elements of sexual excitement in her feeling for Chloe, who has become her best friend. Other aspects of Val's life are included, but not quite enough to give balance to a book that is more a development of a relationship than a development of action. It's capably written, and it explores in honest fashion the confused turbulence of the adolescent who, physically aroused, feels unsure of her sex role. What Val and Chloe, in a frank discussion, decide is that they are not lesbian; they feel that they simply share a love that includes a physical component. "We don't have to fit into any slots," says Chloe, "so let's stop trying."

589 **Hays,** James D. *Our Changing Climate.* Atheneum, 1977. 77-5055. 101p. illus. $6.95.

7- A geologist explains the causes of climatic conditions and the factors that cause changes in them, in a meticulously organized and lucid text. Hays describes first the major influences on earth's temperature and then proceeds to those factors that affect local variations; he also discusses the Ice Ages and theories of future world conditions at length, concluding with separate chapters on man's impact on climate and on the impact of climatic change on man. Skilled at making complicated scientific phenomena clear to the layman, Hays moves from the broad issues to specific matters in exemplary fashion. An index is appended.

590 **Haywood,** Carolyn. *Eddie's Valuable Property;* written and illus. by Carolyn Haywood. Morrow, 1975. 74-17499. 192p. Trade ed. $5.95; Library ed. $5.11 net.

2-4 An inveterate collector of junk, Eddie is dismayed when his father announces that, since they are moving, Eddie must get rid of some of his treasures. Details of Eddie's efforts, his garage sale, and his acquisition of a dog constitute the first third of the story; the second half is set in Eddie's new home. Eddie makes straight for the barn, where he runs into Jimmie (black) who becomes his best friend; together they bring an old cigar-store Indian to school, and together they form a club to which they invite a petulant boy who benefits from their friendship and becomes more amiable. The story ends with a barn party for Eddie's friends, old and new. Like other Haywood books, this is realistic in reflecting children at school and play; there are never serious problems: life is always sunny, and the emphasis is on small events. But they are events that may loom large to children, and concerns are familiar ones, and the style is unassuming and easy to read.

591 **Hazen,** Barbara Shook. *Amelia's Flying Machine;* illus. by Charles Robinson. Doubleday, 1977. 76-51861. 60p. $6.95.

3-4 Based on an incident in Amelia Earhart's childhood, this is a nicely structured story told chiefly through dialogue. Robinson's line drawings echo the breezy style of the writing in sketches that have some Ardizzone-like economy and humor. Left in her grandmother's care, Amelia is resolved that she, her sister, and her cousins will stay out of mischief so that she can earn a promised trip to the World's Fair in Chicago. But the Kansas day is hot, there isn't much to do, and the enterprising Amelia decides to build her own roller coaster, even though she's taunted by her neighbor Jimmy. It is Jimmy, in the end, who keeps Amelia from being punished by insisting that he egged her on. Nice to have a story in which girls are adventurous and in which the author lets the message permeate by osmosis rather than punching it.

592 **Heide,** Florence Parry. *Fables You Shouldn't Pay Any Attention To;* by Florence Parry Heide and Sylvia Worth Van Clief; illus. by Victoria Chess. Lippincott, 1978. 77-14253. 62p. $6.95.

2-4 Although repetitive in pattern, these seven short fables have a bland humor that should appeal to children, for they are the reverse of moral tales. All the other children are careful with their clothes and toys, but careless Genevieve gets all the loot at Christmas because her parents see that the others don't need new belongings. All the other fish eat moderately, but greedy Gretchen says "It pays to be greedy," because the hungry fish pursue worms and are caught. Muriel, a discontented cow, strays over to where the grass looks greener, on the other side of the fence, and it *is* greener, and the farmer's wife gives Muriel a diamond collar. And so on, blithe fables give added zest by the slightly macabre Chess drawings.

593 **Heide,** Florence Parry. *Growing Anyway Up.* Lippincott, 1976. 75-40033. 128p. $5.95.

5-7 Florence Stirkel, who tells the story, is a withdrawn and disturbed child whose undemonstrative mother, a widow, decides to move to Pennsylvania to be near her sister-in-law, Nina. Florence dislikes the private school in which she has been enrolled, and she dislikes the man who courts and later marries her mother. Only Aunt Nina, volatile and affectionate, awakens Florence's interest and gives her self-confidence. Nina, in fact, is Florence's bridge to a stability that is only beginning to be evident by the end of the book. The adult characters are convincing enough but not explored in depth; Florence is. Her fears, her compulsive patterns of behavior (saying words backwards, feeling unsafe unless she looks in certain directions in a certain way a certain number of times) her self-denigration, are depicted with sharp perception.

594 **Heide,** Florence Parry. *When the Sad One Comes to Stay.* Lippincott, 1975. 75-9747. 74p. $4.95.

5-6 It is usually the male who is depicted in our literature as the ruthless person whose successful career has been built on a calculated program of taking care of Number One. In this poignant story told by Sara, it is her shrewd and beautiful mother, Sally, whose goals in the political arena are meant to be achieved by the perfect setting and the right people. And for Sara that means separation from a father deemed "a lazy, slow, stupid ox" by Sally. But her father was love, warmth, laughter, and security to Sara; she finds a substitute adult in Maisie, an old woman who is sloppy and loving. Sally doesn't know about Maisie; they've just moved to a new home where Sara can go to a "good" school, meet the "right" girls, and help bolster Sally's perfectionist image. In a poignant dénouement, Sara not only rejects Maisie but derides her when she must choose between defending the friendship or jeering at it to cement a bond with the "right" girls her mother has arranged an acquaintance with. Sara's careful comments on her mother and her acceptance of Sally's materialistic values are beautifully contrasted with the freedom she enjoys with Maisie and the remembrances of the gaiety and affection in her relationship with her father. Subtle, and perhaps not for every reader, this is a sensitive and convincing study of a child who—torn between two value systems—responds to pressure and example, and chooses the expedient.

595 **Hellberg,** Hans-Eric. *Grandpa's Maria;* tr. from the Swedish by Patricia Crampton; illus. by Joan Sandin. Morrow, 1974. 189p. Trade ed. $4.95; Library ed. $4.59 net.

3-4 Translated from the Swedish, the story of a seven-year-old whose grandfather is the dear and stable person in her life is written in a direct style and with an ingenuous tone that echo the personality of its protagonist. Maria finds it a little difficult to understand why Mama has to go to a rest home, but she feels secure as long as Grandpa is there. She feels somewhat uneasy with her divorced father's second family, but accepts the situation. Hellberg's artistry lies in the fidelity with which he captures the essence of a child who is basically happy: Maria does miss her mother, but that doesn't keep her from being ecstatic at learning to ride a bicycle. Warm, candid, gently humorous, it's a story that has, despite the difference in locale and situation, some of the cozy intimacy of the Moffatt stories.

596 **Hemming,** Roy. *Discovering Music;* Where to Start on Records and Tapes, the Great Composers and Their Works, Today's Major Recording Artists. Four Winds, 1974. 379p. illus. $12.95.

7- Intended for the beginning collector with little or no knowledge of classical music or of the artists who record it, this is a useful compendium of facts and opinions, although there is perhaps more here than a beginner might need or want. A record reviewer for Scholastic Magazines, Hemming prefaces his well-annotated list of "Fifty Composers and Their Major Works," which includes pronunciation of names and advice on recommended recordings, with a series of interviews with musicians, each of whom responds to the proposition that a beginner who can afford only five or six records should buy . . . . and why. The latter section gives such varied opinions that it may be of less value than the author's summary of the suggestions. A final section discusses major music makers on discs and tapes; a glossary and an index are appended.

597 **Hentoff,** Nat. *This School is Driving Me Crazy*. Delacorte, 1975. 75-8003. 160p. $6.95.

5-8 Sam Davidson is a bright, energetic boy with a Big Problem: he doesn't want to attend the school of which his father is headmaster. Father insists. Sam, always in some minor scrape or up to some mischief, is his teachers' despair. When a smaller boy, lying, accuses Sam of being the bully who forced him to steal, matters come to a head; the trio of real bullies is unmasked and expelled, the attitudes of teachers are exposed, and the relationship between Sam and his father improves—with Sam's impending transfer decided on by the end of the story. Sam is an engaging character, and the writing style—in particular the dialogue—is pungent. And a good thing, too, because the messages almost overbalance the narrative. Hentoff is concerned not only about the relationships between father and son, but about the role of the school, the responsibility of the teacher, and relationships between students and teachers. To make his points, he has overdrawn some characters, such as the adamantly hostile teacher Kozodoy or the glib, mendacious brother of one of the three expelled. Yet the issues affect all children in school, public or private, and the minor imbalances of the book are more than compensated for by humor, action, and setting. Note for the shockable: the language is what you might expect in a school for boys.

598 **Heyman,** Anita. *Exit from Home.* Crown, 1977. 234p. $7.50.

6-9 In a novel set in a Russian village just before the revolution, Samuel is a young adolescent whose father is deeply religious and rejoices when the boy is admitted to the Yeshiva, the school where rabbis are trained. But in going to a larger town to attend the school, Samuel meets other young people who have liberal ideas. He not only becomes disenchanted with the strictures of the Yeshiva and drops out, but also becomes involved in the activist movement that preceded the revolution. Witnessing his first pogrom, Samuel decides that he will go to America; the book ends with his hopeful anticipation as he travels. While the message is somber, the writing is not; it is enlivened by good dialogue and by the vivid picture it gives of the Russian Jewish community and its reaction to the first stirrings of rebellion.

599 **Hickman,** Janet. *The Stones;* illus. by Richard Cuffari. Macmillan, 1976. 76-11037. 116p. $6.95.

4-6 In a story set during World War II, a group of boys in a Midwestern town decide that an elderly and eccentric German-American is an enemy. They had already been teasing old Jack Tramp, but when Garrett, the protagonist, learns that Jack's real name is Adolph Schilling, he and his friends really persecute the man. Chasing the boys, old Jack stumbles and his gun goes off, killing a dog that had followed one of the boys. Garrett is indignant along with the others, but he is uncomfortably conscious of the fact that Jack was justifiably provoked: they had been taking cans from his storage shed. Garrett's family invites Jack to dinner, and Garrett sees that the old man is odd but harmless. When Jack and Garrett rescue the latter's small sister, trapped in swirling waters on a stone ledge, Jack goes to a hospital and is destined for the County Farm. And Garrett knows, in his pity for old Jack, that his own actions were reprehensible; he has learned something about prejudice and he has lost a measure of the innocence of childhood. Hickman's characters are strongly delineated, her plot believable, and her message about human relationships and bias convincing and clear without being pushed.

600 **Hieatt,** Constance, ad. *The Castle of Ladies;* illus. by Norman Laliberte. T. Y. Crowell, 1973. 72p. $4.50.

5-7 Another romantic quest of Sir Gawain is adroitly retold in a graceful and flowing style, the material adapted from several threads of the Arthurian fabric. Spurned by the Lady Maudisante, Gawain nevertheless sets out to rescue her sister, who is the captive of a wicked enchanter and is guarded by a fearful monster. Sir Gawain has several adventures en route, all of them tied neatly into his major quest. Naturally, he triumphs over adversity, overcomes a manticore and a basilisk, wins the respect and love of the disdainful Maudisante, rescues the prisoner, and gains the magical Sword of the Strange Scabbard for his own. Wonderful to read alone, to read aloud, to use for storytelling.

601 **Hieatt,** Constance, ad. *The Minstrel Knight;* retold by Constance Hieatt; illus. by James Barkley. T. Y. Crowell, 1974. 99p. $5.95.

5-7 A version of the story of Orpheus blends elements of previous variants, and the author, a medieval scholar, adds some embellishments of her own—and in her flowing, grave style the legend gains a stern reality that is a firm base for the magic and the romance of the tale. The illustrations echo both elements; they are intricate and delicate in detail but strong—at times stark—in composition. Sir Orfeo, visiting at Camelot and charming the court with his minstrelsy, is called home by his loyal follower because a wicked steward has seized power and imprisoned the lady Etain, Orfeo's wife. The steward is sent away and is killed by the Wild Hunt of the Faerie Folk. No "little people" these, but a band ruled by the cruel fairy king who captures Etain, rescued by Orfeo after a long search. Orfeo's harping is a major part of the tale: this is how he gains Etain, this is how he wins her back from Midir; and it is by his harp that his people know him when he returns, a ragged minstrel, to test their devotion.

602 **Hildick,** Edmund Wallace. *Louie's Ransom.* Knopf, 1978. 77-21240. 184p. Trade ed. $6.95; Library ed. $6.99 net.

5-7 In a fourth book about the terse disciplinarian Louie, an English milkman whose "boys" have remembered him with deep affection as they moved from being his helpers to being famous actors or lawyers, Louie comes to the United States and is kidnapped. Ransom is demanded for him and for the daughter of a wealthy American; the two English boys who've come over with Louie are also taken. It's a race against time as Louie's influential friends, the F.B.I., and the shrewd protagonist match wits with the mysterious organizer of the kidnapping. Hildick doesn't ever mean the reader to quite believe the excesses of his tale, but there's enough realism and suspense to make it almost credible and certainly exciting; there are no comic lines, but there's ample humor in the situation.

603 **Hildick,** E. W. *Louie's Snowstorm;* illus. by Iris Schweitzer. Doubleday, 1974. 198p. $4.95.

5-7 Remember Louie, the English milkman who so rigorously screened and disciplined his assistants that they were super-efficient, devoted to their leader, and loyal even when they were famous years later? Taciturn and demanding as ever, Louie is appalled when he is saddled by a company official with a newcomer he hasn't tested and chosen. Worse, an American. Worse still, a girl! Tim and Smitty, his helpers, are delighted with Pat; she's pretty, bright, and willing to work as hard as they must. Although Pat makes a few errors during the busy day-before-Christmas rush, she proves herself a heroine repeatedly, since she has gone to an extraordinary school where she's learned judo (good for repelling rival milkboys and thieves) and delivering babies (good for delivering babies). Fast-paced and funny, with lively characters, a good setting, a distinctive writing style, and the added appeal of being a Christmas story—with a difference.

604 **Hill,** Helen, comp. *New Coasts & Strange Harbors;* Discovering Poems; selected by Helen Hill and Agnes Perkins; illus. by Clare Romano and John Ross. T. Y. Crowell, 1974. 283p. $5.95.

7- Although there is little representation here of protest poetry, the anthology does—as the jacket claims—contain much of the best work of poets of the mid-twentieth century. The poems are grouped under such headings as "Looking at People," "Listening to People," "Still Lifes and Moving Pictures," "The Swift Seasons Roll," and "With a Hey, Ho, the Wind and the Rain." Most of the selections are brief and lyric, few are humorous. The standard of quality is pervasively high; some of the poets most heavily represented are Robert Hayden, Seamus Heaney, Donald Justice, Archibald Macleish, Theodore Roethke, Mark Van Doren, and Richard Wilbur. Separate author, title, and first line indexes are appended.

605 **Hilton,** Suzanne. *The Way it Was—1876.* Westminster, 1975. 74-20665. 216p. illus. $6.95.

6- A detailed discussion of what life was like in the year the United States became one hundred years old ought to be informative and dull; it has no right to be as entertaining as Suzanne Hilton makes it as she describes clothing, education (the incident in which an elocution teacher trains her class to lilt is hilarious), sports, medicine, clothing, home manufacture (one concoction for soft skin sent a girl to bed, the author says, "smelling like a macaroon.") and travel. And much, much more. Based on thorough research but written with spontaneity, the book is both amusing and useful. An extensive bibliography and an index are appended.

606 **Hirsch,** S. Carl. *Meter Means Measure;* The Story of the Metric System. Viking, 1973. 126p. $4.95.

6-10 With the slow but imminent change that will take place in the United States when the conversion to the metric system begins, books like this and Branley's *Think Metric!* for younger readers, can pave the way for comprehension both of the need for change and of the system itself. The first part of the text discusses the various systems of measurement that obtained in history, including the plan for revision, drawn up by Jefferson and never adopted, that would simplify and codify measurements in the new United States. The metric system was used throughout most of the world, but America's ties were to Britain and the British system of measurement. In 1866, a law was passed that permitted use of the metric system here, but it took years before the National Bureau of Standards came up with a report (1971) that recommended adoption of a metric system. Hirsch describes some of the ways in which we have already incorporated the system and discusses its advantages. The text is occasionally discursive, but it is sprightly in tone and informative. A set of metric tables, some suggestions for additional reading, and an index are appended.

607 **Hirsh,** Marilyn. *Could Anything Be Worse?* A Yiddish tale retold and illus. by Marilyn Hirsh. Holiday House, 1974. 28p. $4.95.

K-3 A tale found in many cultures, here adapted from the Yiddish version, is nicely told and illustrated. Dissatisfied with the way his family behaves, a man takes the advice of a friend and goes to the Rabbi for counsel. The Rabbi will answer no questions, but tells the man to bring chickens into the house, then a cow, then some relatives. The small house is noisy and crowded. Again the man goes to the Rabbi; the relatives are sent off, then the cow, then the chickens. The family throws open the windows and cleans and polishes, and settles down in peace. "Shalom," says the father to his happy family, "Our home is a paradise now." One of the most durable of the count-your-blessings tales, gently humorous, is pleasant to read alone or aloud, although the format indicates wider read-aloud use.

608 **Hitchcock,** Gordon, comp. *Let Joybells Ring; Carols for Christmas From Many Nations;* arranged by Ian Copley. David and Charles, 1975. 74-82826. 96p. $8.95.

4- This isn't at all the traditional collection of familiar songs; most of the best-known carols of the English language are missing. But those are easily obtainable elsewhere, and for devoted singers who want to extend their repertoire, this should be a delightful addition. It contains the melodic line, fairly simple piano accompaniment, and often one added feature such as notation for chime-bars, castanets, or descant recorder. The songs have been gathered from sixteen countries; unfortunately, there is no index or access to the songs by language or country of origin, although such information appears on the music page. Occasionally there are explanatory notes; for example, one such note describes the manner in which St. Lucia's Day is celebrated in Sweden, another explains a Latin phrase used in a carol. The small print unfortunately makes the music hard to read.

609 **Hoban,** Lillian. *Arthur's Honey Bear;* story and pictures by Lillian Hoban. Harper, 1974. 64p. (I Can Read Books) Trade ed. $2.95; Library ed. $3.43 net.

1-2 The engaging pictures may show Arthur and his sister to be chimpanzees, but they're really children in disguise, funny enough to entertain beginning independent readers and childlike enough to evoke empathy. Arthur decides to sell all his old toys, and he puts a price tag on everything except his old bear. The sale is a failure, since all the goods are dilapidated and the one attractive item—Honey Bear—is the one thing Arthur balks at selling. His sister bribes him into selling his dearest toy, and Arthur regrets it, but he adjusts nicely after conceiving the thought that he is now Honey Bear's uncle, and uncles take their nephews out for treats and play with them. The writing is simple, the dialogue natural, and the gentle humor icing on the cupcake.

610 **Hoban,** Lillian. *Arthur's Pen Pal;* story and pictures by Lillian Hoban. Harper, 1976. 75-6289. 64p. (I Can Read Book). Trade ed. $3.95; Library ed. $3.79 net.

K-2 Another story about that beguiling child in chimpanzee form, Arthur. Here he wistfully contrasts his sister Violet, who squabbles and teases, with the sibling relationship enjoyed by his pen pal, Sandy. Sandy has a big brother who does karate with him. They Indian wrestle. All that little Violet can do is skip rope. Then Arthur discovers that Sandy is a girl, that she beats her brother at karate. Suddenly Violet seems satisfactory to him, and he writes his pen pal a letter that boasts of Violet's prowess at skipping Red Hot Pepper and double loop-the-loop. A conventional view of sex roles, but a very funny one, is given in a story told very simply, with dialogue that is truly childlike and pictures that capture the busy enthusiasm of childhood.

611 **Hoban,** Lillian. *Arthur's Prize Reader;* written and illus. by Lillian Hoban. Harper, 1978. 77-25637. 64p. (I Can Read Books) Trade ed. $4.95; Library ed. $5.79 net.

1-2 All things change, and in this fourth book about the small chimp Arthur and his little sister Violet, Arthur must reluctantly accept the fact that Violet has learned to read. A light but amusing fictional framework (little Violet is more discerning than her brother in spotting the prize in a contest) shows how quickly the beginning independent reader can move from "easy" to "hard" words, as Arthur challenges Violet's ability. An amiable little story provides good practice for the beginning reader and has enough humor and action to hold the attention of the lap audience as well.

612 **Hoban,** Russell C. *Arthur's New Power;* illus. by Byron Barton. T. Y. Crowell, 1978. 77-11550. 39p. Trade ed. $5.95; Library ed. $5.79 net.

K-3 Remember Arthur, who had *Dinner at Alberta's?* Arthur's into guitar-playing now, but when his Dracula Hi-Vamp amplifier is added to the other electrical gadgets, the fuse blows. The family tries to get along without plugging in anything, but they tire of going out for Chinese food just because the stove doesn't work. Anyway, there's a power cut and the waiter brings a candle. This amusing thrust at the electronic age ends with Arthur's discovery that he can play the guitar without plugging it into anything. Barton's illustrations aren't his best, but they are adequate, and the story has enough humor and pace to stand on its own.

613 **Hoban,** Russell C. *Dinner at Alberta's;* illus. by James Marshall. T. Y. Crowell, 1975. 73-94796. 36p. Trade ed. $5.50; Library ed. $6.25 net.

K-2 Other illustrators have worked successfully with Russell Hoban,
* but it would be hard to envision a better matching of text and illustration than he and James Marshall achieve here. The pictures have a rakish flair that fits the sensible nonsense of the story admirably; the crocodile characters have a seriocomic blandness. Arthur is—let's face it—a slob, the despair of his family. And then love finds a way. His sister's friend Alberta, with whom he is smitten, invites Arthur and his sister to dinner. Arthur practices his table manners, which have been ghastly, and delivers a stellar performance, taking a brief time out to teach Alberta's obnoxious brother a lesson in how to treat a guest. That's the best part, he concludes, teaching manners to others. Hoban's humor lies both in the situation and in the writing style. When Arthur's mother and a friend are exchanging condolences on their children's behavior, for example, "'I suppose we all have our troubles,' said Mrs. Crocodile, and both ladies bought new hats." Arthur's week of practicing table manners is hilarious, and if he's meant to teach a lesson to the audience, they won't mind knowing about it.

614 **Hoban,** Russell C. *How Tom Beat Captain Najork and His Hired Sportsmen;* illus. by Quentin Blake. Atheneum, 1974. 30p. $6.95.

3-5 Hoban in a frolicsome-sophisticated mood is perfectly matched by the tearaway panache of Blake; although some younger children may enjoy hearing the book read aloud (the publishers suggest a K-4 audience) there seems so much that an independent reader can appreciate in wordplay and concept that it is more appropriate for the middle grades. Given to compulsive fooling around, Tom is repeatedly threatened by his cast-iron aunt (Fidget Wonkham-Strong) with retribution and discipline in the form of the hearty captain and his team. When they appear, the games they play—intended to belittle Tom—are all to do with mud, or climbing, or teetering, all the things Tom has perfected in his fooling around. So Tom offers to trade Aunt Fidget for the captain's pedal boat if he wins. Tom wins 85 to 10, the captain weeps, and the champion fooler-around goes off to live with Aunt Bundlejoy Cosysweet. Very tongue-in-cheeky, great fun.

615 **Hoban,** Russell C. *A Near Thing for Captain Najork;* illus. by Quentin Blake. Atheneum, 1976. 75-29464. 30p. $7.95.

3-5 A sequel to *How Tom Beat Captain Najork and His Hired Sportsman* is just as delightfully daft a tale, with Blake's vigorous paintings a medley of ersatz Victoriana and *Punch* cartoon style. Tom, the boy who knows how to putter about, builds a jam-powered frog vehicle; he is spotted and followed by the captain (traveling, with his stalwarts, in a mechanical snake) who is still smarting from the defeat suffered in the first book. Somehow the chase gets complicated by the fact that the captain's militant wife suspects him of dallying with the headmistress at a girl's school and challenges her supposed rival at arm wrestling. And through it all, Aunt Bundlejoy Cosysweet amicably drifts about with flowers springing wildly from her hat and her long, long hair floating in the breeze. Written and illustrated with comic genius.

616 **Hoban,** Russell C. *Ten What? A Mystery Counting Book;* illus by Sylvie Selig. Scribner, 1975. 75-2747. 21p. $6.95.

3-5 yrs. Perhaps it takes a poet to conceive a counting book that is also a mystery story; the versatile Mr. Hoban has, with the collusion of an artist equally tongue-in-cheek, produced a book that should amuse as much as it instructs. An urgent message, "Get Ten," is passed up from a manhole to a beak-nosed detective (who is, in fact, a bird) and the chase is on. The ending is a surprise, but in the course of the search, animals romp through surreal urban scenes. On the page for "7," for example, the text reads, "Seven houses were searched," and there are also seven police cars, seven large shoes, sets of seven windows per house, seven outsize butterflies, seven chairs out on the sidewalk, et cetera.

617 **Hoberman,** Mary Ann. *Nuts to You & Nuts to Me;* illus. by Ronni Solbert. Knopf, 1974. 26p. Trade ed. $4.95; Library ed. $5.59 net.

3-6 yrs. Short poems that have a lilting breeziness are illustrated by lively pictures (unfortunately printed in rather flat colors) that capture the mood of the writing. Sample: "Balloons to blow/ Balloons to burst/ The blowing's best/ The bursting's worst!" or "Pockets hold things/ Pockets hide things/ Special private dark inside things/ Pockets save things/ Pockets keep things/ Secret silent way down deep things." Visually, there is no emphasis on the letters of the alphabet, but the reader-aloud can stress them, and the poems are child-centered, pleasant to read aloud, and eminently memorizable.

618 **Hoberman,** Mary Ann. *The Raucous Auk; A Menagerie of Poems;* illus. by Joseph Low. Viking, 1973. 43p. $4.95.

K-3 One of the most engaging collections of poems about animals to be published in a long time is illustrated with raffish drawings that echo the cheerful tone of the writing. Some of the poems are haiku-brief, some are free verse, some patterned, and almost all of them give information that is accurate and unobtrusive—but any lesson to be learned is ancillary; this is a book that's full of wit and humor, these are poems that are deft and memorable.

619 **Hobson,** Sam B. *The Lion of the Kalahari;* by Sam B. and George Carey Hobson; tr. and ad. from the Afrikaans by Esther Linfield; 3rd ed. Greenwillow, 1976. 76-3432. 118p. Trade ed. $6.95; Library ed. $5.94 net.

5-8 Long a popular tale in southern Africa, this saga of survival is smoothly translated by a South African now resident in the United States. Skankwan, when an evil schemer took over the leadership of the tribe of Bushmen of which Skankwan's grandfather was leader, was left alone in the desert when his father was murdered. Only eight, the boy had already learned many of the hunting and survival skills necessary for a desert existence, and he lived for the day when he could avenge his father. He does; at sixteen he becomes the Lion of the Kalahari, young but a leader of men. The Hobsons create the desert setting and the desert lore most vividly, and in their taut story they show both respect for the Bushmen and knowledge of the culture. An illustrated glossary is appended.

620 **Hobzek,** Mildred. *We Came a-Marching . . . 1, 2, 3;* illus. by William Pène du Bois. Parents' Magazine, 1978. 78-7793. 29p. Trade ed. $5.95; Library ed. $5.41 net.

4-7 yrs. The distinctive palette and engaging details of Pène du Bois' painting add beauty to a rhyming narrative that teaches its young audience how to count 1, 2, 3 in twelve languages. Sample: "On a sunny morning / We were called for duty / We came a-marching, one, two, three / Sacha, Stanislav and me / We came a-marching one, two, three / Sacha, Stanislav and me!" Next the three digits are in German, next in Russian, then Polish: "We must see those birdies / But we had no ladder / How could we do it, jeden, dwa, trzy / Sacha, Stanislav and me / How could we do it, *YEH-den, dvah, tshee* / Sacha, Stanislav and me." Italics are used here to show the words printed in red in the book. The story follows three children in their imaginative play as they examine the nest of a huge bird and have other adventures; based on a German folktale, the poem is set to the music of a traditional Slavic marching song, the notation of which is provided at the back of the book. Great fun.

621 **Hodges,** Cyril Walter. *Plain Lane Christmas;* written and illus. by Cyril Walter Hodges. Coward, 1978. 77-17233. 29p. $7.95.

4-7
*
A small, quaint English street sandwiched between a busy, modern business district and major highway, Plain Lane has small shops above which the residents live. And one empty shop owned by a woman who tries to sound refined and says "naice" for "nice" and "taidy" for "tidy." Threatened by demolition, the children of Plain Lane follow a reporter's suggestion that they try to save the street. A massive Christmas celebration is organized (no plastic trees or reindeer, only the genuine articles) and the quaint little street with its bow windows and gables gets publicity, sympathy, and reprieve. "May goodness," says the refined Mrs. Maidey at the end of the tale, "we were only just in taim!" Hodges' paintings are superb, especially those in color; the architectural details are exact, and the crowd scenes seem full of vitality rather than seeming simply crowded. The story is told with a light touch, and has convincing dialogue, good structure, and a believable contribution by the children, who organize a very popular children's bazaar.

622 **Hodges,** Cyril Walter. *Playhouse Tales;* illus. by the author. Coward, 1975. 168p. $7.95.

7-10 Six tales of the Elizabethan theater are written in a sedate style; despite the fact that many have action, the expository passages tend to be long-winded. However, the stories are about such eminent figures as Burbage, Shakespeare, and Jonson; they are full of authentic details and language, they are historically based, and they are written by an authority on the subject. And the author-artist's sketches are lively and humorous, so the book's strength far outbalances its weakness of writing style. The most entertaining of the six tales describes the legal battle between the Burbage family and Giles Allen, who owned the land on which the first of the theaters was built and who refused to renew the lease—so the Burbages cunningly dismantled "The Theatre," the original building, and put it up again on the south bank of the Thames. They called it "The Globe."

623 **Hodges,** Margaret. *The Freewheeling of Joshua Cobb;* illus. by Richard Cuffari. Farrar, 1974. 111p. $5.95.

4-7 It was a marvelous plan, Josh thought. His former camp counselor, Dusty, would be the leader of the bicycle camping trip and Dusty's friend Muff would use one of her family's farm trucks as the supply truck. Best of all, the girl with whom Josh was smitten, Helen, would be one of the group. But Helen had to have a tonsillectomy and her sister Cassandra turned out to be not unlike Helen but—in Josh's opinion—a freak. A natural food nut. Insisted her name was Crane, not Cassandra. Mixed with the irritation of getting along with Crane were the many joys of being with friends, camping, seeing the sea for the first time, and feeling that he could cope with trouble—and by the end of the trip, Josh realized he had even learned to enjoy Crane for being different, the very thing he'd found irksome. Primarily this is a sunny vacation story filled with small adventures and new experiences, but—as in the earlier books about Joshua Cobb—there's a realistic steady growth toward maturity as Josh learns to compromise, not to prejudge. The writing style has vitality, the characters individuality.

624 **Hodgson,** Mary Anne. *Fast and Easy Needlepoint;* by Mary Anne Hodgson and Josephine Ruth Paine; photographs by Michael Pitts and Richard Fowlkes. Doubleday, 1978. 76-56302. 96p. $5.95.

4-7 An exemplary do-it-yourself book gives helpful general directions and clear step-by-step instructions for seven simple projects; explanations and diagrams for basic stitches are integrated into the projects. The authors continue with a section on making your own designs and they include tips on coping with mistakes, finishing off needlepoint work or adjusting it if it is out of shape. Both text and photographs indicate that this is an occupation for both girls and boys.

625 **Hogrogian,** Nonny, ad. *The Contest;* ad. and illus. by Nonny Hogrogian. Greenwillow, 1976. 75-40389. 27p. $7.95.

3-5 Hogrogian's illustrations (some brisk little black and white line drawings; some ebullient, richly colored pencil drawings) have an earthy humor; her retelling of an amusing folktale is direct and unassuming, letting the humor emerge without directing the reader's attention to it. Two robbers, one of whom operates by day and the other by night, discover, when they meet on their journeys, that they are both engaged to the same perfidious girl. They decide to see which of them is more clever, and most of the story is concerned with the ploys they pull off in this contest, which concludes with the two clever robbers deciding they are too good for the faithless girl and that they will go into business in their new high-potential territory.

626 **Holl,** Adelaide. *The Parade;* illus. by Kjell Ringi. Watts, 1975. 72-3840. 32p. $5.90.

3-6 yrs. First of all, there are the parade participants: a flamboyantly-uniformed leader, a flag-bearer, four musicians, three dignitaries, and a row of identical tubby gentlemen. Second, they march dauntlessly up a giraffe's neck (they're tiny) or down a steep rock to the sea, and into the sea, and so on. The martial verse asserts their purpose and drive: "The drummer's beat / Speaks loud and clear / We never stop / We know no fear / Plinkety plonk / Tideli plonk / Nothing can stop us / Nothing can stop us!" But there's a surprise ending, something does stop the parade, a small thing so lovely that they all must stop to admire it. The verse is bouncy, the idea fresh, and the pictures bright and humorous.

627 **Holland,** Isabelle. *Alan and the Animal Kingdom.* Lippincott, 1977. 76-55371. 190p. $6.95.

5-7 In the twelve years he's lived, Alan has been shunted from one relative to another. An orphan, he is living with a great-aunt who dies, unidentified, in a New York hospital, and Alan decides he's going to keep her death a secret because he's convinced that the authorities will dispose of his beloved pets. Since Aunt Jessie was active in her church and community, there are many inquisitive friends to whom Alan lies, but his inventions about her absence from home and the fact that she doesn't respond to telephone messages become more and more suspect. He tells one classmate and, in desperation, a veterinarian to whom he's taken a sick pet. Dr. Harris, an alcoholic vet, becomes fond of the boy, even giving up liquor to win Alan's respect and confidence; even with his help, Alan is not able to keep up the pretense, and the school head finds out the truth. The book ends on an encouraging note but a realistic one, and the somber plight of the lonely child is alleviated by some deftly woven minor themes and even some lighter moments. What Holland has achieved here is the creation of a believable character in an unusual situation, and her book is rounded out by a group of strongly depicted minor characters, a convincing picture of an urban neighborhood community, and the depth and polish of the writing style.

628 **Holland,** Isabelle. *Dinah and the Green Fat Kingdom.* Lippincott, 1978. 78-8612. 189p. $7.95.

5-7 There have been other books about fat children, but few have explored causes and reactions with as much depth and perception as this. Dinah's twelve, the only girl in a family of four; her father is understanding but her mother (well organized, determined, and "task-oriented") nags and nags about Dinah's weight and diet. Having a puppy helps a bit, but not enough to compensate for sharing her bedroom with an irritatingly perfectionist cousin, Brenda, recently orphaned, or for the teasing of her brothers and classmates. While getting counseling with Sister Elizabeth, a nutritionist, who works at a school for special children, Dinah becomes friendly with a handicapped boy and finds some consolation in that friendship; her real consolation, however, is in the dreaming (some of it vengeful, some optimistic) and writing she does: her "Green Fat Kingdom." When a combination of circumstances makes her plight seem unbearable, Dinah erupts; she pours out her bitterness at the dinner table, including her anger at her brothers, her dislike of Brenda, her resentment against her parents, and her belief that her mother doesn't love her, certainly cares more for Brenda—and then she runs out of the house. Hours later, her father brings her home and she has long, candid talks with each parent in turn. There's a clearing of the air that promises better future relations, but Holland never promises Dinah a rose garden; she's lost only five pounds, there's been no change in the behavior of her peers, and the new parental rapport is a hopeful sign but not an unrealistic capitulation. The writing style is smooth, with good dialogue and excellent characterization; it is, however, an insight into motivations and relationships that the author excels.

629 **Holland,** Isabelle. *Of Love and Death and Other Journeys.* Lippincott, 1975. 159p. $5.95.

7-10 Meg's parents had been divorced before she was born, and she had lived happily with her mother in Europe, helping guide sightseers, becoming familiar with the languages and the culture of half a dozen countries. She liked her stepfather, she doted on the young artist, Cotton, who was part of their household—but she was curious about her father. She knew that her mother had had an affair and left her father; she learned that he had not known there was a child. Meg is appalled when she learns that her mother has cancer, doubly appalled after the operation, when the doctor gives no hope. And then her father comes to Perugia. It is hard enough, at fifteen, to accept a stranger as father; it is even harder, when her mother dies, for Meg to go to New York with him and start a new life in a strange place. This is a sophisticated book; Holland does not talk down to her readers by explaining references made by the cosmopolitan characters. They are superbly drawn, and the relationships are equally strong. The book ends on a hopeful note, as Meg is helped by her stepmother to face her grief, and it is lightened by the humor of the dialogue throughout all but the ending of the story.

630 **Holman,** Felice. *The Drac;* French Tales of Dragons and Demons; by Felice Holman and Nanine Valen; illus. by Stephen Walker. Scribner, 1975. 75-4029. 84p. $6.95.

4-6 The authors have deftly synthesized, in five fantastic stories from French folklore, material from all of the versions they found. Although most of the tales get off to a start that is slowed by rather elaborate descriptions (The Drac is described: "There in the river some terrified folk might glimpse him occasionally, enormous and lizard-like, naked as a worm, willowy as a lamprey, with two fins of transparent blue lace on his back, webbed feet like the flamingo of the Camargue, and long greenish hair which floated like algae on the waves,"), they soon move into action and they are told in high style. Each story is followed by notes on its source and by bibliographic references.

631 **Holman,** Felice. *The Escape of the Giant Hogstalk;* illus. by Ben Shecter. Scribner, 1974. 96p. $5.95.

3-6 While there have been other fantasies about forms of plant life that run amok, none has the wry humor of this tale, Holman's style is bland and smooth, an effective foil for the nonsensical events of the plot; while her major character seems exaggerated (fumbling amateur chemist who is tolerated by his wealthy family, Anthony Wilson-Brown is a bit too silly to be believable) he is undeniably funny. The illustrations are amusing, too. Anthony W-B and his young nephew Lawrence stumble on the giant hogstalk while on a Caucasian holiday, present seeds to the staff at Kew Gardens, and are honored. The giant hogstalk malevolently grows and bursts through the top of the greenhouse, scattering its seeds, it starts an avalanche of severe rashes. Anthony and Lawrence, each working on a project (Elixir of Life and False Fox-scent) throw their mixtures out of a window and discover that they have found a cure for the rash that has puzzled doctors and aroused parliamentary concern. Anthony again receives a medal from the Society of Royal Biologists. The giant hogstalk bides its time.

632 **Holman,** Felice. *I Hear You Smiling and Other Poems;* illus. by Laszlo Kubinyi. Scribner, 1973. 62p. $4.95.

3-5 Delicate line drawings illustrate a collection of poems that are varied: lively or wistful, thoughtful or ebullient, the poems capture a child's mood or the avanescence of natural beauty. Some are metered, some free verse, all are charming to read alone or aloud.

633 **Holman,** Felice. *Slake's Limbo.* Scribner, 1974. 117p. $5.95.

5-7 Small, myopic, a target for bullies, thirteen-year-old Aremis Slake, a tenement latch-key child, was running from a pursuing gang in the subway when he jumped to the track bed—and that's how he found his limbo, his hideaway. A miscalculation in construction had created a chamber under New York's Commodore Hotel. Slake stayed there for four months, his occupation ending with his illness and the announcement of tunnel repair that would mean the discovery of his secret limbo. The story of his tenure is a remarkably taut and convincing account of resourcefulness and tenacity, with something of a Crusoe appeal. The setting is novel (save for Selden's animals), the protagonist depicted vividly, and the writing style smooth and sophisticated, with Slake's forays out of his subway home affording variety and contrast.

634 **Holz,** Loretta. *Mobiles You Can Make;* illus. with drawings by the author; photographs by George and Loretta·Holz. Lothrop, 1975. 75-8994. 128p. Trade ed. $5.95; Library ed. $5.11 net.

5-9 A very good book for the beginner, with helpful diagrams, clear explanations, and step-by-step instructions for making variants of three kinds of mobiles: string-hung, wire-armed, and base-hung. The author lists materials and describes techniques, encouraging the reader to design original mobiles; in the chapters on the three types, the examples progress from simpler projects to those more difficult. A bibliography, a list of sources of supplies, and an index are appended.

635 **Honig,** Donald. *Way to Go, Teddy.* Watts, 1973. 147p. $4.95.

6-9 Ted's father wanted his boy to be not just good, but the best. The best lawyer in town, that is. What Ted wanted was to play professional ball, and he finally managed to overcome his father's objections. Ted's brief career with a minor league team was pure glory, but when he was moved up to a better team, he slumped—and invented an impressive record for his father's benefit. When his father brought a busload of friends to see the "star", Ted was trapped—but his father was unexpectedly encouraging when he learned the truth, and Ted faced going back to the Class D team with courage and equanimity. This has more depth than most baseball stories, and the details of a rookie's life are lively and authentic. The author was a professional ball player.

636 **Hoople,** Cheryl G., comp. *As I Saw It: Women Who Lived the American Adventure.* Dial, 1978. 78-51324. 187p. $8.95.

6-
* A series of letters, journal and diary excerpts, and other historical documents gives varied and absorbing accounts of some of the

adventures and accomplishments in the lives of women in American history. A few are well known—such people as Narcissa Whitman, Abigail Adams, or Clara Barton—and in the statements by them and others (slaves, doctors, spies, pioneers, early colonists in California or New England) there are both personal troubles and triumphs, and a broad view of American history. Each excerpt is prefaced by the compiler's introduction, and the whole has a wonderful vitality, from Lady Margaret Wyatt's despondent letter to her sister, written in 1623, to the commentary by Mary Antin, a Jewish immigrant who came to America in 1894.

637 **Hoover,** H. M. *The Lion's Cub.* Four Winds, 1974. 211p. $5.95.

6-9 Jemal-Edin, son of the Imam Shamil, yearns for the day when he will be old enough to join his father's forces in the holy war (1800–1859) against the detested infidel Christians, the Russians. Trapped in their mountain fortress, the remnants of the Imam's forces are forced to yield Jemal-Edin as hostage to the Czar, and the boy goes from a backward civilization to the luxury of the St. Petersburg court. Recalcitrant and bitter at first, he becomes softened by the kindness of Nicholas I and the affection of the family with whom the Czar has placed him; he decides to learn as much as he can so that he can help and guide his own people when he returns to the mountains. This historical novel has an impressive consistency of period detail, historical fact, and dialogue; it has action, contrast, an exotic setting and a strong protagonist. *And* a powerful ending. A bibliography is appended.

638 **Hoover,** H. M. *The Rains of Eridan.* Viking, 1977. 77-23533. 183p. $7.95.

6-8 A science fantasy is set on an earth-type planet, peaceful and beautiful, and inhabited by odd beasts. Theo, camping alone in the hills while doing biological research, is horrified to see the Orlovs, eminent scientists, killed by laser rays; the murderers flee, leaving the Orlov's only child, Karen, hiding behind a rock. The woman and the girl become close companions, and they discover a strange creature in a cave. Back at the base settlement, Theo learns that the obsessive fear that has affected most of the staff (and apparently caused the Orlovs' death) is linked to the beautiful crystals that most of them have been hoarding, and they—in turn—are linked to the cave creature. The author has knit deftly the two threads of the plot, the solution to the crippling fear, and Theo's desire to adopt Karen despite prohibitive regulations. The writing is smooth, sophisticated, and at times slowed by descriptive passages; it poses a dramatic situation, however, with a good building of suspense.

639 **Hoover,** H. M. *Treasures of Morrow.* Four Winds, 1976. 75-28098. 171p. $6.95.

5-7 A sequel to *Children of Morrow* in which two children from a primitive and harsh community of the future run away and find that they have been in telepathic communication with the people of a highly civilized culture. Now Tia and Rabbit live with the Morrowans, refining their parapsychological powers and enjoying the peace, prosperity, and learning of their new home. The story concludes with an exciting episode in which a scientific expedition is made to the children's old home, where the fearful, ignorant villagers attack the Morrowans, and where Tia realizes that she need no longer feel guilt about her new loyalty to Morrow. Hoover has created a most convincing world of the future, a believable Utopia, and her story has impact and impetus.

640 **Hopf,** Alice. *Biography of an Ostrich;* illus. by Ben F. Stahl. Putnam, 1975. 72-95562. 63p. $4.29.

2-4 Ozzie has a name, but there is no anthropomorphism in this smoothly written continuous text that describes the life cycle of an ostrich. The simple prose has a narrative flow, and the text incorporates facts about mating and breeding, parental care, predators, diet, and the elaborate courtship display of the male who has chosen a mate and a nesting site. Details about other animals of the African veld are included; the illustrations are attractive.

641 **Hopf,** Alice. L. *Misplaced Animals and Other Living Creatures;* illus. with photographs and drawings. McGraw-Hill, 1976. 75-10952. 136p. $5.72.

6-9 A survey of the problems that can arise when alien fauna and flora are introduced into a stable ecology. Although the cactus and the water hyacinth are imported pests, most of the creatures described are animals, and they have caused damage to buildings, livestock, food crops, industries, and human beings. Hopf also discusses a few imports that have been benign: pheasants, brown trout, and striped bass. In each case there is an explanation of breeding habits and of the methods of control that have been tried with varying degrees of success. The text is written in crisp but not oppressively dry style; the print is somewhat crowded. A substantial bibliography and an index are appended.

642 **Hopkins,** Lee Bennett. *Mama.* Knopf, 1977. 76-47628. 90p. $4.95.

3-5 You'll remember Mama. Tough, cheerfully vulgar in her tastes (she scorns real flowers, preferring plastic; she scoffs at African violets because they're foreign flowers), passionately dedicated to seeing that her two sons whose father has decamped have everything they need. But Mama also wants the boys to have everything they want, so she steals. When she works for a butcher, she steals steaks; when she works in a department store, she steals clothes; when she works at the five-and-ten, she steals more Christmas tree ornaments than a single tree can hold. The story is told by the older boy (the children are never named) in a convincing narrative; he becomes aware of Mama's thievery and anguishes about it, but he knows it is done for love. The ambivalence he feels is perceptively portrayed, and the strength and tenderness of his mother's love is touching, but it is in the character of Mama, made vivid through her words and deeds as well as through her son's troubled love, that Hopkins excels.

643 **Hopkins,** Lee Bennett, comp. *On Our Way;* Poems of Pride and Love; photographs by David Parks. Knopf, 1974. 60p. Trade ed. $4.95; Library ed. $5.49 net.

4- While there are many excellent anthologies of black poetry, this is well worth adding to a collection; the poems have been carefully chosen and grouped, and the photographs are of a superior quality, the soft brown and white (rather than the usual black and white) harmonizing with the mood created by the poetry. This is not meant to reflect the spectrum of black life, but the love and joy and pride in blackness. A few of the selections are rather widely anthologized, but who would omit Nikki Giovanni's "Nikki-Rosa" or Langston Hughes' "Daybreak in Alabama" from an anthology of celebration?

644 **Horace** (Quintus Horatius Flaccus). *Two Roman Mice;* retold and illus. by Marilynne K. Roach. T. Y. Crowell, 1975. 74-32416. 37p. $5.50.

K-3 A translation of a portion of Horace's *Satire II* tells the now-familiar story of the city mouse and the country mouse. Urbanus, after visiting his friend Rusticus, invites the latter to taste the joys of city life. They dine in indolent Roman style, but are subsequently chased by ferocious dogs. Rusticus decides that the splendors of city life aren't worth its hazards, and returns with relief to the quiet, simple joys of the countryside. The adaptation is direct and simple, the black and white drawings are pleasantly filled with authentic details of ancient Roman architecture and objects and with ornamental side-drawings that include foods referred to in the story. Not the most dramatic telling, but adequate. The Latin original and notes on Horace and on the story are appended, and these are directed to an audience older than that for which the adaptation is appropriate.

645 **Horvath,** Joan. *Filmmaking for Beginners.* Nelson, 1974. 162p. illus. $5.95.

6-10 Recipient of many awards, Horvath is an experienced filmmaker and reviewer; her knowledge of every aspect of technical procedures is matched by her enthusiastic belief that the personal, creative approach is essential. Well-organized, the text discusses film stock, cameras and how they operate, preparing the script, shooting and lighting a film, special effects, using sound, et cetera. This is written in a straightforward style, dignified enough for adult neophytes but simple enough for young readers. The print is unfortunately crowded but this is mitigated by the clean, modern type face. A relative index is appended.

646 **Horwitz,** Elinor Lander. *Contemporary American Folk Artists;* photographs by Joshua Horwitz. Lippincott, 1975. 75-14353. 143p. $7.50.

6- A most intriguing book because of the subject matter, this is given additional appeal by the informality and vigor of the writing style. Horwitz discusses folk art in an excellent introductory chapter, describing its popularity and those imitators who deliberately abandon perspective and accuracy to achieve (or attempt to achieve) the spontaneity and intensity, even the awkwardness of the real thing. The rest of the book describes the work of individual folk artists in this country, with the text divided into painting, carving, and the work of "Total Environmentalists" like Simon Rodia, the creator of Watts Towers. Amply illustrated by photographs of the works discussed, the book concludes with a list of suggestions for further reading, a list of American museums with outstanding folk art collections, and an index.

647 **Horwitz,** Elinor Lander. *Madness, Magic, and Medicine; The Treatment and Mistreatment of the Mentally Ill.* Lippincott, 1977. 76-54760. 191p. illus. $6.95.

7- Comprehensive and objective, this closely-written text gives a detailed history of both treatment and theories of mental illness, from the magic rituals of primitive peoples to the diverse and sophisticated forms of therapy practiced today. In the course of the book, Horwitz describes the ideas of major physicians, so it should be of interest to readers who are curious about medical history as well as those with a specific interest in the mentally ill. The final chapters discuss various forms of lay therapy (dance therapy, transcendental meditation, or Alcoholics Anonymous) as well as the therapy practiced by professional people, and the various legal implications of our laws that deal with mental illness: property rights, criminal responsiblity, and the right to freedom.

A list of suggestions for further reading and an index are appended.

648 **Household,** Geoffrey. *Escape into Daylight.* Atlantic-Little, Brown, 1976. 76-10162. 139p. $5.95.

6-9 A kidnapping story is set in England, where the daughter of a film star is being held for ransom and a boy who has stumbled on a clue to the identity of the kidnappers is picked up, drugged, and taken also. Mike and Carrie are in a dungeon; once a day a man opens a grating above them to bring them food. When an old well caves in as a result of the children's loosening bricks, Mike is caught. Carrie and the kidnappers assume he is dead, but Mike makes his way above ground. There is a double sequence of chase-and-evade when Carrie later gets away, and Mike eventually reaches a village to get in touch with parents and police. Even after they come, Mike's role is important in the capture of one of the three kidnappers; both he and Carrie are intelligent and inventive within the bounds of credibility in a story that has firm structure, action and suspense, and an ingenious setting.

649 **Houston,** James. *Frozen Fire;* written and illus. by James Houston. Atheneum, 1977. 77-6366. 149p. $6.95.

4-6 Based on the true and dramatic ordeal of an Eskimo boy in the 1960's, this adventure story is set—as are other books by Houston, a Canadian who lived with Arctic Eskimos for many years—in the far north. Kayak, a classmate of Matthew Morgan's in their Baffin Island school, suggests to his new friend Mattoosie (Matthew) that they take a snowmobile and go to the rescue of Mattoosie's father when the latter, a prospector, disappears. The spare can of gasoline leaks, and the two boys face a homeward trek through seventy-five miles of whirling snow and bitter cold. While the characterization has little depth and the dialogue is rather stiff, the combination of suspense, danger, vivid setting, and the appeal of man against the elements triumphs.

650 **Houston,** James. *Koviok's Magic Journey; An Eskimo Legend;* written and illus. by James Houston. Atheneum, 1973. 38p. $5.25.

3-5 A retelling of one of the most popular legends of an Eskimo folk hero, Kiviok, is illustrated by the author with drawings that are vigorous and dramatic. The tale is one that has several variants in other cultures: a bird-maiden weds a human, later flies off to join her kind, and—after her husband has sought and found her—renounces her animal form forever. Here the story contains both the milieu of the culture and some other folk characters peculiar to the North American continent, particularly Raven. Raven steals the white feather coat of the snow goose while she is in human form, and Kiviok takes her as his wife; she cannot resist the calls of the migrating geese seven years later, and uses feathers to improvise wings for herself and her children. Helped by the giant Inukpuk and the magic fish that carry him to his family, Kiviok goes south and fights the wicked Raven; the fish carry the family homeward and the geese-children and wife fly for the last time, Kiviok clutching their feet, to their home in the far north.

651 **Hovey,** Tamara. *John Reed: Witness to Revolution.* Crown, 1975. 75-4933. 227p. illus. $6.95.

7-10 A free spirit, an outstanding journalist, a man whose circle of friends included brilliant and colorful authors and artists, Reed is a figure to excite the imaginations of the young. Coming from a wealthy Oregon family, Reed found his mentor in a Harvard professor who was a major influence in his life, Charles Copeland. He then moved to New York, where he became increasingly interested in radical causes and increasingly adept as an investigator, covering the Paterson strike from the workers' viewpoint (in fact, from jail) and the Mexican war from the viewpoint of the troops of Pancho Villa, with whom he traveled. Best known for his *Ten Days That Shook the World,* based on Reed's presence during the tumultuous changeover from the Kerensky government to a Bolshevik victory, Reed was spurned for his sympathies by most of the great men who had been his friends. He died at thirty-three, castigated by many, honored by others for his dedication to social justice. The author, as his major editor's daughter, had access to personal documents, so that this is an intimate and personal biography; it is marred somewhat by Hovey's tendency to be effusive: ". . . there was always a third eye at the back of her head which watched over her delicate son," "And John Reed would always remain, in some deep and inviolate way, a boy from Oregon." Still, the book gives good and balanced coverage, the subject emerges vividly as a person, and the treatment is candid. A bibliography and an index are appended.

652 **Hovey,** Tamara. *A Mind of Her Own; a Life of the Writer George Sand;* illus. with photographs. Harper, 1977. 76-24310. 211p. Trade ed. $7.95; Library ed. $7.89 net.

7- A mature, perceptive biography is written in polished style and is
* distinctive for the smoothness with which Hovey incorporates quoted material into the text; all of the dialogue and quotations are from original sources. The life of the distinguished French author is intrinsically dramatic, both because of Sand's flouting of nineteenth century conventions and because of the unusual role she played as a woman who moved in, and became intimate with,

cultural circles that included some of the great figures of literary, artistic, musical and political worlds. There is no adulatory tone; the writing is informed and objective, and the characters are vividly recreated.

653 **Howard,** Moses L. *The Ostrich Chase;* illus. by Barbara Seuling. Holt, 1974. 118p. $5.95.

5-7 Howard, who has also written under his Ugandan name, Musa Nagenda, writes a story of the Kalahari desert that is not restricted in time and is timeless in its theme. An adolescent, Khuana knows that it is against the code of the Bushmen for a girl to hunt—even to want to hunt; yet she has secretly collected a bow and arrows, has learned how to make arrow poison, has practiced. She yearns to kill an ostrich, knowing that it is dangerous. All the tribe disapprove of Khuana except her grandmother, who remembers that she too had wanted to hunt when she was a girl, and so old Gaushe helps her grandchild. When a drought forces the Bushmen to move to a new waterhole, Gaushe, ill, is left behind in tribal tradition; Khuana steals off to join her, and the combined skills of the two defeat the "angry desert". Convincing characters, a colorful setting, good pace, and an ending that is both logical and satisfying give strength to the unusual story of feminine protest in an aboriginal culture.

654 **Hughes,** Shirley. *David and Dog;* written and illus. by Shirley Hughes. Prentice-Hall, 1978. 77-27070. 29p. $6.95.

2-5 yrs. A touching story comes from England, but it has qualities that should make it universally appealing, since a child's attachment to a favorite toy is universal. David takes his battered stuffed dog, named Dog, everywhere; while his sister takes seven teddy bears to bed every night, David takes only Dog. In the excitement of watching a fairground set up and having an ice cream cone, David unwittingly leaves Dog behind. At bedtime, all the family help hunt, but to no avail. Despair! How David gets Dog back is told in a realistic ending that's warmed by sister Bella's generosity. Familiar concepts, a plot nicely gauged for small children's interest and comprehension, and a credible happy ending should satisfy listeners, while the beautifully detailed paintings, touched with lightly comic details, should engage both readers-aloud and their audiences. Under the original (English) title, *Dogger,* this won the Greenaway Medal for the best-illustrated book of 1977.

655 **Hughes,** Shirley. *George the Babysitter;* written and illus. by Shirley Hughes. Prentice-Hall, 1978. 29p. $6.95.

4-7 yrs. George comes to babysit for a mother of three who works afternoons in this engaging picture book by one of England's most eminent children's book illustrators. The deft, realistic paintings have fine use of line and color, and the simple story describes, with understated humor, the vicissitudes of the daily round, as George copes with a disorderly kitchen and bedroom, three lively children, and a procession of chores. The children help, but when Mother comes home and wonders how George could have managed without them, Hughes pictures an exhausted George slumped in an armchair, hand pressed to harried brow.

656 **Hughes,** Ted. *Moon-Whales and Other Moon Poems;* drawings by Leonard Baskin. Viking, 1976. 76-6168. 86p. $7.95.

6-9 In an explosion of fantasy, the eminent British poet envisions the creatures, the customs, and the landscape of a lunatic world; his icy, eerie imagery is echoed by the grotesque, adroit pen and ink drawings of Baskin. The title poem begins, "They plough through the moon stuff / Just under the surface / Lifting the moon's skin / Like a muscle . . . " Here, and in some others of the poems, there is a sonorous felicity of phrase and conception. There is, however, a less familiar playfulness in some selections, an extravagance of concepts that almost leads to a suspicion that Hughes is having one on. It's not an even collection, but it is ebullient in a mood that is often macabre. Intriguing, at times awesomely splendid.

657 **Hughes,** Ted. *Season Songs;* pictures by Leonard Baskin. Viking, 1975. 74-18280. 73p. $10.00.

6- Old and new poems by the eminent British poet are grouped by
* seasons and are superbly illustrated by paintings and drawings that have a grand simplicity of composition, subtle use of color and line, and a felicitous evocation of mood. The latter quality is one of the most notable achievements of the poems as well; in the autumn poem, "The Seven Sorrows," for example, Hughes creates a vivid picture of the faint melancholy, the stillness of dying life forms, the end of the golden time of year. All of the poems have a singing quality and an awareness of the natural world that is communicated through sharp, illuminating phrases concepts.

658 **Hunter,** Evan. *Me and Mr. Stenner.* Lippincott, 1976. 76-24810. 157p. $6.95.

5-8 "He certainly had a lot to learn about eleven-year-old girls," Abby reports in her story of adjustment to Mr. Stenner, who moved in when her parents separated and later became her stepfather. She didn't like him. His sons didn't like her mother. Abby loved her father, she resented Stenner's efforts to be friendly, and she was convinced it would be disloyal to relent, but in the course of a European trip for three, Abby changes—and she finally admits that she has come, not just to accept, but to love her stepfather. And well she might, since Hunter has created a warm, intelligent character in Stenner. The writing has vitality, conviction, and polish; the dialogue is natural and occasionally spicy, and the message comes across without didacticism: it is possible to love a stepparent without diminishing one's love for a natural parent. A "good read."

659 **Hunter,** Kristin. *Guests in the Promised Land.* Scribner, 1973, 133p. $4.95.

7-10 Eleven short stories examine facets of the problems of the black child in a white world. Some of the problems that face the protagonists are, of course, those that any child faces in growing up, but they are intensified and sharpened by being black. The title story, about a group of boys who are invited to spend a day at a white country club, exposes the superficiality of a "charitable" gesture; "Two's Enough of a Crowd" is a tender love story; in "Hero's Return" a young teenager who is a fringe delinquent learns a forcible lesson from an older brother who is just out of jail and determined to keep his younger brother from following in his path. The collection has vitality and variety, the stories ranging broadly in tone and mood.

660 **Hunter,** Mollie. *A Furl of Fairy Wind; Four Stories;* illus. by Stephen Gammell. Harper, 1977. 76-58732. 58p. Trade ed. $7.95; Library ed. $7.89.

3-5 Four magical tales are included in a book illustrated with soft, mysteriously tenuous pencil drawings. In the title story a lonely orphan gains a family, in another a household Brownie makes a skeptical farm wife with a degree in household management believe in him. The Queen of the Fairies is a major character in the other two stories; in one, she bewitches a boy for a year and a day, and in the other she teaches a lesson in what true happiness is, to a peddler whose integrity has been briefly threatened by a spasm of dishonest greed. The writing style is fluid, the structure spare in these original tales conceived and told in felicitous adherence to the oral tradition.

661 **Hunter,** Mollie. *A Stranger Came Ashore.* Harper, 1975. 75-10814. 163p. Trade ed. $5.95; Library ed. $5.79 net.

6-8 Mollie Hunter's stories are as evocative of Scotland as Eilis Dillon's are of Ireland: the same strong, spare casting; the creation of mood and setting; the use of just enough cadence in dialogue to give authentic flavor. Here she deftly mingles the reality of the lives of fisherman-crofters and the legends of the Selkies, the seal-folk of the Shetland Islands. A young man, Finn Learson, appears during a fierce storm. Is he the lone survivor of a shipwreck or is he—as young Rob suspects—a seal-man who plans to take Rob's sister to his ocean home? The folklore of the Selkies and the customs of the islands are woven through the tale, which culminates in a suspense-filled struggle between the forces of good and evil.

662 **Hunter,** Mollie. *The Stronghold.* Harper, 1974. 259p. Trade ed. $5.95; Library ed. $5.79 net.

6-10 Mollie Hunter creates a story set in ancient times with a conviction and vigor that are impressive. Her fictional explanation of the brochs, the heavy towers that are found along the shores of northern Scotland, is deftly merged with an exciting plot and interesting historical background. Coll, who had been crippled in a Roman raid, conceives the idea of a fireproof structure that would be impregnable; his plan is not immediately accepted, but when it is, and the Romans attack, Coll is vindicated. Much of the book has to do with the power struggle between the tribal chieftain and the Druid leader, a contest that reveals—as the men and their adherents debate the issues—both the details of the culture and the timeless battle between the progressive and the reactionary. There's a love story, plenty of action, and a high dramatic sense in the writing style.

663 **Hunter,** Mollie. *The Wicked One.* Harper, 1977. 76-41515. 128p. Trade ed. $5.95; Library ed. $5.79 net.

5-7 In a story set in the Scottish Highlands, Colin Grant lives with his wife and three sons; a forester, he also has a small croft that supports his family nicely. But Colin has a terrible temper, and when he loses it and strikes at a supernatural creature, the Grollican, his troubles begin. His outbuildings are torn down, his haystacks ripped apart, and—worst of all—he falls in love with a beautiful, mischievous fairy. But there's a truce between the fairy folk and human beings, and his enchantress helps Colin by giving him an enchanted horse that never tires, a horse that later proves to be a bewitched girl who is loved by the youngest son. Seeing no way to escape the Grollican, Colin goes to America. And guess who's come over on another boat? And is tricked into serving the Grant family for all time? A vigorous tale that incorporates many familiar folklore motifs, this is soundly supported by its realistic base and is told with fluent competence.

664 **Hurwitz,** Johanna. *Busybody Nora;* illus. by Susan Jeschke. Morrow, 1976. 75-25921. 64p. Trade ed. $4.95; Library ed. $4.59 net.

K-2 Six-year-old Nora lives in a New York apartment building and wants to know everybody in the building; most of the people to whom she introduces herself are friendly, but one woman calls her a busybody. Nora's dreams of a big, big party are realized when all the neighbors unite to give one in honor of old Mrs. Wurmbrand. The big event of the text preceding the party is a neighborly dinner, on a smaller scale, that begins when Nora's little brother insists that it's his turn to choose the menu and that they will have stone soup, just the way it's done in the story. The episodes are linked very slightly, but each is pleasantly positive; the party, the dinner, Daddy's birthday celebration, etc., are all mildly humorous and the book is permeated by the affection within the family and the cordial relationships with neighbors. The book takes a sunnier view of urban life than do many stories for children.

665 **Hurwitz,** Johanna. *The Law of Gravity;* illus. by Ingrid Fetz. Morrow, 1978. 77-13656. 192p. Trade ed. $6.95; Library ed. $6.43 net.

4-6 Margot, who's just finished fifth grade, tells of her summer project. Assigned by the teacher to describe something new she's learned or accomplished by the time school starts, Margot decides she's going to change her mother's living pattern. Mom does have a peculiar habit: she never goes downstairs, staying four flights up in the apartment or gardening on the roof. Margot gives a lively account of her plans (what goes up must come down—some day) and her activities. The story ends with a possibility that Margot's goal will be achieved, but she's spent a more profitable summer than she expected: she and Mom can talk openly, she's made a new, stimulating friend (in one of the nicest boy-girl friendships to come along in many a book) and she's learned something very important. She's learned that she loves Mom just the way she is, that Mom's idiosyncrasy is superficial, and that it isn't her (Margot's) job to change her mother. That's up to her mother.

666 **Hussey,** Lois J. *Collecting for the City Naturalist;* by Lois J. Hussey and Catherine Pessino; illus. by Barbara Neill. T. Y. Crowell, 1975. 73-17293. 72p. $5.95.

4-6 While no section of the book gives extensive guidance to observation and preservation of specimens, this covers many kinds of collections and gives quite adequate advice on how to collect and preserve either data about specimens of animal, vegetable, and mineral forms. The text, dry and businesslike, stresses careful recording and labeling, avoidance of trespassing on property or rights, and careful respect toward living plants and animals. Among the topics covered: rocks, sand, trees and other plants and plant parts, birds, insects, and pond life. A selected, divided bibliography, a list of supply houses, and an index are appended.

667 **Hutchins,** Pat. *The Best Train Set Ever;* written and illus. by Pat Hutchins. Greenwillow, 1978. 76-30672. 56p. (Read-alone Books) Trade ed. $5.95; Library ed. $5.49 net.

1-3 Three short stories, illustrated with pictures that have precise details, restrained color, and a high sense of design, show family cohesion without any sentimentality. In the title story, various members of the family buy parts of the expensive train set Peter craves for his birthday; each has made the purchase independently, so they all share Peter's surprise and pleasure. In the other stories, Peter's sister makes a Hallowe'en costume out of her siblings' leftovers, and an extended family Christmas party is postponed until July because all the children have measles. The writing is bland, but the combination of special days, happy outcomes, and quiet but solid family feeling add substance and appeal.

668 **Hutchins,** Ross E. *The Bug Clan;* illus. with photographs by the author. Dodd, 1973. 127p. $4.25.

5- For the amateur entomologist, this comprehensive and well-organized survey of the insect orders Hemiptera and Homoptera provides a ready reference guide and superb magnified photographs that can be used for identification. The author, after making distinctions between the true bug and other orders of insects, methodically describes the families of the two orders of bugs, giving facts about the life cycle, habitat, habits, and the usefulness (or harmfulness) to people or plants. Succinct and lucid, the text is a model of its kind; a classification outline, a bibliography, and an index are appended.

669 **Hutchins,** Ross E. *A Look at Ants;* illus. with photographs by the author. Dodd, 1978. 77-16867. 48p. $4.95.

3-5 An eminent science writer and entomologist, Hutchins also has supplied the many photographs for a simply written text that describes the structure and life cycle of ants, discusses their classification, and then focuses on some of the many varieties of ants. In so doing, he makes clear the complexity of the social structure in the ant world, the division of labor and the several roles (workers, queens, soldiers) played by individual ants, and the amazing varieties of life styles of different ant communities: the farmers, the herdsmen, the honey gatherers, and the various creatures with whom these social creatures have established host, symbiotic, or antagonistic relationships.

670 **Hyde,** Margaret O. *Hotline!* 2nd ed. McGraw-Hill, 1976. 75-42331. 212p. Library ed. $5.72 net.

7- The revision in this edition is substantial in some sections of the book, and several chapters have been added, including one on hotlines for runaways (followed by a list of runaway centers, divided by states). As before, a general discussion of hotlines—how they began, how they operate—precedes separate chapters on hotlines for different needs, such as drug help, rape crisis, suicide, etc. Some sources of help are cited within the text, but full information is given in the appendices: a bibliography, an index, a national directory of hotline services, a directory of child protection hotlines, and a list of newsletters and publications. Case histories and examples of telephone conversations are included in a book that is objective, informative, and well organized.

671 **Isadora,** Rachel. *Max;* story and pictures by Rachel Isadora. Macmillan, 1976. 76-9088. 26p. $4.95.

K-2 On Saturday mornings Max, en route to the park to play baseball, walks his sister to her dancing class. One day he strolls in to observe, and becomes intrigued by the class exercises. At the teacher's invitation, he takes off his shoes and joins the class: he tries barre work, does a split (well, almost), and a pas de chat. Time for one leap across the floor, and he's off to the ball park, where he hits a homer after two strikes. Now Max has joined the dancing class, having found that it's the best kind of warmup for a ball game. The illustrations are amusing, the simply told story encourages readers to think of ballet as not only enjoyable but also appropriate for sports-minded boys.

672 **Italiano,** Carlo. *Sleighs: the Gentle Transportation;* written and illus. by Carlo Italiano. Tundra Books, 1978. 28p. $9.95.

4- Under the title *The Sleighs of My Childhood,* this was published in Canada, where it won the award for the best illustrated children's book of 1974. Meticulously detailed and colorful paintings depict a type of sleigh on every page, with a descriptive text below; for example, the baked bean sleigh passed on certain days of the week, and housewives would come with their empty bean pots and exchange them for a full pot of baked beans that had been kept in an insulated section of the sleigh. The sleighs are drawn from the author's memory and from pictures, for Montreal in the 1920's and 1930's depended almost entirely on sleighs for transportation and deliveries through the deep winter snows. Now only the sightseeing sleighs remain, so that this book has historical value in addition to its beauty.

673 **Jackson,** Jesse. *Make a Joyful Noise Unto the Lord!* The Life of Mahalia Jackson, Queen of Gospel Singers; illus. with photographs. T. Y. Crowell, 1974. 160p. $5.50.

6-9 Mahalia Jackson came up to glory on a rough road. She wouldn't change her style to fit the ideas other people had of how music should be sung; she didn't have vocal training; she wouldn't sing in a night club or a theater; she had to overcome Jim Crow, poverty, lack of education, a disastrous marriage, and the depression. But she became a musical phenomenon, a rich woman able to help in the struggle for black equality, a defender of gospel music who helped preserve the black heritage. For those who know her music—as many young readers do—this is a moving biography; for those who do not, Jesse Jackson has captured the drive, the vitality, and the integrity of the late, great singer. A small section of photographs is bound into the book; an index is appended.

674 **Jacobs,** David. *Chaplin, the Movies, and Charlie;* illus. with picture portfolios. Harper, 1975. 75-6291. 142p. Trade ed. $6.95; Library ed. $6.79 net.

7- Horatio Alger never invented a better rags-to-riches plot than the life of Charles Spencer Chaplin: deserted by an alcoholic father, the two Chaplin boys were taken to a workhouse by their indigent mother (Charlie was six) who later suffered a nervous breakdown from which she never really recovered. At nine, the boy joined a vaudeville troupe. Oscar winner, millionaire, recipient of a knighthood, Charlie the Tramp is enthralling a new generation of film fans today. His biography is as much a tribute to his skill as a director and innovator in film-making as to his creativity as a performer. There is an occasional note of adulation, but the book is remarkable for the detailed information it gives about the early days of the film industry as well as for the revealing picture of a lonely, shy comic genius. The style is vigorous, the treatment balanced. A list of all the films made by Chaplin, divided by the studios that produced them, precedes the index.

675 **Jacobs,** William Jay. *Roger Williams;* illus. with authentic prints and documents. Watts, 1975. 74-12280. 56p. $4.90.

5-6 Oh, he was a trouble maker, Roger Williams. He didn't believe in swearing oaths in civil matters, he upheld the theory of separation of church and state, he thought all religions equally valid, and he even believed that the king had no right to grant land, that it belonged to the Indians and should be fairly purchased from them. As a brilliant young scholar and ordained minister, Williams had been welcomed to the colonies, but his doctrines were held anathema by the church leaders and he was banished from Massachusetts. He learned the languages of the neighboring tribes after he'd established the new town of Providence, which became a haven for oppressed religious minority groups. This is not a complete biography of Williams, and it does not bring the man to life, but it is a fully detailed account of his role in New England colonial history. The writing is serious but not arid, the material smoothly put together and authoritative. The author, an eminent historian, provides no bibliography; an index is appended.

676 **Jagendorf,** Moritz Adolf. *Folk Stories of the South;* illus. by Michael Parks. Vanguard, 1973. 355p. $6.95.

4-7 A collection that will interest adult lovers of folklore as well as children, this is arranged by states, the emphasis therefore on source rather than motifs or types, since within each group of stories from an individual state there may be tall tales, noodlehead tales, Indian legends, tales of magic, tales of ghosts or witches, and "why" stories. The style is colloquial, often jocular, the majority of the tales humorous. Sources—often first-hand—are cited in an appended section of notes.

677 **Jahn,** Mike. *How To Make a Hit Record.* Bradbury, 1976. 76-9939. 118p. $7.95.

7- Radio commentator and newspaper critic of rock music, Jahn uses, in addition to his own advice, the comments of ten other professionals in the music business to add validity to the account of the career of an imaginary singer. The book, written in easy, informal style, follows the career of the singer-composer from an amateur interest in guitar playing, to a part-time job in a small restaurant, to a concentration on making a living by his music, with a move to New York, the services of an agent, and eventually making a hit record. Through the comments of a disc jockey, a sound engineer, a composer, the owner of a restaurant-club, a producer, and other specialists in the music business, Jahn gives a full picture of the usually-tedious route to success. The book does not give easy access to its information, but almost any fact a hopeful performer might want to know is answered at some point in the text.

678 **James,** Elizabeth. *The Simple Facts of Simple Machines;* by Elizabeth James and Carol Barkin; photographs by Daniel Dorn; diagrams by Susan Stan. Lothrop, 1975. 64p. $4.50.

4-6 Clear diagrams and photographs that show jointed wooden mannikins expand a text that explains the ways in which force and distance are balanced in using six basic machines: the lever, the inclined plane, the wedge, the pulley, the screw, and the wheel-and-axle. The simple, lucid text discusses principles and gives several examples of function, suggesting home experiments in changing direction of force or in changing distance to find the effects of altering the balance. Just enough repetition to enforce concepts, and no extraneous material here. An index is appended.

679 **James,** Elizabeth. *What Do You Mean by "Average"?* by Elizabeth James and Carol Barkin; illus. by Joel Schick. Lothrop, 1978. 78-7227. 60p. Trade ed. $5.95; Library ed. $5.71 net.

5-7 James and Barkin do a better than average job of putting information into a narrative framework; using the device of a group of students planning an election campaign, they introduce believable if purposeful discussions as the group works. Jill, the candidate, and her friends base the campaign on the fact that, being an average person, Jill will best represent others. But what is average? Lucidly, step by step, the text describes the differences between mean, median, and mode; it discusses percentages and graphs, random sampling, and the pitfalls in sampling and questionnaires that should make one aware that claimed results can show bias or distortion, conscious or unconscious. Clearly and logically presented, the information is supplemented by helpful examples.

680 **Jameson,** Cynthia, ad. *The Clay Pot Boy;* illus. by Arnold Lobel. Coward, 1973. 56p. $4.29.

K-2 A favorite tale for storytellers is nicely adapted here and given added dimensions by the illustrations. Lobel's clay pot boy *looks* like a piece of pottery, and he grows larger and larger as he goes on his voracious path. Baked in an oven by an old couple who are childless and want a son, the clay pot boy demands food, food, and more food. Having eaten all the food there is, he eats the old couple. And a hen. And a bull. And a woodchopper with his ax. And a farmer and his wife. And a barn, which is only a mouthful for the now-gigantic creature. When he meets a goat, the clay pot boy makes his usual threat, but the goat is more clever than he and manages to smash the clay. All the meals step out, brisk as ever, leaving the barn standing amidst a rubble of clay. A competent retelling of a good tale and illustrations that are more than competent.

681 **Jansson,** Tove. *The Summer Book;* tr. from the Swedish by Thomas Teal. Pantheon Books, 1975. 171p. $5.95.

6-8 Translated from the Swedish, this idyll of an island summer is quite unlike the author's beloved stories of Moominland. Slow-moving and self-contained, the book describes the small events of sun-filled days spent by Sophia and her grandmother, and it is permeated by the love and the rare understanding between them. Sophia's friend comes to visit, but she does not enjoy the simple things that give Sophia such pleasure; Papa is there some of the time, as are other adults. But it is Grandmother with whom Sophia has long discussions about island flora and fauna, about superstition and death and faith. Grandmother is a marvelous character, candid and wise and earthy. The writing style has flow and vitality, and while there is no plot and not enough action for some readers, this is a treasure for those who appreciate nuance, depth and percipience.

682 **Jarrell,** Randall. *Fly by Night;* pictures by Maurice Sendak. Farrar, 1976. 76-27313. 31p. $5.95.

3-4 Completed shortly before his death, Jarrell's last story for children is illustrated in the grave, serene style used by Sendak in *The Juniper Tree* and *The Light Princess.* David is a quiet, solitary child who cannot remember during the day that at night he flies, floating from his bed, naked, into the still night where only the birds and beasts see him. He meets an owl who takes him to see its nestlings, tells him "The Owl's Bedtime Story," and flies him home. It looks at him with such shining eyes that the next morning, when his mother looks lovingly at him, he has a misty memory of something . . . someone . . . he cannot remember. There is little action, and the story will probably not appeal to all readers, but the gentle, dreamy quality and the message of parental tenderness should captivate some children.

683 **Jatakas.** *Jataka Tales;* ed. by Nancy DeRoin; illus. by Ellen Lanyon. Houghton, 1975. 74-20981. 82p. $5.95.

3-5 Although these do not have quite the cadence of the two collections of Jataka tales retold by Ellen Babbitt, they are a welcome addition to any storyteller's list of sources, since there are new animal stories included. The illustrations, brown on cream, are often too busy with detail although they are nicely integrated (visually) with the text on the page. The stories, each of which concludes with a rhyming moral, form a body of practical advice on interpersonal relationships, but they are also lively and humorous tales, brief and pithy, that have been popular for over 2,000 years and were first translated into English in the nineteenth century.

684 **Jenness,** Aylette. *Along the Niger River; An African Way of Life;* text and photographs by Aylette Jenness. T. Y. Crowell, 1974. 135p. $6.95.

5- A superb photographic documentary about the peoples living in the savanna lands along the Niger as it flows through northern Nigeria. The author lived in Nigeria for several years, so that her text has the vitality and color given by personal observation, but this is not just a travelogue: the book is sympathetic, thoughtful, and objective. Well-written, well-organized, and informative, it gives historical background for a discussion of the life styles of tribes that are fishers or herders or farmers or town dwellers, commenting perceptively on cultural integration, mores and patterns of individual and group life. A bibliography and a relative index are appended.

685 **Jenness,** Aylette. *The Bakery Factory; Who Puts the Bread on Your Table;* written and illus. with photographs by Aylette Jenness. T. Y. Crowell, 1978. 77-8094. 71p. Trade ed. $6.95; Library ed. $6.79 net.

4-7 Clear photographs and a casual, almost conversational, writing style make this more palatable than books in the let's-visit category. Jenness follows each step of the procedures in a bakery factory and participates in some of them; what she adds to give this a special flavor is the same kind of curiosity and concern for the people she meets that have distinguished her books for older readers. She discusses with some of the factory workers why they like their jobs, or why they don't, or why they are working at a factory when they've trained for other work. She concludes with a discussion of different kinds of work and suggests trips like her own, advising readers on how to obtain permission to make such visits; she gives some instructions for icing a cake and a recipe for making bread. An index is included.

686 **Jenness,** Aylette. *A Life of Their Own; An Indian Family in Latin America;* text and photographs by Aylette Jenness and Lisa W. Kroeber; drawings by Susan Votaw. T. Y. Crowell, 1975. 75-15964. 133p. $8.95.

4-7
* Profusedly illustrated with well-chosen photographs, this is—like the earlier books by Jenness—a documentary based on personal and sympathetic observation of a way of life. The authors spent a great deal of time with one family but also explored the health clinic, the school, the market, and the government of a Guatemalan town. Although the native language of the Hernandez family was Cakchiquel, they spoke some Spanish, as did the authors, and were able to communicate without too much difficulty. The book is informative and well-written, but it is even more distinguished for two qualities inherent in the writing; one is the attitude of interested respect—nothing in the Hernandez home is deemed odd, quaint, or inferior—and the other is a warmth that clearly permeates the relationships between the

authors and those they interviewed, a warmth that does not preclude objectivity. The last section of the book is called a "Workshop" and gives instructions for weaving, cooking, making festival figures, running a market (with Spanish words for numbers and often-used phrases) and other projects that can enable the reader to learn exactly how the Hernandez family and their neighbors live. A vocabulary and a relative index are appended.

687 **Jensen,** Niels. *Days of Courage; A Medieval Adventure;* tr. from the Danish by Oliver Stallybrass. Harcourt, 1973. 188p. $5.25.

5-7 Awarded the Danish Children's Book Prize in 1972, this is a story set in medieval Denmark after an epidemic of the Black Death. Published in England under the title *When the Land Lay Waste,* the book describes the adventures of two children who meet after each has survived the plague. Hanna is an orphan who has no family; Luke is seeking an uncle in a distant village and asks Hanna to travel with him. While they meet some rascals, the children are treated kindly by other survivors, and when they find Uncle Nicholas (a monk) it is decided that they will all return home together and start life afresh. While the book gives a convincing picture of the desolation and tragedy left in the wake of the plague, and the courage of the children convincingly symbolizes the strength of any stricken people who put the past behind them and start afresh, Hanna and Luke never come alive as characters. The book is adequately written, more impressive for its setting and pace than for its structure.

688 **John,** Timothy, ed. *The Great Song Book;* illus. by Tomi Ungerer; musical arrangements by Peter Hankey. Doubleday, 1978. 77-74707. 112p. 12.50.

all ages Pleasant arrangements vary in difficulty and include chording for guitar in a song book that consists entirely of familiar music included in many other collections. The arrangement of material is occasionally arbitrary, "The Cuckoo" being included under the heading of "Morning Songs," and some folk songs in the "Fireside Songs" section rather than in the "Folk Songs" section. In fact, the one distinctive quality of the book is in the illustrations, which are Ungerer at his comic, dramatic, and colorful best.

689 **Johnson,** Dorothy M. *Buffalo Woman.* Dodd, 1977. 76-53436. 247p. $6.95.

8- A long novel, trenchant and poignant, that follows the life of a
* woman of the Oglala Sioux. Her childhood name is Whirlwind Girl, and she marries the man she has loved since she first saw him, White Thunder. Their lodge is full, a many-generation family

that is happy, generous, busy, and peaceful. Then come the white men with their trading posts, their demands for land, their worthless treaties, their reservations. Whirlwind, who has become a Buffalo Woman in the ceremony of adulthood, sees her people decimated and cheated, her family dispersed and improverished. After the battle of Little Big Horn, she is grief-stricken, but she remains proud and strong until her death; her people are too poor, too few to honor her with traditional observances—but they honor her. The author, an adopted member of the Blackfeet Tribe, has done painstaking research into costumes, customs, mores, and religious beliefs and observances, and these are smoothly incorporated into a story that has historic and sociological significance, but that above all is a moving depiction of a courageous woman who saw tragic changes come to her people.

690 **Johnson,** Eric W. *V.D.;* illus. with photographs by Eric E. Mitchell, Rev. ed. Lippincott, 1978. 78-8666. 126p. $6.95.

7-12 No superficial revision, this. New material has been added, material from the 1973 edition has been revised, the index is more extensive, even the section on questions and answers about venereal disease has been brought up to date. The contrast between the statistics cited in the two editions makes the book potentially more useful; in 1973 the estimate was that 7,000 more people would be infected each day; in 1978, that figure had risen to 27,000. Forthright and comprehensive, the text does not dramatize, moralize, or threaten; Johnson simply describes the most common venereal diseases; gives the facts about prevalence, prevention, and treatment; discusses the volunteer group that maintains a hot line, Operation Venus, and gives information about the ease and anonymity with which an individual may get help.

691 **Johnston,** Johanna. *Harriet and the Runaway Book; The Story of Harriet Beecher Stowe and Uncle Tom's Cabin;* illus. by Ronald Himler. Harper, 1977. 76-24305. 80p. Trade ed. $5.95; Library ed. $5.79 net.

3-5 A smoothly fictionalized biography is printed in large type on spacious pages, illustrated by softly drawn black and white pictures, and written in a direct, informal style. While the book's emphasis is on the writing of *Uncle Tom's Cabin,* it gives balanced treatment to other aspects and periods of Stowe's life.

692 **Johnston,** Norma. *Strangers Dark and Gold.* Atheneum, 1975. 74-19463. 240p. $7.95.

7-12 A stirring, lyric retelling of the mythological adventures of Jason in
* his quests and of the tragic love of Jason and Medea is based on

the three earliest accounts that have survived intact; the author discusses these in her very helpful notes and points out that the three (Apollonius, Pindar, and Euripides) were telling tales that were familiar to their audiences and that therefore they differed in details and approach. *Strangers Dark and Gold* is a synthesis of the early versions, smoothly woven, told with a high sense of narrative and written with the strength and dignity befitting an epic tale. A glossary is appended.

693 **Jones,** Adrienne. *The Hawks of Chelney;* illus. by Stephen Gammell. Harper, 1978. 77-11855. 245p. Trade ed. $7.95; Library ed. $7.89 net.

7-9 In a primitive civilization, one who does not conform can easily become an outsider, even a pariah. And this is what happens to Siri, only son of an elderly couple in an isolated fishing village. Siri is enthralled by the birds, especially the hawks, that swoop and nest on the cliffs; his parents cannot understand their lonely, intense child and reject him. And so Siri, suspected by the villagers of causing the poor fishing they've had, takes refuge in a cave and lives alone. Alone, until Thea comes; a shipwrecked waif who distrusts men, she is infinitely slow to respond to Siri's patience and tenderness, and even when they find comfort in tender mating, she cannot tolerate their complete isolation. She and Siri are killed by the vengeful villagers—or are they? The bodies are never found—but the sea hawks are still nesting. . . . The veiled ending adds a mystic note to a story that has the mournful dignity and passion of a saga. The style is strong, the characters as harshly-drawn and vivid as the bleak setting, but this is a book written by a craftsman: style, setting, story line, and characters are in complete harmony.

694 **Jones,** Diana Wynne. *Charmed Life.* Greenwillow, 1978. 224p. Trade ed. $6.95; Library ed. $6.43 net.

5-7 In a refreshing fantasy from England, the hypothesis is that with every historic event, there are alternative outcomes, so that divergent worlds exist simultaneously. In Eric (Cat) Chant's world, witches and wizards and warlocks are quite accepted; children with natural talent take lessons in witchcraft. Cat's sister Gwendolen, for example, is ready for a course in Advanced Magic. But when the two orphaned Chant children are taken in by a wealthy enchanter, everything goes wrong. Selfish and spoiled, Gwendolen antagonizes the entire household and is deprived of her magic powers as a punishment. She sends a "double" from an alternate world to take her place, and poor Janet tries to pretend she is Cat's sister. The ending is rather complex; suffice it to say that it proves to be Eric who has the true potential for greatness as an enchanter, and that it is not without a great deal of magical turmoil that his affairs are settled. Nothing macabre here; it's a good-natured romp.

695 **Jones,** Diana Wynne. *The Ogre Downstairs.* Dutton, 1975. 191p. $6.95.

5-6 Adroitly blended realism and fantasy, this story of the adjustment of two sets of children to living together uses the results of magic potions to further compatibility. Caspar, Gwinny, and Johnny detest their new stepfather, the Ogre, and he is indeed detestable: an impatient, self-centered bully; they dislike almost as much his two sons, Douglas and Malcolm. The Ogre gives Johnny and Malcolm identical chemistry sets—with spectacular results. The children fly, they bring inanimate objects to life, and one vial puts Casper and Malcolm into each other's bodies. Sharing troubles and the wrath of the Ogre produces more understanding, and when an angry mother decamps, all unite in an effort to improve the family situation. The Ogre's conversion to comparative sweetness and light isn't quite convincing, but this weakness is outweighed by the strengths of the story: action, variety, humor, strong characterization, and sprightly, polished writing style.

696 **Jones,** Hettie. *Big Star Fallin' Mama; Five Women in Black Music.* Viking, 1974. 150p. $5.95.

7- Five biographies of outstanding singers (Ma Rainey, Bessie Smith, Mahalia Jackson, Billie Holiday, and Aretha Franklin) are written with candor and sensitivity, objective in viewpoint and vigorous in style. The book gives, incidentally, a great deal of information about popular music in this country and the contributions of many black performing artists as well as of the five biographees. A bibliography, a discography. and an index are appended.

697 **Jordan,** June. *New Life: New Room;* illus. by Ray Cruz. T. Y. Crowell, 1975. 73-9755. 53p. $5.95.

K-3 Rudy and Tyrone were nine and ten, and Linda was six, and their apartment was already fairly full without a new baby. What would they do for space? Linda liked sleeping in the living room, but her parents said it would be too noisy after the baby came, they'd be going through the room to reach the kitchen at night for baby's bottles. Linda no more wanted to move in with her brothers than they wanted her in their bedroom. But one good idea led to another, and by the time the three children had finished rearranging furniture, painting their room, and weeding through their toys, it had all become a game and they'd started off their joint tenancy on the right note, as a team. A good family story, this stresses compromise and adaptability as well as the value of cooperative effort, yet there's no didactic note. The illustrations, black and white, are simply composed, have considerable vitality, and show touches of humor in the activities of three enterprising black children.

698 **Joseph,** Joan. *Black African Empires.* Watts, 1974. 87p. illus. $3.95.

5-7 Despite a heavy style of writing, this is a book that is useful for the information it gives and interesting because that information is so infrequently assembled in books for young people. It complements the books on individual leaders like Sundiata or Piankhi, and supplements those African histories that go into little detail about great empires that flourished from the time of ancient Kush to the Zimbabwe civilization of the nineteenth century. While this covers too much ground to go into great detail, it gives a competent overview of the wealth and culture of the black African empires, with adequate historical background and descriptions of outstanding rulers. A bibliography (brief, chiefly of adult books published in England) and a relative index are appended.

699 **Kalb,** Jonah. *The Easy Hockey Book;* illus. by Bill Morrison. Houghton, 1977. 77-9917. 64p. $5.95.

3-5 This is not, the author states firmly, a book intended to teach readers to play hockey, but a compilation of advice on individual aspects of the game (skating forward, skating backward, passing, shooting, and the most common mistakes in all of these) so that the reader can be a better player. This is written more simply than *Hockey Talk for Beginners* by Liss or *Be A Winner in Ice Hockey* by Coombs, and it doesn't give game rules, but it does discuss equipment, it gives sensible advice and it fills a need for a book about ice hockey techniques for readers in the middle grades. The text states that "The teacher won't mind" if you wear out your hockey skates during figure skating lessons. Some might. It would be slightly more useful were there an index or a table of contents—but perhaps all young players will want to read it cover-to-cover anyway.

700 **Kalina,** Sigmund. *How to Sharpen Your Study Skills;* illus. by Richard Rosenblum. Lothrop, 1975. 75-22295. 95p. Trade ed. $4.95; Library ed. $4.59 net.

6-10 Advice on improving study skills begins with such general suggestions as charting and scheduling study time, spacing out homework, keeping materials together and available, reviewing class notes, using flash cards, listening closely, skimming easy material, etc. Separate chapters are devoted to suggestions for sharpening skills in specific subject areas or in taking tests; one chapter discusses use of library resources. It's all very practical, common sense, crisply given advice; inevitably, some of the suggestions will seem extraneous to individual readers. The rather choppy style does not provide smooth reading, but the same quality plus the short paragraphs and marginal comments ("read, plan, think . . . check it over . . . get the most out of your answers") may appeal better to the poor student than would a more cohesive but heavier looking text. An index is appended.

701 **Kaplan,** Bess. *The Empty Chair.* Harper, 1978. 243p. Trade ed. $7.95; Library ed. $7.89 net.

6-8 First published in Canada, this is a cozy realistic story about Jewish family life told by eleven-year-old Becky. When her mother died, almost every woman in the family decided that Becky and her brother needed a woman to raise them, and a succession of candidates was introduced to poor Papa. The basic plot is not highly original (a child's adjustment to death and eventual acceptance of a stepmother) but the story has color and warmth, and the family scenes are often very funny. A glossary of Yiddish words used in the story is appended.

702 **Karen,** Ruth. *Kingdom of the Sun; The Inca; Empire Builders of the Americas.* Four Winds. 1975. 75-9886. 255p. illus. $9.95.

7-
* A superb study of the Inca is based on thorough research although this is not obtrusively evident in the fluid and often witty writing style. The author gives a historical review of the Inca empire, then devotes chapters to various aspects of the society: the contributions from conquered peoples that were assimilated into the massive structure of the Inca civilization; the legal, political, military, and agricultural attainments; the regimented lives of the ordinary citizens, the art and architecture—and above all, pervading all, the worship of the sun, and of the Inca ruler who was son of the sun. A second section of the book describes, in narrative form, the lives of the two people of privilege: a "chosen woman," Ima, and a Chimú prince, Huaman, whose paths cross once. And in the stories of Ima Sumac and Huaman many of the facts that appear earlier in the text are incorporated. Comprehensive, detailed, and quite fascinating. A glossary, an index, a list of important place names, and a list of cities and museums, entitled "Tracking the Inca," are appended.

703 **Karen,** Ruth. *Song of the Quail; The Wondrous World of the Maya.* Four Winds, 1973. 222p. illus. Trade ed. $6.95; Library ed. $6.72 net.

6- Profusely illustrated with photographs of Mayan architecture, art, artifacts, and ideograms, a handsome book gives a vivid account of the impressive achievements of the Maya Indians of Central America. The text describes the social, educational, religious, political, and recreational patterns of the past and the artistic and scientific accomplishments of the Maya. A second section is written in narrative form; it follows first a young man, then a young woman, through a full day, and incorporates many of the facts about the culture that are given in the first part of the book. Competently written and well-researched, covering the same information that is in Von Hagen's *Maya: Land of the Turkey and the Deer* but adding the appeal and the informational value of the photographs. A bibliography, a glossary, and an index are appended, as is a list of major Maya sites and museum collections.

704 **Karl,** Jean E. *Beloved Benjamin Is Waiting.* Dutton, 1978. 77-25286. 150p. $7.95.

4-6 Lucinda didn't know why her parents fought so bitterly, but she did know, now that she was the only one left at home, how much it had helped to have older brothers and sisters around. Nervous as she was about bullies, it was still better to be out of the house. And, once outside, Lucinda found the abandoned caretaker's house in a nearby cemetery, and that's where she went when both parents went off, separately and apparently permanently. Benjamin is the name carved on a memorial statue . . . and when Lucinda hears a voice it seems to come from the statue, but it is a voice of an essence, a being from another galaxy. It—or they—can make the statue glow, and the rapport is strongest when Lucinda is touching "Beloved Benjamin, . . . born 1882 . . . aged 7 years . . ." And so Lucinda and Benjamin talk, a neglected child and a corporate entity from another world, trying to learn as much about this world as there is time to learn before departing. With this farewell and with the burning of her home, Lucinda knows her hiding place will soon be discovered—and she is ready for the foster home she had long feared. On the last visit to the cemetery house, she finds that the statue has disappeared. The reality and the fantasy do not really affect each other, save for the fact that dialogues with Benjamin keep Lucinda from being lonely; the relationship is simply another dimension in a tale told with skill and a strong dramatic sense.

705 **Katz,** Bobbi. *The Manifesto and Me—Meg.* Watts, 1974. 87p. $4.95.

4-6 No secret messages about sexism here, but an open affable story about an eleven-year-old who decides to start a consciousness-raising group. Meg describes the difference between her mother, a doctor, and her Aunt Francie, who likes cooking lessons (but not cooking), shopping, and the status quo. Meg is nervous about the publicity her announced meeting gets, still more nervous when elderly Abigail Witherspoon shows up—but it's Abby who's the heroine. A liberated woman from her youth, Abby insists on going to jail for the girls when a policeman announces the group has committed a misdemeanor—burning without a permit. Burning what? Taffy Teen dolls. There's quiet humor in the writing, a good picture of familial relationships, and a trenchant plea for the cause; while the first-person technique at times is weak, with Meg sounding either naive or coy, what she does and how she reacts are convincing.

706 **Kavaler,** Lucy. *Life Battles Cold;* illus. by Leslie Morrill. Day, 1973. 160p. $6.50.

6-10 A comprehensive examination of the ways in which living things adapt to extreme cold concludes with a discussion of the possibility of human hibernation in times of stress. Like other books by Kavaler, this is distinguished by its objectivity, its accuracy, and its logical organization of material; the style is straightforward and dignified, the illustrations are attractive and informative. The text describes the adaptations men have made to cold, both in their bodily processes and in their way of life; it examines the effects of cold on flora and fauna, and their adaptations to it; it surveys the mechanisms used by living things to adjust while active and while dormant. An index is appended.

707 **Keats,** Ezra Jack. *Dreams.* Maxmillan, 1974. 30p. illus. $5.95.

3-5 yrs. Collage and paint are used to contrast bold, large figures and swirling backgrounds, both bright with color. The story is very simple: Roberto makes a paper mouse, puts it on his window sill at bedtime, and retires. He cannot sleep and goes to the window, knocking off the mouse, and the shadows it casts, huge and angular, frighten off a dog that is menacing a cat. Pleased, Roberto goes to bed. And dreams. The story line is not substantial, but it is satisfying, and the writing is direct and simple.

708 **Keats,** Ezra Jack. *Louie.* Greenwillow, 1975. 75-6766. 32p. illus. Trade ed. $6.95; Library ed. $5.81 net.

3-6 yrs. * Set in the same urban neighborhood that has been the background for many recent books by Keats, this story is illustrated with the same glowing colors—no white space at all, but wise choice of backgrounds for print—and with some of the postercollage that is the artist's trademark. The aura is touching without being maudlin, the writing simple and informal. Louie, a silent child, is so intrigued by a puppet in a show being put on by two other children, that he disrupts the performance and, after it, clings to the puppet. The producers gently disengage Louie from the puppet; he goes home for a nap and a dream; his mother wakes him to say that there's a surprise at the end of a long green string.

When he follows the trail, Louie finds the puppet. Ecstasy! The elements of kindness to others, imaginative play, and a fervent wish granted should have a strong appeal to the picture book audience.

709 **Keller,** Beverly. *Fiona's Bee;* pictures by Diane Paterson. Coward, 1975. 75-7560. 48p. $4.69.

2-3 Written in a direct and simple style for the young independent reader, this story of a shy child who finds friends deviates from the single-daring-act pattern in that Fiona gets attention and makes new friends almost by chance. Having rescued a drowning bee, Fiona stands rigidly still when the bee climbs from her hand up to her shoulder. It stays. She stays. Finally, desperately, she decides to move slowly to the park, where the bee will—she hopes—fly off to investigate a flower. Other children see her, assume the bee is a pet, and talk to her admiringly. In fact, they all walk her home and make future engagements before they leave. The book has the appeals of a wish granted and of overcoming a fear; it is logical and satisfying, and it's laced with an understated humor: "If anything got that bee excited, he might be mad enough to sting the nearest thing. The nearest thing was her wrist."

710 **Kellogg,** Steven. *Much Bigger Than Martin;* story and pictures by Steven Kellogg. Dial, 1976. 75-27599. 27p. Trade ed. $5.95; Library ed. $5.47 net.

K-2 Little Henry is depressed by the fact that his older brother Martin is given to saying things like, "You're too small to swim to the raft," or, "The biggest person gets the biggest piece," when he's slicing the cake. Or, even worse, saying in front of other boys, "Better luck next year, shorty," when Henry misses a basket. Henry then envisions dreams of glory in which he towers over Martin, and he tries several paths to instant growth, one of which makes him ill. His parents discover how unhappy Henry is; Martin overhears this; Henry's get-well surprise is a new basket mounted lower than Martin's. So there's amity between brothers. Nevertheless, Henry takes no chances, for on the last page he appears on a pair of stilts. True, funny, and nicely integrated with a splendid set of pictures, both realistic and fanciful, that depict Henry's daydreams.

711 **Kent,** Jack. *There's No Such Thing as a Dragon;* story and pictures by Jack Kent. Western, 1975. 73-93309. 28p. $3.50.

K-2 Billy wakes one morning to find a small dragon sitting on his bed and beaming, but his mother, when informed of the dragon's appearance, says there is no such thing as a dragon. The creature wags its tail and cuddles close while Billy is dressing, but Billy doesn't pat it as he did at first. "If there's no such thing as something, it's silly to pat it on the head." The dragon grows rapidly, eventually carrying the house along with it when it runs after a bakery truck. The ending? Suffice it to say the problem is solved, in this nursery tall tale, by affection. The ridiculous situation is just the sort that appeals to young children; the pictures are consistent with the combination of exaggeration and blandness of the text: "Cleaning the downstairs took Mother all morning (yes, Mother is an aproned housewife) what with the dragon in the way . . . and having to climb in and out of windows to get from room to room," is amusing in itself, but more amusing to children because Mother is still maintaining that there is no such thing as a dragon.

712 **Kerr,** Judith. *The Other Way Round.* Coward, 1975. 75-4254. 256p. $7.95.

7-9 In a sequel to the autobiographically-based *When Hitler Stole Pink Rabbit,* Kerr describes Anna's late adolescence: her first job, her difficulty in accepting her own status as a German refugee in London, her adjustment to bombing, her first love, and her training as an art student. Wartime London and parents who are struggling emotionally and financially are a background to Anna's maturation. The setting is vividly drawn, the characters well-rounded, and the plot moves briskly although there is no defined story line. A good read.

713 **Kerr,** M. E. *Dinky Hocker Shoots Smack.* Harper, 1972. 198p. Trade ed. $4.95; Library ed. $4.79 net.

7-10 Dinky Hocker spent all her money on food, she looked it, and who would want to date her? But Tucker, who was smitten by Dinky's visiting cousin, had to get her a date or Natalia wouldn't go to the dance with him. So he found P. John, the plump school square —and there was instant rapport, with Weight Watchers an added bond. The young romance is blighted by Dinky's parents, who cannot take P. John's open espousal of reactionary ideas, and who are too busy running home encounter groups for drug addicts to see that their child is miserable. The title phrase is one that Dinky paints on walls and sidewalks in angry protest—she doesn't use drugs. This is both hilariously funny, with sparkling dialogue, and sharply observant. The characterization, the relationships (particularly those between parents and children) and the writing style are excellent.

714 **Kerr,** M. E. *Gentlehands.* Harper, 1978. 77-11860. 192p. Trade ed. $6.95; Library ed. $6.79 net.

7-9 Buddy's mother would have nothing to do with her father; he had
* ignored her and her mother all her life, and just because he had moved to the United States and lived nearby in Montauk she

wasn't about to forgive him. Therefore it was odd that Buddy should take Skye, the very rich girl he had just begun dating, to his grandfather's. She was truly impressed; like Buddy, she didn't believe Grandfather Trenker was the same Trenker that the newspaper article called "Gentlehands." Gentlehands, because in the concentration camp where he'd been in charge, the Italian Jews had called him that; he'd played the opera aria "O dolci mani" to taunt them. And there were other accusations under the heading "Montauk Man Accused of Being Nazi." By the time the situation reaches a crisis, Buddy has quarreled with his parents, left home, and been living with his grandfather, whom he knows as a gentle, cultured man devoted to taking care of stray animals. Can a person have changed so completely? Buddy's grief and dismay are not alleviated by the fact that all the summer he's been so smitten by Skye, he's known it would end by autumn and he's learned that she's biased, snobbish and self-indulgent. In fact, Buddy has learned that people are complex and that one can love despite faults. Characterization and dialogue are first-rate, the story moves at a good pace, and the book is remarkable for the percipience of its relationships.

715 **Kerr,** M. E. *I'll Love You When You're More Like Me*. Harper, 1977. 160p. Trade ed. $6.95; Library ed. $6.79 net.

7-10 You don't think Kerr would ever do anything as simple as just boy meets girl, do you? Wally Witherspoon, by the time he meets Sabra St. Amour, has been rejected by Lauralei Rabinowitz and picked up (and firmly clutched) on the rebound by Harriet Hren. Sabra (a professional name) is an adolescent television star and very much resented by Harriet, who doesn't realize that Sabra's never had a date. Too busy. Sabra and her mother are a cozy twosome—or are they? The story, told alternately by Wally and Sabra, reveals, with Kerr's special blend of sophistication, percipience, humor, and poignancy, that Sabra is lonely, insecure, and tied irrevocably to her own glamorous image. Mama's having an affair with a younger man? Sabra can't take it. Mama suggests quitting the grueling life of TV stardom? Sabra can't give it up. Woven through the relationship of the two protagonists are a series of brilliant characterizations: the whining, possessive Harriet; Sabra's tough, cheerful mother; Wally's friend Charlie, who had decided at sixteen that he will make no secret of the fact that he's gay; Wally's undertaker father, who can't understand why his son wants to follow another career. An all-star cast.

716 **Kerr,** M. E. *Is That You, Miss Blue?* Harper, 1975. 112p. Trade ed. $6.50; Library ed. $5.79 net.

6-9 Flanders Brown has her own problems, like being angry at her mother for leaving home, apparently for love of a much younger man. Like wondering if her father has really sent her to Charles School, an Episcopal boarding school, to get rid of her. But she becomes immersed in the concerns of school life: of living with an angry, beautiful deaf girl who cannot talk, of coping with an arranged date, of sympathizing with Carolyn Cardmaker, a charity student, of watching knowingly the two teachers who love each other, and above all of being under the wing of Miss Blue, an exciting science teacher, a religious fanatic who calmly insists that Jesus visits her. Flan's pity for Miss Blue, when she is discharged, softens her adamant resentment toward her mother, and she stops in New York, en route to her grandmother's, to see her mother, discovering that the young man was only a friend, that her mother simply wanted an independence she couldn't achieve as a wife. While the book ends with an improvement in Flan's own life, there is her wistful note (the story is in first person) in closing, her hope that some day she may see Miss Blue. Flan's learned that others need love, and that she can forgive and love them. This is a sophisticated book, one that demands understanding from its readers and can, at the same time, lead them toward understanding. There are some acid portraits: the arrogant head of the school, the lesbian teachers who bicker with each other, and some scheming classmates, but they are shrewd and convincing portraits, and the book evokes with remarkable conviction the closed world of a private girls' school.

717 **Kerr,** M. E. *Love is a Missing Person*. Harper, 1975. 75-6299. 112p. $5.95.

7-10 While Suzy Slade, the fifteen-year-old who tells the story, is a strongly delineated character, she functions primarily as the commentator on the problems of the other people with whom she is involved: her sister Chicago, the librarian who clings to her love for a man who married someone else, the pathetic young woman her father's just married, and the girl she works with in the library, Nan. Chicago, who had been living with their divorced father and been idolized by him, has come to live with Suzy and their mother, hurt by Daddy's love for the young girl (Enid's nineteen) whom he later marries. Chicago falls in love with Nan's boyfriend Roger (Nan and Roger are black) and precipitates a tragic disruption of all their lives. This is one of Kerr's best, honest and poignant and perceptive. She gives no easy answers to the intricate problems in the lives of her characters, offers no lulling conclusions. The characterization and the dialogue are convincing and trenchant; while the ending is (as it was in *Is That You, Miss Blue?*) left open (Chicago and Roger disappear, Nan is hostile, Daddy ambivalent) it is the right ending, but what is left is not bitterness, it is an aching compassion.

718 **Kerr,** M. E. *The Son of Someone Famous.* Harper, 1974. 226p. Trade ed. $4.95; Library ed. $4.79 net.

6-10 Brenda Belle Blossom! What a name for a fifteen-year-old who refers to herself as a flat-chested tomboy. Brenda Belle is astounded when a new boy in town seems interested; Adam Blessing, who has come to stay with his grandfather, is easy to talk to and ready to form a defensive alliance. (Brenda Belle calls it going steady.) Adam is the son of a celebrity and doesn't want anyone in town to know it; when his loving ex-stepmother visits him, she—being an actress—is recognized; but Adam keeps his secret. He and Brenda have drifted into relationships with others by the time he leaves town, and she knows but wouldn't betray a friend. The chapters are written alternately by the two ("From the journal of A." and "Notes for a Novel by B.B.B."), a device that functions smoothly in a lively, convincing story that has strong characterization, excellent dialogue, and a novel, convincing story line. The author is particularly deft in depiction of the relationships between adult and juvenile characters, in striking a contemporary note, and in drawing the shifts and balances within the adolescent community so that they are wry and touching without being either cute or sentimental.

719 **Kesselman,** Wendy Ann. *Time for Jody;* pictures by Gerald Dumas. Harper, 1975. 75-6295. 40p. Trade ed. $5.50; Library ed. $4.79 net.

4-6 yrs. Girl Groundhog Makes Good. Always sleepy, little Jody is surprised when she is invited by the animals of Distant Field to come and be their groundhog who wakes them in the spring. A family farewell party nets twenty-seven alarm clocks, and Jody finds—on February 2—that they all work. It's a sunny day, however, and she goes back to sleep without resetting the clocks; she's wakened by dripping snow and goes above ground to spread the good news that spring has come, the sun is shining, the grass and flowers are up. Scientific inaccuracy notwithstanding, this is a sunny little story, nicely told and illustrated. It captures both the delight in having a responsibility and the apprehension, it has a poignant note in Jody's sudden qualms about leaving her family, and it echoes the ebullience a child feels (well . . . people feel) at being outdoors on the first balmy day.

720 **Kevles,** Bettyann. *Watching the Wild Apes; The Primate Studies of Goodall, Fossey, and Galdikas.* Dutton, 1976. 75-38939. 164p. illus. $8.95.

6- Illustrated with photographs, this interesting survey of three long-term primate studies is written in a smooth, straightforward style. Each of three accounts is divided into three parts: the first gives information about the scientist in charge of the project; the second describes the setting, the base camp, the methodology, and the apes with which the scientist was working; the third describes an imaginary day of tracking. An excellent final chapter discusses Louis Leakey's leadership in encouraging Goodall, Fossey, and Galdikas to pursue their studies and gives a comparative survey of their findings—not evaluating the studies, but comparing the behavior of chimpanzees, gorillas, and orangutans. Charts that compare characteristics and behavior, a bibliography, and an index are appended.

721 **Kidd,** Virginia, ed. *Millennial Women: Tales for Tomorrow.* Delacorte, 1978. 77-86299. 305p. $8.95.

7- In a science fiction anthology, six women writers describe women of a future time. In "No One Said Forever," by Cynthia Felice, a story that is somewhat obscured by the author's use of alter ego, a young mother faces decision about staying with her family or accepting an assignment in Antarctica; in Cherry Wilder's "Mab Gallen Recalled" an older woman faces mandatory retirement. Nicely structured short stories by Diana Paxson and Elizabeth Lynn envision how life styles and familial patterns have changed. Joan Vinge's novelette, "Phoenix in the Ashes," uses the familiar sf device of a society that has gone back to primitive ways, and tells a touching story of two pariahs who marry for convenience and find affection. The star of the collection is LeGuin's new short novel, "The Eye of the Heron." Like Paxson's tale, it has an off-planet setting; like Vinge's, it envisions a post-holocaust society. The style is polished, the story line compelling, and the struggle between good and evil—exemplified by the confrontation between a ruthless, brutal culture and a band of colonists with a tradition of peace and non-violent resistance—is timeless.

722 **Kingman,** Lee. *Head Over Wheels.* Houghton, 1978. 78-15650. 186p. $7.95.

7-10 Seventeen-year-old identical twins Kerry and Terry are in an automobile accident; Kerry is not hurt, but Terry suffers multiple injuries, including a damaged spinal cord. He will not walk again. Terry, bitter and fearful, rejects his twin; Kerry feels guilty for being unscathed, despondent over the rift, and worried about his brother's future. He's also worried because Jen, his girl, seems to be closer to Terry than anyone else—will he lose her too? Not until Terry is home, hostile and self-absorbed, does his healthy twin rebel and make it clear that he too is suffering—and for the first time the brothers really talk frankly, so that the story ends on an encouraging note. Kingman does an excellent job of showing the grief and stress within a family when one of its members is suffering a traumatic disaster. Medical details are smoothly incorporated, the characterization and relationships are perceptively drawn, the writing serious but not melodramatic.

723 **Kipling,** Rudyard. *How the Rhinoceros Got His Skin;* illus. by Leonard Weisgard. Walker, 1974. 28p. Trade ed. $4.95; Library ed. $4.85 net.

K-3 Of course the Just So stories are not limited to a read-aloud audience of only young children, but the felicity of Kipling's humor is complemented by Weisgard's colorful and effective illustrations in a picture book format. The pictures are faithful to the story, the Parsee clad only in the hat that reflects the sun in "more-than-oriental splendor" and the greedy rhinoceros rolling in frustration and making folds in his skin against a background of tropical—but uncluttered—foliage. The humor of an animal being trapped with cake crumbs under its skin makes this an especially good choice for the silly-humor age.

724 **Kirk,** Ruth. *Hunters of the Whale; An Adventure in Northwest Cost Archaeology;* by Ruth Kirk with Richard D. Daugherty; photographs by Ruth and Louis Kirk. Morrow, 1974. 160p. Trade ed. $5.95; Library ed. $5.11 net.

6- An absorbing account of an archaeological project is described in straightforward prose. Written by the author of *The Oldest Man in America* (reviewed in the September, 1971 issue) with the professor of anthropology who directed the project, Richard Daugherty, the book gives not only the same insight into the work of archeologists that the earlier book did, but also the sense of excitement and fulfillment that the scientific team enjoys. The project is the excavation of Ozette, an abandoned Makah Indian site on the Pacific coast; it has gone on for many years and was instigated and assisted by the Makah Tribal Council. Excellent reportage, a real contribution to the reader's understanding of the work of anthropologists and the methodology of archeology. An index is appended.

725 **Klein,** Aaron E. *Beyond Time and Matter; A Sensory Look at ESP.* Doubleday, 1973. 117p. illus. $4.50.

7-10 A study of psychic phenomena, from the sporadic manifestations and reports of the eighteenth century to the more disciplined investigations of contemporary scientists, this survey includes an evaluation of the scientific method as opposed to hypotheses. The text discusses telepathy, clairvoyance, psychokinesis, and other parapsychological manifestations, with emphasis on current research. Serious and sedate in style, the book is objective about its fascinating subject. A bibliography and an index are appended.

726 **Klein,** Aaron E. *The Electron Microscope;* A Tool of Discovery. McGraw-Hill, 1974. 86p. illus. $4.72.

8- A survey of the earliest microscopes and a description of the principle on which the light microscope functions serve as background for a discussion of the electron microscope. Klein describes its structure and use, the preparation of specimens, the improvements that have been made in the electron microscope since it was first invented, and other kinds of tools such as the microtome and the scanning electron microscope. A brief final chapter comments on the sorts of information obtainable from the use of the electron microscope. The photographs of nuclei, strands of DNA, or magnifications of familiar substances are fascinating; a picture-essay on electron microscope techniques is informative although some of the processes would be clearer in magnified pictures. The pages are solid with crowded type, and the text is serious and scientific, so that the reader with no scientific background has a double handicap, but the writing is impeccably clear and authoritative. A brief bibliography of adult books and an index are appended.

727 **Klein,** Mina C. *Hitler's Hang-Ups; An Adventure in Insight;* by Mina C. and H. Arthur Klein; illus. with photographs and caricatures. Dutton, 1976. 76-9817. 162p. $8.95.

7- The Kleins have divided their text into two parts: in the first, titled "The Surface," they record the events of Hitler's life, and in the second, "The Depths," they discuss unofficial reports and comments, with analyses (their own and those of scientists) of the causes, motivations, aberrations, and inadequacies of Hitler's personality. There is, of necessity, a certain amount of repetition in the second section, but it is not burdensome, and the book as a whole succeeds in being as objective and as moderate in tone as could be expected, given the subject. The authors' stated purpose is to arm readers against the blandishments or threats of other political figures by exposing the weaknesses in, and the growing legendry about, one dictator whose reputation (they say) as a political and military genius has grown since his death. The writing style is competent, the material sequential, the research evident. A list of suggested additional reading and an index are appended.

728 **Klein,** Norma. *Confessions of an Only Child;* illus. by Richard Cuffari. Pantheon Books, 1974. 93p. Trade ed. $4.95; Library ed. $5.49 net.

4-6 "'Boy, your mother's really getting fat!" Libby said. 'She's not fat, dope,' I said. 'She's pregnant.'" The prospect of a baby did not enchant Antonia. She liked things just as they were, a family of three. Having Mom to herself most of the time, having Dad to herself on the nights Mom went to law school, being an only—and happy—child. Toe waits for the baby's birth with trepidation and, when a premature brother is born and dies, is surprised at her own sense of loss. The story ends with the safe arrival of another brother the following year and a delightful scene in which Toe and her classmates (the class is celebrating the birthday of Toe's best friend) have a candid discussion of birth, suggesting to the teacher that she get pregnant and have her baby at school so that they can all watch. What the author achieves in this book, as she has in her books for older readers, is a completely convincing picture of real people. The dialogue is natural, the characterization skilled, and the relationships between children and adults particularly deft.

729 **Klein,** Norma. *Girls Can Be Anything;* illus. by Roy Doty. Dutton, 1973. 26p. $4.50.

4-7 yrs. Amusing cartoon illustrations show Marina and her friend Adam in imaginative play. Marina, bothered by Adam's statements that she has to be the nurse, not the doctor, and has to play stewardess to his pilot, complains to her parents. In each case they assure her that women doctors and pilots exist. Then Adam wants to play at being President. That's a poser; Mother and Daddy admit there hasn't been a woman president yet, but point out what important work is done by Mrs. Gandhi and Mrs. Meir. Marina announces to Adam that she is going to be the first woman president and he can fly her to places where she will give talks. Adam agrees, if she will then fly him to give his talk. Peace and equality are achieved, and both presidents give a delicious banquet of candy, gum, potato chips, etc. The illustration shows an impressive state banquet, a light touch that is sustained through both the text and the illustrations of a very pleasant story that makes its point in a convincing manner.

730 **Klein,** Norma. *It's Not What You Expect.* Pantheon Books, 1973. 128p. $4.95.

7-9 As she did in *Mom, the Wolf Man, and Me,* Norma Klein adds another dimension to the junior novel by having living, breathing adults as well as adolescents. Carla describes a summer in which her parents are separated; her twin brother Oliver, a gourmet cook at fourteen, opens a French restaurant; her older brother finds that his girl is in trouble and that Carla and Oliver have offered to help financially; parents can have a past life; she realizes that she herself has never been a realist as Oliver is, accepting people and events as they come. "Things will never be the same again! Never!" says Carla in closing. Calmly Oliver answers, "They never were." The writing style is lively, the characters vividly drawn, the treatment balanced.

731 **Klein,** Norma. *Mom, the Wolf Man, and Me.* Pantheon Books, 1972. 128p. $4.50.

5-7 Brett knows and calmly accepts the fact that she is an illegitimate child. Since her mother is unconventional in every way, their easygoing household suits Brett admirably and she hopes her mother never will marry and become fussy and organized. When the "wolf man"—an acquaintance who has an Irish wolfhound—courts Brett's mother, the possibility of marriage looms, and Brett hopes to prevent it. She doesn't, and she adjusts. What gives the story its vitality are the warm relationships: Brett's special love for her grandfather, the easy and candid friendship she has with her mother, the attitude of mutual respect between the child and her mother's suitor. The characters are perceptively drawn, the dialogue realistic and often very funny.

732 **Klever,** Anita. *Women in Television.* Westminster, 1975. 75-22352. 142p. illus. $5.95.

7- A series of women working in a broad range of jobs in the television industry discuss their jobs, first describing the work and then, in subsequent chapters, discussing the ways in which they obtained those jobs and became successful. A final chapter is devoted to the "Superpros," women like Pauline Frederick and Joan Cooney. In all, thirty-seven women were interviewed for their comments, which are candid and diverse, giving a solidly informational text to readers who may be interested in television careers. A glossary and an index are appended.

733 **Knotts,** Howard. *Great-Grandfather, the Baby and Me;* written and illus. by Howard Knotts. Atheneum, 1978. 78-2940. 30p. $5.95.

4-7 yrs. A small boy tells the story, and Great-Grandfather's story is folded within it. The boy is feeling sad, because his father has gone off to the hospital to bring home Mommy and the new baby sister. The new baby has been named Mary Alice, but the boy feels strange about her: Mary Alice means nothing; "I didn't know who she was," he says. Great-Grandfather puts a consoling arm around the boy and tells him a long anecdote about when he was sixteen, working on a Canadian wheat farm, and about how he rode miles and miles on a hot summer Sunday just to see a new baby. People did that then, he said. The life was such an isolated one, and everybody was so happy when a baby was born. And the child is comforted; he hears the car in the driveway and goes, hand-in-hand with Great-Grandfather, to see the new baby. Fine-textured line drawings capture the gentle quality of the writing; there is tenderness implicit in the relationship between the very old man and the child, and the story gives a fresh treatment of the dethronement problem.

734 **Koehn,** Ilse. *Mischling, Second Degree; My Childhood in Nazi Germany.* Greenwillow, 1977. 77-6189. 240p. Trade ed. $7.95; Library ed. $7.35 net.

7-
* One of the best books, fictional or autobiographical, about Germany under the Nazi regime, this is told in retrospect by an author who did not know why her loving parents separated until after the war, when she learned that it had helped her and her mother avoid the consequences of the fact that her father had one Jewish parent. Liberals and intellectuals, the Koehns coped, as many did, with a government and a philosophy they detested. And Ilse, a young adolescent, was drafted into the Hitler Youth, forced to go through the motions of devotion. Like Anne Frank, she had youth's resilience; she accepted what she could not change and found moments of excitement or pleasure despite fear, loneliness, and the harsh regime of the Hitler Youth camps. What sets the book apart is the intensity of Ilse Koehn's experience; her memory is as sharp as her observation, and the writing has both candor and integrity.

735 **Kohn,** Bernice. *Communications Satellites; Message Centers in Space;* illus. by Jerome Kuhl. Four Winds, 1975. 74-26872. 58p. $5.95.

4-6 After discussing the work of early science fiction writers, the investigations by such space flight pioneers as Goddard and Tsiolkovsky, and the development of the liquid fuel rocket, Kohn describes the telstar and synchronous satellites, explaining the principles by which they function. She notes the improvements that have been made in communications satellites, and anticipates, in a final chapter, the many ways in which they will serve mankind. The writing is clear, the material well-organized, and the illustrations helpful. A glossary and an index are appended.

736 **Konigsburg,** E. L. *Father's Arcane Daughter.* Atheneum, 1976. 76-5495. 118p. $5.95.

5-9
* Beginning this unusual story, and alternating with the longer sections of the narrative, are passages of dialogue in italics. The speakers are not identified until the very end of the book, providing an element of surprise that adds to its suspense. They are speaking in the present, referring always to the unfolding tale told by Winston, son by a second marriage of a very wealthy man, and older brother to Heidi, an awkward, often uncouth, and

apparently retarded child. Winston is torn between his protective love for Heidi and his resentment at the demands she makes of him and that their mother makes on Heidi's behalf. Then comes father's other daughter, Caroline, who has been missing for seventeen years. Kidnapped, she had disappeared. *Is* the woman who claims to be Caroline genuine—or is she an imposter who knows that a large fortune is at stake? Winston's mother is dubious and jealous, but Caroline passes every test and is accepted by their delighted father. The children love her, but her stepmother, irritated by Caroline's efforts to have Heidi tested and helped, decides that the child should no longer visit her stepsister. The conclusion is strong and dramatic, the characterizations and relationships drawn with depth and perception, and the story line original and beautifully crafted.

737 **Konigsburg,** E. L. *A Proud Taste for Scarlet and Miniver;* written and illus. by E. L. Konigsburg. Atheneum, 1973. 201p. $5.95.

6- One of the most fresh, imaginative, and deft biographies to come along in a long, long time, this story of Eleanor of Aquitaine is unusual both in format and in the sophisticated vitality of the writing style. The story begins with a scene in Heaven, where Eleanor is waiting (". . . she had done things on Earth for which there had been some Hell to pay, so she had not arrived in Heaven immediately . . .") for Henry II. Eleanor, due to the influence of her friends, has made it to Heaven; Henry has been held up in the admissions office. Eleanor's companions each describes a portion of her life, the sections interspersed, and the book concluding with episodes in Heaven. The style of telling is beautifully adapted to each speaker, the biography of the amazing Eleanor is vivid, the historical complexities of French and English history are made lucid, and—bonus—the author's wit is both delightful in itself and eminently suitable for the volatile, shrewd heroine.

738 **Konigsburg,** E. L. *The Second Mrs. Giaconda.* Atheneum, 1975. 75-6946. 153p. illus. with photographs. $5.95.

6-9 An interesting fictional treatment of Leonardo da Vinci focuses on his pert young apprentice Salai, often amusing but—alas—not always truthful. Much of the story has to do with the familial jealousies and bickerings of Beatrice d'Este and her mother and sister; Salai was devoted to Beatrice and was a great stimulus to Da Vinci. He supported his master in his firm resistance to painting the portrait of Beatrice's beautiful and importunate sister Isabella. The theory is advanced here that Salai will persuade the artist (for the story ends before the painting is done) to paint the wife of the humble merchant Giaconda because the woman reminds him of the dead Beatrice, whom he, Salai, adored. However highly fictionalized, this is a warm and intimate picture of Leonardo, of the court circles in which he moved, and of the role of an artist in those circles in Milan and Florence. Reproductions of some of the artist's work are included.

739 **Kooiker,** Leonie. *The Magic Stone;* tr. from the Dutch by Richard and Clara Winston; illus. by Carl Hollander. Morrow, 1978. 78-1713. 224p. Trade ed. $6.95; Library ed. $6.43 net.

3-5 In a smooth translation from the Dutch original, this fantasy deftly blends exotic and prosaic elements, for the witches who are members of the Fine Thread Association (they communicate by crocheting intricate messages) are also ordinary citizens: a wizened grandmother, a deaf and placid cafe owner, a doctor, a truck driver. And the very ordinary boy they draw into their affairs has some quite extraordinary adventures when he finds and keeps a pretty stone that proves to be the most powerful magic object owned by any of the Association. It's the old grandmother of one of Chris's school friends who has lost the stone and who decides that Chris is the logical inheritor because of his tenacity in keeping it and because he so clearly wants to work no evil magic after he has discovered its power. In fact, Chris decides he isn't interested at all, even when all the members who have been pursuing or thwarting him eventually agree with Grandmother that Chris is their heir. The ending gives indication of a possible sequel, but the story stands firmly on it own, its bland style an effective foil for the fantasy and magic of the plot.

740 **Korinetz,** Yuri. *There, Far Beyond the River;* illus. by George Armstrong; tr. by Anthea Bell. O'Hara, 1973. 223p. Trade ed. $5.95; Library ed. $5.97 net.

5-7 A story told as a boy's remembrance of his uncle is permeated with the vitality of Uncle Petya himself. First published in Russia, where it was deemed the Russian Children's Book of the Year, the translation by Hans Baumann was a runner-up for the 1972 German Children's Book Prize. Anthea Bell's English translation is excellent, smooth and idiomatic. Uncle Petya is a bear of a man whose imaginative stories captivate Misha, whose presents enchant him, and whose charm and vigor are especially demonstrated when the two go off on a long trip to northern Russia that is filled with action, adventure, and Uncle Petya's boisterous reunion with an old friend from the days when they were young political activists.

741 **Korty,** Carol. *Plays From African Folktales;* illus. by Sandra Cain; music by Saka Acquaye and Afolabi Ajayi. Scribner, 1975. 74-24418. 128p. $6.95.

3-6 Four tales that can be presented separately or, with interludes, as a unit, have been wisely chosen and nicely dramatized. A narrator is used to introduce characters and make interpolated remarks; occasionally these seem unnecessary ("NARRATOR: Then the snake said: LITTLE SNAKE: Good-bye, dear friend. NARRATOR: And the man said: . . .") but most of the time they are functional. The dialogue is crisp, and the tales have action and humor. The author, a children's theater specialist, gives useful suggestions for scenery, costumes and masks, rehearsing, and performing. All the tales have to do with animals, although there are some human characters, and the author gives advice on ways to use the scripts and on incorporating music and dance. Entertaining, not too long or difficult, and flexible, the plays are easy to mount. A glossary of terms precedes the plays; they are followed by an excellent divided bibliography.

742 **Kraske,** Robert. *The Story of the Dictionary;* illus. with photographs. Harcourt, 1975. 74-23177. 67p. $6.50.

5-9 A useful source of information for the general reader, this is the equivalent of the Golden Fleece for the young person who's enthralled by words. Kraske says of lexicographers, in sum, that they are not the dusty, dry characters one might believe; well, this book is a far cry from the dessicated treatment of the subject one might expect. Lively, varied, often amusing, the text explores the first dictionaries, the great ones and their compilers, the laborious and gigantic task of putting together the O.E.D., the first dictionaries for children and how they differ from adult dictionaries, the two schools of thought about preserving standards in the English language, and the prevalence and richness of that language today. A bibliography and an index are appended.

743 **Kraus,** Robert. *Owliver;* illus. by Jose Aruego and Ariane Dewey. Windmill/Dutton. 1974, $6.95.

3-6 yrs. Kraus at his sunniest, Aruego and Dewey at their most beguiling: Owliver, a small owl, should appeal tremendously to the preschool set and those who read to them. Imitating, role-playing, acting, Owliver impresses his mother with his artistic ability and she gives him lessons in acting and tap-dancing. "Better he should be a lawyer or a doctor," Owliver's father says, and gives him doctor toys and lawyer toys. The engaging owlet uses everything with gusto, and puts on a play in which he has two parts, doctor and lawyer. Both parents are convinced their offspring will follow the bent he or she has selected, but Owliver's choice is a surprise. The pictures are gay and funny and the story is fresh and funny, a nice combination of fancy and reality, written in a blithe, direct style.

744 **Krementz,** Jill. *A Very Young Dancer.* Knopf, 1976. 76-13700. 121p. illus. $8.95.

4- * Profusely illustrated by the work of a skilled photographer, this is a record of a ten-year-old dancer's participation in the preparation and performance of the New York City Ballet's *Nutcracker.* Stephanie is in her fourth year of study at Balanchine's School of American Ballet, and she is the speaker in a candid, conversational text that is extremely effective in conveying the dedication and affection in the ballet dancer's life. Stephanie prattles knowledgeably about her classes, her friends and family (mother was a dancer, older sister is a student also), the rigors of training, the excitement of auditions, and the sober task of learning her role (Mary) when she is chosen. The book is full of the professionalism of serious dancers, however young, and of the excitement of backstage events. Terrific.

745 **Krementz,** Jill. *A Very Young Gymnast;* written and photographed by Jill Krementz. Knopf, 1978. 78-5502. 122p. $8.95.

4- As her followers already know, Krementz is an excellent photographer, and, in following the format of the texts of *A Very Young Dancer* and *A Very Young Rider,* she has again achieved the casual intimacy of a child's conversation. It is ten-year-old Torrance York who is the narrator, describing her training, explaining the execution and judging of gymnastic performances. She's an attractive child, wholly dedicated to gymnastic training, taking ballet lessons, working out at a summer gymnastics camp, travelling to Germany to compete in a meet, taking diving lessons, and apparently filling every spare moment with participation in any gymnastic event she can get to. The author spent a year with Torrance, so the coverage is full; an appended author's note includes the information that Torrance qualified for the A.A.U. Junior Olympics just as the book was going to press, and the quality of the book is such that many readers will feel a sense of gratification that someone they know has made it.

746 **Krementz,** Jill. *A Very Young Rider;* written and photographed by Jill Krementz. Knopf, 1977. 77-74996. 119p. $8.95.

4-7 The sense of happy dedication that was part of the charm of *A Very Young Dancer* is present here, the text again in first person, as ten-year-old Vivi, whose older brother and sister are also riders, describes her work. And to Vivi, although she enjoys riding, it is indeed work; she is serious about training, methodical and responsible about caring for horses and gear, and hopeful that she may some day ride on the national equestrian team. Although the photographs can't capture an equivalent of the beauty of ballet, as they did in the earlier book, they do convey the pleasures and rigorous discipline of Vivi's equestrian passion; technically they are outstanding.

747 **Kumin,** Maxine. *The Wizard's Tears;* by Maxine Kumin and Anne Sexton; illus. by Evaline Ness. McGraw-Hill, 1975. 75-8822. 42p. Trade ed. $5.95; Library ed. $5.72 net.

3-4 The old wizard of the town of Drocknock had given up and gone into retirement; his spells just didn't work any longer and he couldn't end the drought, couldn't cure the townspeople of their chickenpox, couldn't retrieve the cows that had vanished. A new wizard was brought in, young but diligent, who solved all of Drocknock's problems but, in his youthful zeal, caused a worse problem still; everyone turned into a frog. Young readers can, thanks to Evaline Ness, enjoy anticipating the outcome as the wizard (a bespectacled boy) searches for the answer to a riddle when it's literally right under his nose. Blithe and nonsensical, this nicely written fantasy has some piquant surprises, a yeasty humor, and the appeal of a double problem-solution in its structure. The illustrations capture the mood of the story and have a vitality of their own.

748 **Kurelek,** William. *Lumberjack;* paintings and story by William Kurelek. Houghton, 1974. 39p. $6.95.

5- A distinguished Canadian painter describes life in a lumber camp, his text and pictures based on his own experiences in 1946 and in 1951. The prose is simple but vivid, giving a quite full picture of the work of lumbering and of camp life; Kurelek concludes with a brief comment on some of the changes in lumbering technique and machinery since that time. The pictures are stunning: nicely detailed, nicely composed, soft but strong in use of color. In fact, the book has a rare combination of handsome format, striking illustrations, and an informative text.

749 **Kurelek,** William. *A Northern Nativity; Christmas Dreams of a Prairie Boy.* Tundra Books, 1976. 76-23274. 40p. illus. $9.95.

5- * Using as a vehicle a series of dreams that come to a Canadian prairie boy, Kurelek writes a lyric text to accompany twenty paintings of the Holy Family. Or, rather, a series of Holy Families: a fisherman turned away at a wharf, an Eskimo mother and her Child, three radiant figures housed in a service station because there is no room at the motel, an Indian Holy Family at the door of a trapper's cabin. Beautiful.

750 **Kurelek,** William. *A Prairie Boy's Summer;* written and illus. by William Kurelek. Houghton, 1975. 40p. $7.95.

3-5 Since summer is the time that farm children work hardest, this has less about playtime activities than did the author-artist's *A Prairie Boy's Winter,* but it has enough variety to be interesting. Each painting is faced by a page of descriptive text, very simply written and rather more personal than the earlier book, since Kurelek, using third person, reveals that he was poor at games and sports, and was a child conscious of his inadequacies. It is, of course, the pictures by this distinguished Canadian artist that give the book its distinction; each full-color page glows with life and vigor, and the paintings have both a felicity of small details and a remarkable evocation of the breadth and sweep of the Manitoba prairie.

751 **Kurelek,** William. *A Prairie Boy's Winter;* written and illus. by William Kurelek. Houghton, 1973. 40p. $5.95.

3-5 Twenty handsome full-color paintings by an eminent artist show scenes—chiefly chores or recreation—remembered from his boyhood on a Manitoba dairy farm in the 1930's. There is no story line, each page of text that faces a picture being a simply-written description of such winter activities as making a hockey rink, watering the cows, playing in snowdrifts, skiing behind a hayrack, or hauling firewood. The writing has an unpretentious spontaneity, the pictures are evocative.

752 **Kuskin,** Karla. *Near the Window Tree;* poems and notes by Karla Kuskin. Harper, 1975. 74-20394. 63p. illus. Trade ed. $5.50; Library ed. $5.79 net.

3-4 After an introduction addressed to adults, the author prefaces each poem with a note, addressed to children, that gives some background for the poem; this is a response to the questions children have asked about where a poet gets the ideas for poems. The poems are light, lilting, and child-oriented; they speak of cows and cats and toys and children, and they can be used for reading aloud to preschool children as well as by the independent reader.

753 **Lamb,** Geoffrey. *Secret Writing Tricks.* Nelson, 1975. 75-20473. 88p. $6.50.

6-8 A British author explains various systems for writing secret messages, using letters, colors, pinpricks, numbers, and symbols as well as invisible ink. He describes some famous ciphers of the past and suggests ways to break and read encoded messages, giving practice activities in a last section. The material covered in the book is substantially the same as that of Martin Gardner's *Codes, Ciphers and Secret Writing;* this is more formally written although equally lucid. The print here is more spacious, the illustrations rather less informative than in the Gardner book.

754 **Lampman,** Evelyn Sibley. *Squaw Man's Son.* Atheneum, 1978. 77-17503. 172p. $6.95.

7-9 Thirteen-year-old Billy Morrison's white father has sent Billy's mother back to her people, a Modoc tribe, and has married a white woman who treats the boy with contempt. Billy runs off to live with the tribe; he is not fully accepted by some of its members, but his allegiance is to the Modocs when white aggressiveness leads to open warfare. Most of the book is about the struggle of the Indians against white treachery although the author makes it clear that there were heroes and villains in each group. As for Billy, who is captured and then released to his father, he takes off for the coast with a white boyhood friend. The book gives a portion of Oregon history in stirring fashion, history seen primarily from the native American viewpoint, and is based on actual events. Some of the characters are historical figures; an author's note is appended.

755 **Lampman,** Evelyn Sibley. *Rattlesnake Cave;* illus. by Pamela Johnson. Atheneum, 1974. 185p. $6.25.

4-6 An only and overprotected child, eleven-year-old Jamie is determined that he is going to learn to ride while he's visiting Aunt Nora in Montana. Bookish Jamie is anxious to learn everything he can from an old Cheyenne whose grandson works on the ranch, but old White Fang does not give friendship or information to a white boy easily. Jamie does become friendly with another grandson his own age, and the two boys together risk their safety to restore a medicine bag to its proper burial site. Jamie has had visionary dreams that lead to this, and his courage has an unexpected reward. Jamie's attitude, reflecting the author's, is respectful toward the Indian culture and its people. Lampman deftly merges the actual events and the dreams in which Jamie sees the events of the past that make him aware of the solution to the source of the mysterious medicine bag. Good style, good pace.

756 **Lang,** Andrew, comp. *Blue Fairy Book;* edited by Brian Alderson. Kestrel/Viking, 1978. 77-28343. 373p. $12.95.

4-6 One of the first three volumes in new versions (the others are the *Red Fairy Book,* illustrated by Faith Jacques, and the *Green Fairy Book,* illustrated by Antony Maitland) of Lang's color series, this has been revised by an eminent British folklore scholar to be closer to original versions, since Lang was adapting for children of the Victorian era. Alderson has not simplified the writing; indeed, it is often more difficult: in the beginning of the story of Jack the Giant-Killer, for example, Lang's Jack "was a boy of bold temper and (who) took delight in hearing or reading of conjurers, giants and fairies." Alderson says "He was brisk and of a ready lively wit, so that whatever he could not perform by force and strength he completed by ingenious wit and policy." Alderson also consolidates material so that the new version often has longer and heavier blocks of print. In the story of Jack there are a considerable number of changes, primarily the reinstatement of material; in other tales there are comparatively few alterations. In appended notes, the editor explains the reasons for his changes in texts, describes Lang's sources, and discusses the versions adopted. Also included is a reprint of Lang's introduction to the 1889 edition. The black and white illustrations have an appropriately antique air, varying in degrees of the macabre and the romantic to suit the tale being illustrated.

757 **Langone,** John. *Human Engineering; Marvel or Menace?* Little, 1978. 77-26030. 158p. $6.95.

8- Langone explores those frontiers of medical progress in which scientific ability to manipulate living things genetically moves into controversial areas of medical and biological ethics. Should human beings be cloned? Genetically altered? Mentally modified electronically, surgically, or chemically? If we prolong life, can we sustain a population in a world already facing drastic depletion of resources? Langone provides background information, reports on conflicting theories, and cites research in a comprehensive and lucid survey of the potential and the problems. Artificial insemination of anonymously donated sperm has already aroused censure by some on several grounds. There are dangers possible in the escaping of germs engineered to fight environmental pollutants. Langone doesn't offer solutions; he presents the issues lucidly and lets readers take it from there. An index is appended.

758 **Langstaff,** John M. comp. *The Season for Singing; American Christmas Songs and Carols;* musical settings by Seymour Barab. Doubleday, 1974. 124p. illus. $5.95.

All ages Simple arrangements for guitar and piano, and a first line index make this a useful book for children or adults. The songs are grouped under the headings of "Folk Carols," "Shaker, Moravian, Indian," "Black Tradition, Spirituals and Gospel," "Shape-Note Hymns and Composed Songs," and "Part Songs." All carry only the melodic line save for the last group, in which some of the earlier selections are repeated. Many of the songs are of European origin, but Langstaff has included them because the melodies are American variations.

759 **Langstaff,** John M. *Shimmy Shimmy Coke-Ca-Pop! A Collection of City Children's Street Games and Rhymes;* by John Langstaff and Carol Langstaff; photographs by Don MacSorley. Doubleday, 1973. 95p. $4.95.

2-5 Good action photographs add to the appeal of a book that includes the games, songs, rhymes, and chants most familiar to urban children. The text is divided into sections on jump rope games, tag games, clapping games, ball bouncing rhymes, et cetera. As variants of one kind of folk material, the rhymes should be of interest to adults; as a guide to no-cost recreational play, it should be of use to adults and children. Musical notation is included for singing games.

760 **Lapp,** Eleanor J. *The Mice Came In Early This Year;* pictures by David Cunningham. Whitman, 1976. 76-45629. 29p. (A Self-Starter Book). Trade ed. $4.00; Library ed. $3.00 net.

1-2 The small child who tells the story explains that Grandmother's remark about the mice coming in early meant that winter was near. The text consists of a listing of all the seasonal changes they observe, and of tasks they and neighbors did: taking a boat out of the water, picking and storing apples, gathering potatoes. Preparing, as the mice did, for the cold season ahead. The writing is spare and direct, the water color illustrations effective in composition and in use of color, and the pages spacious in format. A very nice story indeed to help reinforce environmental concepts or an understanding of seasonal change, or to stimulate interest in nature study. Simple enough for beginning readers, this may also interest the read-aloud audience.

761 **Lapsley,** Susan. *I Am Adopted;* illus. by Michael Charlton. Bradbury, 1975. 74-22852. 23p. $4.95.

2-5 yrs. Huzzah and hurrah for a book about adoption that accentuates the positive. A simple text, first published in England and suitable for small children the world over, is illustrated with pleasant, conventional watercolor pictures of family scenes. The adopted child speaks: "My name is Charles. I am adopted. So is my sister, Sophie. She is only little. I have a tractor. It was a birthday present," and he goes on to speak of family affairs and his friend and his rabbit and, incidentally, being adopted. That means, he ends, belonging. What emerges is an impression of a happy child who knows he is adopted, finds it mildly interesting, but is so busy with other concerns and so secure that the adoption is presented casually as one of the facts of life, not as a problem. Nicely done indeed.

762 **Larkin,** David, ed. *The Art of Nancy Ekholm Burkert.* Harper, 1977. 76-54103. 92p. illus. $15.00.

7- Although the tone of the text and the small print size indicate that this is primarily a book for adults, it should be of interest to young art students and, like any art book, can be used for browsing by children too young to be interested in the text. It should be especially appealing to children who will recognize some of the pictures from books like *The Scroobious Pip* or *The Nightingale;* also included are some family portraits, photographs of Burkert's sculpture, some pencil drawings, and—the majority of selections—brush and colored ink illustrations in reproduction. Danoff's introduction discusses the artist's career, her theories about art, and the techniques and qualities of her art. The oversize format of the book offers a splendid showcase for the plates that follow.

763 **Larrick,** Nancy, comp. *Crazy to Be Alive in Such a Strange World; Poems About People;* photographs by Alexander L. Crosby. Evans, 1977. 76-49667. 171p. $6.95.

5- This is not an unusual anthology in the sense that much of it is new; most of the selections have been anthologized elsewhere. But it is unusual in the sense that it is permeated with loving appreciation of the variety and complexity of humankind. It is the poets—most of whom are living—who speak wistfully, joyously, sadly, compassionately, curiously—but this collection bears the mark of the compiler: it is Larrick who has loved the poets who loved the people. Author-title and first line indexes are appended, as are notes on the poets whose work is included.

764 **Larrick,** Nancy, comp. *Room for Me and a Mountain Lion; Poetry of Open Space;* illus. with photographs. Evans, 1974. 187p. $5.95.

5- The title phrase, from D. H. Lawrence's "Mountain Lion," reflects to a nicety the theme of this poetry anthology: man's need for the space and beauty of nature and the creatures of the wild. The poems are grouped into such areas as woods, mountains, sea, fields; the representation is broad, although a majority of the poems are by American writers, and the editor has been both catholic and discriminating in her choices. There is an index of first lines and another of poems and poets, the latter including each poet's life dates and nationality. This would be a valuable collection at any time; now, when there is a such a strong interest in ecology, preservation of natural resources, and endangered species, the book should have wide appeal.

765 **Lasker,** Joe. *He's My Brother;* story and illus. by Joe Lasker. Whitman, 1974. 36p. Trade ed. $3.95; Library ed. $2.96 net.

2-4 There are a number of stories about retarded children, very few about the child who is simply slow and who suffers the constant knowledge that he isn't keeping up with achievements of his peers. Often the teasing and irritation such a child provokes exacerbate the situation. Here's an antidote: a simply written book that can help young children understand and sympathize with the slow child. It is written from the viewpoint of Jamie's older brother, and it makes very clear the fact that Jamie's family love and respect him. There is no story line, but the situation is touching (and there's comfort for all children in the knowledge that non-achievement isn't damning) and the style casual. The illustrations are also casual, simple, and pleasant.

766 **Lasker,** Joe. *Merry Ever After; The Story of Two Medieval Weddings;* written and illus. by Joe Lasker. Viking, 1976. 75-22017. 46p. $7.95.

3-5 Basing his richly colored and detailed pictures on medieval paintings, Lasker has illustrated his text in a way that can help readers visualize the costumes, architecture, and customs of aristocrats and peasants of medieval Europe. First he describes the arranged marriage of a merchant's daughter and a nobleman's son, from the first discussions between the fathers, through the years in which the children grew old enough for marriage, to the ceremony and celebration that followed. Then, on a simpler scale, Lasker describes the betrothal arrangements made by a blacksmith and a plowman for their son and daughter, and the subsequent ceremony and feasting. The text, like the illustrations, gives many facts about medieval life styles; the writing is direct and informal; the pictures are handsome.

767 **Lasson,** Robert. *If I Had a Hammer; Woodworking with Seven Basic Tools;* photographs by Jeff Murphy. Dutton, 1974. 75p. $7.95.

5-8 Clear photographs of procedures, correct and incorrect, add to the usefulness of a very good book for the beginning woodworker. The author discusses seven basic hand tools and how to use them, then gives step-by-step directions that are crisp and lucid for making several simple projects; much of what Lasson says in discussing the use of tools or handling of woods in giving project directions is applicable to doing woodwork generally.

768 **Lauber,** Patricia. *Tapping Earth's Heat;* illus. by Edward Malsberg. Garrard, 1978. 78-6283. 64p. $4.74.

3-5 Following a lucid description of volcanic action and geothermal eruptions, Lauber discusses the ways in which geothermal sources are being, or can be, used to provide heat and electricity for people. Examples of use, such as the heating of buildings in Iceland, or the conversion of geothermal energy to electrical energy in Italy are cited, and the book closes with a chapter envisioning the tapping of sources of geothermal energy in the future. Some suggestions for home experiments and an index are included; maps and diagrams are adequately placed and labelled; the book's one weakness is in the print, which is large and clear but with so much space between words that the pages have a fractured appearance.

769 **Lauré,** Jason. *Joi Bangla! The Children of Bangladesh;* by Jason Lauré with Ettagale Lauré; photographs by Jason Lauré. Farrar, 1974. 149p. $7.95.

6-9 A journalist-photographer, Jason Lauré had joined the long trek from Calcutta to Bangladesh in 1971 after the fall of Dacca; a year later he returned to interview and photograph a cross-section of the children of Bangladesh. One is a Bihari whose family's wealth and business were commandeered by the authorities; another is an orphan of eleven who serves as foster mother to the many children of a teacher; a third is a country boy who came to Dacca and earns a meagre living as a rickshaw wallah . . . and all of them, living in a country with a literacy rate of less than 20%, an abysmally low standard of living, corruption, inflation, and little food, are tough and resilient—the hope of a nation that lost most of its potential leadership in a mass extermination of intellectuals during a bitter war. Very occasionally, Lauré wanders from the interviews to discourse about customs or to provide background; for the most part, the text consists of descriptions of the children, their reports of wartime experiences and their present situations, and their hopes—or fears—for the future. The photographs are interesting although not outstanding either as documentary art or as sources of information; the text is candid, moving, and dramatic, as bitter an indictment of war as it is a defiant statement of courage.

770 **Lavin,** Mary. *The Second-Best Children in the World;* illus. by Edward Ardizzone. Houghton, 1972. 48p. $4.95.

K-2 If you have the very best parents in the world and you fear that they are so busy working for you and playing with you that they may get tired and cross, what do you do? Ben, Kate, and Matt decided the answer was to take a long trip around the world to give their parents a rest. The bland quality of the tall tale is evident from their first divulgence of the plan. "If you go on a long trip you will wear out the soles of your shoes," mother says. Ben, who is ten and the oldest, says, "Do not worry, I HAVE A PLAN—we will walk on our heels." Father thinks it would be only kind to give them the car, but the car soon stops dead. So they bury it, naturally. They have some placid, silly adventures, and return with a fine car a kindly old gentleman has given them. Called the best children in the world by their joyful parents, they refuse the title. That would be stuck-up. They are content to be second-best. "But I think they were the best," the author concludes, "What do you think?" Mild and amiable nonsense, delightfully illustrated.

771 **Lavine,** Sigmund A. *Wonders of Terrariums;* illus. with photographs and line drawings by Jane O'Regan. Dodd, 1978. 77-6493. 96p. $5.95.

6-9 With restrained enthusiasm, Lavine gives advice on every aspect of successful terrarium gardening. Following some historical material, he explains why the closed environment of the terrarium facilitates the processes of respiration and photosynthesis. The ensuing text describes containers, placement, natural and artificial light, soil, nutrition, and the selection of plants (flowering, nonflowering) and their temperature requirements. There's advice on planting and maintenance (including therapy for ailing plants) and even a chapter on terrarium zoos. Lucid and comprehensive. A one-page index is included.

772 **Lawrence,** Ann. *The Half-Brothers.* Walck, 1973. 172p. $5.50.

6-9 A courtly romance in the fairy tale tradition is given zest by the pointed wit of the writing and the saltiness of some of the characters. Once upon a time (naturally) in an imaginary land (of course) three half-brothers who shared a kingdom each came to woo the young Duchess, Ambra, whose rich lands would be an enhancement to their own. Only one of the three princes was willing to accept Ambra's terms, that his own inheritance be given up to prove that it was she who was desired rather than her lands, and so Prince Clovis won the girl he truly loved. All of this would be standard plot, but it's enlivened by the descriptions of the efforts of each prince to influence and educate Ambra and by that independent young woman's efforts to enrich and stabilize her small country, with especially amusing developments as her surrogates adjust to the importation of musicians, the establishment of a university, and other schemes that revolutionize their lives.

773 **Lawrence,** Louise. *Star Lord.* Harper, 1978. 77-25674. 170p. Trade ed. $6.95; Library ed. $6.79 net.

6-9 In a time-shift novel set in the Welsh countryside, Rhys finds an injured young man who seems to be about his own age; his name is Erlich, and he has come from a far star. Erlich knows—as do Rhys and his family—that if the authorities find him, he will never escape. And the authorities are searching, for the sound of the crashing ship, which disintegrated on contact with the earth, had been heard for miles around. By a deft fusion of reality and fancy, by fine characterization and polished style, and by a vivid evocation of the Welsh setting and the mystic beliefs in the personality of the brooding mountain where the ship crashed, Lawrence achieves a compelling story with a too-good-to-tell surprise ending.

774 **Laycock,** George. *Beyond the Arctic Circle.* Four Winds, 1978. 77-15844. 116p. illus. $7.95.

5-9 Laycock's text is informal and multi-faceted, covering geological, biological, sociological, and historical aspects of the arctic region. He describes the traditional lifestyle of the Eskimo peoples and the ways in which it has changed with the advent of white settlers and their technology and industries; he gives the historical background of European exploration; he describes the plants and animals of the region and the impact of industrial development and the changes in hunting patterns on the wildlife. Throughout the text, the author emphasizes the need for conservation and for preservation of ecological balance. Several personal anecdotes are included, and the photographs are of good quality and well placed. The glossary of Eskimo terms is not impressive, including some words that are found in the index and some that are not; "muktuk" is defined as "whale skin, and Eskimo food," while it is defined in the text as "the favorite layer of fat lying just beneath the skin" of the beluga whale. A bibliography and an index follow the glossary.

775 **Lea,** Alec. *Temba Dawn.* Scribner, 1975. 75-4346. 134p. $5.95.

5-7 The calf Temba Dawn is Rob's tenth birthday present in a contemporary story set in Scotland. Rob gives her the good care he's promised when she was born, he's dismayed when he learns that his father must sell the farm, and relieved when he learns that he may take his pet with him. A simple story, really, but the book is filled with small incidents that attest to the author's familiarity with farm life, the story of the calf is balanced by Rob's growing interest in a girl who periodically comes to visit the family, and the treatment is realistic and sympathetic without ever becoming sentimental. The characters are firmly drawn, although the characterization is less important than the writing style, which is smoothly colloquial, with a good balance between dialogue and exposition.

776 **Leach,** Maria. *The Lion Sneezed; Folktales and Myths of the Cat;* illus. by Helen Siegl. T. Y. Crowell, 1977. 77-3665. 102p. $6.95.

4-6 Black and white woodcuts with fine detail illustrate a good collection of a long poem, tales, and sayings about cats. Chosen by an eminent folklorist, the book has notes for adults, giving sources and information about each selection; there is also a fairly extensive bibliography. Selections are from many countries and are varied in length and style. Because of the scholarly introduction and notes, the book can be used by older readers as well.

777 **Leach,** Maria. *Whistle in the Graveyard; Folktales to Chill Your Bones;* illus. by Ken Rinciari. Viking, 1974. 128p. $5.95.

4-6 A collection of folk traditions (the many ghosts who are reported to inhabit the White House or the regional ghosts who have been seen repeatedly and about whom a body of belief has grown) and ghost stories. Some of the latter have a flat ending, but others are satisfyingly macabre, and the whole book should delight readers who are going through the stage of happiness-is-a-cold-chill. The bibliography and the notes by the author, an eminent folklorist, should prove useful to adults.

778 **Lee,** Dennis. *Alligator Pie;* illus. by Frank Newfeld. Houghton, 1975. 64p. $6.95.

K-2 An eminent Canadian poet, Dennis Lee wrote the first poems in this collection for his own children, and the published book won the award for the most outstanding children's book published in Canada in 1974. There are nonsensical narrative poems, rhymes for games, humorous and rhythmic four-liners, tongue-twisters, and verses based on Peter Rabbit and Winnie-the-Pooh. Jingly, sunny, silly poems. The illustrations have verve and variety, although some may be limited in appeal because of the dull greens that are combined with white. Not great poetry, but facile poetry that is great fun.

779 **Lee,** Dennis. *Garbage Delight;* illus. by Frank Newfeld. Houghton, 1978. 78-14836. 64p. $6.95.

K-4 Recent winner of the annual prize for the best Canadian children's book in English, this is a collection of nonsense poems that only rarely go beyond humor to achieve mood or imagery. Some are brief four-liners, others are longer narrative poems, and they all have the appeals of rhyme, a pronounced rhythm, and exaggeration. Samples: "Quintin and Griffin," "Quintin's sittin' hittin' Griffin ' What will Griffin sit 'n' do?" and, an excerpt from the title poem, "I'm handy with candy / I star with a bar / And I'm known for my butterscotch burp / I can stare in the eys / Of a Toffee Surprise / And polish it off with one slurp / My lick is the longest / My chomp is the champ / And everyone envies my bite / But my talents were wasted / Until I had tasted / The wonders of Garbage Delight."

780 **Leen,** Nina. *The Bat.* Holt, 1976. 75-32252. 79p. illus. $6.95.

4-7 A professional photographer who overcame her prejudice against bats when sent on an assignment, Leen became fascinated by the varieties and abilities in the bat world, and has published *World of Bats* as well as this book for children. The text consists of captions for photographs, which include some unusual species and some excellent action shots. While the book does not give full information about the bat (nothing on distribution or on reproductive processes) all of the facts it gives are accurate and interesting, and they corroborate the author's plea, in the preface, that the bat is useful rather than harmful.

781 **LeGuin,** Ursula K. *The Farthest Shore;* illus. by Gail Garraty. Atheneum, 1972. 223p. $6.25.

6-9 More ornate than *The Tombs of Atuan,* to which it is a sequel, this third volume of the magic lands of Earthsea ends the story of Ged and introduces a new hero, Arren, the young prince who travels with the Archmage Ged on his last perilous mission. The writing has, as the concept has, a majestic intricacy; to appreciate it the reader must enjoy ornate language, the grave discussion of life and death and love and courage, and the tongue-rolling exotic names of a legendary land. In traveling together to the far reaches of Earthsea, Ged and Arren seek the evil spirit who is choking the land, taking the mystic powers from the mages and dragonlords. Using all of his magic in one heroic effort, Ged seals the breach through which potency is being drained and gives up his life in the effort.

782 **LeGuin,** Ursula K. *Very Far Away From Anywhere Else.* Atheneum, 1976. 76-4472. 89p. $5.95.

7-10 Owen is not an all-American boy. Seventeen, he's not particularly interested in sports, and he can't bring himself to tell his father that he doesn't want the sports car he's received for his birthday. He can't bring himself to tell his mother that he wants to go to M.I.T., not her alma mater, which is an hour from home. He's not even very interested in girls, not until he meets Natalie. She's a serious musician, a supportive friend, and a firm believer in the fact that sex and romance are simply obstacles in one's path. There isn't a lot of surface action in Owen's story, but the depth of characterization, the complexity of human relationships, and the problems of the young intellectual are seen with laser vision and described in a flowing, forthright prose style.

783 **L'Engle,** Madeleine. *Dragons in the Waters.* Farrar, 1976. 76-2477. 293p. $7.95.

7-10 Poly and Charles O'Keefe (*The Arm of the Starfish*) become involved in another mystery when the new friend they have made en route to Venezuela is kidnapped. Simon's cousin—who is later proved an imposter—has been murdered during the voyage and one of the ship's crew is suspected. While there's a bit too much coincidence (several of those on board have known and detested

Cousin Forsyth), the story has pace and suspense, a colorful if crowded collection of characters, and judicious doses of religion and extrasensory perception. Canon Tallis appears at the end to solve problems, as he did in the earlier book, and there's an Indian tribe that hails Simon as their long-awaited leader. Too Much? No, not as L'Engle does it.

784 **LeRoy,** Gen. *Emma's Dilemma.* Harper, 1975. 75-6293. 123p. Trade. ed. $5.95; Library ed. $5.79 net.

4-6 Emma loves her dog. She also loves her grandmother, who has just come to live with Emma's family. The dilemma: Grandmom proves to be violently allergic to dogs, and the sheepdog, Pearl, has to go. Emma's comfort comes from an unexpected source, six-year-old Herbie, for whom she baby-sits, and the relationship between the two is drawn with warmth and humor. Balancing these aspects of the book are some delightful scenes and dialogue between Emma and her friend Lucy, especially the episode in which the two experiment with beauty aids. Not a dramatic story, but nicely constructed and written, with the appeal of everyday problems and the satisfaction of a happy but realistic conclusion.

785 **LeShan,** Eda. *Learning to Say Good-by; When a Parent Dies;* illus. by Paul Giovanopoulos. Macmillan, 1976. 76-15155. 85p. $5.95.

5-7 Serious but not somber, LeShan's text is candid about grief and encouraging about its eventual diminution; this is, however, not written simply to solace the child, but to describe honestly and fully all of the emotions aroused by the death of a parent, the stages of numbness, anger, resentment, mourning, and acceptance of the bereavement as a fact. Brief anecdotes illustrate the ways in which children may react or adjust to special circumstances: guilt suffered because there is a momentary relief after a long illness or because of a hasty word; fear of one's own death or that of the remaining parent; the need for other people; the need for understanding the grief-reactions of others in the family; relationships with other children, et cetera. The writing is direct, sympathetic but never saccharine, in this excellent addition to the growing literature on death for children and young people. A divided bibliography is appended.

786 **Levine,** Edna S. *Lisa and Her Soundless World;* illus. by Gloria Kamen. Behavioral Publications, 1974. 30p. $4.95.

3-5 One of a series of books on "psychologically relevant themes" is written in second person, reminding the reader of how he or she learned to talk, use other senses, and to appreciate the pleasure of being able to see, hear, taste, etc. The text suggests that the reader watch only the picture on a television set to understand how frustrating it is to be unable to understand; it describes eight-year-old Lisa, whose parents realized something was wrong and, on taking her to a doctor, found that Lisa was deaf. It describes the ways in which Lisa and other hard-of-hearing children learn, with various degrees of success, to cope with their handicap. While the writing style is repetitive and occasionally pedestrian, and while the reader may wonder why Lisa's parents took so long (to judge by the illustrations) to realize that something was drastically wrong with their child, the book accomplishes several things: it makes the deaf child's plight explicit, it makes clear the difficulty a deaf child has in learning to speak, it explains why a child so handicapped may feel angry and unloved, and it stresses the fact that the halting speech of the deaf may be governed by physical limitations, that it is not due to a lack of intelligence.

787 **Levitin,** Sonia. *The Mark of Conte;* illus. by Bill Negron. Atheneum, 1976. 75-23041. 226p. $6.95.

6-9 Conte Mark has just moved to California, had just entered the freshman class at Vista Mar high school, and had just discovered that the computer had made a mistake. He had two program cards, one for Conte Mark and one for Mark Conte. Since he was a good student and a hard worker, Conte came up with the brilliant idea of taking a double course and graduating in two years. This is a spoof, of course, but it's a spoof just this side of reality, because all the daft, hilarious things that happen and the people in Conte's life could be true. The author writes with zest and vitality, poking fun at everything in sight, but doing it with affection, and while Conte's rocky path is strewn with some peculiar stony obstacles, the problems he and his friends cope with are very real concerns for most adolescents.

788 **Levitin,** Sonia. *Reigning Cats and Dogs;* illus. by Joan Berg Victor. Atheneum, 1978. 77-15811. 151p. $7.95.

6- What better combination for a book about personal experiences with animals than a love for them, a no-nonsense approach that eschews sentimentality, a sense of humor, and a yeasty writing style? The author and her family had one dignified and aging German Shepherd and decided to get a pup of the same breed; little did they know that the pup would be beset with fears, disobedient, wilful, hostile, and in dire need of discipline (finally acquired at obedience school, where he flunked and had to take the course over) or that the two newborn kittens that were to stay for one night would become permanent and dominating members of the household. What Levitin does is make rueful fun of herself as a soft-hearted dupe, an easy mark whose facile rationalizations are easily seen through by her affectionate family, all of whom are almost as easy marks as she. Delightful for animal lovers and even for those who aren't, but who appreciate effervescent humor.

789 **Levitin,** Sonia. *Roanoke; A Novel of the Lost Colony.* Atheneum, 1973. 213p. illus. $6.25.

6-9 A convincing and well-written fictionalized account of the Roanoke colony is told by one of the younger members, sixteen-year-old William Wythers. William describes the long and arduous journey, the futile attempts to build a permanent settlement, the dissent among the colonists, and the lack of understanding between the settlers and the Indians. In love with an Indian girl, William has become friendly with the members of her tribe and warns the other colonists that he has heard of an impending attack from another, hostile tribe—but they take no heed. All save William and the baby who is his godchild, Virginia Dare, are killed. A lively adjunct to a historical unit on colonial settlement, and an excellent adventure story, this has the same immediacy and solidity as did *Constance,* Patricia Clapp's story of the Plymouth Colony.

790 **Levitin,** Sonia. *A Single Speckled Egg;* illus. by John Larrecq. Parnassus, 1976. 75-4189. 31p. Trade ed. $5.95; Library ed. $5.79 net.

K-3 A tale in the folk tradition is told in an easy, colloquial style and is illustrated with framed pictures of rustic scenes, the muted colors and strong composition especially effective in combination with the rough texture of the background. Larrecq echoes the sly humor of the story, as three noodlehead farmers are outwitted by their wives, who have gone to the village sage for help. The men had exaggerated the import of small things until each had convinced himself that he would have to sell his farm; one, for example, had gloomily predicted that since his hen had laid only one speckled egg, it was a sign of bad luck—therefore the hen house would burn down—therefore it would be necessary to burn the farm. The story is as pleasant to tell as it is to read aloud.

791 **Levitin,** Sonia. *Who Owns the Moon?* illus. by John Larrecq. Parnassus, 1973. 31p. Trade ed. $3.95; Library ed. $3.87 net.

K-2 A tale in the folk tradition is told in sprightly style, the illustrations (very handsome indeed) capturing both the earthy peasant flavor and the noodlehead humor of the story. Three farmers who argued incessantly about everything claim ownership of the beautiful full moon; when it wanes they are furious: a piece has been stolen! Even when it completes its phases and is full again the three foolish men dispute ownership. Their harassed wives hatch a scheme; each convinces her husband to talk to the sage of the village, the Teacher. He decides that the moon will belong to each man for two days a week, and that on Sundays it will belong to everyone; each man must stay home on the nights he owns the moon and on Sundays they must all sit together in peace. Result: contented wives, pacified farmers, and an engaging story to read or tell.

792 **Levoy,** Myron. *Alan and Naomi.* Harper, 1977. 77-41522. 192p. Trade ed. $6.95; Library ed. $6.79 net.

6-8 Naomi is a refugee from France, one of the victims of Nazi oppression; she is silent, fearful, a disturbed and lonely child. When his parents and Naomi's hostess beg Alan to make friendly overtures to her, he agrees reluctantly. "She's a girl; and she's crazy; and I *won't,*" he's said, but he's really a kind boy, and once Naomi responds to his friendliness, he begins to feel fond of her, although he makes very sure none of his friends know about the relationship. Slowly, very slowly, Naomi stops her compulsive tearing of paper, gets over her fear, and begins to confide in Alan. She even goes to school. And then one of the prejudiced toughs at school bullies the two friends; to Naomi it is a repetition of her own persecution and her fragile hold on stability is gone. The ending is poignant and dramatic, especially because such progress had been made, but it is a more effective ending than a happy one would have been; Levoy has been forthright about prejudice (as Alan has been exposed to it) thoughout thebook, and he preserves his artistic integrity. Good writing style and characterization, and a true ear for dialogue add to the merit of a deeply perceptive story.

793 **Levy,** Elizabeth. *Lawyers for the People; A New Breed of Defenders and Their Work.* Knopf, 1974. 120p. Trade ed. $4.95; Library ed. $5.59 net.

6-10 Biographical sketches of nine men and women who believe that lawyers can work for changes that improve society, rather than for the status quo, are included in a book that is based on interviews. The major part of the text is devoted to the cases and causes which the lawyers who have defended the poor or worked for the public interest have championed: the rights of the young, the consumer, the prisoner, the home owner, the welfare recipient, the activist. Each of the nine lawyers has a special field of interest, so the book has diversity as well as giving a broad and exciting picture of the growing segment of the legal profession that is making a commitment to justice for all, often at great personal sacrifice. Good colloquial style, good reporting.

794 **Levy,** Elizabeth. *Something Queer Is Going On;* illus. by Mordicai Gerstein. Delacorte, 1973. 48p. Trade ed. $4.95; Library ed. $4.58 net.

2-4 This gives promise of being a boundary-breaker, a story about girls that boys will read—it's too much fun to miss. Jill's languid basset hound is missing, and she and her friend Gwen ring doorbells looking for Fletcher. One man, a producer of television commercials, says he hasn't seen Fletcher *before* they show him the identifying picture, so the sleuths are soon in hot pursuit. It works—Fletcher has been stolen ("borrowed," the embarrassed Mr. Fernbach says) for a dog food commercial in an effort to avoid paying for his use. Pay is offered. Fletcher lies limp and docile, the payment is used for a tremendous neighborhood party. Bonuses: light, breezy style; deduction by girlpower; understanding working mother who takes a day off to help track Fernbach; contrast of frenzied hunt and indolent dog; the cartoon-style illustrations, which extract every bit of possible humor from the situation.

795 **Lifton,** Betty Jean. *Jaguar, My Twin;* illus. by Ann Leggett. Atheneum, 1976. 76-4475. 114p. $6.50.

4-6 Descendents of the Maya, the Zinacantec Indians of Mexico remain an entity within the country, following their own gods, their own rites. This is the story of Shun, who found his jaguar, the twin animal spirit that comes to lucky ones in dreams. When Shun's father convinces the majority of the community to accept the electrical service offered by the government, his enemy strikes, through an evil shaman, at Shun, who falls ill suddenly. He is cured by a stronger shaman, and all through the progress of the therapy, his lot and the jaguar's are tied, although Shun is on the earth and his twin lives with the gods. Lifton does not write from an outsider's viewpoint but accepts the legends and beliefs as the Indians do. The conviction of the writing is based on research and observation; it does not belittle the traditions of the Zinacantec. The only weakness in the story is the lapse, for six pages, into past tense, when the rest of the book is written in present tense.

796 **Linevski,** A. *An Old Tale Carved Out of Stone;* tr. from the Russian by Maria Polushkin. Crown, 1973. 230p. $5.95.

7-10 Written by a Russian archeologist and smoothly translated, this is a story set in Siberia in its Neolithic Era. While the pace of the story is slowed by some incidents that seem more valuable as evidence of cultural patterns than as narrative developments, the action moves fairly steadily; the inclusion of cultural details is not jarring. Seventeen-year-old Liok, who longs to become a hunter, is destined to become his tribe's new shaman; he has enemies within the tribe who fight his power, and he himself is uneasy at the fact that he has never seen the spirits with whom he supposedly communes. Eventually Liok and his brother run away, join another tribe and take wives; Liok's wife is killed when she violates a taboo; Liok decides that he will return to his village to share the knowledge he has acquired for new weapons and other new ideas, so that the story is both a fine picture of a Stone Age tribe and an indication of a path of cultural diffusion.

797 **Lingard,** Joan. *Across the Barricades.* Nelson, 1973. 159p. $4.95.

6-10 A sequel to *The Twelfth Day of July* (reviewed in the April, 1973 issue) brings Kevin and Sadie together several years after their first hostile encounter when, as Catholic and Protestant children of beleaguered Belfast, they had fought about demonstrating on the anniversary of the Battle of the Boyne. Now they are adolescents, and their first tentatively friendly chance encounter leads to falling in love. Opposition from both families forces them to meet secretly in the home of an understanding former teacher, Mr. Blake. Reprisal against him leads to his death, and Kevin and Sadie decide there is no solution for them but to go to England together. This has more focus than the earlier book, and better construction; like *The Twelfth Day of July* it gives a vivid if depressing picture of the trouble in Ireland and of the tragedy of prejudice.

798 **Lingard,** Joan. *Hostages to Fortune.* Nelson, 1977. 76-49646. 158p. $6.95.

7-10 In a sequel to *A Proper Place* and three earlier books about Sadie and Kevin McCoy, the young couple who had come from Ireland to England to give a better chance to their Protestant-Catholic marriage, the McCoys lose their place when the farm where they work is sold. They fill in for a Welsh pubkeeper who is ill, and then decide to settle in that village, but they do not have an easy time. There are still abrasive differences; Sadie is angry, for example, when Kevin leaves her alone on Christmas Eve to go to midnight mass. But they are beginning to be able to face such differences and talk about them. They are also burdened with the insolent presence of Kevin's runaway younger sister and—for a brief time—by a visit from Sadie's intractably biased mother. Lingard has created well-defined, sympathetic characters in this series, she writes about them with practiced ease and consistent candor, and she touches on problems that are discussed in few books for young readers.

799 **Lingard,** Joan. *The Pilgrimage.* Nelson, 1977. 76-40902. 158p. $6.95.

6-9 Third in a series of stories about doughty Maggie McKinley, a Glaswegian lass who has been enthralled by the stories her

Granny tells about the family's Highland background. Here Maggie and her boyfriend James go off to bike and hike in the north country; James is less interested than Maggie in local history, and he's jealous when a Canadian hiker, Phil, shares Maggie's enthusiasm. In fact, Maggie finds that she responds more to Phil's one kiss than all the protestations of love and pressure for an early marriage from James. Maggie really wants to go to college, but her family feels they need her help—so Maggie gets a job. As always, Lingard treats issues that concern young people—independence, life goals, peer relationships—and, as always, she is realistic in maintaining the credibility of events as they are proscribed by social and financial pressures. The characters and dialogue are convincing, the writing style competently restrained.

800 **Lingard,** Joan. *A Proper Place*. Nelson, 1975. 75-6591. 159p. $5.95.

6-10 Like the preceding books in this well-written sequence of stories about a young Irish couple, *A Proper Place* gives American readers a vivid picture of the depth of religious prejudice existing in Ireland today. Kevin is Catholic, Sadie is not; there has been no way to sustain their marriage but leaving home. Here they are parents, living in a Liverpool slum; while the story takes them to a new life on a Cheshire farm, with a difficult adjustment for the gregarious Sadie, it is just as interesting for the problems it poses about familial acceptance of the marriage when the couple are visited first by Sadie's bigoted mother and then by Kevin's surly younger brother.

801 **Lingard,** Joan. *The Resettling*. Nelson, 1976. 75-35985. 166p. $6.95.

6-9 A sequel to *The Clearance* in which Maggie McKinley's summer with her grandmother ends with a return to Glasgow and the discovery that her family has had an eviction notice. Mrs. McKinley detests the highrise apartment in the suburb to which they've moved—but there is no other place to live. Maggie decides that the solution is for her father, a plumber, to open his own shop so that they can live in an apartment above, and she works doggedly to achieve this: coaxing her parents, hunting for a suitable site, getting out publicity, renovating the premises, and working in the shop. Offered a part in the firm, Maggie decides against it; she'd rather go to college, a decision her parents accept. This is a sturdy, realistic story of the problems of a hardworking family; characterizations and relationships are strong, and the book gives a convincing picture of an adolescent who is happily in love and concerned about her future but conscious of responsibilities to her family.

802 **Lingard,** Joan. *The Twelfth Day of July; A Novel of Modern Ireland.* Nelson, 1972. 158p. $4.25.

6-8 Even before the present trouble in Ireland, the anniversary of the Battle of the Boyne, July 12, was a day fraught with tension between Catholics and Protestants. While the increasing hostility between two groups of children, in a story set in Belfast, is convincing, the ending—in which the children, appalled at the lengths to which violence has carried them, spend the 12th together in amity—is not. The pace and plot are animated: Sadie and Tommy, Protestant, see a Catholic boy, Kevin, painting "Down with King Billy" on a wall, retaliate later with "No Pope Here." These first skirmishes lead to planned reprisal and Kevin's sister—who has been less hostile than Kevin—is hit by a brick and hospitalized. Not a great story, but a good one, and for American readers one that may clarify to some extent the bitterness rampant in Northern Ireland today.

803 **Lionni,** Leo. *In the Rabbitgarden.* Pantheon Books, 1975. 74-15295. 28p. illus. Trade ed. $4.95; Library ed. $5.99 net.

4-6 yrs. Two little rabbits have been told not to eat apples or the fox will get them. When the old rabbit leaves the garden he reminds the little ones—but later, when they can't find any carrots, they accept a snake's offer of a nice, ripe apple. (Garden of Eden, hm? Not at all.) The rabbits and the snake become friendly, and many apples are consumed by the time the old rabbit returns; not only are apples safe, but the snake has frightened the fox away. No moral is cited, but there's a definite note of never-too-old-to-learn. The collage illustrations are bold in composition, excellent for group showing because of their scale, and the use of color is restrained and effective. The story line isn't strong, but it is firm, and the message that adults aren't always right will surely please the read-aloud audience.

804 **Lipsyte,** Robert. *One Fat Summer.* Harper, 1977. 76-49746. 151p. Trade ed. $5.95; Library ed. $5.79 net.

6-10 * Adolescent Bobby Marks hates the summer, when it's more difficult to cover his fat body; he's the butt of malicious teasing by acquaintances, and the only person he's comfortable with is Joanie—partly because they've been friends since age three and partly because she has a big nose that she's taunted about. Bobby describes the rough time he has with a summer job, working for a penny-pinching tyrant, and trying to evade the bully who feels Bobby's taken his job away. Joanie gets a nose job; Bobby loses weight and gains confidence, and he learns that his hero, Pete, is fallible. This is far superior to most of the summer-of-change stories: any change that takes place is logical and the protagonist learns by action and reaction to be both self-reliant and compassionate, understanding Pete's weakness as well as the bullying persecutor's motivation. The plot elements are nicely balanced and paced, the characterization is developed with insight, and the writing style is deft and polished.

805 **Liston,** Robert A. *Terrorism*. Nelson, 1977. 77-10565. 158p. $6.95.

8- Commenting on a terrorist's remark that there are no innocent victims, Liston says "These words have echoed through the vacant corridors of a terrorist's mind ever since." After describing some of the incidents of terrorism in the last decade and noting the escalation and universality of them, he discusses the development of terrorist movements, reactions to terrorism and some ways to combat it, and—sadly—the fact that it is unlikely that international action to stop terrorist acts can be achieved. Serious, objective, thorough, and informative, the book has an excellent divided bibliography and an index.

806 **Liston,** Robert A. *The United States and the Soviet Union*. Parents' Magazine, 1973. 281p. Trade ed. $4.95; Library ed. $4.59 net.

7- A clear and objective assessment of the relationship between two major world powers is preceded by the author's analysis of the reasons for the mutual distrust between the U.S. and the U.S.S.R. and the growing similarity that he sees today. Liston's thesis is that the opposition to communism in this country has been unsuccessful historically, that our support of anti-communist governments has not gained any advantages for us in the outcome of that support, that we have maintained friendly relations with other countries that have degrees of Socialistic structure, and that both countries have had erroneous ideas about the other. The major part of the book is devoted to an analysis of events from the time of the Russian Revolution to today, and concludes with an evaluation of the present situation in light of trade agreements, conferences between heads of state, and agreements on armaments and scientific research. Well written and documented with notes on sources; a bibliography and a relative index are appended.

807 **Liston,** Robert A. *Who Really Runs America?* Doubleday, 1974. 207p. $4.95.

7-10 An analysis of the complexities of the power structure in American life scrutinizes the growing power of the president, the political power of office holders at all levels, the collective expertise of The Process, the titans and lobbyists of big business and of organized pressure groups. The author takes no position on issues that are controversial but restricts himself to explanations of structure and operation in objective commentary. A list of readings and an index are appended.

808 **Little,** Jean. *From Anna;* illus. by Joan Sandin. Harper, 1972. 201p. Trade ed. $4.95; Library ed. $4.43 net.

4-6 Seeing what the Nazis were doing to his Jewish friends, and convinced that things would get worse in Germany made Papa decide that the family must emigrate to Canada. The other children faced the change with varying degrees of equanimity; for Anna it meant disaster. Always the awkward ugly duckling of the brood, unable to learn reading, she dreaded both the new language and the prospect of another set of scornful teachers. Although it seems not quite believable that it occurs to nobody that the child needs glasses, and the change from duckling to swan has moments of sentimentality, this does show convincingly what a sympathetic teacher, a special class, and new friends who are understanding can do to help a child gain self-confidence; the glasses Anna gets after an eye-test are, of course, half the battle won. The writing style and the characterization are excellent, and the double themes of loving freedom and understanding the handicapped are values sustained throughout the story.

809 **Little,** Jean. *Listen for the Singing.* Dutton, 1977. 76-58323. 215p. $6.95.

5-7 In a sequel to *From Anna,* the visually handicapped German expatriate girl and her family encounter anti-German prejudice when World War II starts. They are just adjusting to the fact that the oldest boy, Rudi, has enlisted when he comes home, blinded by an accident. Anna, who knows better than the others what it means to be unable to see, helps her brother adjust to his handicap. The characterization is as discerning here as in the first book, and the author is just as adept at picturing the wartime atmosphere in Canada as she is in describing the warmth and mutual supportiveness of the family circle. Good pace, good style.

810 **Little,** Jean. *Stand in the Wind;* pictures by Emily Arnold McCully. Harper, 1975. 73-5486. 247p. Trade ed. $5.50; Library ed. $5.79 net.

4-6 Prevented by a broken arm from going to camp, Martha is already disgruntled, and she is not cheered by the fact that her parents are going back to the city to entertain guests. Then her sister Ellen suggests that the guests' two daughters come out to the cottage, so that the adults will be in town and the four girls at the lake cottage. There's no strong story line, but the small incidents are eventful enough to sustain interest, and the changes in attitudes of each of the four (who haven't hit it off in the beginning) are convincing. Characterization and relationships are well drawn, the dialogue is easy and natural, and the whole has the sympathetic perception of earlier books by Jean Little.

811 **Lively,** Penelope. *Boy Without a Name;* illus. by Ann Dalton. Parnassus, 1975. 74-28699. 47p. Trade ed. $4.50. Library ed. $4.59 net.

4-6 A quiet, graceful story is set in England during the reign of Charles Stuart—although the nameless foundling who is the protagonist is unaware of kings and thrones. The boy knows only that he had been born in the village of Swinfield and, the master to whom he had been apprenticed having died, he has come there because he belongs nowhere. Caught by the beauty of the stonework when he comes to the village church, named Thomas by the poorhouse overseer, the boy asks to be apprenticed to a stone mason. As his skill grows, Thomas feels increasingly secure; he learns to print and then to inscribe stone, and he puts his name down for all to see: "Thomas Mason." Then, knowing he belongs, Thomas as last feels he can play with other children. The delicately detailed illustrations correspond nicely to the chiseled subtlety of Lively's style, grave and direct, and the story has a timeless quality in its perception of a child's emotional needs.

812 **Lively,** Penelope. *The Driftway.* Dutton, 1973. 140p. $4.95.

5-6 An English boy who is hostile toward his stepmother, Paul is buying equipment so that he can stay in his room and make his own meals, when he is accused of shoplifting. Innocent but terrified, Paul decides to hitch a ride to his grandmother's house. The genial carter who picks the boy and his small sister up is sympathetic to Paul's revelation that he is, off and on, drawn into the past as they ride along an ancient driftway, or cattle road. Each experience brings Paul closer to seeing his relationship with his stepmother in better perspective, although this change is not quite convincing; the remarks of the carter are perhaps more provocative. The fantasy episodes are varied and skillful but quite distinct from the realistic situation, also adroitly handled.

813 **Lively,** Penelope. *The Ghost of Thomas Kempe;* illus. by Antony Maitland. Dutton, 1973. 186p. $4.95.

4-6 When James Harrison's family moved into the old house in an English village strange things began to happen: the alarm clock rang through the night, china rattled on the shelves, objects mysteriously disappeared. And there were notes and messages written in old script: "Goe and tell they that are dyggynge for treasure . . . they must give me one halfe of what they finde . . ." In fact, there was a ghost. Thomas Kempe, he signed his notes, and everything he did James was accused of. If your parents don't believe in ghosts, how do you explain that a long-deceased sorcerer is doing all the mischief? The fanciful element is so matter-of-fact in mood that it blends perfectly with the realistic passages about irritating sister, loquacious old neighbor, exasperated parents, and one sympathetic but dubious friend. Good setting, good style, good story.

814 **Lively,** Penelope. *The House in Norham Gardens.* Dutton, 1974. 154p. $5.95.

6-9 Her cousin felt sorry for Clare. Fourteen years old and there she was saddled with an enormous, dilapidated house, two great-aunts, two lodgers, and very little income. But she didn't understand the way it was; Clare adored the aunts, enjoyed the roomers, and had a sense of kinship with the house, crowded with old family possessions. The aunts had been academicians and liberated women at the time when to be either was considered unwomanly, and they were still concerned with world affairs although unaware of contemporary fads and mores. The story, beautifully written (but in unfortunately small print), has two themes: Clare's concern for her beloved aunts and her recurrent lapses into another time and place, New Guinea, a bond created by her interest in a shield she's found in the attic. These dream-episodes are nicely integrated into the realistic story; the occasional passages in italics that narrate directly, incident by incident, the story of the shield, are less smoothly handled.

815 **Lively,** Penelope. *A Stitch in Time.* Dutton, 1976. 76-23118. 140p. $6.95.

4-6 An only child, sedate and shy, eleven-year-old Maria cannot tell her preoccupied parents that she is sure she hears noises from the past: a creaking swing, a barking dog. And when she sees a sampler made—but not finished—by a child who lived in the same house a century earlier, Maria suspects an old tragedy. This borderline fantasy has a logical and surprising ending, and it develops along with a most realistic story line in which Maria makes friends with one of the children in a noisy, large family next door. Nicely structured and smoothly written, this English story has suspense and momentum, sharp characterization, and natural dialogue.

816 **Lively,** Penelope. *The Whispering Knights;* illus. by Gareth Floyd. Dutton, 1976. 75-33670. 160p. $6.95.

4-6 Three children, conducting an experiment, have assembled frogs' legs, the tongue of a toy dog, and other ingredients ("Eye of newt, and the toe of frog . . .") for a witch's brew. Only gradually do they realize that they have indeed conjured a witch: Morgan le

Fay, who persecutes and frightens them. Their refuge is an elderly woman, Miss Hepplewhite, who functions as a white witch, helping them to evade and at last to defeat the wily Morgan with the help of the circle of stones that come alive in the last, desperate battle of good against evil. The children and the fantasy are believable, but the plot is rather slow-paced for all its dramatic moments; this has neither the evocative quality of *The House in Norham Gardens* nor the tempo and humor of Lively's Carnegie Medal book, *The Ghost of Thomas Kempe*, but it does have her polished style.

817 **Livingston,** Myra Cohn, ed. *O Frabjous Day! Poetry for Holidays and Special Occasions*. Atheneum, 1977. 76-28510. 205p. $6.95.

6- A seasoned and discriminating anthologist, Livingston has chosen a broad range of poetry from English language and other sources, arranging the material by the headings "To Celebrate," "To Honor," and "To Remember" rather than the more usual calendar sequence. She includes some moving poetry about assassinated leaders in the middle section, and some interesting notes on the poems in addition to indexes for authors, translators, first lines, and titles.

818 **Livingston,** Myra Cohn. *4-Way Stop and Other Poems;* drawings by James J. Spanfeller. Atheneum, 1976. 75-28068. 40p. $4.95.

5-9 From one of the best contemporary children's poets, this new collection offers variety of mood, subject, and form, with a consistently high quality. Livingston is equally proficient at writing a lyric poem like "October," a humorous piece like "Revenge" (a declaration of vengeance against whoever took the last cooky in the jar), or a sharp comment on current concerns like "Pollution." The illustrations, more decorative than interpretive, are gravely handsome.

819 **Livingston,** Myra Cohn, ed. *One Little Room, an Everywhere; Poems of Love;* woodcuts by Antonio Frasconi. Atheneum, 1975. 75-8859. 136p. $5.50.

7- Chosen with discrimination, varied in mood and style, and representing a dozen countries and a broad time span (from Biblical days to contemporary decades), this fine collection is divided into "Hopes," "Joys," and "Sorrows." There are poems from fourth-century China, the Song of Songs, a Browning sonnet, an Irish ballad, a jaunty dialogue from sixth-century Greece, many favorites from major poets, and some bittersweet poems of today. There are separate indexes for titles, first lines, translators, and authors.

820 **Livingston,** Myra Cohn. *The Way Things Are and Other Poems;* illus. by Jenni Oliver. Atheneum, 1974. 40p. $4.95.

4-6 A collection of brief poems most of which are clearly written from a child's viewpoint, poems about school and friends, objects in museums, keeping one's room neat, etc. Some of the selections seem very simple, some mildly humorous; a few are lyric, and some, like "Dinosaurs" or "Ocean Dancing," are sharply evocative.

821 **Livingston,** Myra Cohn, ed. *What a Wonderful Bird the Frog Are; An Assortment of Humorous Poetry and Verse.* Harcourt, 1973. 192p. $5.25.

4- A cheerful anthology comprises poems and jingles chosen from authors who range from the fifth century A.D. to contemporary, and from sources other than the English language. Just as varied are the subjects and styles, from haiku and couplets to extracts from plays and mock-serious odes. There's a title index, an author index that includes birth dates, an index of first lines, and—small but significant—an index of translators. The selections have been made with Mrs. Livingston's usual discrimination.

822 **Lobel,** Arnold. *Grasshopper on the Road;* written and illus. by Arnold Lobel. Harper, 1978. 77-25653. 62p. (I Can Read Books) Trade ed. $4.95; Library ed. $5.79 net.

1-2 In a series of short, cheerful stories that are simply written, an itinerant grasshopper meets a series of other small creatures. There are three butterflies who are friendly until they find out that Grasshopper doesn't share every one of their likes and dislikes, and a mosquito who is so insistent that the only way to get across a puddle is in his tiny boat that our hero carries the mosquito, boat and all, across the puddle rather than argue. Each brief tale has a bit of provocative lampooning in it, but can be enjoyed even if the reader doesn't get this message. The illustrations are soft, natural colors and have a gently humorous quality.

823 **Lobel,** Arnold. *Mouse Soup;* written and illus. by Arnold Lobel. Harper, 1977. 76-41517. 64p. (I Can Read Books). Trade ed. $4.95; Library ed. $4.79 net.

1-2 Scheherezade lives again! Caught by a weasel who plans to make soup of him, a wily mouse convinces his captor that the soup would taste better with stories in it. He tells a few tales: a clever mouse gets away from doting bees, a rosebush grows out of a chair, two rocks wonder what's on the other side of the mountain, a mouse and some crickets have trouble communicating. Fine, says the weasel, how does he get the stories into the soup? The mouse sends the noodlehead off to catch bees, crickets, et cetera, and quietly goes home. Robust little tales-within-a-tale are nicely framed by the soup story, with its satisfying ending. The deft pictures echo in color and mood the smooth understatement of the stories, simply told for beginning readers, but also suitable for reading aloud to younger children.

824 **Lobel,** Arnold. *Owl at Home.* Harper, 1975. 74-2630. 64p. illus. (I Can Read Books). Trade ed. $2.95; Library ed. $3.79 net.

1-2
*
Owl is obviously an escapee from Chelm, an inspired idiot who refutes all the legendry about wise old owls. In five short stories, Lobel exposes the lovable silliness of this bird who opens the door on an icy winter's night to let the poor, cold winter in; who races frantically up and down stairs trying to be both places at once; who assures the moon, when it follows him home from the shore, that there's no need to escort him; who is terrified by the two strange bumps in his bed (his feet). The soft lines of the brown pictures befit the soft, brown feathers of the bird, and the preschool audience should enjoy them as much as the beginning independent readers will; for both, the joy of the stories is the simple, childlike humor.

825 **Lorenzo,** Carol Lee. *Heart-of-Snowbird.* Harper, 1975. 74-2628. 227p. Trade ed. $5.95; Library ed. $5.79 net.

6-8 Laurel is thirteen, and she dreams of the day when she can get away from the southern town of Snowbird Gap. Until her friendship with Hank Bearfoot, her only joy had been her pet opossum; Laurel knows that townspeople are prejudiced against Hank's family, new residents of the mountain town, but she finds him gentle, forbearing, and more wise than most of the people she knows. After her stepmother dies and her sister marries, Laurel realizes that her father will not let her go—but she also has matured enough to realize that she has some obligation to him and that she can adjust to the narrow parameters of her life, that escape is not the only answer. Realistic, with good characterization and dialogue, the story is smoothly written; although it starts slowly and has little action, there are taut moments and a satisfying but open ending.

826 **Lowry,** Lois. *Find a Stranger, Say Goodbye.* Houghton, 1978. 78-10204. 187p. $6.95.

6-9 Natalie knows she was adopted as an infant, and she loves her sister and parents dearly. There are no problems in her life; she's been accepted at college, looks forward to medical school, accepts the fact that she and her boyfriend will be parted for most of their college years. Her parents are dismayed when she firmly insists that she wants to find her natural mother, but they make it easy for her, even giving her money to travel in order to pursue her goal. It takes several weekends of journeys and telephone calls, but Natalie finds her mother. There's no high drama; her mother had been fifteen when she became pregnant, and she's now married and has two small boys. She's friendly, she's beautiful, Natalie is relieved to have the mystery ended, but there is no comparison between the satisfying of curiosity and the deep, satisfying love for the family that is truly hers. Not an unusual plot, but Lowry gives it depth and poignancy in a story that has perception and sensitivity but no sentimentality.

827 **Lund,** Doris Herold. *Eric.* Lippincott, 1974. 345p. $7.95.

7- Just a week earlier, Eric had passed the medical exam for entering college freshmen. "Mom," he said now, "I don't feel right." Eric was seventeen, and it was discovered that he had leukemia. His mother's story of the years in which Eric fought his illness, in and out of the hospital, going on to college, being elected captain of the soccer team, falling in love, learning to enjoy each day for what it could bring, is so honest, so touching, so beautifully written that it is a tribute—without sentimentality, without self-pity—to all human courage. Doris Lund can see, as Eric saw, the humor of a situation or the imperfections of people; her perspective is true, her appraisal unflinching.

828 **Lundbergh,** Holger, tr. *Great Swedish Fairy Tales;* illus. by John Bauer; comp. by Elsa Olenius. Lawrence/Delacorte, 1973. 239p. $7.95.

4-6 An anthology illustrated in romantic turn-of-the-century style by one of Sweden's major illustrators. The trolls are misshapen but not ferocious, the princesses slim and shining fair, just as they are in the stories, which have—despite the varied authorship—a gentle quality that pervades the tales of magic. Most of the stories in the book, first published in Sweden in 1966, are by Anna Wahlenberg, and the translations are smooth and idiomatic.

829 **Lundgren,** Max. *Matt's Grandfather;* tr. by Ann Pyk; illus. by Fibben Hald. Putnam, 1972. 20p. $4.95.

K-2 Like Blue's *Grandma Didn't Wave Back,* this story describes a child's adjustment to a grandparent who is in a nursing home and is senile. Here the child is much younger, however, and has not been abraded by the separation but comes to visit. It is Grandfather's eighty-fifth birthday, and Matt has been told that his grandfather is almost like a baby—but he finds that Grandfather has his own way of keeping in touch with reality, and that it is a way that a small child can understand and feel empathetic about. The story, translated from the Swedish, is gentle and affectionate, told with grace and simplicity. A very good introduction to the concept of the changes that come with old age.

830 **Luttrell,** Guy L. *The Instruments of Music.* Nelson, 1977. 77-11968. 127p. illus. $6.95.

6-9 A music educator, Luttrell describes standard orchestral instruments, American folk instruments, the human voice, and electronic instruments. There are separate chapters on strings, horns, woodwinds, percussion, and harp and keyboard instruments. In each case, the author gives some historical background, explains how the instrument operates, and often describes how it sounds or is used in ensemble playing. The diagrams and photographs are adequate, although some of the latter give no indication of comparative size; for example, the violin and viola look the same size and the separate pictures are preceded by a diagram that shows the outlines of four string instruments but doesn't indicate which is which. On the whole, a good introduction that covers a great deal of material with celerity and accuracy. An index is appended.

831 **McCaffrey,** Anne. *Dragonsinger.* Atheneum, 1977. 76-40988. 264p. $7.95.

6-8 * A sequel to *Dragonsong,* a science fantasy in which young Menolly, who yearns to be a harpist, is roughly treated by her sexist father and runs away to another community of the planet. Her identity as the composer of music that has excited the Master Harper is unmasked, and in this novel Menolly comes to Harper Hall as an apprentice. Her talent and her brood of nine fire lizards stir admiration in some and envy in others, as she struggles through her first term and becomes a journeyman. McCaffrey has constructed a believable fantasy world; the characterization is excellent, the writing style fluent and vigorous, and the plot soundly constructed and briskly paced.

832 **McCaffrey,** Anne. *Dragonsong.* Atheneum, 1976. 75-30530. 202p. $7.95.

6-8 On an imaginary planet periodically assailed by a fall of corrosive Thread, the inhabitants are protected by tamed dragons whose flames destroy the Thread as it falls. In an isolated district of the planet, fifteen-year-old Menolly lives, her talent as a harper suppressed and derided by her stern father as unseemly for a girl. Running away, Menolly acquires, by imprinting, a band of fire lizards; when she arrives at the planet's ruling community, her skills at composing and at teaching her lizard brood to sing bring her the career she has longed for. Despite a plethora of characters and a rather heavy-handed preface, this is a science fantasy that is cohesive and briskly paced, with sturdy characterization and a fully-conceived society with its mores and customs.

833 **Macaulay,** David. *Castle;* written and illus. by David Macaulay. Houghton, 1977. 77-7159. 79p. $8.95.

5- It's always been hard to evaluate Macaulay's work without
* overindulgence in superlatives; it's hard now to find superlatives that haven't been used. They are well-deserved: the line drawings are meticulous in detail, lucidly illustrating architectural features described in the text and injected with a refreshing humor (a series of pictures of workmen on the master engineer's staff concludes with a view of his dog) that is never overdone. The pictures are equally impressive whether they show small stonework details or a broad view of castle and town. The writing is clear, crisp, and informative, with a smooth narrative flow as Macaulay describes the planning and building of an imaginary but typical Welsh castle and town of the late thirteenth century, including not only construction details but providing a great deal of information about function, historical background, and medieval life. The book concludes with a rousing description of a siege of the castle, for it had been built by the English as part of a military program to subdue and dominate the Welsh. Superb.

834 **Macaulay,** David. *Cathedral; The Story of Its Construction.* Houghton, 1973. 80p. illus. $6.95.

6- In describing, step by step, the construction of the Chutreaux cathedral, the author gives information useful for the understanding of the architectural details of all Gothic cathedrals. This is told in narrative outline, the sequential material slowing to admit architectural details. Although the illustrations are not labelled, they are well placed in relation to the text, so that the terms and procedures are clear. This does not have the flow and continuity of Anne Rockwell's *Glass, Stones & Crown* which has more text of historical interest, but it is far more detailed in explaining and illustrating cathedral construction, and the spacious pages give a better impression of the grandeur and intricacy of the Gothic cathedral. A glossary of architectural terms is appended.

835 **Macaulay,** David. *City: A Story of Roman Planning and Construction.* Houghton, 1974. 112p. illus. $7.95.

6- Like his impressive *Cathedral,* a Caldecott Honor Book of 1973, Macaulay's *City* is large in concept as well as size, profusely illustrated with fascinatingly detailed drawings, and written with clarity and authority. *City* is both less cohesive and more varied than the earlier book, since it describes not one building but a whole planned community; it therefore includes more cultural details and may be valuable to students of history as well as those interested in art or architecture. The text and illustrations are nicely integrated, describing the planning and building of a city meant for a population of predestined size and varied occupations. Macaulay makes a real contribution, and his books will probably appeal to younger children also, those who may not understand every detail but can browse through the text and pore over the pictures.

836 **Macaulay,** David. *Pyramid.* Houghton, 1975. 75-9964. 80p. illus. $7.95.

5- He's done it again, put together a fascinating account of one of the
* great structures of the past, giving in the clearly written text and wonderfully detailed drawings a step-by-step account of its construction. Macaulay prefaces his description of the pyramid tomb of an imaginary Pharaoh with an explanation of the concepts of death and an afterlife held by the ancient Egyptians, concepts that led to elaborate preparations for their entombment and—if families could afford it—mummification. The architectural details are the more impressive in view of the rudimentary tools used in building pyramids, the ingenuity of the planners, and the sheer massiveness of the project that demanded so many years of so many laborers. The diagrams of details of construction are as impressive as the sweep and grandeur of the long-range drawings. An outstanding book.

837 **Macaulay,** David. *Underground;* written and illus. by David Macaulay. Houghton, 1976. 76-13868. 112p. $8.95.

5- In an extensive and intensive examination of the intricate support systems that lie beneath the street levels of our cities, Macaulay explains the ways in which foundations for buildings are laid or reinforced, and how the various utilities or transportation services are constructed. The text is clear, comprehensive and detailed, and the drawings are impressively meticulous. The illustrations vary in the amount of identifying labels they carry, but they are always close enough to the related text to be comprehensible. Here and there are touches of Macaulay's humor: a dog labelled "dog" or an alligator barely visible in the depths of a sewer system.

838 **MacClintock,** Dorcas. *A Natural History of Zebras;* pictures by Ugo Mochi. Scribner, 1976. 76-12630. 134p. $7.95.

7- As they did in *A Natural History of Giraffes,* the author and the
* illustrator have each done a splendid job, the whole indeed greater

than its parts. Mochi's cutouts are perhaps even more striking here, the dramatic striping of the zebra an excellent subject for the medium. MacClintock, a mammalogist, examines every aspect of zebra species, structure, history, and behavior with quiet authority and a related but brisk writing style. A glossary, a list of suggestions for further reading, and an index are appended.

839 **McClung,** Robert M. *Mice, Moose, and Men; How Their Populations Rise and Fall.* Morrow, 1973. 64p. Trade ed. $4.25; Library ed. $3.94 net.

4-7 In a clear and well-organized text, McClung describes the cycles of population growth and decline among animals that are affected by introduction of new species, overpopulation that uses up food supplies and the consequent starvation that lowers the population, and natural disasters. Man is the great enemy, because of deliberate efforts to control species and because of the encroachment into territory, the pollution he introduces, and the changes he makes in the environment through his own expansion. McClung then turns to a brief examination of the problems of human population growth, touching on the psychological effects covered so thoroughly by A. H. Drummond in *The Population Puzzle* but emphasizing the intricate problems of territory, food supply, and the scientific progress that has increased longevity. Lucid and objective, this is a good overview of a complex problem of our time. A divided bibliography and an index are appended.

840 **McClung,** Robert M. *Peeper, First Voice of Spring;* illus. by Carol Lerner. Morrow, 1977. 77-2410. 30p. Trade ed. $5.95; Library ed. $5.49 net.

2-4 Beautifully detailed black and white drawings show the metamorphoses in peepers and other creatures in their environment as the direct and lucid text follows one tiny frog through its life cycle. McClung writes with authority and simplicity, giving a picture of the ecological balance of the peeper's environment as well as an explanation of the stages of its life and reproductive processes. The pages are spacious, the print large and clear, the text and illustrations nicely balanced on the pages in a fine example of bookmaking.

841 **McClung,** Robert M. *Sea Star;* written and illus. by Robert M. McClung. Morrow, 1975. 75-2247. 48p. $4.95.

2-4 McClung describes the structure of a starfish, its eating habits, its reproductive pattern, and the way it can turn over or regenerate a lost arm. Without anthropomorphizing, he follows one starfish through its yearly cycle. Since there is really little more to say about this simple creature for the primary grades audience, the text is stretched by discussions of the creatures that are in the food chain of which the starfish is a part; it concludes with a brief description of other echinoderms. Large print and plenty of white space make the book visually appropriate for the young independent reader.

842 **McCord,** David Thompson Watson. *Away and Ago;* illus. by Leslie Morrill. Little, 1975. 83p. $5.95.

3-6 McCord's playfulness never becomes cute or whimsical; he rejoices in words, he savors them, he teases them—and he is a master craftsman. That's why this, like his earlier collections of poems, is delightful to read aloud or alone. The occasional serious poems are never heavy, and even those speak to a child's concerns, but most of the selections in *Away and Ago* are light in tone whether they are nonsensical or witty. And all of them have a quality of sunny affection, as though the poet were sharing his fun with a friend. Here there are poems for Christmas and for Hallowe'en and Easter, poems about balloons and baseball, parties and pumpkins and people, and—of course—words themselves.

843 **McDermott,** Gerald, ad. *Arrow to the Sun; A Pueblo Indian Tale;* ad. and illus. by Gerald McDermott. Viking, 1974. 36p. $6.95.

K-3 An adaptation of a Pueblo legend is handsomely illustrated with stylized designs that effectively supplement and complement the story. Black, brown, and glowing shades of gold and orange are used throughout most of the book; when the later pages erupt into other colors as the crux of the action is reached, the effect is stunning. The style of the adaptation is direct, almost staccato; the story describes the birth of the Boy to "a young maiden," engendered by a spark from the Lord of the Sun, tells of the Boy's search for his father, his transmutation into an arrow to visit the mighty Lord, and his return to earth bringing the spirit of the Lord of the Sun to his pueblo.

844 **McDermott,** Gerald, ad. *The Magic Tree; A Tale from the Congo;* ad. and illus. by Gerald McDermott. Holt, 1973. 34p. Trade ed. $5.95; Library ed. $5.59 net.

K-2 The brilliant colors, the stunning designs based on African motifs, and the dignity of the stylized figures combine to illustrate effectively a Congolese tale that has many elements traditional in the folk genre. Rejected, a young man whose twin brother has been loved and favored leaves home. He releases an enchanted people from the magic tree in which each had been a leaf, and he weds the princess and lives in wealth, having promised never to reveal this. Visiting his family, Mavungu tells of his experiences;

suddenly he remembers that he has sworn secrecy and he rushes back to his wife and the beautiful village she magically created. But there is nothing left—only a grove of silent trees. The adaptation is terse and simple, the ending abrupt but with great visual impact.

845 **McDermott,** Gerald, ad. *The Stonecutter;* ad. and illus. by Gerald McDermott. Viking, 1975. 74-26823. 28p. $5.95.

K-3 Brilliantly colored, stylized collage paintings illustrate a familiar Japanese folktale retold in a direct, simple style. A stonecutter, content until he saw the splendid retinue of a prince, wished that he were wealthy. The spirit of the mountain, who had been pleased with Tasaku's diligence, granted the wish, and the stonecutter became a prince. Observing the power of the sun, he wished to become the sun, and his wish was again granted; then he became a cloud, then a mountain. And, mighty and solid, the new mountain felt the chisel of a stonecutter—and, the story ends, "Deep inside, he trembled." The pictures are dramatic, using traditional Japanese motifs but unified in interpretation, and their richness is a good foil for the unadorned style of the adaptation.

846 **McFall,** Christie. *Underwater Continent; The Continental Shelves;* with illustrations by the author. Dodd, 1975. 75-11851. 120p. $5.50.

7-10 An examination of the continental shelves includes a description of their formation, structure, and composition as well as the various uses made by man for fishing, mariculture, mining, and marine archeology. This covers much the same material as does Waters' *The Continental Shelves,* but adds discussion of defense projects and legal jurisdiction (and disputes) so that the book has a slightly different emphasis, also reflected in the many diagrams and in the bibliography, which is laden with government reports and bulletins. The writing style is dry but not difficult; material is logically arranged. An index is appended. This is not quite as readable as the Waters book, but it is competently written, good in coverage, and reflects the author's special interest as a member of the staff of the Naval Photographic Center.

847 **McGough,** Elizabeth. *Dollars and Sense; The Teen-Age Consumer's Guide;* illus. by Tom Huffman. Morrow, 1975. 75-19109. 160p. Trade ed. $5.95; Library ed. $5.11 net.

7-12 Based on a questionnaire in which adolescents were asked what aspects of use of money most interested them, this practical guide discusses jobs and allowances, shopping and credit, savings and checking accounts, legal rights, all of the pitfalls in advertising claims, and tips for wise shopping. The text, written in brisk, informal style, neither talks down to readers nor preaches to them.

This covers the same material as does *Smart Shopping and Consumerism* by Rubie Saunders but adds the very useful chapter, "It's the Law." An Index is appended.

848 **McGovern,** Ann. *The Secret Soldier; The Story of Deborah Sampson;* illus. by Ann Grifalconi. Four Winds, 1975. 75-15819. 62p. $5.95.

3-5 Although the first two chapters of this biography are rather heavily fictionalized, it is on the whole a capably written book, objective in tone. Deborah Sampson Gannett's story (described for older readers and in greater detail by Cora Cheney in *The Incredible Deborah*) is exciting as adventure, appealing because of the protagonist's departure from a conventional sex role, and timely because of the current emphasis on the revolutionary period in American history. This describes very simply—with adequate background information about colonial dissent and rebellion—Deborah's successful plan to pose as a man and join the Continental Army, her service as a soldier, the discovery that she was a female after she was wounded, and her career as a lecturer in later years, after she had married and her children were grown.

849 **McGowen,** Tom. *Odyssey From River Bend.* Little, 1975. 74-34216. 166p. $5.95.

4-6 In a story set in the far future, McGowen envisions a world inhabited only by animals, few of whom know more of the past than the fact that there were other, mightier creatures with an advanced civilization. One old badger, Kipp, has a thirst for knowledge; he gathers others who are willing to face the possible dangers of the Long Ago place, the Haunted Land, and they set forth. There's enough excitement and adventure en route to satisfy readers' love of action, and the animals are quite believable and well-differentiated. Well-plotted, although there are frequent broad hints that the "hidden treasury" Kipp seeks is the public library; the chimpanzees he meets in the city tell him that the human beings of Long Ago died out not because of the (usual in such tales of the future) war, pollution, and overcrowding but because they gave up science to lead a simpler life and could no longer cope with drought and disease.

850 **McGraw,** Eloise Jarvis. *Master Cornhill.* Atheneum, 1973. 204p. illus. $6.25.

6-9 Michael was eleven when the plague struck London and he was sent into the country; returning eight months later, he found that the foster family with which he had lived had all succumbed.

Alone and adrift in the city, he was taken up by a vagabond ballad singer and later served as servant and student to old Master Haas, a map maker. While Tom's welfare is the primary concern of the plot, the setting outshines the action; London, after the plague and during the great fire, is made marvelously vivid in a story told with brisk pace, colorful characters, and a wealth of historical detail, with many places, characters, and incidents based on fact.

851 **McHargue,** Georgess, comp. *Hot and Cold Running Cities; An Anthology of Science Fiction.* Holt, 1974. 245p. $6.50.

7- An interesting assortment of science fiction stories about cities of the future, each author envisioning the controls or stresses of a society unlike the one we know. Van Vogt's "Enchanted Village" is set on Mars, Heinlein's spunky heroine lives contentedly in a lunar city, contemptuous of Earthdwellers (although some of her best friends are from Earth) and in Keith Roberts' "The Deeps" the earth has become so crowded that there are scores of underwater cities. Other stories envisage the vicissitudes of life on Earth; in Kornbluth's "The Luckiest Man in Denv" there is war between the city-states, and in Damon Knight's "Natural State" there's war between city and country dwellers. James Harmon's "The Place Where Chicago Was" seems contrived, but the other seven stories and Benet's poem "Metropolitan Nightmare" are excellent. The consensus of the authors and of the compiler, in her interesting preface, is that we are strangling ourselves, although this is not unanimous.

852 **McHugh,** Mary. *Law and the New Woman.* Watts, 1975. 75-15584. 120p. $5.90.

7- A solid compendium of information about women in the legal profession includes advice on preparation for, and choice of, a law school as well as descriptions of fields of law and types of careers. McHugh discusses teaching of law, private practice, government service, corporation work, political life, public interest jobs and feminist law firms; throughout the book she quotes the opinions or experiences of women lawyers, and she also discusses combining a career with motherhood. In addition to the index, there are a list of approved law schools and a bibliography; within the text many sources for obtaining information are cited. Brisk but informal, well-organized and broad in scope.

853 **McKinley,** Robin. *Beauty; A Retelling of the Story of Beauty & the Beast.* Harper, 1978. 77-25636. 256p. Trade ed. $7.95; Library ed. $7.79 net.

6-9 Youngest of three daughters, Honour Huston had been
* nicknamed "Beauty" as a child, and she tells the story of growing

up to be an awkward, ungainly young woman in love only with books, while her two sisters had swains galore. When her father's fortune collapsed, the offer of a home from sister Hope's suitor was gratefully accepted. So begins a version of the familiar story, written with polished, dry wit; Father does ask his daughters what they want when he sets off on a journey, Beauty does ask for seeds for a rose garden, but the sisters' request for jewels is made in fun. Father comes back bemused, bringing a scarlet rose, and tells the tale of the Beast and the bargain. So Beauty goes off to the enchanted castle, where her greatest delight is the library full of books that haven't yet been written, books by people named Browning and Kipling and C. S. Lewis, and so the ritual begins of Beauty and the Beast reading aloud to each other. Beauty goes home not because her father is ill, but to tell her sister Grace that the man she loves (seen by Beauty in a nephrite plate) is still alive although long reported lost at sea; she brings gifts for her beloved sisters—no jealousy in this version. All the rest is as in the original tale, and the whole thing is delightful.

854 **McNeill,** Janet. *We Three Kings.* Little, 1974. 181p. $5.95.

4-6 A Christmas story set in an English coastal village is beautifully put together, with the story of a school play adroitly interwoven with the major plot, the story of Dan Agnew's grief about his father's depression and his suspicion that his swaggering cousin Roger was the cause of an accident for which Dan's father holds himself responsible. Dan and Roger have always been wary rivals, and Dan is elated when he realizes that Roger has been bullying smaller boys and was surely the instigator of the bicycle accident which caused the child's hospitalization. When he brings the news to his father, Dan is baffled by the fact that Dad refuses to tell Roger's parents, and he later realizes that Roger's bullying is a reflection of his fear of his own father. Meanwhile, the carefully rehearsed Nativity play is almost ruined by a delinquent gang—and in working for a hastily-salvaged performance, Roger and Dan at last find themselves in accord. The closing episode, the performance, is touching; it has honest sentiment rather than sentimentality, and it strikes just the right note after the abrasion and tension of the rest of the book.

855 **McNulty,** Faith. *Mouse and Tim;* illus. by Marc Simont. Harper, 1978. 77-11845. 47p. Trade ed. $5.95; Library ed. $5.79 net.

K-2 There are many stories about children who let a pet go, when it matures, so that it can join its kind; this book does that but adds another dimension. Using a different type-face for the two speakers, it gives concurrent accounts of an experience from the viewpoints of a boy and of his pet mouse. Tim finds the baby mouse, feeds and cossets her, plays with her, and prepares her, by giving her the sort of food she will find in the wild, for her release. The mouse comments on the strange and strong-smelling thing that held her, on the growing familiarity of her boy, on the foods he gives her, and on the strange, sweet-smelling dark into which he releases her. Simont's illustrations, clean and softly-colored in a subdued orange and blue, add a note of explicit tenderness to a simply written text.

856 **Madison,** Winfred. *Call Me Danica.* Four Winds, 1977. 76-48243. 203p. $6.95.

5-7 Danica, living in a small Croatian village where her family farms and operates a restaurant, yearns to go to Canada every time there's a letter from relatives living there. Her parents have no intention of emigrating, but when her father dies (acute appendicitis, untended) the financial situation dictates the wisdom of doing so. Danica's older sister is desolate at leaving her fiancé, but her younger brother is delighted. Life is hard at first, with a crowded basement apartment in Vancouver, little money, and—worst of all—the feeling that she's a foreigner who doesn't belong, speaks with an accent, and has no friends, but Danica eventually adjusts. She gets some part-time jobs, makes some friends, and becomes fluent enough in English to feel that it may, after all, be possible to achieve her goal of a career in medicine. The book has some marked strengths and some weaknesses; it gives an excellent picture of village life as it is now rather than the more usual quaintly rustic depiction, and it gives a vivid picture of the difficulties of the newcomer to a new culture and language; on the other hand, the structure of the story is crowded by sub-plots and minor characters.

857 **Maestro,** Betsy. *Where Is My Friend?* by Betsy and Guilio Maestro; illus. by Guilio Maestro. Crown, 1976. 75-15902. 28p. $6.95.

2-5 yrs. Although told in narrative form, this has but a miniscule plot: Harriet looks for her friend, finally finds her. Harriet's an elephant, the friend a mouse. The writing is simple enough to be read by beginning independent readers, with large print and one short sentence on each double-page spread: "Harriet was looking for her friend," "She climbed *up* a tree," "She came *down* again," "Harriet looked *between* two trees," and so on. The letters italicized here are in heavier type, not italicized, on the pages. The illustrations are bright, poster-simple, spacious, and stylized in elementary fashion, so that they do not take attention away from the print. This achieves nicely its purpose, stressing words that can give young children concepts of position and direction.

858 **Mahy,** Margaret. *The Boy Who Was Followed Home;* pictures by Steven Kellogg. Watts, 1975. 75-4866. 27p. $5.90.

K-2 An amusing, nonsensical story is told in a bland, direct style, and the illustrations echo both qualities; Kellogg's softly-tinted pictures have delightful details, especially in the scenes of the protagonist's classroom during the production of an opera. Robert, small and bespectacled, likes hippopotamuses and is quite pleased when one of them follows him home from school. His parents are not pleased. They are especially not pleased when the next day four, the day after that nine (it mounts to forty-three) hippopotamuses are sporting amiably on the front lawn. They call in a witch, who tries repeatedly to tell them, even as she is giving Robert a hippo-cure pill, that they should be warned—but they cut her off every time. As readers will see, they should have listened. Nice, nice.

859 **Mahy,** Margaret. *The Witch in the Cherry Tree;* illus. by Jenny Williams. Parents Magazine, 1974. 31p. Trade. ed. $4.50; Library ed. $4.19 net.

K-2 Outside David's house an anguished witch sits in the cherry tree, drawn by the delicious smell of cakes baking; she tries tricks to get into the house and tricks to get David outside. But David and his mother are too wise, they calmly bake their cakes (David's burn and he throws them out and the witch loves them) and discuss the dangers of being bewitched; they happily sit together and eat fragrant, still-warm cake. The dialogue between mother and son is bland and amusing, and the author's use of the witch as a foil for the cozy scene within is deft. Mother, forgetting the game for a moment, sees a big, black bird fly off. Indignant, David says it is the witch. "I'm sorry," his mother says meekly, "I just saw her from the corner of my eye." Witch-caused rain over, David goes out to play. Pleasant enough pictures, engaging story.

860 **Manchel,** Frank. *An Album of Great Science Fiction Films.* Watts, 1976. 76-15252. 96p. illus. $5.90.

6- In another excellent survey of an aspect of film history, Manchel discusses the science fiction film, as distinguished from fantasy and horror films, both from the viewpoint of the film's relation to the prevalent interests of the time in which it was produced and from the viewpoint of popular themes in science fiction. The arrangement is chronological, with many photographs illustrating comments on special effects and the artistry or accuracy of the producers. The pictures will probably intrigue browsers too young to understand the text; the book should interest any film or science fiction fan, since the author is both fluent and knowledgeable. A bibliography and an index are appended.

861 **Mann,** Peggy. *The Man Who Bought Himself; The Story of Peter Still;* by Peggy Mann and Vivian W. Siegal. Macmillan, 1975. 75-15514. 215p. $7.95.

7-10 The life story of a slave is based on Kate Pickard's *The Kidnapped and the Redeemed,* published in 1856, in which the author told Peter Still's biography as he had told it to her. It is a remarkable story and it is nicely retold here in smoothly fictionalized form. Peter was six when he and his brother were kidnapped and sold; he firmly (and erroneously) believed he came from a free family and he was determined to gain his freedom even if it took most of his life to earn the money. In the end he did; without knowing any more than his parents' first names, not even where he had lived when he was stolen, Peter Still walked into a Anti-Slavery Office in Cincinnati and met his brother. The details of his life and the abuses they reveal among even "good" slave owners are grim—but the authors never reach for sensationalism; they let the facts speak. An extensive list of sources is appended.

862 **Mann,** Peggy. *There Are Two Kinds of Terrible.* Doubleday, 1977. 76-42372. 132p. $5.95.

5-7 It's one kind of terrible to break your arm just as summer vacation starts, Rob finds. But the other kind of terrible is immeasurably worse: having your mother die. Although Rob loves his father, he hardly knows the man he thinks of as a "cold fish," while he has been, as an only child, very close to his mother. Mom goes to the hospital for tests—and she never comes back. Cancer. The author perceptively describes, through Rob's telling, the stages of anguish: waiting, fearing, knowing, and facing the fact, and the reactions of fear, anger, and grief. Rob tells of the separate burdens of the service, the funeral, the gathering after the funeral, and the utter loneliness after all these. The story ends on a note of encouragement, as Rob and his father move toward a new closeness, a change that is attained gradually and believably. Not a happy story, but an honest and sympathetic depiction of a child's adjustment to illness and bereavement.

863 **Manniche,** Lise, tr. *How Djadja-Em-Ankh Saved the Day; A Tale from Ancient Egypt;* tr. and illus. by Lise Manniche. T. Y. Crowell, 1977. 16p. Folded form $5.95; Scroll form $8.95.

4-6 A most intriguing book. Printed in scroll form on paper that resembles that made from the papyrus plant, available in rolled form in a codex-style tube or folded in accordion style and slip-cased, the ancient Egyptian fantasy is on pages that progress from right to left; translated by an Egyptologist from hieratic, the story is also told in hieroglyphs. On the back of the pages (reading from left to right) are Manniche's comments about the scribes and the writing (hieroglyphs) of ancient Egypt, some facts about beliefs and customs, and a citation for the sources of illustrative detail for the story, written 3,500 years ago. The story itself, a brief tale about how a magician kept his king from boredom (young girls row a boat) and saves the day (he folds back the water to find a lost amulet, since the helmswoman won't row until it is retrieved) is not substantial, but the book itself is handsome, the material unusual, and the information that accompanies the story authoritative.

864 **Manning-Sanders,** Ruth. *Tortoise Tales;* illus. by Donald Chaffin. Nelson, 1974. 95p. $4.95.

K-3 First published in England in 1972, a collection of very short folk tales about animals is particularly suitable for a read-aloud audience. The stories have simple plots, several use such devices as a refrain or cumulation, and most of them are humorous. One or two tales seem flat, lacking either humor or drama, but the rest have good pace and movement. The country of origin and each story is cited, and several of the tales are versions of familiar patterns—a Creole tale, "Hyena and Hare," for example, ends with Hare in the briar patch.

865 **Manning-Sanders,** Ruth. *A Book of Magic Animals;* illus. by Robin Jacques. Dutton, 1975. 74-28306. 127p. $5.95.

4-6 First published in England, a selection of eleven folktales from eight countries are illustrated by the delicate precision of Jacques' distinctive drawings. All but one of the stories are about animals that use magical powers to intervene in the lives of people; several are divided into sections and are actually two or three sequential stories. Although Manning-Sanders varies her style to suit the story, she is always fluid, colloquial and aware—as are all good storytellers—that the story is of paramount importance and the teller only a communicator. In one tale, "Elsa and the Bear," the bear is actually a prince under a spell, but in most of the stories the animals—a varied lot—are truly animals and either function as helpers to human protagonists, as in "The Little Humpbacked Horse" or love as well as help people, as in the three-part "The Dolphin," in which the dolphin helps a princess and her husband Peter but also weds Peter's sister. Expectably, another discriminating Manning-Sanders anthology.

866 **Manushkin,** Fran. *Bubblebath!* pictures by Ronald Himler, Harper, 1974. 27p. Trade ed. $4.50; Library ed. $4.79 net.

3-5 yrs. A minimum of text is used, and it suffices, in a small book in which two self-sufficient little sisters indulge in a favorite indoor sport. "I'm dirty," says one; and Little Miss Echo says, "Dirty too." "I need a bubblebath." "Bubblebath!" And they're off, climbing in and out of the tub, splashing, squabbling over bath toys, hugging, and even washing. Eventually they climb out and dress, complacent over their cleanliness, go out to play, and promptly get dirty. It isn't quite convincing to have no adult on the scene, and the story is slight, but the whole should appeal to small listeners who have enjoyed the procedure themselves.

867 **Maralngura,** N. *Djugurba; Tales from the Spirit Time;* by N. Maralngura and others; rev. ed. Indiana University Press, 1976. 64p. illus. $6.95.

3-5 First published in Australia, a compilation of myths and legends collected by Aborigine students in a teacher training program is illustrated with colorful drawings that have the vigor and awkwardness of children's work. The stories, many of them *pourquoi* tales, incorporate familiar folk motifs and devices; many of them are about animals ("How the Kangaroo Got His Tail"), explain natural phenomena like the rainbow, or describe the adventures of supernatural creatures. The writing has the directness and cadence of oral tradition, and the tales are excellent for reading aloud or telling.

868 **Marcus,** Rebecca B. *Survivors of the Stone Age; Nine Tribes Today;* illus. with photographs. Hastings House, 1975. 75-6843. 124p. $6.95.

7- A fascinating array of studies of contemporary tribes leading lives of primitive simplicity, fascinating not because the author takes the attitude that these peoples are "quaint" or "exotic," she is too scientific for that, but because in their varied ways the tribes show the influence of climate and location on living patterns, because each has a structure and a code (not unrelated to the problems of climate, location, food supply, etc.), and each has reacted in a different way to its contact with a technocratic society. Marcus is dignified and objective in her writing, although never stiff; the text has variety in coverage, since the tribes are from scattered areas in South America, Africa, Australia, and Pacific Islands. Photographs are informative, if not always of high quality technically; a divided bibliography and an index are appended.

869 **Marshall,** James. *Going, Going, Gone? The Waste of Our Energy Resources.* Coward, 1976. 75-44014. 94p. illus. $5.49.

7-10 Marshall takes a sober look at the energy needs and resources of our society and particularly of the United States, pointing out that we have gone back—after the oil embargo of 1974—to the same wasteful practices and indulgent use of automobiles and of labor-saving devices in homes, of lavish use of electricity and power outside the home. He discusses the roles of individuals as well as of government and industry in taking conservatory steps or prohibitive legislation, and describes alternate sources of energy. In the final chapter, "Energy in the Future," the author pleads for a reassessment of priorities, but this approach is implicit, also, in much of the rest of the book. The writing style is dry but informal, the information given in succinct, well-organized style. Suggestions for further reading and an index are appended.

870 **Martin,** Sarah Catherine. *Old Mother Hubbard and Her Dog;* tr. from the Swedish by Virginia Allen Jensen; illus. by Ib Spang Olsen. Coward, 1976. 75-21967. 24p. $6.95.

3-6 yrs. This translation from the Swedish (a version by Lennart Hellsing based on the 1805 publication by Sarah Catherine Martin) is delightfully illustrated by ebullient, comic pictures of Olsen's typically raffish figures. The rhymes have some variants from the set of verses most familiar to English-speaking children, but they're just as jaunty; the most significant variant is the last verse, which has Mother Hubbard flying off into the night, not to return until it is light (with the last, wordless doublepage spread showing a Poppins-like little woman against a vast sunset sky) rather than the more usual "The Dame made a curtsey/The dog made a bow . . ."

871 **Mathis,** Sharon Bell. *The Hundred Penny Box;* illus. by Leo and Diane Dillon, Viking, 1975. 74-23744. 47p. $5.95.

3-5 Soft, misty pictures in brown and white reflect the tenderness that is the prevailing note of a touching story about a child and a very old woman. Great-great-aunt Dew had raised Michael's father, John, when he was orphaned and bereft. Now she had come to live with them. Aunt Dew was a hundred years old; frail and sometimes querulous, she used her big box of a hundred pennies to tell Michael the events of each year of her life, a game the child loved as much as she did. Mother wanted to get rid of the box, but Michael fought to protect Aunt Dew's dear possession, knowing that the old woman was convinced that if the box went, she would go too. He wanted to be able to give her the next penny. Most of the story consists of dialogue, much of it between Aunt Dew and Michael, and while the author gives a strong picture of family relationships and family continuity, it is the love and trust between the two protagonists that is the dominant theme. Beautifully written, the restraint of the style makes the book's message of the love the more effective.

872 **Mathis,** Sharon Bell. *Listen for the Fig Tree.* Viking, 1974. 175p. $5.95.

7-10 Muffin is black, sixteen, and blind. Blindness she is used to, but it does make it harder to cope with Momma. Since her husband's death, Momma had turned to drinking, and Muffin knows that this first Christmas alone will be a bad time for both of them. She had planned so long for her first celebration of the Black African Kwanza. A friend is helping her make a dress, but Momma isn't interested. Muffin is beautiful in her dress, too beautiful; a neighbor attempts rape. Other neighbors come to her rescue, protect and soothe her; one makes a new dress for her and Muffin goes in splendor to the Kwanza. What's beautiful about this book is its fierce integrity, a candor that permits no magic change in Momma, for Muffin comes home from the party to find her mother still craving liquor, still insisting that her husband will be coming back. The characterization and dialogue are excellent, and the writing has an easy flow.

873 **Mayer,** Mercer. *AH-CHOO.* Dial, 1976. 75-9205. 30p. illus. Trade ed. $3.95; Library ed. $3.69 net.

3-5 yrs. An elephant smells a vendor's flowers and sneezes so hard that he blows a house down; taken to court, he sneezes at exhibit A (the flowers) so hard he blows the judge down; taken to jail . . . et cetera. At this point children can guess the next step and add the pleasure of prediction to the appeals of action and humor. And it ends with the elephant's winning a lady hippo's affection, beating his rival the policeman (a rhino) because the latter has given the hippo a bouquet. She's allergic. She sneezes! Only the trumpeting "AH-CHOO's" are in print, otherwise the story is told by the lively, amusing black and white pictures.

874 **Mayer,** Mercer. *Frog Goes to Dinner.* Dial, 1974. 30p. illus. Trade ed. $2.95; Library ed. $2.96 net.

3-5 yrs. Fifth in a series of wordless picture books about a boy who owns several pets, among them an affable, large frog. Here Frog slips into the boy's pocket as he prepares to go off to an elegant restaurant with his parents, and once there he wreaks havoc as he hops into a musician's instrument, leaps into a dowager's salad, and takes a dive into a man's cocktail. The ride home is a picture of gloomy disgrace—but once inside their own bedroom, boy and frog dissolve into whoops of joy. The drawings are funny indeed, and the book passes with flying colors the test for wordless stories: the plot is crystal-clear. Animals, action, humor, disruption—what more could any child want?

875 **Mayer,** Mercer. *Hiccup;* written and illus. by Mercer Mayer. Dial, 1976. 76-2284. 29p. Trade ed. $3.95; Library ed. $3.69 net.

3-5 yrs. Mr. Hippo, the sneezing hero of *Ah-Choo,* takes his lady love out rowing in this almost-wordless sequel. Her persistent hiccups are attacked by her swain as he tries throwing water over her, hitting her on the head, and shouting "Boo!" to startle her. By the time they reach shore the entente is not very cordial, but Ms. Hippo has her revenge when Mr. Hippo begins to hiccup; hastily she gives him the full treatment and trots off, satisfied. The story line is easy to follow, the black and white drawings are amusing (Mayer is very good at such things as simpering, coy animal faces), and there's action on every page.

876 **Mayer,** Mercer. *One Frog Too Many;* by Mercer and Marianna Mayer; illus. by Mercer Mayer. Dial, 1975. 75-6325. 26p. Trade ed. $3.50; Library ed. $3.39 net.

3-5 yrs. The happy foursome of *A Boy, a Dog, and a Frog* (and a turtle) has its harmony threatened when the boy is sent a gift: another frog, a very small one. Everyone is delighted except Frog, who glowers jealously at the intruder and makes several attempts to get rid of it; the last attempt is successful, and they all trail home, the boy weeping and the dog and turtle looking balefully at guilty Frog. A flying leap brings the baby frog in the window and down on Frog's head; last picture in this wordless picture book: little frog cuddling up to big frog. One picture seems abruptly cropped, but the illustrations—as always in this series—tell the story very clearly, and Mayer uses grouping of characters and facial expression with a deft comic sense.

877 **Mazer,** Harry. *The Dollar Man.* Delacourt, 1974. 204p. $5.95.

6-9 In his daydreams Marcus Rosenbloom is no longer fat or clumsy or stupid or without a father. He's a hero, Marcus the Magnificent, or he's Mr. Spaghetti who can perform amazing acts of benevolence by his physical ability. But daydreams are not wholly satisfying, and Marcus yearns to know his father. He doesn't want to disrupt his wonderful relationship with his mother, who doesn't want to talk about it; neither his grandmother nor his mother's friend Bill will tell him. Marcus envisions his father as generous—the Dollar Man. And then after wringing his father's name out of his mother, Marcus finds him: comfortably settled into suburban life, willing to admit that Marcus is his son but anxious to get rid of him, and a Dollar Man all right; he gives Marcus some money, buys him a watch, and puts him on a bus, glad to get this unexpected nuisance out of his life. Marcus, whose mother had loyally defended him when he was falsely accused of smoking marijuana, trusts him implicitly. The Dollar Man's comment has been, "I don't believe a kid can be as big as you and be so dumb . . . Didn't anybody ever tell you that in this world you watch out for number one?" So Marcus rides home a bit wiser, and sadly he leaves the watch and the money on the seat of the bus—unbought. Perceptive, sensitive, and often funny in a bittersweet way, the book draws a believable and touching picture of an unhappy child who only slowly comes to awareness of the integrity of his mother and to the realization that he has absorbed her ethical standards.

878 **Mazer,** Norma Fox. *Dear Bill, Remember Me? and Other Stories.* Delacorte, 1976. 76-5592. 195p. $6.95.

7-12
*
A collection of stories that are varied in mood and style and alike in their excellence, the book has the bittersweet period of adolescence as its binding theme, although one tale, "Zelzah," carries the protagonist into maturity. The title story is a series of letters—or tries at starting a letter—in which a girl writes to congratulate a young man whose engagement has been announced; through the letters she reveals the love she felt when, four years earlier, he had dated her older sister. It's touching without being too sentimental, and it's a good foil for the focus on parent-child relations in "Mimi the Fish" and "Peter in the Park," and the groping for independence and self-confidence that are so sensitively depicted in those and other stories.

879 **Mazer,** Norma Fox. *A Figure of Speech.* Delacorte, 1973. 197p. $4.95.

6-9 Jenny seemed to be the only one in the family who really loved Grandpa; her mother complained that Jenny spent more time in Grandpa's basement apartment than she did with her family. But Grandpa *was* her family, Jenny said. In this touching, realistic story of a child's love of her grandfather, the author shows a situation that is common in our time: the old person who is tolerated, unwanted, and then pushed aside. With acid touch, Mazar describes the son who brings a young wife home and the persistent pressure that results in Grandpa being moved out of his apartment into a single room. When Jenny finds that her parents are planning to move him to an old people's home, she runs off with him to the ramshackle farmhouse of his youth where, exhausted, Grandpa dies. And Jenny cannot get over the hypocrisy of her parent's praise of Grandpa ("Wonderful old man . . .") after his death. Good dialogue, excellent characterization; the book might be stronger if it gave some indication that the other members of the family were occasionally sympathetic or compassionate.

880 **Mazer,** Norma Fox. *Saturday, the Twelfth of October.* Delacorte, 1975. 75-8006. 247p. $6.95.

6-8 Zan (Alexandra) is fourteen, worried about her relationships with other people, about the difficulty of communicating, about the fact that she is fourteen and not yet menstruating. When she finds her brother reading her diary to two of his friends, Zan flees in rage and despair to a favorite spot in a nearby park—and she wakes in another time to find herself the strange outsider in a prehistoric community of cavedwellers. Most of the book is devoted to a convincing and dramatic account of Zan's life with "the People," of the tribal superstitions and living patterns, of the simple acceptance of bodily functions, and of the warmth and loyalty of the larger family. When Zan is—as suddenly as she left—returned to a New York Park, she is stunned to find that her months away have taken a single day, disturbed by the realization that nobody believes any part of her story. She tries to bring into her life the simplicity and candor she had known with the People, wistfully vows never to forget them. This is an effective handling of the time-shift device; although the first shift is abrupt, the second (back to today) successfully integrates the dual experience, and the portion of the book that describes the People has strong characterization and story line.

881 **Mazer,** Norma Fox. *The Solid Gold Kid;* by Norma Fox Mazer and Harry Mazer. Delacorte, 1977. 76-47238. 219p. $6.95.

6-9 Derek Chapman, waiting in the rain for a bus, asks a couple in a van—which he's seen parked up the street—for a ride; he offers a pretty blond girl the same opportunity, and three other adolescents hop in also. Not until they find the doors locked and realize they are being driven out of town do the five worry—and Derek has the answer: they are being kidnapped. The others have been caught accidentally; Derek is the intended victim, the son of a very wealthy man. The harrowing experience brings out the best and the worst in the five young people, as they quarrel and snipe at each other, filled with fear, and suffering from sadistic treatment. The Mazers create a believable situation and explore actions and reactions with percipience; the characters are sharply defined, and their relationships develop logically. But this is more than a perceptive analysis of people under stress, it is also an adventure story with a strong plot, good pace, and well-maintained suspense.

882 **Meade,** Marion. *Free Woman; The Life and Times of Victoria Woodhull.* Knopf, 1976. 174p. $6.95.

7-10 Although the author of this biography slows her text by the inclusion of unimportant details and is less than objective about her subject, she has compiled a detailed study based on research. There has been no need to add dramatic details, for Victoria Woodhull's life is as colorful as the most lurid melodrama. One of a large, poor, and not at all respectable family, she grew up to become this country's first female presidential candidate, an advocate of free love, a champion of women's rights, a wealthy newspaper owner, a writer and lecturer, a stockbroker, the first woman to address a Congressional body, and many times a litigant in trials that shocked and titillated the public. Reviled and in poor health, she went to England, married a wealthy man, and died in 1927, at the age of eighty-eight, the grande dame of a rural estate. A bibliography is appended.

883 **Meltzer,** Milton. *Never to Forget; The Jews of the Holocaust.* Harper, 1976. 75-25409. 217p. Trade ed. $6.95; Library ed. $7.11 net.

8-
* The young people for whom this book was written will not remember the unbelievable horror that the world outside Europe felt, learning of the tragically successful story of Hitler's program to exterminate the Jews, but they may have read of the Holocaust. They will never have read a more moving and explicit documentation. Meltzer has searched sources, marshalled the facts, quoted from eyewitnesses, survivors, contemporary commentators, diaries, and court testimony. His text is meticulously organized and written with an inexorable flow; it describes not only the persecution, pogroms, and death camps, but also the resistance workers of the ghettos, the camps, and the labor force. A chronology, an extensive divided bibliography, and an index are appended.

884 **Meltzer,** Milton. *Remember the Days; A Short History of the Jewish American;* illus. by Harvey Dinnerstein. Doubleday, 1974. 114p. $3.95.

7- Although no bibliography of sources is included, there is little doubt that this judicious and balanced survey of Jewish participation in American history is based on thorough research. Meltzer's writing is serious but not dry, his material well-organized, and his viewpoint broad, so that the problems of Jewish immigrants are seen as part of the whole immigrant problem, his account of Jewish activism in the labor movement seen against the background of the whole labor movement. The text discusses Jewish cultural life, discrimination, the life the immigrants fled and the conditions they found in the United States, Jewish contributions to causes and to public life, and support of Zionism in this country. An index is appended.

885 **Meltzer,** Milton. *Taking Root; Jewish Immigrants in America.* Farrar, 1976. 76-18169. 262p. illus. $7.95.

7- In a companion volume to *World of Our Fathers: The Jews of Eastern Europe* Meltzer examines the lives of those Eastern European Jews who came to the United States between the 1880's and the 1920's. Describing the pogroms, poverty, and prejudice that they fled, the author uses source material to corroborate and color his account of the difficulties of the passage and the adjustment to a new life. He is comprehensive in scope and serious in tone, surveying every aspect of the immigrant experience: the sweatshops and child labor, education and cultural life, involvement in the labor unions, problems of housing, et cetera. Well-researched, the book has an impressive bibliography and an extensive index.

886 **Meltzer,** Milton. *Underground Man.* Bradbury, 1973. 220p. $5.95.

7- Although fictionalized, the life story of Joshua Bowen, the "underground man," is based on fact; the sources cited in the author's postcript are evidence that Milton Meltzer has done the thorough research that distinguishes his nonfiction titles. Bowen was white, but his devotion to the antislavery cause, especially to guiding black people to freedom, earned him more than one jail sentence and bitter persecution by the southern slaveholders whose slaves Bowen helped escape. Spare in construction, the book has historical interest, dramatic appeal, and an aura of suspense and danger that emanates from the events rather than by the declaration of the author.

887 **Meltzer,** Milton. *Violins and Shovels;* illus. with photographs. Delacorte, 1976. 75-32916. 99p. $6.95.

8- To young adults who know WPA only as an acronym of the past, Meltzer's splendid documentary can bring to life not only an agency but an era. Based on his usual meticulous research, the book describes the fervor, both personal and artistic, that permeated the writers, artists, folklorists, actors, and musicians for whom the project meant not only a livelihood in a time of deep financial crisis but an opportunity to experiment and expand. As one of the writers, Meltzer (whose WPA job was his first, after he had been subsisting on relief—less than $30 a month) is particularly knowledgeable about the work of other writers and the censure of some of the writing projects, but he gives full, vigorous coverage to other aspects of the program. A divided bibliography is included.

888 **Meltzer,** Milton. *World of Our Fathers; The Jews of Eastern Europe.* Farrar, 1974. 274p. illus. $7.95.

7- A serious almost scholarly book based on thorough research gives a detailed and comprehensive picture of Jewish life in Eastern Europe in the nineteenth century. Meltzer gives historical background but focuses on the problems and concerns of Jews, rural and urban, up to the period of heavy migration to the United States. The text describes both the common people and the leaders; the pervasive motifs are persecution, which affected Jews politically, economically, and personally, and the tenacious courage that was bolstered by religious conviction (even when there were dogmatic differences) and family unity. The rabbis, the radicals, the writers, the Zionists, the peasants, the students, all are included in a broad and vivid canvas. A glossary, a bibliography of sources, and a relative index are appended.

889 **Meriwether,** Louise. *Don't Ride the Bus on Monday; The Rosa Parks Story;* illus. by David Scott Brown. Prentice-Hall, 1973. 30p. $4.95.

R
3-5 Although Rosa Parks' role in the civil rights struggle has been described many times, there have been few accounts for younger children that have given any more information about her than her role in the Montgomery bus boycott. Well-written, this is useful not only because it gives a fuller picture about Rosa Parks but because it exemplifies the quiet courage of many black citizens and because it dramatizes by terse understatement the bitter experience of discrimination that black children have suffered.

890 **Merriam,** Eve. *Out Loud;* designed by Harriet Sherman. Atheneum, 1973. 50p. illus. $4.95.

R
5-9 If a young reader were to get nothing from Eve Merriam's poetry, it would be worth reading and rereading for the way in which words are relished; her writing sparkles with freshets and cascades of words used for meaning or just for the pleasure of their sound. In this new collection there is more, however: bright imagery, fresh ideas, humor, and—while there is some lyricism—a stress on here and now.

891 **Merrill,** Jean. *Maria's House;* illus. by Frances Gruse Scott. Atheneum, 1974. 56p. $4.95.

R
3-5 Maria loved Miss Lindstrom, who taught the Saturday art class at the museum, but she hated the latest assignment: drawing a picture of your house. Nobody at art class knew that Maria was poor and lived in a tenement, and she didn't want them to know, so she had drawn a big white house set among large lawns. It looked like a magazine picture, Mama said, but it wasn't true, and art must be true. Maria loved Mama and knew how much she gave up so that there could be art lessons—and so she tore up the picture and drew her own house. And Miss Lindstrom thought it was beautiful. A slight vehicle, but speaks clearly of the integrity and sense of values that a child can absorb from her parents, it's nicely structured and simply written.

892 **Merrill,** Jean. *The Toothpaste Millionaire*. Houghton, 1974. 89p. illus. $5.95.

4-6 Kate tells the story, which is laden rather heavily with arithmetic and business details, but rises above it. She had just moved to East Cleveland, and Rufus was the first friendly sixth-grader she met; he didn't even seem to mind that she was white, and he quickly impressed her as being a genius. Sensible and sharp, Rufus had decided that toothpaste was unnecessarily expensive, so he mixed his own and sold it for three cents a tube. Honest commercials popularized the product (which was just called "Toothpaste") and forced competitors out of business, a plant was soon in operation, and Rufus soon had stockholders and a board of directors. He also grew bored. And the last Kate heard of him was a postcard, while he was on vacation, asking her to investigate the cost of blow-up rafts and 100-pound bags of dried soup. "If America hadn't already been discovered," Kate concludes, "it wouldn't surprise me at all if that was what Rufus had in mind." The illustrations are engaging, the style is light, the project interesting (with more than a few swipes taken at advertising and business practices in our society) and Rufus a believable genius.

893 **Meyer,** Carolyn, *Amish People; Plain Living in a Complex World;* photographs by Michael Ramsey, Gerald Dodds, and Carolyn Meyer. Atheneum, 1976. 75-28272. 138p. $5.95.

7- Meyer creates an imaginary but very convincing family to illustrate the roles and problems of various positions in an Amish family and in their community, and to describe such events as a wedding, a religious service, a school day, et cetera. The text includes adequate information about the history of the Amish people, their differences from other "plain people" (Mennonites) and the variations from one Amish group to another. The writing is objective in tone, sympathetic, modestly colorful, and informal, and the book gives a wealth of detail about Amish beliefs and custom and about the problems of adjusting to a larger society which has practices and mores so at variance with the firm convictions of the Amish.

894 **Meyer,** Carolyn. *C. C. Poindexter.* Atheneum, 1978. 78-6102. 208p. $7.95.

7-9 In her first book of fiction for young people, Meyer, who has produced several excellent informational books, presents a fifteen-year-old who copes with being over six feet tall, with the problems of a mother who hasn't adjusted well to divorce, and with the difficulty of accepting her father's new wife—and especially with the disagreeable children of her father's new wife. C. C. (Cynthia), who tells the story, is strongly influenced by an aunt who's a militant feminist. The diversity of problems gives the book balance; the strength of the characterizations and relationships gives it substance. While there is no strong story line, the several plot threads (mother's growing self-confidence, Dad's efforts to bring his own children and his bride's into a harmonious group, and C. C.'s collusion in a plan that helps her friend Laura gain independence) knit together nicely.

895 **Meyer,** Carolyn. *Christmas Crafts;* Things to Make the 24 Days Before Christmas; illus. by Anita Lobel. Harper, 1974. 138p. Trade ed. $4.95; Library ed. $4.79 net.

5- Anita Lobel's decorative illustrations are charming and her pictures demonstrating techniques are useful; the text of this attractive "how-to" book is logically arranged and clearly written. It begins with instructions for making an Advent banner and gives one project for each succeeding day of December, ending with a chocolate Yule log on the day before Christmas. The projects are varied enough in type, difficulty, and media to serve a wide audience, including use of the book by adults with younger children; each project begins with a paragraph describing traditional use of the object.

896 **Meyer,** Carolyn. *Rock Tumbling;* by Carolyn Meyer with Jerome Wexler; photographs by Jerome Wexler. Morrow, 1975. 74-22346. 96p. Trade ed. $5.95; Library ed. $5.11 net.

5-9 Logically organized and direct in its businesslike approach, this is an excellent how-to-do-it book for beginners. The author gives ample advice on finding or buying stones and on the equipment needed, and the information in the step-by-step procedures is very full and clear. There are tips on how to judge dealers, how to fix broken stones, how to judge rocks in the rough, and how to test the hardness of a stone. Meyer also gives facts about using the stones in making jewelry, with pictures that show exactly how to "cage" a stone or make neckbands and rings out of twisted wire. Rock tumbling is slow and noisy, but it has two great advantages as a hobby for children: it's easy and it's inexpensive. Suggestions for sources of materials are included in the text; an index is appended.

897 **Meyer,** Carolyn. *Saw, Hammer and Paint; Woodworking and Finishing for Beginners;* illus. by Toni Martignoni. Morrow, 1973. 127p. Trade ed. $4.95; Library ed. $4.59 net.

6- This is everything a "How-to" book ought to be: logically organized, explicit, progressing from easy to difficult projects in nice gradation, simple enough to be used by younger children with some help, dignified enough for adults—and useful. The author describes materials and how to use them, discusses tools and includes helpful hints on what kinds to purchase, and repeatedly gives reminders about safety and about working neatly. The projects are sensible, too. The second part of the book is devoted to finishing procedures: stains, oils, paints, putty, ways to mend damaged spots, how to paint and decorate, sanding, et cetera; it, too, includes advice on selecting materials and tips on using them to best advantage.

898 **Mezey,** Robert, ed. *Poems from the Hebrew;* illus. by Moishe Smith. T. Y. Crowell, 1973. 159p. $4.50.

7- A new volume in the "Poems of the World" series, with an excellent introduction in which the compiler, who has also translated many of the modern poems, gives historical background and discusses the reasons for his choice of selections. The text is divided into three parts: poems from the Bible, poems of Moorish Spain (a brief section), and—the longest section—contemporary poems, with translators' names included. Robert Mezey has chosen an impressive array of beautiful poems, most of them introspective and lyric, with little social commentary or humor. Title, first line, author, and translator indexes are appended.

899 **Miles,** Betty. *The Real Me.* Knopf, 1974. 122p. Trade ed. $4.95; Library ed. 5.59 net.

4-6 Barbara didn't think she was a women's liberation nut. She admits that the subject used to embarrass her ("All those jokes about burning bras. The only bra I had was called Little Miss Beginner . . .") but she found that her opinion on one thing was firm. Company rules or no company rules, she wanted to take over her brother's newspaper route. She'd filled in for him once and done a good job; her brother backed her and so did her parents. In fact, it is due to parental backing that Barbara achieves her goal, in a story that is modestly realistic, balanced by other interests, and given warmth by the solidity of family affection and support.

900 **Miles,** Miska. *Chicken Forgets;* illus. by Jim Arnosky. Atlantic-Little, Brown, 1976. 76-12458. 31p. $5.95.

3-5 yrs. Knowing her chick, the mother hen adjures him not to forget this time: he is to fill the basket with wild blackberries. Each animal he meets advises a better food, but—fortunately for Chicken—his last advisor is a robin who says berries are better. So they go off to a berry patch, eat and pick, and Chicken comes home to be congratulated. "It's easy to remember when you really try," says Chicken, with mendacious modesty. Young children can see the joke and share the pride of achievement in a story in which brevity, simplicity, and subject interest are suited to the audience, as are the uncomplicated, framed drawings.

901 **Miles,** Miska. *Swim, Little Duck;* illus. by Jim Arnosky. Little, 1976. 75-30700. 32p. $5.95.

2-5 yrs. Soft illustrations in brown, black, and white are framed and face each page of text; the book has a quiet, spacious look that fits the mood of the story, which adds to the appeals of the animal characters with repetition in the pattern of the events. A little duck goes out to see the world and is joined by a frog, a pig, and a rabbit. The pig and the rabbit offer to show her the best places in the world; the pigpen is nice, the little duck decides, but she doesn't dare get underfoot to approach the feed box, and rabbit's field has lots of rabbits but nothing to drink. The frog's similar offer is something else, again. Cool and wet, his place, with lots of frogs but also filled with ducks. . . . "a little duck here and big duck there. Little ducks, big ducks everywhere." (Same pattern as the pigs and rabbits.) The little duck happily swims, plays, eats, and then tucks her weary head under her wing and sleeps.

902 **Miles,** Patricia. *The Gods in Winter.* Dutton, 1978. 77-16704. 140p. $7.50.

5-7 First published in England, a story that blends fantasy and reality most effectively is based on the idea that Demeter still roams the earth mourning her lost daughter and rejoicing when she finds her child. Thus the cold, dreary winter; thus the effulgence of spring. Here the goddess comes in the guise of a housekeeper to the Bramble family, who have just moved to a new home in the English countryside. The story is told by Adam, one of the three Bramble children, and he is relieved when he learns that his sister (and later his mother) have also begun to suspect that Mrs. Korngold has supernatural powers and that there is a connection between her and the unusually raw winter they've had. The writing style is polished and the narrative flow even; the dialogue, exposition, and characterization are equally distinctive.

903 **Millard,** Adele. *Plants for Kids to Grow Indoors;* photographs by Glenn Lewis and Bud Millard; drawings by Gregory Thompson. Sterling, 1975. 75-14509. 124p. Trade ed. $5.95; Library ed. $5.69 net.

5-8 Illustrated with drawings and photographs, this succinct guide to growing house plants strikes a nice balance between the carrot-top/sweet potato books for beginners and the complete books of house plant care that are published for adults. There are some projects as simple as carrot-tops, but the author also includes terrarium, bottle, and deep-dish planting as well as the more usual potted plants, window boxes, and water plants. Directions are simple, and although the book does not contain comprehensive advice on such topics as propagating and fertilizing plants, it is quite adequate. An index is appended.

904 **Mills,** John FitzMaurice. *Treasure Keepers.* Doubleday, 1974. 160p. illus. $7.95.

7- Profusely illustrated with photographs of art objects (many in color) and of techniques in analysis and restoration, this stunning book, first published in England, should be of interest to any reader and should be enthralling to art lovers. Mills discusses forgeries and detection, restoration and the human or natural forces that make it necessary, the devices and techniques used in analysis of art objects, the problems the museum curator faces in protecting, displaying, and establishing provenance of items in his collection, and the changing styles of mounting exhibits in museums. Authoritative, well-written, well-organized. A glossary and an index are appended.

905 **Minard,** Rosemary, ed. *Womenfolk and Fairy Tales;* illus. by Suzanna Klein. Houghton, 1975. 74-26555. 163p. $5.95.

4-6 Eighteen stories have been chosen for this anthology that celebrates women or girls who are decisive, active, clever, or courageous. Most of the selections are old favorites: "Clever Grethel," "The Husband Who Was to Mind the House," "Three Strong Women," and "Molly Whuppie." All the stories are available elsewhere, but this anthology serves a specific need in bringing them together. The material is time-tested, the book is timely.

906 **Mitchison,** Naomi. *Sunrise Tomorrow; A Story of Botswana.* Farrar, 1973. 120p. $4.50.

7-10 One of the best of the stories of conflict and resolution between the old ways and the new, this gives a vigorous and balanced picture of the young people who move, in different ways, toward roles in which they can contribute to their nation. The protagonists here, Seloi and Mokgose, come from different villages and meet as students; while there is a love interest it is a minor theme. Each wants to retain the best of the traditional in African life, each wants to play a part in making Botswana strong and self-sufficient, to see children educated and roads built and the sick taken care of. Both the major characters and the minor ones—the brother who is mechanically adept rather than book-oriented—the young hoodlum who changes when he joins a work group and finds his skills appreciated—the African nurse who feels that there are some advantages in the old ways—the father who still believes in witchcraft—are convincingly drawn.

907 **Moffett,** Robert Knight. *Going on a Dig; A Guide to Archaeological Fieldwork.* Hawthorn Books, 1975. 74-342. 107p. illus. $6.95.

7-12 Although this is directed specifically at young people who are interested in participating in archeological digs, it's a book with appeal for any reader who finds the drama of discovery in real life as alluring as any fiction. Moffett discusses some of the problems of site selection and salvage archeology, the procedures used on a dig (especially the role of the amateur), interpretation of artifacts, methodology, and the appeals as well as the uses of archeology. The chapter entitled "Getting Started as a Volunteer" is practical and realistic, the advice on what to do and what to take along is very useful; much of the material pertains to British digs, since there are organized field schools there, but a chapter is devoted to digs in the United States. The coverage is good, the writing style casually conversational. Suggestions for reading material and an index are appended.

908 **Mohr,** Nicholasa. *In Nueva York.* Dial, 1977. 76-42931. 208p. $7.95.

8-12 In a series of interrelated short stories set in a Puerto Rican neighborhood of Manhattan, Mohr creates a remarkably vivid tapestry of community life as well as of individual characters. Lali, the young bride of Rudi, who is twice her age and who has brought her to New York to help him run his luncheonette, goes to night school English classes with the dwarf William, who secretly adores her. William has just come from home to see Old Mary, who had not seen her illegitimate child since his infancy. The self-reliant Raquel, who works at times for Rudi, is independent enough to make her children feel comfortable attending the wedding of a gay friend, Johnny, who for a practical reason marries a lesbian. Jennie and Angie, who have a reunion at the luncheonette, are former schoolmates, one of whom is going on to college, the other trying to achieve a normal life after being a prostitute and drug addict. Tough, candid, and perceptive, the book has memorable characters, resilient and responsive, in a sharply-etched milieu.

909 **Mohr,** Nicholasa. *Nilda;* illus by the author. Harper, 1973. 292p. Trade ed. $5.95; Library ed. $5.79 net.

6-9 Born in Spanish Harlem, Nicholasa Mohr draws a sharp and candid picture of the life of a barrio child, each major character distinctively pictured, the story more a reflection of a life-style than a series of linked events, although these happen. Nilda is ten, curious about people, eager to learn and grow, disturbed by the ideological conflict between her devout mother and her Socialist stepfather. There is a series of jolts to the pattern of Nilda's life: her brother's pregnant mistress moves into the already-crowded apartment, having been thrown out by her mother; her stepfather dies and then her mother; Nilda goes to live with an aunt. The writing style is sometimes heavy, but the verisimilitude of the setting and the strength of the characterization compensate for the occasional stiffness of the prose.

910 **Monjo,** Ferdinand N. *Grand Papa and Ellen Aroon; Being an Account of Some of the Happy Times Spent Together by Thomas Jefferson and His Favorite Granddaughter;* illus. by Richard Cuffari. Holt, 1974. 54p. $5.50.

2-4 As he did in *Poor Richard in France, The One Bad Thing about Father,* and *Me and Willie and Pa,* Monjo pictures a major American historical figure from a child's viewpoint. Here the commentator is Ellen Aroon (Ellen Wayles Randolph), a favorite grandchild of Thomas Jefferson. Her candid remarks about Grand Papa give a great deal of information about Jefferson, but they also have an ingenuous charm of their own, as Ellen prattles on about what Grand Papa is like, and what he thinks of other people, and what other people think of him, and all the things that keep him so busy. Monjo's special ability to invest history with grace and humor adds enjoyment to the usefulness of a book that can give young children accurate information about Jefferson and about the period of his tenure in office.

911 **Monjo,** Ferdinand N. *King George's Head Was Made of Lead;* illus. by Margot Tomes. Coward, 1974. 47p. $5.95.

3-5 The story of the American revolt against its British rulers is told from a new viewpoint, as the petulant voice of George III gives his account of the unreasonable and disobedient colonists who simply wouldn't cooperate. It is not King George, actually, but the head of his statue, and there really was such a statue (erected, during a temporary respite in taxation, by grateful colonial citizens of New York) that was melted down for lead to make bullets. This is a nice adjunct to the more familiar versions of colonial protest told from the American point of view; there's characterization in the monarch's self-description and the irritable monologue, and there's humor in both the text and the illustrations.

912 **Monjo,** Ferdinand N. *Letters to Horseface; Being the Story of Wolfgang Amadeus Mozart's Journey to Italy 1769–1770 When He was a Boy of Fourteen;* illus. and designed by Don Bolognese and Elaine Raphael. Viking, 1975. 74-23766. 91p. $7.95.

5-7 * The versatile Mr. Monjo moves to a new form with great success in this collection of putative letters from the young Mozart to his sister; it is based on actual letters written by Mozart and his father while making a triumphal tour of Italian cities. The letters are ebullient, teasing, and boyish when they are about personal matters; they are amusing and informative, but to some readers their greatest appeal will surely be in Mozart's calm acceptance of his own musical ability. He is aware, when he writes Horseface (his older sister Maria Anna) that ". . . Papa is up to his old tricks! It's not enough for me to be a good musician . . . I must still do tricks and improvisations to surprise the donkey's ears, in the audience," that he's being shown off, but he takes it quite for granted that he should conduct his own symphony, improvise a harpsichord sonata, compose a fugue and variations on a theme given on the spot, and improvise on the violin his own part in a string trio—all in one concert. Fascinating for students of music history and Mozart lovers, this is lively enough to attract other readers as well, and the illustrations (crayon pencil / pen and ink) are meticulously accurate in architectural and costume details. Notes on the Mozart family, sources for the research that is so smoothly incorporated, and a bibliography are appended.

913 **Monjo,** Ferdinand N. *Me and Willie and Pa; The Story of Abraham Lincoln and His Son Tad;* illus. by Douglas Gorsline. Simon and Shuster, 1973. 94p. $5.95.

3-5 The story of the Lincoln years in the White House is told by a putative Tad Lincoln and illustrated with soft, realistic drawings that capture the serious and formal air of contemporary engravings. Tad's account is ingenuous but not cute, appropriately casual and conversational, and nicely balanced between personal anecdotage and historical coverage. Monjo's special talent is in his selectivity; his child's-viewpoint books of biography of historical fiction are convincing because his children remember the sorts of things that are of natural interest to children; the books are also valuable because, however informally presented, their facts are accurate. A bibliography of sources is appended, preceded by an author's note that gives background information.

914 **Monjo,** Ferdinand N. *A Namesake for Nathan; Being an Account of Captain Nathan Hale by His Twelve-Year-Old Sister, Joanna;* illus. by Eros Keith. Coward, 1977. 76-58325. 127p. $6.95.

5-8 Nathan Hale's young sister Joanna tells the story of her family's life in 1776, when Nathan and five of their brothers were serving in the Continental Army. Although the focus is on Nathan's visits, his absences, and then the long wait to learn if the terrible rumor that he'd been shot as a spy were true or not, the book's greater impact is in the vivid way it pictures how the war impinged on families and communities. Joanna's language and attitudes are convincingly those of a twelve-year-old, the story has firm structure and an even flow, and the author's closing note defines fictional additions to the facts he has drawn from what is—as usual—careful research.

915 **Monjo,** Ferdinand N. *Poor Richard in France;* illus. by Brinton Turkle. Holt, 1973. 57p. $4.95.

2-4 Three cheers for the team of Monjo and Turkle, who have produced an easy-to-read history book that is as engaging as it is informative. The drawings are authentic in detail and attractive; the text is historically accurate and lively, convincingly told by Benjamin Franklin's small grandson, who accompanied his distinguished grandfather on a 1776 mission to France to urge French intercession in the American Revolution. Seven-year-old Benny's comments are lively and humorous, and in a perfectly natural way they give a good bit of information about Franklin and about the rebellion against the British.

916 **Monjo,** Ferdinand N. *Zenas and the Shaving Mill;* illus. by Richard Cuffari. Coward, 1976. 75-32531. 48p. $5.95.

4-7 Monjo makes history come alive once again in a deftly written monologue by a seventeen-year-old Quaker lad of Revolutionary War times. Zenas is sailing back home to Nantucket from the mainland, and he describes the plight of the island Quakers. Refusing to fight, they are the enemy and the prey of patriots, British, and Tories. Their possessions are seized, their ships taken, and their actions suspect. "Shaving mills," Zenas calls the

American ships, because they shave their victims of everything they own. Experienced at navigating in his home waters (a map of the shoals and sandbars precedes the text), Zenas cleverly evades a "shaving mill" by taking his sloop over a bar and enticing the pursuing ship to do the same—knowing that he can get across but that his pursuers cannot. The speech Zenas uses is appropriate for the period and the locale, plain talk flavored by his Quaker background. And the whole gives a vivid picture of the plight of the Quakers, a people depicted as firm in their convictions without being self-righteous about them.

917 **Moore,** Lilian. *See My Lovely Poison Ivy and Other Verses About Witches, Ghosts and Things;* illus. by Diane Dawson. Atheneum, 1975. 75-8581. 42p. $4.95.

3-5
*
A rollicking collection of poems, some of which have a wistful touch, is illustrated with black and white drawings that capture the eerie-merry mood of the writing very nicely. The poetry is fresh, deft, and imaginative. A sample, "Bedtime Stories," " 'Tell me a story,' / Says Witch's Child / 'About the Beast / So fierce and wild / About a Ghost / That shrieks and groans / A Skeleton / That rattles bones / About a Monster / Crawly-creepy / Something nice / To make me sleepy.' "

918 **Moore,** Lilian, ed. *To See the World Afresh;* comp. by Lilian Moore and Judith Thurman. Atheneum, 1974. 102p. $4.95.

5- Marianne Moore's poem, "Poetry," says ". . . there is in it after all, a place for the genuine," and it is clear that the compilers of this brief anthology have used such a touchstone in their selection. They have chosen poems that are strong and honest, often deceptively simple, and the title of the book is an indication of the fact that they sought for vision, for that illuminating shaft of insight that makes it possible for the reader to see people and snow and fireflies and emotions and relationships more clearly. There are some familiar selections: Randall Jarrell's "The Bat," Langston Hughes, "The Negro Speaks of Rivers," Robert Frost's "Nothing Gold Can Stay," but this is far from a ho-hum assortment. Brief notes on some of the poets and poems are appended, as is an author-title index.

919 **Moorman,** Thomas. *How To Make Your Science Project Scientific.* Atheneum, 1974. 94p. illus. $5.50.

5-9 A very welcome addition to the many books that give advice on specific science projects, usually for science fairs, this is a serious but not formal discussion of the scientific attitude and scientific methods. Some of the testing methods described are controlled, blind, or double-blind experiments, observation, surveys, and the case study. The text also considers measurement, keeping records and statistics, and the problems of framing and reporting research, but its most valuable contribution to readers may be the pervasive insistence on lack of bias and on rigorous scientific attitude. Smoothly written, carefully organized, logical and lucid, a most useful book. A glossary, a bibliography (divided into material for advanced or beginning experimenters) and a relative index are appended.

920 **Morey,** Walt. *Year of the Black Pony*. Dutton, 1976. 75-33805. 152p. $6.95.

5-7 Set in Oregon at the turn of the century, the story of a boy's love for a pony is smoothly meshed with a family story. Chris had yearned for the wild, beautiful pony in a neighbor's herd, but he had never expected his stepfather to buy the animal. Chris's father had died, and his doughty mother had proposed a marriage of convenience to Frank Chase, a proposal instigated by her fear that she would not be able to support her children. The children become fond of Frank, and Frank becomes fond of Ma—but to Ma it remains a business deal. Or it does until a crisis (the pony's severe illness) follows several episodes in which Ma has learned that Frank really cares for Chris and his sister and that the pony she so disapproved of because he was dangerous fills a real need in Chris's life. The characters are convincing, and the changes in relationships are gradual and credible. If the ending is slightly sugarcoated (pony recovering, Ma softening at last toward Frank, Christmas Day) it is more than balanced by the sturdy, earthy realism of the whole book.

921 **Morgan,** Alison. *A Boy Called Fish*; illus. by Joan Sandin. Harper, 1973. 201p. Trade ed. $4.95; Library ed. $4.79 net.

4-6 The story of a boy and his dog is set in rural Wales, deftly written and, although quiet in mood, nicely paced. Fish is quickly established by the author as an outsider; the story is told by another boy, Jimmy, who describes Fish's awkwardness in a ball game, his strange reluctance to get dirty, and—most telling—the fact that another boy's mother "would have asked us to come in to tea too, but with Fish hanging about . . ." When Fish picks up a stray dog, all the love he has been unable to express is given to Floss; his dour father and stepmother are disinterested in the boy. When Floss is suspected of killing sheep, Fish's father decides to kill her, so Fish runs off to hide in the hills. Jimmy brings food and candles, and he is trapped with Fish in a severe snowstorm; it is Floss, sent by the boys, that brings a rescue party. While the plot is not highly original (in David Walker's *Big Ben* a dog is accused of killing sheep and is proved to be innocent) the story has characterization and dialogue that are sturdy, good construction, and more depth than most child-animal stories.

922 **Morgan,** Alison. *Pete.* Harper, 1973. 241p. Trade ed. $4.95; Library ed. $4.43 net.

5-7 First published in England, a story about one of the minor characters in *A Boy Called Fish.* Pete, whose family had scrimped so that he could join a school tour group, had been eliminated when the travel agents made a short booking. Disappointed, he decides to run off to Scotland and join his father, who's on a job there, letting his mother think he is with his classmates. Robbed and without funds, Pete is taken in by a gentle hippie couple and helped by a friend to get to Scotland, and joins his surprised father. The final episode is pure theater, dramatic yet completely believable, the story line remarkably smooth in a book so divided structurally. The writing is restrained and smooth, the characterization and dialogue deft.

923 **Morgan,** Alison. *Ruth Crane.* Harper, 1974. 244p. Trade ed. $5.95; Library ed. $5.79 net.

6-9 A sequel to *A Boy Called Fish* and *Pete* focuses on the problems of Pete's half-American cousin Ruth, who had come with her family to vacation in her mother's birthplace in Wales. An automobile accident had taken her father's life; her mother and sister were in separate hospitals, and Ruth was bearing the burdens of a whining younger brother and her own feelings of ineptitude in addition to grief. Pete gives physical and moral support while Ruth tries to learn housekeeping and keep track of her brother Tony, but it isn't until Tony runs off to see their sister that Ruth realizes how much the situation has burdened him and how much he means to her. An honest and perceptive story, written with restrained vigor, has solidly drawn characters and relationships.

924 **Morrison,** Lillian, comp. *Best Wishes, Amen; A New Collection of Autograph Verses;* illus. by Loretta Lustig. T. Y. Crowell, 1974. 193p. $4.95.

4-8 A companion volume to Morrison's earlier collections of autographs, *Yours Till Niagara Falls* and *Remember Me When This You See,* this comprises over three hundred new bon mots, jibes, complimentary verses, and includes some Spanish selections with translations. There are many that demonstrate the self-conscious humor of young autographers who felt comfortable only when taking a dig at a friend's expense, some impersonal quips, a few that reflect the changing times, and a modest number that admit to affection: in fact, exactly what one finds in children's autograph books; this should prove as popular as its predecessors.

925 **Morrison,** Lillian. *The Sidewalk Racer and Other Poems of Sports and Motion.* Lothrop, 1977. 77-907. 62p. illus. Trade ed. $5.95; Library ed. $5.21 net.

5- While many of the poems in this collection have been previously published, it's nice to have them pulled together for the same audience that enjoyed Fleming's *Hosannah the Home Run!* although this has less variety of style. The poems are written from the viewpoint of the participant or of the spectator; all are crisp, sharp, brief impressions of a memory, a mood, or a high moment, and most of the poems have a fluidity that are admirably suited to their subjects.

926 **Morton,** Miriam. *The Making of Champions; Soviet Sports for Children and Teenagers.* Atheneum, 1974. 136p. illus. $6.25.

5-8 In what may be considered a companion volume to her *Pleasures and Palaces,* a study of the after-school activities of Soviet children, Miriam Morton again writes with enthusiastic appreciation of the massive programs that are subsidized by organizations, unions, or government agencies at various levels. In addition to other sports-training programs, there are over 3,500 sports schools, with their diversified specialties supported by official sanction and popular approval. Excellent (and occasionally amusing) photographs illustrate the variety of sports that are being taught both in the special schools and in the sports programs of ordinary schools and camps. Despite a sustained note of admiration, the direct and brisk text reads well, perhaps because—unless a reader disapproves of heavy emphasis on sports—it would be hard not to share such admiration for a program so comprehensive and diversified.

927 **Morton,** Miriam, ed. *Russian Plays for Young Audiences;* ed. and tr. by Miriam Morton. New Plays, 1977. 77-82856. 401p. photographs. Hardbound $11.95; Paperback $7.50.

6- Five plays are included in a volume intended for use by adolescents or adults; the plays range from a dramatized Baba Yaga story, "The Two Maples," and an engaging fantasy about a clown who ends the cold, grey life styles of the people in "The City Without Love" to three more serious plays intended for older audiences. In "Hey, There—Hello!" a boy and girl have a dialogue that will remind some readers of a Nichols and May conversation (very funny but very pithy) and, in the background, four mimes act out the boy's imaginary thoughts. "The Young Graduates" face the same kind of decisions about their future that are encountered by adolescents worried about college entrance the world over;

"The Young Guard" is a taut drama about young partisans in World War II. The translations are colloquial, and the plays have more substance than most collections compiled for young audiences.

928 **Mosel,** Arlene, ad. *The Funny Little Woman;* retold by Arlene Mosel; pictures by Blair Lent. Dutton, 1972. 36p. $5.95.

K-3 An engaging tale for telling or reading, the story of the little old woman comes from Japanese folklore. Deftly retold, it is illustrated in soft green and dun, with its impish characters, the wicked oni, in icy blue. The oni capture the little old woman when she runs after an escaping rice dumpling, and set her to cooking for them. One grain of rice, stirred by a magic paddle, produces a full pot; since the giggling woman loves to cook, she enjoys her work—but she misses her own home, and makes a dash for freedom. The trip is not without its hazards, but the little woman escapes from the pursuing oni, and with the magic paddle she has taken soon becomes the richest woman in all of Japan.

929 **Moser,** Don. *A Heart to the Hawks.* Atheneum, 1975. 208p. $6.95.

7-10 His parents wished that Mike were not so wrapped up in natural science, his younger brother alternately whined to be included in Mike's investigations or teased him about them, and the girl he adored was more interested in movie magazines than in Mike's passionate hobby. Alone in the woods for the first time at night, what boy would have deserted the nubile Angeline to catch a rare pond creature? Mike. Part of the story focuses on Mike's patient training of a wounded redtail hawk that he teaches to hunt and of his angry act of retribution (he tries to blow up a bulldozer) when the hawk is killed hitting a power line, part on his efforts to save the piece of wild land back of his home. Mike's a loser on both counts, but he's young and resilient, and the story ends on an upbeat: convalescent, still mourning his beloved pet, he goes to a picnic given by Angeline's father. This may have special appeal to the conservationists and nature lovers, but it is a story for all readers: as convincing in characterization and the concerns of the young adolescent male as it is vivid in depicting the setting.

930 **Moskin,** Marietta D. *Waiting for Mama;* illus. by Richard Lebenson. Coward, 1975. 74-21068. 91p. $5.95.

3-5 A moving little period piece concerns a Russian Jewish immigrant family at the turn of the century, but the family solidarity, the problems of adapting to a new situation, and the satisfactions of achieving a goal and gaining recognition have universal application and appeal. Papa had decided, two years earlier, that he would take his family to America before the children were old enough to suffer Czarist persecution. Mama had had to stay behind because the baby became ill, and for two years the family had scraped and saved to pay for her passage. Becky, the youngest, went to school; her older sister and brother had to work since they were twelve and ten years old. Becky loved learning English, but she wanted so much to contribute to Mama's ticket; through helping her sister, very late at night, do piece work, Becky earned enough to buy the buttons for the surprise coat for Mama. What joy, when Mama arrived, to say that she had helped, to show that she had learned more English than the others! The story is simple and sweet, giving a good picture of the immigrant community of New York's East Side as well as of warm family relationships.

931 **Moss,** Elaine, comp. *From Morn to Midnight;* verses chosen by Elaine Moss; illus. by Satomi Ichikawa. T. Y. Crowell, 1977. 77-2548. 28p. Trade ed. $6.95; Library ed. $7.95 net.

3-7 yrs. Twenty-odd traditional poems (Blake, Farjeon, Aldis, Hood, Stevenson, and a few—Pepler, Lester—lesser known poets) are chosen in a mini-anthology for young children. The pictures are tidily framed, softly colored and detailed, with just a bit less of the Boutet de Monvel influence than has appeared in Ichikawa's earlier illustrations.

932 **Mother Goose.** *Granfa' Grig Had a Pig and Other Rhymes Without Reason from Mother Goose;* comp. and illus. by Wallace Tripp. Little, 1976. 76-25234. 96p. Trade ed. $7.95; Paper ed. $4.95.

3-6 yrs. * Oh, they're the same rhymes, all right, but what Wallace Tripp does with his hilarious illustrations makes this Mother Goose collection very different. There are a few representational (even one romantic) illustrations, but most of them are ingeniously conceived and so bedecked with side comments that the book should be highly enjoyed by adults or older children who have the happy task of reading the verses aloud. For example: Old King Cole's conductor is Toscanini, who is saying, in a balloon caption, "Ignorante! Imbecile! Molto cantando . . . Bitte da capo!" "Terrible." An apple a day keeps the doctor away? "Scram, you quack! You hippocratic oaf!" The scene for "Robbin and Bobbin" is a rural pie-eating contest, complete with scoreboard, groaning contestants, and a quack doctor hawking his cure-alls. Great fun.

933 **Mother Goose.** *Gregory Griggs and Other Nursery Rhyme People;* selected and illus. by Arnold Lobel. Greenwillow, 1978. 77-22209. 48p. Trade ed. $7.95; Library ed. $7.35 net.

3-6 yrs. Eschewing the better-known figures of nursery lore (No Willie Winkie, Humpty Dumpty, or Simple Simon here) and the many animals, Lobel has chosen to illustrate men and women less well known. Gregory Griggs, whose magnificent collection of wigs, shown in frames, yields pride of place to the final frame, a bald and simpering Gregory, is one; another is the ragged and complacent dirty old man, another is Hannah Bantry, gnawing savagely on a bone in the privacy of her pantry. Lobel's pictures give fresh interpretations to many of the rhymes, and all of them are brimful of vitality and humor, the raffish ebullience of the pastel paintings looking as casual as though they were not dependent on a polished technique.

934 **Mother Goose.** *Three Jovial Huntsmen;* ed. and illus. by Susan Jeffers. Bradbury, 1973. 26p. $5.95.

K-2 In a delightful new version of an old rhyme, Susan Jeffers contrasts three bumbling, comic figures against the beauty of woodland and meadow scenes. The huntsmen argue endlessly about what they see: one is sure that a large object, half-glimpsed, is a ship; another sees it as a house. All this, and similar incidents, take place in a country landscape populated by birds and beasts, none of which the hunters bag. The drawings, delicate in color and firm in line, are imaginative and lovely, especially the cool lavender night scenes in which the men wander about while night creatures peer, amused, from the trees.

935 **Murphy,** E. Jefferson. *Understanding Africa;* illus. by Louise E. Jefferson; Rev. ed. T. Y. Crowell, 1978. 77-11560. 208p. Trade ed. $8.95; Library ed. $8.89 net.

8- Murphy begins with a geographical survey, discusses the language groups of Africa and describes the people of major regions, and proceeds to a succinct history of the continent, moving from ancient times through the colonial period and then, in more detailed coverage, to Africa today. Substantially revised from the 1969 edition, this gives a clear picture of the leaders, the conflicts, the pride of the emergent nations, the relations with major powers, and the diverse problems facing African countries today. In the concluding chapter, "Africa Faces the Future," Murphy deplores the paucity of foreign aid and concludes that many nations will remain dependent on agricultural resources for many years, that new educational systems are needed, and that African leaders are gaining ability and experience and are aware that their constituents will demand both strong leadership and better communication. A competent and informative introduction, this has an extensive divided bibliography and an index.

936 **Murphy,** Jim. *Weird & Wacky Inventions.* Crown, 1978. 77-15859. 92p. illus. $7.95.

4-6 The author has combed the files of the United States Patent and Trademark Office for some of the odd devices registered there, and his material is grouped under such headings as "From the Neck Up" or "Down on the Farm." The material is interesting, often amusing, and Murphy has given added interest by showing pictures of each invention, presenting multiple choices for guessing what it is or does, and giving the answer and a fuller explanation with a turn of the page. Quite useless and totally fascinating, an entertaining book for browsers.

937 **Murray,** Michele. *The Crystal Nights.* Seabury, 1973. 310p. $6.95.

7-10 There is no conflict for Elly in the fact that her father is Jewish and her mother Greek Orthodox; growing up on a Connecticut farm, her conflict is between staying where Mama is happy and moving into town. The situation is sharpened when Papa's relatives arrive, refugees from Nazi persecution. This sensitive and realistic story of adjustment and compromise explores both the balances within family relationships and the adolescent's concern about love, friendships, career plans (Elly wants to be an actress) and status; it is particularly adept in its depiction of a strong grandmother and of Elly's aunt, who had led a life of wealth and prestige before Hitler and is now bitter, critical about farm life, and less than grateful for the kindness with which she has been received by Elly's family.

938 **Musgrove,** Margaret. *Ashanti to Zulu; African Traditions;* pictures by Leo and Diane Dillon. Dial, 1976. 76-6610. 27p. Trade ed. $8.95; Library ed. $8.44 net.

3-5
*
A paragraph of text on each page of an oversize book describes some aspect of the cultures of twenty-six African tribes. The writing is dignified and the material informative, but it is the illustrations that make the book outstanding. Beautifully framed, the mixed-media paintings glow with rich color against the soft greige pages; the pictures are stunning both in details and in composition.

939 **Myers,** Walter Dean. *Fast Sam, Cool Clyde, and Stuff.* Viking, 1975. 74-32383. 190p. $6.95.

6-9 One can almost hear the strains of "That Old Gang of Mine" as background for this nostalgic, funny, first-person account of Stuff's friends. He was twelve, he had just moved to 116th Street, where he met Cool Clyde and Sam, Gloria, and Binky and all the other who formed a tight-knit gang who stuck together, helped and teased each other, were twice picked up by the police when they had committed no crime, solaced each other about delinquent parents or relied on parents who were supportive. Stuff falls in love, plays basketball, and goes to a party where others smoke pot, but this Harlem odyssey is as much about the others as it is about him. There's no story line, but there's plenty of action in the many episodes and abundant vitality in the dialogue.

940 **Myers,** Walter Dean. *It Ain't All for Nothin'.* Viking, 1978. 78-57516. 217p. $7.95.

7-10 Twelve-year-old Tippy tells, in completely convincing fashion, the story of a crisis in his life. When his beloved grandmother becomes too old and ill to go on taking care of him, Tippy goes to live with his father, Lonnie. A drifter and a petty criminal, Lonnie is rough and domineering; he insists that Tippy play a part in planned robberies. Brought up to be pious and honest, Tippy cooperates, partly through fear and partly—to his own shame—because he finds it exciting. But when one of the robbers is mortally wounded, Tippy goes to an adult friend and the police; the ethical concepts he's had for his twelve years are stronger than Lonnie's influence. Myers doesn't soften the scene; while with Lonnie, Tippy drinks, he gets beatings, he lies when he goes to the hospital to visit Grandma. Yet he remains a sympathetic character, and in this first really serious book by Myers, that is one of the strengths: none of the characters is superficially drawn as all good or bad. Not a happy book, but a trenchant and touching one, and it ends on a poignant but hopeful note when Tippy visits his father in jail and Lonnie not only concedes that his boy did the right thing but hopes wistfully that they can be friends when he gets out.

941 **Myers,** Walter Dean. *Mojo and the Russians.* Viking, 1977. 77-23454. 151p. $6.95.

5-7 Most of the gang Dean prattles about are black: timid Wayne, sensible Kitty, articulate Kwami, Leslie, Anthony, and Judy, who is white. They're about eleven, they live on the upper west side of New York, and they engage in a series of ploys that are often ridiculous but always funny. Suspicious about the Russian men who visit their friend Willie, they lay elaborate plans to trap them; their plans are confused by the fact that Willie's woman, Drusilla, has them all convinced that she can—and probably will—wreak Mojo (occult) vengeance on Dean because he knocked her down while cycling. The plot is far-fetched, but the gang is marvelous: they tease each other and squabble, but they present a united front to the adult world, and there's a great deal of affection and loyalty and humor in their relationships with each other.

942 **Myller,** Rolf. *From Idea Into House;* drawings by Henry K. Szwarce. Atheneum, 1974. 64p. $6.95.

5-9 Set within a narrative framework, a meticulously detailed explanation of the planning and building of a house makes clear the complexity and thc technicalities of an architect's job. The narrative describes a family of four who find a piece of land they like, negotiate its purchase, and call in an architect to discuss their needs and hopes for the new house. A full set of architectural drawings—from plot plan to finish schedule—is included, with explanations of what is entailed in each. And at the end—a photograph, for this is an actual house that was designed for a real family. Readers may not understand all the minutiae of the drawings, but they will certainly have a thorough introduction to architectural specifications and the order in which a house is constructed.

943 **Myller,** Rolf. *Symbols;* written and illus. by Rolf Myller. Atheneum, 1978. 77-17015. 91p. $9.95.

R
4-6 This isn't the first or only book about signs and symbols, but it's one of the best, for several reasons; the text moves from simple symbols to more complicated ones, it's written with clarity and humor, it gives a broad conception of the many different kinds of symbols used for quick communication or labelling, and it is very handsome. The pages are red, black, and white, laid out with a fine sense of design.

944 **Nabokov,** Peter, ed. *Native American Testimony; An Anthology of Indian and White Relations.* T. Y. Crowell, 1978. 77-11558. 242p. illus. Trade ed. $8.95; Library ed. $9.79 net.

7- Sources are cited for this excellent anthology comprising statements by native Americans of many tribes over four centuries. The focus is on Indian-white relations, and the material is arranged under such headings as "Premonitions and Prophecies," "Face to Face," "The Long Resistance," "Exiles in Their Own Land," and—the last, "The Nation's Hoop is Broken and Scattered." Nabokov provides background material that is varied and dramatic, but above all he has chosen material that represents a viewpoint seldom evident in traditional texts but presenting cultural conflict within a framework that makes the historical record deeper and broader. It is a tragic record, and it is eloquently expressed. An index is appended.

945 **Nagenda,** John. *Mukasa;* illus. by Charles Lilly. Macmillan, 1973. 120p. $4.95.

4-6 A story based on the author's memories of life in Uganda is illustrated with strong, realistically detailed pictures in black and white. Mukasa is an only child whose mother tends to protect him and to dream of a great future; she convinces his father to send the boy to school, and Mukasa falls in love with learning. The story doesn't have a strong line, but includes episodes about school, friends, a death in the family, and Mukasa's delight when his father, after visiting the school, not only agrees that the boy shall continue but asks if Mukasa will teach him. The writing style is smooth, quiet, and serious; the story has little dramatic impact, but it gives a good picture of Ugandan family life and the changing attitudes toward education in the 1940's.

946 **Namioka,** Lensey. *The Samurai and the Long-Nosed Devils.* McKay, 1976. 76-12744. 153p. $6.95.

7-9 Set in sixteenth-century Japan, this is the story of two *ronin* (samurai whose liege lords had been ousted and who were available for service) who come to the city of Miyako. Zenta and Matsuzo take on the job of protecting a Portuguese missionary and his soldier-companion at the behest of Hambei, an old friend of Zenta's, since Hambei's master dare not openly espouse the cause of the foreigners. Embroiled in the political intrigue of Miyako, the ronin investigate a murder and become even more deeply involved in the power struggle going on between a powerful monastic order, local nobility, and Hambei's lord, Nobunaga (a warlord who is a historical character) who is trying to unify the divided country. The story is heavily saturated with complex currents and cross currents, but it has a lively plot with an abundance of derring-do, and the setting is intriguing; the historical research underlying the book is fairly unobtrusive; an author's note describes Nobunaga's subsequent record and brings the story of Japan's relationship with other countries up to 1858 in a brief survey. A selected bibliography is appended.

947 **Navarra,** John Gabriel. *Supertrains.* Doubleday, 1975. 74-18820. 80p. illus. $5.95.

4-7 With dwindling energy resources, increasing pollution, and the continuing difficulties of providing and maintaining roads for automobile traffic, the train systems of many countries are being improved, and new kinds of trains and train transportation systems are being planned. Some are in use (and profitable) and others have been found too expensive to maintain. Navarra examines the problems and solutions in a comprehensive text arranged in brief topics, describing some of the new trains and systems as well as those in the planning stage. Although some of the topics are treated so briefly (a page or two of text) that they leave questions unanswered, the book is on the whole informative and the prospects it raises are exciting. An index is appended.

948 **Naylor,** Penelope. *Black Images; The Art of West Africa;* photographs by Lisa Little. Doubleday, 1973. 95p. $6.95.

7- Penelope Naylor does for older readers what Shirley Glubok has done in her series of art books of many cultures: show how the art objects of people reflect their beliefs and traditions. In the traditional West African societies in which the ritual objects, so beautifully photographed here, are treasured and used, the masks and carvings and bronzes are even more closely meshed with the lives of the peoples whose religion permeates their day-to-day activities as well as being observed in special ways. The book is graphically stunning; on spacious page layouts, the pictures are matched with explanatory and descriptive text and often with poetry.

949 **Naylor,** Phyllis Reynolds. *An Amish Family;* illus. by George Armstrong. O'Hara, 1975. 73-16813. 181p. Trade ed. $5.95; Library ed. $5.97 net.

6- Naylor gives a really excellent survey of Amish life, using descriptions of the members of a three-generation family to illustrate living patterns, attitudes, roles, and relationships. Beyond this, she provides full historical background, assesses the problems of an isolate group in disparate society and those within the Mennonite religion and the Amish sects that sprang from it. The tone is sympathetic, respectful of the tenets of the Amish but objective about dissident elements within their community. As useful as it is interesting, the book can serve as a minor reference source. A bibliography and an extensive index are appended.

950 **Ness,** Evaline, comp. *Amelia Mixed the Mustard and Other Poems;* selected and illus. by Evaline Ness. Scribner, 1975. 47p. $6.95.

3-5 Evaline Ness has chosen twenty poems about girls, poems ranging from A. E. Housman's flippant title poem and Keats' "Meg Merrilies" to Nikki Giovanni's "Poem for Flora" and Myra Cohn Livingston's "Pandora." Other selections are by Gertrude Stein, Ogden Nash, Eleanor Farjeon, Kaye Starbird, and Edna St. Vincent Millay, so that the book has variety, discrimination, and a vitality that is echoed by the vigor of the handsome illustrations.

951 **Newton,** James R. *The March of the Lemmings;* illus. by Charles Robinson. T. Y. Crowell, 1976. 75-42491. 34p. (Let's-Read-And-Find-Out Book). $5.95.

2-3 In direct, simple prose, Newton—a teacher in the middle grades—describes the changes in behavior of lemmings in a community that has become overpopulated. Once friendly, the animals are now hostile and restless; they begin their inexorable march across the countryside to the sea, where they drown. And those lemmings left in the colony, with ample room and food, begin the cycle again. Newton discusses briefly the theories held by scientists as to what triggers the suicidal procession, making it clear that there are no answers yet. A succinct and lucid treatment; this could be used as a companion volume to Alan Arkin's story *The Lemming Condition.*

952 **Nilsson,** Lennart. *How Was I Born?* A Photographic Story of Reproduction and Birth for Children. Delacorte Press/Seymour Lawrence, 1975. 75-24725. 31p. $5.95.

3-6 First published in Sweden under the title *Så Blev Du Till,* this unusual and informative book uses diagrams, photographs, and magnified color photographs of egg, sperm, and fetus to augment the direct, clear text. Nilsson shows and explains how the fetus changes and develops, how it is nourished and disposes of wastes, how it begins, in utero, to hear, to kick, to suck a thumb. After describing the birth process, the author-photographer goes back to describe mating and fertilization in informal but dignified fashion, concluding with a brief note on parental care and hereditary characteristics. An excellent addition to the many sex education books for children.

953 **Nixon,** Joan Lowery. *Danger in Dinosaur Valley;* illus. by Marc Simont. Putnam, 1978. 77-6397. 47p. (See and Read Books) $5.29.

2-3 A time-shift story for young independent readers should have added appeal because of the dinosaur characters and because of the humor of the concept and writing. If readers also get a glimmer of how different things look to someone from another culture and time, so much the better, but this isn't didactic. Little Diplodocus, gentle and herbivorous, knows that his family's biggest enemy is Tyrannosaurus Rex. With a skill that is newly acquired from another culture, he and his parents fight the terrible carnivore. What's the skill? Well, some space-age time travellers had brought along a "something," and one of the two-legged creatures had watched something called "Giants" who hit a round thing with a stick. (Television set; baseball game.) Practicing hurling rocks held in their mouths, Dip and his parents drive off their enemy. Dip does wonder if the tiny "Giants" have driven off *their* Tyrannosaurus Rex, too.

954 **Norman,** James. *Ancestral Voices; Decoding Ancient Languages.* Four Winds, 1975. 75-14426. 242p. illus. $7.95.

8- There have been many fine books about the major finds of archeologists, and most of them give information about objects like the Rosetta Stone or the carvings on the Behistun Rock, but not often do they focus on the extinct writing systems of the ancient world. This does, and it describes in lucid detail the problems that literary archeologists, amateur and professional, have and had in deciphering and interpreting ancient languages lost for centuries. Complicated as some of the material is, the author clarifies the problems facing those who have attempted to decode the records, and he gives due credit to those who failed but contributed some clues as well as to those who, like Champollion or Rawlinson, succeeded in spectacular fashion. A divided bibliography and an extensive index are appended.

955 **Norris,** Leslie. *Merlin & the Snake's Egg;* illus. by Ted Lewin. Viking, 1978. 77-15558. 48p. $6.95.

5-8 In his first collection of poems for children, Norris demonstrates his ability to write with breadth and clarity, with vivid imagery, and with a lyric tenderness that never moves toward sentimentality or obscurity. Many of the poems are about animals ("Walking," "The Old Dog's Song," "The Pit Ponies") or about the beauty of natural things, such as the sand rose or the fossil fern. "Kevin Scores!" captures the tension and triumph of a boy's scoring a goal; the title poem is a contrast to the others, a narrative of quest and magic. A fine collection.

956 **Norton,** Andre. *Wraiths of Time.* Atheneum, 1976. 75-43607. 210p. $6.95.

7-10 A young black archeologist, Tallahassee, identifies an ancient box, its presence in a locker detected by a Geiger counter, as African. Within the box is an ankh and, when it is exposed, there is a supernatural explosion and a time shift, and Tally finds herself in the old Nubian kingdom of Meroë, where she is forced by a priestess clan to impersonate Ashake, the slain princess who is heir to the throne. In her new identity, she fights by wile and magic against the forces of evil, and when she wins, Ashake learns that she has been fully accepted as princess even by those who know she is from another time. The fantasy has an intricate plot, but the setting and the wholly conceived details of the culture are nicely developed, with good pace and suspense.

957 **Nöstlinger,** Christine. *Fly Away Home;* trans. from German by Anthea Bell. Watts, 1975. 75-16255. 134p. $6.95.

6-9 First published in German under the title *Maikäfer Flieg!* and based on the author's experiences as child during the German and Russian occupations of Vienna, this lively story of the way one family coped is told by eight-year-old Christel. It has pathos without being pathetic; it has drama without being melodramatic. With food and clothing at a premium, and with housing a problem that increased as buildings were bombed, the Göth family is delighted when a wealthy acquaintance, fleeing the city, offers her suburban house. Christel becomes fast friends with their benefactor's grandchildren and an equally fast enemy of the prissy child next door. She learns to live with the Russian soldiers who are quartered in the house, even learns to love one of them; she frightens her parents by sneaking back into the city to visit her grandparents, one of the most touching episodes in the book, for stalwart, domineering Grandmother has become frail and insecure. The print is very small, unfortunately, but the vitality of the story will no doubt hold readers despite this.

958 **Nöstlinger,** Christine. *Konrad;* tr. by Anthea Bell; illus. by Carol Nicklaus. Watts, 1977. 77-7489. 135p. $6.90.

4-6 * In a deft blend of fantasy and realism, an eminent Austrian author tells the story of a factory-made child of seven who is delivered by mistake to a scatter-brained but delightful woman. Mrs. Bartolotti is a free-wheeling eccentric, and she becomes fond of Konrad, but she can't adjust to his perfection. Konrad is always truthful, helpful, polite, industrious, and sensible. He's been programmed that way. Konrad is not a success with his classmates; if the teacher asks who knows who broke the window, Konrad tells her, of course. He always tells the truth. Offered ice cream, he tells Mrs. Bartolotti that he's sorry, but it should only be eaten for dessert—and then only if one has finished all other food. So—when the factory catches up with its error and comes to reclaim Konrad, the only way for Mrs. B. to keep him is to reprogram him until he's such a scamp that the factory will reject him as not being their product. It's daftness made believable, it's great fun, and the translator has done a very nice job of conveying the author's blithe style.

959 **Oakley,** Graham. *The Church Cat Abroad.* Atheneum, 1973. 34p. illus. $6.95.

K-3 A sequel to *The Church Mouse* is truly delightful. Samson, the church cat who is a friend of all the church mice, sallies forth with two of the mice to find a fortune after they have muffed a chance of making money filming a television commercial. Reason for search: the campaign to raise money for the leaking vestry roof has been going badly. Nothing goes according to plan, but the sojourn on the tropical island is replete with amusing incidents and the way in which the three animals manage to get back to England is ingenious. When they do get back to the church, penniless, they find that the fund has increased by a few halfpennies, but they are warmly welcomed nonetheless. Freshly imaginative, and very funny, the story is illustrated by drawings full of comic details, some of the printed signs visible only by magnification, but it's worth hauling out a magnifying glass.

960 **Oakley,** Graham. *The Church Mice Adrift;* written and illus. by Graham Oakley, Atheneum, 1977. 76-25705. 33p. $7.95.

K-3 A fifth story about the mice of Wortlethorpe Church and their mentor, Sampson, the church cat, has a dashing plot precipitated by a town improvement scheme. Their home demolished, a band of rats moves in on our old friends and ousts them into the cold, wet night. Sampson conceives a brilliant scheme: they will set up a free meal in a moored dollhouse, lure the rats, and set the restaurant adrift. Unfortunately, two of the mice are trapped in the dollhouse; fortunately, the others assist Sampson in a daring rescue. Talk about cliffhangers! The writing has wit and pace, the pictures have action and humor. Warning: it may be necessary to penalize adults who wish to keep the book themselves, for there are delicious bits in the paintings (the crew tearing down lovely old buildings are from the Heritage Demolition Company) and the text ("The Finger of Destiny had beckoned *him* to lead the mice in Triumph back to their Native Vestry, his Sword wouldn't rest in his Hand until Feet had trampled the rats into the Dust and British mice never, never, never would be Slaves.") and the whole thing is a comic masterpiece.

961 **Oakley,** Graham. *The Church Mice and the Moon.* Atheneum, 1974. 34p. illus. $6.95.

K-3 This sequel to *The Church Mouse* and *The Church Cat Abroad* is more sophisticated than its predecessors, in part because some of the story is carried by handprint in the illustrations, in part because some of the humor depends on comprehension of the gibes at adults, an understanding not all of the read-aloud audience possesses. Nevertheless, there's more than enough plot and humor for the unsophisticated child, and Oakley again has created a delightful blend of such appealing elements as bland nonsense, animal friendship, and adventure. Plus, here, the lure of the intricacies of spacecraft and a planned flight, although he's hard on the poor scientists, who are lampooned in *Punch* fashion. Two of the churchmice are captured by scientists and are being groomed for a flight when Samson, the church cat, comes to the rescue. The resultant mission is enjoyable chaos, and much more fun than is usually garnered by the adult reader-aloud is provided here as well as a witty gambol for the read-to.

962 **Oakley,** Graham. *The Church Mice Spread Their Wings.* Atheneum, 1976. 75-15102. 32p. illus. $7.95.

K-2 Convinced by their most bookish member that "They had indeed become Victims of the Rat Race, crushed by the Pressures of Modern Life . . ." the church mice decide that they need an outing, with the church cat going along as escort. Their rural excursion is fraught with danger and they are convinced that they are on foreign soil; they are overcome at being back in England (they've been on the other side of a park lagoon) and the whole bit of nonsense ends with the daring escape of two mice from an owl. Via paper airplane. The illustrations are half the fun, as Oakley shows them, for example, in languid contrast to the "Rat Race," the mice are shown sunning themselves on a tombstone, napping, playing games with flowers, and enjoying a peaceful afternoon. A clever text has pictures with deft, amusing details.

963 **O'Brien,** Robert C. *Z for Zachariah.* Atheneum, 1975. 74-76736. 249p. $6.95.

7- A posthumously published story with a favorite setting of science fiction, a world in which people have survived disaster of their own making, is quite unlike the fanciful and intricate Newbery winner, *Mrs. Frisby and the Rats of NIMH.* It is told in a diary written by a young woman, Ann Burden, who had thought she was the only person left in the world. Ann knows that her home and some of the land around it are safe, that outside the area everyone has died. And then she sees a man. He is masked, wearing a safety suit, carrying a testing device. Will he be friendly? Ann hides in a cave, coming back to the house when she realizes the man is ill; in a state of delirium, he says some alarming things, but he seems a pleasant companion during convalescence, and Ann hopes they can build a life together. The journal form is used by O'Brien very effectively, with no lack of drama and contrast, and the pace and suspense of the story are adroitly maintained until the dramatic and surprising ending.

964 **O'Connell,** Jean S. *The Dollhouse Caper;* illus. by Erik Blegvad. T. Y. Crowell, 1976. 75-25501. 84p. $5.95.

3-5
* A deft fanciful story by a new children's writer has the appeal of the miniature in a family of dolls that come to life when there are no people about. They are almost caught by some thieves who are, as the boy doll Todd explains, "casing the joint." The dolls are worried by the fact that the three brothers who own them are getting along in years and may discard them; they're also worried by the imminent robbery and try to leave clues for their humans. This book has it all: humor in dialogue, a convincing blend of realism and fantasy, good characterization, smooth writing style, a sturdy plot and satisfying ending, and the merest touch of sentiment. AND Blegvad's wonderfully detailed, brisk drawings.

965 **O'Dell,** Scott. *Carlota.* Houghton, 1977. 77-9468. 153p. $7.95.

6-9 Although the Mexican-American war had ended, some of the U.S. Army hadn't heard about it and stumbled into a battle with a privately-organized group of Californios who wanted neither country's supervision. What they wanted was independence and the right to carry on their peaceful, dignified way of life. O'Dell's story based on this event—the battle of San Pasqual—has pace, color, momentum, and a flowing style. Above all, it has a doughty heroine, Carlota de Zubatan, who tells the story. Her widowed father's companion, a crack rider, and knowledgeable about the affairs of their estate, Carlota takes part in the battle and is left in charge of the ranch when her father dies. The book gives a vivid picture of the way of life of the Californios at the close of the last century, and it cries for a sequel.

966 **O'Dell,** Scott. *Child of Fire.* Houghton, 1974. 213p. $5.95.

7-10 The parole officer who tells the story, Delaney, is in Tijuana looking for Ernie Sierra when he sees another adolescent Chicano perform an act that is both brave and foolhardy. Manuel Castillo, when Delaney drives him home, agrees to stop for food—and it soon becomes clear that Manuel's deed was done to impress a girl, the waitress in the restaurant. All that Delaney learns thereafter about Manuel corroborates his feeling that the boy is a gallant, a conquistadore born past his time: his conduct as a gang member and a lover, his fierce pride in his once eminent family, his passionate insistence on justice. Manuel goes to sea, is jailed as a mutineer, escapes and joins the grape-pickers who are protesting the advent of a machine that will take away their jobs. He throws himself in front of the machine and meets his death in the same way he threw himself before a bull the first time Delaney saw him. This is not teen-age bravado but bravery, and Scott brings out—through Delaney's eyes—the bittersweet quality of Manuel. O'Dell's artistry is evident in the unobtrusive way in which Delaney establishes his own character and philosophy as he deals with Manuel and the other Chicano boys with whom he works, the consistency and distinctiveness of the first-person style, and the smooth incorporation of such dramatic events as a cockfight, a killing, the confrontation between gang members, and bullfights.

967 **O'Dell,** Scott. *The Cruise of the* Arctic Star; maps by Samuel Bryant. Houghton, 1973. 206p. $4.95.

R
7-12 A new field for Scott O'Dell, a new triumph, as he describes a voyage along the California coast to Alaska and weaves into his story some early history of the state, remembrances of his boyhood, descriptions of the sea otter, thoughts on conservation, and an anecdote about a dramatic wreck. These vivid bits are held together by the account of the trip in which O'Dell, his wife, a friend, and a hired hand were the crew. The hand, a handsome and undependable young braggart, is a source of increasing tension, and it is a relief when he finally jumps ship. Unabashed,

Rod communicates with O'Dell by radio, and so the writer knows that Rod is taking his new ship on a dangerous course and learns of its capsizing. A truly engrossing book. An index and a bibliography are appended.

968 **O'Dell,** Scott. *The Hawk That Dare Not Hunt by Day*. Houghton, 1975. 17029. 222p. $7.95.

7-9 Based, the author's prefatory note states, on the work of the best known of William Tyndale's biographers, this historical novel describes Tyndale's determined and successful efforts to translate the Bible into English and to publish it so that it would be available to all Englishmen. Many of the characters and the events are actual; the principal characters of the story, Tom Barton and his uncle Jack, are not. There is enough material about Tom, who tells the story, about his and Jack's smuggling, Jack's imprisonment, the ship they sail and the question of its true ownership, to overshadow slightly the story of Tyndale's determined zeal in the face of persecution, his hurried flight to Hamburg, his harried and furtive hidings while the Bible was being printed, and his trial in Belgium. He was turned over to the secular government for punishment, condemned as a heretic, and hung. Although there is more emphasis on Barton than on Tyndale, the personality of the latter is strongly defined, the story has plenty of action and historical detail, and it gives a vivid picture of the confusion and dissension in the turbulent years of the early sixteenth century.

969 **O'Dell,** Scott. *The 290*. Houghton, 1976. 76-42097. 118p. $6.95.

6-8 An American working in a British shipyard during the Civil War, sixteen-year-old Jim is urged by his brother, a Yankee spy, to furnish information about the vessel he's working on, *The 290*, which is being built for the Confederacy. A loyal southerner, Jim joins the crew and sees action on the ship, renamed *Alabama*. While on a raiding mission, Jim seizes a chance to go to Port-au-Prince, where there is a slave warehouse owned jointly by his father and Ruiz Cicerone, and manages to release a large number of slaves. It is a minor flaw that the story of this rescue seems sharply separated from the rest of the book, but it crystallizes O'Dell's point: one can be loyal to a cause without approving of every facet upheld by other supporters of that cause. The characters and the writing style are of high calibre, and the naval details are authentic and exciting.

970 **O'Dell,** Scott. *Zia*. Houghton, 1976. 75-44156. 179p. $7.95.

5-8 A sequel to *Island of the Blue Dolphins* is set in a California mission and is told by Zia, niece of the long-isolated Karana. Zia's mother had come from the island and had, before her death, told her daughter of the sister who stayed behind; now Zia's dream is to find her aunt. After an abortive attempt to sail to the island alone with her brother, Zia convinces an otter-hunter to find her aunt. But when he does come back with Karana, there are problems: she cannot talk to people, she is used to solitude and independence. Karana becomes ill and quietly dies. Zia, who had been involved in the resistance of other Indians to their displacement and to being forced to work for the Mission, had stayed behind (and been punished) in order to see Karana, but after the latter's death Zia leaves. Alone and unafraid, she has gained confidence from Karana's courage, so that Karana had indeed left a legacy for the future. The two parts of the story (Karana-Zia and Zia as a victim of discrimination and oppression by religious and military institutions) do not quite mesh, and the tone of the writing is subdued, but O'Dell gives a convincing picture of Mission life and the conflict for Indians impressed into it, and his writing style is—as always—smooth and graceful.

971 **Olney,** Ross R. *Gymnastics;* illus. by Mary Ann Duganne. Watts, 1976. 75-34478. 64p. $3.90.

4-6 Interest in gymnastics, both for spectators and participants, has grown in recent years, but many of the spectators who enjoyed watching Olympic competition do not understand scoring as much as they appreciate the skill and grace of performances. Olney tells all. He describes the equipment, discusses training, clothing, safety measures, the differences between men's and women's events, and judging. Diagrams (occasionally inadequate) illustrate the descriptions of individual acrobatic feats for men and women, which include difficulty ratings. A lucid and informative text concludes with an index.

972 **Opie,** Iona (Archibald). *The Classic Fairy Tales;* by Iona and Peter Opie. Oxford, 1974. 244p. illus. $12.95.

4- While this is primarily a book for adult students of folk literature, it contains twenty-four familiar fairy tales that should intrigue young readers as well, although the print is small, and—since the stories are given just as they were first published in English—in some cases the vocabulary and spelling are obsolete. However, the tales themselves are of perennial appeal and the illustrations (Bewick, Cruikshank, Dore, Dulac, Greenaway, Rackham, and Rex Whistler pictures have been selected) are enchanting. But all of these aspects will appeal to older readers, and for them the introduction to the text and the headnotes for each selection will afford profit as well as pleasure. A list of sources for background information, a list of sources of illustrations, and an index are appended.

973 **Opie,** Iona (Archibald), ed. *The Oxford Book of Children's Verse;* chosen and ed. with notes by Iona and Peter Opie. Oxford, 1973. 407p. $10.

K-8 A compilation of time-tested poems for or about children compiled by eminent anthologists, is arranged in chronological groupings. In their preface the Opies state firmly that no effort has been made to seek out the unfamiliar but that their goal has been "to make available in one place the classics of children's poetry." So, from Geoffrey Chaucer to Ogden Nash, five hundred years of poetry for children has been skimmed, and this is the Opie's choice of cream. The notes on authors and sources add to the book's usefulness, and an index of first lines and familiar tales as well as an author index are appended. For home collections or for school and library, a bonanza.

974 **Oppenheim,** Shulamith. *The Selchie's Seed;* illus. by Diane Goode. Bradbury, 1975. 74-22854. 83p. $5.95.

4-6 A fantasy based on the Scottish legends of the selchies, the seal people, is illustrated with soft, misty, romantic black and white drawings. Edward and Ursilla Sinclare, fisherfolk who live on the North Sea coast, are apprehensive about their lovely daughter Marian, who seems bewitched by a white whale. Ursilla's fear is enhanced by the knowledge that there are selchies in her ancestory. The family efforts fail; although they throw the magical sealskin belt into the sea, the whale retrieves it, and Marian goes eagerly to her love, wearing the belt that has transformed her into a mermaid. The style is lyric, the tone grave, and the story moves at a deliberate pace.

975 **Orgel,** Doris. *A Certain Magic.* Dial, 1976. 75-9204. 192p. $6.95.

4-6 Jenny, just before she and her parents left for a trip to London, had come across a diary in her aunt's apartment while Aunt Trudl was out. Ashamed of prying, she was so fascinated by the details of the young Trudl's stay with an English family as a refugee from Austria during World War II that she read almost all the entries. Trudl had been so convinced that her emerald ring had magical, evil powers that she had hidden it. By a chain of believable circumstances, Jenny tracked down a member of the host family and found the ring, bringing it back to Trudl and confessing her own guilt about the diary. Both Jenny's story and the diary narrative are vigorous and effective; the two are nicely knit, and the book is notable for its natural dialogue and for the warmth and spontaneity of Jenny's relationship with her parents and her aunt.

976 **Orgel,** Doris. *The Devil in Vienna.* Dial, 1978. 78-51319. 246p. $7.95.

6-8 Although fictional, the events in this story about the Nazi occupation of Austria are based on the author's experiences as a child in Vienna. Inge is Jewish, her best friend Lieselotte is the daughter of a Nazi officer so devoted to Hitler that he had moved his family to Germany, returning only after the anschluss. Although the girls have been forbidden to meet by both sets of parents, Inge knows her friend is loyal; when her parents are having difficulty in leaving the country, Inge turns to Lieselotte's uncle, a Catholic priest, for help. The story ends with the refugees' safe arrival in Yugoslavia. Books about the experiences of Jewish families in Germany or German-occupied territory are not rare, but this is one of the better ones in depicting the erosion, the tension, and the fear in the midst of which Jewish victims found that they still had friends and they still had hopes. The writing style is natural and fluent as Inge tells her story.

977 **Ormondroyd,** Edward. *All in Good Time;* drawings by Ruth Robbins. Parnassus, 1975. 75-1688. 206p. Trade ed. $5.95; Library ed. $5.88 net.

5-7 In a sequel to *Time at the Top* in which Susan had taken an elevator that took her back to the 1880's, Ormondroyd uses the imgenious device of having a narrator who—directed by a peculiar telephone call—discovers Susan's diary. The Walker family she has met in her venture into the past is in trouble, and Susan has convinced her father, on returning home, to go back with her to 1881. Susan loves the period and she hopes her father will wed the lovely, widowed Mrs. Walker. In a lively and convincing fantasy, Susan and the Walker children (who also hope for a merger) thwart a villain, outmaneuver a domineering aunt, and achieve their goal. There's a nice double time-twist at the end, too. A satisfying story, written with pace and humor.

978 **Ormondroyd,** Edward. *Castaways On Long Ago;* with drawings by Ruth Robbins. Parnassus, 1973. 182p. Trade ed. $4.50; Library ed. $4.38 net.

4-6 With high dramatic sense, Ormondroyd saves the most exciting episode and the solution of an unusual mystery-fantasy until the very end of a very good book. Three children are having a five-day stay on a farm while their parents attend a conference. Expecting to be bored, they find that they are wholly caught up in the puzzle of the boy on Long Ago Island; he's clearly trying to get them to visit him—but how did he get there? And how can they? The island is forbidden territory, they have no boat, and there's a guard on the mainland property across the lake. What gives the book substance that goes beyond the plot is the quality of characterization: both the children and their farm hosts are highly individual, sharply drawn and consistent in behavior and dialogue, for which the author has a keen ear.

979 **Otto,** Svend. *Tim and Trisha;* written and illus. by Svend Otto; tr. by Joan Tate. Pelham / Merrimac, 1978. 24p. $5.95.

4-6 yrs. * In the latest book from the latest winner of the Hans Christian Andersen Award for illustration, the Danish artist has created a troll family as beguiling as they are ugly. An only child, little Tim the troll has nobody to play with, so when he sees a small girl playing alone, he offers companionship. His huge, gentle father feels insecure away from the cave, and begs little Trisha to go back with them, promising to take her home when she is ready. They have so much fun that other trolls are invited, and they all have a ball. Trisha's parents don't believe her tale, but she shows them the huge footprints of Father Troll, who had carried her home. And there the story ends, a bit abruptly; nevertheless, it's a happy book, and the paintings of woodland scenes and rollicking, red-cheeked trolls cavorting merrily are wonderfully vigorous.

980 **Oxenbury,** Helen. *Helen Oxenbury's ABC of Things.* Watts, 1972. 52p. illus. $4.95.

2-5 yrs. Pictures that are imaginative and humorous as well as handsome make this a far better than average ABC book. The verso page gives the letter, in big bold type, in upper and lower case; at the bottom of the page the object or objects on the facing page are identified. What adds zest to learning (or helping to learn) the alphabet are the engaging characters in the illustrations and the often-ludicrous combinations. "B" for example: baby, baker, bear, bird, and badger are entwined in affectionate embrace, although the baker looks somewhat bleary-eyed; there's nothing odd about a leopard and a lion in the same tree—except for the jaded expressions of infinite boredom on their faces. Occasionally a word may need explanation ("wedding" of the wolf and weasel) but there isn't enough of this to be a burden.

981 **Oxenbury,** Helen. *Pig Tale.* Morrow. 1973. 30p. illus. Trade ed. $4.95; Library ed. $4.59 net.

4-6 yrs. A rhyming tale in an oversize book; some of the pages have large-scale pictures, others have four small frames with a line of text beneath each, and all of the pictures by Oxenbury, a Greenaway Medal winner, are light and frolicsome and lovely. Briggs and Bertha, two totally bored pigs who dream of wealth and leisure, unearth a box of jewels which they take to a bank. On a mad spending spree, they acquire a house, an elegant car, new clothes, gadgets—everything a pig could want. But luxury palls, the gadgets don't work, the lush lawn needs mowing, and at last the fretful pair run away from their house, shedding clothing as they go, and happily resume their old style of sloth and freedom. The illustrations are the strength of the book, but the tale itself and the style of telling are quite adequate.

982 **Oxford Scientific Films.** *Bees and Honey;* photographs by David Thompson. Putnam, 1977. 76-45849. 26p. $5.95.

3-5 A six-page text, divided into brief topics ("The Hive," "The Queen," "Foraging," etc.) and crisply written, is followed by captioned full-page color photographs, most of which are greatly enlarged. Text and captions give information about division of labor, communication and cooperation, food-making, life-cycle, and the role of the beekeeper. There is no description of the bee's structure, save for photographs and captions that show anatomical details; otherwise this seems as informative as other books on this subject.

983 **Oxford Scientific Films.** *The Butterfly Cycle;* photographs by John Cooke. Putnam, 1977. 76-45850. 26p. $5.95.

3-5 Adapted from a series of educational films on biological subjects, this is as impressive a book for younger children as Eeckhoudt's *A Butterfly Is Born* is for older readers. The excellent color photographs, some magnified many times, follow the life cycle of the cabbage white butterfly in almost-full page format, with only a running line of text at the foot of the page. This portion of the book is also suitable for children too young to read the introduction that precedes this section, an introduction that is in smaller type, gives more information, and can be used by adults to discuss the photographs with younger children.

984 **Pace,** Mildred (Mastin). *Wrapped for Eternity; The Story of the Egyptian Mummy;* line drawings by Tom Huffman. McGraw-Hill, 1974. 192p. $6.95.

5-9 While the subject of mummies and Egyptian tombs is treated in many other books, this is the only one that is completely devoted to the subject—and it's excellent. The writing style is crisp and informal, the organization of material into and within chapters is logical, and the easily-incorporated research is evident in the extensive bibliography. The text describes Egyptian beliefs about death, funeral and burial practices, tombs and tomb robbers, the work of archeologists, the art of mummification and the delicate techniques used by those who unwrap the mummies, and the deductions scientists are able to make about the person who lived so long ago from the mummy examined today. An index is appended.

985 **Parker,** Elinor Milnor, comp. *Echoes of the Sea;* illus. by Jean Vallario. Scribner, 1977. 76-54719. 134p. $6.95.

6- "Time's self it is, made audible," wrote Rossetti in "The Sea-Limits," and it is the quality of eternal presence that permeates an excellent anthology. Parker has drawn from the works of poets old and new, dividing the book into such sections as "The Great Deep," "Sea Serpents," "Shells," "Mermaids and Mermen," and "Swimmers." Except for humorous poetry, the book has a broad range of moods, styles, subjects, and forms; most of the selections are conservative in form; all of them are distinctive in their color and imagery. Author, title, and first line indexes are provided.

986 **Parker,** Nancy Winslow. *The President's Cabinet and How It Grew;* written and illus. by Nancy Winslow Parker. Parents' Magazine, 1978. 77-10090. 29p. Trade ed. $6.50; Library ed. $6.19 net.

4-6 Ink and crayon drawings enliven but do not extend the text of a clearly written book that reinforces the historical account it gives—by presidential action—of succeeding changes in the composition of the cabinet, by describing the functions of each member of the cabinet, post by post. A useful book to supplement a social studies curriculum.

987 **Parker,** Richard. *He Is Your Brother.* Nelson, 1976. 76-6116. 98p. $5.95.

5-6 Eleven-year-old Mike, absorbed in his own interests, pays little attention to his younger brother Orry (Lawrence); an autistic child, Orry is only a mild nuisance to Mike. When he becomes aware that Orry shares his own great interest in trains, Mike takes the younger boy on some hobby-related outings and also goes along when Orry sees a therapist. Increasingly fond of his brother, Mike is also gratified and impressed when he realizes that Orry is responding, not only talking but talking intelligently. He's also protective, knowing that their father's self-centered, casual behavior disturbs Orry, too. The changes in patterns of family behavior as Orry changes and improves are gradual, believable, and perceptively depicted. Within the story of these changes are enough action sequences to give the book vitality.

988 **Parnall,** Peter. *A Dog's Book of Birds.* Scribner, 1977. 77-7194. 43p. illus. $5.95.

2-4 The scruffy mop of a dog who investigated bugs in *A Dog's Book of Bugs* trots, swims, and climbs about investigating birds in this agreeable companion volume. Parnall's pictures are clean, uncluttered, meticulously detailed, and here they have an antic note that adds to the reader's enjoyment and detracts not a whit from the accuracy of comments and illustrations. One double-page spread shows crows in various positions; the text reads, "The Crow is a rascal. He makes a lot of noise . . . and steals things. He can even learn to talk." What the crows are stealing is the dog, held aloft by ears and tails.

989 **Patent,** Dorothy Hinshaw. *Evolution Goes On Every Day;* drawings by Matthew Kalmenoff. Holiday House, 1977. 76-50525. 156p. $6.95.

8- Patent is one of those rare science writers who combine
* authoritative knowledge, a detached and objective attitude, and an ability to write for the layman with fluency and clarity. Her discussion of evolution is neatly organized and comprehensive, embodying both recent developments and the scientific attitude. And when she speaks of theories or conjecture, she carefully distinguishes between them and facts. Here she describes some of the evolutionary changes in progress in contemporary species of fauna and flora, analyzing the various factors that effect change or encourage the emergence of new species. The text also discusses the effects of human interference with natural selection, research findings about resistant strains and linked genetic traits, and the problems and promise of genetic engineering. A bibliography and a relative index are appended; illustrations are informative and are carefully placed in relation to textual references.

990 **Patent,** Dorothy Hinshaw. *Fish and How They Reproduce;* drawings by Matthew Kalmenoff. Holiday House, 1976. 76-10349. 128p. $6.95.

6-9 Patent's books always maintain a high standard; accurate, logically organized and written with clarity, they exemplify and illustrate the scientific approach. Here the text gives, in the first two chapters, adequate general information about the variety of fishes, their intelligence and their habitats, the development of the senses in fish, and some facts about hereditary characteristics and adaptation. Succeeding chapters describe some of the many, and often fascinating, ways in which fish court, mate, spawn and breed, and protect their progeny—including facts about migration, color change, sex change, and defense mechanisms. A glossary, a list of books and magazine articles suggested for further reading, and a relative index are appended.

991 **Patent,** Dorothy Hinshaw. *Frogs, Toads, Salamanders and How They Reproduce;* illus. by Matthew Kalmenoff. Holiday House, 1975. 74-26567. 142p. $6.95.

4-7 Meticulously detailed illustrations add to the usefulness and
* appeal of an excellent text, lucid and comprehensive, logically

organized and written authoritatively. Patent describes the species of amphibians that inhabit various environments, discusses breeding and feeding habits, and describes the developmental stages of frogs, toads, salamanders, and caecilians. Other aspects discussed are adaptation, nesting, and parental care, with particular emphasis on some of the exotic aspects of egg-carrying frogs and toads. A bibliography and an index are appended.

992 **Patent,** Dorothy Hinshaw. *How Insects Communicate.* Holiday House, 1975. 75-6699. 127p. illus. $5.95.

4-7
*
Excellent photographs, many of them highly magnified, show details of insect structure or behavior in amplification of a text that is as well-written as it is informative. Patent, a zoologist, has a marked aptitude for writing lucidly and fully without writing down to a juvenile audience. Here she discusses such intriguing subjects as the bee-dancing that gives directions to hive-mates; the silent pheronomes, chemicals that trigger various reactions of amatory, defensive, or offensive natures; the lights of fireflies and chirring of cicadas. These and many other ways of communicating by sight, sound, touch, smell, and taste enable insects to find mates, defend themselves, feed, and live in social colonies. It seems odd that, given the title, the book concludes with the chapter, "Some Other Invertebrates" (a scant six pages about crabs, scorpions, and spiders), but the text is no less worthwhile for this. A list of books and magazines suggested for additional reading, and a relative index are appended.

993 **Patent,** Dorothy Hinshaw. *Plants and Insects Together;* drawings by Matthew Kalmenoff. Holiday House, 1976. 75-34205. 128p. $5.95.

5-7 Although the material included here has been described in other books for children (those by Rose Hutchins, for example) this well-organized and clearly written text should be useful. It discusses the many ways in which plants and insects have relationships that are either mutually beneficial (pollination) or harmful (the insect-catching sundew plant, the Colorado potato beetle that damages potato plants); it also describes those relationships in which plant and animal adapt to each other in an evolutionary spiral. The illustrations are accurate and well-placed for the most part, but occasionally a picture omits something described in the text (the pollinia of an orchid) or is not placed to best advantage. Although the author's background as a zoologist usually precludes any unscientific attitude, there are a few phrases used in the text that suggest volition; for example, even with the quotation marks, the statement, "The flower 'pretends' to be an insect," suggests purposiveness. A divided bibliography and an index are appended.

994 **Patent,** Dorothy Hinshaw. *Reptiles and How They Reproduce;* illus. by Matthew Kalmenoff. Holiday House, 1977. 77-3817. 119p. $6.95.

6- * Zoologist strikes again! The direct and unpretenious writing has almost a conversational flow, describing the evolution of reptilian species, the characteristics of each, and the characteristics they have in common. Separate chapters then describe patterns of courting and mating, nest-building, and—in some species—care of young, social organization, establishment of territorial rights or individual dominance. The careful drawings are well-placed and adequately labelled, and the writing is scientifically exemplary, using technical terms when necessary and otherwise avoiding them, distinguishing between fact and theory, communicating a sense of appreciation for the intricacies of life forms without becoming rhapsodical about them. A glossary, a list of suggested readings, and a relative index are appended. Patently superior.

995 **Paterson,** Katherine. *Bridge to Terabithia;* illus. by Donna Diamond. T. Y. Crowell, 1977. 77-2221. 128p. $7.95.

5-7 * Jess Aarons, determined to be the best runner in his small rural school's fifth grade, is taken aback when the new girl in school, Leslie, beats him easily. But it is Leslie who becomes his first friend, who opens doors into imaginative play, who leads him into Terabithia—the imaginary land where they are monarchs. One of a large and stolid farm family, Jess has never met parents like Leslie's, people who talk about books and music, people who treat him as an equal. Leslie learns compassion and compromise from Jess; Jess gains security and insight from Leslie. Then, on a day when Jess is on a trip with a teacher, Leslie goes to their secret spot, Terabithia, alone. Swinging over the ravine to their haven, Leslie is killed when the rope breaks. Jess goes through the several agonies of grief, his usually dour parents proving unexpectedly supportive. At the close of the story, Jesse builds a safe bridge to Terabithia and brings his small, doting sister there. This is what he has gained from his friend, the power to pass on the warmth and joy to others that he gained from Leslie's friendship. Quite unlike Paterson's previous books in setting or theme, this is just as beautifully crafted and convincing, but even more touching.

996 **Paterson,** Katherine. *The Great Gilly Hopkins.* T. Y. Crowell, 1978. 77-27075. 148p. Trade ed. $6.95; Library ed. $6.79 net.

5-8 * Labelled a rebellious troublemaker, eleven-year-old Gilly yearns to be reunited with her mother, whose lovely photograph is so affectionately inscribed. A rejected illegitimate child of one of the "flower children," Gilly's been in several foster homes; now she has been placed with slovenly cheerful Mrs. Trotter and a small boy, also a foster child. At first Gilly despises them both, but she succumbs to Trotter's protective love and to the boy's need for love. Paterson's development of the change in Gilly is brilliant and touching, as she depicts a child whose tough protective shield dissolves as she learns to accept love and to give it. A well-structured story has vitality of writing style, natural dialogue, deep insight in characterization, and a keen sense of the fluid dynamics in human relationships. The story is written with a sophistication and dignity that may well appeal to some high school readers.

997 **Paterson,** Katherine. *The Master Puppeteer;* illus. by Haru Wells, T. Y. Crowell, 1976. 75-8614. 179p. $6.95.

6-9 * Like intricate embroidery, Paterson's story has deftly woven threads of several patterns that combine to make a cohesive and dramatic whole. The setting, as in other of her books, is feudal Japan; the milieu is the closed and intricate world of the puppet theater; the contrapuntal plot thread is the mysterious bandit who operates as an Osakan Robin Hood. Jiro, a young apprentice puppeteer, is one of a group of boys who are rigidly disciplined in their new profession; he also stumbles on some clues about the identity of Saburo. The plot is skilfully constructed, the characters are strong, and the historical background is as interesting as the details of the puppet theater. Good style, good story.

998 **Paterson,** Katherine. *Of Nightingales That Weep;* illus. by Haru Wells. T. Y. Crowell, 1974. 170p. $5.95.

6-9 A colorful and romantic story of feudal Japan has as a protagonist Takiko, daughter of a samurai who was a hero in the early days of the long power struggle between the Heike and the Genji clans. After her father's death, Takiko's mother weds a potter, an ugly and kind man, and they send the girl to live at court. Beautiful and vain, Takiko will not come to help her mother because she has fallen in love; she is punished by both guilt and misfortune. No fairytale ending here, but a bitter loss and a slow acceptance of a scarred face and a peasant's life—yet the ending isn't all sad, because Takiko finds love of another kind. The battle scenes are vivid, the details of court life convincing, the characters drawn with some depth; this is unusual and stirring historical fiction.

999 **Paul,** Aileen. *Kids Outdoor Gardening;* illus. by John DeLulio. Doubleday, 1978. 77-80902. 80p. $5.95.

4-6 In a logically organized book for the beginning young gardener,

Paul describes preparation of the seed bed, planning and planting a flower or vegetable garden, and getting advice on soil or best planting dates. For some processes, she suggests adult help; she advises moderation—such as not attempting a compost heap at the start. The text is clearly written, and the book includes a list of sources for further information, a glossary, and an index.

1000 **Pearce,** A. Philippa. *What the Neighbors Did and Other Stories;* illus. by Faith Jaques. T. Y. Crowell, 1973. 130p. Trade ed. $4.50; Library ed. $5.25 net.

4-6 Eight stories about children in a Cambridgeshire village are included in a delightful collection. The writing is direct and simple, the plot lines clean, the characters drawn lightly but with a firm hand; what make the book enchanting are the fluidity of the author's style and the warmth and realism of her conception.

1001 **Pearson,** Susan. *Monnie Hates Lydia;* illus. by Diane Paterson. Dial, 1975. 75-9198. 28p. Trade ed. $5.50; Library ed. $5.16 net.

2-4 Although recommended by the publisher for ages 4–8, this story in picture book format seems to demand more depth of understanding than most very young children have. The setting is a motherless household; there is no explanation. It is Lydia's tenth birthday, and her younger sister Monnie has helped dad bake a cake and plan a surprise party. Monnie has trouble all day with Lydia's surly behavior toward her: showing no appreciation for a present, scoffing at Monnie's efforts to show her participation, patronizing her in the presence of guests. Daddy (a strong character) is sympathetic but won't interfere. Goaded, Monnie finally drapes the cake over her sister's face. Result: Lydia says it's a good cake and they all laugh and eat it. The message may be "Assert yourself" but Lydia's reaction seems inconsistent with her previous behavior, and the ending is weak. As a picture of an abrasive sibling, however, the book is strong, and Monnie is a sympathetic character.

1002 **Pearson,** Susan. *That's Enough for One Day, J.P.!* pictures by Kay Chorao. Dial, 1977. 76-42923. 26p. Trade ed. $5.95; Library ed. $5.47 net.

K-2 Some mothers may cringe a bit, but most children will be delighted with John Philip's quiet triumph over his. Not that J.P. does anything in the way of rebellion; he obeys Mother dutifully, but he gets exactly what he wants, privacy for more reading. Mother has decided that J.P. stays in his room and reads too much, so she sends him out for fresh air and exercise. He breaks a window playing ball, digs up some bulbs (accidentally) while hunting worms, gets paint on a neighbor's rose bush, gets soaked while helping another neighbor wash her car. When he appears at lunchtime, Mother—who has repeatedly come to the door to scold—is horrified by his damp and dirty state and orders him to go to his room, get clean and dry, and stay in. John Philip complacently goes back to reading. The writing style is brisk and humorous, the dialogue casual, and the illustrations witty.

1003 **Peck,** Richard. *Are You in the House Alone?* Viking, 1976. 76-28810. 156p. $6.95.

7-10 Gail, only child of an affluent suburban couple, had a few problems: she didn't like her best friend Alison's boy friend Phil, or his snobbish parents; she didn't like the way her parents acted toward her own boy friend, Steve Pastorini, who wasn't the "right kind"; and she wasn't sure she wanted to continue her affair with Steve. But when she began to get vicious, threatening letters and nasty telephone calls, Gail felt real fear. Babysitting one night, she was surprised to see Phil at the door, and then she recognized the voice of her nightmares. Raped and beaten, she found that she was doubly victimized, for the police shrugged it off with the insinuation that she'd led Phil on and even her lawyer advised that it would be impossible to fight the most powerful family in town. Peck brings the story to a logical, tragic conclusion (Phil's next victim almost dies) but it isn't *what* happens that gives the story impact, although that is handled with conviction, and although the style, dialogue, and characters are equally impressive—it is the honest and perceptive way that the author treats the problem of rape. For Peck sees clearly both the society's problem and the victim's: the range of attitudes, the awful indignity, the ramifications of fear and shame.

1004 **Peck,** Richard. *Father Figure.* Viking, 1978. 78-7909. 192p. $8.95.

7-10 Jim is seventeen, and since his father had walked out when he was nine, it's been Jim who's been a father figure to his eight-year-old brother Byron. Their mother, dying of cancer, has just committed suicide, and their indomitable grandmother decrees that the boys are to spend the summer with their father in Florida. There's no room in Jim's life for a father, he resents Byron's acceptance of the man, and he becomes even more resentful when he gets a crush on a woman in Florida and becomes jealous of his father, sure that there is or was a relationship between the two. The woman, Marietta, is Peck's best characterization to date: level-headed, compassionate, honest, and drawn with fine consistency as she is seen through Jim's eyes and her own words. The situation is complex and sensitive, and it's handled with finesse and percipience in a story that develops with good pace toward a logical conclusion.

1005 **Peck,** Richard. *The Ghost Belonged to Me.* Viking, 1975. 183p. $5.95.

6-8 Only a very good writer could take so many apparently disparate elements and blend them into a story that is smoothly effective, and Richard Peck certainly has done that here. A ghost, restlessly hunting a grave with her loved ones; a mother and sister whose social climbing is vigorous and unashamed; a sprightly old reprobate uncle and an unprincipled newspaperman he outwits; and Alexander himself, a shrewd but guileless boy of thirteen who resists to no avail the advances of a classmate and neighbor, Blossom Culp. Alexander is the only member of the family who has seen the ghost in the barn, and she has warned him of an imminent accident which he averts by leaping, nightshirted, into the path of a clanging trolley. The setting is a small town, the time is 1913, the teller is Alexander, and the story is funny, nostalgic, and witty.

1006 **Peck,** Richard. *Ghosts I Have Been.* Viking, 1977. 77-9469. 214p. $7.95.

6-9 Blossom Culp, the doughty and persistent ghost's companion of *The Ghost Belonged to Me,* now fourteen, tells her own story here, and she's completely convincing. As the daughter of a shabby spiritualist, Blossom not unnaturally thinks of pretending to have second sight when she can use it for retribution against a snobbish, vindictive classmate. Surprise! She can't always summon the power when she needs it, but Blossom actually does have psychic power; she sees the future. She gets involved in strange dramatic situations, becomes famous when her prescience is proven accurate, and takes it all in her stride. Somehow, in this melange of eccentric characters and dramatic, fantastic events, Peck instills in Blossom and her story a sturdy, lively believability.

1007 **Peck,** Richard. *Representing Super Doll.* Viking, 1974. 192p. $5.95.

6-10 Verna had been determined that she would be taken in by one particular group of town girls when she started high school classes at Dunthorpe, even though she lived on a farm, and she was. One of the small group was Darlene, not very bright, not conceited, but beautiful; when Darlene's aggressive mother pushed her into a beauty contest and she won, Darlene was almost a laughing stock at school. Verna (who tells the story) and the others tried to protect her, but Darlene seemed aloof and frozen; it was Darlene's mother who urged Verna to go along to New York as Darlene's companion for the Teen Super Doll contest. Verna, although she didn't like the city, had a good time, especially in meeting her brother's girl and in spending a happy day at the Cloisters. Darlene detested all of it, and decided to drop out and face her angry mother. Peck's writing is admirable. It has vitality and flow, vivid characterization and dialogue, a fresh viewpoint that makes the story convincingly that of an intelligent adolescent, and a deeper treatment of a theme than most beauty contest books achieve.

1008 **Peck,** Robert Newton. *A Day No Pigs Would Die*. Knopf, 1972. 150p. $4.95.

7- A story of a Shaker boy on a Vermont farm is anecdotal, with no story line but with a strong cohesive bond of love and an occasionally-quaint humor in the ingenuousness of the protagonist when he encounters words or practices foreign to the Shaker Way. Given a piglet by a neighbor, Rob raises his pet in hopes that she will be a brood sow, and is disappointed to find her sterile. His father, who is a pork butcher, kills Pinky, and Rob grieves although he knows it must be done. Knowing, also, that his father is near death, he forgives the act. And when his father dies, Rob becomes the man of the family, stoutly assuming his father's burdens. The book gives a vivid picture of the simplicity and goodness of the Shaker Way, but its real strength is in the depth of family love.

1009 **Pelta,** Kathy. *What Does a Paramedic Do?* illus. with photographs. Dodd, 1978. 77-16868. 63p. $5.25.

5-6 In a continuous text, straightforward but dry in style, the author describes the first paramedical programs and emergency units, the training of paramedics, and the different sorts of care they provide. The work of such non-medical personnel, who function in close contact with doctors via electronic communication, requires certification (with fairly frequent examinations to ensure renewal of certification) and has—in the short time that paramedical units have been established—saved many lives. There is no index, but the information is succinctly given and the book should appeal because of the intrinsic drama of the profession.

1010 **Perl,** Lila. *America Goes to the Fair; All About State and County Fairs in the USA;* illus. with photographs. Morrow, 1974. 127p. Trade ed. $5.50; Library ed. $4.81 net.

5-8 Although the writing style is rather monotonous, this survey of fairs gives such a comprehensive picture of the myriad activities that go on at fairs of every size that it is valuable for its information. Preceded by two lengthy chapters on the first fairs of early times and the fairs of early America, the text describes in great detail the prizes and demonstrations at agricultural fairs, the hoopla of the midway, the homemaking exhibits and contests, the youth groups that participate, the sporting events that are a part of many fairs, et cetera. A list of 100 major fairs in the United States and an index are appended.

1011 **Perl,** Lila. *Egypt; Rebirth on the Nile;* illus. with photographs. Morrow, 1977. 76-30729. 158p. Trade ed. $7.95; Library ed. $6.71 net.

7-10 Perl examines the myriad facets of Egyptian life, past and present, in a smoothly written book that is candid, objective, authoritative, and judiciously organized. The text begins with a physical description of the country, and the geographic influences on population distribution, economy, and history; it moves to historical information, and thence to government and politics, including Egypt's relationships with other countries. The analysis of present progress and problems is discerning, and the discussion of the quality of Egyptian life today includes an estimation of future developments. A bibliography and an index are appended.

1012 **Perl,** Lila. *The Telltale Summer of Tina C.* Seabury, 1975. 75-9518. 160p. $6.95.

4-6 Not a book with a strong storyline, this gives a convincing picture of a young adolescent who gains self-confidence, learns a measure of tolerance for the adults in her splintered family, and becomes aware that frankness makes it easier to communicate. Tina is tall, undeveloped, and particularly self-conscious about the fact that she twitches her nose when nervous. In her twelfth summer she has to adjust to her father's announcement that he's engaged to a woman Tina dislikes, to a fight with her best friends, and to becoming reacquainted with her mother, a nonconformist who has just divorced Tina's father and remarried. Tina reluctantly decides to visit her mother and finds that if they speak openly they are more comfortable, and she becomes very fond of her young stepfather. She also meets a Dutch boy who is obviously smitten and—although he goes home—his admiration gives Tina new confidence. Characterization and dialogue are strong, and the writing style is fluent, convincing as the commentary of a preadolescent and lightened by humor.

1013 **Perrault,** Charles. *Puss in Boots;* adapted by Paul Galdone. Seabury, 1976. 75-25505. 28p. illus. $6.95.

K-3 The ebullience and humor of Galdone's pictures are perfectly suited to the tale of the clever cat whose ploys and stratagems produce for his owner, a simple youth, a castle, a title, and a princess. The text is more direct and more jocose than that of what is perhaps the best known picture book version, a free translation illustrated by Marcia Brown, but its directness suits the more vigorous style of Galdone.

1014 **Pesek,** Ludek. *The Earth is Near;* tr. from the German by Anthea Bell. Bradbury, 1974. 206p. $5.95.

7- Winner of the 1971 German Children's Book Prize, capably translated, this story of the first expedition to Mars is far from the usual derring-do in space. Pesek draws a dramatic and convincing picture of the small crew's boredom and trepidation on the long journey. The story is told by a psychologist, one of the ship's two doctors, so that the analysis of motives and reactions is natural and authoritative; he describes the struggles against the desolation and dust of Mar's surface, the conflicts between individuals under stress, the catastrophic breakdown of machines and men. Although the writing style is heavy, the book is engrossing because of the percipience of the author and because the problems of the astronauts are those that have existed for any group of explorers; the reader can better understand Columbus or Coronado and their achievements thereby.

1015 **Peterson,** Hans. *The Big Snowstorm;* illus. by Harald Wiberg; trans. by Eric Bibb. Coward, 1976. 75-7675. 23p. $5.97.

2-4 While the oversize format and illustrations suggest a read-aloud audience, the subject and vocabulary—as well as the pace—of this story about the effects of a rural snowstorm indicate its appropriateness for independent readers. Only a few details suggest the Swedish setting. Ollie describes his grandmother's prediction of a bad storm, the peddler who is followed by wolves, the hasty loading of firewood, the bringing into the warm kitchen of a newborn calf. Direct, simple, and evocative, but not really a story in its structure, the book is illustrated with handsome paintings, particularly those of the outdoors, with trees towering dark in the grey-white twilight.

1016 **Pettit,** Florence H. *Christmas All Around the House; Traditional Decorations You Can Make;* drawings by Wendy Watson. T. Y. Crowell, 1976. 75-37876. 226p. $8.95.

6- A handsome book, and a useful one, describes in clear details the construction of Christmas decorations from different parts of the world, prefacing each set of instructions with an explanation of the origin of the object. Materials are listed first, then step-by-step instructions are given for construction. The illustrations are more detailed than those in the Coskey book, but alternatives are seldom suggested here; both books are excellent. An index is appended.

1017 **Pettit,** Florence H. *How to Make Whirligigs and Whimmy Diddles; and Other American Folkcraft Objects;* illus. by Laura Louise Foster. T. Y. Crowell, 1972. 349p. $6.95.

7- Even if a reader is not interested in following directions for making any of the objects described, this is entertaining reading. Each section begins with background information that describes the use of the object, and is followed by clear step-by-step instructions that are amply illustrated; a list of tools (also illustrated) and materials for each is included. There is also a glossary of tools and materials, a section on "Tricks to Know About Making Designs", a list of supply houses, a bibliography, a list of museums, and a relative index.

1018 **Pevsner,** Stella. *And You Give Me a Pain, Elaine.* Seabury, 1978. 78-5857. 182p. $7.50.

5-7 Thirteen-year-old Andrea, who tells the story, is the youngest of three; her adored brother Joe is away at college and her sister Elaine, sixteen, is the bane of Andrea's life, a sulky and rebellious adolescent who can't get along with Andrea or with their parents. Depressed by her own plodding personality and resentful of the attention Elaine gets when she defies her parents, Andrea is jolted into despair when Joe is killed in a motorcycle accident. This isn't a book with a strong story line, but it is strong in every other way: it is convincing as a first-person record, it is perceptive in establishing the fluctuations in personal relationships, it has excellent dialogue, and it balances nicely the several aspects of Andrea's life: her problems at school, her friendships, her involvement in the production of a school play, and her role in family life. It ends on an upbeat, as Andrea adjusts to Joe's death, acquires a first boy friend, and—having grown in compassion and percipience—begins to establish a more amicable relationship with her sister.

1019 **Pevsner,** Stella. *A Smart Kid Like You.* Seabury, 1975. 74-19320. 216p. $6.95.

5-7 Starting junior high school as one of the few students from a private high school had already made Nina apprehensive, but when she found that the teacher for her transfer group's accelerated math class was her father's new wife, she was really stunned. Her friends tried to help her by hazing the teacher; it didn't work. Nina, who had not adjusted to her parents' divorce, reluctantly realized that her father was much happier now. The story of her acceptance of her stepmother and her mother's suitor is balanced by her budding interest in a boy, her friendships at school, and her successful attempt to persuade her mother that she's no longer a small child. The book has a serious theme, but there are moments of humor; the characterization is convincing albeit not deep, and the changes and developments in Nina are logical.

1020 **Peyton,** K. M. *A Pattern of Roses;* illus. by the author. T. Y. Crowell, 1973. 186p. $4.50.

6-9 Kathleen Peyton's earlier books have been outstanding, whether set in historical or contemporary times, for their realism and conviction; here she moves into fantasy with a sure touch, knitting the story of an adolescent boy of today with episodes from the turn of the century that link the lives of Tom and Netty, children of the Victorian era, with today's Tim. Tim's father is a successful advertising executive, he has given his son all the advantages he lacked, and he cannot understand why Tim wants to go his own way—if necessary, to work with his hands. Tim's new friend Rebecca understands, and in helping him uncover the mystery of the boy Tom, whose drawings he has found and with whom he feels a strange communion, Rebecca helps Tim find his path to independence. The plot is adroitly constructed, the characters well-defined; although the book has some introspective passages that move slowly, this deliberation contributes to the understanding of Tim's slow gathering of enough courage to make his stand for the sort of quiet life he wants.

1021 **Peyton,** K. M. *Pennington's Heir.* T. Y. Crowell, 1974. 229p. $5.50.

7-10 A new novel continues the story of the rebellious English boy whose ability as a pianist has brought him a sponsor who has not withdrawn his offer of a home and lessons although Pat has been jailed for assaulting a policeman. Surly and often withdrawn, Pat is so happy, when he's released, at being with his girl again that he drops his guarded behavior, and makes love to her. Ruth finds she is pregnant; her parents are angry, Pat is stunned, and Pat's sponsor coldly severs their relationship. So Pat and Ruth begin their marriage: poorly housed, with Pat's progress as a musician halted, a baby due, and no prospects. And they are very happy, with Pat's love for Ruth growing, despite their problems. One of their problems is Clarissa, a violinist with whom Pat had had an affair, who uses her considerable charms and her father's eminence in musical circles to attempt seduction. Through all of this Pat practices, snaps at every chance to perform, and goes through the agony familiar to almost every performing artist before each concert. This sequel to *The Beethoven Medal* is equally effective in the vigor and felicity of its characterization, its authenticity of setting, its perceptiveness in depicting the shifting reactions within relationships, and its polished writing style.

1022 **Peyton,** K. M. *Prove Yourself a Hero.* Collins/World, 1978. 78-18802. 182p. $6.95.

6-9 In *The Team,* Peyton introduced an adolescent girl, Ruth, who later became the wife of Pennington, protagonist of *The Beethoven Medal* and *Pennington's Heir.* Here there is another link between Peyton's fictional characters as Jonathan Meredith, one of the people Ruth rode with in The Team, becomes the central character. Son of wealthy parents, Jonathan is kidnapped and held for ransom. The ransom is paid and Jonathan released, but he can't quite get over the fears he'd had while a captive nor the guilt he felt about those fears, the feeling that he should have been cool and heroic. When, by chance, he recognizes the voice of one of his captors, Jonathan trails the man and confronts him alone, expiating his own sense of inadequacy. As is true of other Peyton books, this has a smooth writing style, perceptive characterization, and particularly deft handling of dialogue; as is not always true of earlier books, this has a most dramatic (yet believable) plot.

1023 **Pfeffer,** Susan Beth. *The Beauty Queen.* Doubleday, 1974. 134p. $4.50.

6-9 The whole thing had been her mother's idea. "You're the prettiest girl Great Oaks has ever seen . . . Why, I'll bet you go all the way and make it to the national contest." Kit knew she was pretty, but she wasn't interested in beauty contests; she wanted to be an actress, wanted to join a theater group in Colorado. She tells her own story of winning the local contest, badgered and prodded by her ambitious mother. Entered in the state contest, Kit resists again, is again nagged by her mother; she is supported by her younger sister, but they are no match for Mom. Despite her boy friend's pleas that she stay home, Kit decides to pull out. She takes her savings and, after a caustic scene with Mom, packs for Colorado and the career she really wants. The backstage scenes of the beauty contest are interesting, the dialogue is natural and often pungent, and Kit is a sympathetic character, but it is Mom who steals the show; Pfeffer's portrayal of a tired, embittered, divorced woman whose ambition precludes compassion is biting.

1024 **Pfeffer,** Susan Beth. *Kid Power;* illus. by Leigh Grant. Watts, 1977. 77-1975. 121p. $5.90.

4-6 When Janie's mother loses her job, eleven-year-old Janie decides she's going to stop spending her allowance and save money for the new bike her father says they can no longer afford on a single salary. But that would be slow, so Janie conceives of "Kid Power," and advertises herself as available for any odd job. Although she tackles some she can't quite handle, her business is so successful that Janie's soon hiring her friends and her sister to take over some assignments, and taking ten percent as an agent's fee. Mom, who's been unsuccessful at getting a new job, decides she's going to organize the same sort of services for adult workers, and Janie's father is delighted by the whole thing. Janie tells the story convincingly, her descriptions of assignments are varied and interesting, and the Kid Power incidents are balanced by material about family and friends. The characterization is adequate, the relationships are perceptively depicted, and the dialogue is natural and often amusing.

1025 **Pfeffer,** Susan Beth. *Marly the Kid.* Doubleday, 1975. 46p. $5.95.

6-9 The sequel to *The Beauty Queen* (reviewed in the November 1974 issue) is even better, with more variation to the story line, excellent characterization, and an almost faultless ear for dialogue. Marly, whose beautiful older sister had run off to escape, in part, their mother's vitriolic tongue, follows suit. Kit had gone west to join a theater group; Marly turns up on her father's doorstep and is welcomed by him and by her stepmother, Sally. (No stereotypical situation, this.) It is Sally, even more than Marly's supportive father, who helps Marly adjust to her new life and who comes to Marly's aid when she gets in trouble for being too outspoken at school. No dramatic ending, but a cheerful and realistic note of encouragement as plump, plain Marly gains insight and perspective about herself.

1026 **Phipson,** Joan. *The Cats.* Atheneum, 1976. 75-43608. 168p. $5.95.

6-9 Jim and his brother Willy had carelessly talked about the lottery money their parents had won, and they were kidnapped by two young toughs and taken into the Australian wilderness. Jim is the older, the resourceful one, but it is Willy whose knowledge of the outdoors and whose almost psychic understanding help save the situation when the four are threatened by a group of feral cats. The writing is solid and serious, but the drama of the situation, the well-maintained suspense, and the vividness of the setting give the story vitality.

1027 **Phipson,** Joan. *Horse with Eight Hands.* Atheneum, 1974. 199p. $7.50.

5-7 The "horse" of the title is a German immigrant, the eight hands belong to the four Australian children who take Horst under their wings. Horst has bought an old house which he turns into an antique shop, and the four children help him ready the house and also guard him against repeated instances of malicious mischief on the part of a gang of motorcycle toughs. While the situation seems a bit contrived (the failure to identify or catch the culprits, the complete involvement of the children almost to the exclusion of other interests, the intervention of the local grande dame) each incident is convincing, and both the characters and their relationships are solidly drawn; the additional appeal of the story is in the satisfying development and completion of a project, as Horst and his eight helping hands turn a dilapidated house into an attractive and successful home and shop.

1028 **Phipson,** Joan. *Polly's Tiger;* illus. by Erik Blegvad. Dutton, 1974. 43p. $4.95.

3-4 Blegvad's precise, small-scale drawings go nicely with this story from one of Australia's most popular children's authors; the concepts of adaptability, conquering fear, and an imaginary companion are smoothly woven into the narrative. Polly has just come to a small settlement where her father has a job, and she finds the children rather unfriendly. To bolster her morale, she imagines that a tiger she's admired at a zoo is her companion; when she shows courage at confronting a large dog (and the two indomitable old ladies who own him) Polly's classmates—who've already thawed realistically—are full of admiration—and Polly no longer needs her tiger. Not dramatic, but there is a problem-solution structure, and the style of writing is natural and easy.

1029 **Phipson,** Joan. *When the City Stopped.* Atheneum, 1978. 78-6930. 181p. $6.95.

5-8 There's a perennial appeal in stories of children who cope capably and believably with disaster, and in this tale of a general strike in an Australian city, Phipson has captured the tension and fear of Nick and his sister Binkie most vividly. Nick has only half listened to the warnings of his teachers; when he walks his sister home from school and finds a breakdown in transportation facilities, he still is not prepared for calamity. His mother, injured in a traffic snarl, is in a hospital, unconscious. There are no lights, no water; food stocks are depleted. So the children start off with a woman who cleans for them, her husband, and two others they pick up, joining the exodus to the countryside. The book shows in credible fashion how such a situation brings out the best in some people, the worst in others, and it's a cracking good read.

1030 **Pinkwater,** Daniel Manus. *Fat Men from Space;* written and illus. by Daniel Manus Pinkwater. Dodd, 1977. 77-6091. 57p. $5.50.

3-6 When William discovers that he can hear radio programs on the new filling in his tooth, he proceeds to play tricks on his mother and—to the joy of his classmates—on his tough teacher, Mr. Wendel. When Mr. Wendel accuses the wrong boy, Melvyn protests, "You are persecuting me. I want a lawyer!" "You will have the best defense money can buy," Mr. Wendel says coldly, "After that—Devil's Island. Give me the radio." The scene will be a high point for many readers, but they can look forward to William's encounter with the fat men from space, invaders who plunder the earth of all junk food and disappear in search of a giant potato pancake that has been launched into space. William, who has been captured and then released by the space men, manages to subsist on lean meat, fresh produce, and other healthful foods. And what do you know? When the dentist checks William, he has no cavities. There's been no sugar for a year; nobody has cavities! Message books aren't usually this much fun, but Pinkwater makes his a polished romp.

1031 **Pinkwater,** Manus. *Blue Moose;* written and illus. by Manus Pinkwater. Dodd, 1975. 75-12575. 47p. $5.25.

K-3 An ingratiating piece of nonsense, adequately illustrated in black and white, is successful primarily because of the bland blend of nonsensical situation and straightforward writing. The blue moose who came in out of the cold became first, the only customer that had ever expressed appreciation of Mr. Breton's culinary skills; second, a helper in the restaurant; third, a promotion manager par excellence. But spring comes, and the moose gets moody and wants to leave. Mr. Breton reluctantly accepts the inevitable, as will most readers. After all, we've all read a dozen back-to-one's-own-kind endings. Not at all, the moose is horrified at the idea: "Chef, do you have any idea of how cold it gets in the wild, free places? And the food! Terrible!" The idea is affably silly, the writing style pseudo-simple (really, rather sophisticated).

1032 **Pitseolak,** Peter. *Peter Pitseolak's Escape from Death;* written and illus. by Peter Pitseolak; ed. by Dorothy Eber. Delacorte, 1978. 77-83236. 43p. Trade ed. $7.95; Library ed. $7.45 net.

3-5 Pitseolak, artist and historian of the Southwest Baffin Island, wrote two accounts in Eskimo syllabics of the true story of being caught in a swiftly moving ice field with his son. Translated, both versions were drawn on for this book, illustrated by Pitseolak with bold, clean, primitive paintings. The writing is direct and simple, a moving narrative that reveals the author's courage, piety, and modesty. It is contemporary (Pitseolak died in 1973) but the story has a timeless quality in its evocation of the isolated wastes, and the stoic and dignified Eskimo acceptance of Arctic life.

1033 **Plath,** Sylvia. *The Bed Book;* pictures by Emily Arnold McCully. Harper, 1976. 76-3825. 36p. Trade ed. $5.95; Library ed. $5.79 net.

K-2 A nursery extravaganza, written by Plath for her children, is illustrated with appropriately ebullient, imaginative paintings that echo the spirit of the poem. Spurning the ". . . white little / tucked-in-tight little / nighty-night little / turn-out-the-light little / bed . . ." in conventional use, Plath invents beds that produce food at the touch of a button, submarine beds, elephant beds, beds that serve as launching pads into space, even a tiny portable bed that grows when it's watered. No story here, but a happy romp of inventive fancy.

1034 **Platt,** Kin. *Chloris and the Creeps.* Chilton, 1973. 143p. $4.95.

5-7 Any man who wants to marry her mother is a creep, Chloris thinks, her bitter resentment recorded by her sister Jenny. Chloris is eleven, Jenny eight and unable to remember clearly the father Chloris idolizes. Nor can Jenny—who was two when their parents divorced and five when their father died, dispute the romantic figure Chloris has built up. When their mother marries the gentle, patient Fidel Mancha, Chloris is venomous. With great skill, Kin Platt develops the slow, reluctant shedding of Chloris' fantasies about a hero-father and her acceptance of Fidel, whose intelligent sympathy does more to help Chloris than her mother's exasperated love or Jenny's careful allegiance to her sister. While the style is not convincing as that of a child of eight, the fidelity and insight of the author's conception and development far outweigh that one flaw in a moving and realistic story.

1035 **Plotz,** Helen, comp. *As I Walked Out One Evening; A Book of Ballads.* Greenwillow, 1976. 76-10306. 265p. Trade ed. $7.95; Library ed. $6.71 net.

6- A substantial and informative introduction discusses the form, appeal, and origins of the ballad, and the book is divided into six areas: Magic and Miracles, Narratives, Broadsides and Satires, War, Work, and Love. This is an anthology with breadth and discrimination, including among its selections of the traditional ballads, story songs of the Depression Era, cowboy songs, political ballads, songs of tall tale heroes, and many others. Separate author, title, and first line indexes are included.

1036 **Plotz,** Helen, ed. *The Gift Outright; America to Her Poets.* Greenwillow, 1977. 77-8555. 204p. Trade ed. $7.95; Library ed. $7.35 net.

7- Another fine book from an eminent anthologist, this is a judicious balance of traditional favorites (Frost's "The Gift Outright," Roethke's "Night Journey," Lindsay's "Abraham Lincoln Walks at Midnight") and poems that are less often anthologized, the selections made with informed discrimination. Poems are grouped in sections under the headings of Columbus, Indians, Settlers, Regions, History and Idea of America; author, title, and first line indexes are appended.

1037 **Plotz,** Helen, comp. *Life Hungers to Abound: Poems of the Family.* Greenwillow, 1978. 78-5829. 181p. Trade ed. $7.95; Library ed. $7.63 net.

7- One of the major compilers of anthologies for children and young people, Plotz adds another fine anthology to those she has already published. The poems represent all aspects of family life and are arranged under five rubrics: "Marriage," "Parent to Child," "Brothers & Sisters," "Ancestors & Descendants," and "Child to Parent." Some of the selections are from ancient Rome or China; many English and American poets of the past are included; such contemporary writers as Carruth, Ginsberg, Rukeyser, Sarton, and Clifton are represented. Author, title, and first line indexes are provided.

1038 **Poignant,** Axel. *Bush Walkabout.* Addison-Wesley, 1974. 55p. illus. Trade ed. $5.50. Library ed. $4.13 net.

3-5 Published for the first time in the United States, a book that won the prize for the best Australian children's book of the year (original title in 1972 was *Piccaninny Walkabout*) is a translation of an Aborigine tale by Raiwalla. Raiwalla acted as interpreter for the author, a photographer, and his anthropologist wife, who were living with the tribe, and his story is about two real children. Nullagundi and Rikili, a ten-year-old boy and his younger sister, play with their friends, go off into the bush looking for their parents, stay the night when they are lost, light a fire and are found, and participate in a celebratory corroboree when they return. The children are beautiful, the photographs of good quality, and the book gives interesting information about the Aborigines' way of life—particularly the ways in which children's play prepares them for the responsibilities and tasks of maturity. One page layout, in which the text is split into two columns horizontally and also divided vertically by a picture, may confuse readers, but other pages are nicely laid out; occasionally the text reads stiffly, as when the children's mother says, "I do hope they're both all right," but on the whole the text reads easily and smoothly enough, although it is more a documentary than a narrative.

1039 **Poole,** Josephine. *Touch and Go.* Harper, 1976. 176p. Trade ed. $5.95; Library ed. $5.79 net.

7- The omniscience of the young, in many of the mysteries written for them, is usually not believable. Here, because one of them—Charles—is with his father, who is a policeman pretending to be on holiday but actually on a security mission, the knowledge Charles has shared with Emily makes it credible that they should realize that a major crime is being planned. Emily, who tells the story, is on a farm holiday in Devon with her mother; kept overnight in a hospital after a car crash en route to the farm, Emily has already worried about the old woman in the hospital and the man with icy, threatening eyes who sat by the woman's bed. The characterization is adequate, the dialogue unusually good, the plot tight, and the suspense delightfully unbearable.

1040 **Pratson,** Frederick J. *The Special World of the Artisan.* Houghton, 1974. 120p. illus. $5.95.

6-8 While not comprehensive in the sense of including all crafts, this has enough variety to communicate the fact that all craftsmen share the same pleasure in being creative and the same satisfaction in the beauty (or utility) of what they produce. The artisans whose work is discussed are a potter, a woodcarver, a glassblower, an instrument maker, and a weaver. This is not a how-to-do-it book, but it gives considerable information about the procedures of each craft and, through comments by the artisans, a real feeling for the patience and skill that go into their work. The woodcarver, for example, explains that his work is slow and deliberate, the outcome shaped in part by his own preconception, in part by the way the wood patterns emerge. The text describes the qualities of some woods, the tools of the woodcarver, and the fact that the work is affected by its being seen in three dimensions.

1041 **Prelutsky,** Jack. *Nightmares; Poems To Trouble Your Sleep;* illus. by Arnold Lobel. Greenwillow, 1976. 76-4820. 39p. $6.95.

5-9 Deliciously awful, a collection of poems is calculated to evoke icy apprehension, and the poems about wizards, bogeymen, ghouls, ogres (well, one poem apiece to each or to others of their ilk) are exaggerated just enough to bring simultaneous grins and shudders. Prelutsky uses words with relish and his rhyme and rhythm are, as usual, deft. Lobel's illustrations are equally adroit, macabre yet elegant.

1042 **Prelutsky,** Jack. *The Queen of Eene;* illus. by Victoria Chess. Greenwillow, 1978. 77-17311. 32p. Trade ed. $6.95; Library ed. $6.43 net.

K-3 Prelutsky's poems about a series of peculiar people are merrily ghoulish, stylishly nonsensical, and most appropriately illustrated by the nicely macabre drawings by Chess. There's no relationship among the poems, they simply form a gallery of oddities described in verse that has rhyme, rhythm, and humor that are well controlled. Example: "Pumberly Pott's unpredictable niece / declared with her usual zeal / that she would devour, by piece after piece / her uncle's new automobile." Or "Curious Clyde was out walking one day / when he chanced on a porcupine coming his way / He knelt to examine the porcupine's hide— / they're still pulling quills out of Curious Clyde." Great fun.

1043 **Preussler,** Otfried. *The Satanic Mill;* tr. by Anthea Bell. Macmillan, 1973. 250p. $4.95.

6-9 First published in Germany under the title *Krabat,* this compelling fantasy was given the German Children's Book Prize in 1972 as the the best children's book of the year. A beggar and a vagrant, fourteen-year-old Krabat comes to a mill whose master is a strange magician and whose apprentices are doomed to death after they have served the Master. Krabat has watched the older apprentices go, each one in his turn; he escapes through the power of love, and through his struggle saves those who are left. The story has pace and suspense, its mood created with skill, its characters strong; it also has running through the events the message of brotherhood.

1044 **Price,** Christine. *Made in West Africa;* illus. with photographs and drawings. Dutton, 1975. 150p. $9.95.

6- This is certainly one of the most beautiful of Price's series of books about the arts and crafts of various countries or regions, in part because the objects shown are so striking, in part because the book itself is handsome and dignified in layout. The photographs and drawings are of high quality, the text written with grave simplicity and as informative about the cultural context as about the art forms it describes and pictures. Material is grouped by technique and medium: metal sculpture, clay sculpture, textile arts, pottery, etc. The final chapter discusses work of contemporary artists. A list of notes on illustrations (including location if the object is in a museum), a bibliography, and a relative index are appended.

1045 **Price,** Christine. *Talking Drums of Africa*. Scribner, 1973. 43p. illus. $5.95.

3-5 Vigorous, stark woodcut illustrations swirl through the pages of a text that describes the drums of the Ashanti and the Yoruba peoples. Some of the patterned prose describes the drums themselves, some the dances and the songs; both in the portrayal of the ceremonial procedures and in the stately chants are evidences of cultural patterns. In discussing the various drums, Price explains how the drummers achieve different tones and how these imitate the inflections of the spoken language.

1046 **Pringle,** Laurence. *The Economic Growth Debate; Are There Limits to Growth?* Watts, 1978. 77-4695. 86p. $4.90.

8- Pringle takes a long, hard look at the intricate problems of economic growth and at various viewpoints held by experts on whether or not there are—or should be—limits imposed. With calm and thoughtful objectivity he examines such factors as population growth, pollution, depletion of natural resources and possible substitutes for them, food supplies, the gap between rich and poor, recycling, and inequality among the world's nations. Some scientists have predicted disaster resulting from inertia in making policy changes; others regard the future more optimistically. Pringle describes some of the agencies concerned, some of the programs in operation or proposed. A serious and provocative book. A glossary, a bibliography, and an index are included.

1047 **Pringle,** Laurence. *Energy; Power for People.* Macmillan, 1975. 74-19033. 146p. illus. $6.95.

6-8 A competent survey of the problems of diminishing sources of energy, pollution by fuels, and the difficulties and expense of obtaining fuel from new sources. Pringle discusses conservation and recycling briefly, but his emphasis is on current practices (and malpractices) and future possibilities; solar, wind power, hydroelectric, geothermal, and trash-conversion energy. Objective and comprehensive, the book is competently written, authoritative, and logically organized. A glossary, a list of books and articles suggested for further reading, and a relative index are appended.

1048 **Pringle,** Laurence. *Follow a Fisher;* illus. by Tony Chen. T. Y. Crowell, 1973. 42p. $3.95.

2-4 Laws protecting the fisher were passed in many states in the 1930's, since which time there has been an increase in the numbers of this once-plentiful member of the weasel family. Decimated by fur trappers, the sleek brown animal is so elusive that its habits are not as well known, one of which is that the fisher has an unusually long gestation period, almost a full year, and another that it is one of the few beasts that preys on porcupines, which has proved a boon to people who live in areas where the destructive porcupine is found. The text, written in brisk, clear style, gives facts about habits, habitat, procreation, and distribution.

1049 **Pringle,** Laurence. *Wild Foods;* written and photographed by Laurence Pringle; illus. by Paul Breeden. Four Winds, 1978. 78-1910. 182p. $9.95.

7- Following a general discussion of the profitable pleasures of gathering wild plants for food, recognizing them, identifying them, and collecting them, or their parts, Pingle gives approximately twenty examples. For each, he describes ways to find, recognize, harvest, and prepare the plant, occasionally giving more than one recipe, and often giving warnings (with illustrations) of harmful look-alikes. A photograph (not adequate for identification) and a drawing (adequate for identification but not in color) are provided for each plant. The writing style is smooth and conversational, the recipes are clearly presented and enticing. A final chapter describes ways of preserving wild foods for winter use; a glossary, a bibliography, and an index are appended.

1050 **Provensen,** Alice. *My Little Hen;* by Alice and Martin Provensen. Random House, 1973. 29p. illus. Trade ed. $3.95; Library ed. $4.59 net.

2-5 yrs. A story for the very young is just substantial enough for the audience and is illustrated with pictures in frames, in the style of a family album; some of the text is, indeed, written as captions to the pictures. When her pet hen lays an egg, Emily decides that it should be hatched rather than eaten; soon there is a fluffy chick named Neddy. Emily's cat may be a menace to Neddy, but her dog dotes on him. He (Neddy) turns out to be a hen, so she is renamed and proceeds to have a chick of her own. The pictures are less static than the format might imply, with Neddy teasing the dog, the dog looking sheepish and funny, the cat being rebuffed by Neddy's indignant mother, and a last picture of dozens of yellow chicks, all descendants of the original little hen.

1051 **Provensen,** Alice. *Our Animal Friends at Maple Hill Farm;* by Alice and Martin Provensen. Random House, 1974. 56p. illus. $3.95.

2-6 yrs. Surprise, surprise. How often does one find an oversize book with animal-filled pages and no story line at all that is fun to read? Well, here it is. All of the animals at Maple Hill Farm have personalities, and they are described with humor in the captions for the several-to-many pictures on each page. For example, one of the two Siamese cats is Willow, who is beautiful but not interesting. On a double-page spread about the four cats, there are small pictures, each with a caption: "Eggnog is eating an umbrella plant," and then, "Willow is not interested in umbrella plants." "Willow is sitting still," "Willow is washing, although she is never dirty." Periodically, after describing the vagaries of a group of animals, the authors say kindly "Oh, well, no horse is perfect . . ." or "That's the trouble with geese, who otherwise are nearly perfect," after divulging the fact that they are greedy, grabby, grouchy, etc. Even the animals' names are fun. And the pictures are delightful: bright, lively, and drawn with affectionate humor.

1052 **Provensen,** Alice, illus. *A Peaceable Kingdom: The Abecedarius;* illus. by Alice and Martin Provensen. Viking, 1978. 78-125. 40p. $8.95.

4-7 yrs. Published as "Animal Rhymes" in the Shaker Manifesto of 1882, this newly-illustrated version adds appropriately quaint, prim people, details of Shaker artifacts and costumes, and an enchanting variety of animals to the original text. Twenty-six rhymed lines have a lilting appeal; at the start of each line the first letter of the first animal is written boldly: "ALLIGATOR, Beetle, Porcupine, Whale / BOBOLINK, Panther, Dragonfly, Snail . . ." and so on. The pages are pale beige, stained to look like old paper, and the pictures, in a running frieze, are in soft colors, so that the whole looks like an old book. An afterword by Richard Barsam, student of Shaker life, gives some background information about the Shaker community.

1053 **Pursell,** Margaret Sanford. *A Look at Adoption;* photographs by Maria S. Forrai. Lerner, 1978. 77-13080. 30p. $4.95.

K-3 Although this isn't couched in simple language, it is a book appropriate for young children because of the simplicity of concepts. Here a series of photographs, some of interracial families, reinforces the main thrust of the text: people adopt children to love and be loved, and their families are like all other families. There are straightforward explanations of why some people don't have their own children and why some people give up their own children, and there is some discussion of the legal complexities and safeguards in the adoption process.

1054 **Pushkin,** Alexander. *The Tale of the Golden Cockerel;* tr. by Alessandra Pellizone; illus. by J. Bilibin. T. Y. Crowell, 1975. 24p. $5.95.

3-5 * The story will be familiar to opera-lovers as "Le Coq d'Or," which Rimsky-Korsakov based on Pushkin's retelling of a folktale. Here the tale is retold from the Italian edition translated by Pellizone with the illustrations from the original edition published in 1910. The Czar Dadon, whose kingdom had been protected by the warnings given by the golden cockerel, had promised the sorcerer who had given him the bird, that he would grant any wish. But when that time came, the czar, entranced by the beautiful young queen who had made him forget his two dead sons, refused to give the sorcerer his wish, for it was the queen the man desired. The story ends tragically: the czar kills the sorcerer, the golden bird kills the czar, the queen vanishes. (Made for opera, you say?) The tale ends with a moral, "Do not make a promise you are not willing to keep," and is dramatic enough to hold readers even without the illustrations. The illustrations, however, are spectacular: richly embroidered and ornate, the pictures have intricate details of costumes and furnishings; they have a quality of Oriental opulence, a similarity to Persian miniatures, and a romantic, almost medieval aura, especially in those pictures that are in frieze form.

1055 **Putnam,** Peter Brock. *Peter, the Revolutionary Tsar*; maps and illus. by Laszlo Kubinyi. Harper, 1973. 269p. Trade ed. $7.95; Library ed. $6.79 net.

7- A biography of the Russian ruler whose friendships with European residents of his country and travels to other European countries led him to radical measures that he hoped would bridge the gap between them and his own backward land. A robust and volatile man, Peter the Great had unlimited power, but inadequate means to carry out his plans, hampered as he was by widespread corruption, resistance to change, and the handicaps of both intrigue in Russia and shifting nuances in the European struggle for dominance. The writing style is competent, the characterization vigorous, and the biography has a balanced coverage of necessary background information, personal details, and the achievements and failures of Peter's reign. Appended materials include a diagram of the Romanov family tree, notes on the major figures of the book, lists of important dates in early Russian history and in Peter's life, a divided bibliography, and a relative index.

1056 **Rabe,** Berniece. *The Girl Who Had No Name*. Dutton, 1977. 76-56768. 149p. $6.95.

6-8 Set in rural Missouri in the Depression Era, the story of twelve-year-old Girlie is both grim and touching. After ten girls, Papa said, he couldn't think of another name. But did he want to? Did he think Girlie wasn't his? Why had he buried Mama, two months earlier, in the old graveyard at Sand Hill instead of the regular graveyard? And, most of all, why did he insist that Girlie go off and live, turn and turn about, with her married sisters when she so wanted to stay with him and help him? Dour and taciturn, Papa lives alone and Girlie gets shunted from one family to the other. In the end, Girlie comes to understand that Papa's remoteness comes from his own fear that he had (through repeated pregnancies) caused Mama's death, that it was easier to believe Girlie was another man's child even though he has no proof of infidelity. Girlie's maturity and compassion are evident in her decision, when she realizes that she is Papa's daughter, not to tell him of an inherited trait. That would make him feel guilty again. So she accepts the fact that he has softened at last, given her a name (Glencora) and decided that he'll adopt her and take her home.

1057 **Rabe,** Berniece. *Naomi.* Nelson, 1975. 75-4599. 192p. $6.95.

6-9 Writing out of her own experiences, the author sets her story on a
* Missouri farm during the depression era, with superstition and religion strong influences in the lives of her characters. Naomi, eleven, firmly believes that she will die before her fourteenth birthday, since other predictions made by the fortune-teller who has said so have come true. Her mother is more concerned with the fact that Naomi can't do household tasks properly, and the dour woman repeatedly reminds her daughter that she *must* be able to get a husband, she *must* work to be marriageable. One local resident, a nurse, has had more education than most of the neighbors and she helps Naomi see that a firm purpose and schooling may help her achieve a career. By the end of the story, Naomi is fourteen (and still alive) and has lived through several embarrassing incidents, has learned to bear the intolerance of her stern, pious mother, has had a boyfriend and a job. This is a discerning portrait of a young adolescent who is beginning to come to terms with her individuality and to gain perspective about her family; it's also a vivid portrait of a place and a time and a way of life.

1058 **Raskin,** Ellen. *Figgs and Phantoms.* Dutton, 1974. 153p. illus. $5.95.

4-6 It's a mad, mad, mad, mad book. With cheery ebullience, Raskin has assembled a cast of dafties with silly names like Figg Newton, Fido the Second (son of a dog-catcher) and the two main characters, Mona Lisa Newton and her maternal uncle Florence Italy Figgs. Mona is, of course, a Figg-Newton. All the members of the family have dreamt of Capri as their Utopia, and when Uncle Florence dies Mona is convinced that she can find him in Capri. In a shift to fantasy, Mona goes to "Caprichos" and finds a happily married Florence—or is it a dream? She wakes in a hospital. Yeasty style and high humor should appeal to all readers except those who like their fiction served up with sobriety.

1059 **Raskin,** Ellen. *The Tattooed Potato and Other Clues.* Dutton, 1975. 74-23764. 170p. $7.50.

5-7 "A spoof of Sherlock Holmes," states the book's jacket, but this is a spoof of detective fiction in general, and a rollicking good one. A baffled Chief of Detectives in New York City turns repeatedly to the painter Garson, who uses brilliant deductive powers to solve a series of crimes (all ridiculous) while apparently oblivious to the menacing tenants who frighten his assistant, Dickery Dock (she's seventeen and the protagonist) and who bear such names as Shrimps Marinara and Manny Mallomar. And there's a mystery about Garson himself. A bit of murder, which it is hard to take seriously since the whole book is such a rummy soufflé. Humor, action, zany characters, and a blithe style; a palpable hit.

1060 **Raskin,** Ellen. *Twenty-Two, Twenty-Three;* written and illus. by Ellen Raskin. Atheneum, 1976. 76-5475. 19p. $6.95.

K-3 In a most ingenious contrivance, Raskin concocts a holiday message with nonsensically dressed animals who speak in a rhyming text and who cumulate on pages 22 and 23 in an imaginative puzzle-pastiche. A small mouse, seeing a goat in a coat and an ape in a cape, and other creatures, wants to join the fun. She dons a muumuu but is criticized; neither a tutu nor a parka satisfies the owl in the cowl or the pig in the wig, but they all accept the mouse in a blouse. Finally they group to form a Christmas tree. But *what* a Christmas tree! It's composed of bits and pieces of the animals on the preceding pages, many recognizable only by the pattern of their clothes. Santa stands by as page 22 wishes readers a happy Christmas; on the facing page, animals fit into letter patterns to spell out "Merry New Year." Imaginative, fresh and amusing, this is both a marvelous encouragement to visual perception and a beautiful piece of bookmaking, with handsome pages, intriguing endpapers, and some graphic information about the construction of a book.

1061 **Raskin,** Ellen. *The Westing Game*. Dutton, 1978. 77-18866. 185p. $7.95.

5-8 Lured by specially prepared ads to a new, attractive apartment building, six tenant families take residence in Sunset Towers, next to the old Westing house. When the eccentric millionaire Westing dies, the tenants learn that they are heirs to a large sum apiece, but that they must play a devious game—clues left by Westing and distributed by a lawyer—to win the major part of the estate. Complicated doesn't begin to describe the convolutions of the plot or the idiosyncratic deviance of the players, as sixteen people play detective, suspecting each other and stealing clues and trying to guess the identity of the person who is planting small-scale bombs. And one of them has several identities. Raskin's style is staccato, her characters well-defined, her story line a bit labored—but the device of the game should intrigue readers, and the whole thing is more fun than its parts.

1062 **Rau,** Margaret. *The People of New China;* written and photographed by Margaret Rau. Messner, 1978. 78-960. 128p. $7.79.

5-7 This can serve as a companion volume to the author's *The People's Republic of China* although it covers some of the same material. In the earlier book the author, who was born in China and lived there for many years, provided a history of the country and described many aspects of contemporary life; here the focus is on contemporary life, with chapters devoted either to life in a town or a village, or to life in such a major city as Peking or Shanghai. In discussing the living patterns of residents, Rau covers such aspects of modern life as education, industry, familial relationships, and the arts. The tone is not laudatory, but it is sympathetic; the writing style is direct and the material well-organized. A pronunciation guide and an index are appended.

1063 **Rau,** Margaret. *The People's Republic of China;* illus. with photographs. Messner, 1974. 128p. Trade ed. $7.25; Library ed. $6.64 net.

5-7 A brisk and objective overview, by an author who was born in China and lived there for many years, includes both historical background and a description of life in China today. Rau deals competently with historical material and discusses internal politics and international relations lucidly. Such topics are covered in many other books about China, however; what is less usual is the coverage (at this reading level, particularly) of the contemporary scene: education, military training, widespread interest in sports and the revival of ancient crafts, the patterns of urban and rural family life, medicine, agriculture, and other aspects of the problems, prowess, and activities of the 700,000,000 citizens of the People's Republic. An index is appended.

1064 **Ravielli,** Anthony. *What Is Bowling?* written and illus. by Anthony Ravielli. Atheneum/SMI, 1975. 75-13572. 29p. $5.95.

4-6 A model how-to-do-it book is illustrated with impeccably drawn stop-action figures of bowlers and is preceded by a history of the development of the game from ancient times to today. Ravielli gives a clear step-by-step explanation of how the game should be played, and describes the correct way to hold the ball, the way the game is scored, and rules for play, as well as the correct equipment and standards for bowling alleys.

1065 **Ray,** Mary. *Song of Thunder.* Faber, 1978. 206p. $8.95.

7-10 Kenofer, a promising young bard, had left his Aegean island after a volcanic eruption in which his widowed mother lost her life and his younger sister, Theano, disappeared. The boy is taken in by a master harper on the Cretan shore where his boat lands; later he finds his sister being cared for in the home of an older friend, Prince Geryon. It is Geryon's son who, years later, accompanies Kenofer—by then a famous harper—and Theano on a return visit to the island. In a dramatic conclusion to a deftly-crafted story, the visitors are endangered and horror-stricken when they witness an even more violent "song of thunder," for this time the volcanic eruption is so violent that the ash lays waste vast stretches of other islands nearby. This is an exciting story, and the period details are so smoothly incorporated that the author's manifest erudition and her research are never obtrusive.

1066 **Rayner,** Mary. *Mr and Mrs Pig's Evening Out*. Atheneum, 1976. 30p. illus. $7.95.

4-6 yrs. There was immediate objection from the ten children when Mother Pig announced that she and father were going out, but that a very nice lady was coming to take care of them. The children were all in bed when Mrs. Wolf came, and she kept busily knitting until she felt like a snack. The snack she felt like having was little Garth Pig, and she snatched him out of bed; his protesting noises woke the others, and his oldest sister Sorrell quickly worked out a plan to save Garth and make Mrs. Wolf inoperable. So they did. The illustrations have a breezy quality and plenty of action, and the story has a felicitous blend of familiar situation, drastic crisis, and resourceful solution by a team of children.

1067 **Reiss,** Johanna de Leeuw. *The Journey Back*. T. Y. Crowell, 1976. 76-12625. 214p. $6.95.

5-8 In a sequel to her autobiographical novel, *The Upstairs Room,* Reiss describes the aftermath of war: the broken or alienated families, the scarcity of food and clothing, the ruptured relationships with friends and neighbors, the people still weak or ill. Or missing. For Annie, there is the tragedy of parting from the beloved Oosterveld family who had sheltered her, the pain of seeing her older sisters leave home, the problems of adjusting to a new stepmother whom she cannot seem to please. And, on visits to the Oostervelds, Annie realizes that she is torn between her desire to be with them and her desire to adhere to her stepmother's snobbish standards. A vivid evocation of the bittersweet lot of survivors in wartime, and a poignant, trenchant picture of a young adolescent in a fragmented Jewish family in Holland.

1068 **Reiss,** John J. *Shapes*. Bradbury, 1974. 29p. illus. $5.95.

3-6 yrs. Absolutely luscious in its spectrum of vivid colors, this is one of the most attractive of the several books that present to young children examples of such shapes as oval, circle, triangle, rectangle, and square. Reiss carries it a bit farther, showing how squares form a cube, or circles a sphere, and he tosses in a few more complex shapes at the close of the book to intrigue the audience: a hexagon, an octagon, a pentagon. Examples of each shape are included; for rectangles, for example, there are doors, wooden planks, and sticks of gum. Animals cavort among the shapes, adding interest to the visual appeal and the clearly presented concepts.

1069 **Reit,** Ann, comp. *Alone Amid All This Noise; A Collection of Women's Poetry*. Four Winds, 1976. 75-38705. 118p. $6.95.

6- A fine collection, arranged by birth dates of the poets, includes authors of many countries and centuries, from ancient Greece to today. Some of the poets are as well known as Dickinson, Millay, Plath, or Giovanni; others are little known either in the original or in translation. The selections have been chosen to reflect images and concerns of women, and they have been chosen well. An author-title index is appended.

1070 **Remini,** Robert V. *The Revolutionary Age of Andrew Jackson*. Harper, 1976. 74-2623. 205p. illus. $6.79.

7- In the years between the War of 1812 and the Civil War, the United
* States changed from a young country with a frontier philosophy to a nation with intricate problems, a "transportation revolution," as roads and canals and railroads proliferated, and an economy that was increasingly industrialized. Its central focus for many years was Andrew Jackson, the epitome of the "self-made man," the war hero who had been an orphan, became a lawyer, and rose to the Presidency. Remini is not adulatory, but his esteem for Jackson is evident in his descriptions of the Latter's handling of political and financial problems; he shows clearly how many of the Jacksonian theories and decisions affected and influenced the contemporary and future directions of national policies. The author, a history professor, has an easy, lively writing style, he uses material based on primary sources, and he adroitly balances detailed explanations of some events with a presentation of broad movements and issues. He discusses, in the annotated list of books suggested for further reading, books of differing viewpoints and provides an extensive relative index.

1071 **Resnick,** Michael. *Gymnastics and You; The Whole Story of the Sport*. Rand McNally, 1977. 77-8345. 96p. illus. Trade ed. $3.95; Library ed. $4.97 net.

6-9 Since Korbut and Comaneci made headlines, there has been a spate of books about them or about women's gymnastics; this book gives that coverage and more. Resnick describes the moves in various areas of women's gymnastics and in men's gymnastics, gives detailed information about scoring, and discusses training, financial aspects, sources of information, and other forms of gymnastics now and in the past. The tone is light, the writing style casual, the information specific. Lists of Olympic gold medalists and an index are appended.

1072 **Resnick,** Rose. *Sun and Shadow; The Autobiography of a Woman Who Cleared a Pathway to the Seeing World for the Blind.* Atheneum, 1975. 74-32614. 274p. $10.00.

7- * No self-pity, no dramatizing, no lecturing are in this fascinating autobiography of Rose Resnick who, at the age of two, lost her sight. Lifetime prognosis: she would see, at best, light and shadow. One of eight children in an immigrant family, Rose was not over-protected. She went to a New York City public school, learned to skate, dance, ski, and play piano—the latter so well that she became a professional musician. Educated and qualified for teaching, she was denied a job because of her blindness; having had the happy experience of attendance at the New York Lighthouse for the Blind, she later worked for the blind in San Francisco, organized a successful camp, and was instrumental in having blind children admitted to the California public schools. While the author's comments on attitudes of and toward the blind will be of great interest to most readers, the book would be appealing enough without that aspect because of the casual, conversational writing style and the sense of humor that emerges in Ms. Resnick's descriptions of, for example, herself as a child actress or as a member of a road company.

1073 **Rettich,** Margret. *The Silver Touch and Other Family Christmas Stories;* tr. from the German by Elizabeth D. Crawford; illus. by Rolf Rettich. Morrow, 1978. 78-6817. 191p. Trade ed. $6.95; Library ed. $6.67 net.

4-6 The translator has provided smooth, colloquial writing; the author has provided a wonderfully differentiated assortment of stories that are pithy, realistic, and nicely constructed, some tender, some humorous. All of the tales are brief, all are contemporary, and they include such topics as staying up late as a special treat, writing thank-you letters, making up after a family quarrel, putting up with the hospitality of a boastful relative, coping with a household disaster (minor), comparing Christmas dolls (one boy owner, one girl owner) and other delights of the season.

1074 **Rice,** Edward. *The Five Great Religions;* photographs by the author. Four Winds, 1973. 180p. Trade ed. $6.95; Library ed. $6.72 net.

7-10 A survey of Buddhism, Christianity, Hinduism, Islam, and Judaism covers the same material as does *Religions* by James Haskins but gives more background, since the author feels that the traditions and the mystical aspects of each faith are rooted in their beginnings. Rice concentrates on the essence of each belief and, in more flowing a style than Haskins or Seeger, reviewed below, goes into great detail about doctrine and worship, and discusses the relationships among the major religions. A relative index is appended.

1075 **Rice,** Edward. *The Ganges; A Personal Encounter;* photographs by the author. Four Winds, 1974. 189p. Trade ed. $7.95; Library ed. $7.46 net.

7- Although the chapters of this impressive book are not logically arranged, the material in them is so diverse, perceptive, and informative that this weakness is far outweighed by the strength of the whole. The author states that in his visits to India he has moved away from the Western viewpoint, and he does accept the mythic and religious beliefs and rites that are an integral part of the Indian way of life and of the sacred status of the Ganges—yet in his observations he sees as a Western man, albeit percipient and sympathetic. The book contains much background information (a section on geology, another on the British in India) but what gives it significance is the description of personal encounters that are an avenue to understanding the variety of peoples, their concepts, their practices, and their problems. The writing style is rich and flowing, the photographs are excellent. A relative index is appended.

1076 **Rice,** Eve. *Papa's Lemonade and Other Stories;* written and illus. by Eva Rice. Greenwillow, 1976. 75-38754. 56p. (A Read-alone Book). Trade ed. $5.95; Library ed. $5.21 net.

1-2 The five "stories" in this book for beginning independent readers actually are a continuous narrative, although they are loosely linked. Mama and Papa and their five children (who seem to be a cross between dogs and bears) lead a pleasant life, the tempo set by the amicable parents who adjust easily to any situation. Papa and Mama go for a food-gathering walk but forget the food as they greet friends? Nice friends are better than onion soup, says Papa. The youngest child has used all the lemons? Papa, who has announced he is going to make lemonade, makes orangeade instead. Save for the youngest child, the children have little part in the action; however, the book has mild humor, good family relationships, and a writing style that is nicely gauged for the audience.

1077 **Richardson,** Ben Albert. *Great Black Americans;* by Ben Albert Richardson and William A. Fahey. Rev. ed. (Formerly titled *Great American Negroes.*) T. Y. Crowell, 1976. 75-12841. 344p. illus. $7.50.

7-12 A revision of the 1956 title, *Great American Negroes,* a collective biography; six of the original inclusions have been dropped, and several new subjects added to total thirty-one. The biographies are grouped under such headings as theater, literature, education and public affairs, and sports. In addition to new material, the text has been carefully revised, and to considerable advantage. In the biography of Duke Ellington, for example, such florid phrases as ". . . playing . . . the common C scale with the languid fluidity of an andante movement," becomes simply, ". . . playing even the common scale of C major slowly, with great expression." And a rather tedious imagined dialogue about piano practice has been dropped. A useful and interesting book, this contains photographs of each biographee, and an index.

1078 **Richardson,** Fayette. *Sam Adams: The Boy Who Became Father of the American Revolution;* illus. by William Sauts Bock. Crown, 1975. 42p. $5.95.

3-5 Familiar as the story of Samuel Adams and his role in the American Revolution is, this account adds a facet that is seldom included in books for younger readers: the economic difficulties of the colonists. Richardson describes the establishment of land banks, the banning of them by the British Parliament, and the resentment against the authorities when they attempted to sequester property. Although Adams doesn't emerge vividly as a personality, the biography is smoothly written, balanced in coverage, and not overly fictionalized despite some imaginary dialogue in the first half of the text. The illustrations, buff and blue added to the black and white, are both attractive and informative in giving details of costume, architecture, and household objects.

1079 **Roberts,** Willo Davis. *Don't Hurt Laurie!* drawings by Ruth Sanderson. Atheneum, 1977. 76-46569. 166p. $6.95.

4-6 This is the most trenchant of the few stories for young readers on the subject of child abuse; while written in third person, it consistently sees developments from the viewpoint of the eleven-year-old protagonist, Laurie. Laurie's father never communicates with her; her mother, who has remarried, periodically assaults her daughter viciously, although she does it only when they are alone. Laurie's stepfather, Jack, is a pleasant man but often away on business trips: her younger stepbrother,

Tim, is sympathetic, knowing that Annabelle (Laurie doesn't think of her as "mother") is cruel to his stepsister. The pattern of Laurie's life has been that as soon as she makes a friend or is taken to one emergency room too many times, Annabelle moves. Matters come to a head when Tim witnesses a beating that leaves Laurie insensible. The children take refuge with Tim's grandmother, and when Jack learns the whole story he takes Annabelle away for treatment. The events are inherently dramatic in a shocking sense, but Roberts deals with them matter-of-factly, and the book—which has excellent characterization and an easy narrative flow—is both realistic about the problem and realistically encouraging about its alleviation: first, Laurie learns that people do believe her story when she finally tells it and second, they help her. Roberts also closes with an encouraging note by having Jack explain to Laurie some of the causes of her mother's illness, the changes that therapy should produce, and the fact that he still loves Annabelle, leaving the possibility that she will be a lovable mother when she recovers.

1080 **Roberts,** Willo Davis. *The View from the Cherry Tree.* Atheneum, 1975. 75-6759. 181p. $6.50.

5-9 Although written in a direct and unpretentious style, this is essentially a sophisticated story, solidly constructed, imbued with suspense, evenly paced, and effective in conveying the atmosphere of a household coping with the last-minute problems and pressures of a family wedding. (There are actually a few too many of these for credibility, the one weakness of the book.) Everybody's too busy to listen to Rob when he tries to tell them that, from his perch in the cherry tree, he has seen their crotchety old neighbor die and that she didn't fall, but was pushed. He'd seen two big hands push her out of the window. Everybody's too busy, that is, except for the murderer; he tries repeatedly to trap Rob (nobody will listen to Rob's stories of near-misses, either) and finally does so in the empty house next door. While the ending is exciting, it may disappoint readers that, although Rob is proved right, there's little evidence of any chagrin on the part of his family. However, on the whole, this is a smooth, well-constructed story.

1081 **Robertson,** Keith. *In Search of a Sandhill Crane;* illus. by Richard Cuffari. Viking, 1973. 201p. $5.95.

5-8 Because his widowed mother was taking a summer course in computer operation, fifteen-year-old Link had had to accept an aunt's invitation to visit her in Michigan. He had promised an uncle that he would use his borrowed camera to take pictures of a sandhill crane. Link was sure he would be bored to distraction in the Michigan woods, but his first desultory interest in finding the crane grew to a passionate curiosity, and his first disdain for a summer spent with an elderly aunt and her Indian friend to a vigorous appreciation of their knowledge and abilities. While there is a small element of suspense in Link's search for the sandhill crane, the story as a whole is quiet and contained, its strength in the economy of structure, the convincing characterization, the wealth of natural lore, and the evocation of the setting of the beautiful North Woods.

1082 **Robinson,** Adjai. *Singing Tales of Africa;* illus. by Christine Price. Scribner, 1974. 80p. $5.95.

4-6 Illustrated by dramatic black and white woodcuts, seven stories are told by an author who had a storytelling program on Radio Sierra Leone. His preface explains the role of the participating audience in these song stories, each of which is preceded by the musical notation and words of the chorus or response. The tales —some "why" stores about animals, one that resembles "Jack and the Beanstalk," some that have no magic elements ("Ayele and the Flowers"), and some that have humorous aspects—all have the flavor of the oral tradition. Notes on the stories are appended.

1083 **Rock,** Gail. *The House without a Christmas Tree;* illus. by Charles C. Gehm. Knopf, 1974. 88p. Trade ed. $3.95; Library ed. $4.59 net.

4-6 Adapted from a television program, a story about the communications gap between a father and daughter is nicely balanced by ten-year-old Addie's affairs at church and school and by her loving but candid descriptions of her grandmother. Addie can't understand why Dad is so adamant about not having a tree (it's because of his memory of the last Christmas with his dead wife) and she defiantly brings the school tree home. Dad is furious, Addie miserable. During the night she takes the tree to the home of a classmate who is poor, and leaves it on the porch. The ending is TV-predictable: Dad buys a tree, gets out the old ornaments, and they talk about Addie's mother for the first time. Grandma is a marvelous character, the class scenes and the Christmas pageant are funny and convincing, and it is clear that the author is wasted on script-writing, her natural forte is writing for children. Excellent realistic pictures show costume details of the 1940's with felicity.

1084 **Rockwell,** Harlow. *I Did It.* Macmillan, 1974. 56p. illus. (Ready-to-Read Books). $4.95.

1-2 A how-to book for the beginning reader has big print, plenty of restful blank space and clean-lined drawings in shades of brown and green. Best of all, it has projects that are truly simple, save for the last, breadmaking, and even that is broken down into easy-to-follow instructions. The projects are varied: making a paper airplane, writing a message in invisible ink, making a picture out of dried foods, making a papier mâché fish, making a paper bag mask, and baking bread. Good format, clear instructions, and a variety of things to do.

1085 **Rockwell,** Harlow. *Look at This;* written and illus. by Harlow Rockwell. Macmillan, 1978. 77-12716. 64p. (Ready-to-Read Books) $6.95.

1-2 Rockwell presents three very simple projects for younger children, each incorporated into a pleasant narrative framework, each told by a different child. In the first, a girl makes a paper dancing frog for a younger child, in the second two children make applesauce with parental guidance, and in the third a boy follows a magazine's directions for making a New Year's Eve noisemaker. It isn't New Year's Eve, but the boy thinks the house is too quiet. Directions are clear, projects inexpensive, and the author makes the projects sound easy and fun to make.

1086 **Rockwell,** Harlow. *My Dentist;* Greenwillow, 1975. 75-6974. 30p. illus. Trade. ed. $6.95; Library ed. $5.81 net.

3-6 yrs. A calm, matter-of-fact text describes the equipment in a dentist's office and the steps of a routine visit: tartar-scraping, polishing and cleaning, and an adjuration to avoid candy and to brush regularly before the selection of a parting gift. No mention of drilling, save for a comment on the equipment. The illustrations are just right: big, clean pages that have poster-simple line-and-watercolor depictions of all that fascinating machinery. An especially good book for the nervous child.

1087 **Rockwell,** Harlow. *My Nursery School.* Greenwillow, 1976. 75-25871. 22p. illus. Trade ed. $6.95; Library ed. $5.81 net.

2-5 yrs. Clear, simple pictures with no clutter and plenty of white space illustrate the activities described by a small girl who, delivered by father and picked up by mother, spends a happy morning. She speaks of her teachers and of the other nine children in the class, what she and they best like to do, of the plants and pets, playground activities, classroom equipment, marching and singing, and she closes with, "Now it is time to go home. But I will come again tomorrow." A good soft-sell for the pre-nursery set, since the setting is alluring, the attitude positive, and the sense of achievement pervasive.

1088 **Rockwood,** Joyce. *Long Man's Song.* Holt, 1975. 74-14937. 207p. $6.95.

6-9 A novel about a young Cherokee who is an apprentice medicine man is set in pre-Columbian times and is imbued, unobtrusively, with details about tribal culture and belief. Soaring Hawk, whose sister is ill, works desperately to cure her of a malady he is sure has been induced by a member of the tribe, and his efforts, his chants and visions, are treated with sympathetic respect. Woven through the smoothly-written story are a love interest, the intricacies of clan loyalties, matriarchal lineage, and the deep affinity for nature felt by these ancient Indians. The foreword is rather heavy-handed and seems to be addressed to an adult audience.

1089 **Rockwood,** Joyce. *To Spoil the Sun.* Holt, 1976. 76-10568. 180p. $6.95.

6-9 Rain Dove, a Cherokee of the sixteenth century, begins her story with a cycle of four evil omens that were seen by members of her village. She describes her family, the People of the Seven Clans who live in her village, her marriages, and the terrible scourges of illness and persecution that came with pale-skinned strangers who were so inexplicably hostile. Rockwood has that gift of the best writers of historical fiction, of immersing herself so completely in the spirit as well as the facts of a past culture that the details that give color and verisimilitude are incorporated into the story with no obtrusion on the narrative flow. She does not tell us that the Cherokee were a peaceful, gentle people; it emerges from this moving novel.

1090 **Rodgers,** Mary. *A Billion for Boris.* Harper, 1974. 211p. Trade ed. $4.95. Library ed. $4.79 net.

4-6 The sprightly and articulate heroine of *Freaky Friday* reports another fantastic adventure that seems completely believable; Mary Rodgers has to a remarkable degree the ability to blend fantasy and realism. Spiced with humor, sophisticated dialogue, and an unusual mother-son relationship, the story is, in the British sense, a "good read." Boris is Annabel's friend and neighbor, a level-headed boy whose extravagant, eccentric mother needs (in his eyes) reform as well as tender loving care. One of the things he does in his mother's absence is to refurbish their apartment, a ploy that brings about her wrathful rejection of his attempts to change her life and a subsequent clearing of the air from which all hands benefit. But how does Boris propose to pay for all this? Ah, there's the fantasy: he has an old television set that gives the next day's news, which enables him to know race results, forestall crimes, predict stock market changes . . . the possibilities are endless, and *A Billion for Boris* takes advantage of many of them.

1091 **Roethke,** Theodore. *Dirty Dinky and Other Creatures; Poems for Children;* selected by Beatrice Roethke and Stephen Lushington. Doubleday, 1973. 48p. illus. $3.95.

3-6 Almost all of the poems that Beatrice Roethke Lushington has chosen for inclusion in this collection are about animals, almost all are nonsensical; the silliness conceals a pithy thought here and there, but most of the poems are sheer, lilting fun and it is as such that they appeal to readers. Too few selections have the grave tone and sharp imagery of "The Bat" and "The Snake"; it's a delightful collection, but it gives a canted perspective of the breadth of Roethke's poetry.

1092 **Rogers,** Pamela. *The Stone Angel.* Nelson, 1976. 76-5481. 96p. $5.95.

4-6 There is a conviction of distinction that comes to many children. For Susan, it came when a gravestone angel seemed to point the way—and Susan knew her fate. She would be a saint. The only person she told was Rab Banerjee, the small boy who had just come to England; bullied by the others, Rab had attached himself to Susan. Rab, therefore, was privy to each disastrous attempt to Do Good. Like the time she decided that, like St. Francis, she could tame animals by love, and ended in a tree after being chased by a ferocious dog. The story is light and funny, but it has a solid base, both in Susan's change from irritated acceptance of Rab to her appreciation of his loyal friendship, and in her acceptance of her family. For Susan is at an age when she feels dissatisfied with her parents, embarrassed because her father is a gravedigger, resentful because her older sister is married, aloof toward her brother-in-law, and jealous because her mother is giving so much attention to her older child, who is pregnant. Rogers sees and describes a stage of childhood with affectionate perception.

1093 **Rose,** Anne K. *How Does a Czar Eat Potatoes?* illus. by Janosch. Lothrop, 1973. 26p. Trade ed. $4.50; Library ed. $4.14 net.

2-4 There's an old-country lilt to the language of a non-storybook that contrasts wealth and poverty as a Russian peasant child might see it, and the pictures fit the text nicely, with alternations of color (for the extravagant ways of the czar) and black and white (for the modest, hard-working peasant). How *does* a czar eat potatoes? A soldier shoots them through a wall of butter into the czar's mouth. Then, "Tell me, child, how does your father eat potatoes?" He grabs a handful and eats them fast, with cabbage—if there is any. So the pattern repeats: how does a czar drink tea, how does your father drink tea, et cetera. But in the end, when it comes to the question of happiness, it is the poor farmer with his many children who can leap and dance and sing, his face shining, happier than any czar.

1094 **Ross,** Laura. *Mask-Making With Pantomime and Stories From American History;* drawings by Frank Ross; constructed mask photos by George Haddad. Lothrop, 1975. 75-11960. 112p. Trade ed. $5.95; Library ed. $5.11 net.

4-6 As clearly written as her books on puppetry, a new book by Ross gives instructions for making several simple kinds of masks, instructions that can be adapted for plays other than the ones included, each using a narrator as well as a small cast. There are instructions for miming and for miming with masks; there are sections on the history of pantomime and the history of the mask as used in ritual, religious ceremonies, and the theater. A bibliography and an index are appended.

1095 **Ross,** Pat. *What Ever Happened to the Baxter Place?* illus. by Roger Duvoisin. Pantheon, 1976. 75-22251. 38p. $4.95.

2-4 Although this does not have high narrative interest, it is a cohesive text that explains, via a fictional framework, how rural land can disappear into the urban sprawl. The Baxter Place is a thriving Maryland farm, but some acres are sold off to accommodate a friend, since the Baxter children for whom it was being saved don't plan to be farmers. When the weather is bad and a crop fails, the Baxters sell a field to a realty company so that they can pay the mortgage. Not being able to afford equipment and compete with mechanized dairy farms, the family sells most of their herd . . . and so on. The story ends with the farmhouse and a small acreage surrounded by a shopping center, a housing development, and a motor lodge. Useful for the social studies curriculum, the book is given warmth and vitality by the handsome illustrations.

1096 **Rounds,** Glen. *The Day the Circus Came to Lone Tree.* Holiday House, 1973. 34p. illus. $3.95.

3-6 Illustrations that are lively, scribbly, and comic add to the appeal of a robust tall tale. "Hardly a day goes by," it begins, "that someone doesn't stop me on the street to ask why the circus never comes here to Lone Tree." Well, the circus did come. Once. The people flocked from miles around, and cheered enthusiastically, applauded, sat spellbound—there'd never been such an audience. Then Linda the Lady Lion Tamer fired a pistol at a recalcitrant, threatening lion, and the cowboys came to the rescue; they didn't realize it was part of the act, and the circus animals were so upset that in the ensuing uproar they all broke loose, ripped tents, and took off. Roped by eager cowboys, they all tied themselves and the pursuers in a tangle of ropes. Disaster. The people of Lone Tree couldn't understand why the circus people wouldn't even wave good-bye. Good style, great fun.

1097 **Rounds,** Glen. *Mr. Yowder and the Steamboat;* written and illus. by Glen Rounds. Holiday House, 1977. 76-43089. 43p. $5.95.

3-6 Rounds' scratchy, vigorous line drawings are exactly right for the ebullient humor of his tall, tall tale about Mr. Yowder, a luxuriantly mustachioed character who, while visiting New York City, feels an urge to go fishing. Well, one thing leads improbably to another, and our hero finds himself on a huge liner, playing cards with the captain. Having won the poor man's license and that of the tugboat pilot, Yowder decides only he can dock the boat. And that's how a steamboat gets stuck under an elevated track in Manhattan.

1098 **Roy,** Cal. *The Legend and the Storm;* illus. by the author. Farrar, 1975. 75-17931. 212p. $6.95.

8-11 The extensive and bitter student uprising in Mexico in 1968 is seen from the viewpoint of fifteen-year-old Rafa, who tells the story. Son of a conservative, wealthy family in Mexico City, Rafa is drawn into the movement when his older cousin Nicolás comes to visit. Disobeying his uncle (Rafa's father) Nicolás persists as an activist and is killed; the story ends with Rafa's letters to a friend (written between 1969–1973) in which it is made clear that he has been receiving therapy after an emotional breakdown. The writing is at times turgid, but the book gives both an authoritative (and rare) picture of the intricacies of political and philosophical conflict in modern Mexico and a sympathetic picture of the tradition and dignity of family life and customs with which the rebellious young are often in conflict.

1099 **Ruben,** Patricia. *True or False?* illus. with photographs. Lippincott, 1978. 77-25285. 32p. Hardbound $6.95; Paperback $3.50.

4-6 yrs. A book of black and white photographs, each with a true-false question, can be used to heighten acuity of observation and to suggest or reinforce concepts of shape, size, texture, numbers and even simple logic. For most questions, the answer is either "true" or "false," but for some the answers are partly true and partly false, or false because of a more complex reason than a simple fact like the wrong number of circles on a butterfly's wing; for example, "Chickens lay eggs because people like to eat them for breakfast." There's even one slightly tricky question. A good book for stimulating discussion.

1100 **Ruben,** Patricia. *What Is New? What Is Missing? What Is Different?* written and illus. with photographs by Patricia Ruben. Lippincott, 1978. 78-8109. 31p. $6.95.

3-6 yrs. A book of photographs encourages observation, and moves from simple differences to some that are more complicated. In the first set of facing pages, for example, one picture is missing from one page; in the second set, the same thing, only it's missing from the recto rather than the verso page. By the end of the book, there are changed actions, changes in the numbers of things, and—in the last set—changes of more than one kind. The text consists of simple questions like "What is missing? What was on page 6 that isn't on this page?" or "Something is different here. What is it?" The book offers some challenge to young children but not so much as to be discouraging.

1101 **Rudström,** Lennart. *A Home;* with paintings by Carl Larsson; tr. by Lone Thygesen-Blecher. Putnam, 1974. 29p. $5.95.

5- A beautiful book in every way, *A Home* is illustrated with reproductions of watercolors by a distinguished Swedish artist and designer of the late 19th century. Alternating with full-page pictures that have the sunny charm of a Bonnard, the verso pages describe Larsson's life and work, with a right-hand column (clearly differentiated from the text) that comments on the pictures and gives background information. In an era when interiors were gloomy, Larsson painted his rooms in soft, bright pastels and designed his own functional but light and graceful furniture. The period details of the pictures are charming, the draughtsmanship impeccable. The text, first printed in Sweden in 1968, describes the family activities, the artist's wife and children, and the ways in which he decorated and beautified his home. It also gives, as do the right-hand columns, a considerable amount of information about Larsson's technique. Although the text may not be of interest to very young readers, the book will—like any art book—undoubtedly be enjoyed by them as well as by children who can read the text and by adults.

1102 **Ruskin,** Ariane. *History in Art.* Watts, 1974. 307p. illus. $14.95.

7-10 A comprehensive history of art, from cave murals to pop, covers most major artists and their work; while Ruskin discusses to some extent the backgrounds of the periods and/or countries in each chapter, the bulk of the text is devoted to analyses of art styles and techniques, the work of the artists of the period, and the ways in which they were influenced or in which they influenced each other. The title is misleading if one reads it as meaning "history as it can be seen in works of art," a fact that is even more obvious in examining almost any sequence of illustrations. However, the writing is fluent and authoritative, and the many illustrations are of excellent quality. A bibliography and an index are appended.

1103 **Russ,** Lavinia. *The April Age*. Atheneum, 1975. 119p. $5.25.

7-10 Peakie Maston is not quite eighteen when she sets off for a year in Europe. Never a conformist, Peakie had failed to graduate from boarding school, and her trip with five other girls and a chaperone was—she was convinced—not a gift, but a solution for parents who didn't know what else to do with her. Written in first person, the story bubbles along like the effervescent Peakie herself, as she plunges through Europe so busy falling in love (it's the Real Thing each time) that she hardly has time to absorb the culture of the Old World. The time is 1925, and there are some piquant period details (one that is erroneous), but the emphasis is on romance, and the romance is tempered by humor. An engaging romp, cover to cover.

1104 **Russell,** Solveig Paulson. *Like and Unlike; A First Look at Classification;* illus. by Lawrence Di Fiori. Walck, 1973. 47p. $4.95.

3-5 A simply written book on classification of flora and fauna, nicely illustrated and logically organized. The text explains clearly the divisions of classification, introducing the subject by a discussion of the need for order and grouping of objects. A brief mention of ecological, nutritional, and library classification systems can stimulate the reader's curiosity about other groupings, systems, and accepted conventions in classification. Nothing new here, but the writing is lucid and the subject handled with crisp authority.

1105 **Sabin,** Francene. *Women Who Win;* illus. with photographs. Random House, 1975. 74-20835. 171p. Trade ed. $3.95; Library ed. $4.99 net.

6-10 Biographical sketches of fourteen women athletes focus on their training, their careers, and their special problems as women in being accepted as major sports figures. There's one biography for each sport, save for skiing and swimming; in those sections the author describes a swimming team of four and a trio of skiing sisters. Many of the women have competed at an international level, some in the Olympics; most of them have become professionals; some of them have fought for women's rights in the sports world. While the style of writing often verges on journalese, it is smooth and informal, and the subject—which has been given little coverage in books for young people—has appeal.

1106 **Sachs,** Marilyn. *Dorrie's Book;* illus. by Ann Sachs. Doubleday, 1975. 74-33688. 136p. $4.95.

5-6 Their apartment was delightful. Their rapport was delightful. An eleven-year-old never had a happier home life than Dorrie O'Brien, only child of handsome, intelligent parents who doted on her and included her in many of their activities. Dorrie knew that her mother had been disappointed by several miscarriages, but that was long ago. And then—disaster! Not just a baby, but triplets. Goodbye to the lovely, small apartment and lazy, happy Sunday mornings and the concerts and dinner parties. And peace. They moved to a dilapidated old house, the rooms full of crying babies and their equipment, and Dorrie's parents were always tired and often quarrelsome. The final blow came when two rejected children gradually moved in and were proposed as permanent wards: her parents left the decision to Dorrie, and she was faced with weighing values and ethics: to turn away the two dependent children selfishly or to accept the fact that space and parental attention would be even less available? Marilyn Sachs is especially adroit in describing tensions and problems within a familial situation and, while this isn't primarily a humorous story, the book is lightened by intrinsic humor and by the vitality of the characters and the directness of the writing style.

1107 **Sachs,** Marilyn. *A Pocket Full of Seeds;* illus. by Ben Stahl. Doubleday, 1973. 137p. $3.95.

5-7 Nicole Nieman is eight when she leaves the foster home in which she and her small sister have been living, and rejoins the parents who had not until then been able to afford a home big enough for four. Self-assured and rather self-satisfied, Nicole is baffled by the hostility of some of her classmates, a hostility that presages the persecution that French Jews suffered during World War II. When her parents are taken by the Nazis, Nicole goes to her foster parents; since it is unsafe there, she goes to school, where the teacher, who Nicole has disliked, shows unexpected compassion and takes Nicole in as a boarding pupil. A touching story, realistic in the way Nicole adjusts to the drastic changes of war and changes from a blithe eight-year-old to a mature adolescent. Style and characterization are deft, and the atmosphere of the place and period are convincingly recreated.

1108 **Sachs,** Marilyn. *The Truth about Mary Rose;* illus. by Louis Glanzman. Doubleday, 1973. 159p. $3.95.

4-7 Remember Veronica Ganz? This is her daughter's story. Mary Rose has been named after Veronica's sister, who died in a burning apartment building when she was a child, and Mary Rose

Ramirez idolizes the memory of her aunt, having seen the newspaper pictures of the girl who alerted other people in the building at the cost of her own life. Now Mary Rose and her family are living at Grandma's while they look for a new home, and she is very anxious to find the one thing the first Mary Rose left behind—a box of "treasures." When the box is found, Mary Rose begins to understand something more of the family heroine; she learns still more when she overhears a conversation between her mother and her uncle as they discuss the past and the night of the fire. Woven through and around the story of Mary Rose is a rich and perceptive picture of the intricacies of family relationships, a picture peopled with vivid characters. Particularly telling: the obdurately prejudiced grandmother, who repeatedly makes slurring remarks about Mary Rose's father (Puerto Rican) and then asks, "But what did I *say?*" when her daughter remonstrates, who has made a saint of the dead Mary Rose, and who blindly idolizes all her grandchildren.

1109 **Sarnoff,** Jane. *The Code and Cipher Book;* by Jane Sarnoff and Reynold Ruffins. Scribner, 1975. 74-24419. 40p. illus. $5.95.

4-7 An entertaining compendium of ciphers, codes, and such variants as pig Latin and cockney slang concludes with a page of advice on breaking ciphers and some messages to decode, with keys to the numbers used for cipher systems in the book. Each of the ciphers is explained, and sentences to encode and decode follow. Here and there throughout the book are double-page spreads that offer little bits of information about codes used in history, rules about who was permitted to use them, signs used by hoboes, etc. Great fun for the child who enjoys puzzles.

1110 **Sasek,** Miroslav. *This is Historic Britain.* Macmillan, 1974. 60p. illus. $6.95.

3-6 Another in the series of oversize books filled with beautifully detailed pictures of sights and sites of a city or a country. Sasek's text is, as always, packed with facts that would be interesting to a sightseer, and the book can serve as an adjunct to a historical unit of the curriculum, but the primary appeal is visual: carefully detailed and accurate paintings in restrained color of the period architecture found in castles, cathedrals, and historic buildings throughout England, Scotland, and Wales.

1111 **Saunders,** Dennis, comp. *Magic Lights & Streets of Shining Jet;* photographs by Terry Williams. Greenwillow, 1978. 76-20519. 142p. Trade ed. $7.95; Library ed. $7.35 net.

4-7 An interesting selection of poems includes some by writers as eminent as Rossetti, Yeats, Longfellow, Millay, Brownjohn, and Wordsworth, and some by children. First published in England, the book is divided into four sections: "Creatures Small," "Weathers and Seasons," "Colours," and "Sea and Shore." Facing each poem is a color photograph; the pictures are of good quality and nicely matched with the poems. There's little that's complex, little that's humorous, but the level of the selections is high, and it's as pleasant a conservative collection of poems about natural things as one could find for young readers. Author and first line indexes are included.

1112 **Scheffer,** Victor B. *A Natural History of Marine Mammals;* illus. by Peter Parnall. Scribner, 1976. 76-14820. 157p. $7.95.

6- An eminent marine biologist, Scheffer is distinguished also as a writer of pellucid prose; he communicates his zealous appreciation of natural marvels without embellishing fact. The text is logically arranged, thoughtful and informative: the illustrations by Parnall are impeccably detailed and beautifully drawn. Scheffer describes the evolution of the six groups of marine mammals (sea otters, walking seals, crawling seals, sirenians, toothed cetaceans, and baleen cetaceans) and then discusses them in relation to adjustment to ocean living, food preferences, reproduction and growth, intelligence, migration patterns, and hazards such as disease. He also describes the ways in which marine mammals are studied and considers their possibilities for survival. Appended material includes a list of places where marine mammals can be seen, a classification chart, an extensive bibliography, and an index.

1113 **Schick,** Alice. *Kongo and Kumba; Two Gorillas;* pictures by Joseph Cellini. Dial, 1974. 82p. Trade ed. $4.95; Library ed. $4.58 net.

3-5 Alternate sections describe the first years of one gorilla's life in the wilds and of another's in captivity. While zoo-born Kumba is taken from her increasingly careless mother and raised by attendants, Kongo is learning gorilla behavior from the adults of his group. The writing is direct and informal, affectionate but not sentimental, and the book shows clearly the meticulous care given by zoo personnel. Ms. Schick points out that life in captivity is not preferable to the freedom and independence enjoyed by gorillas in the mountain jungles but that, as men encroach on their territory, the wild gorilla may disappear and the zoo gorillas be the last survivors of this fierce-looking but gentle endangered species.

1114 **Schick,** Alice. *The Peregrine Falcons;* illus. by Peter Parnall. Dial, 1975. 79p. $4.95.

6-10 As she did in *Kongo and Kumba,* Schick describes actual forms of animal life to give validity and color to a text that makes a creature's life cycle both comprehensible and fascinating. Named (by a watcher) Zeus and Artemis, two peregrine falcons courted and mated on the west bank of the Hudson River Palisades in the 1940's. Here they made a nest, raised and trained their three eyasses, and returned another year to mate and breed again. Then they disappeared, as peregrines were disappearing everywhere, victims of DDT. Conservationists and ornithologists, alarmed, began trying to breed peregrines in captivity, and the last section of the book describes the successful breeding program at Cornell as vividly as its beginning depicted the soaring, swift flights of Zeus and Artemis. Beautifully written, and most beautifully illustrated.

1115 **Schick,** Alice. *The Remarkable Ride of Israel Bissell; Being the True Account of an Extraordinary Post Rider Who Persevered;* by Alice Schick and Marjorie N. Allen; illus. by Joel Schick. Lippincott, 1976. 75-29179. 38p. $5.95.

3-4 Text and illustrations are nicely wedded as the former describes a true incident, Bissell's long journey carrying news of the Revolution through the colonies two hundred years ago. The tale is told by Bissell's pet crow, a fictional addition to fact; it is illustrated with deft, amusing drawings, filled with action and authentic details of costume, clothing, and architecture. Bissell, a post rider, galloped from Boston to Philadelphia via New York, spreading the Call to Arms (a document that is in Independence Hall). The story is told in a brisk, straightforward manner; the pictures add invented mishaps. This can also be enjoyed by the read-aloud audience.

1116 **Schick,** Alice. *The Siamang Gibbons; An Ape Family;* pictures by Joel Schick. Raintree, 1976. 75-38550. 81p. Trade ed. $5.97; Library ed. $5.95 net.

4-6 A description of the siamang gibbon is given in narrative form, first through an account of a family in the Sumatran jungle, then by a factual account of the particular gibbon in that family that was to be named "Unk," a resident of the zoo and the first siamang to breed in captivity. Rescued when his mother was killed in a fall, the infant siamang was picked up by the Hoffmans, animal collectors, who later sold him to a zoo in Hanover, Germany. Purchased by the Milwaukee County Zoo, Unk became the father of a thriving family. The information is accurate, detailed, and on occasion as amusing as it is interesting, giving many facts about modern zoo practices as well as about the animals' behavior.

1117 **Schick,** Alice. *Viola Hates Music;* by Alice and Joel Schick. Lippincott, 1977. 76-46566. 44p. illus. $4.95.

3-6 yrs. The Osborne family makes music: father plays in a string quartet, mother sings, son's in a combo, daughter is taking piano lessons, Consuelo the housekeeper is devoted to the saxophone. With each performance the dog, Viola, howls in anguish; in fact, she bites little Cynthia's piano teacher. She hates music. They think. But wise old Uncle Bert sees the real problem, and plays patron to the thwarted Viola, who goes off to take lessons and returns an accomplished bagpipe player. Again thwarted, because nobody will let her join their performances, Viola is again pacified when Uncle Bert writes a rock opera version of "Lassie Come Home" and Viola plays the lead. The pictures are brisk and amusing, each character a different animal. Only the dog is a dog; all the Osbornes are moose (Cynthia plays "Indian Moose Call"), Bert is a duck, the string quartet and combo members are a bear, a rabbit, chicken, lion, etc. The story is as crisp and funny as the pictures.

1118 **Schlein,** Miriam. *Giraffe the Silent Giant;* illus. by Betty Fraser. Four Winds, 1976. 76-7922. 58p. $6.95.

3-6 Attractive, realistic drawings are nicely combined with blocks of print in a handsome book that is competently written. While not comprehensive, the text gives most of the pertinent facts about the habits, behavior, and appearance of giraffes; it also gives some developmental history, some anecdotes and theories about giraffes in relation to people of earlier times, and it pleads for the preservation of this unusual animal. An index is appended.

1119 **Schlein,** Miriam. *I, Tut; the Boy Who Became Pharaoh;* illus. by Erik Hilgerdt. Four Winds, 1978. 78-15603. 43p. $7.95.

3-5 "Am I a lucky boy? I do not know," begins the six-year-old prince, Tutankhaton, third son of the Pharaoh Amenhotep the Magnificent, as he describes his life. At the age of nine, he inherits a land that is in rebellion against the regime of his oldest brother, Akhenaton, and the boy pharaoh changes his name to Tutankhamun. He has been married for a year, he is helped by two advisers, and he brings peace and prosperity to Egypt. The story is taken up by his friend Hekenefer, for the beloved young ruler has died at the age of eighteen, having been pharaoh for half his life; his friend describes the mourning, the mystery of his sudden death, and his burial in the sealed tomb in the Valley of the Kings where, Hekenefer concludes, "Tut, alone in his tomb, found his way to eternal life in the Land of the Dead." Simple and dignified, the story should appeal to the many children who know of the tomb and its treasures; the writing is carefully factual, the illustrations faithful to the known art and decorative motifs of ancient Egypt. The author's notes, a glossary, and bibliography of sources are appended.

1120 **Schneider,** Herman. *Laser Light;* illus. by Radu Vero. McGraw-Hill, 1978. 77-26620. 114p. $7.95.

7-10 In a lucid explanation of a complicated phenomenon, Schneider describes the technique by which scientists built the intense, coherent, focused beam of the laser. His description is preceded by a discussion of the nature of light and of atomic structure and behavior, and is clarified by simple examples and by suggestions for home experiments, some of which could do with safety warnings. The text concludes with a survey of some of the special tasks that lasers can do: remove tumors without surgery, cut or weld obdurate materials, make intricate measurements, etc. An index is appended.

1121 **Schneider,** Herman. *Science Fun For You in a Minute or Two; Quick Science Experiments You Can Do;* by Herman and Nina Schneider; illus. by Leonard Kessler. McGraw-Hill, 1975. 75-20175. 64p. $5.72.

2-5 How nice to have a book of experiments and home demonstrations that are simple to do, require little equipment, and take only a few minutes. The authors have grouped their suggestions: things to make, things to do at bath time, quick tricks, etc. Some of the projects are explained, some are open-ended, and they demonstrate physical phenomena without getting too technical. An index "for adults only" gives labels to the principles, phenomena, or devices covered, including fluid friction, equal expansion, Bernoulli's Law, surface tension, electrolytic action, and differential vision.

1122 **Schreiber,** Elizabeth Anne. *Wonders of Terns;* illus. with photographs by Elizabeth Anne and Ralph W. Schreiber. Dodd, 1978. 77-16862. 64p. $5.95.

5-9 Illustrated with photographs that are nicely placed and labelled, a text in a good series ("Wonders of . . .") is written most capably by an ornithologist. Schreiber's material is accurate and logically arranged, moving from general information about tern species and their physical characteristics to chapters that deal with such particulars as migration, feeding habits, or courtship and nesting. A final chapter discusses problems in the environment, especially those caused by people, that threaten the tern population; an index is appended.

1123 **Schulman,** Janet. *Jenny and the Tennis Nut;* illus. by Marylin Hafner. Greenwillow, 1978. 76-51763. 56p. (Readalone Books) Trade ed. $5.95; Library ed. $5.49 net.

2-4 The tennis nut is Jenny's father, who enjoys the game so much that he buys his daughter a racket and gives her her first lesson. Jenny is more interested in doing cartwheels on the sidelines. Daddy's encouraging, but Jenny convinces him, by demonstration of the gymnastic feats she's taught herself, that she's already found a sport she enjoys. So (three cheers for Dad) he announces he's going to get her some equipment, she's really good, and yes, she may take gymnastic lessons. Maybe someday she'll want to play tennis, too. The style is light and breezy; the father-daughter relationship is admirable; and the story line, although spare, is nicely structured.

1124 **Schulman,** L. M., ed. *A Woman's Place; An Anthology of Short Stories.* Macmillan, 1974. 264p. $5.95.

7- Although most of the stories included in this sobering anthology may be familiar to older readers, they should prove exciting reading for the young adults to whom they are new. Chosen with discrimination, the stories all reflect the theme of woman's role (and her conception of it) in a world in which she is not treated as man's equal; the authors, all women, include Hortense Calisher, Doris Lessing, Carson McCullers, Katherine Anne Porter, and Katherine Mansfield. None of the selections is light in tone, although some have humor, but the book has variety and depth.

1125 **Schwartz,** Alvin, comp. *Kickle Snifters and Other Fearsome Critters Collected From American Folklore;* illus. by Glen Rounds. Lippincott, 1976. 75-29048. 63p. $6.95.

3-5 All of the "fearsome critters" are imaginary beasts of the tall tale variety, and this is a list of illustrated definitions, with notes on sources included at the back of the book. The scratchy, vigorous illustrations by Rounds extend the text and often add a humorous note that exists textually more in the name than in the definition. For the goofus bird, for example, the text reads, "The goofus bird likes to see where it has been, not where it is going. So it flies backward. It also likes to sleep upside down. So it builds its nest bottom-side up." This sort of bland exaggeration can be very effective when used in narration, but in bald definition it is often flat. Some of the entries which *do* have some stories added are more amusing than the example cited. The combination of nonsensical terms, silly concepts, and diverting pictures should appeal to the middle grades audience.

1126 **Schwartz,** Alvin, comp. *Tomfoolery;* Trickery and Foolery with Words; illus. by Glen Rounds. Lippincott, 1973. 127p. $4.95; Paperback ed. $1.95.

3-6 Ebullient illustrations add vitality to the folksy and often childlike humor of the tricks, jokes, stories with no ending, nonsense tales, and puns that are collected in a volume that is a companion piece to the compiler's *A Twister of Twists, A Tangler of Tongues.* Samples: "Pete and Repeat went for a boat ride. Pete fell in. Who was left? Repeat. Pete and Repeat went for a boat ride . . ." or, "What does a duck do when it flies upside down? It quacks up." or, "Would you hit someone after he surrenders? No. (Hit your friend, then announce:) I surrender!" A section of "Notes and Sources" and a bibliography are appended.

1127 **Schwartz,** Alvin, comp. *Witcracks; Jokes and Jests from American Folklore;* illus. by Glen Rounds. Lippincott, 1973. 125p. Trade ed. $4.95; Paper ed. $1.95.

3-6 A section of sources and notes and a bibliography that stars books in which young people might be particularly interested are appended to a collection of riddles, shaggy dog stories, Tom Swifties, hate jokes, noodlehead humor, ethnic humor, and knock-knock jokes. The selections represent the range of American folk jest, and the book should be of interest both to young readers and to the serious student of folklore.

1128 **Schwartz,** Sheila. *Like Mother, Like Me.* Pantheon, 1978. 77-26695. 166p. Trade ed. $6.95; Library ed. $6.99 net.

7-10 Jen, sixteen, tells the story of the year in which she and her mother struggled to adjust to the fact that Dad had gone off to Denmark with one of his students. Mom, who also was a college teacher, cast desperately around looking for a man to fill the gap in her life, and slowly came to realize that she could manage very well on her own. Jen, reacting to a series of surrogates, is candid: she feels uncomfortable knowing that the first substitute, Percy, sleeps in her mother's bed; she shares her mother's uncomfortable feeling that Henrik—nice as he is—is a cut below them socially. Jen acquires a first boyfriend, but this is really her mother's story, and to some extent the story of any woman who has been convinced that she must have a man at any cost to her self-esteem—and it's nicely told if a bit redolent of Message. Style and dialogue are very good in this promising first novel, and the mother-daughter relationship is a warm one. In the end, Jen has learned, along with her mother, not to make "compromises" that are injurious to one's own growth, and she is wholly understanding when Daddy comes back, blithely expecting to move in, and Mom says she loves him but can't live with him.

1129 **Scoppettone,** Sandra. *Trying Hard to Hear You.* Harper, 1974. 264p. Trade ed. $5.95; Library ed. $5.79 net.

8-12 The story of a crucial summer in the lives of a group of adolescents is told by Camilla, who has fallen in love with Phil, a newcomer to the group. Phil and Camilla date, he kisses her, she's thrilled—but he doesn't really seem to respond. And then, at a party, Phil and

Jeff, who's been Camilla's lifelong neighbor and friend, prove to have a homosexual relationship. Camilla is stunned and disbelieving, trying to be understanding—but she's heartsick, both on her own account and because the reactions of some of the group are so vicious. This goes farther than other books in explaining the homosexual relationship since Jeff is willing to talk about his love for Phil, about the fact that it is not merely physical, and since Camilla can discuss it with her mother, a psychiatrist. The story ends with the deaths of Phil and Penny (with whom he's forced to go out on a date) but this car accident is not used as a convenient device, since Jeff later tells Camilla that he's met another man, but nobody will take Phil's place. The story is written with dignity and perception and is balanced by family and peer relationships.

1130 **Scott,** Jack Denton. *Canada Geese;* photographs by Ozzie Sweet. Putnam, 1976. 76-871. 64p. $6.95.

5-
*
"The hounds of heaven," the Cree call the Canada geese, flying in perfect V formation as they migrate, honking their wild cries. Into a smoothly flowing text, Scott incorporates information about migration theories and flight patterns, biological clocks and conservation, predators and sanctuaries. He describes mating, nesting, parental care, courtship, and other aspects of the behavior of individual geese, families, and flocks, as well as the physical features of the geese. There is no obtrusive introduction of facts, but they emerge with quiet authority in a book written with no sentimentality but great appreciation. The photographs, carefully placed in relation to textual references, are clear and handsome, whether they are informative close shots or stunning pictures of a skein of geese silhouetted against a moonlit sky.

1131 **Scott,** Jack Denton. *Discovering the American Stork;* photographs by Ozzie Sweet. Harcourt, 1976. 75-41393. 64p. $6.50.

5- As is true of other books by Scott, this is profusely illustrated with handsome photographs, and the fluent, deceptively casual text is authoritative, lucid, and up to date. Until recent years the American stork was mistakenly identified as the wood ibis and was, along with its habitat, endangered by drought and lumbering. With the establishment of a sanctuary, Corkscrew Swamp Sanctuary, the American stork and other wading birds have protection, seclusion, and implemented food resources. Scott describes nesting, courtship, and mating procedures (the male chooses a nest site, the female then woos him), and the care and feeding of the young when they hatch. Also discussed are flight patterns and feeding habits. Fascinating.

1132 **Scott,** Jack Denton. *The Gulls of Smuttynose Island;* photographs by Ozzie Sweet. Putnam, 1977. 77-7870. 63p. $6.95.

5- * Sweet's photographs are beautiful, varied, clear, and informative; Scott's writing is lucid, authoritative, skillfully organized and often poetic in its phrasing and vision. In his description of the herring gulls and black-backed gulls that take over an Atlantic island rookery each summer, Scott includes every aspect of the gulls' lives: mating and breeding patterns, group behavior, territorial prerogatives, flight, feeding and nesting. . . . it's a superb book.

1133 **Scott,** Jack Denton. *Island of Wild Horses;* illus. with photographs by Ozzie Sweet. Putnam, 1978. 78-17380. 61p. $7.95.

5- Profusely illustrated by Sweet's action photographs of the coastal island of Assateague, the text describes the lives of the small, sturdy horses that live, free and protected by law, on the windswept island, low and marshy. Scott discusses the several theories as to the horses' origins, the most popular of which is that the original band swam to the island when a Spanish ship was wrecked. He describes the hierarchy within each herd, the yearly competition between stallions who seek, at breeding time, to start or enlarge their herds, and the way in which a foal is born and raised until it gains independence. A staunch conservationist, Scott discusses, as he has in earlier books, both the environmental adaption of the animals he is writing about and the protective legislation that enables them to continue to have their freedom and comparative safety. The writing style is straightforward, the information accurate, the tone sympathetic but not saccharine.

1134 **Scott,** Jack Denton. *Loggerhead Turtle; Survivor from the Sea;* photographs by Ozzie Sweet. Putnam, 1974. 58p. $6.95.

5- Like Victor Scheffer's *Little Calf,* this is both a poetic essay and an impressively informative book about a marine creature. The photographs are excellent and are nicely integrated with the text. Scott describes in vivid prose the lumbering, ferocious looking loggerhead turtle on land, laboriously scraping a nest and laying her eggs—and waddling back to the sea to move with grace and power in her watery element. As background for his description of the habits and habitat of the loggerhead, he discusses the endurance of a creature that has survived almost unchanged for 150 million years, the dangers it faces today, and the conservation work that is being done to protect it. A fine book.

1135 **Scott,** Jack Denton. *Return of the Buffalo;* photographs by Ozzie Sweet. Putnam, 1976. 76-19019. 64p. $6.95.

5- * Although he explains that the animal we call the plains buffalo is in fact the bison, Scott uses the more familiar term in another volume in the excellent photo-essay series in which text and pictures are of uniformly high quality and carefully correlated. The text gives a great deal of information about the buffalo's habits, habitat, appearance, growth, and patterns of mating and breeding; it also describes the many ways in which the Plains Indians used the buffalo, but did not abuse it, killing only enough to provide food, clothing, and shelter from meat and hide. With the western immigration came the white settlers' slaughter: between 1870 and 1890, the buffalo population was reduced from 60 million to less than 600 animals. The thriving buffalo herds today are due to the efforts of a few conservationists rather than to legislation, although the movement now has many supporters. Scott lists the preserves where buffalo can be seen in the United States and Canada.

1136 **Scott,** Jack Denton. *The Survivors; Enduring Animals of North America;* illus. by Daphne Gillen. Harcourt, 1975. 75-10132. 110p. $7.50.

5-9 As is evident from his earlier books, *Loggerhead Turtle* and *That Wonderful Pelican,* Scott has both a profound knowledge of the animal world and writing style that is both spontaneous and fluent. The admiration he feels for wild creatures is never excessive; his views on conservation or respect for animals never become didactic. Here he examines, in separate chapters, some of the creatures that have flourished in a time when so many species have become endangered or extinct; in the descriptions of the twelve survivors (chipmunk, cottontail, coyote, crow, whitetailed deer, gull, opossum, porcupine, raccoon, short-tailed shrew, skunk, and woodchuck) the reasons that they have been successful emerge. A full-page black and white drawing, realistic and handsome, precedes each chapter.

1137 **Seed,** Jenny. *The Great Thirst.* Bradbury, 1974. 188p. $5.95.

7-10 A story set in Africa in the 1830's describes the conflict between the Hottentots and the Hereros, or Cattle People, after the long drought of the previous decade brought the latter to Hottentot country, Namaland, in search of grazing land for their beasts. Seen through the experiences of a Nama boy, Garib, the dramatic tale describes the leadership of "The Lion of Africa," Jonker Afrikaner, his downfall, and the impact of the white missionaries on tribal patterns. Garib, captive of the Cattle People and later an aide to Jonker Afrikaner, grows to detest the recurrent warfare and leaves to make his own life. Much of the material is based on records kept by traders and missionaries, but the historical value of the book is outweighed by the sweep and color of the story; the writing style is solid and mature, the characters have vitality, and tribal cultures are described with dignity.

1138 **Seed,** Suzanne. *Saturday's Child; 36 Women Talk about Their Jobs;* interviews and photographs by Suzanne Seed. O'Hara, 1973. 159p. $6.95; Paper ed. $4.95.

7-12 A useful book for the girl who is undecided about a career, this gives both information about fields of work and some idea of the varieties of occupations in which women are successful today. The text is in first person, each piece based on an interview and accompanied by a photograph. The 36 women who are included give facts about their childhood and their first interest in a chosen field, discuss their education and training, and describe the work they do. A list of sources of further information and an index are appended.

1139 **Seeger,** Elizabeth. *Eastern Religions.* T. Y. Crowell, 1973. 213p. illus. $4.95.

7-10 An authoritative and well-written discussion of five of the major eastern religions: Buddhism, Confucianism, Hinduism, Shinto, and Taoism. The author gives excellent historical background and describes for each religion the beliefs, the rituals, the legends, the religious leaders or founders of the faith, the holidays, and the historical development of each religion. An annotated bibliography and an index are appended.

1140 **Selden,** George. *Harry Cat's Pet Puppy;* illus. by Garth Williams. Farrar, 1974. 168p. $5.95.

3-6 Hooray! The characters who delighted readers in *The Cricket in Times Square* are back—not Chester Cricket, who's still in his rural retreat, but Harry Cat and Tucker Mouse, still residing in comfort in a drainpipe in the Times Square subway station. Here they adopt a bedraggled puppy, and their problem is that their darling grows too big for the drainpipe. So Harry Cat sets about wooing a supercilious Siamese whose master might be induced to take the pup in and save him from a life with the gang of raffish strays that hang out in Bryant Park. Everything about the book is appealing: the humor, the dialogue, the characterization, the yeasty style, the setting, and the beguiling illustrations.

1141 **Selfridge,** Oliver G. *Trouble with Dragons;* illus. by Shirley Hughes. Addison-Wesley, 1978. 77-22441. 86p. $6.95.

5-6 "Look, Ma! There's another one," says a child as the oldest of three royal sisters gallops off, armor glinting, to slay the dragon that will procure the hand of the prince. It's an old routine to observers: a princess comes, she and the prince fall in love, she goes off to earn his hand, and is eaten by the dragon. And the Prime Minister is delighted, because he runs the goblet factory that makes sapphire goblets that come from sapphire dragon eggs, and *they* can only be produced if a dragon eats people. When the two older sisters have been eaten, the youngest, Celia, agrees with the prince that it is her turn to fall in love and change her blue jeans for dragon-fighting garb; but Celia begins by doing some research in the library, and she takes advice when she can get it, and—with a bit of help from a fairy godmother—she uses wit instead of brawn and conquers the dragon. Delightfully illustrated, delightfully told, witty and sophisticated.

1142 **Selsam,** Millicent (Ellis).*The Apple and Other Fruits;* photographs by Jerome Wexler. Morrow, 1973. 48p. Trade ed. $4.50; Library ed. $4.14 net.

3-5 A model of botanical instruction, this lucidly describes the reproductive organs of an apple flower, pollination, and the changes that take place as the fertilized seed grows to a ripe sphere of familiar fruit. Other fleshy fruits are also described, both those that have multiple seeds and those that develop from a single pistil into a fruit with a single seed, as do the peach or plum. There is no extraneous text, and the magnified photographs are handsome, clear, and nicely placed.

1143 **Selsam,** Millicent (Ellis). *A First Look at Insects;* by Millicent E. Selsam and Joyce Hunt; illus. by Harriett Springer. Walker, 1975. 73-92451. 31p. Trade ed. $5.50; Library ed. $5.39 net.

2-4 One in a series of nature books designed to encourage children's powers of observation and to give them some sense of how animals are classified, this is carefully structured to those ends. Repeatedly, the text calls attention to details that distinguish insects from other animal forms (a lobster has an exoskeleton but is not an insect because . . .) or points out body parts (wing shape, antennae, wing position) by which one insect can be distinguished from another. The careful drawings are nicely integrated with the text, and the authors use them to suggest matching words and pictures: Find the insect that looks like a stick with wings, look at the way the wings are held when the insect is at rest, et cetera. The book, useful but less fluid than Selsam's solo work, concludes with suggestions for ways to collect and care for insects.

1144 **Selsam,** Millicent (Ellis). *A First Look at the World of Plants;* by Millicent E. Selsam and Joyce Hunt; illus. by Harriett Springer. Walker, 1978. 77-78088. 32p. Trade ed. $5.95; Library ed. $5.85 net.

1-3 Just enough material, just enough classification in the plant world is included in an excellent book for the primary-grades reader. Clear pictures, adequately labelled, show the differences among bacteria, algae, bryophytes, fungi, ferns, gymnosperms, and angiosperms. The text and illustrations are nicely coordinated to give children repeated opportunities to observe and to differentiate among botanical species.

1145 **Selsam,** Millicent Ellis. *The Harlequin Moth; Its Life Story;* with photographs by Jerome Wexler. Morrow, 1975. 75-17862. 48p. Trade ed. $5.95. Library ed. $5.11 net.

2-4 Excellent photographs (some enlarged, some in color) are carefully placed in relation to textual references in another impeccable science book for young readers. The writing is succinctly informative and carefully sequential as the many stages of molting are followed by cocoon, pupa, and finally the resplendent moth emerging to dry its expanding wings, fly off, and mate to begin the cycle again with the caterpillar and its molting. Selsam concludes with a brief discussion of the fact that some caterpillars are useful, some harmful, some innocuous.

1146 **Selsam,** Millicent (Ellis). *How Kittens Grow;* photographs by Esther Bubley. Four Winds, 1975. 28p. $4.95.

4-7 yrs. Photographs of a litter of four appealing kittens are nicely integrated with a simply written text that is straightforward in describing the stages of the kitten's growth. There's no sentimentalizing or cuteness (who needs it, with pictures?) but a crisp record of the gradual acquisition of full use of the senses, developing motor skills, training by the mother cat, and acquisition of permanent teeth. And there they are, eight weeks old, affectionate and playful at the age when, the text ends, it is "the best time to get a kitten."

1147 **Selsam,** Millicent Ellis. *Mimosa, the Sensitive Plant;* illus. with photographs by Jerome Wexler. Morrow, 1978. 78-15090. 48p. Trade ed. $6.95; Library ed. $6.67 net.

3-5 * The impeccable team of Selsam and Wexler have produced another excellent book on a botanical subject: the photographs are of fine quality and beautifully integrated with the text, the text is written with simplicity and clarity, and the information is accurate and comprehensible. After a brief discussion of other plants that have moving parts (usually leaves or flowers that fold at night) Selsam describes the mimosa plant, the leaves and stems of which droop almost instantly when threatened by heat or when touched. In a fine example of the scientific attitude, the author then discusses what is known, what is a matter of theorizing, and what is still unknown about the way in which the message of danger is communicated from part to part of the plant—and, in so doing, includes an explanation of the plant structure. Suggestions for growing a mimosa plant and description of a home demonstration of its sensitivity are included.

1148 **Selsam,** Millicent (Ellis). *Land of the Giant Tortoise; The Story of the Galápagos;* illus. with photographs by Les Line. Four Winds, 1977. 77-4897. 55p. $7.95.

4-7 * Photographs in black and white and in color illustrate a text that describes the fascinating flora and fauna of the Galápagos Islands. Selsam, in her usual impeccable style, discusses the creatures and plants that are found on these volcanic islands and presents the theories of their evolution in a way that exemplifies scientific teaching: disciplined, lucid, organized logically, and careful to distinguish between fact and conjecture. An index is appended.

1149 **Selsam,** Millicent (Ellis). *Popcorn;* photographs by Jerome Wexler. Morrow, 1976. 76-26627. 48p. Trade ed. $5.95; Library ed. $5.21 net.

2-5 After giving some facts about evidence of corn in pre-Columbian times and distinguishing popcorn from other varieties, the text suggests a home experiment in which the reader can grow a popcorn plant. Excellent enlarged photographs show plant parts as the author explains structure, fertilization, and development of the plant; the text concludes with a discussion of some of the many uses of corn in foods, as animal fodder, in manufactured products, in medicine, in chemicals. Impeccably organized and lucidly written, as Selsam's books usually are, this is also outstanding for the quality of the photography and the handsomeness of the format.

1150 **Sendak,** Maurice. *Some Swell Pup; or Are You Sure You Want a Dog?* by Maurice Sendak and Matthew Margolis; illus. by Maurice Sendak. Farrar, 1976. 75-42870. 26p. $5.95.

K-4 For primary grades independent readers as well as for the read-aloud audience, this amusing and instructive picture book stresses the fact that it is normal for a puppy to be destructive and make messes, that a pup is best trained with patience and kindness. No yelling, no hitting. Sendak uses humor in dialogue and pictures to make the message palatable; Margolis is director of the National Institute of Dog Training. The pictures are in cartoon style, full of action and humor, showing a boy and girl (one insisting the dog is male, the other persistently calling it "she") who mistreat their pup, are scolded and taught by a mysterious cloaked bear, and learn that formal training shouldn't start until the puppy is twelve weeks old.

1151 **Serwadda,** W. Moses. *Songs and Stories from Uganda;* transcribed and edited by Hewitt Pantaleoni; illus. by Leo and Diane Dillon. T. Y. Crowell, 1974. 81p. $6.50.

3-5 A delightful mingling of songs, stories, and games, and even instructions for dance steps is illustrated with strong woodcut pictures in black, rust, and white. The first story, for example, has within it a song that includes solo and group response; another, "Purrrr Ce!" uses a chorus after the story has been told. There are action and humor in both songs and stories; the Luganda words for the songs, all traditional music from and Baganda people of Uganda, are given with English translation, so that the words can be understood but sung in the original. Children can use the book alone, and it is ideal for group use (especially with younger children) under adult guidance.

1152 **Shannon,** Terry. *Windows in the Sea; New Vehicles that Scan the Ocean Depths;* by Terry Shannon and Charles Payzant; illus. with photographs and drawings. Childrens Press, 1973. 78p. Trade ed. $6.39; Library ed. $4.79 net.

5-8 A description of the new panoramic view submersibles that have been constructed and operated since the authors' *The Sea Searchers* (1968). Profusely illustrated with photographs, the book gives details of the machines that have been used for various scientific purposes in exploring the flora and fauna of the ocean depths; some submersibles have been designed to investigate pollution, some are used for sight-seeing, and one project uses trained sea lions in conjunction with a manned observation vehicle for retrieving objects on the sea floor. Fascinating stuff. An index is appended.

1153 **Sharma,** Partap. *The Surangini Tales;* illus. by Demi Hitz. Harcourt, 1973. 126p. $4.75.

4-6 A collection of tales in folk style, some of which have been previously published in India, uses an Arabian Nights format that links the stories together. Here, the beautiful Surangini has disappeared into the carpet that was woven for her by the poorest and humblest of her suitors. A wise judge proposes a storytelling contest to bring her back, since Surangini loved stories so much. The framing story gives impetus and is nicely concluded; the tales are truly in the folk tradition, stressing the ethics and mores of the culture, mingling talking beasts and magic with the foibles and graces of men. The writing has vitality and originality, and the stories are as good for telling as they are for reading aloud.

1154 **Sharmat,** Marjorie Weinman. *I'm Not Oscar's Friend Anymore;* illus. by Tony DeLuna. Dutton, 1975. 25p. $5.95.

K-2 In a wistful monologue, a small boy mulls over the fight he's had with his ex-best friend Oscar. He envisions Oscar moping, Oscar penitent, Oscar bored, finding the humor has gone out of television and the joy out of life. In fact, all the feelings he's having himself. He decides to give Oscar one more chance, and walks by his house. No result. He gives him still one more chance and telephones; Oscar doesn't even remember the fight they had—but that's immaterial, Oscar is going to come over and life is back to happy normal. The illustrations are competent, but the book is carried by the humor of the writing and the affectionate perception of the author.

1155 **Sharmat,** Marjorie Weinman. *I'm Terrific;* illus. by Kay Chorao. Holiday House, 1977. 76-9094. 26p. $5.95.

3-6 yrs. * Sharmat and Chorao are both at their best in a story that is as endearing as it is amusing. Jason, a bear cub, thinks he's marvelous. He does all the things he should do, complacently awards himself gold stars, and is not averse to telling other small bears how terrific he is. The other bears somehow do not find this an attractive trait, and Jason decides that he'll have to change if he wants friends. So he tries being nasty. That doesn't work either. Conclusion: Jason gives away his gold stars, announces that he'll be himself (with no boasting) and is quickly accepted by the other cubs. The relationship between Jason and his mother is exemplary: Mrs. Bear is loving, moderate, wise, and patient encouraging Jason's independence and supportive toward his experiments. The pictures are softly drawn and amusing, and the text is written with bland humor.

1156 **Sharmat,** Marjorie Weinman. *Morris Brookside, a Dog;* illus. by Ronald Himler. Holiday House, 1973. 43p. $3.95.

K-3 Mr. and Mrs. Humphrey Brookside are a quiet elderly couple whose children have grown up and left home; into their peaceful lives comes a stray dog, amiable and persistent about the fact that he belongs to them. So they adopt him, name him Morris, and encourage him to make friends with other dogs. Morris resists until he meets another stray, a very dirty dog. The Brooksides close the door. Morris howls. Finally they relent; she can come in for one meal. Next meal, Morris is back with his friend. "That's the last dog in the world I would have chosen for Morris," Mr. Brookside says. They're beaten, and they know it. They name her Princess, on the theory that it might give her something to look forward to. Finale: a picture of Princess joins those of Morris and all the grandchildren on the piano. This is that oddity, a successful child's story with no children in it; the quiet humor, the appealing characters, and the bland, ingenuous style are echoed in the attractive illustrations.

1157 **Sharmat,** Marjorie Weinman. *Morris Brookside Is Missing;* illus. by Ronald Himler. Holiday House, 1974. 29p. $3.95.

K-3 A sequel to *Morris Brookside, A Dog* has the same bland, ingenuous approach to people-pet relationships and the same affectionate tone. Here Morris is baffled when Mr. Brookside uses the dog's blanket to cover his own legs, since he is chilly and his legs ache. Morris tries to snuggle on his owner's lap, but that's bad with aching legs. Rebuffed, Morris disappears and the Brooksides hunt anxiously, even calling the police. (The policewoman is a pleasant character.) Found in the basement, Morris is at first tentative about a rapprochement, but all ends in love and kisses. It isn't an impressive plot, but the style of writing is easy and natural, and the story has warmth and a sweetness that stops far short of sentimentality.

1158 **Sharmat,** Marjorie Weinman. *Walter the Wolf;* illus. by Kelly Oechsli. Holiday House, 1975. 29p. $6.95.

K-2 An amusing story, pleasantly illustrated with bright pictures of a young wolf who learns to walk the middle of the road. Walter is perfect, a fact acknowledged by all, especially his mother. He has two perfectly matched fangs but never bites, he practices violin assiduously and writes poetry, he takes singing lessons and he likes peace. Under the malevolent influence of a sly fox, Walter sets himself up as a professional biter, but he encounters resistance and gives up his career. He decides, however, that he is no more perfect than he is a biter. "That's all right," says his mother, "Nobody's perfect forever. You lasted a long time." The pacific message is not belabored, and it's lightened by the yeasty style and humor; for example, after Walter has his first experience of being bitten for his own good (by Naomi the beaver, who has just fed him cake) his hostess sighs, as he scampers off, "Eat and run, eat and run."

1159 **Sharpe,** Mitchell R. *"It is I, Sea Gull," Valentina Tereshkova, First Woman in Space;* illus. with photographs. T. Y. Crowell, 1975. 214p. $5.95.

6-10 Valentina Tereshkova didn't dream of space flight as a youngster, didn't even dream of being a pilot. One of the three children of a war widow, she worked in a factory and attended night school; she was twenty when a school friend urged her to join a parachuting club. The details of her training as a parachutist and later as an astronaut are most interesting, and those of the historic flight are fascinating. The biography goes on to describe her marriage to astronaut Andrian Nikolayev, her further training as an aerospace engineer, her travels about the globe. While some segments of the text (a visit to Leningrad, for example, in the year before she became a parachutist) read like a travel brochure, most of it is capably written, giving a good picture of Tereshkova's personality and a considerable amount of information about the history of space science in the U.S.S.R. as well as about the subject's training and her mission. A bibliography, a list of references, and an index are appended.

1160 **Sheffield,** Margaret. *Where Do Babies Come From?;* illus. by Sheila Bewley. Knopf, 1973. 33p. $3.95.

K-2 Adapted from a B.B.C. program, a first sex education book is illustrated with softly colored paintings, each picture facing a pastel page of text. The information is given in serious, forthright style, with all the facts included and with the use of correct terminology. What makes this book different from (and, for the most part, better than) other such books is the tone; without a specific reference to the beauty and intricacy of birth, the mood of reverence for life is created in a harmonious complementing of text and illustrations.

1161 **Shoemaker,** Robert H. *The Best in Baseball;* rev. ed. T. Y. Crowell, 1974. 274p. $5.50.

5- Shoemaker skims the cream off baseball history with lively sketches of baseball greats, brought up to date since the 1962 edition. Ty Cobb and Babe Ruth lead the procession, Steve Carlton and Johnny Bench end it. Not every great player is included, and some of the material went to press too soon to be up-to-the-minute, but on the whole this is one of the best of the collective biographies about baseball players, enthusiastic rather than adulatory, and it gives a good overview of the game. An extensive index is appended.

1162 **Showers,** Paul. *Sleep Is for Everyone;* illus. by Wendy Watson. T. Y. Crowell, 1974. 33p. (Let's-Read-and-Find-Out Books). $3.95.

1-3 One of the most adept and dependable contributors to a series notable for the succinct treatment of limited areas of information, Paul Showers writes with simplicity and smoothness about an intricate subject. His text discusses the ways in which different forms of living things sleep, the fact that people need sleep and that their behavior becomes aberrant when they feel that need strongly, and that the amount of sleep needed varies among individuals. The illustrations are attractive, adding humor especially to a description of an experiment in which four scientists stayed awake as long as they could. Nicely done.

1163 **Shulevitz,** Uri. *Dawn;* words and pictures by Uri Shulevitz. Farrar, 1974. 28p. $5.95.

5-7 yrs. Beautiful, beautiful. A text as hushed and simple as the still, cool hour it describes is almost a poem of dawn. And the pictures, in soft, dark blue that springs into lush, brilliant green and blue when daylight comes, are lovely and evocative. An old man and his grandson sleep, curled in blankets, by the shore while the mountains are reflected, immobile, in the motionless water. The sleepers stir as a slight breeze ruffles the grey-blue water; they silently pack and launch their boat, gliding into the middle of the lake. The sun's rays suddenly bring the colors of the day. That's all, and it's glorious.

1164 **Shulevitz,** Uri. *The Magician;* ad. from the Yiddish of I. L. Peretz. Macmillan, 1973. 32p. illus. $3.95.

K-2 Set precisely on every page, 3x4 pictures in black and white capture the homely quality of peasant life and the raffish charm of the magician who comes to visit the village, in a Passover story based on a Yiddish folk legend. It is customary, at the Passover feast, to set an extra wine goblet for the unexpected guest—Elijah's cup. The magician who has appeared in the home of a poor old couple and magically produces a magnificent meal is gone when they return after a hasty check with the rabbi. What is real, he has told them, must be sent from heaven. The food is real, the wine is real, the soft pillows the magician has conjured up for their comfort are real. "Only then," the story ends," did they know that it was not a magician but the prophet Elijah himself who had visited them." Nicely retold, handsomely illustrated, a story to read alone, read aloud, and tell.

1165 **Shuttlesworth,** Dorothy E. *To Find a Dinosaur.* Doubleday, 1973. 113p. illus. $4.95.

4-7 A good introduction to one area of paleontological research encourages young readers to take an active interest in the hunting of fossils. The text describes the Age of Reptiles, then briefly discusses the evolution of dinosaur species and their eventual extinction; this is not a book about dinosaurs, however, but about the way men have discovered and interpreted evidence about the dinosaur. A major portion of the well-written text is devoted to the ways in which specimens are treated on the discovery site, wrapped for preservation, and mounted as museum exhibits. The author, who has long worked in the field of natural history, writes with easy competence and communicates her sense of excitement about the satisfactions of fossil-collecting. A relative index is appended.

1166 **Shuttlesworth,** Dorothy Edwards. *Zoos in the Making;* illus. with photographs. Dutton, 1977. 76-54782. 117p. $8.50.

5-7 Covering much the same material that is in Shannon and Payzant's *Zoo Safari* or Halmi's *Zoos of the World,* this equally thoughtful and competent book not only describes major zoos and animal parks, but also stresses the importance of conservation and breeding of rare or endangered species that are part of the programs of such institutions. Like the other books, this has photographs that extend the textual information about the ways in which modern facilities are laid out and the provisions that are made for the comfort and safety of their inhabitants. Separate chapters describe individual creatures ("The One and Only Panda") or groups of them ("Giant Vegetarians") and the final chapter discusses the various jobs at zoos and the educational function. A brief reading list is appended.

1167 **Shyer,** Marlene Fanta. *Welcome Home, Jellybean.* Scribner, 1978. 77-17970. 152p. $6.95.

5-7 The story is told by Neil, who is twelve; his sister, a year older, has come home after years of living in institutions for the retarded. Neil and his parents knew that there would be problems, but they hadn't envisioned the debilitating effect of the constant strain: the screaming, the late night noise when Gerry rocked and banged her head, the messes she made—such as pulling labels off every can in the pantry, or getting applesauce all over the piano keys. Dad moved out, and Neil was all set to move with him until he noticed that Gerry was learning a few things, was improving—and it was in part due to things he himself had taught her. So Neil changed his mind: ". . . she was the way she was, and she was my sister." Painful, honest, and convincing, this is quietly written and very effective in evoking sympathy and understanding for retarded children and for their families.

1168 **Siegel,** Beatrice. *A New Look at the Pilgrims; Why They Came to America;* illus. by Douglas Morris. Walker, 1977. 76-57060. 82p. Trade ed. $5.95; Library ed. $5.85 net.

5-7 Siegel really does go beyond the usual compilation of information gathered for the upper elementary reader in describing the theological differences of Puritans and Separatists, and the persecution that led to schism and emigration. She gives a vivid picture of the Separatists' stay in Holland and the generation gap between parents and those children who, having spent most of their lives in Holland, felt more Dutch than English. She also points out that the majority of those sailing on the *Mayflower* were not Separatists but "Strangers," people recruited by the journey's commercial sponsors and who did not necessarily share the views of the smaller group. The question-and-answer format may annoy some readers, but the material in the book does give solid information in a readable prose style. A list of books suggested for further reading is included.

1169 **Silverberg,** Robert, ed. *The Aliens; Seven Stories of Science Fiction.* Nelson, 1976. 76-147. 189p. $6.95.

7- Stories by Frederic Brown, Carol and Terry Carr, Damon Knight, William Tenn, James White, and the editor have as a unifying theme the encounter between human beings and alien creatures; although they describe reactions to such aliens, they also have implications for the problems of the adjustment of men and women to sharp cultural differences within the society. The plots and styles are as varied as the creatures described; most of the stories are cheerful in approach and positive in attitude, and they range from a humorous monologue by a Jewish father (Carol Carr's "Look, You Think You've Got Troubles") whose daughter has married an extraterrestrial "plant with legs" to William Tenn's "Firewater," a long story about aliens who invade the earth and change some of its inhabitants. An old hand at science fiction compilation, Silverberg has done a particularly good job here.

1170 **Silverstein,** Alvin. *Gerbils; All About Them;* by Alvin and Virginia B. Silverstein; photographs by Frederick J. Breda. Lippincott, 1976. 75-34390. 159p. $6.95.

5-8 Although there have been several excellent books about gerbils published for children (those by Dobrin and by Shuttlesworth among them) none is as extensive as this. The Silversteins, who are noted for their simply written and authoritative books in the natural sciences, describe gerbil behavior in detail; give background information about the way in which these animals, brought into the country for research purposes, quickly became a popular pet; discuss the care, feeding, and housing of gerbils; describe the mating cycle and give advice on breeding gerbils; and conclude with an explanation of the many ways in which gerbils are used in laboratory experiments, with particular stress on their potential contribution to medical knowledge when scientists discover why the gerbil accepts transplants or is resistant to high cholesterol levels. A brief bibliography, an index, and two sources for obtaining gerbils are included.

1171 **Silverstein,** Alvin. *So You're Getting Braces; A Guide to Orthodontics;* written and photographed by Alvin and Virginia B. Silverstein; illus. by Barbara Remington. Lippincott, 1978. 77-16588. 112p. Hardbound $6.95; Paperback $3.95.

5-9 With increasing numbers of young people experiencing orthodontic therapy, there should be widespread (no pun intended) interest in a book that has been made as informal as is consistent with the subject matter. This is in part due to an occasional humorous remark and in part to the cheerful faces, in many photographs, of the three Silverstein children, all of whom have gone through or are still coping with corrective treatment. The text describes the structure of teeth and jaws, the ways they change, the causes and varieties of malformation, and the devices used in orthodontics and how they work. A crisp text gives useful facts and sensible advice about cooperation, dental hygiene, and care of orthodontic devices. Sources of further information and an index are included.

1172 **Silverstein,** Shel. *Where the Sidewalk Ends; The Poems and Drawings of Shel Silverstein.* Harper, 1974. 172p. Trade ed. $7.95; Library ed. $6.89 net.

3-6 Comic drawings in cartoon style sound the note for a big, breezy book of poems, almost all humorous; some are nonsense poems, some have a pointed message, and most of them are both funny and sensible, often expressing the fears or dreams of childhood. The rhyme and rhythm of Silverstein's writing indicate the appropriateness of the collection for reading aloud to younger children as well as for the independent reader in the middle grades.

1173 **Simon,** Hilda. *The Date Palm; Bread of the Desert;* illus. by the author; photographs 1910-1914 by Henry Simon. Dodd, 1978. 77-14244. 158p. $8.95.

7-9 A substantial portion of the text here is based on the work of the author's father, who brought date palm shoots from Africa to California to contribute to the founding of a new industry. Simon describes the date palm's importance through the ages as a staple food in desert regions, and—accompanied by the meticulous drawings for which she has been noted—describes the plant botanically. She also discusses the spread of the plant, since other growers had sent agents like her father to obtain offshoots; their place in the ecology of which they became a part; and the date industry in the United States. The small print is a handicap; the photographs and drawings add greatly to the value of the book. An index is appended.

1174 **Simon,** Hilda. *Frogs and Toads of the World;* written and illus. by Hilda Simon. Lippincott, 1975. 75-14095. 128p. $6.95.

5- * Written in a straightforward but informal style laced with humor, logically organized, comprehensive, and illustrated with meticulously detailed colored pictures of many species, this excellent book is more enjoyable reading than most books with comparable reference use. The first chapter gives general information about the evolution, morphology, and physiology of toads and frogs; succeeding chapters describe varieties of each, and a final chapter discusses unusual breeding habits. A bibliography; a list of species illustrated, giving common and scientific names; and an index are appended.

1175 **Simon,** Hilda. *Snails of Land and Sea;* written and illus. by Hilda Simon. Vanguard, 1976. 75-18423. 143p. $6.95.

6- As in other books by this naturalist and artist, the text is competently organized, comprehensive, clear, and authoritative, and the softly colored drawings are impeccably detailed and handsome. Simon begins with a discussion of the collecting of shells and the products used by people (snails as food, purple dye from the Murex group, shells used as money or ornaments) and provides two chapters of general information, "Evolution and Anatomy," and "Growth and Structure of the Shell," before discussing groups of snails in succeeding chapters: land, fresh-water, and marine snails as well as those gastropods that are less well known because they have no shells. Throughout the text, Simon describes structure, reproduction, habitat, diet, and—extensively—shells and shell color. Either the pictures or the text would stand alone; together they provide a valuable resource and an aesthetic tour de force. The writing style is direct and serious but not dry. A bibliography, a glossary, and an index that includes common and scientific names are appended.

1176 **Simon,** Hilda. *Snakes;* The Facts and the Folklore; illus. by the author. Viking, 1973. 128p. $6.95.

6-10 Meticulously detailed, handsome drawings add to the beauty and the usefulness of a book that is smoothly written, well-organized, and informative. There are separate chapters on giant, rear-fanged, venomous, and non-venomous snakes, profusely illustrated with pictures that will enable the reader to identify species; these chapters are preceded by one on "Snakes in Myth, Folklore, and History," and followed by a very sensible chapter on keeping a pet snake, with emphasis on the snake's well-being. A final chapter gives the ranges of familiar snakes of North America, with maps in color; and an index is appended.

1177 **Simon,** Seymour. *The Optical Illusion Book;* drawings by Constance Ftera. Four Winds, 1976. 75-33873. 78p. $6.95.

4-6 Optical illusions are fascinating to most people, and there have been other books that consisted of drawings that confuse the eye—but few authors have explained as diligently and as lucidly as Simon does, *why* we think, seeing lines of equal length, that one is longer or why one circle seems larger than another of the same size. An experienced science teacher, Simon is careful to distinguish between conjecture and proven theory; he discusses how what we think we see may be affected by past experience, familiarity with perspective, how light or color can effect illusion, and how much of our visual impression may be determined by the brain rather than the eye. There is also an interesting chapter on optical illusions in art, and several suggestions for readers' experiments. An index is appended.

1178 **Simon,** Seymour. *The Rock-Hound's Book;* illus. by Tony Chen. Viking, 1973. 80p. $5.95.

4-6 An excellent book for the beginning collector or the reader who is being introduced to the subject of rocks. The text gives basic information about the kinds of rocks and the minerals in them, describes the qualities that identify kinds of minerals, rocks, and gems, and includes tables that help in identification. The suggestions for where to hunt for rocks and how to collect them include safety warnings and comments on cooperation; an index, a bibliography, and a list of sources for materials are appended.

1179 **Singer,** Isaac Bashevis. *Naftali the Storyteller and His Horse, Sus and Other Stories;* pictures by Margot Zemach. Farrar, 1976. 76-26971. 129p. $6.95.

5-
* Singer at his best, Zemach at her best, and a pleasure all around, this collection of stories has verve and variety. Three have been published previously; two are autobiographical; several are set in Chelm, the town where fools outdo each other in inanity; the title story is gentle and tender. A little magic, a little affection, a lot of humor, and a zest for the absurd would make the stories palatable even without the distinctive writing style that makes them delightful.

1180 **Singer,** Julia. *We All Come from Puerto Rico, Too;* written and photographed by Julia Singer. Atheneum, 1977. 76-46600. 71p. $6.95.

3-5 Although one adult speaks, most of the commentary is by children; the text and photographs together give a rich and varied picture of Puerto Rican life. A boy talks about his prowess as a baseball player, a girl describes her training in ballet classes, a group of cousins visits their grandfather's farm. What the book achieves can be an antidote to the image that appears in most children's stories set in Puerto Rico, which is that of a place where poor people emigrated from to live in (usually) urban barrios in the United States.

1181 **Sivulich,** Sandra Stroner. *I'm Going on a Bear Hunt;* illus. by Glen Rounds. Dutton, 1973. 28p. $4.50.

3-5 yrs. With the help of amusing illustrations and the use of brown print for directions, a participation game translates nicely into book form. "I'm going on a bear hunt . . . And I'm not afraid . . . Goodbye, mother . . . Off we go through the tall jungle grass . . ." is accompanied by brown-type instructions to "pound legs like you're walking, wave, hands together sliding-swish sound." The boy and his dog climb a tree, swim two lakes, cross a swamp, and find the glowing eyes of a bear in a cave, so they back hurriedly off and reverse the whole pattern. Not a story, but a game that leans on storyteller's art and that uses words (in the directions) with an appreciation of humorous effect.

1182 **Skorpen,** Liesel Moak. *Bird;* pictures by Joan Sandin. Harper, 1976. 75-25399. 41p. Trade ed. $5.95; Library ed. $5.79 net.

K-3 The boy had found the nestling in the grass, put it back in the nest, and decided to raise it when he found the small creature in the grass a second time. "Bird," the boy named his pet, who grew plump and tame. But Bird didn't fly, even when the boy flapped his arms to show what flying was. "He's ready to fly," the boy told his father, "he's just too dumb to know it." He put Bird into an old nest—and he flew! In fact, he eventually disappeared, to the boy's grief. One day the boy found a nesting bird, and it was Bird. "I was right," the boy said to an egg. "Your mother's dumb." Happily he went off, saying "Stupid bird. He doesn't know beans about being a mother. I'll probably have to bring them up myself." The quiet humor is echoed in the illustrations, and the story, nicely constructed, has the double appeals of subject interest and of letting readers feel satisfaction because the author doesn't feel they need the boy's mistake explained.

1183 **Skorpen,**Liesel Moak. *His Mother's Dog;* illus. by M. E. Mullin. Harper, 1978. 76-58707. 46p. Trade ed. $6.95; Library ed. $6.79 net.

K-2 Three-color illustrations, subdued in tone and mood, are a nice match for a quiet, perceptive story about a small (nameless) boy who is given the puppy he's long wanted. The dog, however, is chosen by his mother: a spaniel like the one she'd had as a girl, rather than the Newfoundland he'd wished for. The dog follows his mother about and ignores him. When his mother goes to the hospital to have a baby, the dog mopes; when she comes back and is busy with the baby, the boy mopes. What could be more natural than the two who are feeling rejected turning to each other? The story is told in dry style and kept at a low key, and in two places the text moves abruptly ("He missed his mother. She took him in her arms and hugged and hugged him.") but it captures the wistful longing of a child, it is nicely structured for a young audience, and it has the appeal of a wish granted.

1184 **Skorpen,** Liesel Moak. *Mandy's Grandmother;* illus. by Martha Alexander. Dial, 1975. 74-20383. 28p. Trade ed. $4.95; Library ed. $4.58 net.

K-2 Mandy didn't understand why her mother was cleaning so furiously just because grandmother was coming for a visit; she knew, from one of her books, what grandmothers were like: gentle and kind, they held children on their laps and took them for walks. To the zoo, even. But Grandmother came and she wanted Mandy to eat oatmeal. She thought the baby was precious. She didn't like Mandy's frog. Grandmothers, Mandy decided, were boring. But one day her grandmother was sad, and she wanted someone in her lap as much as Mandy wanted to sit there. And they talked, and told secrets, and taught each other things, and became friends. No drama here, nor any sentimentality; the neat little pictures fit the cozy text, slight but realistic, and the blandness of the style is alleviated by very mild, occasional humor.

1185 **Skurzynski,** Gloria. *Bionic Parts for People: the Real Story of Artificial Organs and Replacement Parts;* illus. by Frank Schwartz. Four Winds, 1978. 78-54678. 147p. $7.95.

7- An excellent survey of the subject is written with clarity in a style that is straightforward and mature but not dry; the author uses simple but accurate terminology, not medical jargon. The text describes some of the devices, both bionic parts and machines, that can help those suffering because of malfunction or loss of a body part. The descriptions of some of the devices that help people who are blind or deaf, for example, are prefaced by precise descriptions, with good diagrams, of the way the normal eye or ear functions. Coverage is comprehensive, and the book closes with an explanation of the pace of scientific research, the problems in choosing or inventing materials that will not damage the body or be damaged by it, and brief biographical sketches of some of the major medical contributors in the field. An index is included.

1186 **Skurzynski,** Gloria. *The Poltergeist of Jason Morey.* Dodd, 1975. 74-25516. 178p. $4.95.

6-9 Disruptive? Disturbed? Jason was the most quiet, well-behaved eleven-year-old his cousins had ever seen. Too quiet. The girls had agreed with their parents that orphaned Jason should come to live with them; he'd been expelled from yet another school, and their parents were sure that what the boy needed was loving kindness. Yet Jason always seemed to be breaking and throwing things. True, they didn't see him do it, and he denied it, but how else could dishes shatter and pictures fall off a wall? One by one, the family members witness the frenzied mischief of Jason's poltergeist and are convinced; they call in a psychologist and then the clergy, but that is not what solves the problem. The scenes of exorcism (a Catholic priest) and blessing (a bishop in the Church of the Latter Day Saints) are the weak points of the story, but it's strong enough to accommodate them: convincing characters, a robust style, a psychic phenomenon taken seriously—and a good family story.

1187 **Sleator,** William. *House of Stairs.* Dutton, 1974. 166p. $5.95.

7-9 One by one, five sixteen-year-old orphans discover each other in the strange, frightening building that consists only of endless flights of stairs and landings. They cannot get out; they discover that a mechanical device will feed them if they behave in certain ways: they must do a highly patterned, ritualistic dance—and they are rewarded when they show cruelty to each other. Two of the five rebel and withdraw, taunted and persecuted by the other three; eventually the scientists who are using the five in a thought-control experiment bring them out, they let the two dissidents go, and the others remain for further conditioning. The story closes on a note that sustains its boding quality: the three victims, seeing a familiar signal, stop. "Without hesitation they began to dance." The setting is bleak, dramatic and convincing; the interaction and development of the five young people as characters trapped in an abrasive situation are compelling. A very effective and provocative suspense story that can be read for plot alone or doubly enjoyed for the mystery and the message.

1188 **Slote,** Alfred. *Hang Tough, Paul Mather.* Lippincott, 1973. 156p. $4.95.

4-7 When Paul begins his story, he is in the hospital and talking to his doctor. Very deftly the author makes it clear that Paul's prime interest in life is baseball; he's been a star batter on two Little League teams, and has just moved to town. Paul's retrospective account is without sentimentality or self-pity, but the tragic fact is that he has leukemia and knows it. He has, against orders, seized a chance to play baseball and it has exhausted him. There are some baseball scenes, but these are balanced by the family sequences and the conversations between Paul and Dr. Kinsella. Both the doctor-patient relationship and the bond between Paul and his younger brother are beautifully developed, and the story of Paul's candor and courage is convincing, sad but never morbid, in a book that has depth and integrity.

1189 **Slote,** Alfred. *Matt Gargan's Boy.* Lippincott, 1975. 158p. $5.50.

4-6 All of Slote's baseball stories have clear, colorful game sequences and believable characters with real, soluble problems. As in earlier books, the two are nicely meshed in a book that is sturdily structured and smoothly written. Danny is the best pitcher in his league, proud of being the son of a major league player, and convinced that when Matt Gargan retires he'll come home and remarry Danny's mother. Danny is doubly disturbed when his mother's new supervisor turns up as her escort at a game and when it develops that the man's daughter wants to be on the team. When the girl makes it, he quits. Then he learns that his father is to be married to the divorcee and he nervously shows up at the ball park, aware that the team needs him but not sure that they want him. The ending is low-keyed, logical, and satisfying—a sports story with real substance.

1190 **Slote,** Alfred. *My Trip to Alpha I;* illus. by Harold Berson. Lippincott, 1978. 78-6463. 96p. $5.95.

4-7 A science fantasy and a mystery are neatly packaged in a crisp and ingeniously plotted story. Jack, who tells the tale, is sent to help his Aunt Katherine pack. The gimmick: he travels by VOYA-CODE, an interplanetary system in which the "traveller" sleeps in storage while a duplicate is activated by a computer at the receiving terminal. So Jack sleeps in New Jersey and his alter ego arrives in Alpha. Very strange. Aunt Katherine, a wealthy mine owner, tells Jack that she's decided not to pack and move back to earth, and also that she's turning over all her property to two servants, Frank and Ruth Arbo. Jack doesn't like the fawning pair, suspects them of chicanery and indeed discovers that his real Aunt Katherine is in VOYA-CODE storage while the one he's with is a dummy. Like him. There's pace and suspense in Jack's plot to outwit the Arbos, logic within the fantasy, and good structure and style in the telling.

1191 **Smith,** Doris Buchanan. *Kelly's Creek;* illus. by Alan Tiegreen. T. Y. Crowell, 1975. 75-6761. 71p. $5.95.

4-6 Kelly O'Brien is nine, and he has a physiological malfunction that inhibits coordination. Adults think he isn't trying; his classmates tease him; only the friend he has met while poking about the tidal marshes seems to take Kelly on his own terms. Phillip is a biology student at a nearby college, and he shares with Kelly all the fascinating discoveries he has made while studying marsh life.

Although his parents forbid Kelly to waste time in the marshes, it is this very pursuit that enables him to gain status in the classroom—and thus he gains enough confidence to try some of the physical tasks that had before seemed impossible. A bit slow-moving, the story is perceptive without being at all sentimental about Kelly's handicap. Dialogue and characterization are believable, and the story is nicely structured.

1192 **Smith,** Doris Buchanan. *Kick a Stone Home.* T. Y. Crowell, 1974. 152p. $5.50.

6-9 The title phrase is literal: fifteen-year-old Sara has an almost compulsive habit of kicking a stone home all the way from school, a habit that gives Sara an outlet for her emotional stress. She hasn't yet fully adjusted to her parents' divorce three years before, she certainly hasn't accepted her father's new wife, and she really hasn't accepted herself. She wants to date, but the boys with whom she plays football don't interest her. And then she meets a new boy, and falls hard. Doris Smith handles this without resorting to formula: Sara has an unsuccessful date with a boy she then avoids, the new boy is friendly but finds another girl, her football buddy stays a pal—but she notices another boy who's been in her class all along, and she invites him to a party. She finds it a boost to her morale when the other girls voice their admiration—and all of this seems to fall into a new pattern, one in which Sara can cope with a teacher who's been harsh, can respond to the overtures of her step-mother. There are many stories about the difficulties of adolescence, but there is always room for another that is written with insight and honesty, that can eschew melodrama and still have vitality and pace.

1193 **Smith,** Betsy Covington. *Breakthrough; Women in Religion;* illus. with photographs. Walker, 1978. 78-3016. 139p. $7.95.

5-7 Smith examines the lives and the philosophy of five contemporary women who have broken the barriers that have traditionally barred women from religious leadership. Perhaps the most remarkable is Jeanette Picard, who began her theological study for Episcopalian priesthood at the age of 77; also an Episcopalian priest is Daphne Hawkes, whose four children participated in her ordination ceremony. Rabbi Sandy Sasso is the first woman rabbi to serve a Conservative congregation; Patricia Green is a minister in the African Methodist Episcopal Zion Church; Sister Jogues Egan is a reformer within her order and her church, an ardent pacifist who was jailed for refusing to testify at Philip Berrigan's trial. The writing is brisk and straightforward, prefaced by an introduction that gives historical background and discusses the emergence of women as religious leaders as a part of the feminist struggle and as a phenomenon of progress in contemporary religious life.

1194 **Smith,** Doris Buchanan. *A Taste of Blackberries;* illus. by Charles Robinson. T. Y. Crowell, 1973. 58p. $3.95.

4-6 Jamie is given to exaggeration and to dramatizing whatever happens to him, so when he writhes on the ground after a bee sting, while the other children simply run off screaming, his best friend—who tells the story—is mildly bored and goes home. Then he is smitten with dismay when he learns that Jamie has died, victim of an unsuspected allergy. This is touching rather than depressing, a candid picture of a child's reaction to death, a story that shows the perception and sensitivity of children. The story ends with the never-named child bringing Jamie's mother blackberries, just as he and Jamie has planned to do, and she understands that he is offering more than the berries . . ." And you be sure to come slam the door for me now and then," Jamie's mother says gently.

1195 **Smith,** Gene. *The Hayburners;* illus. by Ted Lewin. Delacorte, 1974. 64p. Trade ed. $4.95; Library ed. $4.58 net.

5-8 "Hayburner" is, literally, a second-rate racehorse; here it's a term used for two creatures that are deficient in different ways. One is a steer that has been picked by lot as Will's 4-H project; the other is a hired man who is retarded, Joey. Joey has come to work for Will's parents for the summer, he is gentle and industrious, he has the mind of a ten-year-old, and he adores Will's ungainly steer. At the end of the summer, there is an auction of all the 4-H steers, and Will's beast gets honorable mention; its development is all due to Joey's assiduous, loving care and he is thrilled. Will and his parents don't know whether Joey, when he goes back to the state mental home where he lives, knows that the animal he loves is to be butchered. Will, who had been callous about Joey, has learned respect and compassion for this good, childlike man. In a brief epilogue, Will is shown telling his own son, years later, about Joey. And he weeps. While the story is touching, it is written without sentimentality; the characters—particularly Joey—and dialogue are strong, and the implicit message is deftly conveyed: it is not necessary to be a winner to achieve, shown in the contrast between Joey's delight and confidence and Will's pessimism and irritation at having drawn by lot an animal that can't be a winner.

1196 **Smith,** Jim. *The Frog Band and Durrington Dormouse;* written and illus. by Jim Smith. Little, 1978. 77-9187. 31p. $6.95.

2-4 Running from a member of a press gang, Durrington stumbles into the lair of Mad Maud the Toad and gratefully accepts a soporific. One hundred years later he wakes to the drumbeat of the frog band, who give him a life home, explain that a century has passed, and help him chase evil Squire Fox. That dastard has been evicting Durrington's descendants, and he snatches the dormouse's proof of title out of his hand and takes off. The chase is a successful and exciting one, and the story ends with a nice twist: the evil fox, on the run and exhausted, stumbles into the lair of Mad Maud and accepts a drink. This has, albeit to a lesser extent, one of the weaknesses of the earlier Frog Band book, illustrations that meet jarringly at the inner edges of the pages, and it has some writing flaws ("I'm a might stiff this morning!") but it's a better structured story, with good pace, humor, and deft watercolor illustrations.

1197 **Sneve,** Virginia Driving Hawk. *Betrayed.* Holiday House, 1974. 125p. $5.95.

5-7 Based on historical documents, this story of Indian-white conflict during the Civil War has a quiet and convincing intensity, drama and danger, and an abrupt, bitter ending. Destitute, angry at the treachery of the whites with whom they had been dealing, the Santee tribe under the leadership of White Lodge raided a Minnesota settlement, killing the men they could catch and taking women and children prisoners. A small group of Teton braves, pitying the prisoners, pleaded for the captives and traded valuable goods for them, their effort aided by White Lodge's son, Black Hawk; the Tetons were amazed that the captives felt affection for some of the Santee, and the captives equally amazed at the altruistic compassion of their rescuers. A final episode describes a mass hanging of some Santee, their executioner the father of some of the rescued captives.

1198 **Sneve,** Virginia Driving Hawk. *When Thunders Spoke;* illus. by Oren Lyons. Holiday House, 1974. 95p. $4.95.

5-6 A story of cultural conflict within the family of Norman Two Bull, a Sioux of fifteen; Norman follows his mother's lead in rejecting the traditional beliefs but changes his rigid stance when a sacred ceremonial object he has found loses its worn and faded look after Norman refuses to sell it. Even Norman's mother can see that the coup stick glows again with bright color and that an eagle feather now hangs from the once bare staff. This element of magic weakens a story that is otherwise strong in defense of the dignity and validity of the old ways, is candid in depicting the relationship between the Sioux and the white storekeeper with whom they trade, and is rich in cultural detail.

1199 **Snow,** Richard F. *The Iron Road: a Portrait of American Railroading;* illus. with photographs by David Plowden. Four Winds, 1978. 78-5388. 90p. $8.95.

6- Full-page photographs of good quality illustrate a history of railroads in the United States, a survey that concludes with a cautiously hopeful appraisal of a renaissance of train travel in the future. Snow incorporates facts about inventions and inventors, such legendary feats as the last ride of Casey Jones, background history, and information about the builders and the workers into a smooth, lively text. He indulges in an occasional moment of lyricism or nostalgia, but the book as a whole has straightforward writing with a good narrative flow.

1200 **Snow,** Richard F. *Freelon Starbird; Being a Narrative of the Extraordinary Hardships Suffered by an Accidental Soldier in a Beaten Army During the Autumn and Winter of 1776;* illus. by Ben F. Stahl. Houghton, 1976. 75-43901. 209p. $7.95.

7-9
* Freelon hadn't really planned to enlist in the Continental Army, but he and his friend Jib had been drinking, and somehow they thought it a lark to volunteer. No lark, they found. The Pennsylvania Militia was scattered; the British forces were well equipped, well organized, well trained; Washington's army was composed of recruits who were always hungry, ill-clad and cold, ill and often frightened. Freelon participates in the surprise attack on Trenton, a desperate, disorganized, somehow successful foray. His account never strikes a false note, it is always that of a participant and adheres, both in language used and in attitudes, to the period. Tart, funny, lively, and percipient, this fine example of historical fiction gives a more vivid picture of the Revolutionary War than do many ponderous histories.

1201 **Snyder,** Zilpha Keatley. *And All Between;* illus. by Alton Raible. Atheneum, 1976. 75-29315. 216p. $6.95.

5-7 In the second volume of an intricately conceived fantasy, the pending conflict of *Below the Root* becomes confrontation. Snyder uses an interesting overlap of events, picking up the story from the viewpoint of Teera, the Erdling child who lives in the cavern community below ground, a people cast out from the ordered, peaceful life of the planet Green-Sky. Teera's people have been lied about and portrayed as evil by the ruling group on Green-Sky, and when she escapes from Erda and is taken in by a family whose daughter Pomma is the same age, both girls learn about each other's cultures. Some of the ruling council also learn, having been duped by their leaders, that there is no difference between themselves and the Erdlings, and they instigate a move for rapprochement, a move that is fought bitterly by some of the council, who kidnap Teera and Pomma and hold them hostage. Like the first book, this has some passages that move slowly, long monologues or explanatory passages, but they are compensated for by the imaginatively detailed conception of the light and dark worlds of Green-Sky and its deported citizens who live below the magic, ice-cold Root and by the suspense of the conflict that seems resolved by the end of the book. The two children have united their Spirit-power, and the weapon that the malevolent leader has planned to use, the single weapon left from the days before the hegira to Green-Sky from the home planet, falls to the ground: evil has been conquered by good.

1202 **Snyder,** Zilpha Keatley. *Below the Root;* illus. by Alton Raible. Atheneum, 1975. 231p. $7.50.

5-7 Using a favorite science fiction theme, after-the-holocaust, Snyder has created a world of tree-dwellers, the Kindar, ruled by the Ol-zhaan and governed by principles of Love, Joy, and Peace. No violence, not even words for violence, exist in the planned society. Thirteen-year-old Raamo, newly chosen as one of the Ol-zhaan, learns from a colleague that the dreaded people who live below the ground may be a fiction contrived by an inner circle of Ol-zhaan; with two friends, Raamo dedicates himself to finding the truth; they learn that those who live below are Kindar like themselves, people who are exiled because they were dissidents. While the writing is at times heavy with protocol or explanatory passages, the book has a strong story line, action and suspense, and interesting characters. What may have extra appeal for today's readers is the philosophy with which the story is imbued: the detestation of war, the disapproval of killing animals for food, the belief that children can be brought up to develop their talents and to become men and women to whom brotherhood is not a word but a way of life.

1203 **Sobol,** Harriet Langsam. *Jeff's Hospital Book;* photographs by Patricia Agre. Walck, 1975. 74-25982. 42p. $6.95.

K-2 As in Arthur Shay's *What Happens When You Go To the Hospital,* this is a photo-documentary that follows a child from admittance to discharge and recovery. Jeff is cross-eyed, and his doctor has decided it's time to operate to correct the condition. Jeff's nervous but finds, as he goes through the preparatory procedures, that the bloodsampling is not very painful, that each step is over quickly, that parents are there before and after surgery, that the medical staff is kind and willing to explain what is going on. This has one edge on Shay's book: the change in Jeff is visible in the last picture

(Shay's child had her tonsils removed) as he rides his bicycle, beaming and clowning just a bit for the photographer.

1204 **Sobol,** Harriet Langsam. *My Brother Steven Is Retarded;* photographs by Patricia Agre. Macmillan, 1977. 76-46996. 26p. $5.95.

2-4 Direct and candid, illustrated with photographs that seem unposed, this is a good introduction to the problems of retarded children and their siblings, in a text that is perceptive and sympathetic. Eleven-year-old Beth talks about her ambivalent feelings about Steven, who is an older retarded brother: the relief she feels at being normal mingled with her guilt at feeling that way; the embarrassment she feels when her friends see Steven, the relief when they accept him; the resentment she feels because her parents have to spend so much time with her brother, tempered by compassion because he can't help it. Brain-injured during his birth, Steven cannot walk or talk normally, and Beth sees the limitations of his adult life with somber clarity. In sum, no dodging of the disadvantages of having a retarded sibling, but to balance this, the book is pervaded by Beth's love, her knowledge that Steven needs her patient understanding, and the open way in which she and her parents have acknowledged the problems they share.

1205 **Sobol,** Rose. *Woman Chief*. Dial, 1976. 76-2289. 108p. $6.95.

6-8 Although no sources are cited, the jacket for this biography states that it is based on the reminiscences of a fur trader who knew the Crow warrior and chief. The writing style is direct and the tone objective; despite a fairly heavy use of dialogue it has no aura of being unduly fictionalized. The character delineation is not deep but it is clear and consistent; the author is candid about the fact that Lonesome Star, born a Gros Ventre and captured and raised by Crow Indians, lived as husband and wife with another woman. The book is sound as a biography, and it also gives a sympathetic and detailed picture of the Plains Indians, particularly of the Crow culture and the importance of horse stealing. Lonesome Star, who won the name of Woman Chief, was murdered, while on a peace mission, by some Gros Ventres.

1206 **Southall,** Ivan. *Benson Boy;* illus. by Ingrid Fetz. Macmillan, 1973. 137p. $4.95.

5-7 Ivan Southall is at his best in a story like this: a dramatic setting, a tense situation, only a few characters, and a child who calls on unexpected courage and resourcefulness to cope with a problem. Here the child is Perry Benson, who is wakened late on a stormy night and told by his father that Mum must go to the hospital immediately to have her baby. Tripping over Perry's toy, Dad falls, hits his head on a stone and lies unconscious; it is Perry who must pull Dad to shelter and who must go for help to the nearest neighbor, dour Mr. Morgan with whom Dad has had a relationship of deep hostility. The story's span is the one night, but it encompasses problem, conflict, and resolution most deftly constructed and the sometimes-staccato Southall dialogue is just right in the situation. Believable and exciting.

1207 **Spence,** Eleanor. *The Devil Hole.* Lothrop, 1977. 77-909. 215p. Trade ed. $6.50; library ed. $5.61 net.

6-9 A teacher of autistic children, this award-winning Australian author depicts the effects on a family when the fourth child proves to be autistic. Spence is neither didactic nor sentimental, although she gives an authentic and heart-wrenching portrayal of little Carl, and she avoids the case-study-fictionalized by focusing on Douglas, the second son of the Mariner family. A quiet and compassionate child, Douglas takes more responsibility for the beautiful infant (so angry, so unresponsive) than do his brother or sister. By the time Carl is three, his destructive violence leads the Mariners to take him in for testing. When the diagnosis is made, they move from the small town they love to Sydney so that Carl can attend a special school. But he lives at home, and it affects every member of the family: Mother is exhausted, Father changes jobs, family finances are drained, few friends come to the home, and days and nights are permeated with Carl's screaming and his destructive behavior. The oldest boy leaves home; Douglas becomes a student at a special school for the musically gifted. The ending, in which Douglas has a long talk with one of Carl's teachers, is sober and realistic in appraising the future, but it is weak in a literary sense. The story has great dramatic impact and, while it deals with a serious topic, provides enough action and development to have pace; the style, characterization, and dialogue are excellent.

1208 **Spence,** Eleanor. *The Nothing Place;* illus. by Geraldine Spence. Harper, 1973. 228p. Trade ed. $5.50; Library ed. $4.79 net.

5-7 Glen, the new boy who had just moved to Sydney was strange, Shane thought. He stared at one so . . . and sometimes he ignored the person speaking to him. It wasn't until another friend, Lyndall, told Shane that she'd discovered that Glen was deaf and embarrassed about it that he understood and sympathized. When Glen learned that his friends' project, a commemorative museum, was to raise money to buy him a hearing aid, he was furious; when he learned of parental investigation of a special school, he left home. It was an elderly friend he'd made, old Reggie, who convinced Glen to go home and compromise: to get a hearing aid and be able to stay on at school with the friends who had only tried to help. The characters are well-drawn, the dialogue natural; the friendship between Glen and Reggie is particularly well developed. Although the story is set in Australia, it has a quality that transcends locale, and the situation—a handicapped child who is resentful and self-conscious but who comes to realize the fact that others accept his handicap and that he must do so as well—is depicted with honesty and moderation.

1209 **Spier,** Peter. *Bored—Nothing to Do!* written and illus. by Peter Spier. Doubleday, 1978. 77-20726. 40p. Trade ed. $6.95; Library ed. $7.90 net.

K-3 Spier's perky, colorful paintings are full of small details and action, and his story is told via short sentences or captions. Told by their mother that she was never bored at their age, two boys who have nothing to do pick up an instruction book while poking about a barn. Depleting the house of sheets, the car of engine, the baby's pram of wheels, the TV of its antenna wire, etc. etc. they put together an airplane and fly it. Wrathful and worried, their parents talk them down, spank and kiss them, order them to put things back. Conclusion: parents congratulating themselves, "Some boys." "Clever too!" while the boys, sent to their room early, mope about. Nothing to do. They're bored. A teasing, nonsensical, but amusing book.

1210 **Spier,** Peter. *Tin Lizzie;* written and illus. by Peter Spier. Doubleday, 1975. 74-1510. 38p. $5.95.

4-6 An affectionate and nostalgic look at the life history of one Model T Ford is illustrated with marvelously detailed drawings with Spier's exuberant humor visible in almost every picture. The text describes vehicles of 1909, when the horse reigned supreme and those who "knew" scoffed at the idea that the horseless carriage would go on being popular. Our particular tin lizzie is bought from a small-town dealer and affords a great deal of pleasure to its family for eleven years; then it is sold to a young couple who use it for touring (pictures of mountains, buttes, desert, etc.) and then, after the third owner has used the car for farm work, Tin Lizzie is left in a field to rust. Happy ending: an antique car buff buys and repairs the old car, and it's much admired by one and all. The story is told in pleasant, jocund style; it is marred slightly by the fact that the car suddenly becomes "she" well along in the text, and there are such statements as ". . . Lizzie saw parts of the world she did not even know existed . . ." Nevertheless, the book has charm, it can be used for an attractive supplement to social studies, and it will be especially enjoyed by avid young fans of motoring history. The endpapers show diagrams of the Model T.

1211 **Spier,** Peter, illus. *The Star-Spangled Banner.* Doubleday, 1973. 48p. $7.95.

3-6 All of the verses of the national anthem are illustrated with handsome pictures, full of vivid and historically authentic details; most of the pictures show the battle scenes that inspired Francis Scott Key to write the words of "The Star-Spangled Banner" in 1814, but others reflect aspects of life in the United States today. Following the illustrated lyrics are a photograph of the manuscript, a discussion of the War of 1812, the music for the anthem, and a double-page spread that shows official flags for government agencies and officers.

1212 **Srivastava,** Jane Jonas. *Averages;* illus. by Aliki. T. Y. Crowell, 1975. 75-5927. 33p. Trade ed. $4.50; Library ed. $5.25 net.

2-4 A good addition to an excellent series of books that explain mathematical concepts and terms for the primary grades reader. The text is lucid and simply written, describing the differences in the terms "median," "mode," and "mean," explaining how each is deduced and how it is used. Aliki's pictures extend the text, and they are also amusing, often using cartoon-style balloon comments to add humor.

1213 **Srivastava,** Jane Jonas. *Statistics;* illus. by John J. Reiss. T. Y. Crowell, 1973. 34p. Trade ed. $3.75; Library ed. $4.50.

2-4 A book that tells, in very simple terms, what statistics are and how they are gathered is illustrated with bright, clear pictures that use color to full advantage. The text shows how statistics can be translated into bar, line, and circle graphs and tables; it discusses polls and samples, suggests ways that the reader can gather statistics, and it points out the important fact that how, when, and where the facts are gathered—or by whom—can affect the results. Crisp, clean, and informative.

1214 **Starkey,** Marion Lena. *The Tall Man from Boston;* illus. by Charles Mikolaycak. Crown, 1975. 75-9970. 47p. $5.95.

3-5 The author, who has written impressively about the Salem hysteria of colonial times, has adapted and simplified the story for younger readers; Mikolaycak has illustrated the account with dramatic black and white pictures that are as subtly simple as posters, strongly outlined, with no background detail, and stark in mood. Starkey gives some background information about the piety and superstition, the winter boredom and the childish guilt, that led to the witch-hunting; she focuses on the involvement of

John Alden, accused at random by the troubled girls, who had spoken vaguely of "a tall man from Boston" first mentioned by the accused slave Tituba. A competent version for the middle grades; a handsome book.

1215 **Steel,** Flora Annie (Webster). *Tattercoats; An Old English Tale;* pictures by Diane Goode. Bradbury, 1976. 76-9947. 27p. $7.95.

K-3 A romantic tale from Steel's collection, *English Fairy Tales,* is beautifully illustrated in soft, floating pastel water colors. All the paraphernalia of the Cinderella theme are here: the beautiful waif, the besotted royal suitor, and the magic that changes the rags Tattercoats is wearing to ballgown and crown. The grandchild of a lord who rejects her because her mother died at Tattercoats' birth, the girl is happy only when a gooseherd pipes his music, and it is the gooseherd who plays a magical tune that enables the prince—and later the assembled company—to see the true beauty beneath the rags. Goode picks up every nuance of the story, including one picture in which the geese, who have accompanied the gooseherd to the ball, are echoed by a group of simpering courtiers.

1216 **Stefansson,** Evelyn (Schwartz) Baird. *Here Is Alaska;* rev. ed. Scribner, 1973. 178p. illus. $6.95.

5-9 Even handsomer than the original edition, this revision of an authoritative survey of Alaska has been brought up to date throughout the text and includes new illustrations. The book explores all aspects of Alaskan life, agricultural and urban, geographic and historical, and industrial; it discusses the Eskimos, the Indians, the oil rush and the struggle between industrialists and environmentalists. Useful, well-organized, and well-written. A relative index is appended.

1217 **Steig,** William. *Abel's Island.* Farrar, 1976. 75-35918. 119p. illus. $5.95.

4-6 Abel is a mouse who lives in cultured comfort on an inherited income and dotes on his bride Amanda. Ever gentlemanly, Abel leaves the safety of a cave (they've taken shelter while on a picnic) to rescue Amanda's gauzy scarf. He is swept off by wind and rain, catapulted into a torrent of water, and lands on an island. This is really sort of a Robinson Crusoe Tale, as the heretofore pampered and indolent Abel learns to cope with solitude, find food and shelter, avoid a predatory owl, and eventually find his way back—a year later—to his loving wife and luxurious home. There are comic touches, but the book depends more on situation and style for its appeal than on humor. And, of course, the major appeal is that of mouse-against-nature.

1218 **Steig,** William. *The Amazing Bone.* Farrar, 1976. 76-26479. 28p. illus. $7.95.

K-2 Steig has come up with the ideal pet: a guardian, a conversationalist, something that you don't have to feed or worry about. Something your parents let you take to bed, *and* something that can do magic! Of course piglet Pearl doesn't know all this when the bone first speaks to her, but then it frightens off some robbers by making snake and lion noises, and it causes a fox to shrink to mouse size when he threatens to eat Pearl (the bone's last owner had been a witch). Steig's improbably vernal setting makes a nice contrast to the nonsensical story, which is told with sophisticated nonchalance.

1219 **Steig,** William. *Caleb & Kate.* Farrar, 1977. 77-4947. 27p. illus. $7.95.

K-3 Caleb and Kate love each other, but they often quarrel; after one spat, Caleb storms off to the forest, where a witch puts a spell on him and turns him into a dog. He goes home and tries to comfort Kate; although she accepts him as a pet, she cannot recognize him as her Caleb. And then . . . thieves invade the house, one of them slashes at the menacing dog, and cuts the very spot the witch had touched to effect her foul enchantment. So the dog turns into Caleb, Kate is overjoyed, and the frightened thieves run away. Steig's vigorous, broken lines and the humor of his characters' faces are droll as ever; although the advent of magic seems fortuitous (the witch just happens by and snickers, "How timely! Here's my chance to test that new spell Cousin Iggdrazil just taught me."). Steig carries it off by combining a bland acceptance of the impossible and a witty writing style that makes few concessions to its audience: if "pondering" seems just right to the author, he doesn't simplify it to "thinking."

1220 **Steig,** William. *Farmer Palmer's Wagon Ride;* story and pictures by William Steig. Farrar, 1974. 28p. $6.95.

K-2 While less subtle and more slapstick than Steig's earlier books, this has some of the same quality of nonsensical situation combined with a bland writing style that assumes it is perfectly ordinary to have as a hired hand a talking ass that wears glasses. The story line comprises a series of minor calamities as Farmer Palmer, a pig, goes to market to sell his produce and buy gifts for his family, and then makes his star-crossed way home. This hasn't the narrative quality of Steig's stories about Sylvester, Roland, or Amos and Boris, but its fun, there's wit in the writing, and the illustrations are engaging.

1221 **Steig,** William. *The Real Thief;* story and pictures by William Steig. Farrar, 1973. 58p. $4.95.

4-5 Proud of his job as guard to the Royal Treasury, loyal to his king (Basil the bear) Gawain the goose is baffled by the repeated theft of gold and jewels from the massive building to which only Gawain and Basil have keys. He is heartsick when the king dismisses him publicly and calls him a disgrace to the kingdom. Sentenced to prison, the goose flies off to isolation. The true thief, a mouse, is penitent and decides that he will go on stealing so that the king will know Gawain is innocent; still suffering guilt, he takes back the loot piece by piece, searches for Gawain, and confesses. They decide to keep it secret, but Gawain goes back to accept royal apologies and greater status than before. The writing style is graceful and the structure of the story taut; although the plot is not strong, the sympathetic characters are appealing both in the text and in the engaging illustrations.

1222 **Steiner,** Jörg, ad. *The Bear Who Wanted to Be a Bear;* illus. by Jörg Müller. Atheneum, 1976. 76-29355. 31p. $7.95.

K-3 First published in Switzerland, this engaging reversal of the familiar theme of the creature who wants to be another sort of animal is nicely told and is illustrated with amusing, sophisticated color pictures in pencil and airbrush. A bear wakes from his winter sleep to find that a factory has been built over his den; when he appears and insists he is a bear, not a man, he is scoffed at. Other bears will corroborate his claim, he says—but the zoo bears reject him (bears don't sit in the audience, they dance), so the bewildered, docile bear dons work clothes and joins a button-pushing crew. Time passes, autumn comes, the bear is sleepy; he is fired for laziness. Turned down by a motel proprietor who says that bears cannot be accommodated, the bear is satisfied to find, at last, someone who acknowledges that he's a bear. He goes off into the snowy forest, and there is a den. Last picture: a heap of clothes outside the den, and paw prints leading to it. The illustrations are handsome, especially one of the snow scenes with a harsh, acrylic blue neon sign, "Motel," and the story has a message about conformity that's a bonus for the child who sees it but that does not lessen the appeal or cohesion of the book for the child who misses it.

1223 **Sterling,** Dorothy, ed. *Speak Out in Thunder Tones; Letters and Other Writings by Black Northerners, 1787–1865.* Doubleday, 1973. 396p. illus. $5.95.

7- The first of three volumes, this impressive book is based on newspaper accounts, correspondence, essays, and diaries; much of the material has not been previously published, and all of the excerpts are linked by explanatory notes. The book gives a vivid picture of black history, particularly of the back-to-Africa movement of the late eighteenth century, of the participation of black people in the North in social movements, and of the courage and tenacity of men and women who fought for their country, their brothers, and their own integrity. A fascinating book, a rich resource. An extensive index is appended.

1224 **Sterling,** Dorothy, ed. *The Trouble They Seen; Black People Tell the Story of Reconstruction*. Doubleday, 1976. 75-19218. 491p. illus. $7.95.

8- While there have been several books that used source material in black history (Julius Lester's *To Be a Slave,* Milton Meltzer's *In Their Own Words*) none has focused, as this does, on the years of Reconstruction, 1865–1877. It is a sequel to *Speak Out in Thunder Tones* which was a compilation of writings by black northerners in the years 1787–1865. This book is equally impressive, both as a research document and as a fresh view of an era that was tragic, turbulent, and exciting, for in the years after the Civil War there was at first a hope for an integrated society, a flowering of black culture, and an emergence of black leaders. But their enemies were stronger than their friends, and the freed black men and women of the Reconstruction were persecuted, their accomplishments expunged from the record. Much of Sterling's material is based on interviews by Congressional investigating committees; other sources are cited in an editorial foreword. An extensive relative index is appended.

1225 **Stevenson,** James. *"Could Be Worse!"* written and illus. by James Stevenson. Greenwillow, 1977. 76-28534. 29p. Trade ed. $6.95; Library ed. $5.94 net.

K-2 Two children comment on the fact that their grandfather, a quiet, harassed-looking gentleman, goes through the same routine every morning. Same food. Same reactions to any reports of trouble by the children: "Could be worse." But one day Grandpa fools them and tells a long, involved story of a dream-fantasy in which he went from one peril to another. "What do you think of that?" And the children gleefully shout, "COULD BE WORSE!" The tale is slight, but the switch from placidity to flagrant desperation should amuse readers, and the pictures of an elderly man in pajamas being attacked by an abominable snowman, chased across a desert by a blob of marmalade, being kicked into the clouds by an ostrich, et cetera, are delightfully comic.

1226 **Stevenson,** James. *The Sea View Hotel;* written and illus. by James Stevenson. Greenwillow, 1978. 78-2749. 42p. Trade ed. $6.95; Library ed. $6.67 net.

K-2 Back in the days of buggies and potted ferns, a family of three (animals, Edwardian vintage) go for a vacation. Hubert's parents sink happily into the plush gentility of the resort hotel, but Hubert is bored to death. He can't swim (annual invasion by stinging jellyfish) and he can't play (not another child there) and the other guests are annoyed by his noise. Then Hubert finds Alf, the handyman. Alf shows him natural wonders, skips stones with him, and reveals his hobby: a home-made flying machine. Comes a windy day and they take the machine out; lifted by a gust of wind, the machine—and Hubert—have a marvelous, dangerous, unplanned ride. So, when they leave, Hubert is already hoping that for their next vacation his parents will choose the Sea View Hotel. The story's told in cartoon strips, with humor and action in both text and pictures.

1227 **Stevenson,** James. *Wilfred the Rat.* Greenwillow, 1977. 77-1091. 30p. illus. Trade ed. $5.95; Library ed. $5.49 net.

K-2 A lonely wanderer, Wilfred finds two friends (Dwayne is a squirrel, Ruppert a chipmunk) in an amusement park that is closed. The three have a marvelously entertaining winter, but when Dwayne and Ruppert make their annual plans to leave for the summer, Wilfred can't resist the lure of carnival lights. He is caught between the owner (in a roller coaster car, going down) and his ferocious dog (on the roller coaster track, going up), jumps, lands in a pail of popcorn, and is offered a job by the owner: a nightly jump in return for all the cheese he can eat and stardom. But Wilfred has learned what's important in life: he turns down the offer and rejoins his two friends. Stevenson is one of the best cartoonists on the scene; his drawings are lively and funny and deft. The story is told in direct, unembellished style and, while the basic plot is not highly original, the setting and the denoument's drama make it a more palatable variant.

1228 **Stevenson,** Janet. *The School Segregation Cases; Brown v. Board of Education of Topeka and others); The United States Supreme Court Rules on Racially Separate Public Education.* Watts, 1973. 61p. illus. $3.95.

5-9 While many of the incidents described here have been included in books about the struggle for equality by black people or in studies of civil rights, this draws together the several aspects of the fight for integrated schools and fair educational opportunities for black students in a cohesive and coherent survey. It begins with the student-inspired strike in a black school in Virginia, a strike for adequate facilities rather than for integration, and covers other major cases through to the momentous Supreme Court decisions of 1954 and 1955. Stevenson concludes with a dispassionate assessment of the failure of the hopes for implementation of the rulings that were meant to establish equal and integrated opportunity "with all deliberate speed." Straightforward, objective, and well-researched, a useful and well-written book. A bibliography of sources and an index are appended.

1229 **Stewart,** A. C. *Ossian House.* Phillips, 1976. 76-9645. 179p. $7.95.

6-8 Used to London life, eleven-year-old John Murray is burdened by the knowledge that his paternal grandfather is bequeathing their ancestral home in Scotland to him. John has little interest in country life, and his widowed mother is appalled to learn, when the will is read, that John cannot sell the property until he comes of age, and that he must spend eight weeks of each year at Ossian House. Most of the story is concerned with John's growing interest in family history, his bickering with two young Murray cousins, and his increasing appreciation of the people, the land, and the beasts of his heritage. The setting is vividly drawn, the Scots dialect written with a true ear for cadence as well as language, and the gradual change in John believably developed. The ploys and problems of the cousins give opportunity for enough action to balance the material about setting and historical background.

1230 **Stewig,** John Warren. *Sending Messages;* illus. with photographs by Richard D. Bradley. Houghton, 1978. 77-26110. 64p. $6.95.

2-4 A noted educator's succinct text is combined with photographs to suggest to children the many ways in which people communicate. Two or three lines of text are centered on each verso page; facing pages carry sets of pictures or diagrams. In addition to speaking, writing, and body language, Stewing points out that there is a language of dance or mime, that there are notation systems for communicating instructions for performers of music or dance, that there are hand-sign languages, Morse code, Braille, chemical symbols, and so on. Although much of the material is available in other books for children, none has as varied a range of media of communication.

1231 **Stolz,** Mary Slattery. *Cat in the Mirror.* Harper, 1975. 75-6307. 199p. Trade ed. $6.50; Library ed. $5.79.

5-8 Although Erin's unhappiness stems from other causes, she escapes, like Zan in Mazer's *Saturday, the Twelfth of October,* at a moment of stress to another point in time, and she returns to the world of today with clear memories of her other life and her other self. Unlike Zan, who remains herself in a prehistoric world, Erin becomes Irun, a girl in a wealthy household of ancient Egypt, and all of the major figures in her real life are duplicated in the Egyptian sequence, even her cat. Erin's greatest problem is her mother, who usually nags, ignores, or belittles her; her comfort comes from her father and from the housekeeper, Flora. She has no friends, although a new classmate, an Egyptian boy named Seti, has been friendly. Her crisis comes when she overhears a group of classmates talk of her with contempt during a museum visit. Because of her acquaintance with Seti and her father's shared interest in Egyptology, the long episode in ancient Egypt (in which Erin, as Irun, has disturbing memories of her real life) there is logic within the fantasy. Like Mazer's Zan, Erin comes back to find only a few hours have passed—but when she has recovered and sees Seti (the only person who is in both sequences under the same name) he greets her softly, "Hello, how are you, Irun?" A strong ending for a book that deals deftly with the twin-image and time-shift devices and that depicts with percipience and honesty the mother-daughter relationship and the pecking order within the peer group.

1232 **Stolz,** Mary Slattery. *The Edge of Next Year.* Harper, 1974. 195p. Trade ed. $6.95; Library ed. $6.11 net.

5-8 The Woodwards were a happy family. Orin was fourteen and Victor ten the October day the car skidded after avoiding a driver in the wrong lane, the day that their mother was killed. And after that, their father slowly, steadily immersed himself in drinking until he knew that he might lose his job, knew that he must get help. The story ends on a realistically hopeful note, but for all three Woodwards it has been a slow painful, adjustment—not only to bereavement but to the ways in which each of them reacted. It demands the skill of a writer like Mary Stolz to write a story so honest and perceptive that the nuances of shifting relationships and the conflicts between love and resentment are solid and believable enough to compensate for the lack of action—no lack is felt.

1233 **Storey,** Margaret. *Ask Me No Questions.* Dutton, 1975. 74-23926. 142p. $5.95.

5-7 A kidnapping story first published in England under the title *Keep Running* is economically structured and remarkably well sustained. Imogen wakes to find herself captive and sedated, guarded by a nurse and a terse, abrupt man called Keen. When she manages to get to a telephone and call the police, Keen takes her off to another place, and from then on they are on the run. Imogen is convinced that the kidnapping has been engineered by a man who is using her safety as a threat against her father; this aspect of industrial espionage is not fully developed, but it is not intended as the major facet of the story, which is the relationship between Imogen and Keen. Despite his role and his occasional cruelty, she has become fond of him and feels enough loyalty to try to protect him when she is rescued. The characterization is adequate, the dialogue excellent, and the story has good pace and suspense.

1234 **Storr,** Catherine. *The Chinese Egg.* McGraw-Hill, 1975. 75-11575. 302p. Trade ed. $6.95; Library ed. $6.84 net.

7- Because of its length and the density of small and rather light type face, this may intimidate younger readers, but once into the story they may well be captured by the book. Set in London, where it was first published, the story has a taut, suspense-filled kidnapping; it is seen from the viewpoints of the kidnappers, the distraught parents, the police, and three children who have a special interest. The facets are smoothly meshed; the children are Stephen, Vicky, and Chris. Stephen has bought a wooden puzzle-egg; Vicky has found a lost piece of the egg; together they have precognitive flashes that enable them to see aspects of the kidnapping. They are not believed at first, but soon convince the police superintendent that their visions are genuine and are asked to help in the search. These aspects are nicely balanced by home problems, with sharply etched characterization, especially in the character of Stephen's father, a garrulous and rather obtuse psychologist.

1235 **Streatfeild,** Noel. *When the Sirens Wailed;* illus. by Judith Gwyn Brown. Random House, 1976. 75-38326. 176p. Trade ed. $5.95; Library ed. $6.99 net.

4-6 First published in England as *When the Siren Wailed,* this is the story of a Cockney family separated during the London Blitz. Dad serves in the Navy, Mum gets a factory job, and the three Clark children are evacuated and are billeted with elderly Colonel Stranger and his housekeeper in a Dorset town. The children adapt well to the new and more rigorously disciplined way of life, but when the Colonel dies, they rebel against their second sponsor and run off to London to find their mother. Mum, bombed out and in a hospital, is happy to see them but sends them back to the country; the story ends happily when Dad returns, wounded, and they all are reunited and settle in a cottage left by the Colonel. Some of the terminology will be unfamiliar to readers (the wartime trains "is something chronic," a woman complains) but can usually be understood because of the context. Streatfeild's style is lively and her descriptions colorful; the characters are well-drawn and the dialogue is excellent. While the problems and fortunes of the children should engage readers, it is the atmosphere of wartime England—both in London and in the country—that gives the book its strength.

1236 **Streatfeild,** Noel. *A Young Person's Guide to Ballet;* drawings by Georgette Bordier. Warne, 1975. 74-81666. 123p. $7.95.

4-7 This most interesting book has enough variety and action for the general reader and a wealth of detail for the confirmed balletomane, with photographs of great dancers in stellar roles and diagrams of ballet positions and exercises. The story of two children, Anna and Peter, who enter ballet classes, covers three years of training and is nicely carried off as a frame for ballet history (given, logically, by the teacher as part of the children's schooling) and discussions of the rigorous details of ballet basics and practice sessions.

1237 **Suhl,** Yuri. *The Merrymaker;* illus. by Thomas di Grazia. Four Winds, 1975. 45p. $5.95.

4-6 The place and time are not specified, but this story of a poor Jewish family is set in a European village early in the 20th century. Ten-year-old Shloimeh knows that there is little food at home even for the three of them, but he is so enchanted by the rhyming speech of the stranger visiting the synagogue that he points him out to Papa. Having heard his parents argue about whether or not they could afford hospitality, Shloimeh knows that Mother may not welcome a guest. But the stranger proves to be grateful and appreciative, he enthralls the family by examples of his art, for he is a merrymaker, a badchen who entertains the guests at weddings by impromptu rhyming. And Mother finds that her hospitality is more than repaid. The illustrations have a soft warmth that echoes the mood of the story, which is told with graceful simplicity and gives a vivid picture of family life and the Jewish community life of Mitteleuropa.

1238 **Suhl,** Yuri. *On the Other Side of the Gate*. Watts, 1975. 74-13452. 149p. $5.95.

7-9 Based on a true episode, this story is a young Jewish couple's successful plan to smuggle their infant son out of the Warsaw ghetto is both a tale of danger and courage and a grim picture of the plight of Polish Jews during the German occupation of World War II. Starving and stifled in their barbed wire compound, Warsaw Jews were being sent off to labor details and concentration camps. Hershel and Lena risk their lives to save their child's by asking a Polish Catholic acquaintance to "find" him on their doorstep and adopt him. The dangers are shared by the Polish friends and their family, and the story shows the range of attitudes among Poles from anti-Semitism to defiant compassion. Suhl creates the atmosphere with caustic conviction and constructs the plot and the characters with solidity.

1239 **Suhl,** Yuri. *Uncle Misha's Partisans.* Four Winds, 1973. 211p. Trade ed. $5.75; Library ed. $5.92 net.

5-8 A World War II story, set in the Ukraine, describes the activities of a colony of Jewish partisans who live in a forest. Motele is twelve, and he comes to Uncle Misha—as have so many others—because the Nazis have killed all his family. He knows that his violin playing is welcomed by the forest dwellers, but Motele yearns to go out on a real mission. Since he is one of the few who can speak Ukrainian without a ghetto accent, he uses his Ukrainian name, Mitek, and poses as a peasant boy; established as a German Headquarters musician, he is used as the inside man in a successful plot to blow up the building. Good period details and a convincing plot are the basis for a story that is exciting in its action and moving in the picture the book gives of the bereft but dauntless partisans.

1240 **Sullivan,** George. *Better Softball for Boys and Girls.* Dodd, 1975. 74-25507. 64p. illus. $4.50.

4-9 A model of its type, *Better Softball* explains the game clearly and fully, giving advice on each kind of play (sliding, pitching, bunting, etc.) and on playing each position; it describes the strategy in defensive teamwork, and it gives comprehensive information about clothing, equipment, and the softball diamond. The book is profusely illustrated with action photographs of boys and girls, and has precise diagrams of diamond distances, permitted arc of the pitch, and so on. Instructions for coaching and a brief glossary are included.

1241 **Sullivan,** George. *Queens of the Court;* illus. with photographs. Dodd, 1974. 111p. $4.95.

6-10 After an introduction that describes the recent changes in women's tennis (prize money, publicity, status, attendance) Sullivan goes on to the "queens," Court, King, Evert, Goolagong, Casals, and Wade. The biographical sketches focus on each player's career and include highlights of major matches, but they also give quite vivid impressions of the personalities of the players. The writing style is brisk, informal, and smooth, and the book concludes with a backward look at some of the important women tennis players of the past. Action photographs are included; a list of each woman's championship record follows her biography; an explanation of scoring terms, a glossary, and an index are appended.

1242 **Sullivan,** George. *This Is Pro Hockey;* illus. with photographs and diagrams. Dodd, 1976. 75-38369. 120p. $4.95.

5-
*
This is the best all-around book on ice hockey we've seen. Sullivan, a veteran sports writer, has a lucid style, clear explanations, logical arrangement of material, and fully detailed coverage. A brief history of the game precedes a description of how it is played; the text includes discussion of team play, of positional play, of each of the basic skills (skating, shooting, stickhandling, passing, and checking) and of uniforms and equipment. Included also are descriptions of some of hockey's stars and what their special abilities are, rules of the game, trophies, strategy, and all-time records. The diagrams are clear, the action photographs interesting; a glossary and an index are appended.

1243 **Sutcliff,** Rosemary. *Blood Feud.* Dutton, 1977. 76-58502. 147p. $6.95.

7-9 Jestyn the Englishman begins his tale when he is old, remembering his youth as a captive sold in slavery to a Viking not much older than he. When his master Thormod is ready to leave Dublin, then a Viking stronghold, he gives Jestyn his freedom. Swearing blood brotherhood, Jestyn takes as his own the feud between Thormod and the Herulfson brothers, a feud suspended while they all travel to Constantinople and serve the Emperor Basil, joining the Varangian Guard. After Thormod's death, Jestyn is obligated to kill Anders Herulfson, but by then he has become a man of medicine—and he cannot kill. The small print of the book and the frequent lengthy passages of solid print may look forbidding, but Sutcliff's grasp of history, sustained by unobtrusive research, gives a vivid picture of the period; the dialogue is convincing; the tale has sweep and action that is modulated and offset by periods of quiet.

1244 **Sutcliff,** Rosemary. *The Capricorn Bracelet;* illus. by Richard Cuffari. Walck, 1973. 149p. $5.95.

6-9 The story begins in 61 A.D. when Roman-ruled Londinium is ravaged by the savage Queen Boudicca; young Lucius Calpurnius escapes and goes on to join the Legion and win an award, the Capricorn bracelet. In six episodes that span three centuries, the bracelet passes on to other members of the family who serve Rome in Britain. The stories are exciting in themselves, and they give a vivid picture of the years of Roman occupation and of the gradual merging of the native peoples and the Legionnaires. The vigor and authenticity of the book are yet another testament to Sutcliff's supremacy in the field of historical fiction. An annotated chronology, divided by chapters, is included.

1245 **Sutherland,** Margaret. *Hello I'm Karen;* illus. by Jane Paton. Coward, 1976. 75-25614. 93p. $4.95.

2-3 Each chapter in a book about a small New Zealand child is a brief story, so that the book is excellent for reading aloud in installments as well as for independent readers in grades two and three. Karen's activities are small, familiar ones: playing with a friend, speaking on the telephone, going on an errand, et cetera. There are a few unfamiliar terms ("gumboots") but not so many as to make the book difficult for children in America to understand. Hemi, Karen's friend, is a Maori, and this is discussed very casually and realistically by the two children. There is an occasional note of didacticism, but the book has a pleasantly affectionate tone, the episodes are brief, and added to the appeal of everyday activities is the recurrence of a closing line to each chapter: "And she did."

1246 **Swinburne,** Irene. *Behind the Sealed Door; The Discovery of the Tomb and Treasures of Tutankhamun;* by Irene and Laurence Swinburne; published in cooperation with the Metropolitan Museum of Art. Sniffen Court/Atheneum, 1977. 77-88476. 96p. illus. $12.95.

4-7 Oversize pages afford opportunity for stunning photographs of King Tut's tomb and the treasures it held; many of the pictures are full-page, and many are in color. The text is simply and sequentially written, describing Howard Carter's efforts to discover a tomb that had not been robbed, the careful methods he used when his last venture proved successful, and the objects he found. The text gives a good idea of the procedures archeologists use and of the beliefs and practices of the ancient Egyptians. Photographs are well placed and adequately captioned; although there are minor flaws (some misspellings like "sentinal" and a very abrupt ending) the authors have, on the whole, done a creditable job in describing for the middle grades reader one of the most frequently recorded events in archeological history. Transparent overlays, slipped into the back of the book, show the layers of coffins and the mummified remains.

1247 **Switzer,** Ellen. *How Democracy Failed;* illus. with photographs. Atheneum, 1975. 74-19461. 176p. $7.50.

8- The author, whose father decided to leave Berlin because of the ominous progress of Hitler's domination, became an American citizen; she had left as a teenager, and she went back as a reporter, in 1972 and 1973, to interview those who had been in her age group and had lived in the "Thousand Year" Third Reich. The text is based in large part on interviews, and its purpose is to show

how such a political philosophy affected ordinary people, to examine not only how democracy failed but why it failed. Switzer is objective in analysis, candid in describing the many men and women who, as adolescents, had gloried in and glorified the Hitler regime, vivid in evoking the atmosphere and events that paved the way for Hitler's success: the wild inflation, the bitterness of defeat in the first world war, the reverence for authority, particularly military authority. The writing style is brisk, the material well-organized, and the inclusion of many case histories gives color and variety to a provocative study. An index is appended; a list of important dates (from Hitler's birth to the German surrender in 1945) precedes the text.

1248 **Synge,** Ursula, ad. *Land of Heroes; A Retelling of the Kalevala.* Atheneum, 1978. 77-14489. 222p. $6.95.

7- A splendid retelling of the great Finnish epic, unfortunately printed in very small type, draws the separate tales together into a smooth whole, much as Evslin did for Greek myths in *Greeks Bearing Gifts.* The adventures of the three magician-heroes, Ilmarinen, Leminkainen, and Vainamoinen, are told in a style that makes them more comprehensible to today's readers yet preserves the sweep and grandeur of the genre.

1249 **Syme,** Ronald. *Verrazano; Explorer of the Atlantic Coast;* illus. by William Stobbs. Morrow, 1973. 95p. Trade ed. $3.95; Library ed. $3.78 net.

4-6 A good biography of the Florentine explorer who sailed up the coast of North America searching for a passage to the Pacific in 1524. Sent by the French king, Verrazano was hunting a trade route; his hopes, based on erroneous information about the continent, were not fulfilled, but he did find New York Bay and was treated with great courtesy by the Indians of the region. With records lost, Verrazano's voyages were not acknowledged until the end of the nineteenth century, when an Italian scholar discovered the explorer's manuscript in a private library. Like all of Syme's books, this account of the man for whom the Verrazano bridge is named is lucidly written in a direct, brisk style and is based on careful research. A bibliography is appended.

1250 **Takashima,** Shizuye. *A Child in Prison Camp.* Morrow, 1974. 63p. illus. $6.95.

5- First published in Canada in 1971, the record of a Japanese-Canadian family's internment is based on the author-artist's own experience although (as she explains in an appended note) she has changed some of the details. Sent to a relocation camp from their home in Vancouver, the Takashima family had three years of privation; only after protest from the camp residents were such amenities as running water and electricity added. Takashima writes from the viewpoint of the child she was in 1941, a child who tried to understand the injustice of her lot, who enjoyed the small pleasures she had, who worried about the bitterness of those who—like her father—wanted to return to Japan. A postscript, written in 1964, describes the family in Toronto, reunited; a section of delicate, colorful watercolor pictures is bound in.

1251 **Tapio,** Pat Decker. *The Lady Who Saw the Good Side of Everything;* illus. by Paul Galdone. Seabury, 1975. 75-4610. 30p. $6.95.

K-2 Always cheerful, the little old lady is pleased, after her house washes away in a flood of rain (she needed a new house anyway) to drift to sea in a log (she'd always wanted to see the ocean) and pleased at how peaceful the trip is (behind her back, a shark's gaping jaw) and delighted by arriving in China. She's even pleased when it rains, because it's good for the rice. The story has a merry inanity—but who worries about days without food in a tall tale? Galdone picks up the story greatly: the lady clings to her umbrella throughout, wears her pancake hat imperturbably, changing only in the last picture for a coolie hat, and the cat that travels along is used for contrast—woebegone when his mistress is cheerful, terrified when she ignores the shark. Lightweight, but amusing.

1252 **Tate,** Joan. *Ben and Annie;* by Judith Gwyn Brown. Doubleday, 1974. 79p. $3.95.

4-6 A short and poignant story from England is given immediacy by the use of present tense; the writing style is direct, somehow ingenuous, which is suitable for the quality of the relationship that is the dominant aspect of the book. Ben is eleven, friend and protector of a frail girl of thirteen who lives downstairs in an old house. He takes Annie, confined to a wheelchair, to the store; he plays checkers with her, he talks to her on an intercom his father has installed. Trying to give the invalid more pleasure, Ben takes her out to watch him and his friends play. Annie is so excited by Ben's and his friend's hillsliding that they race her downhill, too; she is screaming with excitement and pleasure when a bystander, misinterpreting what he sees, thinks Annie is frightened. He reports to Annie's parents, who are alarmed and angry, forbid Ben ever to talk to Annie again, and remove the intercom. The story ends with Ben sobbing in frustrated rage, knowing that no adults will ever understand what it meant to Annie to feel the rush of wind past her face, to feel a measure of freedom, to share a joy with friends. The end is shocking in a dramatic sense, but realistic; the book seems unsubstantial, a slow building of a mood and a relationship, and a quick, cruel shattering—a scene rather than a play, a short story that could have been, but wasn't, quite fleshed out enough to be a full book.

1253 **Tate,** Joan. *Wild Boy;* illus. by Susan Jeschke. Harper, 1973. 100p. Trade ed. $4.50; Library ed. $4.43 net.

5-7 In a gracefully written story set in Yorkshire, the author writes with conviction and simplicity a story of the friendship between two boys, both solitary people. But they are very different; Will is an only child of quiet, understanding parents and he is quite happy rambling alone on the familiar, loved moors, while Mart is a hostile runaway from foster homes and urban loneliness. Mart's improvised shelter on the moors serves adequately until he becomes ill, and then Will takes him home. Patiently and gently, Will's parents win the wild boy's trust, and although Mart decides to go back to London, it is clear that he has found a family to love and a home to which he can return.

1254 **Taylor,** Mildred D. *Roll of Thunder, Hear My Cry;* illus. by Jerry Pinkney. Dial, 1976. 76-2287. 237p. $7.95.

7-9 The family of *Song of the Trees* is described more fully in this
* story for older readers, set in Mississippi during the Depression Era. Since he can earn more money for his family by doing railroad work, Papa is away from the farm; Mama teaches school, and most of the chores fall on Cassie and the other Logan children. Two strong themes run through the story: the bitter indignity of suffering persecution and condescension, for the Logans and other black families, at the hands of white people; and the almost equally bitter struggle against the financial strictures of the period. The story has strong characterization and relationships, good pace and dialogue, and trenchant depiction of a time and place—but its greater strength is in depth of the author's compassionate understanding of one family's price and love for each other and for the land they own.

1255 **Taylor,** Theodore. *Battle in the Arctic Seas; The Story of Convoy PQ 17;* illus. by Robert Andrew Parker. T. Y. Crowell, 1976. 75-33655. 151p. $6.95.

7- An engrossing account of a naval disaster of World War II is based
* on careful research and told with a high sense of drama, its somber events given relief by the diary excerpts of one young officer. The United States, Russia, and Great Britain were joined in a massive effort to deliver much-needed supplies to Russia; the convoy sailed from Iceland with seven million dollars' worth of cargo on a motley collection of ships protected by escort vessels. Some of the

chapters are based on German source materials, so that the reader can see the plotting and counterplotting as each of the combatants tries to outdo the other in gathering intelligence and predicting next moves. The key is the Allied fear of the Nazis' great ship the *Tirpitz* which evokes two commands from British officers: one from the First Sea Lord to instruct the convoy to disperse and scatter, the second from Commander Broome to attach his protective force of destroyers to the assisting cruisers rather than to the cargo ships. For the latter, this was a disaster: a quarter of the cargo delivered, twenty-three ships lost. A bibliography and an index are appended.

1256 **Taylor,** Theodore. *The Odyssey of Ben O'Neal;* illus. by Richard Cuffari. Doubleday, 1977. 76-23800. 208p. $5.95.

6-8 In a sequel to *Teetoncey* and *Teetoncey and Ben O'Neal,* the now-orphaned Ben decides he will leave Cape Hatteras and go to Norfolk to join a ship's crew. He has said farewell to Teetoncey (Tee has gone back to England—he thinks) and hopes to catch up, somewhere, with his brother Reuben, who is already at sea and doesn't know of their mother's death. But Ben has underestimated Tee, who shows up on his ship, having told the captain that she is returning to her home in Barbados. Again pursued by the authorities, Tee (who has won the heart of every crew member) is smuggled onto another ship—and both young people do get to England. The background for this plot is a colorful setting of shipboard life at the turn of the century, with a broad and lively assortment of characters. Plenty of action, some humor, and a brief postlude in which, in 1914, Ben explains what happened later; he and Tee are married and are back in North Carolina.

1257 **Taylor,** Theodore. *Teetoncey;* illus. by Richard Cuffair. Doubleday, 1974. 153p. $4.50.

6-8 The first of a trilogy, *Teetoncey* is set in 1898, in a maritime community on the Outer Banks of North Carolina where the residents still use colorful words that stem from their Devonshire ancesters. Eleven-year-old Ben, whose widowed mother hates the sea that took her husband and an older son, is detailed to bring home the one survivor of the shipwreck, a frail girl who emerges from shock as mute and inert as a catatonic. "Teetoncey," they dub her, meaning a small thing, and Ben's mother clings to the belief that she can be helped. Alternately compassionate and irritated, Ben is startled when his mother suggests that he take Teetoncey down to the shore during a storm, that perhaps it will jar her into memory and speech. It does, and there the book ends. The atmosphere and local color are vivid, the characterization sturdy if not deep, and the author's craft evident in the drama and suspense built into a story in which, after the first scene, there is so little action.

1258 **Taylor,** Theodore. *Teetoncey and Ben O'Neal;* illus. by Richard Cuffari. Doubleday, 1975. 74-4875. 185p. $5.95.

6-8 The second volume of a planned trilogy, this is a sequel to *Teetoncy,* the story of a survivor of a shipwreck. The young girl who, stunned, has lost her memory is called "Teetoncey" (small thing) by Ben O'Neal and his mother, who give her shelter and affection; that her real name is Wendy is learned at the very end of the book, when she retains her faculties. Now Wendy is trying to evade the British consul and to help Ben and his friend find the treasure she knows was aboard her father's vessel. This has as much suspense as the first book, much more action, and an effective evocation of time (1898) and place (the Outer Banks of North Carolina). There is a developing affection growing between Teetoncey and Ben, a surprising conclusion to the hunt for treasure, and a hint—as Teetoncey sails for her home in England and Ben goes off to sea—that the two may meet again.

1259 **Terlouw,** Jan. *How to Become King.* Hastings House, 1977. 77-12471. 128p. $5.95.

4-7
* Orphaned Stark had been born, seventeen years earlier, on the night the beloved king of Katoren died; Stark's doting uncle, the palace butler, dreamed that his dear Stark would become the new king. Cheerful, intelligent, and self-confident, Stark offered himself to the ministers who had ruled the land for seventeen years, and to appease the public they set the lad seven impossible tasks. Ho-hum quest story? Not a bit. Terlouw uses wit and satire, he has a vigorous style, his seven tasks are conceived and solved with high originality, and his hero looms engagingly just as large as life, in a book that won prizes as the best book of the year in Holland and in Austria.

1260 **Terlouw,** Jan. *Winter in Wartime.* McGraw-Hill, 1976. 75-41345. 197p. $5.72.

6-9 Set in the Netherlands during World War II, this is the story of sixteen-year-old Michiel, who takes over the care of a wounded British flyer when the friend who has hidden him is picked up by the Nazis. Michiel learns two hard lessons: the resistance worker must operate alone, sharing neither his problems nor his triumphs; one must forgive an act that has just cause. For it develops that the friend and the flyer had killed the German soldier for whose death Michiel's father was shot in reprisal. As taut as it is tragic, the story is a trenchant indictment of war and a convincing argument that war has no winners. Published originally under the title *Oorlogswinter,* the book was named the Best Dutch Juvenile for 1973.

1261 **Terris,** Susan. *Whirling Rainbows.* Doubleday, 1974. 153p. $4.50.

5-7 "I don't suppose you've ever met a fat, blue-eyed Jewish Indian. Well, now you have," Leah Friedman begins. Leah had a Polish father and a Chippewa mother and had been adopted by the Friedmans in her infancy. Leah and her adoptive parents had happily done crossword puzzles and gone hiking, played chess and collected stamps, celebrated Jewish holidays and argued about whose turn it was to mop the kitchen floor. But when Leah was sent to a Wisconsin camp with her cousin Torie she decided this was just the time to find herself, to know her Indian heritage. She finds that Torie is malicious, that an Indian member of the camp staff feels that Leah is working too hard at being Indian, that she is herself—with her Chippewa heritage a part, but only a part—and that she can accept it naturally just as she has accepted being Jewish. This is the dominant theme of the book but Leah's problems and achievements as a camper, her disillusionment about the popular Torie, her affection for a younger camper, all add variety and balance to a capably written story which is unfortunately printed in eye-strainingly small type.

1262 **Terry,** Walter. *Frontiers of Dance; The Life of Martha Graham;* illus. with photographs. T. Y. Crowell, 1975. 75-9871. 177p. $5.95.

6- An eminent dance critic writes with knowledgeable affection
* about an old and dear friend, yet he writes with an objectivity that is as impressive as is his candor. Martha Graham's relationship with Ruth St. Denis and Ted Shawn, who were her first teachers, was a stormy one; Terry is quite objective about Graham's rupture of the relationship: "She was proud, determined, very touchy (her temper grew with her skills) and determined to do exactly what she wanted. Heaven help whoever got in her way." The book not only draws a remarkably vivid picture of Graham as a person and as a dancer, but it gives an authoritative assessment of her repertoire and of the development of contemporary dance. A bibliography and an index are appended; many photographs are included.

1263 **Thaler,** Michael C. *Madge's Magic Show;* illus. by Carol Nicklaus. Watts, 1978. 77-17288. 27p. (Easy-Read Books) $3.95.

1-2 Cartoon style illustrations are repetitive but amusing, taking advantage of a good gag situation. When Madge puts on a magic show for other neighborhood children, she has an enthralled audience save for Jimmy Smith, who heckles from his position at the fence. He is especially caustic when Madge says she's going to pull a rabbit out of her hat, jeering at each unsuccessful try, impressed only when—finally—a rabbit emerges. The joke is (for the reader) that Jimmy is unimpressed and Madge embarrassed by the rabbit's predecessors: a chicken, a goat, a turkey, and a horse. Lightweight but not pretending to do more than amuse, this should prove a pleasant addition to books for beginning independent readers.

1264 **Thiele,** Colin. *February Dragon.* Harper, 1976. 176p. Trade ed. $5.95; Library ed. $5.79 net.

5-7 In the hot, dry summer of Australia, there is always the danger of a bush fire, the "dragon" of February. There's no softening of the blow here, as the Pine family and their neighbors lose their farm crops, their home, and most of their pets after a fire due to one careless picnicker who never realizes her role. In fact, the arrogant Aunt Hester who is culpable is also the first to offer a home to the Pines and their three children, Resin, Turps, and Columbine. Hester's attitude toward animals and rural life is one thread, the threat of fire another, and the courtship between two teachers a third, in a story that is episodic rather than sequential. The Pines go to a fair, Turps gets a pony for her birthday, Resin and a friend are caught smoking, the Christmas dinner is enlivened when Aunt Hester is nipped by a crab, and so on. This is not as cohesive as Thiele's earlier books, but it gives a good picture of family and community life in the Australian countryside, it has variety and action in the episodes, a vigorous style of writing, and good dialogue, with enough idiom to flavor but not burden the conversations.

1265 **Thiele,** Colin. *Fight Against Albatross Two*. Harper, 1976. 75-37104. 243p. Trade ed. $5.95; Library ed. $5.79 net.

6-8 When an offshore oil rig begins operating near a village on Australia's south coast, the young people are curious and excited, but their elders foresee problems for their fishing industry. Link, fourteen, takes a temporary job on the rig Albatross Two, and he's aboard when it blows out and must be abandoned. The townspeople, already angry, are appalled by the damage done to fish and birds by the resultant oil spill. At great expense the rig is towed away. Link's younger sister, who has been working hard to save the local birds, is relieved, but the director of the salvage operation predicts sadly that more rigs will come, now that it is known that oil and gas are there. Man, he fears, will destroy himself, The characters are varied and convincing, the conflict between two concepts of the public good presented quite objectively, and the setting and pace of the story provide color and excitement.

1266 **Thiele,** Colin. *Fire in the Stone*. Harper, 1974. 305p. Trade ed. $6.95; Library ed. $6.79 net.

6-9 A story that has elements of suspense and romantic adventure is set in the Australian opal fields. Living alone with his shiftless father, Ernie Ryan hides gems he finds when he has a lucky strike; he is stunned with dismay when he finds his cache gone. Willie Winowie, an Aboriginal friend, helps Ernie track down the thief in an exciting and dangerous hunt in which the boys are trapped in a mine. Ernie escapes, and later discovers that Willie has been taken to an Adelaide hospital and is in a coma. Heartsick, tired of the greed and deceit of the opal hunters, Ernie packs his belongings and sets off for Adelaide. He does not know that Willie has died. Thiele creates the setting with harsh realism, constructs his tale deftly, and creates believable characters in a fast-paced story that is just as evocative as Mavis Clark's *Spark of Opal*, which also includes friendship with Aborigines, and which has the same setting.

1267 **Thiele,** Colin. *The Hammerhead Light*. Harper, 1977. 76-24311. 128p. Trade ed. $6.95; Library ed. $6.49 net.

5-7 Thiele is adept at creating a convincing, dramatic setting for his stories of Australia; here the characters move against a background of a small town intent on preserving the old, abandoned lighthouse that is on a spit of land dangerously battered by winter storms. Two of the most ardent defenders of the condemned lighthouse are twelve-year-old Tessa and her friend and mentor Alex Jorgenson, who is in his seventies and who shares with the child his love for, and knowledge of, all natural beauty—especially of the wild bird for whom he has carved a plastic leg. When his own shack blows down, Alex moves to the lighthouse; thus it happens that he and Tessa are able to operate the light and help guide Tessa's father home when there is a storm at sea. There's no pat ending: the lighthouse collapses and old Alex, much to Tessa's anguish, is sent from the hospital to a residential home. The structure is taut, the characterization percipient, but the two strong points of the story are the evocation of atmosphere and the deep friendship between the girl and the old man.

1268 **Thiele,** Colin. *The Shadow on the Hills*. Harper, 1978. 77-11829. 216p. Trade ed. $6.95; Library ed. $6.79 net.

6-9 This has, despite some incidents rife with action and drama, less story line than most of Thiele's fiction, but the lack of sustained plot is compensated for more than adequately by the vivid evocation of place—a small town in Australia—and of time—a depression year in which financial stress creates a tension that is a catalyst for dramatic events. Yet the chief appeal of the book is probably in the immediacy of a boy's involvement in the pattern of rural life, the mores of a German-Australian community, the humorous predicaments like being treed by a bull or the more serious ones like being an eye-witness to a crime committed by a miserly man who has had a long-standing feud with an old hermit who thunders Biblical quotations when he encounters anyone.

1269 **Thomson,** Peggy. *Museum People; Collectors and Keepers at the Smithsonian;* illus. by Joseph Low. Prentice-Hall, 1977. 77-3175. 305p. $8.95.

7- A behind-the-scenes view of the Smithsonian Institution is based on interviews with historians, exhibits people, technicians, curators, film-makers, collectors, and many others who collect, conserve, record, and mount the exhibits seen by the public. The book is divided into three sections: the places, the people, and the work, and includes a glossary, bibliography, and index. The author makes it clear in her preface that she is not attempting to give all the facts about the Smithsonian staff nor to give career guidance, but the book serves fairly well in both areas; the writing is informal, the material varied and interesting.

1270 **Thum,** Marcella. *Exploring Black America; A History and Guide.* Atheneum, 1975. 74-19428. 402p. illus. $10.95.

6- An unusual approach to black history in the United States functions as a guide to museums that specialize in that subject. A history of slavery gives background information, and subsequent chapters are on such subjects as the Underground Railroad, military heroes, pioneers and cowboys, et cetera, concluding with a discussion of the struggle for civil rights. Each chapter includes a list of museums and historic sites, descriptively annotated. The book is written in dignified style and with an objective tone, and is profusely illustrated, primarily by photographs. A subject index and a geographical index (by states) are appended to this most informative and interesting book.

1271 **Thurman,** Judith. *Flashlight and Other Poems;* illus. by Reina Rubel. Atheneum, 1976. 75-29442. 35p. $4.95.

3-5 Brisk little black and white drawings illustrate a collection of poems that focus on objects or activities or emotions that are familiar to most children. The fresh viewpoints, the illuminating phrases, and the insight into children's concerns make the book a fine addition to children's poetry collections.

1272 **Titiev,** Estelle, tr. *How the Moolah Was Taught a Lesson & Other Tales from Russia;* trans. and adapted by Estelle Tietiev and Lila Pargment; pictures by Ray Cruz. Dial, 1976. 75-9200. 53p. Trade ed. $5.95; Library ed. $5.47 net.

3-5 Four tales, each from a different part of the U.S.S.R., are smoothly retold and are illustrated by black and white pictures that have interesting small details yet bold composition, so that the eye focuses on the strong peasant faces. The stories carry the morals of their culture: be kind, faithful, and ingenious; they follow familiar folktale patterns, with "Chilbik and the Greedy Czar" a variant of "Molly Whuppie," even to the slaying of her own three daughters by a witch who has been tricked and the device of a bridge she cannot cross. Good for reading aloud or alone, this will be a welcome addition to the storyteller's sources.

1273 **Titus,** Eve. *Anatole in Italy;* illus. by Paul Galdone. McGraw-Hill, 1973. 32p. Trade ed. $4.95; Library ed. $4.72 net.

K-3 Every proper hero of an adventure story should be brave, cunning, and personable, loyal to his friends and lofty in his cultural standards. Especially if he's a mouse. Another tale of derring-do takes Anatole to Italy to discover why the friend of his employer is losing his cheese business. Anatole is a professional cheese-taster, but it takes the help of all the mice of Rome to outwit the fiendish rivals (named, of course, Borgia) who are engaged in sabotage. There are a few more spicy bits of sub-plot, but they are frosting on the cake. A light style, a good plot, humor in the situation, and totally engaging drawings keep up the standard of the several Tales of Anatole.

1274 **Titus,** Eve. *Basil in Mexico;* illus. by Paul Galdone. McGraw-Hill, 1976. 75-10827. 96p. Trade ed. $5.95; Library ed. $5.72 net.

3-5 Basil, the detecting mouse of Baker Street, is again called upon to solve a baffling mystery. Who has stolen the art treasure, recently acquired by a Mexican museum, and put a clever forgery in its place? And where is the real portrait, the true *Mousa Lisa?* Basil, who is accompanied by his faithful Dr. Dawson, not only solves the problem of the theft but also—with the help of seven young Mexican mice, the Pandero Street Irregulars—rescues Dawson when he is kidnapped. That is, mousenapped. Galdone's drawings are lively and funny, and the story is the usual Titus blend of mock Conan Doyle, tongue-in-cheek use of coincidence, plenty of action, and humor.

1275 **Tobias,** Tobi. *Arthur Mitchell;* illus. by Carole Byard. T. Y. Crowell, 1975. 74-13730. 33p. $4.50.

3-5 Arthur Mitchell had always wanted to be a dancer, but he had not considered ballet until one of the founders of the New York City

Ballet invited him (Mitchell had just graduated from the High School of Performing Arts) to study at the company's training school. Black ballet dancers were rare, but Mitchell was determined and dedicated, and his later success was a testament to his tenacity as well as to his ability. Known internationally as the director of the Dance Theatre of Harlem, Mitchell now devotes his time to helping and teaching young aspirants. The author prefaces this account with a description of Mitchell's childhood in Harlem; her writing is direct, objective, admiring but not adulatory.

1276 **Tobias,** Tobi. *How Your Mother and Father Met, and What Happened After*; illus. by Diane de Groat. McGraw-Hill, 1978. 78-7966. 38p. $6.95.

3-4 Written as if told by an elderly friend of the family, illustrated as if the pictures were in a family album, this is a rather sentimental but not mawkish story about the parents of Jimmy, to whom the book is addressed. Jeanie McLaren was nineteen when she met William Singer; he was older than she and dedicated to his medical career, but they fell in love. He went off to serve in the Korean War, and when he came back they were married. The book closes with pictures of Jimmy as a baby, as a graduate, as a bridegroom, and then there's a last picture: Jimmy Jr. Tobias handles the interreligious aspect with gentle candor and the pacific feelings of the young soldier (which increased when he, a man dedicated to saving lives, saw the carnage of the front lines) with directness and dignity. The book can help younger children to whom it may be read aloud understand concepts of family relationships and generations.

1277 **Tobias,** Tobi. *Isamu Noguchi: The Life of a Sculptor*. T. Y. Crowell, 1974. 46p. illus. $5.95.

4-6 A biography written in a grave, direct style is illustrated with many photographs of the sculptor's work, and a few of his studios. While the book has a subdued tone, it is candid about the unhappy aspects of Noguchi's life and makes a very strong statement about the isolation and dedication of the artist. Noguchi's mother, an American, moved to Japan when her son was two although his Japanese father had left them. Always conscious of being only half Japanese, the boy did not feel he belonged wholly to either culture. Sent to the States when he was eleven, Noguchi was displaced by the war and felt rejected by his mother; always he felt that he was alone, and in many of his sculptures there is a sense of isolation and strength. Much of the text describes Noguchi's years of study, of moving toward his own style, and of his techniques in working in different media. An interesting and unusual biography, this should be of special concern to readers who are students of any art form.

1278 **Tobias,** Tobi. *Petey;* illus. by Symeon Shimin. Putnam, 1978. 76-25515. 31p. $5.95.

2-4 Shimin's soft, realistic two-color paintings are a bit repetitive, but they reflect admirably the tender quality of a nicely-told story about the death of a pet. Emily describes her apprehension on finding her gerbil Petey unresponsive one afternoon; her father gently tells her that Petey is old for a gerbil, that he's had a happy life due to Emily's loving care, that the pet book states there is nothing that can be done. Petey dies and is buried; when offered new gerbils, Emily decides she isn't ready. Maybe later. Not unusual in structure, the book still is one of the better stories about accepting death, especially for the reader to whom it is a new experience.

1279 **Tolan,** Stephanie S. *Grandpa—and Me.* Scribner, 1978. 77-18254. 120p. $6.95.

5-7 In dated entries, eleven-year-old Kerry tells the story of her anguish as she realizes that her beloved grandfather is becoming senile. Grandpa had lived with them for many years, had been a companion and teacher to her and her brother, had helped make home a happier place. With working parents, Kerry knew that sending Grandpa away was a possibility, and she hid from them some of the evidence she'd had of Grandpa's senility. The more Kerry learns about Grandpa's past, the more she sympathizes, for he reverts at times to childhood and she sees what his childhood problems were. All the family are torn about making a decision, but it is Grandpa who, in a lucid period, takes matters into his own hands; having seen his own father become senile, Grandpa commits suicide in such a way that it looks like an accident. This is a realistic and sympathetic depiction of one pattern of old age, convincing save for Kerry's tenacity in hiding from her parents that she's seen Grandpa do such things as urinate outdoors, wear his pants inside-out, and mistake her for his dead sister. The writing style is smooth, the dialogue well-written.

1280 **Tolkien,** John Ronald Reuel. *The Father Christmas Letters.* Houghton, 1976. 44p. illus. $8.95.

3-5 J. R. R. Tolkien's children were, for twenty years, the fortunate recipients of an annual letter from Father Christmas, the British equivalent of Santa Claus. They even included envelopes with carefully simulated North Pole stamps, and they describe the tribulation of preparing for Christmas when your chief assistant is a bumbling polar bear. Tolkien's daughter-in-law has selected some of the letters and most of Tolkien's pictures; the stories can be read by independent readers, but they can also be used for reading aloud to younger children, and many of the author's adult or young adult fans will probably enjoy recitals of amusing woes. There are elves, snowmen, and goblins; as he grows older, Father Christmas, age 1936, has one of his elves write on his behalf. Inventive, amusing, and—because each letter can be read separately—excellent for installment reading.

1281 **Torre,** Frank D. *Woodworking for Kids.* Doubleday, 1978. 77-76264. 132p. Photographs. Trade ed. $6.95; Library ed. $7.90 net.

5-7 Principal of a technical high school, Torre devotes the first section of the book to a description of basic tools and an explanation of how to use them—and how not to use them. The rest of the book gives directions for making a series of projects. The step-by-step directions are illustrated by well-placed photographs that would be more helpful if they bore numbers or captions. The text is usually clear, although little guidance is provided for the final assembly in most projects; for example, "Assemble sides, shelves and brace, and fasten together . . ." An index is appended.

1282 **Townsend,** John Rowe, comp. *Modern Poetry;* photographs by Barbara Pfeffer. Lippincott, 1974. 224p. $5.95.

6- A diversified anthology of poetry chosen for its reflection of the concerns of the years of the 1940's through the 1960's (according to the jacket flap) has many poems that are timeless, like Randall Jarrell's "The Bat" or the poignant "Adrian Henri's Talking After Christmas Blues." There are some often-anthologized poems, like Henry Reed's "Naming of Parts," but not too many—and who would want "Naming of Parts" omitted? The arrangement is roughly in order of the years in which the poems were written, with author and first line indexes. This is an anthology of poems the editor enjoys rather than one of important poets, but by virtue of Townsend's discrimination this becomes an important anthology.

1283 **Townsend,** John Rowe. *Noah's Castle.* Lippincott, 1976. 75-30709. 256p. $6.95.

7-10
* In a compelling story of a realistic future, Townsend envisions a world in which food is so scarce that people commit acts of desperation in order to eat. Barry, who tells the story, is puzzled when his father buys a huge house and barricades it, refusing to admit visitors. He takes some food for a sick woman; his sister moves out. Father is adamant. His food is for his family. Barry sympathizes with a group called "Share Alike" who are opposed to hoarding, and he is torn between his sense of justice and loyalty to his father. The book ends with an exciting confrontation, having maintained pace throughout. Provocative and adroitly structured, it has strong characterization and insight.

1284 **Townsend,** John Rowe. *The Visitors.* Lippincott, 1977. 77-7197. 221p. $7.95.

6-9 Published in England under the title *The Xanadu Manuscript,* this is a tight-knit, smoothly written science fiction novel in which Townsend has deftly meshed realistic and fanciful elements. John, adolescent middle child of a Cambridge academic family, is perturbed by some strange newcomers to the city, the Wyatts and their daughter Katherine, who had suddenly appeared during a dizzy spell shared by John and his friend Alan. They are reserved people who claim to be ordinary tourists—yet they seem to find ordinary things (traffic, money) strange. They finally admit they are an investigative team from the future; since they have been detected, they are recalled. Katherine and John's older brother have fallen in love, however, and she insists she must stay in the present; when her parents point out that those from their time who have stayed have never lived long, being susceptible to 20th century illnesses, Katherine realizes she would bring only unhappiness, and she goes back to her own time. The transportation device is believable, the plot strong, the dialogue and characterization polished.

1285 **Travers,** Pamela L. *About the Sleeping Beauty;* illus. by Charles Keeping. McGraw-Hill, 1975. 75-12893. 111p. Trade ed. $7.95; Library ed. $7.71 net.

4-6 Travers has written her own version of the familiar tale, basing it on the Grimms' variant, which she considers the purest of the many versions of the story of the sleeper wakened by the magic of love. The story is followed by an essay—addressed to adults rather than children—on the theme of the sleeper in particular, although there is some general discussion of fairy tales. Following the essay are five other variants of the tale: "Dornroschen," "La Belle au Bois Dormant," "Sole, Luna, e Talia," "The Queen of Tubber Tintye," and "The Petrified Mansion," which are briefly discussed, with sources and chronology cited, in the essay. Few children will read the latter, and probably few will be interested in comparing variants, but the stories are classic, the illustrations handsome, and the essay a bonus for adult students of children's literature.

1286 **Tripp,** Wallace, illus. *A Great Big Ugly Man Came Up and Tied His Horse to Me; A Book of Nonsense Verse.* Little, 1973. 46p. $5.95.

2-4 Although the selections in this volume are neither unusual nor impressive by their numbers, the standard fare is given new vigor by the hilarious drawings. The cover picture, for example, has a surprised horse peering down at the very small animal (with a

"Don't blame *me*" look on his face) around whom the reins have just been wrapped. What Tripp achieves are pictures that are funny when taken at face value and that also entertain because they embody a silly idea—such as tying a very large animal to a very small one serving as a totally insecure hitching post. Most of the characters are animals, but occasionally there is a human being whose caricature may not be evident to the young reader.

1287 **Tripp,** Wallace. *Sir Toby Jingle's Beastly Journey;* story and pictures by Wallace Tripp. Coward, 1976. 75-10455. 32p. $6.95.

3-5 Recommended by the publishers for kindergarten to fifth grade, this can certainly be read to prereaders, but much of the humor lies in use of language ("My kinsmen have many a score to settle with this tin soldier," a dragon hisses.) and some rather sophisticated signs printed within the illustrations. Tripp's animals have marvelously expressive faces, and he uses comments in balloons in comic strip style. The story is ridiculous but sturdy. Sir Toby's long record as an aggressive knight has led the animals to believe he has magical powers. When they decide to unite and trap him, there is a series of narrow escapes (Sir T. always unaware but safe) that frustrates the entourage even more. They are, finally, trapped in Sir Toby's castle courtyard where they are exhibited as a collection and find that the living is easy and that it's fun to gain audience attention by pretending ferocity. Funny story, funny pictures.

1288 **Trivett,** John V. *Building Tables on Tables;* illus. by Giulio Maestro. T. Y. Crowell, 1975. 74-11263. 33p. $4.50.

2-4 A mathematics teacher presents, with lucid simplicity, the concepts of substituting and reversing numbers in the process of multiplication, showing the reader how to construct diagrams of related products to arrive at the same common names; i.e., 3×4 is related on the diagram to $3 \times (5 - 1)$ and to $(1 + 1 + 1) \times 4$ et cetera, and demonstrating the satisfying function of simple tables. Trivett doesn't suggest that mathematics is a game, but his text makes the subject just as intriguing.

1289 **Tunis,** Edwin. *The Tavery at the Ferry;* illus. by Edwin Tunis. T. Y. Crowell, 1973. 109p. $6.95.

4-7 As all Tunis books are, this is profusely illustrated with pictures that give, in their meticulous detail, authoritative information about clothing, buildings, weapons, vehicles, and other artifacts of the period. And they are handsome both because of their precision and because of the restraint with which the artist used black, white, and shades of grey. The text describes a New Jersey ferry and tavern belonging to a Quaker family; in following the changes in the family and in the property, the author used both text and illustrations to give information about the Colonial way of life. The pace is stately through most of the book, but excitement is added in the final pages, in which the events preceding the Battle of Trenton, and the battle itself are described. Useful for social studies, fascinating for the history buff or the reader interested in Americana, well organized and written, this is a handsome book with minor reference use. An index is appended.

1290 **Turkle,** Brinton, illus. *Deep in the Forest.* Dutton, 1976. 76-21691. 29p. $5.95.

3-6 yrs. Once upon a time there was a story about Goldilocks and the three bears, remember? Well, here's a switch: an inquisitive bear cub wanders into a cabin in the forest, finds it deserted, and pokes about. There are three bowls on the table (labelled for Papa, Mama, and Baby) and three chairs and three beds, and pillows that burst and emit an intriguing cloud of feathers. The family comes home, they see the destruction, the child with golden locks weeps bitterly, and they chase the frightened cub away. The last scene of an engaging wordless book shows the bear cub happily touching noses with its mother. The softly drawn pictures are clean in composition, humorous, and quite effective in telling the story.

1291 **Turkle,** Brinton. *Rachel and Obadiah;* written and illus. by Brinton Turkle. Dutton, 1978. 77-15661. 28p. $7.95.

3-4 In another story about the impish Quaker boy of Nantucket, Obadiah finds that girls can be as determined and active as boys. He and his small sister Rachel know that a friend has received a silver coin for being the first to let a captain's wife know his ship was sailing into port. They both want the coin, and they race to see who'll have the chance to tell the news when another ship is sighted. In hare-and-tortoise fashion, Obadiah is diverted (a patch of ripe berries) and Rachel wins the race. The grateful recipient of the news gives Rachel two coins, and the story ends with a hint that the second one will go to Obadiah. Turkle's softly shaded, realistic paintings give authentic architectural and costume details of the sailing days, and the story is nicely told; the historical setting, the use of Quaker forms of address, and the latent content about sailing indicate an independent reading audience rather than the preschool group, but the story can also be used for reading aloud.

1292 **Turska,** Trystyna. *The Woodcutter's Duck.* Macmillan, 1973. 32p. illus. $5.95.

K-3 An old Polish tale is illustrated with paintings that are romantic, beautifully composed, and full of action. The townspeople make fun of young Bartek, the woodcutter who takes such tender care of his pet duck, but his kindness to animals is appreciated by a frog that he rescues. A magic creature, the frog rewards Bartek with a secret power: he can whistle up a storm and stop it by whistling again. When a blustering army officer demands his duck for dinner, Bartek uses the magic to frighten him; again the man insists on having a duck dinner, again Bartek calls forth a storm. The officer's soldiers, realizing that their leader is not a man of his word (he had promised, while frightened, to forget his demand) strip him and make Bartek their commander. Although the last action strikes a dubious note, since such investiture usually came from above, the tale otherwise is typical of the folk genre: the reward for virtue and the use of a magic token. Very nice.

1293 **Uchida,** Yochiko. *The Birthday Visitor;* illus. by Charles Robinson. Scribner, 1975. 74-14076. 28p. $5.95.

K-3 There is always, in Uchida's books, a happy blend of verisimilar details that evoke vividly Japanese or Japanese-American life and a universality that speaks for and to all children. Here Emi, who lives in California and is periodically bored by eminent visitors from Japan, is just a little sulky because one man, a minister, is going to stay with her family on the night of her birthday dinner. She complains to the elderly Wadas (who function as grandparents) and is told she may be pleasantly surprised. Emi doubts it. But the lively young minister turns out to be very understanding, and he helps with a bird's funeral so that it's the best service Emi's ever held. In fact, she decides, her seventh birthday is nice in every way. The story, illustrated with soft, realistic pictures, is appealing both because of the ever-entrancing subject of birthdays and because of the familiarity of the situation of boring (or potentially boring) adult visitors—but it also has the subtler appeal of being imbued with the gently firm, loving discipline that is so characteristic of Japanese family life.

1294 **Uchida,** Yoshiko. *Journey Home;* illus. by Charles Robinson. Atheneum, 1978. 78-8792. 131p. $7.95.

4-6 In a sequel to *Journey to Topaz,* the story of a Japanese-American family's internment in a Utah camp during World War II, Yuki (now twelve) and her parents are released. They stay in Salt Lake City briefly, then learn that they may go home to California—but their home is gone, as is Father's job. Taken in by a church group, the family arranges the purchase of a grocery store in cooperation with Grandma Kurihara and Mr. Oka—but the store is burned. Yuki has known that not all the neighbors are hostile, indeed some are supportive friends, but it hurts her that some white people feel so bitter. She's also upset when her beloved brother Ken comes home; he's moody, aloof, and depressed. At a Thanksgiving dinner at the Olssen's, Ken learns that their only son was killed, yet they feel no bitterness toward the Japanese. And so he gains perspective, and with his recovery, Yuki feels that at last she has come home. Based on the author's experiences, the story is poignant, and it lacks the sharp edge of bitterness. Written in a fluent, simple style, the book gives a candid picture of a shameful episode in our history.

1295 **Uchida,** Yoshiko. *The Rooster Who Understood Japanese;* illus. by Charles Robinson. Scribner, 1976. 76-13450. 29p. $6.95.

3-4 Both the story and the illustrations have a direct simplicity and warmth in this guileless book about a small girl who worries about her neighbor's problem. Miyo's mother is a widow and a doctor, so she has arranged that Miyo stay with Mrs. Kitamura after school each day, a plan that suits both Miyo and the friendly Mrs. K. But their peaceful routine is disrupted when a new neighbor, Mr. Wickett, threatens to call the police because Mrs. K.'s rooster, Mr. Lincoln, crows so early. (With the growth of the town, the street is now within the city limits.) Miyo and her mother try to think of an answer, but Mrs. K. is determined that Mr. Lincoln should be where he is happy. Of all her pets, he's the only one who understands Japanese, she insists. The solution is quite credible and satisfies everybody; the plot has just enough suspense and pace to appeal to children's love of action, but its real charm is in the gentle humor of the writing and the pervasive aura of neighborly affection and concern. This is also a good choice for reading aloud to younger children.

1296 **Unstead,** R. J. *Living in a Medieval Village;* illus. by Ron Stenberg. Addison-Wesley, 1973. 44p. $4.50.

4-6 One of a series of books about medieval times (others are *Living in a Castle, Living in a Crusader Land,* and *Living in a Medieval City*) is adequately illustrated and historically accurate; the writing style is brisk and straightforward. Unstead describes the people of Benfield, a small village owned by an absentee noble and administered by his absentee steward. The bailiff does the actual work of coordinating the work of the villeins and cottars who till the lord's demesne. Although Unstead doesn't give as full or vivid a picture as did Alfred Duggan in such books as *Growing Up in Thirteenth Century England,* he manages to inject some life into the characters, and the division into short books about one aspect of medieval life makes the subject easily assimilable. The books should be especially useful as supplementary curricular material.

1297 **Valencak,** Hannelore. *A Tangled Web;* tr. from the German by Patricia Crampton. Morrow, 1978. 78-16715. 189p. Trade ed. $6.95; Library ed. $6.67 net.

5-7 First published in Austria, a smoothly translated story written with perceptivity and depth; despite a slow pace, the book has enough beautifully crafted episodes and enough insight into a child's imaginative processes to hold the reader. Annie, a timid and lonely child is victimized by a domineering classmate, Josepha, into belief in her own powers; having told Josepha a lie, she becomes more and more enmeshed in the consequences. For Annie firmly believes that, as in an old legend, there is a treasure somewhere in the deserted mill nearby, and she's told Josepha that she can work a magic spell and now is fearful because Josepha threatens to tell everyone she is a witch. Forced to toady to Josepha and to lie to her mother, Annie is increasingly wretched. Not until she has blurted out the whole story to a chaplain and has realized that she's been more foolish than wicked is Annie able to find peace.

1298 **Van Der Horst,** Brian. *Rock Music.* Watts, 1973. 90p. illus. $3.95.

7-12 An informative survey for those who are ignorant about rock, a trip down Memory Lane for the cognoscenti, this describes the various kinds of music that contributed to rock and the various types of rock music. Much of the book, chronologically arranged, is devoted to individual performers, composers, and groups, and the contributions or musical deviations of each; Van der Horst, a music critic, also discusses the changing attitudes toward rock music and the effects it has had on the recording industry. Lucid, well-written, with a touch of defensive fervor. A list of suggested readings and an index are appended.

1299 **Van Leeuwen,** Jean. *The Great Christmas Kidnapping Caper;* illus. by Steven Kellogg. Dial, 1975. 75-9201. 133p. Trade ed. $5.95; Library ed. $5.47 net.

3-5 Shades of Damon Runyon (with a dash of Selden) color this story told by a tough mouse, Marvin the Magnificent, who has learned to fend for himself and his "gang" in New York. Discovering the joys of living in a dollhouse in Macy's toy department, Marvin brings the other members of the gang, Fats and Raymond, to share the wealth. They become fond of the department's Santa Claus and appoint themselves sleuths when the genial gentleman disappears. They're sure he's been kidnapped, and they're right; they solve the problem—and only Santa realizes their role. Much is made of the gluttony of Fats (with some improbable achievements in the way of opening cans) and the quiet wisdom of

Raymond, the scholar of the group, for whose sensible ideas Marvin takes all the credit, and the story has a happy blend of humor in dialogue, Christmas setting, local color, and silly situations. Tough Marvin becomes as sentimental about Santa as his friends are, and—while there are some points at which the story line sags or becomes improbable even within its fanciful boundaries—it's a merry seasonal romp on the whole.

1300 **Van Stockum,** Hilda. *The Borrowed House.* Farrar, 1975. 75-8853. 215p. $6.95.

5-6 Twelve-year-old Janna misses her parents, who are on a theatrical tour, but she enjoys being part of a Hitler Youth group so much that she feels ambivalence when her parents ask her to join them in Amsterdam. Although one German officer, who is in love with her mother (a theme that seems perhaps unnecessarily stressed and culminates in a fight between Janna's father and the Baron), is just and kind, it is from observing the cruelty of others, from getting to know a boy in the Dutch underground, from learning how much false propaganda she had been fed, and from her feelings of sympathy from the evicted family in whose "borrowed" home she is living, that Janna comes to understand what has really happened to her native Germany. The setting is interesting, the characters varied and believable, and the writing style deft, particularly in dialogue.

1301 **Van Woerkom,** Dorothy, ad. *Abu Ali; Three Tales of the Middle East;* illus. by Harold Berson. Macmillan, 1976. 76-8401. 64p. (Ready-to-Read). $6.95.

2-3 Three short tales for the primary grades reader are illustrated with bright pictures in Berson's typical flowing line; the pictures echo the humor of the stories. In the first, "Abu Ali Counts His Donkeys," the silly Abu Ali gets confused by forgetting to count the donkey he's riding. In the second tale, he outwits the friends who think they've outwitted him; in the last tale, he fills the pockets of a borrowed coat with food, but the owner comes to retrieve the coat and mistakes Abu Ali's greed for a surprise gift to the lender. The tales are retold in a direct style that has, despite its simplicity, a breezy zest.

1302 **Van Woerkom,** Dorothy, ad. *Alexandra the Rock-Eater; An Old Rumanian Tale;* illus. by Rosekrans Hoffman. Knopf, 1978. 77-13778. 27p. Trade ed. $6.95; Library ed. $6.99 net.

K-3 In an entertaining retelling of a Rumanian variation on a favorite folktale theme, Van Woerkom describes Alexandra's outwitting of a young dragon and his mother. The familiar device: convincing the dragon of her terrible might by, for example, squeezing a cheese and claiming she's squeezing buttermilk from a stone. Our heroine has sought the dragon because a shepherd has promised her animals if she'll get rid of the predatory dragon. And why does she need animals? Because she has one hundred hungry children, all magic results of having wished for them. Alexandra's tricks should amuse readers and Hoffman's freshly imaginative paintings intrigue them, but the strength of the book is primarily in Van Woerkom's yeasty style.

1303 **Van Woerkom,** Dorothy. *Becky and the Bear;* illus. by Margot Tomes. Putnam, 1975. 74-16628. 45p. $4.69.

1-3 A good book for beginning independent readers is simply written and nicely illustrated, has plenty of action in a well-constructed, brief story, and has a doughty eight-year-old heroine who uses her wits and merits the compliment for bravery that she's wanted. The setting is colonial Maine; her father and brother have gone hunting, her grandmother is called away to help an injured neighbor, and Becky has to cope with a bear. She's run from the huge animal and barricaded herself in the cabin, but the bear was prowling and scratching about. So Becky resourcefully mixed a bowl full of strong drink, set it outdoors, shut herself in and waited. Outcome: sleeping bear ready to be shot by Father, which meant meat for meals and fat for lamps and a warm rug.

1304 **Van Woerkom,** Dorothy, ad. *The Friends of Abu Ali; Three More Tales of the Middle East;* retold by Dorothy O. Van Woerkom; illus. by Harold Berson. Macmillan, 1978. 77-12624. 64p. (Ready-to-Read Books). $6.95.

1-3 In three short tales for the beginning independent reader, Van Woerkom adapts some Middle Eastern noodlehead stories in a style that has vitality and humor despite its simplicity. Abu Ali, Musa, Nouri, and Hamid bicker about such weighty matters as who should be entitled to sit in a donkey's shadow (while the donkey runs away), whether or not too much sniffing will make a cake fall (the cake falls), and whether or not Musa's donkey should be allowed to cross Hamid's bridge, which he doesn't really own (Abu Ali loses the rice he's just borrowed). Berson's illustration, distinctive for their fluid line, echo the humor of the stories.

1305 **Van Woerkom,** Dorothy. *The Queen Who Couldn't Bake Gingerbread;* illus. by Paul Galdone. Knopf, 1975. 26p. $5.50.

K-3 The dash and ebullience of Galdone's bright pictures add to the vigor and humor of an adapted German folktale, but the story holds up nicely on its own. Van Woerkom's retelling doesn't have the oral cadence of the folktale, but it has a brisk vitality that makes it fun to read or hear. King Pilaf of Mulligatawny searches from kingdom to kingdom for a princess who can bake gingerbread properly. He finally settles for Princess Calliope, more wise than beautiful, who makes it clear that if he will give up the gingerbread stipulation, she'll give up *her* condition: she wants a husband who can play the slide trombone. They wed, the honeymoon ends in a quarrel, and each retires to a wing of the castle. Smells of burnt food and horrible noises are heard; when the two are reconciled, each has learned a new art. Surprise: it's the king who has learned to bake gingerbread, the queen who has learned to play the slide trombone.

1306 **Ventura,** Piero. *Piero Ventura's Book of Cities.* Random House, 1975. 74-4927. 54p. illus. $4.95.

3-5 The oversize format affords the author-artist an opportunity of which he takes full advantage: big double-page spreads that have intriguing details but that are, on most pages, not too crowded because he uses so much white space. In a London scene, for example, the trees are green but there is no indication of grass, so the houses, vehicles, and small (often comic) figures are distinct. Ventura uses a paragraph or two of text for each of six major cities, then moves on to getting around in a city, having fun in a city, working in a city, etc. While this doesn't give the information that is found in the Sasek books on individual cities, it shows some striking differences and quite a few similarities between widely dispersed places and varied cultures.

1307 **Vestly,** Anne-Cath. *Aurora and Socrates;* tr. from the Norwegian by Eileen Amos; illus. by Leonard Kessler. T. Y. Crowell, 1977. 76-43038. 144p. $6.95.

3-5 In a sequel to *Hello, Aurora,* Vestly explores further the small problems of a child of a nuclear family in an urban setting. Aurora's mother is a lawyer; father, who has been taking care of the household, is a student who, in the course of the story, successfully defends his doctoral dissertation. His last weeks of intensive study make it necessary to bring in friends to look after Aurora and little Socrates, and there are many quasi-comic mishaps that spring from the adjustment of sitters and children. Vestly deals smoothly with such common problems as separation anxiety, peer jealousy, a friend's moving away, and a child's reaction to parental quarrels, incorporating all of them in an easy, anecdotal flow. The book, capably translated from the Norwegian, is also a good choice for reading aloud to younger children.

1308 **Vestly,** Anne-Cath. *Hello, Aurora;* tr. from the Norwegian by Eileen Amos; adapted by Jane Fairfax; illus. by Leonard Kessler. T. Y. Crowell, 1974. 135p. $4.95.

3-5 As the book's jacket says, "Pioneers never have an easy time," and Aurora and her father suffer more than Mother because Mother is away at her law office. Father, who is a doctoral candidate, keeps house and takes care of Aurora and the new baby. Everybody had known this in their old home, but in the huge new apartment complex to which the family has just moved, several snooping ladies are horrified. And so are most of the children Aurora meets, although one boy who competently cooks and shops for himself and a working mother takes Aurora's situation for granted. The story, first published in Norway under the title *Aurora in Blokk Z* and adapted for American readers from the British translation, would be interesting from the feminist viewpoint alone, but it has much, much more to offer readers: it is written in a smooth, casually deft, and lightly humorous style, it has good characterization and warm family relationships, and it gives a sympathetic picture of the child who has just moved and is adjusting to other children and their life-styles. A nice book, too, for installment reading to children too young to read it independently.

1309 **Vlahos,** Olivia. *Far Eastern Beginnings;* illus. by George Ford. Viking, 1976. 76-5855. 292p. $10.95.

8- In a fascinating exploration of the early cultures of Asia, Vlahos brings together the findings and theories of archeologists, anthropologists, and other scientists. She distinguishes between concrete clues, recorded or visible, and those that are legendary or conjectural, taking into account differences or similarities in language, rites, customs, diet, et cetera. From the book one can get both a broad picture of cultural diffusion and detailed pictures of individual cultures. Her catholic approach, historical and sociological, is based on solid research, but her fluency of style and objectivity fuse the mass of facts into a readable whole. An extensive bibliography of sources, divided by chapter, and an equally detailed index are appended.

1310 **Waber,** Bernard. *But Names Will Never Hurt Me.* Houghton, 1976. 75-40473. 32p. illus. $6.95.

4-7 yrs. A busy immigration official had changed "Voonterlant" to "wonderland," and that was Alison's last name. Teased by her classmates when a family move brought her to a new school, Alison protested unhappily to her parents. So they told her the story of how they had named her, and she did feel better. In fact, when she grew up she could joke about it. The story is amusing and ruefully tender, but Waber makes a point: name-calling can wound a child.

1311 **Waber,** Bernard. *I Was All Thumbs.* Houghton, 1975. 75-11689. 48p. illus. $6.95.

K-2 Legs is a small octopus who has never known any home except a laboratory tank. He's told he will be happy in the sea, and Legs is apprehensive. "Why complain, I thought. Why make waves. Leave well-enough alone." So Legs is taken to the sea and sent crashing down into a new, strange world. Everyone stares, and poor befuddled Legs does all the wrong things, like squirting ink in the wrong direction. He finds a hiding place but suspects it might be better to be sociable and join a group. (Somehow he doesn't fit into a school of fish, a "very fast crowd.") Life improves, however, with the advent of a friend and the conviction that the sea offers more action and variety than the dear old tank. The illustrations have color, movement, and a merry quality; the story has a felicitous blend of bland treatment of a silly situation and a witty use of cliché phrases when they are delightfully inappropriate to the situation.

1312 **Waber,** Bernard. *Lyle Finds His Mother.* Houghton, 1974. 46p. illus. $5.95.

K-2 Save perhaps for Paddington the Peruvian bear there is no animal character in contemporary picture books who is so happily ensconced in a family's affections as Lyle the crocodile. Here he is disturbed in the happy pattern of his life by the calculating Hector P. Valenti who has come on hard days and wants to lure Lyle back into a theatrical life that will benefit Valenti; as bait he uses the thought that Lyle might meet his "dear, sweet mother." Lyle's never thought about it before but it occurs to him that he must indeed have had a mother, and eventually he gets Valenti to fly him down to the "land of the crocodile." Naturally, they immediately meet Lyle's mother. She doesn't turn out to be the sweet, solicitous, indulgent mommy he's envisioned—but she and Lyle prove to have much in common. The familiar characters, the combination of bland style and nonsensical situation and the conflict-resolution of the plot, however silly it is, are as fetching as they are in earlier books about the amicable crocodile of 88th Street.

1313 **Waber,** Bernard. *Mice on My Mind;* written and illus. by Bernard Waber. Houghton, 1977. 77-9050. 48p. $5.95.

3-5 Although Waber's books are usually for the picture book audience and this is in picture book format, it would be a rather sophisticated prereader who'd appreciate the latent content and sly innuendo of *Mice on My Mind.* The characters are all cats, the protagonist an adult male, and the problem the absence of mice. "I jog . . . I took up needlepoint . . . I pay my taxes . . . I give at the office . . ." He tries everything to rid himself of the obsession, but all he can think about is mice, mice, mice. Why aren't there any? Scattering cheese about the house and drilling holes in the baseboards produce only a smelly house and drafts. A psychiatrist doesn't help; in fact, he gets carried away along with his patient. Cleverly and sprightly in style, the book could well become a favorite of older readers.

1314 **Waber,** Bernard. *The Snake: A Very Long Story;* written and illus. by Bernard Waber. Houghton, 1978. 78-60495. 45p. $7.95.

2-4 yrs. The wider-than-tall pages of this silly but engaging book are used nicely to show a snake that carries over for pages and pages, its rippling green body moving over an assortment of running friezes at the foot of each double-page spread. There are a string of telephone poles and wires (with conversation), a blurred photograph of night traffic, a pattern of road signs, one of flowers, one of snowflakes, etc. The text is simple: the snake travels for days and nights and months; it's the longest trip ever undertaken by a snake and it wonders if it will ever reach its destination. Wiggling with joy, it sees the end ahead. Alas, the snake discovers it is right back where it started. Not much there? Yes, there is: the concepts of time and distance, the appeals of exaggeration and humor, and the visual variety of the pages.

1315 **Wagner,** Jenny. *The Bunyip of Berkeley's Creek;* illus. by Ron Brooks. Bradbury, 1977. 77-73826. 26p. $7.95.

K-2 A familiar figure in Australian folklore, the bunyip seeks his identity plaintively in a story illustrated with beautifully detailed pictures, imaginative in concept and handsome in composition; the pictures capture the serene idiocy of the text. Emerging from the mud, the creature asks those whom he meets what he is and, when he learns that he is a bunyip, what he looks like. Every anatomical feature he brings up is contemptuously dismissed, " 'Fine, handsome feathers,' and the bunyip hopefully. 'Horrible feathers,' said the wallaby firmly . . . 'Handsome webbed feet?' called the bunyip, but there was no answer." But all is not lost; another creature emerges from the mud, and our hero is delighted to tell her she's a bunyip and she looks just like him.

1316 **Waldron,** Ann. *The Integration of Mary-Larkin Thornhill.* Dutton, 1975. 75-15505. 137p. $6.95.

5-8 Legislation and school district rezoning cause consternation among a group of white southern children who learn that they must go to a black junior high. Some cheat; some move; some go to private schools. Mary-Larkin's parents feel strongly that integration is right; in fact, her father wishes that the members of his church would welcome black people. Mary-Larkin is ambivalent, and her first experiences at Wheatley Junior High are discouraging. When she does make a black friend, she brings Vanella into her own church choir and causes a schism amongst her father's parishioners. While there is hostility on the part of many black students at Wheatley and contempt on the part of many former white classmates, Mary-Larkin eventually finds her niche. The story is believable and the writing style adequate; it is burdened to some extent by the repeated passages of dialogue between Mary-Larkin and her aggressively idealistic parents, passages that at times seem more a vehicle for propounding a philosophy than a conversation.

1317 **Waldron,** Ann. *The Luckie Star.* Dutton, 1977. 76-30371. 165p. $7.50.

5-7 Quincy—or Ducky, as her family calls her, irritatingly—is a misfit. All of the other Luckies are creative and artistic; Quincy is interested in science, particularly in astronomy. She'd always loved their summer home on the Florida coast of the Gulf of Mexico, but she did feel that once, just once, they could stay in Houston for a summer so that she could take courses in computer programming and astronomy. The story of the summer includes a hurricane, finding sunken treasure, putting on a traditional Summer Show, and making a new friend—but this is far better than most it-happened-one-summer books: the characters are drawn with depth and insight, the dialogue has vitality, and the writing has pace and polish. It isn't as cohesive as Waldron's *The Integration of Mary-Larkin Thornhill,* but it's just as lively and readable.

1318 **Walker,** Alice. *Langston Hughes, American Poet;* illus. by Don Miller. T. Y. Crowell, 1974. 33p. $3.95.

2-4 A simply written biography that is sympathetic but not adulatory begins in the poet's sixth year, with the dramatic episode of a visit to his father in Mexico and his mother's decision, experiencing an earthquake, that she will continue to live in the United States without her husband. The author, who knew and revered Hughes, describes most of the incidents that are in other biographies, but she includes a candid assessment of the poet's bitter, biased father that is not usually found in books about Hughes written for children. The illustrations are adequate, the biography as substantial as one for the primary grades reader can be.

1319 **Walker,** Greta. *Women Today;* Ten Profiles. Hawthorn Books, 1975. 74-22925. 174p. illus. $6.95.

6-10 Ten profiles in a collective biography are based on interviews and therefore have long comments by the subjects, who include Steinem and Friedan, an orchestra conductor, a policewoman, an obstetrician, a television producer, an actress, a day care center advocate, a consumer action advocate, and the New York City

Commissioner of Human Rights. Some of the women are black, one came from a Mormon and several from Jewish backgrounds; in different ways many of them had experienced prejudice for these reasons as well as being discriminated against because of their sex. Each profile gives some biographical information about the subject's personal life and her career experiences; all of them include some discussion of the subject as a woman. The writing style is competent, the material varied. A list of suggested additional readings and an index are appended.

1320 **Wallace,** Barbara Brooks. *Palmer Patch;* illus. by Lawrence DiFiori. Follett, 1976. 76-2185. 218p. Trade ed. $5.95; Library ed. $5.79 net.

4-6 For children who love animal stories, this has a sure appeal, since the author's affection for them permeates the book without ever descending to sentimentality. Palmer is a skunk who, after an operation, is acquired as a pet by the Patch family. He is accepted quickly by the other Patch pets (a duck, a goat, two dogs, a cat) but he neither accepts nor makes overtures to Jonathan Patch and his parents. Overhearing a remark that "They'll have to be farmed out," Palmer instigates a mass departure from the Patch home, and the animals head for the forest. Their adventures strengthen the bonds of affection and loyalty, so that when Palmer is injured the others manage to bring him to the attention of some people who heal him and the story ends with a reunion with the Patch family (the "farming out" had been a plan to have the animals boarded while a move to a new home was made) and Palmer's realization that he could trust and love people. The animals talk to each other; they understand human speech but do not talk to people. The dialogue is brisk and funny, only occasionally verging on the cute.

1321 **Wallace,** Daisy, ed. *Giant Poems;* illus. by Margot Tomes. Holiday House, 1978. 77-21038. 32p. $5.95.

K-3 Fresh, imaginative line drawings make marvelous use of page space and add to the humor of an intriguing minianthology of poems about ogres and giants. Some of the poems have been published previously; others were written for this collection; among the contributors are Dennis Lee, Lilian Moore, Laura Richards, Walter de la Mare, and Shel Silverstein.

1322 **Walsh,** Gillian Paton. *Children of the Fox;* illus. by Robin Eaton. Farrar, 1978. 78-8138. 115p. $7.95.

5-8 Three stories that are linked by their association with the Athenian hero, Themistokles, are told by three young people who lived during the time of the Persian Wars and the shifting relationship between Athens and Sparta. Aster, the first narrator, helps Themistokles when the Athenians have fled to Salamis; the second tale is told by Demeas, who makes a long run to Sparta to bring a message to the leader; in the third story, Themistokles is a fugitive whose life is saved by a young princess who helps him reach Persia and safety from the Spartans and Athenians who have accused him of bribery. The historical details are meticulously researched, smoothly incorporated in stories that are nicely constructed and told, each tale salted by the heroism and enthusiasm of the protagonist. A map and some clarifying historical commentary are appended.

1323 **Walsh,** Gillian Paton. *The Huffler;* illus. by Juliette Palmer. Farrar, 1975. 75-25917. 84p. $5.95.

5-7 Jill Paton Walsh's historical fiction has previously been more broad and sweeping, but here she shows her versatility by creating a cameo, for *The Huffler* is a Victorian adventure, the story of a properly beruffled English miss who escapes to pose as a servant so that she can better fit into the life of a canal boat family. Or, rather, part of a family, for young Bess and Ned Jebb are making a cargo delivery alone because of a family crisis. The characters and dialogue have vitality but it is the setting that especially delights: the lore of the canal, the intricacies of the locks, the conviviality of the canal travelers.

1324 **Walsh,** Gillian Paton. *The Island Sunrise; Prehistoric Culture in the British Isles.* Seabury, 1976. 75-4666. 128p. illus. $8.95.

7- A serious study of the wanderers and settlers of British prehistory covers the millennia from the earliest migrants of interglacial times to the end of the Iron Age and the coming of the Romans. The author smoothly integrates the ebb and flow of influences and cross-cultural diffusion in discussing the artifacts and art of the early peoples, the archeological evidence of their increased skill at making and using tools, the growing agricultural stability and diversification of labor that laid the groundwork for a civilization possible only because of a food surplus. A well organized, informative, and competently written book, this has a base of solid research. It has good illustrations, but some of the plates are far removed from textual reference; for example, Plate 11 faces page 49 but is referred to on page 102 (not by name, but there is a mention of mirrors as part of the metalworker's art, and there are photographs of two mirrors on pages 102 and 103, while the color plate—a third mirror—is fifty pages away). A bibliography and an index are appended.

1325 **Walsh,** Gillian Paton. *Unleaving.* Farrar, 1976. 76-8857. 145p. $5.95.

7-10 The young Madge of *Goldengrove* is again living at the house by the
* sea, for in this sequel Gran has died and Madge has inherited

Goldengrove. Most of the rooms have been rented for the summer to two Oxford professors, their families, and some of their students. Madge becomes friendly with Patrick, one professor's son, who is a moody boy, unhappy about a retarded small sister who is laughed at by the others and who has a bleak future. In the child's death and Patrick's guilt (unable to bear the bitterness of the burden, he has pushed little Molly over a cliff—and both she and the man who tries to rescue her are drowned), Madge acts as Patrick's comforter and then sees clearly that she loves him, that their lives are tied. Only she knows of his guilt—and she does not tell. Throughout the story there are scenes that seem to be flashbacks, scenes with a grandmother and her family, but it is only toward the end of the book that it becomes clear that the grandmother is Madge herself and that the viewpoint is prescient. Beautifully crafted, the story is written with bittersweet perception; the characterization is strong, the style polished.

1326 **Wangerin,** Walter. *The Book of the Dun Cow.* Harper, 1978. 241p. Trade ed. $7.95; Library ed. $7.49 net.

5-7 Chauntecleer the Rooster, an eloquent and proud ruler of the barnyard as well as the coop, is the hero who fights against the evil perpetrated by Wyrm, who lives deep under the land, so huge he "could pass once around the earth and then bite his own tail ahead of him." Wyrm's disciple is the cockatrice, spawner of invading serpents, and it takes all of Chauntecleer's minions (John Wesley Weasel, the Ants, Mundo Cani Dog, Corningware Turkey, etc.) to win the battle. The Dun Cow is a great mother figure who gives aid and comfort through the terrible struggle, but—since she appears late in the story and is only one of the heroic characters—the book's title seems rather puzzling. In its length, its complexity, its creation of a whole and vivid animal world, this is superb and is likely to appeal to the same kind of reader who enjoyed *Watership Down.* Yet it is an animal fantasy, and it is a moot point whether the book is appropriate for the middle grades readers who will be interested in the subject or for older readers who can appreciate the most distinctive quality of the book, its style: witty, sophisticated, and polished, with dialogue that is as dramatic as it is entertaining.

1327 **Warner,** Lucille Schulberg, ad. *From Slave to Abolitionist; The Life of William Wells Brown.* Dial, 1976. 76-2288. 135p. $6.95.

6-9 Based on Brown's autobiography, published in 1847, this extends the story of his life to the end of the Civil War, continuing to use the first person form. Born a slave in 1814, William saw his mother and sister sent to the slave markets, and he vowed to become free; in 1834, he escaped, later taking the name of Wells Brown to honor a Quaker who helped him reach Buffalo. Here he worked on a lake steamer, helping many other black refugees reach Canada. Self-educated, Brown became an author and lecturer, speaking in the United States and England in support of the abolitionist movement. His story is candid and dramatic, and Warner interprets it forcefully, continuing the account of his later years in the same vein of matter-of-fact reportage as is in the portion based on the autobiography. The later years, when Brown became the first black author of a play, a novel, and a history in this country, are filled with references to luminaries here and abroad, but it is as an indictment of slavery that the book, in its first half, is most effective. A list of Brown's major works is appended.

1328 **Warren,** Lee. *The Theater of Africa; An Introduction;* photographs by Judith Bernstein. Prentice-Hall, 1976. 74-20728. 112p. $6.95.

7- A companion volume to *The Dance of Africa* and *The Music of Africa* (the latter written in collaboration with Fred Warren) is equally vivid, varied, and informative. While some forms of theater such as storytelling, miming, and ritual drama are traditional, theatrical performances in western style are found primarily in university companies. Warren describes some of the special aspects of African theater, such as audience participation or the reflection of problems of censorship and apartheid in contemporary dramatic writing and performance. Most of the chapters focus on a single facet: storytelling, ritual drama, folk opera, puppetry, et cetera; a discussion of drama in television and film is included, as are excerpts from two plays. A bibliography and an index are appended.

1329 **Warren,** Ruth. *A Pictorial History of Women in America.* Crown, 1975. 74-83212. 228p. illus. $7.95.

7- Although the book is profusely illustrated with print reproductions and photographs, it is not a picture history but an extensive survey of the role of women and the contributions of individual women to all aspects of life in the United States, from colonial times to today. Despite the recurrent note of fulsome praise, the book provides varied and interesting information about well-known and lesser-known women in all fields, with emphasis on those who participated in the battle for the vote. A lengthy bibliography and a full index add to reference use.

1330 **Warrick,** Patricia, ed. *The New Awareness; Religion Through Science Fiction;* ed. by Patricia Warrick and Martin H. Greenberg. Delacorte, 1975. 74-22631. 480p. $7.95.

8- In the belief that an increasing knowledge about the universe has led to a new awareness, to self-understanding by individuals and new levels of spiritual insight, the compilers of this interesting anthology have chosen stories that illustrate (and each story is so heralded in the table of contents) such facets as moral behavior, the need to believe, the problem of good and evil, the power of the religious vision, religious institutions of the past and future, et cetera. Some of the selections are familiar anthology inclusions like Walter Miller's "A Canticle for Leibowitz" or Arthur Clarke's "The Nine Billion Names of God," and others are less well known. A few of the selections are pedestrian in style or weakly structured, but most of them are written with skill and insight, and a few are brilliant.

1331 **Waters,** John F. *The Continental Shelves.* Abelard-Schuman, 1975. 75-6697. 142p. illus. $5.95.

6-10 Comprehensive treatment and good organization of material are the strong points of a book that describes the formation and variety of the oceans' continental shelves and the slopes and canyons that extend or divide them. The writing style is straightforward and clear but the solidity of print on the pages is a bit overwhelming. Separate chapters discuss such subjects as mining, fishing, gathering (Irish moss, kelp, etc.), and the continental shelves in relation to man: creatures that furnish medicine, sponges, glue, or opportunities for research. One chapter deals with the ways in which ocean exploration is carried on; the final chapter is on the very important topic of offshore gas and oil. A bibliography and an index are appended.

1332 **Watson,** Aldren Auld. *Country Furniture;* illus. by the author. T. Y. Crowell, 1974. 274p. $7.50.

6- In the early days of America, there were few specialists. Most of the furniture was made by men who were farmers or blacksmiths or millers who could turn a hand to many tasks and whose furniture was simple, at times crude, and functional. In time there were craftsmen who specialized and whose techniques and styles reflected those of the past. Watson describes and illustrates in detail the tools used in furniture-making, with clear pictures of—for example—each step in making a combback Windsor chair or a scrolled cornice. One chapter is devoted to woods, another to tools, another to woodworking methods; the discussion of all of these facets of furniture-making is prefaced by a description of the world in which the early artisans lived. This isn't a book for the general reader to browse through, it is much too detailed and too concerned with a special interest, but for those who are themselves hobbyists or craftsmen, or for the student concerned with history—especially the history of the colonial period—the book should be valuable despite the rather heavy writing style. The illustrated glossary, the bibliography, and the index add to the book's usefulness as a reference tool.

1333 **Watson,** Clyde. *Binary Numbers;* illus. by Wendy Watson. T. Y. Crowell, 1977. 75-29161. 33p. $5.95

2-4 An unusually lucid explanation of the binary system begins with several examples of the simplicity and scope of doubling sequences. Watson then presents a chart with numbers 1–15 in a left-hand column, and columns to the right that have spaces for translating (under headings for 8, 4, 2, and 1) into binary numerals; a few are filled in and the rest are left for the reader to figure out. A filled-in chart gives the answers on the next page. With the suggested secret-message code that follows, it would have been useful to have (or describe) a fifth column (16) to take care of translating numerals over 15, but even with the omission, this stands as one of the simplest descriptions of the binary system yet published for beginners, and the text is nicely integrated with the helpful illustrations.

1334 **Watson,** Jane (Werner). *Whales; Friendly Dolphins and Mighty Giants of the Sea;* illus. by Richard Amundsen. Western, 1975. 73-94379. 61p. Trade ed. $4.95; Library ed. $9.27 net.

4-7 An oversize book, profusedly and informatively illustrated, is logically arranged, broad in scope, and written in a brisk style that is—for the most part—straightforward but that occasionally has a note of coyness: "But to a baby Humpback, its mother looks just right," or, ". . . no one can really understand the dolphins' language. Do you suppose the dolphins, with their large brains, can understand ours?" Watson describes kinds of whales and ocean and river dolphins, their habits and habitats, anatomy and reproduction. A full relative index is appended.

1335 **Weber,** William J. *Wild Orphan Babies; Mammals and Birds;* photographs by the author. Holt, 1975. 74-23811. 158p. $5.95.

5- A veterinarian discusses the ways in which one should handle, feed, and house abandoned or injured wild baby mammals and birds. The advice is detailed and specific for each kind of creature, permeated with a sense of respect and affection for the animals, but with no trace of sentimentality. Weber is very firm about the rights of wild creatures, about making the needed effort to provide them with exactly the right foods and medication, keeping them clean, and handling them gently. An informative and useful book, and the photographs are beguiling. Several lists are appended (kinds of migratory birds, regional offices of the Fish and Wildlife Service, etc.) as are a bibliography and an index.

1336 **Weiss,** Ann E. *News or Not? Facts and Feelings in the News Media;* illus. with photographs. Dutton, 1977. 76-54920. 136p. $8.95.

7-9 In a serious look at what affects the news received by the public, Weiss examines editorial bias and policy, the restraints by official agencies or advertisers, the conscious or unconscious coloring by reporters and broadcasters, and the fact that what is considered news changes from place to place and from period to period. Although the chapters, after the introductory discussion of what news consists of, deal separately with each mass medium, there is a certain amount of overlap in the text. Weiss is specific about examples, candid about people, and usually objective, aware throughout of the responsibility of the news media and of the conflicting theories about the public's right to know. A bibliography and an index are appended.

1337 **Weiss,** Harvey. *Carving; How to Carve Wood and Stone.* Addison-Wesley, 1976. 75-2337. 72p. illus. $6.50.

6- As is true of other books on arts or crafts by Weiss, this is well organized, succinctly written, and clear in its step-by-step explanations of how to choose materials and use tools. The first projects described are simple, later ones being more complex. While the text gives instructions for making specific objects, it also gives enough general information to enable the neophyte sculptor to strike out alone. Drawings of stages in carving and photographs of finished objects provide added incentives.

1338 **Weiss,** Harvey. *How To Run A Railroad; Everything You Need To Know About Model Trains.* T. Y. Crowell, 1977. 76-18128. 127p. illus. $7.95.

5- In his usual meticulous fashion, Weiss gives a full and logically arranged sequence of facts about buying, building, and operating a model railroad. The diagrams are adequately labelled and are nicely placed in relation to textual references, and the writing is clear, informal, and authoritative. The text describes the several gauges and the advantages and disadvantages of each; gives advice about power packs, transformers, coupling and track plans; it leaves to the kits (about which Weiss also gives some suggestions) the directions for putting cars and engines together, but every aspect of assembling and running the whole system and of making such ancillary equipment as tunnels or mountains is explained.

1339 **Weiss,** Harvey. *What Holds It Together?* written and illus. by Harvey Weiss. Atlantic-Little, Brown, 1977. 76-54692. 48p. $6.95.

3-5 Weiss, an old and deft hand at "how-to" books, describes some of the ways in which two objects, or parts of an object, are held together: nails, screws, clamps, thread, glue, cement, melting, forging, et cetera. The writing is casual in tone but precise in the information it gives, and the illustrations are placed and labelled carefully. The author does more than simply list devices that hold things together, however; he explains how each method works and gives advice on what to do or what not to do. Simple and clear, this is more enjoyable reading than are many books of comparable usefulness.

1340 **Weiss,** Malcolm E. *What's Happening to Our Climate?* illus. by Paul Plumer. Messner, 1978. 78-15684. 93p. $7.29.

5-7 A clear and well organized text describes the long-range changes in the world's climate and discusses all the factors that have contributed to those changes and that will affect the climate of the future. Weiss points out that the world seems to be growing colder very slowly, and describes some of the aspects of changing climate caused by man, such as increased pollution and the growing amount of carbon dioxide in the atmosphere; he notes particularly that the changes have affected agricultural yield and will do so even more in the future. The tone is not one of dire prediction, but a matter-of-fact acceptance of the need to plan for anticipated changes. Save for one map in which code-colors seem to be reversed, the illustrations are helpful; a glossary and index are appended.

1341 **Weiss,** Peter. *Simple Printmaking;* illus. by Sally Gralla. Lothrop, 1976. 75-31762. 122p. Trade ed. $5.50; Library ed. $4.81 net.

5- Profusely illustrated with examples of prints of many kinds, this excellent book for the hobbyist encourages experimentation but gives enough specific advice to make the neophyte experimenter confident. Weiss describes equipment and techniques for printing by roller, stencil, or stamp pad, explains the procedures for making block prints and monotypes, and gives advice for printing on fabric. The explanations are clear, the material varied; a list of books for further reading and an index are appended.

1342 **Weldrick,** Valerie. *Time Sweep;* illus. by Ron Brooks. Lothrop, 1978. 78-11837. 156p. Trade ed. $6.95; Library ed. $6.67 net.

5-7 An Australian boy of twelve, Laurie has made only one friend since the family's moved to Sydney; He's met Clare in the library, and Clare is the only person he tells about his experiences. At first frightening and then exciting, Laurie's trips in time are spurred by an old bed his parents have bought him; each time he travels, he wakes in London in 1862. Most of the story has to do with Laurie's friendship with a boy his own age; Frank is a poor crossing sweeper who yearns for an education and is delighted when Laurie teaches him to read. The boys traipse about London (lovely period details) and overhear a planned burglary, which they courageously prevent. It's an exciting adventure story, written in fine style and nicely structured. At the close of the story Laurie and Clare discover Frank's great-grandson, a man who is delighted to talk about his ancestor; Laurie and Clare are equally delighted to hear about Frank and to realize that he had come to Sydney because of his friendship, in boyhood, with Laurie.

1343 **Wells,** Rosemary. *Abdul.* Dial, 1975. 34p. illus. Trade ed. $4.95; Library ed. 4.58 net.

K-2 Delightful drawings reinforce the humor of the text in a small book that has a punch-line message. Abdul dotes on Gilda, his camel, and is proud of the three babies she produces each year. Then—disaster! Gilda gives birth to a peculiar-looking child; she won't leave him, and her owner won't leave her, so they're all trapped by a sandstorm. The deformed baby camel is lost and is found at a strange settlement, and there the people laugh at Gilda as much as Abdul's tribe laughed at her baby. They've never seen such a funny looking horse. (The reader has, of course, seen the joke pages ago.) If one can accept a camel giving birth to a horse, it's a merry tale with action and suspense; if one can't, it's an implausible tale with action and suspense.

1344 **Wells,** Rosemary. *Don't Spill It Again, James;* written and illus. by Rosemary Wells. Dial, 1977. 77-71513. 48p. Trade ed. $5.95; Library ed. $5.47 net.

3-6 yrs. Three short episodes with a neatly rhymed text and engaging pictures of two cuddly animal children, drawn with humor and softly colored, have a more gentle note than is usual for Wells. She never becomes sugary, but in the protective love shown by James' older brother as he copes with a- James spilling groceries, b- an adult with reeking pipe who is befouling a train compartment in which he and James are the other passengers, and c- a sleepy James who needs to be put to bed, there's a genuine tenderness.

1345 **Wells,** Rosemary. *Morris's Disappearing Bag; A Christmas Story.* Dial, 1975. 75-9202. 40p. illus. Trade ed. $4.95; Library ed. $4.58 net.

4-6 yrs. A share-the-loot story, seen from the viewpoint of the youngest in a family, is illustrated with uncluttered frames, small and bright, that show a family of rabbits on Christmas Day. (It is true that the tree ornaments move about from page to page, but the picture book audience surely won't cavil at such things.) Morris likes his present, a bear, but as he watches his brother and sisters taking turns using their gifts and telling him he's too young for any of them, Morris gets sulky. Then he finds one more present, a bag that makes him invisible; Morris is instantly offered trades by the others, and he has a satisfying orgy that should appeal to all. Light, amusing, with the one note of fantasy nicely blended with the realistic situation. Young listeners should vibrate sympathetically to the triumph of the downtrodden youngest child.

1346 **Wells,** Rosemary. *Noisy Nora;* written and illus. by Rosemary Wells. Dial, 1973. 34p. Trade ed. $3.95; Library ed. $3.69 net.

3-6 yrs. Frisky pictures and a blithe text describe the plight of the middle child. Nora is a mouse; she has an older sister who can Do Things, and a baby brother who gets a great deal of physical care. Nora's way of establishing herself in the family constellation is by being a nuisance, and when her noise is ignored, she announces loudly that she is leaving. Unfortunately, nobdy notices her dramatic exit, but they are worried when they realize she must be gone because it is so quiet. Nora's return brings such evidence of loving concern that she and the reader can be reassured. An old theme, a new twist; the story is told in rhyme, simply and well.

1347 **Wells,** Rosemary. *None of the Above*. Dial, 1974. 184p. $5.95.

7-10 Marcia is pretty, placid, and not very much of an intellectual, and although she tries to live up to the expectations and standards of her stepmother, she doesn't really care about culture or college. Marcia likes bright colors and wants to work in a beauty parlor, and she knows that her stepmother disapproves of Raymond, her boyfriend. Marcia's a little bothered herself by Raymond—she finds him apt to get edgy and frustrated when they start making love—and when he confesses to impotence, she knows that he loves and trusts her, and she decides that she can't keep up the family pace, doesn't want to, and will marry Raymond. The characterization is strong and consistent, and the complexities of relationships within the family are beautifully developed. Wells is particularly adept at dialogue, using it adroitly to develop both the story line and the characters in a story that is sensitive and candid.

1348 **Wells,** Rosemary. *Stanley & Rhoda;* written and illus. by Rosemary Wells. Dial, 1978. 78-51874. 40p. Trade ed. $5.95; Library ed. $5.47 net.

2-5 yrs. * Three vignettes of a sibling relationship are illustrated with pictures of an animal (vaguely hamsterish) family; the pictures add touches of sly humor to the text, complementing and extending it. The three episodes consist primarily of dialogue, and Wells has a marvelous ear for speech patterns as well as an appreciation of the wiles of the young. Stanley, the elder child, copes in each case with his fractious younger sister: he helps Rhoda clean her room and does most of the work; he sees through Rhoda's simulated agony when she overdramatizes a reported bee sting; and he instructs a babysitter who is baffled by Rhoda's obstinacy, an episode that ends with a nice twist. An entertaining story that invites children to laugh at their own foibles, this is one of those unusual books that can also beguile adult readers-aloud.

1349 **Wersba,** Barbara. *Tunes for a Small Harmonica.* Harper, 1976. 75-25411. 178p. Trade ed. $6.95; Library ed. $6.49 net.

7-10 J. F. is a teenage student at a private school for girls in New York, a chain-smoker who dresses in pants all the time. Her elegant mother thinks J. F. looks like a cab driver and sends her to a psychiatrist, a man who believes all the nonsense J. F. feeds him. Maybe she's a lesbian? J. F. tries kissing her friend Marylou and knows she isn't. She has despised her poetry teacher, Harold Murth, but love strikes suddenly, and J. F. begins hounding and spying; doting, she decides to earn enough money to help Harold go to England to complete his thesis, and she does it by playing the harmonica on the street. Begging, in fact. The end of the love affair, which is quite one-sided, is surprising; disappointing, at first, but then J. F. realizes life goes on. And even that her life's not so bad. Funny, frank, and sophisticated, the story has—despite such exaggeration as the inept, neurotic psychiatrist—memorable characters, brisk dialogue, and a yeasty style. It is consistent and believable as a first-person account, and it faces many broad concerns of all adolescents.

1350 **Westall,** Robert. *The Machine Gunners.* Greenwillow, 1976. 76-13630. 186p. Trade ed. $6.95; Library ed. $5.94 net.

5-9 First published in England, where it won the Carnegie Award,
* this story of World War II recreates vividly the drama and terror of a small town that is strafed daily by German planes and that expects invasion. One of the children, Chas, has stumbled on a machine gun in a downed plane; with the help of four other youngsters and a retarded adult, the gun is hidden (in an underground shelter which the children equip and man) and used. Military authorities suspect the group, but cannot find the shelter. And they never suspect that a German soldier is also there; Rudi had stumbled in, tired and ill, been taken prisoner and become a friend, exchanging his knowledge of gunnery for a promised escape boat. The final episode is taut with suspense;

the entire story is fast-paced and convincing, with strong characterization and dialogue. The writing style is competent and even, its sober realism given variety by moments of pathos or humor.

1351 **Westall,** Robert. *The Watch House*. Greenwillow, 1978. 77-19088. 224p. Trade ed. $6.95; Library ed. $6.43 net.

7-10 In a story set in an English coastal community, Westall knits realism and occult fantasy deftly in a compelling story that has mounting suspense. Anne's selfish, dictatorial mother leaves her with Mum's old nanny for a summer, and Anne is truly frightened when she realizes that her placid visit is being disrupted by a ghost. With two friends, however, she gains courage and begins to explore the background for the obviously restless, plaintive requests for help from the ghost. All this is tied very neatly into some local history about the life-saving brigade (hence the "watch-house," which is used as a storage site for mementoes of the brigade). The solution of the spectral mystery is as logically solved as a fantasy can be, the solution to Anne's unhappiness about being with her mother rather than with her gentle father is solved satisfactorily, and the story is distinctive in characterization, dialogue, and writing style.

1352 **Westall,** Robert. *The Wind Eye*. Greenwillow, 1977. 77-5162. 213p. Trade ed. $6.95; Library ed. $6.43 net.

5-8 An intriguing time-shift story has a solid contemporary base and is at the same time a perceptive story of the adjustment to stepparents of three children who have an affinity that transcends their divided loyalties. Mike is the son of Bertrand, a prosaic and pedantic professor; Sally and Beth are the daughters of Madelene, a volatile and assertive woman. It is the children who discover, on vacation in an isolated part of the English coast, that an old boat is a time ship that takes them back to the medieval period in which the local legendary saint, St. Cuthbert, lived. Sally, the youngest, is marooned in the saint's time and is, in a final time journey, in need of rescue; when she comes back, a miracle has happened, the complete healing of a crippled hand. Then it is Beth who is in danger, and this time it is Bertrand, the unbeliever, who passes through the time warp and finds he is in the midst of a Viking raid. And he understands then that the mysterious "Wind Eye" is a window, that he has been privileged to see through it to another world. Westall's characterization is firm, particularly astute in drawing the petulant, egocentric Madeleine and her relationships with other family members. The plot is tightly constructed and nicely meshes realistic and fantastic aspects, and the story has good pace and a compelling narrative flow.

1353 **Wilbur,** Richard. *Opposites;* written and illus. by Richard Wilbur. Harcourt, 1973. 39p. $3.75.

5-7 A series of verses, deftly explaining opposite terms, should appeal to the word-lover. "What is the opposite of *fleet?* / Someone who's *slow* and drags his feet / Another's an *armada* that'll / Engage the first fleet in a battle." The cartoon-style illustrations echo the humor of the poems. Although younger readers can enjoy the book, some of the terms as used require a fairly sophisticated reader: "The opposite of *post,* were you / On horseback, would be *black and blue . . .*"

1354 **Wilder,** Laura (Ingalls). *West from Home;* Letters of Laura Ingalls Wilder, San Francisco, 1915; ed. by Roger Lea Macbride; Historical Setting by Margot Patterson Doss. Harper, 1974. 168p. Trade ed. $4.95; Library ed. $4.79 net.

6- For all those who have been loving fans of Laura Ingalls Wilder, this compilation of letters should be pure delight. Years before she wrote the "Little House" books, Laura visited her daughter Rose in San Francisco; it was 1915, the year that the city was mounting a world's fair, and Laura spent much time visiting there and getting her daughter's help (Rose was a newspaperwoman) in the craft of writing. Laura thought she might make a little extra money if she could sell some articles. Her letters are to her husband, Manly, and they are enjoyable not only for the Laura they reveal, not only for the small touches that surprise (the nice Austrian musician Rose interviews turns out to be Fritz Kreisler, the "little artist girl" Laura meets proves to be Berta Hader) but also for the vivid way in which the letters reflect the place and the period.

1355 **Wilkinson,** Brenda Scott. *Ludell and Willie.* Harper, 1977. 76-18402. 181p. Trade ed. $5.95; Library ed. $5.79 net.

6-9 A sequel to *Ludell* finds the doughty adolescent still living with her grandmother, who she calls Mama, and more than ever in love with Willie, the very nice boy next door. Although the story line is more substantial than that of the earlier book, this is primarily a facet of the black experience, for Ludell works for a white family and resents the way she is treated, sympathizes with Willie in his worrying about his future, and participates in the mutually supportive life of the black community in her town. While the use of phonetically spelled dialect is more controlled in this second novel, there are still some instances of this ("Everybody dark who be with Lilly nem do,") or of colloquialism in exposition ("He kissed her like he longed to.") Ludell worries about Mama, who is increasingly frail and forgetful, and she is furiously resentful when her mother insists that she come to New York after Mama dies. But

Ludell loses; she must leave Willie, she must leave her classmates just before graduation. While this is a story about a black adolescent, it is a story about problems all teenagers share: loving and being loved, moving towards independence, being concerned about the pattern of adult life that suddenly seems so close.

1356 **Willard,** Barbara. *Harrow and Harvest*. Dutton, 1975. 75-11918. 174p. $7.50.

6-9 * In the fifth and last of a cycle of historical novels that began during the reign of Henry VII, this story of a country manor, Mantlemass, and the Medley family who reside there, ends with the bitter internal conflict of the English Civil War. Two long lost members of the family come, separately, to Mantlemass; Roger Medley takes all but two members of the family back to his home in the New World and young Edmund Medley, converted during his brief stay from a King's man to a supporter of Parliament, dies in the final confrontation in which the great house is destroyed. The author weaves smoothly through the complexities of family relationships, two love affairs, and the vicissitudes of wartime tragedies, but her story never becomes overshadowed by historical details although they permeate the book.

1357 **Willard,** Barbara. *The Iron Lily*. Dutton, 1974. 175p. $5.95.

6-9 Winner of the 1974 *Guardian* Award for children's fiction, this is the fourth in a series of historical novels about Mantlemass, the home of the Medley family. Here the widow Lilias Godman, who conceals the fact that she is an illegitimate daughter of the family, opens an iron foundry near Mantlemass and sends her daughter away when she suspects the girl is in love with a man who may be one of her kinsmen. When Lilias confesses to her father, Piers Medley, that she is his daughter, she also learns that Robin, his daughter's love, is adopted and that there is no bar to the young people's marriage. The plot is substantial and the characterization strong, but it is the powerful evocation of the place and the time (a forest in Tudor England) that are most remarkable.

1358 **Williams,** Barbara. *Albert's Toothache;* illus. by Kay Chorao. Dutton, 1974. 26p. $4.95.

3-5 yrs. While the literal-minded may object to turtles standing erect or wearing boots, or even turtles that appear to have no shells, there can be no doubt of the humor in the illustrations of Albert and his family. Albert won't get up. Albert won't eat. Albert has a toothache. His father scolds, his mother worries, his brother and sister sneer, but Albert persists. Not until Grandmother Turtle comes to visit does toothless Albert reveal his source of woe, and that's because he's been asked the right question: "Where do you have a toothache?" The dialogue—and the story is told almost entirely in dialogue—is very funny indeed, but there's substance in the way it reflects relationships in human families.

1359 **Williams,** Jay. *Everyone Knows What a Dragon Looks Like;* illus. by Mercer Mayer. Four Winds, 1976. 74-13121. 24p. $7.95.

K-3 A tale in the folk tradition is illustrated by pictures that effectively combine the style of Oriental prints and Mayer's more familiar raffish, cozy figures. The illustrations and the text complement each other nicely, yet each can stand alone. In a city on the Chinese border, long ago, the gatekeeper was a small, cheerful boy named Han. He was the only person who was courteous to the fat, bald, old man who appeared one day announcing that he was a dragon and that he could save the city of Wu. For Wu was threatened by invasion. The Mandarin's advisers had agreed that prayer was the one thing that might stop the Wild Horsemen of the north—but it didn't. And the old man was scoffed at, for although each of the ruler's advisers had a different idea of what a dragon looked like, they all agreed he didn't look old and shabby. However, for Han's sake, the old man saved the city; he became a mighty wind and drove off the invaders, and then he changed his shape and sprang into the sky, a glorious and terrible dragon. He was never seen again, but Han was heaped with honors and riches for his part in saving the city, and from then on everybody knew what a dragon looked like, ". . . a small, fat, bald old man," the story ends. Several standard components of the folk tradition are woven into the tale, which is told with brisk humor.

1360 **Williams,** Jay, ad. *The Wicked Tricks of Tyl Uilenspiegel;* illus. by Frisco Henstra. Four Winds, 1978. 77-7884. 51p. $8.95.

3-5 Henstra's distinctive paintings, stiffly medieval yet ebullient, are eminently appropriate for the sly humor of a legendary Dutch hero. Williams retells four tales in which Tyl outwits Spanish soldiers or misers by his wit and cunning; often he steals from the rich and helps the poor, but his chief concern is to fill his own pockets. Here and there the prose is stiff, but for the most part Williams is simple and direct in his writing style, and he does communicate the zest and merriness that have made the Tyl Uilenspiegel stories popular for several centuries.

1361 **Williams,** Ursula Moray. *Bogwoppit.* Nelson, 1978. 78-57534. 174p. $6.95.

5-6 Orphaned Samantha is sent to live with her wealthy Aunt Daisy when Aunt Lily, who's been her substitute mother, goes abroad. Aunt Daisy, alas, ignores and apparently dislikes her niece, but by the end of the story Daisy has made Samantha the beneficiary of all her wealth, and they weep at an upcoming temporary separation. This exaggerated but possible realistic framework is filled by bogwoppits, a cuddly, furry invention of a creature that is supposedly in danger of extinction; the fantasy broadens when the bogwoppits multiply and make Aunt Daisy their prisoner in the drain, although they are kind enough to bring her food. The story line is nonsensical but the yeasty style and humor, the colorful characters (Aunt Daisy is a modern equivalent of Lady Bracknell), and even the bogwoppits should engage readers of this English tale.

1362 **Windsor,** Patricia. *Mad Martin.* Harper, 1976. 76-3837. 119p. Trade ed. $5.95; Library ed. $5.79 net.

5-6 Set in London, this vigorous and touching story describes the changes in the life of a child who hadn't known how lonely he was until he made a friend, who hadn't known what the warmth of family love was like until he lived with a large family. "Mad Martin," the boys at school called him, because he never spoke and never played with them. Martin lived alone with his grandfather, Mr. Drivic. They had few possessions, little communication, no friends; when grandfather became ill and was hospitalized, Martin was taken in by a neighbor, Mrs. Crimp. From the Crimp family he learned what it was to be clean, how to play, and—most important—how to have and be a friend. And so, when grandfather was well and came home, Martin knew what a home should be like and how they could now talk and laugh. Characters and dialogue are powerful, and the smooth writing style carries a story with less plot than incidents.

1363 **Winn,** Marie, ed. *The Fireside Book of Fun and Game Songs;* Musical Arrangements by Allan Miller; illus. by Whitney Darrow. Simon and Schuster, 1974. 224p. $12.50.

all ages A delightful song book for home use and library collections, and a valuable resource for group leaders, this can be used independently by older children and adults and can be used with younger children. The illustrations are amusing, the arrangements are simple, and the songs offer entertainment and participation in varied forms. There are cumulative songs, songs to which phrases or verses can be added on an impromptu basis, parodies, rounds, songs that are narrative or mock-gruesome, songs for action or (joy for the youngest) making funny noises.

1364 **Winther,** Barbara. *Plays from Folktales of Africa and Asia.* Plays, Inc., 1976. 76-15558. 274p. $8.95.

3-5 A collection of short plays that should be useful for schoolroom production or for any group working with children's theater, adapted by a professional in the field. The plays are grouped according to source, are competently adapted from excellent and diverse material, and are preceded by notes that give some background. Some of the plays begin with introductions by storytellers, most of the selections are humorous, and all of them have enough action to quickly catch and hold audience attention. All are one-act plays, royalty-free; they are easy to stage and are provided with production notes.

1365 **Winthrop,** Elizabeth. *Walking Away;* illus. by Noelle Massena. Harper, 1973. 219p. Trade ed. $4.95; Library ed. $5.11 net.

5-7 While Emily loved everything about her grandparents' farm where she spent the summers, it was her special closeness to Grandfather that was so precious. With high anticipation she awaited a visit from her best friend, Nina, to whom she had often described every loved detail of the farm. She knew that Nina and Grandfather would enjoy each other—but they didn't. He didn't even come to the station to meet Nina, and Nina—although she was cheerful about it, thought the farm was rundown. Nina brought cigarettes and they smoked in secret, she kept Emily too busy to spend time with Grandfather, she regarded the local people as odd characters. Forbidden the loft, Nina jumped and broke her leg—and that ended the visit. The story is written in an easy, natural style, with good dialogue and well-defined characterization, but its strength lies even more in the perceptive and lucid development of changing relationships as Emily learns how easily a new factor can upset an established situation.

1366 **Wiseman,** Bernard. *Morris Has a Cold;* written and illus. by Bernard Wiseman. Dodd, 1978. 77-12030. 46p. $5.25.

1-3 In an amusing story about a literal moose, suffering from a head cold, and his friend Boris the bear, solicitous but soon exasperated, Wiseman appeals both to the sense of humor of young children and to their appreciation of the translation of a familiar situation into an animal story; he also provides a pleasant experience for the beginning independent reader who can enjoy word play in this very simply written tale.

1367 **Wolf,** Bernard. *Anna's Silent World;* written and photographed by Bernard Wolf. Lippincott, 1977. 76-52943. 48p. $6.95.

2-4 Photographs of excellent quality capture, in candid shots, the charm and vitality of six-year-old Anna, born deaf. Like Edna Levine's *Lisa and Her Soundless World* this shows how a deaf child learns to talk and makes clear the fact that the limited abilities of those who are deaf are not an indication of limited intelligence. This, however, is more smoothly written than Lisa's story, and the photographs more informative than its drawings. Wolf's pictures and text show vividly the way in which therapy sessions and special equipment have made it possible for Anna to attend classes with children who have normal hearing. The activities pictured and the warmth of the family scenes give variety and balance to the text.

1368 **Wolf,** Bernard. *Don't Feel Sorry for Paul;* written and photographed by Bernard Wolf. Lippincott, 1974. 96p. $5.95.

3-6 Photographs of superb quality illustrate a text written with candor and dignity, describing Paul Jockimo, a seven-year-old who was born with malformation of hands and feet. Paul requires three prosthetic devices. The book describes his activities at home and at school, his riding lessons and participation in a show in which he wins a ribbon, his seventh birthday party, his visits with prosthetic specialists and doctors and rehabilitation therapists. There are moments of discouragement, but the common sense and courage of Paul's family, his own determination and vitality are paramount. At the end of the story, another child's mother says to Mrs. Jockimo, "How does he do it, poor kid? I can't help feeling sorry for him." Paul's mother speaks quietly of the joy that Paul has brought, of what a happy child he is, and concludes, "No, don't feel sorry for Paul. He doesn't need it." No mincing of words, no sentimentality, no appeal for sympathy in this text. It's a fine way to acquaint readers with the problems of the handicapped; even more, it is a beautifully conceived book.

1369 **Wolf,** Bernard. *Tinker and the Medicine Man; The Story of a Navajo Boy of Monument Valley;* written and photographed by Bernard Wolf. Random House, 1973. 67p. $4.95.

4-6 Unlike most of the photo-documentary books that give information about a child of an ethnic, tribal, or national group, this does not attempt to give broad background or to use dialogue, or a visit, or a classroom lecture, to introduce cultural aspects beyond the protagonist's immediate circle. It introduces a small Navajo boy who wants to follow in his father's path and become a medicine man and a peyote chief; much of the text is devoted to Tinker's conversations with his father about training for this gravely important position, to demonstration of the needed skills, and to the intricate details of a peyote ceremony. The author never refers to peyote as a drug, saying only such things as, "After the peyote has been taken for a second time, a new atmosphere of serenity and hope envelops the gathering." The pictures are handsome, there is no sense of text contrived to fit the photographs, and the writing is direct, simple, and serious, with a strong sense of the beauty and pride of the Navajo Way.

1370 **Wolitzer,** Hilma. *Toby Lived Here.* Farrar, 1978. 78-4550. 147p. $6.95.

5-7 Toby and her younger sister Anne are sent to stay with foster parents, the Selwyns, when their widowed mother has a nervous breakdown. Anne accepts the Selwyn's quiet affection easily, but Toby is determined not to like them, not to adjust, not to let friends at her new school know that she is staying in a foster home or that her mother is emotionally ill. But it comes out—and Toby finds that her friends feel only sympathy. She had been intrigued by the fact that a previous foster child had carved her name on a table; later she met and loved that same person, now an adult. She couldn't understand the fact that all her former foster children called Mrs. Selwyn "Mother." Yet when Toby's mother recovered, and she knew she had to leave the Selwyn house, Toby added her carving: "Toby Lived Here." She no longer rejected the Selwyns or pretended that this had not, for a time, been her home. This hasn't the dramatic impact of Paterson's development of a similar situation in *The Great Gilly Hopkins,* but it's a solidly constructed story that's often touching without being bathetic; the characters and dialogue are convincing, the outcome realistic, as Toby accepts—reluctantly—the fact that she can't keep the now-acknowledged security of the Selwyn home and also go back to Brooklyn and Mother.

1371 **Wolkstein,** Diane, ad. *Lazy Stories;* pictures by James Marshall. Seabury, 1976. 75-25781. 39p. $6.95.

4-5 Three tales about lazy people (folk material from Japan, Laos, and Mexico) are retold by a skilled storyteller; helpful notes, which include advice on technique and duration of the tellings, are appended. In "Hikoko," a lazy wife is plagued by the mat fairies who are irritated by her slovenly ways; her problem is solved by her samurai husband. In "The Tatema," there are two familiar themes: reward for kindness, and the failure of an envious imitator to get the same reward as lazy Mario. Only in the Laotian tale does the lazy protagonist receive bounty after becoming industrious. While graded here for independent reading, the stories can be told to younger children or older; Wolkstein suggests, in her notes, the best audience for each of the tales.

1372 **Wolkstein,** Diane, comp. *The Magic Orange Tree and Other Haitian Folktales;* illus. by Elsa Henriquez. Knopf, 1978. 77-15003. 212p. Trade ed. $6.95; Library ed. $6.99 net.

5-
* This collection of tales gathered in Haiti by a noted storyteller is distinguished for its humor, its variety, and the sense of relish that Wolkstein conveys without coming between reader and story by commenting. Although the stories were collected as heard, only a skilled storyteller could transcribe them with such fidelity to the oral tradition. The stories have local color, flavorful dialogue, and a pervasive awareness of magic in daily life. Each tale is prefaced by Wolkstein's notes on the circumstances in which the story was told, and a section at the close of the book gives musical notation

for songs used within the stories. The book may also be used for reading aloud to a younger audience.

1373 **Wood,** Madelyn. *Medicine and Health Care in Tomorrow's World;* by Madelyn Wood and the editors of Science Book Associates. Messner, 1974. 144p. illus. Trade ed. $6.25; Library ed. $5.79 net.

7- A thoughtful and objective assessment of the problems of giving adequate health care today incorporates some of the programs and some proposed changes that may provide more adequate care in the future. Health maintenance organizations that give complete coverage on a prepaid basis, hospital services that extend into the community, shorter and therefore less expensive medical training, the use of auxiliary personnel, the provision of medical social workers and health counseling—all of these programs have been or are being set in operation. The book does not confront the possibility of a national health service such as Britain's or the various medical insurance plans, but it does describe some of the efforts to cope with the inadequacies in our health services. A bibliography, a list of sources of information about health care, and an index are appended.

1374 **Wood,** Nancy. *Many Winters; Prose and Poetry of the Pueblos;* illus. by Frank Howell. Doubleday, 1974. 78p. $6.95.

5- A recording of some of the comments by older members of the Taos Indians is illustrated by strong, realistic portraits, some in color, and some in black and white, of the dignity and beauty of these Anasazi, the "old people." Some of the statements are measured prose, some are poetry; while there is an accent on recollection and remembrance that does not speak directly to the experience of young readers, many of the selections are timeless and universal. "There is a Time for Believing Nothing / So that you do not speak / What you have already heard / There is a Time for Keeping Quiet . . ." one poem begins. Another: "Brother, you fight against me / Brother, you do not see we cannot live / Except as we are / Brother, you have listened to a different song / You have danced a different dance / Brother, how can I hold you to me now / When I do not know your face?"

1375 **Woods,** Gerald, ed. *Art Without Boundaries;* ed. by Gerald Woods, Philip Thompson, and John Williams; with 333 illustrations, 15 in color. Praeger, 1974. 214p. Trade ed. $8.50; Paper ed. $4.95.

9- The work of over seventy artists from many countries is described and illustrated, usually in double-page spreads, in a book that has minor reference use. In some cases, the artist's own statement about his art or his philosophy of art is included. This major portion of the book is prefaced by a lengthy and trenchant introduction that discusses the blurring of traditional boundaries between disciplines and media in the visual arts; the artists exemplify contemporary creativity in communicating graphically. A section of brief biographical notes is appended.

1376 **Worth,** Valerie. *More Small Poems;* pictures by Natalie Babbitt. Farrar, 1976. 76-28323. 41p. $5.95.

4- Fresh and imaginative, Worth's new poems have a combination of vigor and delicacy that is echoed by Babbitt's small, precise drawings. There is no labored quality, the verse is free but disciplined, and the poems—direct and deceptively simple—offer those illuminating perceptions of familiar things that are the essence of the poet's vision and function.

1377 **Worth,** Valerie. *Still More Small Poems;* illus. by Natalie Babbitt. Farrar, 1978. 78-11739. 41p. $5.95.

4- A third collection (*Small Poems, More Small Poems*) is again deftly
* illustrated by small drawings in pen and ink, nicely scaled to the page layouts and the quality of the poems. The poems are evocative and laser-focused, bringing fresh insights into such familiar things as rocks, pigeons, snow, garbage, stars, or an ordinary pail. A sample, "bell," "By flat tink / Of tin, or thin / Copper tong / Brass clang / Bronze bong / The bell gives / Metal a tongue / To sing / In one sound / Its whole song."

1378 **Wriggins,** Sally Hovey, ad. *White Monkey King; A Chinese Fable;* illus. by Ronni Solbert. Pantheon Books, 1977. 76-44281. 113p. $5.95.

4-6 A retelling (with credit to the translator given only in the introduction) of a portion of a longer Chinese classic is simple and jaunty, with illustrations that are, like the print, brown on cream paper. Curious, ambitious, and indefatigably daring, the white monkey takes on legendary creatures, the Jade Emperor, and even the Heavenly Forces. His arrogance and mischief finally bring Monkey King to the throne of the Buddha, where he gets his comeuppance—and five hundred years of penance, from which, as the story ends, he is promised release by the merciful Kuan Yin. A lively prankster tale is modernized enough to have flippant dialogue that independent readers can enjoy, and the book is also a good source for storytelling.

1379 **Wrightson,** Patricia. *The Ice Is Coming.* Atheneum, 1977. 76-45438. 223p. $5.95.

6-9 Some of the creatures of *An Older Kind of Magic* and *Nargun and the Stars* appear again in a memorable fantasy set in Australia and adroitly meshed with the realistic quest by Wirrun, a young

Aborigine, to prevent the terrible destruction that threatens his land. The ancient ice people, the Ninya, are on the march, and the media are filled with reports of strange pockets of ice in summer. Wirrun understands that there are supernatural forces at work, and he calls on other creatures to help him reach the Nargun, the most ancient of them all, a rock-creature with the power of fire, the only hope of stopping the Ninya. Wirrun travels with a wispy, capricious, and delightful rock spirit, a Mimi, and she is an example of Wrightson's powerful writing: the Mimi is completely believable within the parameters of the fantasy. The story has an almost epic sense of adventure, danger, and high deeds, and it is taut with suspense.

1380 **Wrightson,** Patricia. *The Nargun and the Stars.* Atheneum, 1974. 184p. $5.50.

5-7 A particularly deft meshing of fantasy and reality is set in a remote Australian region where orphaned Simon has come to stay with elderly cousins. Charlie and Edie are brother and sister, and Simon feels no affection for them or pleasure in the countryside —until he finds the swamp where a mischievous water creature, the Potkoorok, lives. Then he discovers the Nargun, an ancient, ponderous creature born of fire, a thing of stone that periodically kills. Simon blurts out this story to Charlie and Edie and finds that they too have met the Potkoorok and the elfin Turongs and Nyols (who appeared in *An Older Kind of Magic*) and believe his account of the Nargun. Threatened by the Nargun, the three work with the friendly spirits to frighten the beast by the one means they know it dreads—vibrations in the earth. Characterization and the relationship between the boy and the adults are superb and are effected with remarkable economy; the setting is intriguing, the magic creatures convincing. The story is slow starting, but it has a dignified momentum, a vivid evocation of mood, enough suspense to sustain those passages that do not forward the action, and a polished style of writing.

1381 **Wyler,** Rose. *What Happens If . . ? Science Experiments You Can Do by Yourself;* pictures by Daniel Nevins. Walker, 1974. 48p. Trade ed. $4.95; Library ed. $4.85 net.

2-4 An experienced teacher of science and of science education has compiled some home demonstrations that really are easy, safe, and clearly explained. The text is divided into five areas: experiments with balloons, mixtures, flashlights, shadow pictures, and ice. Materials are simple: a balloon, an empty milk carton, a bulb, a battery, aluminum foil, etc. The instructions are clear; the cartoon-style illustrations, reminiscent of Jeanne Bendick's, lively and informative.

1382 **Wyse,** Anne. *The One to Fifty Book;* by Anne and Alex Wyse. University of Toronto Press, 1973. 100p. illus. $2.75.

3-6 yrs. A counting book, chiefly in black and white but with unexpected splashes of color here and there, that uses a double-page spread for each number from 1 to 50. The book was prepared by a teacher using the pictures drawn by children in her classes over the years, children in England and in Canada, children who were white and Indian. Each set of pages has the number, the number in word form with the name of the objects shown on facing pages: 9 ships, 13 gingerbread men, 30 bananas, 39 girls, 47 beetles. On some pages the unit object is repeated, on others there's an amazing—sometimes amusing—variety. It's different, it's creative, and it's just as useful as any other counting book.

1383 **Yep,** Laurence. *Child of the Owl.* Harper, 1977. 76-24314. 224p. Trade ed. $5.95; Library ed. $5.79 net.

6-9 * Casey's father, Barney, is an inveterate gambler and dreamer; since her mother's death she has become toughened by their wandering life, more protective toward her father than he is toward her. When Barney is hospitalized, Casey is taken over by her uncle's family, but they are horrified by her behavior and sophistication, and she is taken to the Chinese neighborhood of San Francisco to live with a grandmother she hardly knows. There is a story line, and a well-constructed one, but it is Casey's adjustment to her Chinese heritage that is the most trenchant aspect of the story: her growing love for her grandmother, her new perspective on her own childhood, her acceptance of herself as a "child of the owl," a reference to a long folktale told (beautifully) by her grandmother. This is a most impressive book: impressive in its depiction of Chinatown, in its strong characterization, vigorous style, and in its perception.

1384 **Yep,** Laurence. *Dragonwings.* Harper, 1975. 74-2625. 248p. Trade ed. $6.50; Library ed. $6.79.

5-9 At the turn of the century, there were many Chinese and Japanese men in California who worked diligently to earn enough money to bring their families to the "Land of the Golden Mountain." Moon Shadow, who tells the story, is eight when his father sends for him; he comes to San Francisco's Chinatown to find a close-knit community of friends who work together and a puzzling hostility of the "white demons" toward their Chinese neighbors. Moon Shadow does make two white friends, the elderly Miss Whitlaw and her niece Robin; together with Moon Shadow's father, they do rescue work after the earthquake. And then Father is free to do the one thing he really wants: build and fly an airplane. There was a young Chinese flier who, in 1909, flew a biplane for twenty minutes over the Oakland hills, and the incident was a catalyst for the story, although not used as fact in it. Yep very adroitly combines in the book several diverse elements: San Francisco's reaction to the earthquake, the Chinese community and its ties to the old country, the friendship between Robin and Moon Shadow, and the curiosity, persistence and daring of the boy's father.

1385 **Yolen,** Jane H. *The Magic Three of Solatia;* illus. by Julia Noonan. T. Y. Crowell, 1974. 172p. $5.95.

5-7 A four-part fantasy in which the sequential segments can stand alone. The writing is fluent, the mood romantic in the fairytale tradition, and many of the typical elements of the genre are included: the struggle between forces of good and evil, the bestowing of a magical object; wizard's spells that cast people in animal forms, a quest, and the love between a mortal and a superhuman being. The three magic buttons save the situation at crucial moments in the lives of Sianna, the wise and beautiful woman who has learned the magic of a sea creature, and of her son Lann, who uses the magic and his minstrelsy to save the life of an old man and gain the love of a bird-girl whom he rescues from the evil spell of a wizard-king.

1386 **York,** Carol Beach. *Takers and Returners; A Novel of Suspense.* Nelson, 1973. 123p. $4.50.

6-8 Julian, fifteen, was the oldest of a small group of children who had always spent their summers together, and it was he who came up with the idea for a new game. It was hot, they were all bored, and it sounded like fun—although thirteen-year-old Ellen, who tells the story, was dubious about the morality of what Julian proposed. One team would steal something; the other team would have to return it without being caught by adults; it wasn't really stealing, Julian explained. As the children become more and more audacious in their game, the feeling of imminent catastrophe grows. And it comes. The story ends, "We were all losers." Not minatory, but effectively sobering, the story's serious theme is alleviated by the action of the ploys, the sound characterization, and the skillful building of suspense. Problem, conflict, and resolution are adroitly structured in a tight plot.

1387 **Young,** B. E. *The Picture Story of Hank Aaron;* illus. with photographs. Messner, 1974. 64p. $4.79.

2-5 A biography illustrated by good action photographs gives some information about Aaron's childhood, the early prowess that earned a berth with a sandlot team, and the years with the

Indianapolis Clowns and minor league teams before he joined the Milwaukee Braves. The pace of Young's description of Aaron's career broadens at the close of the book, moving from homer to homer (rather than from one highlight or seasonal statistics to another) as the record-breaker draws closer. Big print, easy-to-read style and balanced coverage of personal and professional aspects of Aaron's life are strong points. A chart of Aaron's batting record is appended.

1388 **Young,** Miriam. *Truth and Consequences;* illus. by Diane de Groat. Four Winds, 1975. 74-19038. 101p. $6.50.

4-6 Kim Jones, eleven, is bothered by the fact that telling a lie can get one in trouble and equally bothered by the fact that even the adults she respects occasionally tell social lies. She vows to tell only the truth—and she loses her best friend, Alison. You don't tell a girl who has just had her hair cut that she looks ugly, Kim finds. Most of the story is about Kim's struggle to patch up the broken friendship, but it's nicely balanced by family concerns, especially by her relationship with a six-year-old brother. If you've vowed to tell the truth, what do you say when asked about Santa Claus? The story ends happily, Kim's dilemma solved in a realistic way. No great melodrama here, but a "good read" because of the natural dialogue, familiar situations, and an easy, flowing writing style.

1389 **Young,** Miriam. *A Witch's Garden;* illus. by Charles Robinson. Atheneum, 1973. 156p. $5.50.

5-7 Clover Lake is a community for WASPS, twelve-year-old Jenny realizes, and has several club members who talk kindly about what nice people the Greens are—but, you know, let one Jewish family in . . . and then they'll all pour in. Furious, Jenny damns the whole committee of the club. And then a new family arrives, young and charming, and Mrs. Matthews becomes Jenny's friend. But she's odd: she keeps a rat as a familiar, and her garden is all poisonous plants, and she seems to be taking credit for every trouble that assails the committee members. Is she a witch? Jenny frets and worries, never quite able to ask. Then a storm creates havoc at Clover Lake, and when it is over the Matthews family all seems to have changed and become more conforming. The book ends with Jenny still in doubt, but with a change in the composition and attitude of the club committee, presumably a shift away from prejudice in the offing. The theme is not belabored but is strongly drawn, and the lively episodes carry the story forward at a brisk and well-sustained pace. Good characterization, good style.

1390 **Zemach,** Harve. *Duffy and the Devil;* a Cornish tale retold by Harve Zemach; with pictures by Margot Zemach. Farrar, 1973. 35p. $5.95.

5-8 yrs. A variant of "Rumpelstiltskin" is told with verve and relish and illustrated in a high-comedy style; the pictures are soft in tones and bold in execution, beautifully detailed, echoing the strong style of the text. Duffy is a servant who has been hired by the Squire because she has said that she spins like a saint and knits like an angel. (She lies like a trooper.) A devilish little creature appears who promises to fulfill her tasks but exacts the penalty: if she can't tell his name after three years he will take her away. Three years later, Duffy has become the Squire's lady; she tells her husband the whole story and he cleverly learns the creature's name: Tarraway. So Duffy is spared, but the devil-made garments of the Squire vanish, and the portly gentleman is suddenly left with only shoes and hat to defend his modesty. Very funny, very handsome, this is based on a Cornish dramatization of the folktale and it conveys fully the dramatic flavor of the source.

1391 **Zemach,** Margot, illus. *Hush, Little Baby;* illus. by Margot Zemach. Dutton, 1976. 76-5477. 26p. $6.95.

2-5 yrs. With her usual deft, humorous handling of line, Zemach creates an engagingly frumpy family in tempera paintings of a homely baby, a frowsy mother (never mentioned in the lyrics of the familiar lullaby) and a beefy father who doffs his derby only at bed-time. The music is included at the back of the book, after the cumulated gifts from Poppa to baby have erupted in a glorious collision (no damages sustained) that should delight the lap audience.

1392 **Zemach,** Margot, ad. *It Could Always Be Worse; a Yiddish Folk Tale;* ad. and illus. by Margot Zemach. Farrar, 1976. 76-53895. 27p. $7.95.

K-3 While Zemach retells a Yiddish version of the folktale, this will remind many readers of Sorche Nic Leodhas' *Always Room for One More* or other variants of the story about a house so crowded that the only way to make the owner feel comfortable is to stuff it with even more people or creatures so that when the extra guests leave, the original population seems pleasant by comparison. Here a poor man goes to his Rabbi to complain that a wife, six children, and his mother make home a bedlam; the Rabbi insists that the man bring in all his beasts—and when the latter go, home seems quiet, peaceful, and roomy. Zemach's pictures are always engaging, with strong use of line, subdued and deft use of color, and humor, but this is one of the best vehicles she's used for her distinctive style.

1393 **Zimelman,** Nathan. *The Lives of My Cat Alfred;* pictures by Evaline Ness. Dutton, 1976. 75-35514. 26p. $5.95.

K-3 The pictures of Alfred benign, Alfred wistful, Alfred mysterious, are delightful; the text has an ingenuous blandness; the two are a happy union, each standing alone but complementing the other. Alfred, his boy says, likes dogs (Alfred told him so) and soulful communion with his tree. Alfred likes shrimps and ice cream; they are cat food, he insists, anything a cat eats is cat food. "It wouldn't surprise me," the boy says, "if you smiled that smile for Leonardo. It wouldn't surprise me . . ." and the author lists a series of historical events in which Alfred is shown as a participant, concluding with taking "that step" with Neil Armstrong. Why should it, Alfred asks, when a cat has nine lives? It's nice of Alfred, the boy concludes, to spend one of them with him. Although there is no plot, this has humor and variety enough to appeal to readers. For cat lovers, of course, it's shrimps and ice cream.

1394 **Zindel,** Paul. *Let Me Hear You Whisper;* a play by Paul Zindel; drawings by Stephen Gammell. Harper, 1974. 44p. Trade ed. $4.95; Library ed. $4.79 net.

7- A touching and trenchant short play in two acts, *Let Me Hear You Whisper* was very effective on television but makes technical demands that would strain the capabilities of amateur production. Nevertheless, it reads beautifully, with good dialogue and characterization, an original plot, and a theme that should appeal to young people. A cleaning woman who has just begun working for an experimental biology laboratory learns that the dolphin in a laboratory tank has failed to learn to talk and is therefore to be killed. Helen is a gentle, ingenuous person who has chattered with pity and affection to the dolphin. And it talks to her when they are alone, although it will not speak to the staff. She learns that the dolphin knows it was meant to be used for warfare and would not cooperate; the dolphin tells her of a plan: she must get him into a large hamper and take him to the sea. Helen is caught talking to the dolphin, which she's been told not to do, and dismissed. The dolphin says one word, "love," and everybody hears it. If Helen can be brought back and the dolphin speaks to her again, it will not be killed . . . but it is too late, an angry Helen will not return.

1395 **Zoll,** Max Alfred. *A Flamingo Is Born;* photographs by Winifried Noack; tr. by Catherine Edwards Sadler. Putnam, 1978. 77-13761. 37p. $5.95.

2-3 Only the jacket of the book shows the full beauty of the pink flamingo; the black and white photographs that accompany a brief, direct text are of good quality. First published in Germany, the text describes the mating of a pair of adult flamingos, the nesting and brooding, and the care and behavior of a chick until its down feather begins to turn. The pictures are, as pictures of the young of any species usually are, engaging, and the text simple; the book serves nicely as an introduction to bird behavior for young independent readers.

1396 **Zolotow,** Charlotte. *May I Visit?* with illus. by Erik Blegvad. Harper, 1976. 75-25405. 32p. Trade ed. $4.95; Library ed. $4.79 net.

K-2 Erik Blegvad's precise, blithe drawings capture nicely the direct simplicity and warmth of a quiet, engaging story of family love. A small girl is intrigued by the difference in an older sister, now married, who has come home for a visit. The sister doesn't leave a mess in the bathroom the way she used to, and she doesn't say "Oh Mother!" the way she used to. The little girl asks her mother if she may come back to visit when she's grown if she doesn't use good stationery to draw on, or leave Magic Marker marks on the bedspread, or try on her mother's jewelry? Yes, says her mother, and it will be fun, ". . . just as it is now!" And there's a loving hug.

1397 **Zolotow,** Charlotte. *My Grandson Lew;* pictures by William Pène Du Bois. Harper, 1974. 31p. Trade ed. $4.95; Library ed. $4.79 net.

3-7 yrs. A new approach is used in a story about a child's view of death. Not sentimental, but gentle and poignant, the book is charming in its illustrations, its style, and in Lew's memories of his grandfather and the joyful love his grandfather had shown. "I miss Grandpa," Lew says one night. "You miss him! You were two when he died. Now you're six and you never asked for him before." But as they talk it becomes clear that Lew remembers Grandpa very well; Mother tells him things that she remembers, and says that now that they can remember him together it won't be as lonely for each of them as it would be if each had to remember him alone. On all counts, nicely done.

1398 **Zolotow,** Charlotte, comp. *An Overpraised Season; 10 Stories of Youth.* Harper, 1973. 188p. Trade ed. $4.95; Library ed. $4.79 net.

6- Charlotte Zolotow's name is familiar as a writer of particularly perceptive picture books; she is less well known as an editor of books for older children, but her sensitivity on their behalf is evident here as well. The title is taken from Samuel Butler's, ". . . youth is like spring, an overpraised season." In a varied collection of short stories, the bittersweet problems of adolescents, especially in their relations with parents and other adults, are explored. The authors include Nathaniel Benchley, Doris Lessing, Elizabeth Taylor, John Updike, Kurt Vonnegut, and Jessamyn West.

1399 **Zolotow,** Charlotte. *Someone New;* illus. by Erik Blegvad. Harper, 1978. 77-11838. 32p. Trade ed. $5.95; Library ed. $5.79 net.

K-3 In a subdued text illustrated with simple paintings that have firm line, delicate detail, and quiet color, a child describes his feelings about a turning point in childhood. The boy wonders what it is that's wrong; nothing has changed, his family and home are the same, but he's vaguely dissatisfied, he keeps feeling that someone is missing. He looks about his room and sees a clutter of books and toys and stuffed animals; he realizes that he is curious about some shells and not interested in a teddy bear and a panda. When he packs them in a carton, the answer comes to him. *He* has changed. It is the small boy he was that is missing; he's moved on to new interests and larger horizons. A gentle and perceptive book that may, because it is so quiet, appeal to a limited audience; for that audience, however, it may touch a deep feeling.

1400 **Zolotow,** Charlotte. *The Unfriendly Book;* illus. by William Pène Du Bois. Harper, 1975. 32p. Trade ed. $3.95; Library ed. $3.79 net.

K-3 Breathes there a person who hasn't been irritated by a friend who criticizes everybody? Here the dialogue between Judy and Bertha, as they walk their dogs, shows Bertha carping at every other friend of Judy's, and replying to Judy's defensive statements with a contemptuous ". . . you like everyone." But Judy has the last word. This hasn't a strong line, but it's true and—in a wry way—amusing, and it may even be an eye-opener for other unhappy carpers. As usual Zolotow sees and tells clearly and directly. The artist uses an intriguing device: on the pages that have text are the small figures of Bertha and Judy, usually tangled in their dogs' leashes, and on the facing pages are pictures of each friend they discuss, first as Bertha sees each girl (usually frowsty and disagreeable) and then as Judy sees Jean, Marilyn, Helen, and Mary—nice people.

Appendix

Addresses of Publishers of Listed Children's Books

PUBLISHERS

Abelard. Abelard/Schuman, Ltd., 10 E. 53rd St., New York, N.Y. 10022
Abingdon. Abingdon Pr., 201 Eighth Ave. S., Nashville, Tenn. 37202
Abrams. Harry N. Abrams, Inc., 110 E. 59th St., New York, N.Y. 10022
Addison. Addison-Wesley Pub. Co., Inc., Reading, Mass. 01867
American Heritage, American Heritage Publishing Co., 10 Rockefeller Plaza, New York, N.Y. 10020
Appleton. Appleton-Century-Crofts, 292 Madison Ave., New York, N.Y. 10017
Ariel. Ariel Books. See Farrar
Assoc. for Childhood Education International. 3615 Wisconsin Ave., N.W., Washington, D.C. 20016
Atheneum. Atheneum Pubs., 597 Fifth Ave., New York, N.Y. 10017
Atlantic. Atlantic Monthly Pr., 8 Arlington St., Boston, Mass. 02116
Atlantic/Little. Atlantic Monthly Pr. in association with Little, Brown & Co.
Basic. Basic Books, Inc., 10 E. 53rd St., New York, N.Y. 10022
Beacon. Beacon Pr., 25 Beacon St., Boston, Mass. 02108
Bobbs. Bobbs-Merrill Co., Inc., 4300 W. 62nd St., Indianapolis, Ind. 46206
Bradbury. Bradbury Pr., Inc., 2 Overhill Rd., Scarsdale, N.Y. 10583
Childrens Pr. Childrens Press, Inc., 1224 W. Van Buren, Chicago, Ill. 60607
Chilton. Chilton Book Co., 401 Walnut St., Philadelphia, Pa. 19106
Collins. William Collins Pub., 200 Madison Ave., New York, N.Y. 10016.
Coward. Coward, McCann & Geoghegan Inc., 200 Madison Ave., New York, N.Y. 10016
Criterion. Criterion Books, Inc., 666 Fifth Ave., New York, N.Y. 10019
T. Crowell. Thomas Y. Crowell Co., 10 E. 53rd St., New York, N.Y. 10022
Crown. Crown Pubs., Inc., 419 Park Ave. S., New York, N.Y. 10016
Day. The John Day Co., Inc., 10 E. 53rd St., New York, N.Y. 10022
Delacorte. Delacorte Pr. See Dell
Dell. Dell Pub. Co., 1 Dag Hammarskjöld Plaza, New York, N.Y. 10017
Dial. The Dial Pr., Inc. See Dell
Dodd. Dodd, Mead & Co., 79 Madison Ave., New York, N.Y. 10016
Doubleday. Doubleday & Co., Inc., 245 Park Ave., New York, N.Y. 10017
Duell. Duell, Sloan & Pearce. See Meredith
Dufour. Dufour Editions, Inc., Chester Springs, Pa. 19425
Dutton. E. P. Dutton & Co., Inc., 2 Park Ave. S., New York, N.Y. 10016

For the address of any publisher not listed here consult the latest *Literary Market Place* or Bowker's *Books in Print*.

Elsevier/Nelson Books. 2 Park Ave., New York, N.Y. 10016
Eriksson. Paul S. Eriksson, Inc., Pub., Battell Building, Middlebury, Vt. 05753
Evans. M. Evans & Co., Inc., 216 E. 49th St., New York, N.Y. 10017
Farrar. Farrar, Straus & Giroux, Inc., 19 Union Sq., W., New York, N.Y. 10003
Follett. Follett Pub. Co., 1010 W. Washington Blvd., Chicago, Ill. 60606
Four Winds. Four Winds Pr. See Scholastic
Funk. Funk & Wagnalls, Inc., 10 E. 53rd St., New York, N.Y. 10022
Garden City. See Doubleday
Garrard. Garrard Pub. Co. 107 Cherry St., New Canaan, Conn. 06840
Golden Pr. Golden Pr., Inc. See Western
Greenwillow. Greenwillow Books. 105 Madison Ave., New York, N.Y. 10016
Grosset. Grosset & Dunlap, Inc., 51 Madison Ave., New York, N.Y. 10010
Hale. E. M. Hale & Co., Inc. 128 W. River St., Chippewa Falls, Wis. 54729
Harcourt. Harcourt Brace Jovanovich, Inc., 757 Third Ave., New York, N.Y. 10017
Harper. Harper & Row, Pubs., 10 E. 53rd St., New York, N.Y. 10022
Harvey. Harvey House, Inc., 20 Waterside Plaza, New York, N.Y. 10010
Hastings. Hastings House Pubs., 10 E. 40th St., New York, N.Y. 10016
Hawthorn. Hawthorn Books, Inc., 260 Madison Ave., New York, N.Y. 10016
Hill. Hill & Wang, Inc. See Farrar
Holiday. Holiday House, Inc., 18 E. 53rd St., New York, N.Y. 10022
Holt. Holt, Rinehart & Winston, Inc., 383 Madison Ave., New York, N.Y. 10017
Houghton. Houghton Mifflin Co., 2 Park St., Boston, Mass. 02107
Houghton Mifflin/Clarion Books. 52 Vanderbilt Ave., New York, N.Y. 10017
Knopf. Alfred A. Knopf, Inc., 201 E. 50th St., New York, N.Y. 10022
Lerner. Lerner Pubns. Co., 241 First Ave. N., Minneapolis, Minn. 55401
Lippincott. J. B. Lippincott Co., E. Washington Sq., Philadephia, Pa. 19105
Little. Little, Brown & Co., 34 Beacon St., Boston, Mass. 02106
Lothrop. Lothrop, Lee & Shepard Co., Inc., 105 Madison Ave., New York, N.Y. 10016
McGraw. McGraw-Hill Book Co., 1221 Ave. of the Americas, New York, N.Y. 10036
McKay. David McKay Co., Inc., 750 Third Ave., New York, N.Y. 10017
Macmillan. Macmillan Co., 866 Third Ave., New York, N.Y. 10022
Macrae. Macrae Smith Co., 225 S. 15th St., Philadelphia, Pa., 19102
Messner. Julian Messner, Inc. See Simon & Schuster
Morrow. William Morrow & Co., Inc., 105 Madison Ave., New York, N.Y. 10016
Natural History Pr. See Doubleday
Nelson. See Elsevier/Nelson
Norton. W. W. Norton & Co., 500 Fifth Ave., New York, N.Y. 10036
Norton/Grosset. W. W. Norton in association with Grosset & Dunlap
Oxford. Oxford Univ. Pr., 200 Madison Ave., New York, N.Y. 10016

Pantheon. Pantheon Books, 201 E. 50th St.,New York, N.Y. 10022
Parents' Magazine. Parents' Magazine Pr., 52 Vanderbilt Ave., New York, N.Y. 10017
Parnassus. See Houghton Mifflin
Phillips. S. G. Phillips, Inc., 305 W. 86th St., New York, N.Y. 10024
Platt. Platt & Munk, Inc., 1055 Bronx River Ave., Bronx, N.Y. 10472
Plays. Plays, Inc., 8 Arlington St., Boston, Mass. 02116
Praeger. Praeger Pubs., Inc., 200 Park Ave., New York, N.Y. 10017
Prentice. Prentice-Hall, Inc., Englewood Cliffs, N.J. 07632
Putnam. G. P. Putnam's Sons, 200 Madison Ave., New York, N.Y. 10016
Rand. Rand McNally & Co., P.O. Box 7600, Chicago, Ill. 60680
Random. Random House, Inc., 201 E. 50th St., New York, N.Y. 10022
Ritchie. The Ward Ritchie Pr., 474 S. Arroyo Pkwy., Pasadena, Calif. 91105
Roy. Roy Pubs. Inc., 30 E. 74th St., New York, N.Y. 10021
St. Martin's. St. Martin's Pr., Inc., 175 Fifth Ave., New York, N.Y. 10010
Scarecrow. The Scarecrow Pr., 52 Liberty St., Metuchen, N.J. 08840
Scott/Addison. See Addison-Wesley
Scribner's. Charles Scribner's Sons, 597 Fifth Ave., New York, N.Y. 10017
Seabury. See Houghton Mifflin/Clarion
Simon. Simon & Schuster, Inc., 1230 Ave. of the Americas, New York, N.Y. 10020
Stein & Day. 7 E. 48th St., New York, N.Y. 10017
Sterling. Sterling Pub. Co., 2 Park Ave. S., New York, N.Y. 10016
Time-Life. Time-Life Books, Time-Life Bldg., Rockefeller Center, New York, N.Y. 10020
Tuttle. Charles E. Tuttle Co., Inc., 28 S. Main St., Rutland, Vt. 05701
Univ. of Calif. Pr. 2223 Fulton St., Berkeley, Calif. 94720
Univ. of Chicago Pr. 5801 S. Ellis Ave., Chicago, Ill. 60637
Vanguard. Vanguard Pr., Inc., 424 Madison Ave., New York, N.Y. 10017
Van Nostrand. Van Nostrand Reinhold Co., 450 W. 33rd St., New York, N.Y. 10001
Viking. Viking Pr., Inc., 625 Madison Ave., New York, N.Y. 10022
Walck. Henry Z. Walck, Inc., 3 E. 54th St., New York, N.Y. 10022
Walker. Walker & Co., 750 Third Ave., New York, N.Y. 10017
Warne. Frederick Warne & Co., Inc., 2 Park Ave. S., New York, N.Y. 10016
Washburn. Ives Washburn, Inc. See McKay
Watts. Franklin Watts, Inc., 730 Fifth Ave., New York, N.Y. 10019
Western. Western Pub. Co., 850 Third Ave., New York, N.Y. 10022
Westminster. The Wesminster Pr., Witherspoon Bldg., Philadelphia, Pa. 19107
White. David White Co., 14 Vanderventer Ave., Port Washington N.Y. 11050
Whitman. Albert Whitman & Co., 560 W. Lake St., Chicago, Ill. 60606
Whittlesey. Whittlesey House. See McGraw-Hill
Windmill. Windmill Books, 257 Park Ave. S., New York, N.Y. 10010
Young Scott. Young Scott Books. See Addison-Wesley

Title Index

a

C

i

Developmental Values Index

Curricular Use Index

Reading Level Index

Titles are arranged in order of increasing difficulty, with books for the preschool child and kindergartener first, followed by books for independent reading beginning with grade 1. The reading range is intended to be indicative rather than mandatory.

Subject Index

Type of Literature Index